Practice

These excerpts from Chapter 15, "The Impact of Public Policy: Social Trends, School Reform, and Special Education" give you a glimpse of practice in context — a framework especially provided by Chapters 1 to 6 and 14 and 15 of this book.

Window on Practice

Case Study in Advocacy: Passage of Goals 2000

Goals 2000 is a federal education act that was signed in March 1994. (The contents of the act are discussed later in this chapter.) It is a good example of the power of advocacy groups. For instance, the original draft of the act listed six national goals, but the final law includes eight. Where did the extra two goals come from?

■ During debate on the bill, teacher groups argued that if they were to provide the up-to-date instruction implied by other passages of the act, they would need greater opportunities for professional development and training. Thus, a goal relating to teacher education and professional development was added to the law.

■ Both teachers and parents argued that students could not achieve the national goals without considerable parent involvement and strong linkages between homes and schools. For this reason, a goal concerning parental participation was added.

Other variations between the original and final drafts included the following:

■ The original draft had no specific language to indicate that the law applied to all American children, including those with disabilities. But parents of students with disabilities argued that the high educational standards specified in the act should apply to their children as well as others. In the end, such language was added.

■ The original bill mandated that states establish opportunity-to-learn standards (described later in the chapter). This provision reflected the belief that if we hold students responsible for achieving high standards, we should also hold schools and school personnel responsible for delivering the related instruction. But teacher unions and others actively opposed this requirement. As a result, in the law's final language, the opportunity-to-learn standards became voluntary rather than mandatory for the states.

■ The law's original version mentioned only certain academic subjects. The final version named a number of other subjects, because groups of teachers representing the omitted subject areas successfully lobbied for their inclusion.

These changes were neither unusual nor unexpected. Goals 2000 is merely one recent instance of the major role played by advocacy groups in formulating public policy on education.

Special Education

A Practical Approach for Teachers

Special Education

A Practical Approach for Teachers   Third Edition

JAMES E. YSSELDYKE
University of Minnesota

BOB ALGOZZINE
The University of North Carolina at Charlotte

HOUGHTON MIFFLIN COMPANY   **Boston**   **Toronto**
Geneva, Illinois   Palo Alto   Princeton, New Jersey

Senior Sponsoring Editor: Loretta Wolozin
Senior Project Editor: Carol Newman
Production/Design Coordinator: Jennifer Waddell
Senior Manufacturing Coordinator: Marie Barnes
Marketing Manager: Pamela Shaffer

Cover image and design by Darci Mehall, Aureo Design

Chapter opening photo credits: Frontispiece: Jean-Claude Lejeune
Chapter 1, p. 4, Richard Hutchings/Science Source/Photo
Researchers, Inc.; Chapter 2, p. 38, M. Richards/PhotoEdit;
Chapter 3, p. 60, Bob Daemmrich/The Image Works, Inc.;
Chapter 4, p. 88, Spencer Grant/Monkmeyer Press;
Chapter 5, p. 120, Arthur Tilly/FPG; Chapter 6, p. 160,
Richard S. Orton/The Picture Cube, Inc.; Chapter 7, p. 206, Jerry
Howard/Positive Images; Chapter 8, p. 240, Elizabeth Crews;
Chapter 9, p. 276, James Shaffer/PhotoEdit;
Chapter 10, p. 304, Grant LeDuc/Monkmeyer Press;
Chapter 11, p. 342, Jeff Greenberg/PhotoEdit; Chapter 12,
p. 374, Bill Anderson/Monkmeyer Press; Chapter 13, p. 412, Alon
Reininger/Unicorn Stock Photos; Chapter 14, p. 456, John
Coletti/The Picture Cube, Inc.; Chapter 15, p. 498,
P. Prettyman/PhotoEdit.

**Excerpts from the following material have been reprinted
by permission of the publisher:** Chapter 7, pp. 212–213:
Definition of gifted and talented children from "Minnesota
Standards for Services to Gifted and Talented Students,"
pp. 2–3, April 28, 1988. St. Paul, MN: Minnesota State
Advisory Council for the Gifted and Talented. Used with
permission. Chapter 9, pp. 291–292: Dean, John F. and Karol
D. Hicks, *Games Make Alpha-Betics Fun.* Copyright © 1987
Better Teaching Aid Publications. Used with permission.
Chapter 12, pp. 402–403: Reprinted from *Oser's News in
Print,* Vol. 5, No. 2., Suggestions for Empowering People Who
Are Deaf" from "We Can! Empowerment Of People Who Are
Deaf . . . an Enpowerment Agenda for the 1990's and Beyond"
by P. Singleton, p. 12–15. Copyright © 1992 Osers News in
Print. Used with permission.

Printed in the U.S.A.
Library of Congress Catalog Card Number: 94–76557
ISBN: 0–395–67666-5

3 4 5 6 7 8 9-DH-98 97 96

Brief Contents

Table of Contents

Preface

Education is changing. Special education is changing. More and more students with disabilities are being taught and held accountable for the same content in the same classes as their neighbors and peers. More and more students who are gifted and talented are being identified and expected to demonstrate outstanding achievement as evidence of America's willingness and ability to provide a world-class education to its citizens. More and more, students with disabilities are also being expected to attain world-class standards. We support these changes with one reservation. We believe they cannot and will not happen without providing support for general and special education teachers who will be expected to make them happen. We revised our introduction to special education to meet this need. This is the most practical edition we have written—it contains hundreds of strategies and tactics for teachers working with students with disabilities as well as those who are gifted and talented.

Audience and Purpose

This book is for people who want to learn more about special education. It is for people attending colleges and universities who are enrolled in undergraduate and graduate teacher preparation programs. It is for people who are currently teaching who want to learn more about how to make the educational experiences of their students more productive and successful. It is for people who live and work with people with disabilities, gifts, and talents who want assistance with activities of daily living and transition to the world of work. It is a book for teachers, parents, and other professionals who believe as we do that special education is important, necessary, and deserving of change.

Although this book is changed significantly from previous editions, our purpose in writing it remains the same: to provide a comprehensive, practical overview of the field of special education for people who want to improve the lives of people with disabilities and those who are gifted and talented. To achieve this purpose, we provide fundamental information on definitions and terms commonly used in the field, we describe characteristics commonly associated with people who receive special education, and we provide in-depth coverage of tactics effective teachers use to make educational experiences more successful for students with those characteristics. We also describe laws and legal cases affecting the delivery of special education services, the full range of settings in which those services are delivered, and the principles of assessment and instruction that promote effectiveness in providing the services. To help you understand the impact of disabilities and exceptionality, we explore the subtle factors that influence the personal experiences of people who receive special education and the key areas in which changes are occurring in their lives as they adjust and adapt to everchanging views of who they are and what they can accomplish in contemporary societies.

Features of the Revision

The major change in this edition is an emphasis on practical answers to questions commonly asked by teachers and other professionals who provide special education. This change is most obvious in the seven chapters focused on teaching students with special education needs. Students who are gifted and talented, as well as those included in the most recently adopted set of special education categories, are addressed in these new chapters. Each chapter includes an overview of a widely accepted definition, a discussion of the numbers of these students being served across the country, a description of their characteristics, and a presentation of tactics teachers will find effective in meeting the educational needs of these students.

Equally important, and because special education is a dynamic and rapidly changing field, all other chapters have been updated and changed to reflect the latest thinking and most current information and scholarship available. Coverage has been added to reflect significant trends in areas such as cultural diversity, effective teaching, technology, inclusion, alternative assessment, and changing social policy. Throughout the text, we provide the latest statistical information from the most recent reports compiled by the federal government. All recommended readings and reference citations have been updated whenever appropriate to build on the knowledge base of the former edition. Finally, the resource package accompanying this textbook has been expanded to include an updated print and computerized test bank with on-line testing and ESAGRADE as well as an improved Instructor's Resource Manual with additional resources for both professors and students.

Organization of the Text

The fifteen chapters of the book contain all the information needed to introduce novice or experienced professionals to special education and help them provide it as it is practiced today. The text is divided into four parts.

In Part I, "Fundamentals of Special Education," we describe the foundations of special education. Chapter 1 includes discussion of what special education is, why it is part of America's education system, who receives it, and what it means to be exceptional and receive special education in society today. Special education in contemporary schools, including perspectives on diversity, best practices, and modern approaches to providing services, is described in Chapter 2. In Chapter 3, we analyze the laws and court cases affecting the development of special education and the general treatment in society of people with disabilities and gifts and talents.

"Principles of Instruction and Assessment" is the focus of Part II. We describe essentials of effective instruction in Chapter 4, specific teaching methods in Chapter 5, and assessment practices in Chapter 6. The content in each of these chapters reflects the latest thinking on ways to make special education more effective. It sets the base for detailed descriptions of effective assessment and intervention practices with students with disabilities, gifts, and talents.

Part III presents "Instructional Approaches and Teaching Tactics for Students Who Are Exceptional." Extensive coverage of key information is provided for each of the most current categories of students receiving special education. Chapter 7 defines students who are gifted and talented and discusses their prevalence and characteristics as a background for describing effective instructional approaches and teaching tactics. Similar information is provided in Chapters 8, 9, 10, and 11 for students with learning disabilities, communication disorders, mental retardation, and serious emotional disturbance. Definitions, prevalence, characteristics, and effective instructional approaches and teaching tactics are described in Chapter 12 for students with sensory disabilities (visual impairments, hearing impairments, deafness, and blindness). Part III concludes with a discussion of key information for those who teach students with medical (other health impairments and special health problems), physical (orthopedic impairments, traumatic brain injury, and autism), and multiple disabilities.

In Part IV, "Community and Professional Issues in Special Education," we look beyond the classroom for a fuller understanding of special education. Chapter 14 addresses life-stage and community issues, and Chapter 15 places special education in the context of long-term social, political, economic, and educational trends.

Special Features of the Text

This edition includes the following special features designed to make understanding and mastery of the content easier:

- *Focusing questions* at the beginning of each chapter highlight the content to be covered.
- *Chapter-opening vignettes* provide real-life perspectives about special education.
- *Marginal notations* review central points throughout the text.
- *Bring Your Learning to Life* boxes illustrate key information with examples from real-life classrooms.
- *Perspective* sections at the end of each chapter provide a forum for our observations about topics covered in the text and serve as a basis for discussing key issues and concerns related to them.
- *What Every Teacher Should Know* summaries at the end of each chapter highlight the content that was covered.
- *Projects* are included in each chapter to stimulate class discussions and encourage review as well as to provide opportunities for independent extension of text material.

■ *For Your Information* sections at the end of each chapter provide annotated lists of books, technology, organizations, and journals that reinforce and extend the chapter coverage.

■ *Windows on Practice* offer first-hand accounts by practitioners about what it's like to be in the field.

■ *Point of View* offers an enhanced perspective on issues affecting special education.

■ *Glossary* at the end of the text offers readers definitions of all key terms that appear in boldface type in text.

The text also features examples from two teachers who shared their experiences working with students receiving special education. Descriptions of what Kim Bazan, a fifth grade teacher, and Larry Williams, a secondary school teacher, do appear as illustrative examples of content described in selected chapters. Kim and Larry also helped us compile "top ten" lists of teaching tips that appear in the chapters addressing specific categories of students receiving special education. Appendices at the end of the book include the following useful resource materials: a directory of professional associations providing services to people with disabilities and their families, the code of ethics of the Council for Exceptional Children (CEC), and sections from the CEC's policy statement on standards for professional practices in special education.

Instructional Components that Accompany the Text

■ **Instructor's Resources**   This teaching aid has been expanded and thoroughly updated and revised to reflect new text content.

Part I contains model syllabi for organizing course materials and activities. This is especially useful for new instructors or those who are using the text for the first time.

Part II includes chapter-by-chapter materials for student Study Guide handouts. These include key-terms worksheets with definitions, activities, sample multiple-choice and short-answer questions, and additional resources and readings. For the instructor's convenience, these handouts are formatted for easy photocopying and distribution to students as needed.

Part III offers chapter-by-chapter materials for the instructor, including chapter outlines, annotated lecture outlines with class activities and discussion ideas.

Part IV contains a complete set of assessment materials. The Test Bank provides thirty multiple choice questions, five short answer and essay questions, and ideas for portfolio assessment for each chapter.

Part V includes several case studies written specifically for this text. Accompanying each case are suggestions for discussion and activities.

Part VI offers guidelines for using the videotape "Window on Practice," a day in the life of Lynn Wilcox, a special education practitioner in rural Nebraska.

- **Computerized Test Generator**   The test items contained in the *Instructor's Resources* are also available in an interactive computerized form on adoption of the text. It is formatted for both IBM and Mac versions. On-line testing and ESAGRADE are new features in this program.
- **Transparencies**   A set of colorful transparencies is available to each instructor upon adoption of the text. The transparencies feature figures from the text and highlight key content covered in the chapters.
- **Videotape**   A fifteen-minute videotape entitled "Window on Practice" effectively shows the major themes of the text by portraying a day in the life of Lynn Wilcox, a special education supervisor in a rural cooperative in Nebraska.

Acknowledgements

This revision represents a significant effort to address changes that are occurring in special education. It would not have been possible without the support and assistance of many colleagues and friends.

A number of reviewers made helpful suggestions and provided valuable feedback at various stages in the development of this book. We wish to thank the following people for their efforts and contributions to the content of this edition.

For Their Comments to Surveys

Debbie Schell-Frank, University of Colorado, Denver
Sharon Suritsky, Penn State University
Edmund Coombe, West Virginia University
Joe Wehby, Vanderbilt University
Geoff Schultz, Indiana University
Jeanne Repetto, University of Florida
Tina Oxer, Michigan State University
Janet Spector, University of Maine, Orono
John Wheeler, University of South Dakota
Gary Clark, University of Kansas
Lee Truesdell, Queens College

For Their Evaluations of Manuscript

Peggy Crossley, University of Arkansas
Robert Gable, Old Dominion
Blanche Glimps, Marygrove College
Susan Glor-Scheib, University of Pittsburgh
Placido Arturo Hoernicke, Fort Hays State University
Asha Jitendra, Texas Tech University
Donna McNear, Rum River Special Education Cooperative
Cindy Okolo, University of Delaware, Newark

Geoff Schultz, Indiana University NW
Karen Sniezek, California State University, Stanislaus
Fred Spooner, University of North Carolina, Charlotte
Mary M. Jensen, Western Illinois University
Paul Zionts, Central Michigan University

Professionals associated with Houghton Mifflin have made the work a pleasure. Loretta Wolozin provided perceptive leadership as well as unending support and friendship. Carol Newman and Lisa Mafrici helped us attend to details that sometimes make publishing a book more like a "never ending story" than an "unforgotten classic." Doug Gordon worked tirelessly and seemingly effortlessly to improve what we had written and ensure that the message was not overlooked by the medium. Dr. Mary M. Jensen of Western Illinois University developed an outstanding resource for instructors. Dr. Cindy Okolo of the University of Delaware contributed valuable information on special technology resources throughout the text. Dr. Michael Casby of Michigan State University gave us important material for Chapter 9. The efforts of these people, plus the copyeditor, art, and production staff, are appreciated, and we want to thank them all, one more time.

The patience, understanding, and love of our wives, Faye and Kate, are also a deeply appreciated part of this book as are the dedication and support of our children, Amy, Heather, Kathryn, and Mike, who help us remember on a daily basis that good teaching pays off. Finally, we recognize Kirby and Reggie who seemed to know when "time for a walk" would provide a needed opportunity for content to percolate so we could return to the rigors of writing renewed.

James E. Ysseldyke
Bob Algozzine

Special Education

A Practical Approach for Teachers

Fundamentals of Special Education

What is the kind of education that people call "special," and how does it differ from regular education? To answer these questions, Chapter 1 considers the meaning of concepts like *normality* and *exceptionality* and the ways in which we categorize students who receive special education. The chapter also takes a broad look at our society's reactions to exceptionality and the effects of those reactions on the lives of students who are exceptional.

Chapter 2 focuses on a key feature of today's educational landscape—the great diversity of students in American schools. Because students vary so widely in culture, language, ethnic group, and family background, virtually everyone is "exceptional" in some sense. Yet not every student re-

ceives special education. The chapter explores how special education fits into the spectrum of diversity, how eligibility decisions are made, and how special education services are delivered.

In Chapter 3 we examine another fundamental aspect of special education: the laws and court cases that have expanded the rights of people with disabilities and mandated a free, appropriate public education for all. The chapter discusses the most important legal mandates and illustrates their role in shaping special education today.

Chapter

1

What Is Special Education and What Does It Mean to Be Exceptional?

Focusing Questions

- What is special education and why do we have it?
- What standards do educators use to define normality?
- Who receives special education in today's schools?
- How many students receive special education?
- What is it like to be exceptional?
- How do you react to people who are exceptional?

C. J. rolls himself from class to class in his wheelchair, chatting incessantly with his friends about Saturday's Yankees game. Bobby and his friends stop playing when he has to take a break to use his oxygen tank. C. J. and Bobby are students with disabilities who attend school in regular classrooms in Johnson City, New York. They are included in the general education instructional programs in that city. As recently as 10 years ago students like C. J. and Bobby were educated in set-aside structures, special schools, institutions, or special classes. They did not participate in educational programs with their nondisabled peers. Times have indeed changed. ■

The best for all students

If you are going to be a teacher, you will be expected to get the very best out of your students—*all* of the students you are assigned to teach. Teachers have always wanted to get the best from all of their students, but the nature of "all" has changed over the years. It now includes students like C. J. and Bobby. Their story was featured recently on the front page of the *New York Times*. The education of students with disabilities is front-page news, and this text is about the education of students like C. J. and Bobby.

Kim Bazan is a friend of ours who teaches fifth grade. The enthusiasm she showed in her college education classes is still evident in her teaching. She loves the variety in teaching, and the opportunity to help students of all types grow and develop. She's a good teacher, concerned about her students and informed (through professional associations, books, and journals) about current practices in education. We've written this book for people like Kim.

Darryl is one of Kim's students. Whatever the level or kind of work that Kim assigns him, Darryl demonstrates superior academic performance. He works hard, sometimes redoing an assignment after the final grade has been recorded. Most of his classmates look to Darryl for academic, athletic, social, and emotional leadership during the school day. Kim finds teaching Darryl a challenge because she must always be prepared to stay a step ahead of him and provide him with extra work.

Marti is another of Kim's students. Marti always seems to be behind. Yet she is a joy to have in class, talkative and funny. Many of her classmates enjoy helping Marti because she appreciates that help so much. Kim derives a lot of satisfaction from working with Marti.

Students with special needs

Kim was prepared to teach students with special learning needs like Darryl and Marti. As she learned to become a teacher, Kim took courses in which she learned how to modify her teaching to accommodate the individual differences that are common in most classrooms. But now and again she has a student whose special needs make teaching difficult. Ray is one of those students. He comes from a home where both parents are alcoholics. He does not trust adults and often takes out his anger with them on his classmates. When he is not physically disrupting the class, Ray is "entertaining" his classmates with stories, songs, underarm "rips," or animal noises. The rules that are important to many of Kim's students (asking permission to leave the room, raising a hand to ask a question or offer information) are not important to Ray. The things that many of Kim's students do in school to get her attention (finishing their work quickly, sharing stories) are not the things that Ray does to get attention. Ray's behavior in school is neither expected nor accepted by his teacher or classmates.

Phyllis is another of Kim's students. She is a challenge, not because of what she does, but because of what she does not do. Phyllis was born blind. She needs special help with many of the ordinary things children are expected to do in school. Kim has to consider Phyllis's visual functioning when she plans activities for her.

Definition of special education

Kim is a regular education teacher, but some of her students also receive special education services. They receive instruction from special education teachers and speech and language therapists, and assistance from other school personnel like school psychologists and physical therapists. **Education** is the process of learning and changing as a result of schooling and other experiences. **Special education** is instruction designed for students with disabilities or gifts and talents who also have special learning needs. Some of these students have difficulty learning in regular classrooms; they need special education to function in school. Others generally do well in regular classrooms, but they need special education to help them master certain skills to reach their full potential in school.

Students are considered **exceptional** when they (1) meet the criteria for being classified as exceptional and (2) require a modification of school practices, or special educational services, to develop to maximum capacity. The term *exceptional* includes students like Darryl who are gifted or talented; for legal reasons, however, most of special education is focused on education of students with disabilities. A **disability** results from a medical, social, or learning difficulty that interferes significantly with the student's normal growth and development, such as the ability to profit from schooling experiences or the ability to participate successfully in work activities. Special education is evidence of society's willingness to recognize and respond to the individual needs of students and the limits of regular school programs to accommodate those needs. This book is about responding to individual needs, accommodating students with disabilities, and teaching students with special learning needs.

Definition of disability

The work of a special education teacher

Kim's friend Larry Williams is a special education teacher. He teaches in one of the high schools in the town where Kim lives. Larry became a teacher because he wanted to help people with special needs. Sandy is one of Larry's students. He is an exceptional athlete, with awards in football, basketball, and baseball. He would like to go to college, but his academic abilities are not as keen as his athletic performances. Sandy spends about two hours a day in Larry's classroom working on his reading and mathematics skills, and he is making considerable progress. Janet also goes to Larry's room for special instruction one period a day. She is working on her study skills. Just like the other teachers in his school, Larry teaches five periods a day and has one planning period. His "basic skills" classes help students learn to read, write, and do math better. His "learning strategies" classes help students develop skills they can use when they return to their regular academic classes. He also teaches one class of students who have social and emotional problems.

Even though Kim and Larry teach in different settings, the types of students and the ways they teach are similar. For example, they both structure their teaching to accommodate their students' individual differences. They both use information from tests and classroom observations to plan instruction and to evaluate the effects of that instruction. They both have to deal with discipline in the classroom to be effective teachers. If you teach, whether in a regular classroom or special education, you will probably have students like Kim's or Larry's, and you will need a similar range of skills to make sure that each student receives the best possible education.

This book is about special education. You will learn about people who receive special education, the people who provide it, and assessment and teaching practices. In this first chapter you learn what special education is, who receives it, and what it means to be exceptional.

What Is Special Education?

What is this branch of education that we call "special," why does it exist, and how does it attempt to deal with children who are exceptional? As we prepared this text we asked students in grades 1 to 9 to tell us what special education is. Their responses are shown in the following Window on Practice. They are both enlightening and amusing. Young children have no idea what special education is, but by about grade 4 they begin to view special education as a service that helps students who are experiencing academic difficulty. From grade 7 on, students typically view special education as a set of services for students who are "slow."

As we noted earlier, special education is instruction designed for students with disabilities or gifts and talents who have special learning needs. Students are considered candidates for special education when they have such special learning needs. They are allowed to receive special education when professionals decide they meet specific eligibility criteria. In the present-day United States almost 5 million students receive some form of special education. They are being taught in a variety of instructional environments designed to meet their unique learning needs by specially trained teachers who use many of the instructional approaches and activities used with students who are not considered exceptional. How did this complex system evolve?

The very first schools in this country were established in Massachusetts in the early seventeenth century. But states did not begin to make school attendance compulsory until around 1850; by 1916, children in every state were required to attend school. Although requiring students to go to school was probably a good idea, making it happen was not easy. For one thing, many

Window on Practice

What Is Special Education?

Following are some responses we gathered from students on their views of what special education is.

"It's for learning big jobs, like how to fix cars." (Gr. 1)

"To learn how to do a special job." (Gr. 2)

"It is for people that need extra help on writing, jump rope, writing facts and all that stuff. For people that can't hear, talk, walk, stand, look, feel, run. People that are in wheelchairs and the people that can't write or color. People that can not see very well and the people that cant do anything at all." (Gr. 3)

"My special education is when I am having trouble with something my [teacher] stops what she is doing and help with my problem. Special education means what is your special thing in school that you just like." (Gr. 3)

"It's for kids who are real smart or mentally retarded." (Gr. 4)

"Weard stuff!" (Gr. 5)

"Music, gym, library, art." (Gr. 5)

"It is work that you don't know how to do but you learn how to do it." (Gr. 5)

"If you don't know stuff when you just come to school it will help you figure out stuff." (Gr. 6)

"A learning place for people who are slow or maybe can't walk or people who can not think right but they can learn the same way as us." (Gr. 6)

"It is for learning, like if you need to do better, like if your in the lowest math group having to go to special education will help you do better." (Gr. 6)

"It's top secret." (Gr. 7)

"When some one teachs you in a way that you learn and don't get confused as you allmost allways do." (Gr. 7)

"I couldn't tell you it's too important." (Gr. 7)

"An education for people who have learning problems, or for people who are high potential and are far ahead of others in their grade and age group." (Gr. 7)

"Special education is for kids who are slower in understanding things. They could be 14 and not able to write but they will try to learn as much as possible because they want to be like all the other 14 year olds." (Gr. 8)

"Education for people who are slow in a subject. It is extra help or tutoring if you have trouble in school. If you are in the classes it doesn't mean you are dumb because people are better at some activities and worse at others." (Gr. 9)

"I think S.E. is like a class to help slow learners. And it could also be a class for extra special brainy kids." (Gr. 9)

"Special education is when people need more education than what they are getting." (Gr. 9)

families were not convinced that school was the best place to receive an education. (In fact, today a growing number of families educate their children at home.) Another issue was deciding what to do with students once they were in school. The class-graded system that exists today was one solution to the problem of structuring the school day. Early educators reasoned that students should be taught specific content and that the content could best be organized into graded units.

Students with special learning needs always have been (and always will be) a part of the educational system in America. But before they were required to attend school, they did not attract much attention. Progressive social policy brought them to school. When traditional graded units failed to transmit content to these students, or when teachers and other school personnel argued that the presence of exceptional students was interfering with the training of other students and hindering the education of the exceptional students themselves, physicians and early special educators developed a formal alternative to the regular education system.

Special education as a separate system

By the beginning of the twentieth century, public educational programs therefore began to offer two primary choices: Students were taught in a lock-step graded class or in an ungraded special class. Administrators of that era believed that special education classes were clearinghouses for students who would otherwise be going to institutions for physically, mentally, or morally "deviant" members of society. Once assigned to special classes, students often remained in those classes for their entire school careers. Moreover, students were often placed in special classes on the recommendation of one teacher or on the basis of their performance on one test. This system produced special class enrollments in which minority students were heavily overrepresented. In addition, there were problems with the programs themselves. Some institutions and special schools were substituting harsh discipline for the educational services exceptional students needed.

Inadequacies of the separate system

The basic either/or structure—either regular graded classes or separate, usually ungraded special education—continued for over half a century. With very rare exceptions, today's adults with disabilities who recall segregated facilities or separate classes cannot say enough about the inadequacies of their academic training. When comparing their education with that of siblings or neighbors who were not disabled, they speak only of the gaps. For example, they mention subjects, such as science, that they never studied, maps they never saw, field trips they never took, books that were never available, assignments that were often too easy, expectations of their capacity (by nearly all teachers) that were too low (Asch, 1989).

Challenges to the separate system

By the 1960s parents and professionals had mounted strong challenges to the old system, and special education began a period of rapid change that continues today. The current special education system in the United States has its roots in the methods used to treat disabled people in Europe and Scandinavia more than one hundred years ago. That system entitles exceptional students to a free, appropriate public education. Federal laws now make it illegal to discriminate against people because they are disabled. This means that people cannot be denied an education or a job because of a disabling condition. It also means that records are kept of the types and numbers of students receiving special education in this country. Federal law does not require states to provide special education to gifted and talented students, so the number of those students receiving special education services does not appear in annual reports to Congress. Several states, however, have passed laws mandating special services for this group of exceptional students.

Varieties of special education today

Today's special education takes account of the fact that different students have different special needs. Some need help dealing with the social and psychological problems they face as a result of their exceptionality. Many students who are gifted, for example, feel isolated from their classmates. Special education programs not only challenge them intellectually, but also help them deal with their feelings of alienation. Other exceptional students need special serv-

All students are entitled to a
free, appropriate education.
© *Laura Dwight.*

ices because of what they are *not* able to do, because some disabling condition
limits their ability to learn in the typical educational program. Students who
are blind, for example, may need to be taught to read in braille or by means of
large-print books. Students who cannot hear need instruction in a manual sign
language or some other special communication system. These students also
face social and psychological challenges. They have to learn to cope with not
only the challenge of their handicapping condition, but also other people's reactions to their conditions. For many students whose special needs mean learning in separate educational settings, there's the added knowledge that their
educational experiences are not like those of other people.

By dealing with these diverse needs, special education has become a sophisticated series of educational alternatives that is considered the right of every
student with disabilities. Educators must make choices about who receives special education services, and the choice usually depends on ideas of "normality"
and "abnormality." For instance, when our friend Kim decided that her student Marti was not learning certain subjects at a "normal" rate, Kim recommended that Marti receive special assistance. But how do educators reach such
decisions about normality and abnormality, and what do these concepts really
mean?

Defining Normality and Abnormality

In a diverse society, it is difficult to define what we mean by the terms *normal*
and *abnormal*. Most people have standards on which they make judgments
about others. These standards are based on experience and often change, de-

Normality is a relative concept and deciding when behavior is normal is not a simple task. *Frank Siteman/ Stock, Boston, Inc.*

pending on specific circumstances. Studying how people define normality helps us understand the foundations of special education because definitions of normality serve as the basis for judgments about whether someone is exceptional and what it means to be exceptional.

What is abnormal?

Would you use the word *abnormal* to describe someone who prefers milk in coffee? How about someone who puts ketchup on fried eggs? Is it abnormal to wash your hands twenty-five times a day? Is it normal to refrain from eating for five days or to laugh during a religious ceremony? Behaviors or characteristics, in themselves, are neither normal nor exceptional. They generate actions or reactions by others who judge them to be so.

Changing perceptions of normality

Normality is a relative concept. A person is considered normal in our society or in school as long as he or she behaves like the majority or behaves in ways that parents, teachers, or principals think of as normal. Perceptions of normal and abnormal change over time. As society becomes more and more diverse, perceptions of normality and abnormality change. Behaviors once evidenced by few people (and therefore considered abnormal) become evidenced by more and more people; when a large enough number of people demonstrate the behavior, it is no longer considered abnormal.

Knowledge of normal development

The decisions we make about exceptional people before, during, and after school are based in large measure on what we know about normal development. For example, by the age of 3, most children have been toilet trained, their attention spans have developed enough to listen to stories, and they use their vocabularies of about 200 words to carry on conversations. By 4, most children are running, jumping, and riding tricycles and have the fine motor skills to cut with scissors, do puzzles, and make things. Youngsters this age also are beginning to understand the concept of numbers. By the time they enter first grade, most children have started to learn from books and to play for long periods of time with their peers. Well-developed speech and language skills mark the early school years. By the end of fourth grade, most youngsters can read, write, do math, and solve problems proficiently. By the time they enter middle or junior high school, their independent learning skills are developed and many of the social skills they will have as adults are in place.

Decisions about special needs

Parents and teachers and other professionals use their knowledge of normal development to make decisions about the special learning needs of students. A two-year-old who is beginning to use a few words to get what he wants is normal; a two-year-old who speaks in full sentences is exceptional. What about a fourth-grader who is not reading fluently? Normal or abnormal? It depends. Most of us would agree that the behavior is not normal. But if the child just moved to this country and does not speak English as a first language, the behavior might very well be normal. Or if the child experienced a series of traumatic events in earlier grades, again the behavior might be normal. Our judgment of a behavior thus depends not only on the behavior, but also on the circumstances in which we find it.

Negative connotations of terms

As professionals refine their definitions of normality, they often assign names to behaviors that are not normal. Professionals from differing disciplines use different names in their discussions of abnormality, most of which carry negative connotations. For example, medical professionals use terms like *pathological* and *diseased*. Psychologists talk about people being *abnormal, mentally ill, psychotic,* or *neurotic*. Sociologists and social workers use terms like *deviant*. Educators use terms like *different, exceptional, disabled, special, disordered,* or *handicapped*. Educators try to keep these terms free of negative connotations but are not always able to avoid their harmful effects, as we discuss later in this chapter.

Establishing categories of exceptionality

Within the broad field of exceptionality, special educators assign names to categories of exceptionality. Although some characteristics overlap, each category represents a discrete cluster of attributes. To decide who fits in each category, educators write definitions of the categories. They also state specific criteria to use in deciding whether or not one is a member of a categorical group. Decisions about normality rest on evaluations of the extent to which individual differences vary from accepted standards. These standards, which we use as operational criteria in the decision-making process, are based on statistical, medical, and social norms. In some cases, research data support the decision. Many times, physical or medical information provides a basis for evaluating skills, characteristics, and behaviors. Decisions about normality also are made using conventional wisdom, public opinion, and other socially accepted standards, values, and norms.

Statistical Standards

Statistics track performance, giving us information we need to distinguish between exceptionality and normality. Many human behaviors and characteris-

Figure 1.1
Normal Curve

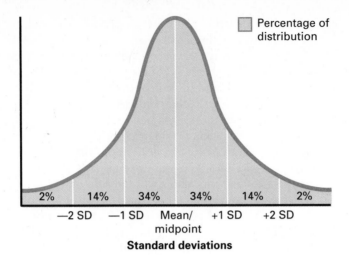

Percentage of distribution

2%   14%   34%   34%   14%   2%

—2 SD   —1 SD   Mean/   +1 SD   +2 SD
midpoint

Standard deviations

Characteristics of the normal curve

tics fall into a pattern of distribution that forms a bell shape (Figure 1.1). This symmetrical distribution is called the *normal curve*.

The shape of the normal curve is exactly the same on either side of its midpoint, so we can predict the area between points on the curve. The midpoint is the *mean* (arithmetic average) of the curve. The degree to which occurrence of a behavior or characteristic differs from the mean is expressed in *standard deviation* (SD) units, each of which contains a fixed percentage of cases above and below the mean. As Figure 1.1 indicates, 34 percent of cases fall between the mean and 1 standard deviation above the mean. If we wanted to know the number of cases that fell within 1 standard deviation on *either* side of the mean, the answer would be 68 percent (34 percent above the mean and 34 percent below).

For example, the scores of high school students on the College Board examinations are normally distributed. The mean score is 500, and the standard deviation is 100. We know, then, that 68 percent of the students score between 400 and 600—that is, between 1 standard deviation above the mean and 1 standard deviation below the mean. This information helps us interpret a student's score. It also helps us predict how a population of students will do on the tests.

Using the normal curve to define exceptionality

The normal curve gives us a numerical basis for making decisions about the probability that a behavior or characteristic will occur. Special educators use these standards in defining exceptionality, focusing on the small percentage of cases at either side of the curve. For example, the definition of mental retardation is based on the idea that intelligence is normally distributed (meaning that it follows the normal curve) in the general population. In this context, IQ scores that are 2 standard deviations below the average on intelligence tests are used to identify students with retardation. Giftedness also is defined in terms of performance on intelligence tests. Here scores 2 standard deviations above the mean indicate exceptionality. When these criteria are applied, we can expect

Bring Your Learning to Life

Distinguishing Disabilities from Special Learning Needs

Bobby and C. J. are considered abnormal from a medical perspective because C. J. walks and Bobby breathes differently from other children. C. J. needs a wheelchair to get about in the environment, has medical needs, but does not have unique learning needs. It is necessary for those who teach C. J. to make modifications or adaptations in their instruction when he is in physical education and on the playground to enable him to participate. But he doesn't receive special education services. In the regular sixth-grade classroom his instruction in mathematics, social studies, and music is just like that of the other students.

Bobby, on the other hand, has academic difficulties in addition to his breathing problems. He is experiencing significant difficulty "catching on to the basics" in kindergarten. His teacher reports that he doesn't know his colors or letters, and says that he has difficulty with basic concepts like up, next to, and begin or start. She has been getting consultation from the special education resource teacher. If Bobby continues to show very slow progress, the kindergarten teacher will refer him to the child study team for psychoeducational evaluation.

that about 2 percent of the population will be identified as gifted and about 2 percent as mentally retarded.

Medical Standards

In medicine, normality means the presence of normal signs or the absence of disease symptoms. The medical standard for normal human body temperature is 98.6 degrees. It was determined by evaluating many "healthy" people. Temperatures above or below that point are one indicator of illness. In the same way, doctors use blood tests to check for abnormal levels of body chemicals, the symptoms of certain diseases or health problems. In the same way, standards in blood pressure, respiration rate, and pulse rate are used to determine physical well-being.

Medical standards of exceptionality

Genetic abnormalities, prenatal problems, infections, and physical trauma can cause special learning needs. You probably remember from high school biology that normal cells contain forty-six chromosomes. Any deviation from this standard number produces physical and biological abnormalities. More than one hundred genetic disorders have been identified. One of them, Down syndrome, causes retardation. Most people with the condition have forty-seven chromosomes instead of forty-six. German measles, encephalitis, and other infectious diseases also can cause retardation if they occur during critical periods of development. Anoxia (insufficient oxygen to the fetus during the birth process) destroys brain cells, producing cerebral palsy, mental retardation, or other exceptional conditions. Malnutrition and lead paint poisoning are physical traumas that increase the risk of mental retardation.

In the beginning of this chapter we talked about C. J. (a boy in a wheelchair) and Bobby (a boy who had difficulty breathing). Both boys would meet the definition of *abnormal* from a medical perspective. C. J. does not walk in a normal way, and Bobby does not breathe in a normal way. The Census Bureau has used a medical definition of abnormality in defining disability: Does this person have a physical, mental, or other health condition that has lasted six or more months and that limits the kind or amount of work this person can do at a job, or prevents this person from working at a job? (Haber & McNeil, 1983).

Medical standards give us a benchmark against which to gauge exceptionality. The logic of using these standards to determine who or what is exceptional is appealing. Specific symptoms appear to be associated with specific problems. But most students who are exceptional are identified through other means.

Social Standards

Normality as a set of rules

Sociologists, psychologists, anthropologists, and educators often define normality in terms of a society's or subculture's code of behavior. Certain behaviors are expected as part of normal schooling. Many of these behaviors are written down or otherwise clarified in the form of explicit rules. But schools also operate with a set of implied rules, rules that although unwritten, require student conformity no less than explicit rules. For example, students are generally expected to demonstrate competence in basic skills (reading, writing, math) by the end of the third grade. Not being able to read, write, or compute to accepted or adopted standards is a form of exceptional behavior, as is performing above those standards.

Variations in social standards

But the rules applicable at any given school may depend on the culture of the school, which varies greatly from one school or community to another. Moreover, social standards change with setting and with the kinds of experiences people have. Research has found high rates of mental illness in inner-city areas. This finding has led some to conclude that community attitudes and standards play a part in how we define normality. Others believe that abnormal behaviors are learned by associating with people who have abnormal lifestyles. Certainly what we know about the person being judged influences at least our initial reaction to that individual's behavior. We expect the younger brothers and sisters of a legendary class clown to act up in class, and we expect the siblings of a gifted student to do well.

Role of teachers

Teachers play an important role in defining exceptionality, both in terms of their expectations for students and in terms of their difficulty handling specific behaviors. Because teachers are individuals and because they are working with individual students, we can't say with certainty how they will respond to their exceptional students. But we do know that in the course of elementary school, 50 to 60 percent of students are perceived to have behavior problems by at least one teacher. We also know that boys are less likely to show teacher-pleasing behaviors (self-control, being prepared for class, complying with teachers' requests); instead, they tend to be aggressive, noncompliant, and active—behaviors that teachers are more likely to have problems handling.

Subjectivity of social standards

Of all the standards used to judge normality, social standards are the most subjective. For example, some teachers believe students should be quiet during school; others believe students should actively communicate about their assignments and work together on them. You may recall the confusion created by two teachers with different standards in your own school career.

Who Receives Special Education?

Students considered exceptional in today's classrooms are those with disabilities and those who are gifted and talented. Using the various standards for defining normality and abnormality, educators and other professionals have established that some students require more and some require less instruction to master the content mastered by their nonexceptional peers. Sometimes they need different instruction than their nondisabled peers. Sometimes they need instruction in environments that are different from general education classrooms.

We believe the similarities between exceptional and nonexceptional students far exceed their differences. We recognize, however, that some of the differences are central to success in school, and so form the basis for the concern of teachers, parents, and students themselves.

Organization by categories

Today, most states organize their special education departments along categorical lines. A **category** is simply a name assigned to a group of exceptional students. Although the names of the categories vary slightly from state to state, special education generally is provided to students within each of the following groups.*

Visual Impairments   These students have special learning needs in areas requiring functional use of vision. (The word *functional* refers to the way an ability is actually used in daily life.) Of the school-age population 0.04 percent are classified in this category.

Hearing Impairments   These students have special learning needs in areas requiring functional use of hearing. Of the school-age population 0.11 percent are classified in this category.

* Throughout this passage the percentage figures are based on U.S. Department of Education (1993) and Office of Educational Research and Improvement (1993).

Deaf and Blind   These students have special learning needs in areas requiring functional use of hearing and vision. Less than 0.01 percent of the school-age population (the number is so small that it is listed as 0.00 percent of the population in the 1993 report to Congress) is classified in this category.

Orthopedic Impairments or Other Health Impairments   These students have special learning needs in areas requiring functional use of hands, arms, legs, feet, and other body parts. This category may also include students who have serious illnesses or medical conditions (for example, heart conditions). Less than 1 percent of the school-age population is classified in these two categories (0.09 percent for orthopedic impairments and 0.10 percent for other health impairments).

Mental Retardation   These students have special learning needs in areas requiring functional use of intelligence and adaptive behavior. About 0.96 percent of the school-age population is classified in this category.

Gifted and Talented   These students have special learning needs in areas requiring functional use of intelligence and artistic ability. About 3 to 5 percent of the school-age population is classified in this category.

Specific Learning Disabilities   These students have special learning needs in areas requiring functional use of listening, speaking, reading, writing, reasoning, and arithmetic skills. This is the largest category in special education, with about 3.9 percent of the school-age population. Half of all students with disabilities are considered learning disabled.

Serious Emotional Disturbance   These students have special learning needs in areas requiring functional use of social and emotional skills. About 0.69 percent of the school-age population is classified in this category.

Speech or Language Impairments   These students have special learning needs in areas requiring functional use of language and communication skills. Often the many varieties of speech and language disabilities are called *communication disorders*. About 1.73 percent of the school-age population is classified in this category.

Multiple Disabilities   These students have special learning needs in more than one area requiring functional use of skills. Less than 1 percent of the school-age population (about 0.17 percent) is classified in this category.

Traumatic Brain Injury   These students have brain injury caused by an external physical force or by an internal occurrence such as stroke. It does not include children born with brain injuries or who suffer brain injury as a result of birth trauma. The number of students classified in this category is so small that it is listed as 0.00 percent in the 1993 Annual Report to Congress.

Autism   Autism is a specific developmental disability that significantly affects communication and social interaction. About 0.01 percent of the school-age population is classified in this category.

Some states assign a consultant or supervisor to each group of exceptional students. In these states, local school districts usually organize their special education programs along categorical lines. Other states have a single administrator who is responsible for all groups of exceptional students. In these states, local programs are organized differently, and most students with special needs receive some part of their education in regular classes.

Variations in names of categories

Different names are used for the different categories, and there are very many abbreviations in special education. The categorical names just listed are used in federal legislation. The names we use in this text, however, vary somewhat from the federal terminology. Table 1.1 lists some common category abbreviations used in the different states.

Table 1.1   Common Categorical Abbreviations in Special Education

DB	Students who are deaf-blind
ECSE	Early childhood special education
GT	Gifted and talented
HH	Hard of hearing
POHI	Physical and other health impairments
HI	Hearing impaired
MR	Mentally retarded
EMR	Educable mentally retarded
SLBP	Specific learning and behavior problems
SLD	Specific learning disabilities
LD	Learning disabled
MI	Mentally impaired
MH	Mildly handicapped
MMMR	Mild to moderate mental retardation
SMR	Severe mental retardation
TMR	Trainable mentally retarded
MH	Multihandicapped
PMR	Profoundly mentally retarded
PH	Physically handicapped
OI	Orthopedically impaired
SED	Seriously emotionally disturbed
BD	Behavior disordered
ED	Emotionally disturbed
SM	Socially maladjusted
CD	Communication disordered
VH	Visually handicapped
VI	Visually impaired

How Many Students Receive Special Education?

Overall, nearly 5 million individuals between birth and 21 years of age receive special education services in school or community settings in the United States every year. That number is roughly equivalent to the number of full-time undergraduates in four-year colleges and universities in this country. In fact, it is about the same as the combined population of North Dakota, South Dakota, Montana, Nevada, Idaho, and Wyoming and exceeds the population of each of thirty-two states.

Rising number of students in special education

The number of students with disabilities receiving special education services has increased steadily in recent years, as shown in Figure 1.2. Between 1977 and 1992, more than 1.2 million new students were identified as needing special education. The average rate of increase during those years was almost 2 percent a year. This substantial increase (almost 35 percent) in the number of students enrolled in special education classes occurred at the same time that enrollment in general education fell by almost 6 percent.

Increase varies by category

Growth in the number of students is different for different categories. The highest growth is in learning disabilities, and there is a decline in the number of students classified as mentally retarded or as having a speech and language disorder. Figure 1.3 illustrates these changes in percentage terms. The numbers served in the various conditions also vary considerably by state.

New teaching positions

The growing number of students in special education programs means that plenty of new teaching positions have been created in the field. Using a conservative average of fifteen students for each special class teacher, about forty-seven hundred new teachers were needed each year from 1977 to 1993. The growth in enrollment also has created challenges for school personnel who

Figure 1.2
Increase in Number of Students Receiving Special Education Services
Note: Based on individuals between birth and age 21.

Source: As reported in U.S. Department of Education (1993). *Fifteenth annual report to Congress on implementation of the Individuals with Disabilities Education Act.* Washington, D.C.: Author; Office of Special Education Programs, Data Analysis Systems (DANS).

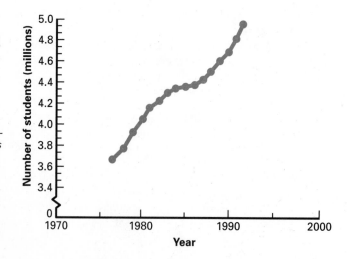

Figure 1.3
Breakdown by Category for Students with Disabilities Who Received Special Education Services, School Years 1976–77 and 1991–92

Note: Graph indicates the number of students in each disability category as a percentage of the total in all disability categories. Data based on children and adolescents ages 6 to 21 who received special education services under guidelines established by federal statutes.

Source: As reported in U.S. Department of Education (1993). *Fifteenth annual report to Congress on implementation of the Individuals with Disabilities Education Act.* Washington, D.C.: Author; Office of Special Education Programs, Data Analysis Systems (DANS).

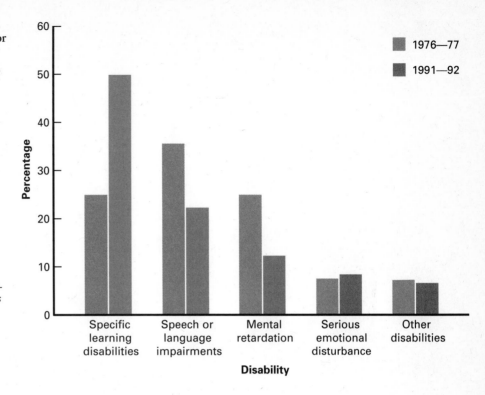

The concept of prevalence

have to decide how to pay for expanding programs. The costs of educating exceptional students sometimes compete with the costs of educating students in regular programs.

In Table 1.2 we have listed each of the categories of exceptionality as defined by the federal government. We show the percentage of all students who are currently classified in each category. This percentage is called the **prevalence.** Gifted- and talentedness may be the most prevalent category of all, although the classification procedures of individual states vary so much that the number of students who are gifted and talented is not exactly comparable to the figures for other categories. Among students with disabilities, the most prevalent conditions are learning disabilities, speech and language impairments, mental retardation, and serious emotional disturbance. As the numbers in the third column indicate, 93 percent of students with disabilities fall into these four categories.

Table 1.2 also indicates the kinds of special education needs that are primary for each of the categories. As we will illustrate when we discuss each of the categories in detail, there is considerable overlap both in characteristics and in special education needs. There is no one-to-one link between category name and educational need or service.

Table 1.2   Overview of Special Education Categories

Federal Category	Prevalence in Total School-Age Population (percent)	Category as Percent of All Students with Disabilities	Primary Special Education Needs
Gifted and talented	3–5	—	Faster pacing in curriculum Broadening curriculum Maintaining positive social relationships
Specific learning disabilities	3.90	49.9	Improving basic academic skills Improving social skills
Speech or language impairments	1.73	22.2	Reducing speech problems Improving language skills Improving academic skills
Mental retardation	0.96	12.3	Improving functional skills Improving social relations Improving academic skills
Serious emotional disturbance	0.69	8.9	Improving social skills Improving social relationships Improving academic skills
Multiple disabilities	0.17	2.2	Improving academic skills Improving mobility skills Improving functional skills
Orthopedic impairments	0.09	1.1	Improving physical skills Improving academic skills
Other health impairments	0.10	1.3	Improving physical skills Improving functional skills
Hearing impairments	0.11	1.3	Improving language skills Improving academic skills
Visual impairments	0.04	0.5	Developing reading skills Improving academic skills
Deaf-blindness	Less than 0.01	Less than 0.1	Improving mobility Developing communication
Autism	0.01	0.1	Improving social skills Developing communication
Traumatic brain injury	Less than 0.01	Less than 0.01	Improving physical skills Improving academic skills

Note: Figures are based on children and adolescents between the ages of 6 and 21.
Source: U.S. Department of Education (1993). *Fifteenth annual report to Congress on the implementation of the Individuals with Disabilities Act.* Washington, DC: Author; Office of Educational Research and Improvement. *National excellence: A case for developing America's talent* (1993). Washington, DC: U.S. Department of Education.

Reactions to Exceptionality

Typical reactions to exceptionality

How do you react to people who are exceptional? Do you look away from the woman in a wheelchair? Do you speak loudly to the blind man who asks you for directions on campus? Are you surprised when your friend who's brilliant in math misspells a word? It's not unusual to be embarrassed by a handicapping condition, to assume that one sensory impairment means another, or to expect that being gifted and talented extends to all aspects of life. The problem is that these typical reactions to exceptionality have enormous impacts on the behaviors of those who are exceptional. They force them to deal not only with the exceptional condition itself, but also with what the condition means to others.

Our reactions to exceptionality—our own or that of others—are influenced by three factors: the nature of our individual tolerance, the cause of the exceptionality, and the label assigned to it.

The Nature of Individual Tolerance

All of us respond in different ways to the things around us. Certain things are more important to some of us than others. For some, a defeat on the basketball court may be just another loss; for others, it may be a critical casualty in a Cinderella season. We react to diversity in much the same way. Some of us are uncomfortable with those who have a physical disability; others are put off by mental or emotional disabilities. Still others have difficulty interacting with those whose disabilities are pronounced.

Different teacher responses

Among teachers, similar behaviors in the classroom can evoke different reactions. For example, the extent to which disruptive behavior is tolerated by teachers varies widely. Students who are outspoken in class may be encouraged, tolerated, or punished by different teachers. Moreover, teachers' responses are likely to depend on the particular type of disruptive behavior under consideration. Some teachers may permit students to speak out in class, but they have difficulty coping with students who are withdrawn and uncomfortable participating in class discussions. Other teachers may prefer their students to behave quietly and to listen attentively—they can't handle aggressive, candid students.

Recognizing similarities

Because exceptional people are all unique individuals, it makes no sense to tell you how to act around them. Because *you* are a unique individual, it is difficult for us to predict how exceptional people will interact with you. But we can tell you one thing: Although exceptional people are different in some ways, they are more like you than not. It is important to understand the differences and to respond to them matter-of-factly; it is even more important to recognize the similarities, to treat people with exceptionalities as you would anyone.

The Cause of the Exceptionality

Infections, physical trauma, prenatal problems, genetic abnormalities, environmental problems, and many other factors can cause a disabling condition.

Often the cause of an exceptionality influences the way people respond to it. C. J., the sixth-grade boy in the wheelchair we described at the beginning of this chapter, is viewed as an "all-right-guy" by both his classmates and his teachers. They enjoy being with him and having him around. Teachers have a different view of Theodore and Ronnie, who are described in the Bring Your Learning to Life feature on page 25. Teachers see those two boys as having difficulty in school not because of physical or mental disabilities but because of environmental circumstances. Even though teachers may sympathize with Theodore and Ronnie, they probably feel less tolerant than they do toward C. J.

Tolerance and "controllability"

Teachers, of course, are not alone in this kind of reaction. Organic impairments—physical problems that are clearly out of the individual's control—seem more acceptable than functional impairments—problems that have no physical cause and therefore appear to be "controllable." For example, most of us do not mind being held up in traffic by a person crossing the street in a wheelchair or with a white cane; however, we react very differently to somebody who deliberately slows us down. Most of us also are more willing to help a person who can't do something than a person who simply refuses to do it.

If you were told these students had a "learning disability," how would you react? What if you were told they were "gifted"? *David Young-Wolff/ PhotoEdit.*

Bring Your Learning to Life

Students from Different Environmental Circumstances

Theodore lives in a one-room apartment just two blocks from school. He shares this space with his mother, who is a prostitute and heroin addict. If Theodore wants room to play, he has to use the parking lot in front of the apartment. Very often his mother works all night and the boy gets little sleep. Mom's heroin addiction leaves her either strung out, euphoric, or asleep; none of these conditions allows for much quality parenting time or maintaining the household. Theodore's clothes are old and dirty. Meals are strictly up to him. As a nine-year-old he learned where to find any money Mom had left over after buying drugs. He shops for himself, buys whatever food suits his fancy, and eats it when he has a chance. The two have lived in the apartment under these circumstances for three years. After three years, Theodore is chronically fatigued, malnourished, underdressed, and depressed. He has no power to change what is going on in his life and no reason to believe that things will ever change. Theodore puts little energy into school. He spends an hour or so sleeping each day there.

Ronnie's dad was a biker. Most often he was gone. When he was away, Ronnie spent time with a family friend. When his dad was home, he shared his sense of values and perceptions of the world with his son. Fighting was a valued activity. The only thing better than fighting was the ability to project such a dangerous presence that others gave in to your demands without a struggle. Ronnie was white, and his dad made it clear that any nonwhites were enemies whose presence required a violent reaction.

Due to the father's alternative lifestyle, Ronnie was not enrolled in school until he was 7. The results were predictable. During the first month, there was a great deal of fighting on the playground and in class. When teachers asked Ronnie to participate in classroom activities, they met with defiance. The boy made it clear to the principal that he had his own set of rules. During conferences with school officials, the dad made it clear that he approved of Ronnie's behavior.

The Label Assigned to the Condition

Negative labels

Labels are names we assign to behaviors, people, or the conditions people exhibit. We use labels to organize the world around us. Yet labels can also lead us to behave toward people in certain ways. To the extent that the labels are negative, especially if they are inaccurate, they may lead us to behave in inappropriately negative ways toward other people. You probably have signed up for courses that are "gifts," avoided professors who are "bears," formed negative impressions before meeting another person you've been told is a "snot," "conceited," arrogant," or a "bully." Students can be labeled early in their school careers as "slow," "disruptive," or "smart." You may have gone through

Point of View

The Importance of Labeling: A Fable

MILO AND TOCK WALKED up to the door, whose brass name plate read simply "THE GIANT," and knocked.

"Good afternoon," said the perfectly ordinary-sized man who answered the door.

"Are you the giant?" asked Tock doubtfully.

"To be sure," he replied proudly. "I'm the smallest giant in the world. What can I do for you?"

"Are we lost?" said Milo.

"That's a difficult question," said the giant. "Why don't you go around back and ask the midget?" And he closed the door.

They walked to the rear of the house, which looked exactly like the front, and knocked at the door, whose name plate read "THE MIDGET."

"How are you?" inquired the man, who looked exactly like the giant.

"Are you the midget?" asked Tock again, with a hint of uncertainty in his voice.

"Unquestionably," he answered. "I'm the tallest midget in the world. May I help you?"

"Do you think we're lost?" repeated Milo.

"That's a very complicated problem," he said. "Why don't you go around to the side and ask the fat man?" And he, too, quickly disappeared.

The side of the house looked very like the front and back, and the door flew open the very instant they knocked. "How nice of you to come by," exclaimed the man, who could have been the midget's twin brother.

"You must be the fat man," said Tock, learning not to count too much on appearance.

"The thinnest one in the world," he replied brightly; "but if you have any questions, I suggest you try the thin man, on the other side of the house."

Just as they suspected, the other side of the house looked the same as the front, the back, and the side, and the door was again answered by a man who looked precisely like the other three.

"What a pleasant surprise!" he cried happily. "I haven't had a visitor in as long as I can remember."

"How long is that?" asked Milo.

"I'm sure I don't know," he replied. "Now pardon me; I have to answer the door."

"But you just did," said Tock.

"Oh yes, I'd forgotten."

"Are you the fattest thin man in the world?" asked Tock.

"Do you know one that's fatter?" he asked impatiently.

"I think you're all the same man," said Milo emphatically.

"S-S-S-S-S-H-H-H-H-H-H-H-," he cautioned, putting his finger up to his lips and drawing Milo closer. "Do you want to ruin everything? You see, to tall men I'm a midget, and to short men I'm a giant; to the skinny ones I'm a fat man, and to the fat ones I'm a thin man. That way I can hold four jobs at once. As you can see, though, I'm neither tall nor short nor fat nor thin. In fact, I'm quite ordinary, but there are so many ordinary men that no one asks their opinion about anything. Now what is your question?"

Source: From pp. 110–114 of *The Phantom Tollbooth.* Copyright © 1961 by Norton Juster. Reprinted by permission of Random House, Inc., and Wm. Collins Sons & Co., Ltd.

school with a "legend." Perhaps you have had the experience of behaving toward another person in ways consistent with a label, only to learn that the label was inaccurate. The labels assigned to individuals can determine how others treat them and relate to them.

Professionals typically assign names like "gifted," "autistic," and "retarded" to conditions of exceptionality. These labels help organize our knowledge, perceptions, and behavior. Yet they also carry with them certain

Labels create expectations

expectations—some good, some bad. These expectations can change the relationships between those who are labeled and those who are not. They influence the ways in which people react to exceptionality.

Considerable debate exists in the special education community about the extent to which labeling is necessary and helpful, and there is no clear resolution of the debate. Many professionals argue that labeling is "bad," that it leads to negative expectations, causes exclusion of individuals from schooling and society, and has the effect of limiting opportunities and making students feel bad about themselves. Other professionals argue that labeling is "necessary" because those who are labeled are entitled to special services and treatment, moneys are allocated to treating and serving them, and researchers can communicate meaningfully about them. State agencies often require that students be labeled in order to receive services.

Deciding whether the effects of labeling are good or bad is not easy. Many factors are at work here. Professionals and parents do not want students to be denied the services they need, they also do not want the students to be treated in negative ways just because of the labels assigned to them. Regardless, the reactions of exceptional individuals to themselves and the reactions of others toward them are often a function of the label assigned to the condition. In the next section we explore in more detail the effects of labels and the expectations they create.

Effects of Perceptions and Expectations

As we have seen, being exceptional means many different things. Not all exceptional people are alike, and few are treated the same way. You need to think about how people who are exceptional are viewed by others and how they view themselves. Think about how you perceive yourself and how others perceive you. In this section we talk about the factors that influence how teachers and parents think about exceptional people, then about how individuals who are exceptional see themselves.

How Teachers Regard Students Who Are Exceptional

The evidence is clear that the perceptions and interactions of exceptional people are affected by their condition. It is also clear that those around them—peers, teachers, and parents—often allow the exceptional condition to affect their expectations for and behavior toward these people.

A number of factors have been shown to influence teachers' expectations of their students. For example, a student's appearance, race, gender, classroom behavior, and even the achievements of older siblings affect teachers' expectations. Those expectations influence the ways in which teachers and pupils interact.

Labels and self-fulfilling prophecies

It's not surprising that category labels ("emotionally disturbed," "learning disabled," "blind," "deaf," "gifted") play a part in shaping teachers' expectations of their students. Most of us believe that students who are gifted will do well on most tasks and that students who are mentally retarded will do poorly.

These beliefs and others like them affect teachers' expectations and, most important, the attitudes they convey to the student. Teachers' expectations often become *self-fulfilling prophecies,* influencing the students' own expectations and behaviors. When students are identified as "retarded," teachers may expect them to complete assignments slowly. Students learn to perform in accord with expectations about their performance. If students learn they are expected to perform slowly, then they may do so, and thus the teacher's prophecies will be fulfilled. This kind of cycle can be a good thing when teachers' expectations are high, but it can be very damaging when they are not.

Our knowledge of what classroom teachers think about exceptional students comes from a number of natural and contrived experiments.

- When classroom teachers view videotapes of students who demonstrate normal behavior, and when they are told the students are "emotionally disturbed," they report seeing behaviors associated with emotional disturbance, like excessive aggression, anger, and hostility (Foster & Ysseldyke, 1976; Foster, Ysseldyke, & Reese, 1975).

- Teachers interact differently with students in different special education categories. For example, teachers interact differently with students who are said to be mentally retarded than with those who are said to be learning disabled (Beez, 1970; Salvia, Clark, & Ysseldyke, 1973; Schain, 1972).

- Teachers rate students lower in terms of social skills and academic potential when those students have been labeled (Algozzine & Mercer, 1980).

How Parents Regard Students Who Are Exceptional

Two sources give us information on the parents of children who are exceptional. The first is the parents themselves, in their descriptions of what it's like to have a special child. The second is studies in which parents' characteristics, thoughts, and expectations for their children are sampled. Both are revealing.

Parents' emotions

It is common for parents to deny that anything is wrong with their child. Often they go from one doctor to the next, looking for a different diagnosis, or they isolate themselves and their child from social interactions. Some parents feel guilty, angry, and afraid, which affects their interactions with each other, their exceptional child and any other children, and their friends and coworkers.

Themes in parental responses

In a work that describes the positive contributions the exceptional child often makes to the family, Ferguson and Asch (1989) point out that having an exceptional child complicates family and interpersonal relationships. They suggest that four themes emerge in the writings of parents of children with disabilities: They shelter their children from the world; they pretend, often through silence and denial, that nothing is wrong; they try to find ways to "fix" the disabilities or minimize the differences of those that cannot be fixed; or they minimize the impact of the exceptionality while working to ensure their child has a full life. These reactions seem understandable to us. We think parents always have the best interests of their child in mind as they adjust to an exceptionality.

Bring Your Learning to Life

"What Did He Say, Lady?"

Amy is a speech and language pathologist who works with young adults who have speech and language problems. One of the young men she works with is Mel. Because Mel's vocal cords were injured during surgery for throat cancer, he is unable to speak. Amy and the engineer at the clinic devised a software program so that Mel could use a computer to speak for him. They are in the initial phases of training.

Amy and Mel work together to program the computer with simple voice commands like "I'd like to have a hamburger with cheese, french fries, and a medium Coke." Amy then takes Mel to social settings, like fast food restaurants, where he can practice using his "electronic voice." Mel is beginning to use the electronic voice well, but what interests Amy most is the way people react to Mel.

Recently Amy and Mel went to a fast food restaurant to place an order. Mel used his machine to say to the clerk "I'd like to have a hamburger with cheese, french fries, and a medium Coke." Immediately the woman taking the order looked at Amy and said "What did he say?" Amy replied simply, "You should ask him," at which point the woman did. Mel once again activated the voice on his computer, reordered, and received his meal.

People often react to individuals with disabilities as if they were incapable of responding, acting, or speaking. They often do not expect them to be able to interact, so they rely on others. We expect certain behaviors of those who are exceptional, and sometimes our expectations get in the way of the individuals' growth.

The "message" . . . is not that parents rejoice in the disabilities of their children. . . . No parent narrative expresses pleasure about the opportunity to deal with a child's physiological limitations. Nor is the message that many parents eventually reach some golden stage of adjustment called "acceptance" by some social workers and psychologists. The limitations of any disability are too much embedded in the biases of the culture to allow some simple acquiescence to the latest professional version of "biology of destiny." The narratives repeatedly express anger, frustration, and resentment not at fate, but at the unnecessary burdens they and their children face because of social attitudes and behavior toward disabilities. (Ferguson & Asch, 1989, p. 113)

A parent's rewards

Despite the difficulties, having an exceptional child can be rewarding. Steve Largent, a former professional football player, described how life changed for his family when his son, Kramer, was born.

That was on Nov. 11, 1985, perhaps the best and worst evening of Steve Largent's life. "I always cry at the births of my children because I get so emotional," he says. "I was making jokes, feeling happy, when the doctor said to me, 'Uh, oh, we've got a problem.'" The newborn had an exposed spinal cord—spina bifida. The possible consequences included paralysis and retardation.

"I was crushed," Largent says. "I broke down, went into a corner and wept. Then I heard Terry [Largent's wife] say, 'God planned Kramer. Having him in our lives will be one of the greatest things that ever happened to us.'"

The day after Kramer was born, he underwent surgery to close his spine. Bowel and bladder problems are common with spina bifida, but so far Kramer has not developed any. Although he must use crutches for longer distances, the 3-year-old can already walk across a room unaided, and doctors say he may eventually gain full use of his legs. "He's been a blessing for me," says Largent. "When you have someone like Kramer, you think about all the things people have to overcome, and it makes you more sympathetic. His brothers and sisters are very protective of him, but they play rough and tumble, too."

With a whoop, Kramer gets up off the floor and toddles unsteadily toward his father. "That's it!" Largent cries. "That's just great, Kramer!" The boy begins to totter, and his father grabs him just in time. Largent is accustomed to spectacular receptions, but it is clear from his expression that, to his way of thinking, this catch ranks as one of his finest. (Friedman & Gallo, 1988, p. 80)

Parents of those who are gifted share some of the concerns of parents of other exceptional children. They also have their own special concerns:

Parents of children who are gifted

Zelda's mother worries that her daughter may be socially ostracized or isolated as a result of negative peer-group reaction to her intellectual gifts. This is a particularly sensitive issue to Zelda's mother, who never was very popular herself and does not wish her only daughter to face the same loneliness that she had had to endure. . . . Sam's mother has very different anxieties. Will Sam turn against her or will he be embarrassed by her lack of education when he himself becomes an educated young man? She will strive for him because she believes so deeply that education is a way for Sam to achieve success in the world, but she often wonders, late at night, as to whether she is not helping him reach his goal at the expense of losing him psychologically. . . . Laura's parents . . . wonder if she follows a career in dance or music whether she can maintain a traditional or reasonable lifestyle, or whether she will be drawn off by persons who will lead her into increasingly atypical patterns of behavior. (Gallagher, 1985, pp. 403–404)

Research on parents

Studies of parents of exceptional children focus on their attitudes and expectations (Turnbull & Turnbull, 1979). Researchers have found that parents of children with learning disabilities hold negative views about their children. They describe them as more difficult to talk to, more anxious, and less able to control themselves than their nondisabled siblings. The parents of these children also tend to attribute success less to ability and more to luck, and failure more to a lack of ability and less to bad luck, than do parents of children who are not learning disabled. Analyses of tape-recorded interactions between mothers and their children show that parents use different kinds of language when they talk to a handicapped child. Finally, mothers of exceptional children generally hold less favorable opinions about their children's experiences in school.

How People Who Are Exceptional Regard Themselves

We all hold expectations for our own behavior. How we've done something in the past shapes our expectations about how well we will do it in the future. If we've done well, we expect to do well; if we've done poorly, we usually expect to do poorly. Past performance and the expectations based on that performance also shape our current behavior. Most of us enjoy the things we do well, and most of us avoid the activities that we don't expect to do well.

Answer this test item:

1. If $1/2x + 2 = B$, then $2x + 2 =$
    a. $2B$.
    b. $2B - 2$.
    c. $4B$.
    d. $4B - 2$.
    e. $4B - 6$.

Expectations for one's own behavior

How well do you think you solved the problem? How many problems like this could you complete in two minutes? Do you think you could do better if you had more time? Do you think you could do better with some practice? Your answers reflect your expectations, and those expectations are based on your experiences.

Like all of us, exceptional people hold expectations for themselves. Those expectations are based on past performance, but they also are influenced by the expectations of others. In the following quote, a man thought to be retarded describes his frustration with what others think about him:

> I don't believe that anyone from the hospital has it easy outside. There's problems from being in that place [the institution]. I mean with people you meet. They take me as if I'm not a smart person. That's what makes me so provoked. And I mean they act like I don't understand things, which I do understand things. . . . Sometimes I'd rather be dead than have people act like I'm not a smart person. (Edgerton, 1967, p. 206)

This man believes that people respond, not to him, but to the institution where he has been. He thinks they respond to him as someone who is "from the hospital," and this influences the way he regards himself.

Self-perception and social behavior

The ways people perceive themselves deeply affect their social behavior. In his book *The Cloak of Competence* (1967), Edgerton described the life experiences of a group of people who had been released from a large institution. Although the book appeared over a generation ago, much of what these people had to say still has relevance. For example, throughout the book evidence is

When people with disabilities are challenged they respond just like everybody else. *Peter Southwick/Stock, Boston, Inc.*

found of the kind of "passing" that is part of the social behavior of many exceptional people: Rather than admit their exceptionality to others, they try to disguise it.

> I don't like to read. It hurts my eyes. I'd rather watch TV. (p. 131)

> When I try to get a job they always ask me where I'm from. I don't tell nobody I'm from there [the hospital]—I say I'm just an outsider like anybody, but I've been working in the East. (p. 151)

> You know old [another ex-patient]. He's always putting on. He went and got these books at the junk shop for ten cents a piece, and now he's got 'em all over his place like he was some kind of millionaire. Well, I went and got me some books too, real classy ones, I paid a dollar for some of 'em. Got all kinds, I think they look real nice. (p. 159)

Defensive or hostile responses

Often those with disabilities avoid social contacts or use defensive covering to reduce the likelihood of having to deal with other people socially. Some use a hostile bravado to protect themselves in social interactions. In these and many other ways, the behavior of people with disabilities is shaped by their feelings and expectations about themselves and their conditions.

Normality, Exceptionality, and Special Education in Perspective

Exceptional people are individuals, each unique. Their exceptionality may give them a common challenge, but they are not all alike. Current federal rules and regulations specify thirteen categories of students who receive special education services. We describe these groups in specific chapters in Part Three.

We believe professionals, especially teachers, are in a unique position to shape the public image of and attitude toward people with disabilities. The words and images they use can create a straightforward, positive view or an inaccurate portrayal that reinforces myths and leads to discrimination, lowered expectations, and negative stereotypes.

Ways to speak about people with disabilities

Throughout this book, we refer to people with disabilities using guidelines recommended by over 100 national disability organizations and endorsed by media and disability experts across the country (Research and Training Center on Independent Living, 1990). Generally, this means putting people (not their disabilities) first, eliminating use of the word *handicap* as a synonym for disability, and not referring to people by a disability name (see Table 1.3). In some cases, this goes against past practices, but we are trying to shape the future, not simply reflect the past.

Lack of absolute standards

We believe the concepts of normality and exceptionality are relative. Our perspective on normality is based on the belief that there are no absolute standards for many of the concepts that shape people's lives. Data collected on the prevalence of a behavior or characteristic in the population can be useful as a reference. But normality is always a relative concept, regardless of the context in which it is evaluated.

A disability (real or perceived) can be both a promise and a burden. For many, their only hope for a full life is classification as exceptional and subsequent special education. But the costs of classification can be high whenever public recognition leads to changed interpersonal interactions, discrimination, or rejection.

Teachers' special responsibility

Teachers have a special responsibility to students who are exceptional. Their expectations shape their students' own expectations and behaviors. When they base those expectations not on what a student can do, but on what a label implies that student can do, they do the student a grave injustice. Students who are exceptional are people first. Yes, in some ways they are different. But each of us is different in some ways. It is very wrong to allow an exceptional condition to be the source of lowered expectations and differential treatment in school.

Perceptions of special education

As this book will demonstrate, special education can be many things to many people. To parents, it promises help, a means for their child to reach his or her full potential. It also involves parents in the decision-making process, because they are considered part of the special education team. For regular classroom teachers, special education is a method for dealing with students whose learning needs are different in some way. For administrators caught up in arranging class schedules, transportation, and conferences, it may be both a source of pride and a logistical nightmare.

Table 1.3   Top Ten List of Tips for Professionals Writing or Speaking About People with Disabilities

1. In speaking of categorical groups, avoid the kind of phrase that emphasizes the condition while disregarding the people: "the retarded," "the deaf and dumb."

2. Generally speak of the person first, not the disability: for instance, say "students with learning disabilities" rather than "learning-disabled students." If you must put the disability term first for brevity, be careful of the implications. You may also want to avoid terms that are obvious euphemisms ("physically challenged").

3. Don't use "handicap" as a synonym for "disability." A handicap, properly speaking, is a condition or barrier imposed by society, the environment, or oneself; it is a problem the person encounters, not a characteristic of the person.

4. Avoid sensationalizing a disability with phrases like "afflicted with," "suffers from," and "victim of." Instead, say simply that the person "has" a certain disability.

5. Avoid medical terminology—"patients," "cases," "symptoms"—unless a particular medical condition or relationship with a doctor is under discussion.

6. Emphasize abilities rather than disabilities: "uses a wheelchair" rather than "is confined to a wheelchair."

7. Don't lavish excessive praise on people with disabilities or on their accomplishments; they don't need to be patronized.

8. Don't portray successful people with disabilities as superhuman.

9. Don't focus on a disability unless it is important to the point being discussed.

10. In describing the lives of people with disabilities, be sure to portray them as interacting with nondisabled people in social, educational, and work environments. In this way you can help break down social barriers, alleviate irrational fears, and open lines of communication.

Sources: Adapted from information in The Research and Training Center on Independent Living (1990). *Guidelines for reporting and writing about people with disabilities,* 3rd ed. Lawrence, KS: Author; and "It's the 'person first'—then the disability," guidelines issued by the PACER Center, Inc., Minneapolis, 1991.

What about special educators? There is considerable diversity in perceptions of special education. Some insist that special education is a separate system for educating students who are exceptional. But most disagree. Special education is a process for helping students with special learning needs, and that process must be an integral part of the general education system. All students—both exceptional and nonexceptional—are more alike than they are different. They need to interact, to share experiences. The importance of that interaction for students with disabilities is clear: To learn to act in expected ways, they must be exposed to expected behaviors. But it is equally important for those who are not exceptional, because the interaction engenders understanding of how little differences matter, of how much alike all people are. And with that understanding comes acceptance.

This book is about teaching and how to modify or enhance it to accommodate people who are exceptional. In the chapters that follow you will learn about the kinds of students considered exceptional, their characteristics, how they are assessed, and many strategies and tactics for teaching them effectively. You will finish this text prepared to make a difference in the lives of all students and prepared to help all students, including those with special learning needs, obtain better results from their educational experiences.

What Every Teacher Should Know

- Special education is education designed to meet the unique learning needs of students who learn more slowly or rapidly than their peers and who, according to professionals, meet state criteria for eligibility for services.
- The decisions we make about exceptional people before, during, and after school are based in large measure on what we know about normal development.
- Normality is a relative concept, and different standards are used to define the concept: statistical, medical, and social standards.
- Nearly 5 million individuals between birth and 21 years of age receive special education services.
- The following categories of individuals are eligible for special education services under federal law (the Individuals with Disabilities Education Act): specific learning disabilities, speech or language impairments, mental retardation, serious emotional disturbance, multiple disabilities, orthopedic impairments, other health impairments, visual impairments, hearing impairments, deaf-blindness, autism, traumatic brain injury. Under separate legislation states are permitted to provide special education services to students who are gifted and talented.
- People have different life experiences as a result of being exceptional. They also have specific feelings about being exceptional.
- Society reacts to exceptionality in ways that differ from reactions to people who are not exceptional. Reactions are influenced by the nature of individual tolerance, the cause of the exceptionality, and the label assigned to it.
- It is preferable to use "people first" terminology in talking about students with disabilities.

Projects

1. Interview three people. Ask them to define special education and to give you one or two examples of students they believe should receive special services.

2. Make a list of the categories of students who are eligible to receive special education in your state. Identify how your state's department of education defines each of these conditions.

3. Start a scrapbook of newspaper and magazine articles about people who are exceptional and their educational experiences.

4. Consult any general introductory special education textbook (a few are given in the following section) and list the definitions the authors give for *special education* and *exceptional students*.

5. Interview either an adolescent with a disability or the parent of such a student. Ask about his or her experiences in school and in society. Specifically, investigate the ways in which others react to the student.

For Your Information

Books

Adams, B. (1979). *Like it is: Facts and feelings about handicaps from kids who know.* New York: Walker.

A group of young people with disabilities share their problems and adjustments. Excellent for upper elementary and middle school students.

Baum, D.D. (1981). *The human side of exceptionality.* Baltimore: University Park Press.

Explores disabling conditions through the use of popular literature. The book contains over forty articles that have appeared in popular magazines, covering a wide range of disabilities. The articles reveal the effects of disabilities in the home, school, and community.

Biklen, Douglas, Philip Ferguson, & Alison Ford. (1988). *Schooling and disability.* Chicago: NSSE; distributed by Paul H. Brookes.

The eighty-eighth yearbook of the National Society for the Study of Education provides an overview of issues in special education today, including relationships between regular and special educators.

Brown, T. (1984). *Someone special, just like you.* New York: Holt, Rinehart, and Winston

A book for preschoolers and young children written to help them accept and become more comfortable with children with disabilities as they are increasingly integrated into everyday classrooms.

Carballo, Julie B., et al. (1990). *Survival guide for the first-year special education teacher.* (Reston, VA: Council for Exceptional Children.

Developed by special education teachers who survived their first five years, this guide offers tips on the many aspects of teaching from organizing your class to managing stress.

Fine, M., & Asch, A. (Eds.). (1988). *Women with disabilities: Essays in psychology, culture, and politics.* Philadelphia: Temple University Press.

This collection of essays from activists in varied academic disciplines grew out of a personal friendship between the editors, and the political commitment they had made to feminism and disability rights. Their objective was to shift the image of girls and women with disabilities from one of passiveness and weakness to one incorporating passion and strength.

Jablow, M.M. (1982). *Cara: Growing with a retarded child.* Philadelphia: Temple University Press.

A mother's account of what it means to live and grow with a child who has a disability.

Kirk, S., Gallagher, J., & Anastasiow, N. (1993). *Educating exceptional children* (7th ed.). Boston: Houghton Mifflin.

A thorough and widely read introduction to special education.

Organizations

Council for Exceptional Children

Founded in 1922, CEC has a membership of about 60,000 teachers, administrators, teacher educators, and related services personnel. CEC advocates for services for students with disabilities and those who are gifted and talented. It is a professional organization that addresses service, training, and research relative to persons with disabilities and those who are gifted and talented. For more information, contact Council for Exceptional Children, 1920 Association Dr., Reston, VA 22091.

National Easter Seal Society

Founded in 1919, NESS has 67 state groups and 98 local groups. It is a federation of state and local societies that operate over 400 service centers that serve over 1 million people. NESS establishes and conducts programs that serve people with disabilities, works with other agencies and government agencies to provide support services for people with disabilities, and publishes information on the professional, medical, and rehabilitation service needs of individuals with disabilities. For more information, contact the National Easter Seal Society, 70 E. Lake St., Chicago, IL 60601.

National Association of School Psychologists

Founded in 1969, NASP has 16,000 school psychologists as members. It works to serve the mental health and educational needs of children and youth, encourages and provides opportunities for professional growth to school psychologists, informs the public on the services and practice of school psychology, and advances the standards of the profession. For more information, contact the NASP, 8455 Colesville Rd., Suite 1000, Silver Spring, MD 20910.

Journals

Exceptional Children

The primary journal in the field, this official publication of the Council for Exceptional Children includes professional perspectives on special education and papers describing research on students with disabilities. For more information, contact Council for Exceptional Children, 1920 Association Dr., Reston, VA 22091.

Journal of Special Education

This is a multidisciplinary publication presenting primary research and scholarly reviews related to special education. Research reported is on students with disabilities, their teachers, and/or parents. The journal is distributed by Pro Ed publishers and the editors are Douglas and Lynn Fuchs. They can be reached at *The Journal of Special Education,* Box 328 Peabody College, Vanderbilt University, Nashville, TN 37203.

Educational Leadership

Educational Leadership is the flagship journal of the Association for Supervision and Curriculum Development. The journal is intended primarily for leaders in elementary, middle, and secondary education but is also geared toward anyone interested in curriculum, instruction, supervision, and leadership in schools. For more information, contact *Educational Leadership,* 1250 N. Pitt St., Alexandria, VA 22314-1453.

Chapter

Special Education in the Context of Increasing Diversity

Focusing Questions

- How much diversity exists in present-day classrooms?
- How are diversity and exceptionality related?
- How does special education relate to diversity?
- How do educators determine eligibility for special education?
- What are the major ways in which special education services are delivered?

Pat and Chris were students in George McMaster's fourth-grade class. Both students were from single-parent families in which the mothers worked but earned very little money. Their homes were in the part of the city that had the highest crime rate and heaviest drug traffic. Both students were considerably behind in academic work. Pat had difficulty with any academic content that required reading, but performance in mathematics was nearly on grade level. Chris experienced academic difficulty across the board, functioning considerably below grade level in all academic areas. Both students behaved in ways that bothered McMaster. Pat tended to act out, repeatedly bothering other students, and nearly always seemed inattentive. In third grade there had been many instances in which Pat was involved in fistfights with other students. Chris, on the other hand, was quiet and seldom interacted socially with the other students.

Throughout their school careers both Pat and Chris had needed extra help. In fourth grade, McMaster had paraprofessional James Alvarez work with them. Academic work was adjusted so that reading was at a first-grade level, and Alvarez used direct and frequent measurement procedures to keep a chart of both students' progress. But improvement was slow for Chris and Pat, and by March they were being considered for special education services. ▪

There are many students like Pat and Chris in today's schools, and many like C. J., Bobby, Theodore, and Ronnie whom you met in Chapter 1. Such students must struggle to acquire the skills and knowledge taught in school, for several reasons. Some have disabilities, some do not. Some receive special education services, some do not. Some students receive other kinds of services (like compensatory education or speech and language assistance). Sometimes they leave the regular classroom to receive special education services, and sometimes the services are brought to them. Some students with severe disabilities spend their entire school day in separate classes. Others attend separate schools. This chapter provides a perspective on today's special education. We describe the diversity that is present in schools and classrooms, and illustrate why some students are declared eligible for special education services while others are not. It is our intent to help you understand why service delivery operates as it does. We also explain the challenges being raised about the ways we decide whom to serve.

Diversity in today's schools

The one word that best describes students in today's classrooms is *diverse*. There is a broader variety of students than in the recent past, and this diversity presents teachers with new and different opportunities and challenges. Think about the many dimensions of the diversity that characterize the classrooms of today. Students differ in gender; race/ethnicity; the languages they and their parents speak; family structure; income level of their parents; activity levels; parental expectations; background experiences; the opportunities they have been given; and physical, mental, and emotional skills and abilities. Many of these characteristics have direct and significant impacts on learning and create unique learning needs.

Dimensions of Diversity

A multicultural society

America and American schools have a fascinating abundance of peoples, cultures, languages, and attitudes. We have a truly multicultural society marked by unparalleled diversity. America's schools are changing as a result of increasing diversity. In the sections that follow we describe the kinds of diversity evident in schools and talk about how it is affecting the delivery of instruction.

Cultural Pluralism

The new face of America

American society is a pluralistic society in which many cultural and ethnic groups blend but at the same time are increasingly less willing to give up their cultural and ethnic heritages. More than 1 million immigrants enter the United States every year. Most are from Asia and the vast Hispanic world (see Table 2.1). Today, more than 20 million people in America were born in another country. Fourteen percent of all adults in the United States and about 20 percent of children under 17 are minorities. By the year 2000 one-third of children under 17 will be minorities, and by 2020 about half of your students will probably represent ethnic and multicultural groups (Hodgkinson, 1993). In many places the historical minorities are already majorities.

Many of your students will speak a language other than English at home. Whatever your own background, some of your students will likely be from cultures or subcultures that are unfamiliar to you. This offers tremendous possibilities for you to learn about others and to broaden your experiences. It also presents some challenges for you as a teacher. Remember, most of the new immigrants share an important characteristic with those who came before them (largely of Anglo and European ancestry). They are self-starters who had the gumption to pack up, move to a new land, and chase their dreams.

Cultural diversity is not restricted to urban areas. There are hundreds of subcultures in rural communities. They differ in racial/ethnic composition (you may have heard of towns called "Little Sweden," or "Little Italy"), in remoteness, economy, language patterns, and language dominance.

Varieties of acculturation

Differences in race, ethnicity, language, and culture can affect school performance and the extent to which schooling experiences are relevant and appropriate for students. An important, relevant concept is **acculturation**—literally the "process of acquiring culture"—which refers to the specific set of background experiences and opportunities that students have. To the extent

Table 2.1	Diversity in American Society: Selected Statistics	

Top 10 places of origin for immigrants:	
Mexico	22%
Vietnam	8.0
Philippines	6.3
Russia and other former Soviet states	4.5
Dominican Republic	4.3
China	4.0
India	3.8
El Salvador	2.7
Poland	2.6
United Kingdom	2.1
Cities where more than half the population is foreign born:	
Hialeah, FL	70%
Miami, FL	60
Huntington Park, CA	59
Union City, NJ	55
Monterey Park, CA	52
Miami Beach, FL	51
Santa Ana, CA	51
School systems in which more than 100 languages or dialects are spoken:	
Washington, DC	
New York	
Chicago	
Los Angeles	
Fairfax County, VA	
Proportion of residents who speak languages other than English at home	13%

Source: Data from "The new face of America: How immigrants are shaping the world's first multicultural society." (Fall 1993). Special issue of *Time.*

that each student's acculturation is different from that of the majority of students in his or her class, teachers must make adjustments in instruction. Students achieve better outcomes when instruction is made relevant to their culture and background experiences and opportunities.

Family Life

Changes in the American family

Many children grow up healthy and happy in strong, stable families. Far too many do not. Dramatic social, demographic, and economic changes over the past twenty-five or thirty years have transformed the American family. A "typical" middle-class child may now have four parents/stepparents, six or eight grandparents, and numerous uncles and aunts. These people may or may not

The diversity in today's classrooms provides a source of richness and sense of pride to many teachers. *Elizabeth Crews.*

live with the child. Families have changed, and students come to class with diverse notions of family, diverse role models, and so forth. Census Bureau reports (Rawlings, 1993; U.S. Bureau of the Census, 1993) indicate some ways in which families are changing.

Census statistics

- The proportion of "family households" (at least two persons related to one another) is declining. It dropped from 81 percent in 1970 to 70 percent in 1992.
- More children are living with single parents. The number of single-parent situations rose from 3.8 million in 1970 to 10.5 million in 1992.
- The vast majority of single parents (86 percent in 1992) are mothers, and single mothers are especially likely to be poor.
- Although the total number of white single parents is more than twice the number of black single parents, in percentage terms single-parent situations are much more prevalent among blacks. Of all black family groups with children at home in 1992, 62 percent were headed by single parents. For whites the corresponding figure was 24 percent; for Hispanics, 34 percent.

Children without adequate supervision at home

More than 60 percent of children live in a family in which both parents work or the single parent works. In such families the parents may be too

Window on Practice

The Multicultural Classroom

On a cloudy winter afternoon, Florann Greenberg, a teacher at P.S. 14 in New York City, noticed that her first-grade class was growing fidgety. One girl, dropping all pretense of work, stared at the snow falling outside the school-room windows. Annoyed, Greenberg asked her, "Haven't you seen snow before?" The girl whispered "No." Her classmates began shaking their heads. Then it dawned on Greenberg: Of course these children had never seen snow; almost all were immigrants from Colombia and the Dominican Republic. Immediately she changed the lesson plan. New topic: What is snow? How is it formed? How do you dress in the snow? What games do you play?

Such moments of cultural dissonance, followed by attempts to learn and teach from them, now take place daily in thousands of classrooms across the United States. The children of the new immigrants, often immigrants themselves, have been arriving at these class-rooms in growing numbers, and more are on the way. They are placing unprecedented demands on teachers, administrators, and already strained school systems. To a heartening degree, however, educators are responding with fresh, pragmatic methods of coping with these new demands.

Isolated numbers hint at the scope of the challenge:

- Total enrollment in U.S. public schools rose only 4.2 percent between 1986 and 1991, according to a 1993 Urban Institute study, while the number of students with little or no knowledge of English increased 50 percent, from 1.5 to 2.3 million.

- In the Washington, DC, school system, students speak 127 languages and dialects; across the Potomac, in Fairfax County, Virginia, that figure is more than 100.

- In California public schools 1 out of 6 students was born outside the United States, and 1 in 3 speaks a language other than English at home. The Los Angeles school system now absorbs 30,000 new immigrant children each year.

Source: Excerpted from Paul Gray, "Teach your children well: But what to teach the newest arrivals in what language still vexes the nation's public schools." (Fall 1993). *Time,* p. 69. Copyright 1993 Time Inc. Reprinted by permission.

stressed and harried to provide caring attention and guidance. There are wide disparities in adult supervision of children and in the extent to which adults are available to help children with homework. Children who do not receive adequate attention at home sometimes seek it elsewhere, often in the form of gang/group membership. Increasingly, children are spending more time alone at home. Some 14 percent of eighth-graders surveyed in 1991 said they usually were home after school without adult supervision for longer than three hours.

Poverty

Many children are living in economically secure circumstances, but far too many are not. One in five children lives in poverty; about 40 percent of the nation's poor are children. More than 25 percent of children ages 0 to 5 live in poverty. Of children under 6 years of age living in families with a female householder (no husband present), 65.9 percent were poor in 1992 (U.S. Bureau of the Census, 1993). Poverty and instability have well-documented negative effects on children: malnourishment, frequent moves, inadequate clothing, substandard housing, and crime-ridden environments. Children who are hungry, tired, or ill or who live in fear are difficult to teach and are at risk for poor performance in school.

Homelessness

For some the situation is even worse. On any given night up to 600,000 people are homeless. They live and sleep on our streets, in parks, in storefronts, in shelters, and on ventilation/heat grates. Some even sleep in darkened corners of bus, train, or subway stations. Many students with disabilities spend their evenings in homeless shelters, some sleep in their cars and do their homework on the steps of a shopping mall, and others live in motels. With no home to return to, they find doing their homework difficult. In 1991 it was estimated that 240,000 school-age children and youths were homeless, over one-third of whom did not attend school on a regular basis. It should not be surprising if such students leave projects half-finished, get depressed over leaving familiar places and friends, withdraw, act aggressively, do not complete their homework, fall behind academically, are restless, fight with other students for control of things, have difficulty with transitions, have poor attention spans, or demonstrate developmental delays.

High-Risk Social Behaviors

Risky behavior

More and more students are engaged in high-risk social behaviors or fail to make healthy lifestyle choices. On the basis of survey data, Hodgkinson (1973) estimated that about 25 percent of adolescents engage in social behaviors (unprotected sex, abuse of alcohol and drugs) that can lead to serious problems. One million teenage girls become pregnant each year. Half have abortions, half deliver. The proportion of teenage births has been going up every year since the 1970s. More than half of young people say they have tried an illicit drug by the time they finish high school. They are committing more serious crimes, and the proportion of young people in jails and detention facilities is increasing. The high-risk social behaviors in which students engage can have negative effects on their performance in school, leading to absence, inattention, and lack of interest. These behaviors also often become the targets of intervention and instruction. Schools are being called on to provide instruction that leads students to make healthy lifestyle choices.

Implications of Diversity

Need for multicultural education

All of the social trends we have noted—positive ones like the growth of cultural pluralism and negative ones like poverty and homelessness—have increased the diversity in American schools. One major implication is that teachers no longer can afford to teach from a monocultural perspective. They need to engage in what is being called multicultural education. **Multicultural education** has as its major goal the transformation of the school "so that students from diverse cultural, social class, racial and ethnic groups will experience an equal opportunity to learn in school" (Banks, 1989, p. 20). Americans are committed to the twin notions of excellence and equity. We believe that our students ought to achieve at very high levels, that they ought to demonstrate excellence. At the same time we believe that all students have the right to achieve at high levels. Banks (1989) identified four major goals in multicultural education:

1. To increase the academic achievement of all students
2. To help all students develop more positive attitudes toward different cultural, racial, ethnic, and religious groups
3. To help students from historically victimized groups develop confidence in their ability to succeed academically and to influence societal institutions
4. To help all students learn to consider the perspective of other groups

Multicultural education involves attitude development and change, equal opportunity to learn the same high-level content, and opportunity for individual students to overcome the possibly deleterious effects of diversities in heritage and home life.

Rising number of exceptional students

Another major implication of diversity is that an increasing number of students may be considered exceptional in one way or another. By grade 4 students already show a range of skills amounting to more than four grade levels (Biemiller, 1993), and this disparity may increase in the future. Such diverse skill levels imply different educational needs, but how many of these needs require special education? Consider the case of Xong, described in the following Bring Your Learning to Life feature. Xong came from a very unusual and strife-filled background, which made it difficult for her to adapt immediately to American schooling. According to the assessment tests, she also appeared to have a disability—mild mental retardation. Yet how sure can we be, in a case like Xong's, that we are measuring a disability?

Problems in labeling students of diverse backgrounds

A disproportionately high number of student with disabilities come from historical minority groups or from culturally diverse backgrounds. This has long been the case, and it continues to be true today (U.S. Department of Education, 1993). For that reason, many have argued that special education reduces diversity in regular education settings; by siphoning off the "different," special education makes regular classes more homogeneous. There is also a great deal of concern that students from diverse backgrounds may suffer from being mislabeled. Xong's case represents typical action on the part of some school personnel. When youngsters experience difficulty, they are referred for professional evaluation, and the focus in such evaluations is on what is *wrong* with the child. Often, the educators may miss what is *right*. Moreover, children from diverse backgrounds are commonly underrepresented in programs for students who are gifted and talented. Many students from ethnic and multicultural backgrounds have gifts and talents that are not valued or nurtured in school (Chinn & McCormick, 1986).

Distinguishing disability from diversity

In making decisions about special education, educators try to distinguish disability from diversity. At the next section illustrates, the prevailing assumption is that special education services should be reserved for students who have

Finding the Right Program for Xong

Xong was born in rural Cambodia sometime during the monsoon season of 1974. Her family led an uncomplicated life centered on growing rice. Xong spent a good deal of her time tending animals and gathering fuel for the fire. For the rest of her day she played with children from the village. Xong loved this life. It was predictable. Dry and wet seasons came and went. Babies were born and old people died. Rice was planted, wood gathered, and both products consumed. She was Cambodian, a member of Asia's "beautiful people."

Xong's fifth year was a disaster. Machines of war appeared overhead, and soldiers came and took away all men and older boys along with any available rice. Resistance, no matter how insignificant, meant instantaneous death. Xong's grandfather was shot, her father taken prisoner, her hut burned, and the family food supply stolen. In one day, the rule of predictability was replaced with chaos.

Over the next two months, the remnants of Xong's family made their way through Cambodia to a refugee camp in Thailand. Observing death became a way of life. Xong's days consisted of standing in line for water, food, or shots. The rest of the days and nights were spent waiting. Eventually Xong and her family were flown to a camp in the Philippines. The plane trip was memorable, but the camp was not—more lines, more waiting.

In 1984 Xong, by then a ten-year-old, left the Philippines with her mother and sister. Later on that same day they arrived in California. Four weeks later they were living in a small town in California's Central Valley.

Xong was enrolled immediately in an elementary school. Due to her age and size, she was placed in the third grade. Due to the absence of other Cambodian families, Xong and her sister were not offered a bilingual or English-as-a-second-language program, but placed in classrooms with English-speaking teachers. As the year went by, Xong's teacher became increasingly alarmed at the child's lack of progress in picking up English and academic skills. A referral was made to the child-study team. The consensus of the group was that Xong was "developmentally deviant." Psychological testing seemed in order. During the assessment process the psychologist thought it wise to use an interpreter and give Xong only the performance subtests on a commonly used intelligence test—after all, Xong couldn't be expected to do well on verbal subtests. The results were shocking. Xong performed very poorly on the test. The psychologist was not comfortable with the results, so he administered a nonverbal test of intelligence. Xong's performance was low enough to qualify her for services as a mildly mentally retarded student. An individualized education program was written; acceptable levels of performance, goals, and short-term objectives were established. Program recommendations were made, and forms signed.

Yet some teachers in the school began to notice elements of Xong's behavior that didn't fit the pattern "developmentally deviant." At recess Xong and her sister had rapid conversations in their native language, during which they seemed to exchange humorous observations about their new surroundings. In the school lunchroom, where she bought small snacks, Xong had no trouble dealing with American coins. Moreover, Xong gradually began to make friends with a few of her English-speaking classmates, even though her English remained limited. Watching Xong gradually adapt, the teachers began to wonder if she had been misclassified.

disabilities that interfere in some way with their ability to meet the objectives of schooling. If problems stem only from the students' cultural or social backgrounds, other educational strategies are considered appropriate, such as bilingual education or compensatory education.

The Special Education Process

Three basic steps

Determining eligibility

The provision of special education involves a three-step process: determining eligibility, delivering special education, and then evaluating whether the education has made a difference in outcomes. In the first stage, determining eligibility, educators must make a number of critical decisions. For a student like Xong, they must try to determine whether a disability is present. If the student does have a disability, they must decide whether it requires special education services. Recall the student named C. J. from Chapter 1. C. J. clearly had a disability—he used a wheelchair—but he had no unique learning needs; therefore, he did not receive special education.

From prereferral to referral

The process begins when a student progresses unusually quickly or slowly at home or in school, or when teachers feel that the student can't learn in a regular classroom setting without special help. Interventions may be used in the regular classroom to improve the student's functioning. These are often called **prereferral interventions** because they take place before the student is referred for formal evaluation. Records are kept of the student's performance. If the student continues to progress at a rate that educators consider unacceptable, a **referral** is made: The teachers formally request a decision on whether the child is eligible for special education services. In response, a team of professionals gathers information and uses it to decide the student's eligibility. Of key importance at this point are the specific eligibility criteria of the particular state. Some students who are having difficulty in school will meet the state's guidelines for special education services; other students, who may appear to be quite similar, will not meet the guidelines and will not be referred for special education.

Role of teams

The next Bring Your Learning to Life feature continues the case descriptions of Chris and Pat, the students introduced at the beginning of this chapter (see page 51). Both experienced considerable difficulty in school, and teachers tried many alternative ways of meeting their needs. When Chris and Pat still made little progress, an intervention assistance team was consulted. The **intervention assistance team (IAT)** is a group of teachers who help regular educators solve problems with individual students. Even with the help of special techniques suggested by the IAT, Chris and Pat continued to progress very slowly, so the two students were referred to the district child-study team. The **child-study team,** which includes teachers, other school personnel, representatives of the school district, and the child's parent(s), is responsible for determining eligibility for special education. (Although the term *child-study team* is common, many districts use other names for this kind of group.) It was at this stage that Chris and Pat went in different directions. Pat, who showed a measurable dis-

Team decision-making is central to special education today. *Carol Palmer.*

crepancy between ability level and performance in reading, met the state's criteria for specific learning disabilities. The team therefore found Pat eligible for special education. Chris, in contrast, did not meet any specific criteria for special education. Chris was given other kinds of help, but Chris was not entitled to special education services.

The eligibility decision

In short, an eligibility decision requires that a child-study team find that the student (1) has special learning needs, and (2) meets the state criteria for a particular special education category. The flow chart in Figure 2.1 uses the cases of Chris and Pat to illustrate this process of determining eligibility.

Delivery of services

Once a student is declared eligible, he or she moves on to the second stage, the delivery of special education. The student receives individualized instruction from trained professionals. Alternatively, special education professionals may work as consultants with general education personnel to design interventions for use in the regular classroom. This phase is guided by a formal document called the *individualized education program (IEP)*, developed by the child-study team in association with other professionals. (The IEP is described in more detail in Chapter 3.)

Evaluation

The final stage of the special education process is evaluation. The student's progress is evaluated to determine the need for continuing, changing, or concluding special services. A student with a disability must be evaluated at least once a year. Every two or three years, a formal reevaluation is necessary to determine if a student is still eligible for special services. Students can be removed from special programs any time they have shown sufficient progress.

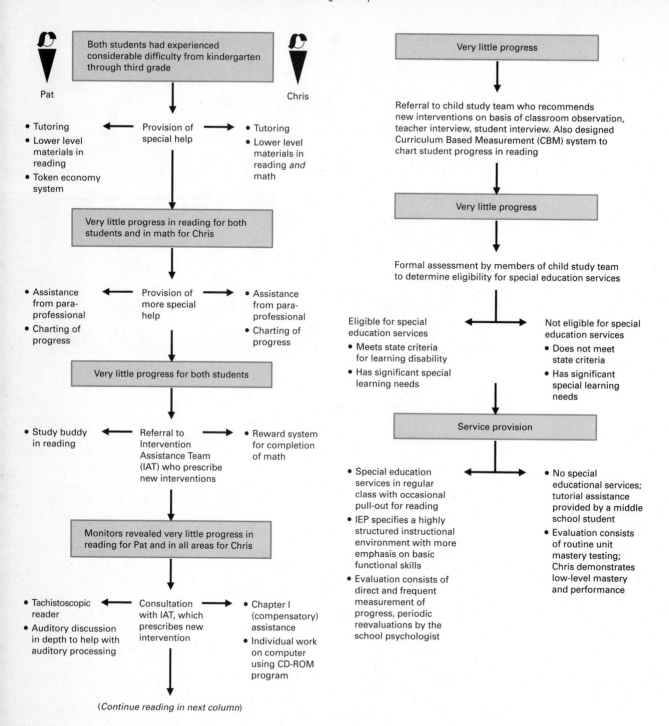

Figure 2.1
Determining Eligibility for Special Education: A Flow Chart for Two Fourth-Grade Students

Referral for Chris and Pat

When Chris and Pat continued to struggle in George McMaster's fourth-grade class, McMaster reviewed their progress with the intervention assistance team, comprising six teachers from the school. The team recommended a reward system to use for Chris's math assignments, and a student buddy, Marie, to work with Pat during reading. But neither student profited much from these interventions. New ones were tried: for Pat, a tachistoscopic reader (a device that aids reading concentration by exposing the words only briefly); for Chris, individual work on a classroom computer.

Still, little progress occurred. Both students were referred to the district child-study team. Two members of the team, the school psychologist and a special education consultant, observed Chris and Pat in McMaster's room. The psychologist also interviewed both students, their mothers, and McMaster. On the basis of these observations and interviews, the child-study team recommended further interventions and began a curriculum-based measurement (CBM) program to gather specific data on both students' reading progress.

After another month, little had changed. At that point, both students were tested by the school psychologist to determine their eligibility for special education services. Pat showed a significant difference between ability level and actual performance in reading, which meant that Pat met the state criteria for a specific learning disability. Since Pat was eligible for special education, the child-study team developed an individualized education program. Each day, Pat was taken from the fourth-grade classroom to a resource room, where special education teacher Laura Minnema provided intensive reading services. In addition, Minnema worked with McMaster to adapt classroom work for Pat.

Chris did not meet any specific state disability criteria. Chris scored low on an intelligence test, but not low enough to meet the state standards for mental retardation. Chris also showed no significant discrepancy between ability level and actual performance. The child-study team concluded that Chris was not eligible for special education services. Chris did continue to receive some help from James Alvarez, the paraprofessional, and from a study buddy, Miguel. Once a week, Chris left McMaster's class to receive assistance from a compensatory education teacher.

Varieties of Special Education Services

Today, special education is a complex system for meeting the special learning needs of exceptional students. Three types of assistance are generally available: direct services, indirect or consultative services, and related services.

Direct services

Direct services are provided by working with students themselves to correct or compensate for the conditions that have caused them to fall behind in school or to enrich or accelerate the progress they are making in school. Teaching a

Special education teachers sometimes work with small groups of students when providing collaborative/supportive direct services. *© Alan Carey/The Image Works, Inc.*

student who is deaf to use sign language, a student with a learning disability to read using a special method of instruction, or a gifted fourth-grader to do algebra are examples of direct services provided by teachers.

Indirect services

Indirect or consultative services are provided to classroom teachers and others who work with exceptional students over a period of time to help meet the needs of the students. Helping a teacher identify the best method for teaching a student with learning disabilities to read, or showing a teacher how to reposition a student with a physical disability, are examples of indirect services provided by teachers and other professionals.

Related services

Related services are provided by specially trained personnel directly (to students) or indirectly (to those who work with exceptional students). Related services include psychological testing and counseling, school social work, educational/occupational therapy, adapted physical education, school health services, and transportation. Related services may also include **assistive technology,** which means equipment designed to improve or maintain the functional abilities of students with disabilities. For instance, the provision of electronic communication aids is often considered a related service.

Types of placement

The types of services students receive as part of their special education program vary according to the level of their learning needs. Placements may also differ for different conditions. Sometimes the children are taken out of regular education classes to other settings to serve them. Sometimes services are taken to the student. **Resource rooms** are settings used to provide special education outside the regular education classroom for 21 to 60 percent of the school day. **Special classes** are settings in which students receive special education and related services outside the regular classroom for more than 60 percent of the school day. Students may be placed in special classrooms with part-time instruction in regular classes or placed in special classes full time on a regular school campus.

Even when students require full-time special services, there are different degrees of "restrictiveness." Some students spend all their time in special education classrooms. Others, because of illness or other medical problems, are educated in hospitals or at home. Still others are taught in residential (institutional) settings, in classes run and staffed by personnel from local school districts. In the most restrictive setting, students live in a residential school or institution and are taught by staff members of that school or institution. In Table 2.2 we show the continuum of settings in which students receive special education, and report the most recent figures on the numbers or proportions of students with disabilities who are educated in each setting.

There is increasing widespread belief that removing students from regular classroom settings to provide services is not a good idea. Rather, whenever possible, services are brought to the student. For example, a speech and language specialist may come into the regular classroom to provide special instruction for those with language needs. Or a resource room teacher may work with the regular classroom teacher to develop instructional strategies and tactics.

Mainstreaming

This process of keeping the student in the regular classroom as much as possible is known as **mainstreaming**. As Chapter 3 demonstrates, it is partly an outgrowth of legal requirements that students be educated in the "least restrictive environment." But advocates of mainstreaming believe in it for more than legal reasons. They believe that students with disabilities profit socially and academically from interactions with their peers without disabilities. Further, they believe the reverse is true: Students without disabilities can benefit from interacting with those who have disabilities. Mainstreaming helps all students develop an understanding and appreciation of the diversity in our society.

The terms *inclusion* or *full inclusion* are increasingly used in place of the term *mainstreaming*. It is common now for state education agency personnel to talk about their state being a "full inclusion state" or about mandating full inclusion of students with disabilities. Some school districts, like Johnson City, New York, are now described as full inclusion districts. The goal of full inclusion is placement and instruction of all students—regardless of type or severity of disability—in their neighborhood schools, in the regular classroom.

There is much debate among educators and policy makers regarding the ethics and efficacy of educating students with disabilities in regular school settings along with their peers. Sometimes the debate consists of strong assertions that placement in set-aside structures limits students' cognitive, academic, and social development. Sometimes it consists of strong assertions that placement in general education settings enhances the cognitive, academic, and social development of students with disabilities, and sometimes the contention is made that it is impossible to meet the special learning needs of students with disabilities without providing a full continuum of services. Most educators now believe very strongly that students with disabilities should be educated as much as possible in regular classrooms with their same age peers, that extra assistance, necessitated by disabilities, should be provided in regular classes, and

Table 2.2	Percentages of Students Who Receive Special Education Services in Six Main Educational Environments	

Environment	Students (percent)	Description
Regular Class	33.7	Students receive a majority of their education in a regular classroom and receive special education and related services outside the regular classroom for less than 21 percent of the school day. This option includes children placed in a regular class and receiving special education within the regular class as well as children placed in a regular class and receiving special education outside the regular class.
Resource Room	34.6	Students receive special education and related services outside the regular classroom for 21 to 60 percent of the school day. This includes students placed in resource rooms with part-time instruction in a regular class.
Special Class	25.2	Students receive special education and related services outside the regular classroom for more than 60 percent of the school day. They may also receive part-time instruction in regular classes.
Separate School Facility	4.9	Students receive special education and related services in separate day schools for students with disabilities for greater than 50 percent of the school day.
Residential Facility	0.8	Students receive education in a public or private residential facility, at public expense, for greater than 50 percent of the school day.
Homebound/Hospital Environment	0.7	Students placed in and receiving special education in hospital or homebound programs.

Source: U.S. Department of Education, 1993. *Fifteenth annual report to Congress on the implementation of the Individuals with Disabilities Education Act.* (Washington, DC: Author).

A Puppet Show Promotes Acceptance of Diversity

C. J., a boy who used a wheelchair, was mainstreamed early in his educational career. Other than a few accommodations for his medical needs, he required no special services. But his third-grade teacher saw his inclusion in the regular class as an opportunity to promote an appreciation for diversity among all the students.

To do so, she used a puppet program called "Count Me In," developed by the PACER Center in Minneapolis. The program features child-sized, multicultural puppets that represent children who are blind, deaf, physically disabled, and mentally retarded, and who have epilepsy or learning disabilities. The puppets perform a dialogue or skit, using different scripts for different age groups. The performance gives students a comfortable opportunity to discover how children with various disabilities feel, think, and function in the world. Students also learn about wheelchairs, hearing aids, braille books, and other adaptive equipment. After the skit, students can ask the puppet characters questions.

C. J.'s teacher found that the program helped students discover that children with disabilities are like everyone else in most ways. Not surprisingly, C. J.'s inclusion in the regular classroom was a smashing success.

Some of the "Count Me In" puppets: Gina, Grandma, Lilly, Jay, Mitch, and Sally. *Reprinted with permission from the PACER Center, Minneapolis, MN.*

that every effort should be made to involve students with disabilities in regular class activities and to encourage their acceptance and social integration. Disagreements come about over defining the phrases "to the extent possible" and "every effort should be made." They also come about because inclusion is implemented in radically different ways in different schools and school districts. Personnel in one district might believe they have met the intent of full inclusion when they "put" students with disabilities in general education classes, even without special education supports. Others believe they have met that intent only when students are placed and the necessary supports are provided. Still others believe inclusion has occurred only if schools are radically restructured to include all severity levels in regular classrooms, there is no separate system called special education, and funds for special education, compensatory education, and general education are pooled.

You will observe in school districts today that full inclusion is both an action and a state of mind. Some educators believe they have to justify the presence of a student with a disability before the student is included; others believe they have to justify the student's separation before the student is excluded. Listen carefully as you hear people talk about full inclusion. Listen to the view they express on inclusion, but listen also to how they define inclusion and the kinds of practices they believe give evidence of it. Clearly, throughout all of the discussion and debate on mainstreaming, inclusion, full inclusion, and placement, there is a move to bring services to students rather than students to services. And this means that regular education teachers need to be prepared to adapt their teaching in many ways. Moreover, their job will involve cooperating with other teachers and professionals, such as speech and language specialists, resource room teachers, and school psychologists.

Diversity and Special Education in Perspective

Reasons for increase in disabilities

Diversity is growing among those who attend our nation's schools. This means that students have more special needs. At the same time, more students are being classified as disabled. The increase in disabilities results in part from the prevalence of very difficult social circumstances. It also stems from the success of Herculean medical interventions, which now save the lives of infants and toddlers who might otherwise have died. It may also result, however, from the difficulty of distinguishing disabilities from the effects of an unusual cultural or social background.

Special education and diversity

Special education is one way to deal with the diversity of students in present-day schools. But diagnostic personnel are faced with a very hard task in deciding who to serve under special education guidelines. Not only must they provide evidence that a student meets state criteria for eligibility, but they also must take diversity and individual acculturation into account as they do so.

Time misspent

We think efforts to separate disability from diversity are doomed to be difficult. Educators and psychologists spend far too much time trying to decide whom to serve or whether a specific student is eligible. They also spend too much time judging why specific students are having difficulty. In contrast, they spend far too *little* time deciding what to do with youngsters who experience difficulty—how to help them.

The job of educators is to make students more competent. This means that educators should spend their time delineating the kinds of competencies students, teachers, and parents want students to achieve; ascertaining gaps between actual and desired competencies; and designing instructional interventions to help narrow the gap between actual and desired behavior.

Increasing competence, not classification

We support efforts that are designed to develop competence in students, but oppose the increased classification of students as disabled. Educators must work diligently along with families and caregivers, and along with entire communities, to understand diversity and to enable more students to achieve the desired outcomes of schooling.

What Every Teacher Should Know

- Present-day schools and classrooms are characterized by considerable diversity—in ethnicity, language, cultural background, and family experience, as well as physical, mental, and emotional skills.
- Because of this diversity, multicultural education is increasingly important.
- Recognition of this diversity means that more and more students are considered exceptional and have special needs.
- Special needs, however, do not automatically qualify a student for special education. The student must fit specific criteria established by the state. The process of determining eligibility for special education and designing a program for a student can be lengthy and complicated.
- Students eligible for special education may receive direct services, indirect or consultative services, and related services. These can be provided in a variety of settings, ranging from the regular classroom to a residential institution or hospital.
- Today's educational movement is toward mainstreaming—educating students with disabilities in the regular classroom as much as possible.

Projects

1. Divide your class into groups and discuss the extent to which education can and should play a role in promoting cultural differences. How can the curriculum of the school be modified to account for cultural differences?
2. Select a minority commonly represented in the United States (Hispanic, Asian American, African American). Through reading and interviewing representatives of the group, prepare a written report describing what the group expects from education, the group's desired educational outcomes, and the extent to which expectations differ for males and females.
3. Prepare a written report describing the kinds of social services available in your community for families and children who are poor.

For Your Information

Books

Baca, L. M., & Almanza, E. (1991). *Language minority students with disabilities.* Reston, VA: Council for Exceptional Children.
> This text discusses issues to consider in providing special education services to students for whom English is not the first language.

Cassie, D. (1984). *So who's perfect! People with visible differences tell their own stories.* Scottdale, PA: Herald Press.
> An excellent compilation of experiences of people with disabilities.

Fanshawe, E. (1975). *Rachel.* Scarsdale, NY: Bradbury.
> Rachel enjoys life and participates fully in many activities at home, at school, and on vacation, illustrating similarities between people with disabilities and their peers.

Golnick, D. M., & Chinn, P. C. (1990). *Multicultural education in a pluralistic society* (3rd ed.). Columbus, OH: Macmillan.
> A useful survey of considerations and practices in multicultural education.

Ortiz, A., & Ramirez, B. (1988). *Schools and culturally diverse exceptional students: Promising practices and future directions.* Reston, VA: Council for Exceptional Children.
> In considering instructional practices for culturally diverse children who are exceptional, this book focuses on ways to improve education in the future.

Phelan, T. (1979). *The S. S. Valentine.* New York, NY: Macmillan.
> Connie, who uses a wheelchair to move around, is a success in the class play. Excellent book for upper elementary school students.

Roy, R. (1985). *Move over, wheelchairs coming through!* New York, NY: Clarion Books.
> Seven young people in wheelchairs talk about their lives with disabilities.

Organizations

Association for Culturally and Linguistically Diverse Exceptional Learners

This organization is a division of the Council for Exceptional Children. Its activities are focused on delivery of educational services to and improving educational outcomes for students with disabilities who are culturally and linguistically diverse. For more information, contact the Council for Exceptional Children, 1920 Association Dr., Reston, VA, 22091.

International Council on Disability

Founded in 1953, ICD is a council made up of 68 nongovernmental organizations granted consultative status by the United Nations Economic and Social Council. The ICD assists the United Nations and specialized agencies in developing a well coordinated program for the rehabilitation of individuals with disabilities throughout the world. For more information, contact ICD, 25 E. 21st St., 4th Fl., New York, NY 10010.

3

The Legal Basis for Special Education

- How have laws and court decisions expanded educational alternatives for students with special needs?

- What is an individualized education program?

- What is an individualized family service plan?

- Why is the equal protection clause of the Constitution relevant to special education?

- What role have parents of children with disabilities played in changing the delivery of special services?

Timothy W. was a thirteen-year-old with quadriplegia and severe mental retardation. He could hear and respond to words, music, and touching, but his school district in Rochester, New Hampshire, decided that he was not eligible for special education services because there was no indication that he would benefit from them. Basically, the school district thought he could not be educated, so there was no point in spending money on a program for him.

His parents and others disagreed, and a suit was filed on his behalf in 1974, alleging that his legal rights had been violated. The case dragged on until 1988, when a U.S. District Court upheld the school district's decision. According to the court, federal law required school districts to determine first whether a child would benefit from special education; if, like Timothy, the child would presumably show little or no benefit, no special education was necessary.

The next year, however, a federal appeals court reversed the decision. Basing their decision on the 1975 Education for All Handicapped Children Act, the appeals court judges declared that all children with disabilities must receive an appropriate public education, regardless of the severity of the disabilities or the achievement level the children might be expected to attain. The judges sent the case back to the district court, demanding that the school district develop an individualized education program for Timothy.

The decision created a good deal of controversy. Some people celebrated the ruling that federal law really meant what it said: All children with disabilities have the right to a free appropriate public education. Others, however—especially public school officials—worried about the financial burden on public schools and on taxpayers. ■

Many legal changes in recent decades

As the case of Timothy W. demonstrates, the courts and federal and state legislatures have become deeply involved in the process of special education over the past twenty-five years. Educators have been compelled to comply with an increasing number of court rulings and laws. In this process of change the primary movers have been the parents of students with disabilities. Much of the legislation and most of the court rulings that have changed the practices of special education are a product of parents' working to redress problems with the education their children were receiving. Parents have formed advocacy groups, acting on behalf of students with disabilities. For example, if a group of parents of children who are mentally retarded believes that their children are being excluded from school programs, the parents go to court to compel the schools to include the children. When many parents in many states start taking legal action on the same issue—such as the inclusion of children who are mentally retarded in public school classes—and when that action reflects a shift in public opinion, Congress may pass a law that addresses the parents' concerns. Over time, special education has undergone radical change as a result of such judicial and legislative actions.

Before 1975 students with disabilities did not have the right to a free, appropriate public education. As a result, many students with severe disabilities were relegated to living at home with their parents, not attending school, often not being taken out of the house. Others were placed in institutions where they were treated in a "custodial" manner. Staff attended to their physical needs, but they received little or no education. Today all students, including those with disabilities, have the right to a free, appropriate public education in a setting that is as normal as possible.

The law continues to change

It is important to recognize that the situation is dynamic. People talk about the law, but the law is always changing. Practices that were followed yesterday may be illegal today. Procedures that are required today may be replaced by others tomorrow. Laws, rules, and regulations change as society's social and economic priorities change. Still, despite the evolutionary nature of the process, at any specific time the laws, practices, and procedures that govern education are expected to reflect the broad principles of freedom and equality that society, through the Constitution, has agreed on. As we write this text—even as you read it—Congress, state legislatures, and the courts are shaping public policy in special education by making and interpreting laws that affect how students are treated in our schools.

Equal protection clause

The fundamental principle that underlies both litigation and legislation on the rights of students who are exceptional is the **equal protection clause** of the Fourteenth Amendment to the U.S. Constitution. The Fourteenth Amendment specifies that "no State shall make or enforce any law which shall abridge the privileges or immunities of citizens of the United States; nor shall any State deprive any person of life, liberty, or property, without due process of law; nor deny to any person within its jurisdiction the *equal protection* of the laws." It was the civil rights movement that pushed the equal protection clause onto national and state agendas. As court decisions and laws addressed the rights of minorities and women, the movement gradually expanded to protect the rights of people with disabilities.

Laws

If you asked one hundred directors of special education why special education services existed in their school districts, more than half probably would answer that state and federal laws required them. If you asked specific questions—Why do you try to educate nondisabled students and students who have disabilities in the same classes? Why do you allow parents to challenge proposed changes in their child's educational program? Why do you make extensive efforts to conduct evaluations that are not racially or culturally biased? Why do school personnel write individualized education programs for students with disabilities?—again, most of the directors probably would say that state and federal laws required these actions. Moreover, most would indicate that changes that have taken place in the education of students with disabilities, changes that have been in response to the courts or legislatures, have been for the good.

Capsule history

The history of legislation to provide services for people with disabilities dates back over 160 years. Before 1950, most laws were directed at providing institutional care or rehabilitative services. For example, in the nineteenth century, legislation was enacted to fund asylums, hospitals, and institutions for those with physical and mental disabilities. In the first half of the twentieth century, laws were passed to support vocational rehabilitation for disabled war veterans, and counseling and job placement for citizens with physical disabilities. In the 1950s, the focus of legislation began to change. Although state and community facilities continued to be funded, there was a new emphasis on research and training, vocational education, assessment, and special education services.

Five important laws

In this section we examine five laws that have had important effects on the current practice of special education: Section 504 of the Rehabilitation Act of 1973 (Public Law 93–112), the Education for All Handicapped Children Act of 1975 (Public Law 94–142), the 1986 Amendments to the Education for All Handicapped Children Act (Public Law 99–457), the Individuals with Disabilities Education Act of 1990 (Public Law 101–476), and the Americans with Disabilities Act of 1992 (Public Law 101–336). Table 3.1 lists the major provisions of these five laws.

Section 504 of the Rehabilitation Act of 1973

Section 504 of the Rehabilitation Act of 1973, which was finally adopted in 1977, prohibits discrimination against people with disabilities.

Discrimination prohibited

> No otherwise qualified handicapped individual shall, solely by reason of his handicap, be excluded from the participation in, be denied the benefits of, or be subjected to discrimination in any program or activity receiving federal financial assistance.

Since states and school districts depend at least in part on federal money to educate students with disabilities, most choose to comply with this mandate.

Equal access

Another important provision of Section 504 is architectural accessibility— the removal of steps and other barriers that limit the participation of people with disabilities. The law does not require that every building be barrier free, or that every method of transportation be accessible to those who are disabled. Instead, it demands equal access to programs and services. For instance, a college does not have to make every building barrier free, but it does have to offer at least one section of every class in a building that is barrier free. If band con-

| Table **3.1** | Major Federal Laws and Their Key Provisions |

Section 504 of the Rehabilitation Act (1973)

- *It is illegal to deny participation in activities, benefits of programs, or to in any way discriminate against a person with a disability solely because of the disability.*
- *Individuals with disabilities must have equal access to programs and services.*
- *Auxiliary aids must be provided to individuals with impaired speaking, manual, or sensory skills.*

Education for All Handicapped Children Act (1975)

- Students with disabilities have the right to a free, appropriate public education.
- Schools must have on file an individualized educational program for each student with a disability.
- Parents have the right to inspect school records on their child, and when changes are made in a student's educational placement or program, parents must be informed. Parents have the right to challenge what is in records or to challenge changes in placement.
- Students with disabilities have the right to be educated in the least restrictive educational environment.
- Students with disabilities must be assessed in ways that are considered fair and nondiscriminatory. They have specific protections.

1986 Amendments to the Education for All Handicapped Children Act

- Extends all rights of the Education for All Handicapped Children Act to preschoolers with disabilities.
- Each school district must conduct a multidisciplinary assessment and develop for each preschool child with a disability an individualized family service plan.

Individuals with Disabilities Education Act (1990)

- A reauthorization of the Education for All Handicapped Children Act.
- Adds two new disability categories (traumatic brain injury and autism) to the definition of students with disabilities.
- Adds a comprehensive definition of transition services.
- Includes provisions to make assistive technology more widely available.

Americans with Disabilities Act (1992)

- Prohibits discrimination on the basis of disability in employment, services rendered by state and local governments, places of public accommodation, transportation, and telecommunication services.

A disability is no reason not to be treated like everybody else. © 1993 Aneal Vohra/ Unicorn Stock Photos.

certs are held in only one building on campus, that building must be accessible to those who are disabled, so that they, like their nondisabled peers, have the opportunity to attend concerts. If the college does not make that building barrier free, any federal funds it receives can be cut off.

Auxiliary aids

Section 504 also mandates the provision of auxiliary aids (readers for students who are blind, interpreters for students who are deaf) for those with impaired sensory, manual, or speaking skills. This does not mean that a school must provide these services at all times; it simply means that it cannot exclude students because it does not have an appropriate aid present.

Most of the provisions of Section 504 were incorporated into and expanded in the Education for All Handicapped Children Act of 1975 and later legislation. But Section 504 still serves a purpose because of its breadth of coverage: Its provisions are not restricted to a specific age group or to education. Section 504 is the law most often cited in court cases involving employment of people with disabilities and appropriate education in colleges and universities for students who are disabled. Also, the accessibility provisions of the law have removed the architectural barriers that limited the full participation of those with disabilities in school and community functions. Recently Section 504 has been used to get services for students who are said to have attention deficit disorders. Since attention deficit disorders are not defined as disabilities by the Individuals with Disabilities Education Act, Section 504 has once again played a major role.

Education for All Handicapped Children Act

On November 29, 1975, then-President Gerald R. Ford signed the **Education for All Handicapped Children Act.** This famous act is often cited simply by its number: **Public Law 94–142.** The law mandated *a free, appropriate public education* for students with disabilities between the ages of 3 and 21. Its objectives were

Objectives of PL 94–142

1. to assure that all children with disabilities have available to them a free, appropriate public education.
2. to assure that the rights of children with disabilities and their parents are protected.
3. to assist States and localities to provide for the education of children with disabilities.
4. to assess and assure the effectiveness of efforts to educate children with disabilities.

The Education for All Handicapped Children Act came about because parents, advocacy groups, and professionals were dissatisfied with certain conditions and brought them to the attention of legislators. Among other things, Congress found that

Problems addressed by PL 94–142

- more than 8 million children with disabilities (from birth to age 21) were living in the United States, more than half of whom were not receiving an appropriate education.
- more than 1 million children with disabilities were excluded entirely from the educational system, and that many others were enrolled in regular education classes where, because their disabilities were undetected, they were not learning as much as could be expected.
- families were being forced to find services outside the public schools because the educational services within the schools were inadequate.

The lawmakers believed that special education could make a difference, that with special education services these children would stand a better chance of achieving their potential. Moreover, they believed that it was in the national interest to fund programs to meet the needs of students who were disabled.

Procedures specified

The law sets forth a number of procedures; states that do not comply with them cannot receive federal funds. Specifically, the law requires each state to have a plan that fully describes the policies and procedures used to ensure a free, appropriate education for all students with disabilities between the ages of 3 and 21, and to have procedures in place for identifying all students with disabilities.

The law makes several very specific provisions about the education of students with disabilities. For example, whenever possible, they must be taught in regular classrooms, along with their nondisabled peers. Also, tests and other evaluation devices used to decide the nature of students' disabilities must be both racially and culturally fair.

We talk about four specific areas of the law in the next subsection to give you a perspective on the magnitude of this landmark legislation. As you read, think about how these provisions affect the work of special education teachers, general education teachers, school psychologists, administrators, counselors, speech-language pathologists, and all the other people who work with students who are exceptional. Think also about how it will affect your work in attempting to achieve maximum educational results for students who are exceptional.

Individualized Education Program   A central concept to the law is the **individualized education program (IEP).** An IEP is a written document that describes

Contents of an IEP

- the student's present levels of functioning.
- the annual goals and short-term objectives of the program.
- the services to be provided and the extent of regular programming.
- the starting date and expected duration of services.
- evaluation procedures and criteria for monitoring progress.

Goals must be measurable

The IEP is the product of a thorough evaluation that begins with information about the child gathered from parents, teachers, and formal and informal assessments, and often ends with a review by a team of professionals. The law states that the instructional goals specified in an IEP must be measurable—observable and based on performance. Figure 3.1 shows the IEP of a fifth-grader with learning disabilities in reading, math, and language skills. Notice that assessment results are specified, along with long- and short-term goals, and a description of the services to be provided. In actual practice, the objectives are often written even more specifically, defining precise levels of desired achievement and ways they will be measured.

Reasons for IEPs

Why was such a formal plan necessary? What were lawmakers thinking when they drafted the IEP provision? First, they recognized the need for a mechanism to keep track of the students' progress. Second, special educators had convinced them that students would benefit more from their education if school personnel had specific objectives for students, a plan of where they were going and how they were going to get there, and a method for evaluating the extent to which the students were meeting individual goals.

The IEP has had a profound effect on the activities of teachers, school psychologists, and other school personnel. Students must be assessed by a multidisciplinary team, and that assessment must form the basis of students' individual instructional programs. These programs can be carried out in a variety of settings (general education classes, self-contained classes, homes, separate schools), and teachers (in both general and special education) are expected to provide instruction that ties in with the goals specified in the IEP.

INDIVIDUALIZED EDUCATION PROGRAM   _11/11/95_

Date

STUDENT: Last Name   First   Middle

_5.3_   _8-4-85_

School of Attendance   Home School   Grade Level   Birthdate/Age

School Address   School Telephone Number

Child Study Team Members   _LD Teacher_

Case Manager

Homeroom   _Parents_

Name   Title   Name   Title

Facilitator

Name   Title   Name   Title

Speech

Name   Title   Name   Title

Summary of Assessment Results

IDENTIFIED STUDENT NEEDS: _Reading from last half of DISTAR II –_
present performance level

LONG-TERM GOALS: _To improve reading achievement level by at_
least one year's gain. To improve math achievement to grade level. To improve
language skills by one year's gain.

SHORT-TERM GOALS: _Master Level 4 vocabulary and reading skills._
Master math skills in basic curriculum. Master spelling words from Level 3 list.
Complete units 1 – 9 from Level 3 curriculum.

White copy – Cumulative folder   Golden rod – Case manager
Pink copy – Special teacher   Yellow copy – Parent

Figure 3.1
An Individualized Education Program
(continued on next page)

Description of Services to Be Provided

Type of Service	Teacher	Starting Date	Amt. of time per day	OBJECTIVES AND CRITERIA FOR ATTAINMENT
SLD Level III	LD teacher	11-11-95	2 1/2 hrs.	**Reading:** will know all vocabulary through the "Honeycomb" level. Will master skills as presented through DISTAR II. Will know 123 sound-symbols presented in "Sound Way to Reading". **Math:** will pass all tests at basic 4 level. **Spelling:** 5 words each week from Level 3 list. **Language:** will complete Units 1–9 of the grade 4 language program. Will also complete supplemental units from "Language Step by Step".

Mainstream Classes	Teacher	Amt. of time per day	OBJECTIVES AND CRITERIA FOR ATTAINMENT
		3 1/2 hrs.	**Out-of-seat behavior:** sit attentively and listen during mainstream class discussions. A simple management plan will be implemented if he does not meet this expectation. **Mainstream modifications of Social Studies:** will keep a folder in which he expresses through drawing the topics his class will cover. Modified district social studies curriculum. No formal testing will be made. An oral reader will read text to him, and oral questions will be asked.

The following equipment, and other changes in personnel, transportation, curriculum, methods, and educational services will be made:

DISTAR II Reading Program, Spelling Level 3, "Sound Way to Reading" Program, vocabulary tapes.

Substantiation of least restrictive alternatives:

The planning team has determined the student's academic needs are best met with direct SLD support in reading, math, language, and spelling.

ANTICIPATED LENGTH OF PLAN _1 yr._   The next periodic review will be held: **May 1996**
Date/Time/Place

☒ I do approve this program placement and the above IEP
☐ I do not approve this placement and/or the IEP   PARENT/GUARDIAN
☐ I request a conciliation conference   Principal or Designee

Figure 3.1
An Individualized Education Program *(continued)*
Source: Reprinted from "Honig v. Doe: The Suspension and Expulsion of Handicapped Students" by M. L. Yell, *Exceptional Children*, vol 56, pp. 60–69. Copyright © 1989 The Council for Exceptional Children. Reprinted with permission.

Parents have a right to challenge school decisions and often do so when services for students with disabilities need questioning. *Bob Daemmrich Photography.*

Rights of parents

Due Process The Fourteenth Amendment guarantees the citizens of the United States due process of law. Public Law 94–142 reaffirms that guarantee for students with disabilities. The law gives their parents, guardians, or parent surrogates the right to examine their child's records. It also gives them the right to independent evaluations of their child. At one time, the practice of testing children and making changes in their educational placement without their parents' knowledge or consent was widespread. Parents had little or no input in their child's education. The due process provisions of Public Law 94–142 bring parents into the system; they give parents an opportunity to be involved, to understand and question what the schools are doing with their child.

Prior written notice

Whenever a school proposes or refuses to change the identification, evaluation, or placement of a child, the parents must receive prior written notice (in their native language, if at all possible). Parents have a right to challenge the school's decision at an impartial hearing. If they are not satisfied with the findings of the hearing, in most states they can appeal the decision to the state education agency, and from there to the civil courts.

Due process hearing

At a due process hearing, parents have several rights: the right to counsel and/or experts in special education; the right to present evidence, cross-examine, and compel the attendance of witnesses; and the right to a written or taped record of the hearing. These due process rights apply whether the hearing is in an educational facility or in a court.

Protection in Evaluation Procedures   The protection in evaluation procedures (PEP) provisions of Public Law 94–142 address assessment practices. Those practices must be fair, with no racial or cultural bias. The provision was put in place because it was thought that students who were inappropriately assessed would be inappropriately labeled and placed. It was thought that they could end up in "dead end" placements, be stigmatized, and have limited life opportunities if they were assessed with tests that were not fair for them.

School personnel must provide state education agency personnel with assurance that they are using fair (unbiased) testing and evaluation materials to identify students with disabilities and to decide where they will receive their educational programs. Tests must be selected and administered in ways that are not racially and culturally discriminatory. There are specific rules and regulations for the implementation of the PEP provisions:

- A "full and individual evaluation" of a student's needs must be made before the student is placed in a special education program.
- Tests must be administered in the child's native language or other mode of communication.
- Tests must be valid for the specific purpose for which they are used.
- Tests must be administered by "trained personnel" following the instructions provided by their producer.
- Tests and other evaluation materials must be relevant to specific areas of educational needs, not designed to yield a single general IQ score.
- The results of tests administered to students who have impaired sensory, manual, or speaking skills must reflect aptitude or achievement, not the impairment.
- Special education placement cannot be determined on the basis of a single procedure. More than one test must be used.
- Evaluations for special education placement must be made by a multidisciplinary team, including at least one teacher or other specialist with "knowledge in the area of suspected disability."
- Students must be assessed in all areas related to their suspected disability, including general health, vision, hearing, behavior, general intelligence, motor abilities, academic performance, and language abilities.

The PEP provisions were included in Public Law 94–142 to address abuses in the assessment process. In the background testimony for this law, parents and their representatives asserted that children were being tested with unfair tests, instruments that were in languages other than their primary languages that included items from cultures other than those to which the children had been exposed. It was argued that a law should be enacted to stop these abuses. The product of that argument was the PEP provisions.

Least Restrictive Environment   Public Law 94–142 also specifies that students with disabilities be educated in the **least restrictive environment** (**LRE**).

Technology and changes in attitudes have helped many more students attend school with their neighbors and peers. *Elizabeth Crews.*

States must have policies and procedures in place to ensure that students with disabilities, including those in public or private institutions or other care facilities, are educated with their neighbors and peers. States must also ensure that students are removed from the regular education environment only when a disability is severe enough that instruction in regular classes with the use of supplementary aids and services is not effective.

The LRE provisions reflect the generally held belief that students are better off and demonstrate better development when they spend as much time as possible interacting with their nondisabled peers. If students can learn in an environment that is relatively nonrestrictive, then they can live and work in that environment as they get older. The provision is sometimes referred to as the *mainstreaming provision* because it specifies that students must be educated in the main stream of education to the fullest possible extent.

Mainstreaming

A massive educational reform

Summary   The intent of Public Law 94–142 was massive educational reform for students with disabilities. Its major provisions target different stages in the three-stage process that characterizes special education: (1) deciding whom to serve, (2) deciding how to serve those students, and (3) deciding whether the services have done any good. The due process and protection in evaluation-procedure provisions obviously relate to the first stage, determining eligibility. They attempt to reduce the problems inherent in deciding who should receive

Public Law 99–457 extends the right to a free, appropriate education and early intervention to preschool children with disabilities and those who are at risk of substantial developmental delays. *David Young-Wolff/ PhotoEdit.*

special education. The IEP and LRE provisions target the second stage, treatment practices. All the provisions address aspects of progress evaluation, the third stage of the process. Of course, passing a law does not guarantee that changes will occur in the ways the law directs. Interpretation of the law—by the courts—influences the effect the law has on practice.

1986 Amendments to the Education for All Handicapped Children Act

In 1986 Congress amended Public Law 94–142, extending all rights and protections of the law to preschoolers with disabilities. Effective in the 1990–91 academic year, all states that applied for funds under Public Law 94–142 had to provide free, appropriate public education to all children with disabilities ages 3 through 5.

Program for early intervention

At the same time, as part of Public Law 99–457, the 1986 Amendments to the Education for All Handicapped Children Act, Congress established a new state grant program for infants and toddlers with disabilities. Eligible for **early intervention** are children from birth through age 2 who are delayed in development or at risk of substantial delay in development. The states have the authority to specify the criteria for deciding whom to serve.

To receive the federal funds available as part of Public Law 99–457, states must have an agency that administers the services and an interagency coordinating council to help develop programs and services. State early intervention programs are required to provide all eligible infants and toddlers with multidisciplinary assessments, individualized programs, and case management services.

As part of the early intervention program, the law specifies that each school district use a multidisciplinary assessment to develop an **individualized family service plan (IFSP)** for each child. The IFSP functions much like an IEP but includes a description of the family's needs and services as well as those of the child. It must include

Changes in language and categories

- a statement of the child's present level of cognitive, social, speech and language, and self-help development.
- a statement of the family's strengths and needs related to enhancing the child's development.
- a statement of the major outcomes expected for the child and family.
- criteria, procedures, and timelines for measuring progress.
- a statement of the specific early intervention services necessary to meet the unique needs of the child and family, including methods, frequency, and intensity of service.
- projected dates for initiation and expected duration of services.
- the name of the person who will manage the case.
- procedures for transition from early intervention into a preschool program.

Individuals with Disabilities Education Act (IDEA)

Civil rights for Americans with disabilities

The **Individuals with Disabilities Education Act (IDEA)** (1990) is a reauthorization of Public Law 94–142. Congress renamed the Education for All Handicapped Children Act and reaffirmed a national intent to support alternative education for students with special learning needs. To reflect contemporary practices, Congress replaced references to "handicapped children" with "children with disabilities." Two new disability categories (autism and traumatic brain injury) were added to the definition of "children with disabilities," and a comprehensive definition of "transition services" (services to ensure smooth movement from school to postschool activities) was added. The law also specified that schools must develop individualized transition plans (ITPs) for students 16 years of age or older.

IDEA further states that individuals with disabilities should have access to assistive technology equipment and associated services, including purchasing or leasing technological devices and training in their use. Calculators for students with learning disabilities, closed-caption television systems for students with hearing impairments, electronic communication aids for students with speech or language disorders—all these are examples of assistive technology supplied under IDEA guidelines. Decisions about a student's need for assistive technology are generally made by the team that develops the IEP.

Americans with Disabilities Act (ADA)

Civil rights for Americans with disabilities

The purpose of the **Americans with Disabilities Act (ADA)** (1992) is to extend to people with disabilities civil rights similar to those now available on the basis of race, color, national origin, gender, and religion through the Civil Rights Act of 1964. ADA prohibits discrimination on the basis of disability in employment, services rendered by state and local governments, places of public accommodation, transportation, and telecommunication services (such as phones). The ADA says that employers cannot discriminate against individuals with disabilities. They must use employment application procedures that enable individuals with disabilities to apply for jobs; in making decisions about whom to hire, advance, or discharge, employers are not allowed to do so on the basis of disability; individuals with disabilities should not be paid differently from others, they have the same rights to job training, and they are to have the same privileges of employment as others.

Court Cases

Impetus from court cases

The laws we have described have brought about a revolution in special education within the last thirty years. Much of the impetus behind these laws came from court cases, especially ones brought by parents to challenge existing education practices. Even after the passage of a law, its effect often depends on the way the courts interpret it. For these reasons, understanding the legal basis of special education requires some knowledge of major court rulings, as well as the realization that courts are continuing to interpret and reinterpret the law every year. Some of the most important court cases that have influenced special education are listed in Table 3.2.

The *Brown* case

Court action before the enactment of Public Law 94–142 in 1975 focused on the individual's right to a free, appropriate public education and on guidelines for the states to follow in educating students. The cornerstone of this litigation was set in 1954, when the U.S. Supreme Court, in *Brown* v. *Board of Education,* ruled that separate schools for black and white students are inherently unequal and therefore unconstitutional. The parents of students with disabilities who later sued school systems for the denial of equal protection—complaining that their children had been assessed inaccurately or had been placed in inferior educational settings—based their legal arguments on the decision in *Brown.*

Issues addressed by the courts

Other issues addressed by the courts before Public Law 94–142 included ability grouping based on test performance, the notion that children are persons under the Constitution and have civil rights, the exclusion of students with disabilities from schools, the misclassification of minority and non–English speaking children, and the exclusion from schools of students with

Table 3.2　Primary Rulings in Court Cases Relevant to Special Education

Case	Ruling
Watson v. *City of Cambridge* (1893)	A student can be expelled for "disorderly conduct or imbecility."
Beattie v. *State Board of Education* (1919)	Students who are physically handicapped can be excluded from school when their presence has a "depressing and nauseating effect" on other students.
Brown v. *Board of Education* (1954)	Segregation in schools is illegal because it denies equal protection and equal opportunity (U.S. Supreme Court).
Hansen v. *Hobson* (1967)	Ability grouping (tracking) based on pupil performance on standardized tests, as employed in the Washington, DC, schools, is unconstitutional, violating both due process and equal protection.
Tinker v. *Des Moines Independent School District* (1969)	Children are "persons" under the Constitution and have civil rights independent of their parents (U.S. Supreme Court).
Diana v. *State Board of Education* (1970)	In a consent decree, the state of California agreed ■ that all children whose primary language is not English should be tested in both their primary language and English ■ to eliminate "unfair verbal items" from tests. ■ to reevaluate all Mexican-American and Chinese students enrolled in educable mentally retarded (EMR) classes using only nonverbal items and testing them in their primary language. ■ to develop IQ tests reflecting Mexican-American culture and standardized only on Mexican-Americans.
Covarrubias v. *San Diego Unified School District* (1971)	A consent decree establishing the right of plaintiffs to monetary damages for misclassification.
Lemon v. *Bossier Parish School Board* (1971)	Ability grouping is unconstitutional.
Mills v. *Board of Education* (1972)	■ Exclusion of students labeled as having behavior problems, mentally retarded, emotionally disturbed, or hyperactive is unconstitutional. ■ Any child with a disability has a right, under equal protection, to a "constructive education," including appropriate specialized instruction. ■ Due process of law requires a hearing before exclusion from, termination of, or classification into a special program.
Pennsylvania Association for Retarded Children v. Commonwealth of Pennsylvania (343 F. Supp. 279, 1972)	In a consent decree, Pennsylvania was enjoined from excluding from schools students with mental retardation. The state agreed to engage in extensive activities to locate and assess children with retardation.

(continued)

Table **3.2**	Primary Rulings in Court Cases Relevant to Special Education *(continued)*

Case	Ruling
Goso v. *Lopez* (1974)	Due process is required before students are suspended or expelled from school.
Hairston v. *Drosick* (1974)	Exclusion of children with disabilities from the regular classroom without procedural safeguards is a violation of their constitutional rights as well as of the Rehabilitation Act of 1973.
Wyatt v. *Stickney* (1971; 1974)	Individuals with mental retardation who are committed to a state school have a right to adequate treatment (education).
Washington v. *Davis* (1976)	When actions result in a discriminatory outcome, one can assume discriminatory intent.
Frederick L. v. *Thomas* (1976; 1977)	Philadelphia schools must engage in massive screening and follow-up evaluation designed to locate and serve students with learning disabilities.
Panitch v. *State of Wisconsin* (1977)	A long delay in implementing a state law designed to give equal education to those with disabilities is sufficient indication of "intentional discrimination," in violation of the equal protection clause.
Lora v. New York City Board of Education (1978)	■ The process of evaluating students to determine if they should enter "special day schools" for emotionally disturbed students violates students' rights to treatment and due process. ■ To the extent that students are referred to largely racially segregated schools, there is a denial of equal opportunity in violation of Title VI. ■ New York City's monetary problems do not excuse violation of students' rights.
Larry P. v. *Riles* (1979)	■ The California State Department of Education cannot use intelligence tests to place black students in EMR classes. ■ Schools in California must eliminate the disproportionate placement of black students in EMR classes. ■ Schools in California must reevaluate all black students currently enrolled in EMR classes.
PASE v. *Hannon* (1980)	Intelligence tests are not biased against black students, and so are appropriate for use in placing black students in EMR classes. (This ruling contrasted with the one in *Larry P. v. Riles*.)
Board of Education of Hendrick Hudson Central School District v. *Rowley* (1982)	It is not necessary for a school district to provide a sign language interpreter in the classroom as part of a deaf child's education program. Schools do not have to develop the maximum potential of students with disabilities; but they must grant them access to educational opportunities.
Irving Independent School District v. *Tatro* (1984)	School personnel must provide related services that enable a child who is disabled to remain at school during the day.

Table 3.2	Primary Rulings in Court Cases Relevant to Special Education *(continued)*

Case	Ruling
Smith v. *Robinson* (1984)	Attorneys' fees are not reimbursable under Public Law 94–142.
Burlington School Committee v. *Department of Education* (1985)	Reimbursement for private school tuition is an appropriate form of relief for a court to grant.
Honig v. Doe (1988)	School officials cannot unilaterally decide to expel or suspend students with disabilities.
Timothy W. v. *Rochester School District* (1989)	All children with disabilities must be provided with educational programs, regardless of the severity of the disability and regardless of whether educators predict the child will benefit from education.

Source: Adapted and updated from Ysseldyke, J. E. and Algozzine, B. (1982). *Critical Issues in Special and Remedial Education.* Boston: Houghton Mifflin Co., pp. 215–217. Copyright © 1982 by Houghton Mifflin Company. Used with permission.

mental retardation. In separate cases, the courts ruled that the exclusion of students labeled as behavior problems, mentally retarded, emotionally disturbed, or hyperactive is unconstitutional; that it is illegal to group students by ability ("track") based on their performance on standardized tests; that all children with disabilities have the right to a "constructive" education; that assessment tests must be in a student's primary language (in California); and that students who are mentally retarded have the right to attend schools with students who are not retarded.

Most of the court cases listed in Table 3.2 are state or federal district court cases. In the remainder of this section we focus on five U.S. Supreme Court cases. The Supreme Court has been involved in defining and clarifying the

The meaning of appropriate education

meaning of *appropriate education* as mandated by Section 601c of Public Law 94–142. In *Board of Education* v. *Rowley* (1982), the Court overturned a lower-court ruling that had required a school to provide an interpreter for a deaf student. The case began when Amy Rowley's parents asked the school to provide a sign language interpreter in their deaf daughter's class on a full-time basis. The school was providing speech therapy, use of a hearing aid, and a tutor for one hour a day, and had offered sign language instruction to those of Amy's teachers who wanted it. But the school refused to put an interpreter in Amy's classroom. The Supreme Court ruled that the school was acting within its rights. In writing the decision for the Court, Justice William Rehnquist stated that schools do not have to develop the maximum potential of students with disabilities; the law was intended only to give students access to educational opportunities.

In *Irving Independent School District* v. *Tatro* (1984), the issue was the re-

Schools are required to provide simple medical services for all students. *Bob Daemmrich Photography.*

sponsibility of a school to provide a medical procedure, in this case catheterization, to a child with a disability. Chief Justice Warren Burger, writing for the majority, reasoned that

> a service that enables a handicapped child to remain at school during the day is an important means of providing the child with the meaningful access to education that Congress envisioned. . . . Services like [catheterization] that permit a child to remain at school during the day are not less related to the effort to educate than are services that enable the child to reach, enter, or exist in the school. (104 S.Ct. 3371 [1984]).

Burger went on to say that services like catheterization, which can be carried out by a school nurse, must be provided by public schools.

Use of private schools

A third case heard by the Supreme Court involved the payment by school districts of tuition and fees for students who are disabled to attend private schools. In *Burlington School Committee* v. *Department of Education* (1985), the lower courts asked the Supreme Court for a ruling on the meaning of appropriate education. Michael Panaco, a first-grader with a specific learning disability, was enrolled in a private school because his parents contended that he was not receiving an education that met his unique needs in the local public school. The Court noted that "where a court determines that a private placement desired by the parents was proper under the Act and that an IEP calling for placement in a public school was inappropriate, it seems clear beyond cavil

Bring Your Learning to Life

A Simple Medical Procedure

Amber Tatro was a child with spina bifida, a congenital disability in which the spinal column is imperfectly closed. To avoid damage to her kidneys, Amber needed a regular medical procedure known as clean intermittent catheterization (CIC), which involves washing a small metal tube called a catheter, inserting it in the bladder to allow urine to drain, pulling the catheter out, and wiping the area. This is a fairly simple procedure that can be done by a person with only minimal training; Amber's parents, her teenage brother, and her babysitters all performed CIC for her.

Her school district, however, refused to include CIC as part of Amber's IEP. CIC was a medical service, according to the school district, not a "related" service as required by Public Law 94–142. Amber's parents protested;

they pointed out that by not offering CIC, the school district was essentially excluding Amber from school.

The argument ended up in the court system, where it eventually reached the U.S. Supreme Court. The Supreme Court distinguished between medical services that require a doctor and those that can be performed by a school nurse. Schools do not have to offer medical treatment by a physician. But since the school nurse could readily perform Amber's CIC, the Court ruled that it was indeed a "related" service and the school district was legally required to provide it.

Legal fees

that appropriate relief include[s] . . . placing the child in a private school" (471 U.S. 359 [1985] p. 231). The Court ruled that the most important element of Public Law 94–142 is an appropriate educational program, wherever it takes place, and that the school district may be obliged to pay for private schooling.

Court actions take time. For example, the *Burlington* case took eight years. They also cost a lot of money. Parents who go to court on behalf of their child incur extensive legal fees. It is not surprising, then, that the fourth case heard by the Supreme Court involved the issue of responsibility for legal fees. In *Smith* v. *Robinson* (1984), the school district had agreed to place Thomas Smith, a youngster with cerebral palsy and physical and emotional handicaps, in a day treatment program at a hospital in Rhode Island. Later the school district informed the parents that the Rhode Island Department of Mental Health, Retardation and Hospitals would have to take over the expense of the program. The state supreme court ruled that the duty of funding the educational program rested with the local school, not the state. The parents appealed the case to a federal district court and, in addition, asked for payment of attorneys' fees. The district court agreed with the parents, but the court of appeals did not. The Supreme Court ruled that parents are responsible for paying attorneys' fees.

So the Supreme Court had ruled that parents could be reimbursed for private school tuition but not for attorneys' fees. In 1986 Congress settled the issue by passing the Handicapped Children's Protection Act, an amendment to Public Law 94–142. The amendment specified that courts could award attorneys' fees to parents who win in current proceedings or in cases that began after July 4, 1984 (coincidentally, the date that the rulings in both *Tatro* and *Smith* were read by the Supreme Court). Parents have the right to collect attorneys' fees. However, they must work in good faith to try to settle their case. Also there are specific conditions under which parents are not entitled to recover attorneys' fees.

Behavior problems

In *Honig* v. *Doe* (1988), the Supreme Court reaffirmed the decision of a lower court that schools cannot exclude students with disabilities, specifically those who have emotional disturbances, because of their behavior. The case involved the suspension of two students who were receiving special education services in the San Francisco School District. The students (called John Doe and Jack Smith in the decision) had been expelled for different reasons:

> Student Doe had been placed in a developmental center for handicapped students. While attending school, he assaulted another student and broke a window. When he admitted these offenses to the principal he was suspended for five days. The principal referred the matter to the school's student placement committee with the recommendation that Doe be expelled. The suspension was continued indefinitely as permitted by California state law, which allowed suspensions to extend beyond five days while expulsion proceedings were being held.
>
> Student Smith's individualized education program (IEP) stated he was to be placed in a special education program in a regular school setting on a trial basis. Following several incidences of misbehavior the school unilaterally reduced his program to half-day. His grandparents agreed to the reduction; however, the school district did not notify them of their right to appeal. A month later Smith was suspended for five days when he made inappropriate sexual comments to female students. In accordance with California law Smith's suspension was also continued indefinitely while expulsion proceedings were initiated by the school placement committee. (Yell, 1989)

The case went through several levels of courts, eventually ending up in the Supreme Court. Justice William Brennan, writing for the majority, stated that schools cannot unilaterally exclude disabled students. When placement is being debated, the child must remain in the current educational setting unless school officials and parents agree otherwise. The decision left a number of questions unanswered (Yell, 1989): In what ways can students with disabilities be disciplined? How should the schools deal with students who are a danger to themselves or others but whose parents do not consent to removal?

The Legal Basis for Special Education in Perspective

Law as the basis of practice

Constitutional provisions, legislation, and litigation have had tremendous impact on the field of special education. Much of current practice in the field has been shaped by them. This means that current changes in special education are less a product of new teaching techniques, new research findings, and new technologies than of new laws or interpretations of those laws.

What effect does this legal basis for special education have on those who work with exceptional students? As a practical matter, most of the changes have meant extra work for special educators—keeping detailed records, filling out forms, meeting with other team members. Another effect is the legal responsibility that has attached itself not only to school districts and schools, but also to educators.

Finding a balance

However, the lawmaking process draws on all kinds of information and opinion in the drafting of new legislation. New teaching techniques and research findings and technologies are examined. Parents, educators, and psychologists are heard. The end product tends to find a balance between earlier practice and ideal possibility, attained through common sense and common decency. That product—the laws that shape special education—has immeasurably improved the delivery of special services to exceptional students.

What Every Teacher Should Know

- New federal and state laws, combined with a number of important court cases, have brought major changes in special education within the last generation.

- The equal protection clause of the Constitution underlies much of the legal framework for special education.

- Major federal laws governing special education include Section 504 of the Rehabilitation Act (1973), the Education for All Handicapped Children Act (1975), the 1986 Amendments to the Education for All Handicapped Children Act, the Individuals with Disabilities Education Act (1990), and the Americans with Disabilities Act (1992).

- Federal laws require a free, appropriate public education for all children with disabilities. For each student who has a disability, educators must develop an individualized education program (IEP). For those receiving early intervention, an individualized family service plan (IFSP) is required.

- Students with disabilities must be educated in the least restrictive environment (LRE); in practice, this often leads to mainstreaming—educating students with disabilities in regular classrooms as much as possible.

- Federal laws also guarantee due process for students and their parents and require that evaluation be conducted in a fair and nondiscriminatory way.

- Court rulings have helped define what kind of educational services meet the requirement of "appropriate" education. The U.S. Supreme Court has determined, for example, that schools must provide simple medical procedures that can be administered by a school nurse and that school districts must pay for private schooling when no appropriate public schooling is available.

Projects

1. Obtain a copy of the Individuals with Disabilities Education Act. Read it and make a list of things school personnel must do to comply with the law.
2. Go to your library and locate a summary of one of the Supreme Court cases discussed in this chapter. Write a report in which you list the plaintiffs, the defendants, and the nature of the complaint. Then describe the arguments made by each side and the Court's decision.
3. Engage in a discussion with your classmates about why it has taken so much legal activity to get school districts to allow students with disabilities to attend school and to provide appropriate services for those students.

For Your Information

Books

Cutler, B. (1993). *You, your child, and special education: A guide to making the system work*. Baltimore: Paul H. Brookes.

A practical guide to special education law and children's educational rights.

Rothstein, L.F. (1990). *Special education law*. White Plains, NY: Longman.

Essential reading for those concerned about legal issues in special education. Rothstein's text is clearly the most definitive treatment of special education law with a focus on how the law affects children with disabling conditions in the public school system. The text contains reviews of all the major judicial decisions, statutes, and regulations with interpretations, explanations of their meanings, and detailed discussions. It contains information that will help teachers and administrators develop policies and make decisions that are consistent with legal requirements.

Wehman, P. (1993). *The ADA mandate for social change*. Baltimore: Paul H. Brookes.

This text provides a summary of the Americans with Disabilities Act and discusses its implications for individuals and organizations.

Organizations

Commission on Mental and Physical Disability Law

Founded in 1976, this organization gathers and disseminates information on court decisions, legislation, and administrative developments affecting people with mental and physical disabilities. It also makes available research tools like article reprints and expert witness lists. For more information, contact the American Bar Association, 1800 M St. NW, Washington, DC 20036.

National Legislative Council for the Handicapped
Founded in 1977, this organization works to ensure barrier-free environments, civil rights, acceptable living conditions, employment, education, and rehabilitation for individuals with disabilities. For more information, contact NLCH, P.O. Box 262, Taylor, MI 48180.

Journals

Individuals with Disabilities Education Law Reporter
This newsletter-type publication contains reviews of legislation and articles about the relevance of the law for students with disabilities. It includes summaries of the results of major national and state court cases. For more information, contact LRP Publications, 747 Dresher Rd., Box 980, Horsham, PA 19044-0980.

Part

II

Principles of Instruction and Assessment

How do we teach students who are exceptional? How do we decide what instruction each student needs, then deliver that instruction, then evaluate its results? Part II addresses these questions by providing an overview of instruction and assessment in special education.

Chapter 4 describes the general principles that guide effective instruction and presents strategies for putting each principle into practice. We believe these strategies are useful for students in all categories of special education—and for those in regular education as well.

Chapter 5 discusses special teaching methods and adaptations for students who are exceptional. This chapter also looks in detail at the use of individualized education programs. After reading Chapters 4 and 5, you should have a good idea of how teachers deliver special education in the regular classroom as well as in resource rooms and other special settings.

Finally, Chapter 6 concentrates on assessment practices in special education. We talk about the types of assessment, the decisions commonly based on assessment, and the methods of collecting information. We also consider the worries that people often have about assessment, and we offer guidelines for good assessment practices.

Chapter

The Process
of Instruction

Focusing Questions

- What are the four major components of instruction?

- Deciding what to teach is a diagnostic process; deciding how to teach it is a prescriptive process. What does this statement mean?

- What is the first step in presenting instruction?

- How do we teach thinking skills?

- How should feedback be used in the process of monitoring instruction?

- Why is task-specific praise important?

- What are four ways in which teachers can adjust instruction to meet individual students' needs?

- What is the difference between formative and summative evaluation?

Greg Olsen, a junior high industrial arts teacher, attended a class taught by Marie Blackburn on effective instruction. She gave those who attended the class the assignment of applying one principle of effective instruction that they had learned in the workshop to make changes in their classroom. The teachers who attended this session had to hand in a written report of their experiences in applying those principles, which were drawn from our resource entitled Strategies and Tactics for Effective Instruction *(Algozzine & Ysseldyke, 1992).*

Olsen had always had trouble having the students in his shop remember the classroom rules. He taught a wide diversity of students, nearly all of whom had special needs and some of whom had been declared eligible for special education services. In studying effective instruction he learned that there should be very few classroom rules and that they should be stated briefly. He also learned that an effective strategy for getting students to remember classroom rules was to arrange them so that the first letters would provide a memory aid. He reduced a list of thirty-three general safety rules to a set of five and used the phrase Safety **W**ill **A**lways **C**ome First *as a memory aid. The rules he stated were:*

S: *Safety first. Always be careful.*

W: *Wear safety glasses at all times during work periods.*

A: *Attend to the operation you are doing. Do not allow yourself to be distracted.*

C: *Clean up after yourself. A clean shop is a safe shop.*

F: *Follow all teacher's directions right away.*

This list made it much easier for Olsen to communicate the rules. When he gave students tests on the rules, the performance of all of the students (including those with quite severe disabilities) improved dramatically. Most important, students followed the class rules, and Olsen had many fewer safety infractions. He wrote up an account of his experiences in Teaching Exceptional Children *(Campbell & Olsen, 1994).* ■

A fundamental goal of teachers is to help students develop to their fullest potential by giving them the necessary skills to function in society. This goal is no different for students who are exceptional. A big part of teaching is deciding which skills to develop and how to teach those skills.

Are the teaching practices unique?

Does special education involve a unique set of teaching practices? Yes and no. For the most part, the things we do to plan, manage, deliver, and evaluate instruction for students who are exceptional are the same as those we do for those who are not exceptional. For example, the tactic Greg Olsen employed to

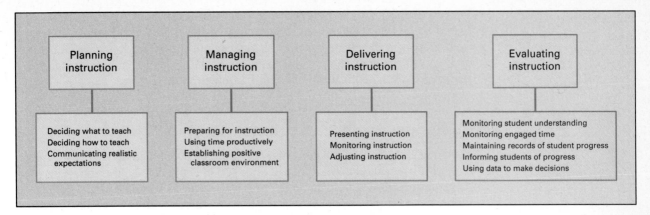

Figure 4.1 **Model of Effective Instruction**

increase students' memory of safety rules would be useful to students with and without disabilities. He would not change the rules for students with disabilities, and he probably would not have to modify the tactic for teaching the rules. Students with disabilities would learn the rules in the same ways as students who were not disabled. However, at times it is necessary to modify teaching practices. Certain students who are exceptional require specialized methods of instruction or instructional materials that have been adapted to their special learning needs. For example, specialized instructional methods using touch and hearing are necessary for students who have profound visual impairments, and their teachers use modified instructional materials (large-type books, raised-line paper, cassette recordings, computerized synthetic speech). But the basic principles of instruction—principles that are critical for effective teaching—continue to apply.

Examples of teaching adaptations

Phyllis is a student in Kim Bazan's class. She is blind. To meet her special learning needs in language arts, Bazan asked a student in a friend's class to tape-record reading assignments so that Phyllis would be able to participate in class discussions. She also had the student record daily quizzes to evaluate Phyllis's understanding of the content. When a unit was complete, Kim evaluated the overall level of Phyllis's knowledge by giving her an oral test, the same as the written test she had prepared for the rest of the class.

We've already discussed the various settings in which students with disabilities can be taught. In this chapter, we describe the components of effective instruction, the principles that make education work for all students. Figure 4.1 is based on an outline we developed to show the four components of effective instruction and the major principles for each component (Algozzine & Ysseldyke, 1992). In this chapter we describe these in more detail and share specific strategies for implementing some of the principles. Certain teaching ideas and suggestions appear in more than one section; although we risk sounding repetitive, it is important to realize that some teaching tactics have implications for several phases of instruction. For example, providing students with direct and immediate feedback is an important part of motivating them, as well as a way to keep them informed of their progress. You may want to refer to a separate publication, *Strategies and Tactics for Effective Instruction* (listed in the For Your Information section at the end of the chapter), to learn even more specific strategies and tactics for putting effective instruction into practice. In the next chapter, we examine some of the instructional variables that make special education different from regular education.

Components of Effective Instruction

Teaching is the systematic presentation of content assumed necessary for mastery within a general area of instruction. When Kim teaches, she first plans her presentations. Based on what her students currently know, she decides what to teach. For example, if the target area of instruction is addition of whole numbers, Kim uses information from formal and informal tests, observations, and interviews to determine her students' present levels of performance. She then decides how to improve their performance using instructional methods she believes will work. She might decide to use basal texts, manipulatives, games, or workbooks as her primary instructional materials. She decides how and when to evaluate the efforts of her instruction and when to modify it based on the results of her evaluations. She also anticipates how she will manage the instruction and any disruptions that occur during her presentations. As she teaches, these various activities overlap and come into play at different times.

Four groups of principles

The many principles of effective instruction can be grouped into four broad areas: **planning** instruction, **managing** instruction, **delivering** instruction, and **evaluating** instruction (see Figure 4.1). Whether they teach students with gifts and talents, mild disabilities, severe disabilities or no disabilities at all, teachers must plan, manage, deliver, and evaluate their instruction. Throughout this text we refer to these four principles as components of effective instruction.

Planning Instruction

If all students in a class were at the same instructional level, and if the goals and objectives of schooling were clearly prescribed and the same for all students, then instruction would consist of doing the same things with all students, being certain to do them in the right order and at the right time. But all students are not alike, and the goals and objectives of instruction are not the same for all students. Schools are becoming increasingly diverse environments, which is why instructional planning is such an important part of teaching.

Diversity necessitates planning

Instructional planning means making decisions—about what content to present, which materials or other activities to use, how to present information, and how to determine if students are learning. In deciding what to teach and how to teach it, teachers set goals and expectations for their students. These goals and expectations help students learn. Instructional planning, then, has three main principles: deciding what to teach, deciding how to teach it, and communicating realistic expectations (shown in Figure 4.1). We talk about each of these principles in the sections that follow, "unfolding" the figure as we do so.

Three principles of planning

Deciding What to Teach

The strategies involved in deciding what to teach are listed in Figure 4.2. In making decisions about what to teach, teachers have to assess their students' skill levels. They have to identify the skills students have and those they do not have. Teachers gather assessment information using tests, observations, and interviews. Much of this assessment occurs during instruction. Teachers sample students' performance by asking them to read aloud from their books, spell the words on their spelling lists, or do the kinds of math problems that are in their math texts. Larry Williams, our friend who is a special education teacher, uses this kind of informal assessment along with formal testing to plan instruction in his resource room. For example, standardized achievement tests tell him what his students know in broad content areas (science, social studies, mathematics). Using norm-referenced tests, he can make judgments about their relative knowledge and estimate the grade levels at which they are performing. Using criterion-referenced tests, he can identify the specific skills his students have and do not have. With an understanding of his students' academic and behavioral strengths and weaknesses, Larry is able to modify his instructional methods to meet the needs of individual students in his classes.

Another part of deciding what to teach is analyzing the instructional task. **Task analysis** consists of breaking down a complex task into its components. For example, to do the problem $105 \div 3$, a student must understand numerals, know the meaning of the division sign, and have a basic understanding of subtraction and multiplication. It's not enough to know what students are able to do; we also must know exactly what we want them to do. Only then can we match activities to the students' levels of skill development.

Task analysis also helps teachers plan a logical sequence of instruction. Students are more likely to learn if teachers present material in a clear, logical sequence. This is especially true when the acquisition of new skills depends on the learning of lower-level skills.

The instructional context or environment plays a part in deciding what to teach. Where will instruction take place? How long will the lesson(s) be? Who will be in the room during instructional presentations? In planning what to teach, Kim considers the instructional groupings that work best in her classroom. Usually she teaches students in a group, but sometimes she teaches them individually. She considers her students' performances, behaviors, and skills when they are in particular instructional arrangements. She also thinks about the physical space and the ways in which students interact in it. For example, if Darryl and Bobby are not getting along and their behavior is interfering with their learning, Kim figures it makes good sense to teach them in different groups. At another time, she would work with the boys on their social relationship.

Finally, in deciding what to teach, teachers must identify any gaps that exist between a student's actual level of performance and the level of performance a student is expected to achieve. By recognizing the difference between actual performance and expected performance, teachers are able to keep instructional goals and objectives realistic—neither too low nor too high.

The elements we've described here—analyzing students' skills, examining

Assessing skill levels

Analyzing the task

Establishing a logical sequence

Considering the context

Identifying gaps between actual and expected performance

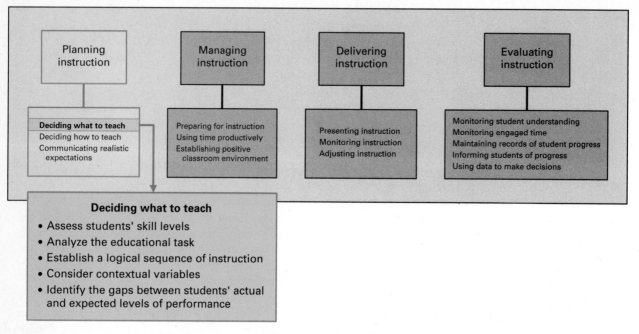

Figure 4.2 Deciding What to Teach

the instructional task, establishing a logical sequence of instruction, considering relevant contextual variables, identifying gaps between students' actual and expected performance—are all parts of planning known as diagnosis. **Diagnosis** involves determining the nature of the educational task or problem. It is a critical part of instructional planning because it allows us to match what we teach to each student's level of skill development.

Diagnosis

Deciding How to Teach

Knowing ahead of time how best to teach is difficult. Teaching is an experimental process: Teachers often try alternative approaches and materials until they find an approach or combination of approaches that works best in moving each student toward instructional objectives. You may have thought, or even been told in courses, that the way to decide how to teach a student is to give a battery of tests, identify the student's strengths and weaknesses, then work to overcome weaknesses or build up strengths. But this is not enough. Yes, it's important to take into account a pupil's level of skill development and to identify learning and behavioral strengths and weaknesses, but simply knowing a student's score on a test cannot help you decide how to teach the student.

Trying alternatives

The "educated guess"

In making decisions about how to teach, teachers must make an "educated guess" about the kinds of approaches that will work, then try those approaches and monitor the results. That educated guess is based on experience, either with a particular student or with others like that student.

The only way to decide how to teach is to teach, then to gather data to determine the effectiveness of the approach. This does not mean that we teach blindly. Our experience gives us a basic understanding of what works and what doesn't work. Also, the literature is filled with guidelines for instruction (cf. Wittrock, 1986). For example:

Sample guidelines

- Beginning with an overview or using advance organizers or lists of objectives to set the stage for a presentation
- Signaling transitions between parts of a lesson and reviewing or summarizing subparts as the lesson proceeds
- Asking questions of varying levels of difficulty throughout a presentation
- Controlling the pace and continuity of lessons by regulating the time allowed for students to ask or answer questions

Setting goals; establishing a sequence

The process of deciding how to teach is shown in Figure 4.3. It begins with setting instructional goals for individual students, then establishing an instructional sequence. Most complex skills consist of combinations of simpler or lower-level skills; these skills must be taught in a logical sequence.

Selecting methods and materials

The next step is to choose appropriate methods and materials, a relatively easy task that can become complicated when students are exceptional. These students may need special methods (sign language, acceleration), or they may need special instructional materials (tape-recorded lessons, advanced reading materials, high interest–low vocabulary reading books). Some of Larry's students have learning disabilities. In the regular classroom they are reading *Macbeth*. In the resource room, Larry has them read from the *Illustrated Macbeth*, then tests their comprehension with verbal quizzes and discussions after each scene of the play. Sometimes he plays a videodisk of *Macbeth*, stops the disk after each scene, and has the students discuss vocabulary, plot development, and the characters' motives.

Pacing

Ratio of known to unknown

Pacing instruction is also part of the process, as are setting a ratio of known to unknown material and setting standard rates of success. Effective instruction should include about 75 percent known and 25 percent unknown material, and students should be expected to demonstrate at least 80 percent mastery of such material before they go on to higher levels.

Monitoring performance and planning subsequent instruction

Probably the most important activities at this stage are monitoring students' performance and using that information to plan subsequent instruction. (We talk more about this later in the chapter.)

Deciding what to teach is a form of diagnosis; deciding how to teach is a prescription, a treatment. If that treatment is not appropriate to the individual's needs, it actually can produce educational problems. Whenever a particular treatment doesn't work, it's time to try another approach.

Communicating Realistic Expectations

Impact of expectations

An important component of instructional planning is setting realistic expectations for students and communicating those expectations to them. In Chapter 1 we talked about expectations and the impact they have on learning. When teachers do not expect much from their students, they are shortchanging them. If they have the skills to do so, over time students learn to perform at the level of expectation teachers hold for them (Good & Brophy, 1984). When those ex-

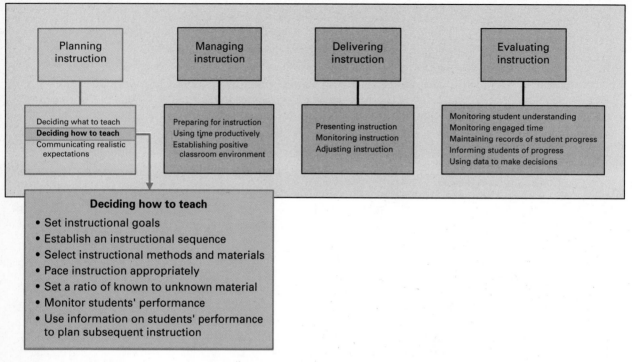

Figure 4.3 **Deciding How to Teach**

pectations are realistically high, students succeed; when they are unrealistically low, students fail.

Getting students involved

Figure 4.4 lists some of the things teachers must do to communicate realistic expectations to their students. First, you have to get students active and involved in learning. Students who do not take part in learning activities cannot be expected to demonstrate high levels of performance on classroom quizzes and tests. This is particularly important when students are disabled. Too often, teachers decide that these students cannot handle the same assignments as other students. By using separate standards in deciding what and how to teach students with disabilities, teachers are setting separate standards for those students' education.

Students who have disabilities and their parents will tell you that too often educators adapt instruction for these students in ways that lead to patronization and lowered expectations. You should work very hard to include students with disabilities in the same activities as students without disabilities. In addition, you should expect similar levels of performance from these students.

Maintaining high standards

Performance standards should be lowered only when each student has been given the opportunity to attempt to meet the expectations set for others and it is very clear that the student cannot realistically meet those standards.

Teaching the consequences

The second part of communicating realistic expectations is teaching students to understand the consequences of success and failure. An example of an effective way to do this is to use a *contingency contracting system* (Algozzine

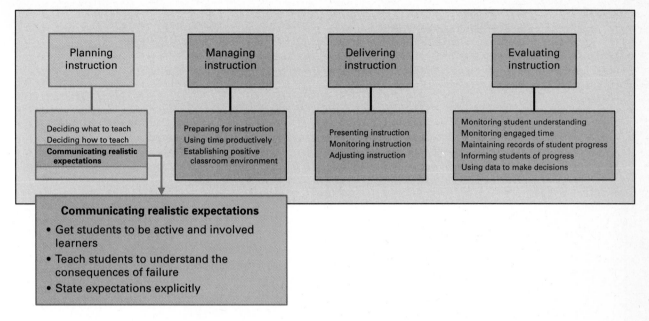

Figure 4.4 **Communicating Realistic Expectations**

& Ysseldyke, 1992). To incorporate such a system, enter into a contract with each student. In the contract specify what the student will do, in response to what stimulus, under what conditions, and with what standards of performance. You should tell students the specific consequences of successful and unsuccessful completion of tasks. In this way they learn to anticipate consequences of their actions.

Finally, there's the communication itself, the process of telling students (and being sure they understand) what they are expected to learn and what they have to do to learn it. Very explicit communication is usually the most effective. Some of the teachers we work with write their instructional goals on the board along with performance criteria and standards for mastery. Others develop and use goal notebooks for each student in their classes. In each notebook they list the specific goals for that student and include a statement of what the student is to do, under what conditions, and at what levels of proficiency. The teachers initial the goals as they are achieved, and they have the students also initial them.

Stating expectations explicitly

Managing Instruction

Few of us are comfortable in chaos. We need a certain order around us. Students, too, need an orderly environment in which to learn. They need structure, and they need rules to follow; they need an understanding of those rules and the consequences of not following them; and they need to see that those

Bring Your Learning to Life

Using Contingency Contracts in the Classroom

Recently one of us had an opportunity to see how Peggy Sokolow, a kindergarten teacher, used a contingency management approach to change the behavior of Stacey, a student in her class. When Stacey began kindergarten, she spent most of her time darting about the room. She ignored all of Peggy's requests and demands to slow down and participate in any group activity. She moved from one center to another spending no more than a few seconds with any toy or activity. Her morning was spent flushing toilets and unrolling toilet paper in the restroom, pulling storybooks off the shelf behind the teacher's desk, and using a cup to remove water from the fish tank. At recess she chose to walk up the slide rather than coming down it in the traditional way. She showed interest in a tricycle by removing the student who was riding it. After spending a few seconds racing it about the yard, she cast it aside and commandeered a ball from a group of children. Within a minute, she managed to throw the ball over the fence along with a number of tools children had been using to make castles in the sand. All the while, Stacey's glowing smile made it clear that she liked being in kindergarten and was having the time of her life.

Peggy was faced with the task of controlling Stacey's behavior without using punishment or tangible rewards like candy, toys, or trinkets. She recalled reading about the Premack principle—a behavior that has a high probability of occurring at time X can be used to reinforce or strengthen any behavior that has a lower probability of occurring at time X. It was clear that Stacey found running very rewarding. Peggy decided to make running contingent on completing work—very small amounts of work at first. When Stacey completed very small amounts of work, she was allowed to run to the end of the school hallway and back. Peggy recognized that having a student running about in the school was not an entirely desirable situation. Yet, she also was aware that the behavior would occur with high frequency because it was natural behavior for Stacey. Using running as a reward for completing work gave Peggy some control over the running behavior. Over time she increased the amount of work that had to be done to get time running. She also slowly replaced running in the hallway with running in place in the classroom. Eventually she was able to restrict the time spent running and engaging in very active behavior to recess and other breaks.

Larry Williams uses a more explicit contingency contracting system with students in his high school classes. With help from parents, he identifies behaviors in which students like to engage at home (like watching TV, being allowed to drive the family car) and writes contracts with students to make engaging in those behaviors (pleasurable events) contingent on performance of homework assignments. The contracts are written in very specific terms. When homework assignments are completed on time and with a specified level of accuracy, Larry writes notes home to inform the parents and indicate the rewards the students have earned. The students in Larry's class like this approach. What Larry wants them to do is clear to them, as is what will happen if they do what Larry wants. Moreover, the rate of homework completion in Larry's class has increased significantly.

Three principles of management

rules are enforced. There are three principles of effective classroom management: preparing for instruction, using time productively, and establishing a positive classroom environment.

Preparing for Instruction

Strategies for establishing rules and handling behavior problems

Several strategies are involved in preparing for instruction (Figure 4.5). Teachers must establish and communicate rules for behavior in the classroom early in the school year. Students must understand the importance of following rules and the consequences of not following them. When disruptions occur, it is important to handle them quickly—as soon as possible after they happen—and consistently. Prompt, consistent action helps the class settle back down and refocus its attention on the work at hand. Teachers are expected to enforce general school rules; students need to know that these rules apply consistently to all rooms in the school, and that it is their job to learn and comply with these rules as quickly and positively as possible. If you get in the position to set classroom rules, set fewer than ten. Each should be clearly stated and reviewed with students early and frequently throughout the school year. You will save yourself much agony if you give students examples of appropriate and inappropriate rule compliance when teaching classroom rules to them (such as "This is what I mean by raising your hand to ask permission to leave the room . . ." and "This is not what I mean . . .").

Figure 4.5 Preparing for Instruction

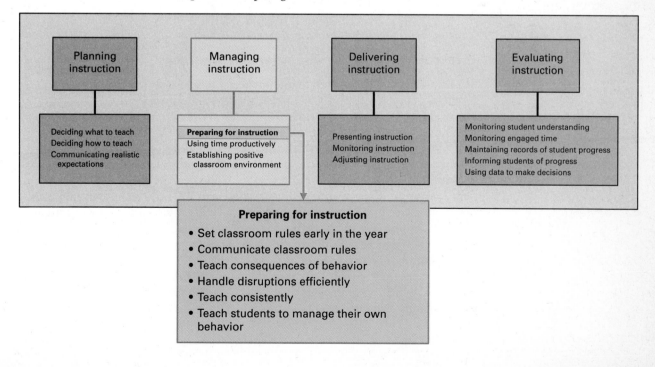

Students managing their
own behavior

One factor that limits the integration of students with disabilities into general education settings is that teachers can become overwhelmed with managing problem behaviors (Algozzine, 1989). One solution is to teach students to manage their own behavior. There are several easy-to-use procedures for doing this. Kim places an index card on some of her students' desks. At the top of each card she writes a question that is appropriate for the student. Sandy has this question: "Am I paying attention?" Pat's is "Did I raise my hand?" Kim has taught Sandy and Pat to check their own behavior periodically and record their performance by making a mark on their card if they are doing what they are supposed to do. She checks the card during the day and gives the students feedback on their self-monitoring and their behavior.

Using Time Productively

Teachers must teach; they must present academic content and other instructional material. But they also must manage learning environments and use time productively so that students are able to learn. What does a well-managed instructional environment look like?

Strategies for productive
use of time

- There are well-established routines and procedures.
- The physical space is organized to facilitate learning.
- Transitions between activities are short.
- Few interruptions break the flow of classroom activities.
- The classroom has an academic, task-oriented focus.
- Sufficient time is allocated to academic activities.

These strategies for using time productively are summarized in Figure 4.6.

Establishing a Positive Classroom Environment

Students are more motivated to learn when teachers accept their individual differences; interact positively with them; and create a supportive, cooperative classroom atmosphere. Students feel better about school and about learning when their teachers demonstrate acceptance and caring.

Ways to make the
classroom a pleasant
place

There are many ways in which teachers can make classrooms positive environments (Figure 4.7). They can make their classrooms friendly places by using background music to support instruction, using general praise to support student learning ("Thanks for always being on time"), listening carefully and being supportive, and greeting students individually. There is an old adage about discipline that suggests that teachers should not smile before November so that they can communicate to students that they really mean business. Unfortunately, the presence or lack of a smile does not maintain good discipline. Consistency in establishing rules, reinforcing rules, and providing consequences is what communicates to students that teachers mean business. It is all right to smile and let students know that you, their teacher, are happy to be there.

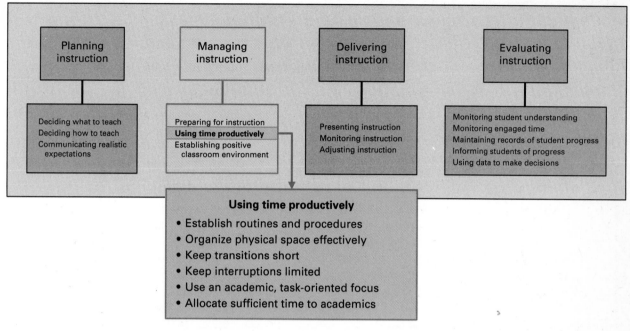

Figure 4.6 Using Time Productively

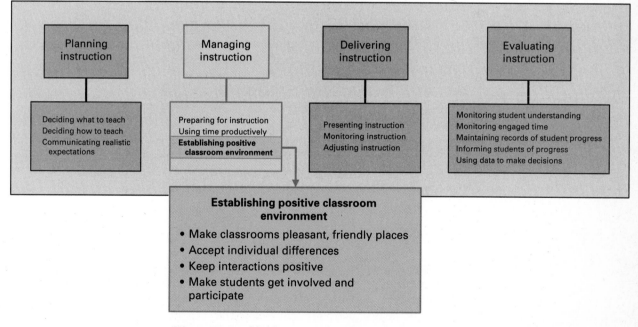

Figure 4.7 Establishing a Positive Classroom Environment

Bring Your Learning to Life

A Technique for Using Time Productively

Bonita Martinez, a friend of ours who teaches first grade, found that taking attendance each morning was a major time killer and provided wonderful opportunities for students to act out. To avoid such problems, she began having students check themselves in each morning.

She put a large posterboard next to the door, placed clear pockets (like those used by libraries to hold the "date due" cards in books) on the posterboard, and wrote a student's name on each pocket. Each student was given an index card with the word "out" on one side and "in" on the other.

As students enter the room Bonita has them turn their cards over to show the "in" side; as they leave the room they turn the cards over to show the "out" side. Bonita can tell at a glance specifically which students are not in attendance. Even more important, the system helps her focus class time on academics rather than routine administrative chores, and it reduces the opportunities for classroom disruptions.

Accepting differences; keeping interactions positive

Effective classroom teachers accept individual differences among their students. They accept the racial, ethnic, home, and ability diversity in today's students. They also keep the interactions between themselves and their students positive. They learn quickly to sandwich any negative statements between positives. ("Kristin, you amaze me. You're always willing to help others, I think that's nice. There are some times when you need help too. For example, this math paper has some mistakes on it. You're so helpful to others, let me help you with these.")

All students should participate

One more aspect of positive classroom environments must be mentioned. It is critical that all students in a classroom are involved, participate, and respond. Effective teachers make it a point to call on everyone, and they may even use rewards to get all students to participate.

Delivering Instruction

Good teaching doesn't just happen. As we have seen so far, it involves strategic planning to decide what and how to teach, and effective orchestration of classroom management principles. Further, good teaching requires some thought about how the instruction is delivered to the students. Delivering instruction is a three-stage process in which teachers present, monitor, then adjust instruction.

Presenting Instruction

Presenting instruction has to do with presenting content, teaching thinking skills, motivating students, and providing relevant practice (Figure 4.8).

Getting attention; reviewing; stating goals

Presenting Content   The first thing teachers must do when they present content is to get their students' attention. Students cannot learn unless they pay attention and get involved in the instructional process. Effective instruction begins with a review of skills students already have or of material they already have learned. New material should be introduced within the context of material with which students are familiar. Those skills necessary to complete new lessons should be reviewed and reinforced. Another important factor is an early statement of instructional goals and their importance. When Larry teaches, he tells students the goals of instruction and the reasons each lesson is important.

Making lessons relevant

Teachers also should make lessons relevant to individual students. To do this, they have to be knowledgeable about the social and cultural environments in which their students live. Students in rural North Dakota have different frames of reference from students in inner-city classrooms. It makes sense, then, to use different examples when teaching them.

Maintaining attention, showing enthusiasm, and other strategies

Making lessons relevant is one way to maintain students' attention; others are to be enthusiastic, to be organized, and to pace instruction. It's also important that teachers and students interact positively and that teachers be supportive of their students, avoiding negative comments and put-downs.

Clear communication of intent

Another component of presenting instruction is clear communication of instructional demands and intent. This means that written or oral directions should be easy to understand, complete, and in order.

Do students understand?

Finally, it's important to check that students understand what's being taught. The best way is to check students' understanding before they start to practice a new skill. This keeps them from practicing incorrectly.

Teaching Thinking Skills   Students should be taught more than how to do something by rote. Most studies of effective instruction contend that the thinking skills used in completing assignments should also be explained to students. There are a number of ways to do this. First, teachers can model thinking skills; that is, they can show students how to do what they expect them to do. Second, they can teach learning strategies directly, explaining how and why students' responses are right or wrong, and the processes that must be used to complete a task. Third, it's important to check that students understand what they are supposed to do. Kim does this by having students go through the steps they will use to solve a problem before they actually do the work. We watched the process in a math lesson. Kim asked her students to describe how they would do a sheet of two-digit addition problems before working on them. Each student described the process he or she would use. Some said they would start at the upper-left-hand corner and work across the first line; others said they would start in different places. Kim told them she didn't mind where they started as long as they did each problem by adding the right column together

Strategies for teaching thinking skills

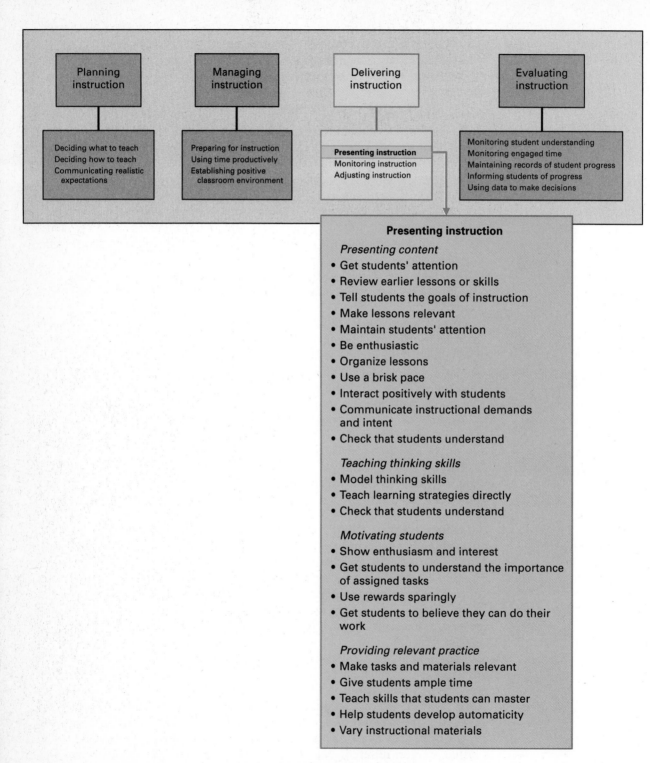

Planning instruction

Deciding what to teach
Deciding how to teach
Communicating realistic
  expectations

Managing instruction

Preparing for instruction
Using time productively
Establishing positive
  classroom environment

Delivering instruction

Presenting instruction
Monitoring instruction
Adjusting instruction

Evaluating instruction

Monitoring student understanding
Monitoring engaged time
Maintaining records of student progress
Informing students of progress
Using data to make decisions

Presenting instruction

Presenting content
- Get students' attention
- Review earlier lessons or skills
- Tell students the goals of instruction
- Make lessons relevant
- Maintain students' attention
- Be enthusiastic
- Organize lessons
- Use a brisk pace
- Interact positively with students
- Communicate instructional demands and intent
- Check that students understand

Teaching thinking skills
- Model thinking skills
- Teach learning strategies directly
- Check that students understand

Motivating students
- Show enthusiasm and interest
- Get students to understand the importance of assigned tasks
- Use rewards sparingly
- Get students to believe they can do their work

Providing relevant practice
- Make tasks and materials relevant
- Give students ample time
- Teach skills that students can master
- Help students develop automaticity
- Vary instructional materials

Figure 4.8 Presenting Instruction

before going to the left. She also carefully monitored the students' remarks about what they would do when the sum of the first column was greater than 9.

Anton Malinowski, a ninth-grade resource room teacher, teaches students to monitor their own thinking. He does so because he has found that his students do not always think, let alone think about what they think. He gives some of the students with whom he works checklists to guide them through their assignments. The checklists for writing assignments include statements like "Capitalize first words," "Put punctuation marks at the ends of sentences," and "Write so it sounds like talking." The checklists for math problems involving subtraction of two-digit numbers include statements like "Is the bottom number bigger? Yes, regroup, no, subtract." Anton also has students predict the number of correct responses they think they can make on a given assignment, then has them compare their predictions with their actual performance. This gives him opportunities to talk to students about how they proceed through tasks, the extent to which they are accurate in their judgments of their own performance, and how they can be careful and deliberate in their work.

Checklists as guides *(margin note)*

Ways to motivate students *(margin note)*

Motivating Students   Students learn better when they are motivated. How do we motivate students? First, we have to show enthusiasm and interest in the material we present. Second, we have to get students to understand the importance of assigned tasks. One way is to design work to reflect individual students' interests and experiences. A third consideration is that rewards can motivate students, but they should be used sparingly. Students who are constantly rewarded for what they do soon lost interest. Instead, rewards should be administered intermittently to maintain attention and behavior. A fourth strategy we use to motivate students is to make them believe they can do the work. Two simple methods work: maintaining a warm, supportive atmosphere, and selecting and using instructional activities at which we know students can succeed.

Guidelines for student practice *(margin note)*

Providing Relevant Practice   Students learn better when they have an opportunity to practice. Whether they practice under the teacher's direction or independently, it's important that the tasks they work on and the materials they work with be relevant to achieving instructional goals. Time is important; students should have ample time to practice skills independently. It's also important to teach skills that students can master at least 80 percent of the time. With relevant practice over adequate time and with high levels of success, students develop automaticity—they complete tasks and demonstrate skills automatically. Finally, teachers should vary instructional materials. Having students engage in extensive relevant practice is important, but if instructional materials are not varied, then practice becomes boring and interferes with instructional goals. Computer-assisted instructional programs can provide interesting variations in practice materials; they also offer immediate feedback and help students develop automaticity.

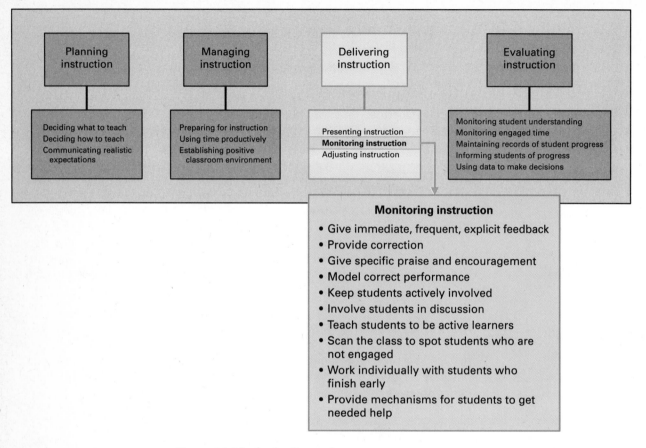

Figure 4.9 **Monitoring Instruction**

Monitoring Instruction

Strategies for feedback

The second major part of delivering instruction is monitoring students' learning (Figure 4.9). Feedback—information about students' performance—is very important. Good teachers give students immediate, frequent, explicit feedback on their performance or behavior. When students do something correctly, they should be told so. When they do something incorrectly, they should be corrected. It's important to use praise and encouragement—**supportive feedback**—tying them to a specific task. Supportive feedback lets the student know that he or she did what was expected; it supports the performance by letting the student know that what he or she did was right ("I like the way you used your number line to add your numbers correctly"). Diffuse praise can leave the student wondering.

Types of feedback

Corrective feedback lets the student know that he or she did not do what was expected; it corrects the performance by letting the student know that what was done was done incorrectly, and it provides a corrective demonstration from the teacher ("Good try, but this is how we do two-digit addition"). One way to provide corrective feedback is to explain the material again. Especially for students with learning difficulties, it is often necessary to explain over and over how to accomplish a specific task. Teachers also can model correct performance. It is often necessary, and almost always helpful, to show students specifically how to complete academic tasks.

Active involvement

Students should be actively involved in responding to instruction. One way to do this is to use their names during instructional sessions or to move around the room during a presentation. Another is to teach students to be active learners. When we described a well-managed classroom, we talked about strategies that increase the time students spend on tasks. These strategies also are important in monitoring instruction. Teachers should keep an eye out for students who are not busy and redirect them. They should work individually with students who finish tasks early. Students should not spend much time waiting for things to happen.

Help mechanisms

Finally, teachers should establish mechanisms for students to get needed help. For example, students who need help can be asked to sit quietly at their desks with hands raised until the teacher is able to help them. Or they can be asked to move to a special workstation where help is provided by the teacher, a paraprofessional, or a peer.

Adjusting Instruction

All students do not learn in the same way or at the same pace. So teachers have to adjust instruction for individual learners (Figure 4.10). We cannot give you specific rules for modifying lessons to meet all students' needs. The process usually is trial and error. We try alternative approaches until we identify one that works. An example: We recently observed Larry teaching a lesson on the characteristics of dinosaurs. During the lesson, he noticed Tim was not paying attention, Susan asked to go to the bathroom, and Marty started drumming on his desk with two pencils. Larry later told us it was clear to him that the students were not interested in the lesson, so he modified it, assigning to each dinosaur the name of one of the students. He saved the most powerful, *Tyrannosaurus rex*, to the end of the lesson and named him Larry. He said this slight change was enough to interest the students in the lesson, and he was right.

An example of modifying a lesson

Providing instructional options

Another way teachers can adjust instruction is to use varied methods and materials, which increases the chances of meeting individual students' needs. Specific materials can be used for each student's level. Teachers can also make certain that the materials they use are culturally relevant—that they incorporate names, places, pictures, and stories that are pertinent to students' cultural backgrounds. For students who are having difficulty, teachers can provide extra instruction and review or they can adjust the pace of instruction. With students who are especially tough to teach, effective teachers build in safeguards. They plan ample opportunities for practice and check student understanding very often. High school teachers use partially completed outlines that students must complete as lectures proceed. This strategy keeps students on

Extra review and different pacing

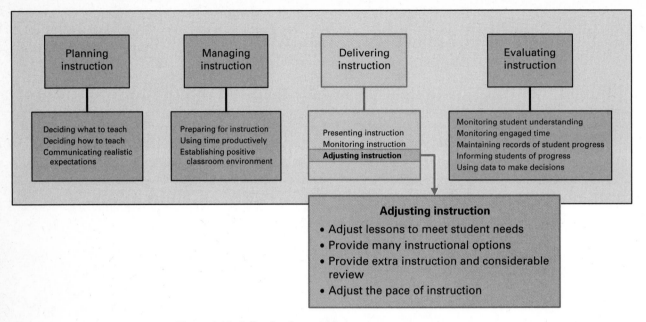

Figure 4.10 **Adjusting Instruction**

track and attending to instruction. Having them hand in their completed outlines helps make them accountable for listening.

Evaluating Instruction

Two kinds of evaluation

Evaluation is an important part of teaching. It is the process by which teachers decide whether the methods and materials they are using are effective, on the basis of individual students' performance. There are two kinds of evaluation: formative and summative. Both involve data collection. **Formative evaluation** occurs during the process of instruction: The teacher collects data during instruction and uses those data to make instructional decisions. **Summative evaluation** occurs at the end of instruction, when the teacher administers a test to determine whether a pupil has met instructional objectives.

There are five principles in the evaluation process: monitoring student understanding, monitoring engaged time, maintaining records of student progress, informing students about their progress, and using data to make decisions. In the sections that follow we describe these principles in more detail.

Monitoring Student Understanding

Monitoring student understanding of directions

Three strategies involved in monitoring student understanding are shown in Figure 4.11. First, students must understand what teachers expect them to do in the classroom, which means teachers must monitor the extent to which they

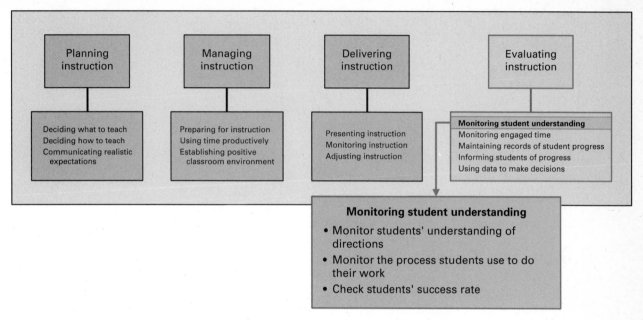

Figure 4.11 Monitoring Student Understanding

understand directions. This involves more than asking a student, "Do you understand what you're supposed to do?" It's too easy for students to say "yup" without having the foggiest idea of what's expected. Instead, ask students to tell you or show you what they are going to do.

Monitoring the work process

Second, students must understand the process they need to go through to complete classroom assignments. You can check their understanding by asking them to show you what they are going to do, or to describe the process of responding to questions or doing problems. As an alternative, you can take them aside and have them show you how they solved problems. This enables you to watch the process they use and pinpoint areas of misunderstanding or misinformation.

Checking success rate

Finally, a handy method to use in monitoring student understanding is simply to check their success rate. Think about it for a moment. If you were to show a student how to solve double-digit addition problems, send her off to solve a page of 20 problems, and find out that she got 8 of 20 correct, what would you conclude? You probably would conclude that she did not have a good understanding of the task. If, on the other hand, she got 19 of 20 correct, you could assume that she did understand the process. Data on student success rate tell us a great deal about the extent to which students understand what we ask them to do. Teachers sometimes find that it takes too much time to monitor student success rate. When they have many assignments to track and a large number of students to account for, the task of monitoring can become unwieldy. We suggest that these teachers show their students how to monitor their own behavior.

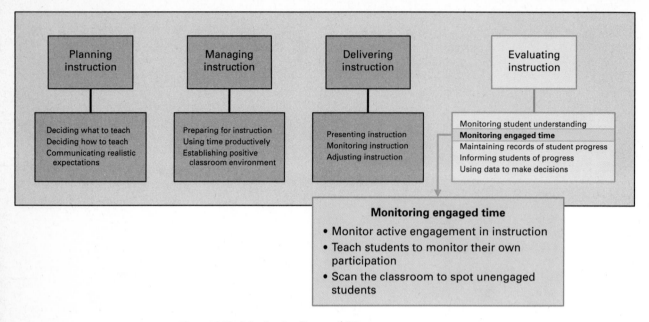

Figure 4.12   Monitoring Engaged Time

Monitoring Engaged Time

Monitoring active engagement

Students who are actively engaged—those who answer direct questions and participate in discussions during instruction—learn more in school. Figure 4.12 shows three strategies teachers can use for monitoring academic engaged time. First, teachers can monitor the amount of time their students are actively involved in lessons simply by noting the extent to which individuals participate in classroom activities. For example, Kim wanted to know whether Mark was actively participating in the class discussion on various types of trees. As an index of involvement and participation, she recorded the number of times Mark raised his hand and the number of times he asked questions.

Self-monitoring

Second, teachers save time by teaching students to monitor their own participation. Kim has a chart in her room that lists each student's name. At the end of every math class, she has the students record the number of times they asked a question during the day's lesson. She also has them place a plus sign, minus sign, or equal sign after the number to indicate if they did better (+), worse (−), or about the same (=) as the previous day. At the end of the week, she has them evaluate their overall performance and write a note to take home describing how they did in math during the week.

Scanning the classroom

Third, teachers can gather data on student engagement by scanning the classroom to see who is actively involved in instruction. Periodically, they record the results of these observations and provide rewards to students who meet criteria they have set for expected levels of involvement.

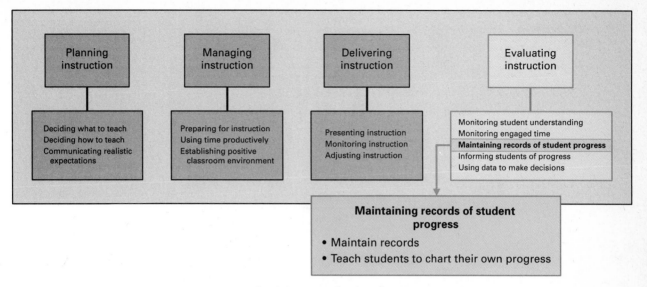

Figure 4.13 **Maintaining Records of Student Progress**

Maintaining Records of Student Progress

Types of record keeping

To know the extent to which students are profiting from instruction, teachers must keep records of their progress (Figure 4.13). Record keeping can be informal or formal. Kim keeps relatively informal records of some students' progress in math, simply by writing down the number of problems completed and the number or percentage completed correctly. In other subjects she keeps more formal records. Figure 4.14 shows a chart on which she keeps track of Bobby's performance in reading words correctly. Along the bottom of the chart are the days she has been graphing his behavior. Along the left side are numbers of words read correctly. The line in the middle of the chart shows progress in the number of words read correctly. As the figure illustrates, a student's performance and goal can be recorded on the same chart. The chart then can be used as a visual aid in making decisions about the student's rate of progress toward meeting specific objectives. For example, visual inspection of Figure 4.14 would lead us to the conclusion that although Bobby has good and bad days, in general he is on target toward accomplishing the goal Kim has set for him.

More and more, teachers are using computer database programs to keep track of students' scores and print out reports to share with students, parents, and other professionals. Graphics programs can make charts like Figure 4.14 relatively easy to produce. Some software packages combine several functions: They maintain records, print reports, produce graphs, and even help the teacher create new assessment measures.

Teaching students to chart progress

Even with the aid of a computer, however, record keeping and charting can

Figure 4.14
Bobby's Reading Performance

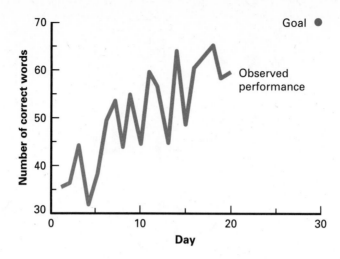

involve much work, particularly in a large class. As in monitoring engaged time, students can share the load by learning to keep track of their own performance. For instance, Kim taught Bobby how to chart the percentage of math problems he solves correctly each day. This frees some of Kim's time but, more important, keeps Bobby actively involved in his own learning and gives him a sense of accomplishment.

Informing Students of Progress

Regular, frequent, quick feedback

Regular feedback is one way to keep students informed about their progress (Figure 4.15). It helps students know what is expected of them and the extent to which they are meeting expectations. Feedback should be frequent and quick. Students learn better when they know how they are doing and when errors are corrected quickly, before they become habits.

Task-specific praise

Again, task-specific praise is most effective. It's not enough simply to tell Manuel that he did a good job; we have to tell him what we mean when we say "Good job." For example: "Manuel, you did a very nice job of filling in the names of the countries on your map; you got them all correct."

Immediate correction by students

When students make mistakes, it's good practice to have them correct the mistakes immediately. Both Kim and Larry are very concerned that students do not practice errors. Kim told us about something that happened when she was student teaching. She had students do a math worksheet while she worked individually with a boy who was having trouble completing the worksheet. She didn't pay much attention to the other students. She figured that because they were quiet and busy, the activity must be instructionally appropriate. Later, when she reviewed the students' work, she found that one student had done all the problems on the sheet using the wrong algorithm $(27 + 43 \neq 610)$. She realized that she should have monitored the student's work.

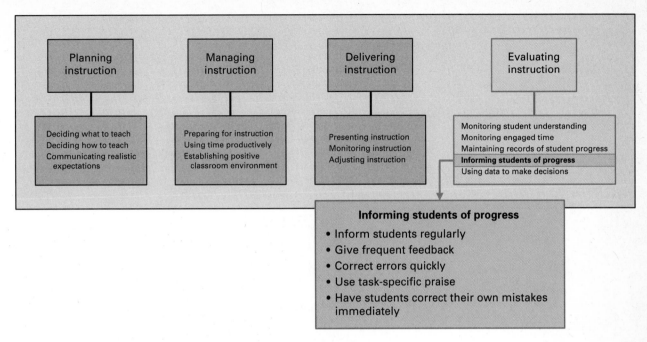

Figure 4.15 Informing Students of Progress

Using Data to Make Decisions

Using data for decisions about services

Records are important, not only for charting students' progress, but also for making decisions about their educational programs (Figure 4.16). For example, suppose the child-study team is considering declaring Bill eligible for special education services. Before they make that decision, members of the team want to know what has been done instructionally with Bill in the regular classroom and the extent to which he has profited from instruction there. If his teacher has kept good records or, better yet, charted Bill's progress, the data are readily accessible. The decision to discontinue special education services also rests on information about the student with special needs and about the student's agemates. If teachers have kept track of the student's progress and if they know the progress of students in the general education classroom, they can make normative peer comparisons, judgments about the performance of the individual student relative to the average performance of his or her peers.

Figure 4.17 shows samples of data on pupil performance that can be used to make instructional decisions. We've plotted the average number of words read correctly by one of the reading groups in Kim's classroom. We also show the rate of reading for three of her students: Rodney, Rachael, and Rozanne. Notice that Rodney's rate of progress is above average for the group, Rachael's performance is about the same as the average for the group, and Rozanne's rate

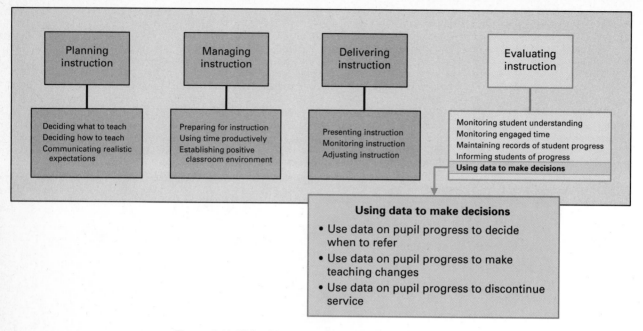

Figure 4.16 **Using Data to Make Decisions**

of progress is below average for the group. Using this information, Kim decided to move Rodney and Rachael to another reading group; she decided to keep Rozanne in the group until her rate improves.

Direct, frequent data on student performance also can be used to make instructional decisions. By keeping track of a student's progress, the teacher can decide whether particular approaches or materials are effective. Although monitoring a student's progress does not tell a teacher how to teach that student, it does tell the teacher the extent to which the student is progressing.

To measure students' performance effectively, teachers must specify their goals for individual students; then they can plot what we call an aim line. An **aim line** shows the rate of ongoing progress that is necessary for a student to achieve a particular goal.

Figure 4.18 shows Courtney's progress relative to a goal that Larry has set. The straight line is the aim line. It denotes the rate of progress necessary for Courtney to achieve the instructional goal. Her actual progress is slower. Larry can use this information to make instructional or placement decisions about Courtney.

Notice that teachers must make a critical judgment before establishing the aim line. Does Larry want or expect Courtney to achieve the same instructional goals that are held for all students in the school? Or does he want Courtney to achieve goals that are specific for her?

Using data to make teaching changes

The aim line

Figure 4.17
Reading Group Performance

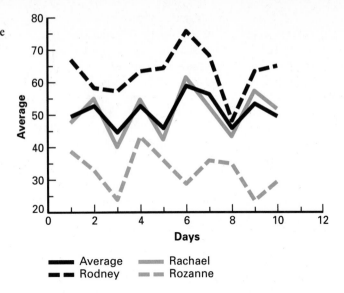

Figure 4.18
Courtney's Reading Progress

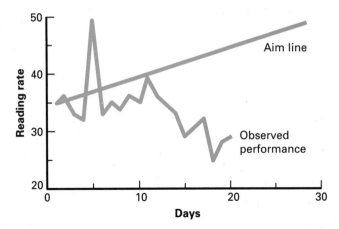

Application of Effective Instruction

Today's educators know a good deal about effective instruction. The principles of effective instruction and improved methods of teaching are being included in teacher training programs. These principles of effective instruction apply to all students—exceptional and nonexceptional. The methods we use for students who are exceptional are much the same as those we use for students who are not exceptional.

Teaching students who are exceptional is a decision-making process in which school personnel decide what to teach, the approach to use, and whether adaptive devices are needed. Once these fundamental decisions are made, the

Same principles for all students

principles of effective instruction come into play. Teachers still have to plan, manage, deliver, and evaluate instruction.

More than ever before, regular and special class teachers are working together to accommodate students with special learning needs in classroom environments that are as much like normal as possible. Through combinations of individualized instruction, small- and large-group instruction, and teacher- and student-directed instruction, teachers are adapting learning experiences for all students.

Normal environments

Teachers are accommodating diversity by doing things like

Adaptations to accommodate diversity

- varying the amounts of instruction on the basis of individual student capabilities.
- using modified instructional approaches, materials, and procedures to enable students to master content at paces suited to their individual capabilities and interests.
- monitoring pupil progress and providing students with immediate feedback. Instruction is then adapted on the basis of student performance.
- teaching students to monitor their own performance and identify modifications they need in order to make satisfactory progress.
- providing students with opportunities to make choices and decisions about their learning objectives.
- using peer teaching, in which students assist one another in mastering subject matter content.

Effective Instruction in Perspective

We have been in special education for more than twenty years. Over that time, some of our beliefs about teaching students who are exceptional have stayed the same and others have changed. We have always believed in a simple axiom: Good teaching is good teaching. We think the principles of instruction are more clearly articulated today than they ever have been, in addition to more and more robust research on good teaching, so we continue to hold this belief.

A teaching model

We think you will be a better teacher if you use a simple teaching model based on what is known about effective instruction. First, *demonstrate* what the student is expected to do. This demonstration can be in the form of a verbal presentation or actual performance of the expected behavior. Next, *have the student demonstrate* that he or she can do what is expected. Your job during student demonstrations is to provide supportive or corrective feedback.

Once students have demonstrated that they can perform the expected behaviors at 80 percent accuracy, we release them to independent practice. During the *practice* stage of our teaching model, teachers monitor the performances of their students and again provide corrective or supportive feedback. This stage provides a final opportunity for the teacher to correct misconceptions and errors. It also gives students a chance to use new skills in different activities (for example, games, problem solving, enrichment activities) in preparation for the final step of the model, which is providing *proof* they have learned the new skill. We believe performance on a mastery test should be 90 percent accurate before a student proceeds to new material within an instructional sequence.

Using the model

This **demonstrate-demonstrate-practice-prove** teaching model can be used when teaching in different content areas. It is an effective way to approach instruction of exceptional as well as nonexceptional students. We would like to see this model or something like it tried before any student is referred or removed from a regular classroom in search of an alternative educational environment designed to meet his or her unique educational needs.

What Every Teacher Should Know

- A teacher's primary goal is to help students develop to their fullest potential by teaching the necessary skills to function in society.
- Whether their students are exceptional or not, effective teachers plan, manage, deliver, and evaluate instruction.
- Planning decisions include deciding what to teach (diagnosis) and how to teach (prescription), and communicating realistic expectations to students.
- To manage instruction effectively, teachers need to prepare for instruction by establishing and communicating rules for behavior in the classroom early in the school year, then enforcing them promptly and consistently. They must also use time productively and establish a positive classroom environment.
- When delivering instruction, teachers present, monitor, and adjust lessons to meet the needs of their students.
- Presenting instruction involves not only presenting content, but also teaching thinking skills, motivating students, and providing relevant practice.
- Teachers monitor instruction by providing supportive and corrective feedback, and keeping students actively involved.
- Adjusting lesson content, offering different instructional options, providing extra instruction and review, and changing the pace of work are four ways in which teachers adjust instruction to meet the needs of individual students.
- Evaluation is the process by which teachers decide whether the methods and materials they are using are effective, based on individual students' performance.
- When teachers collect data during instruction and use those data to make instructional decisions, they are undertaking formative evaluation. Summative evaluation occurs at the end of instruction, when teachers administer a test to determine whether students have met instructional objectives.
- Today more than ever before, regular and special class teachers are working together to accommodate students with special learning needs in classroom environments that are as much like normal as possible.

Projects

1. Interview a regular classroom teacher who is currently teaching special needs students. Ask him or her to describe how he or she plans, manages, delivers, and evaluates instruction for different groups of students in his or her classroom.

2. Interview several special education teachers. Ask them to describe how they plan, manage, deliver, and evaluate instruction for different groups of students in their classrooms.

3. Observe elementary, middle, and high school teachers working with exceptional students. Note any similarities and differences in what the teachers do during instructional presentations.

4. Observe regular class and special class teachers teaching an exceptional student at different times during the school day. Note any similarities and differences in these teachers' methods.

For Your Information

Books

Algozzine, B., & Ysseldyke, J. (1992). *Strategies and tactics for effective instruction.* Longmont, CO: Sopris West.

This resource meets two compelling needs in education: the need to think systematically about effective instructional strategies and the need to generate tactics quickly and easily. It uses the Algozzine/Ysseldyke model of effective instruction and provides teachers with more than three hundred very specific strategies and tactics to use in their classroom.

Kauffman, J. M., & Hallahan, D. P. (1981). *The handbook of special education.* Englewood Cliffs, NJ: Prentice-Hall.

This edited volume includes information on the conceptual foundations for delivering services to students with disabilities, service delivery systems, curriculum and methods, and classroom and instructional management.

Stainback, S., Stainback, W., & Forest, M. (1989). *Educating all students in the mainstream of regular education.* Baltimore, MD: Brookes.

This is a set of edited readings providing educators with theory and practice on educating students with disabilities in general education settings.

Wang, M. C. (1989). Adaptive instruction: An alternative for accommodating student diversity through the curriculum. In D. K. Lipsky & A. Gartner (Eds.), *Beyond separate education: Quality education for all* (pp. 99–119). Baltimore, MD: Brookes.

A description of the adaptive learning environments model, a specific systematic approach to educating students with disabilities.

Wittrock, M. C. (1986). *Handbook of research on teaching* (3rd ed.). New York: Macmillan.

This is the American Educational Research Association's definitive guide to what we know about teachers, teaching, and the learning process. The text includes thirty-five articles that cover virtually all aspects of education. The articles are grouped into five sections. Section one covers conceptual, historical, theoretical, and methodological aspects of research on teaching. Section two explores classroom dynamics. Section three examines the social and institutional contexts of teaching, while section four includes coverage of research on teaching students who are gifted, creative, bilingual, and disabled. Section five is a systematic guide to research on the teaching of subjects and grade levels.

Organizations

Association for Supervision and Curriculum Development

Founded in 1943, ASCD has 150,000 members. It is a professional organization of supervisors, curriculum coordinators and directors, consultants, professors of education, classroom teachers, principals, superintendents, parents, and others interested in school improvement at all levels of education. ASCD provides professional development experiences and training in curriculum and supervision; disseminates information; and encourages research, evaluation, and theory development. For more information, contact ASCD, 1250 Pitt St., Alexandria, VA 22314–1403.

International Reading Association

Founded in 1956, IRA has 93,000 members. It is a professional organization of teachers, reading specialists, consultants, administrators, supervisors, researchers, psychologists, librarians, and parents interested in promoting literacy. IRA seeks to improve the quality of reading instruction at all educational levels. It disseminates research on reading, including information on adult literacy, computer technology and reading, early childhood and literacy development, international education, and literature for children and adolescents. For more information, contact IRA, 800 Barksdale Rd., P.O. Box 8139, Newark, DE 19714–8139.

National Council of Teachers of English

Founded in 1911, NCTE has 120,000 members who are English teachers at all levels. NCTE works to increase the effectiveness of instruction in English language and literature. For more information, contact NCTE, 1111 Kenyon Rd., Urbana, IL 61801.

National Council of Teachers of Mathematics

Founded in 1920, NCTM is an organization of teachers of mathematics in grades K–12, two-year colleges, and teacher education personnel on college campuses. It works to improve the teaching of mathematics at all educational levels. For more information, contact NCTM, 1906 Association Dr., Reston, VA 22091–1593.

Journals

Intervention in School and Clinic

ISC is an interdisciplinary journal directed to an international audience of teachers, parents, educational therapists, and specialists in all fields who deal with the day-to-day aspects of special and remedial education. Most of the articles that appear in this publication are focused on specific intervention approaches and activities. It is a very practical journal. For more information, contact Gerald Wallace, Editor-in-Chief, *Intervention in School and Clinic,* PRO-ED Publications, 8700 Shoal Creek Blvd., Austin, TX 78757–6897.

Teaching Exceptional Children

This journal is available as part of the membership package of the Council for Exceptional Children. It provides information on methods for teaching students who are exceptional. For more information, contact Council for Exceptional Children, 1920 Association Dr., Reston, VA 22091-1593.

5

Individual Plans and Teaching Methods

Focusing Questions

- What is special about special education?
- What is outcomes-based education and how does it relate to instruction of students with disabilities?
- What is the difference between remedial and compensatory instruction?
- What kinds of information should be included in every individualized education program?
- How are the principles of respondent and operant conditioning tied to behavior therapy?
- What are two ways in which ability training can be used?
- What are the key components of crisis therapy?
- What are some of the roles computers currently are playing in special education?

Imagine a typical junior high school—we'll call it Central Junior High—where the teachers use a wide variety of teaching methods. Charles "Bubba" Beam is known as the Steven Spielberg of Central Junior High. He structures his class presentations around a brilliant selection of supportive media. Beam knows the best videos, CD/ROM disks, movies, and guest lecturers. He uses a flashy set of multicolored overheads and slides to present material in his class. Betty Bloomington, in contrast, uses the spoken word to capture content and the attention of her students. She spins tales of intrigue and mystery about advanced algebra and environmental science.

Teachers structure their presentations in ways they believe are interesting. They also use different ways of having students demonstrate their understanding of new material. Mabel Maple divides class time equally among subjects and students. She diligently goes around the room asking each student to read four sentences or recite three lines of a poem. Students know exactly what they are going to have to do during group instruction in her class. Fern Farkle, on the other hand, keeps students on their toes by calling on them at random; students can never predict when their turn will come. Juwalla Komandori is known as "the humanitarian" at Central because he asks questions only of those students he's certain know the answers. This gives "the knowing" an opportunity to demonstrate their knowledge and "the unknowing" an opportunity not to be embarrassed. Yet, he demonstrates good instruction by adapting his questions to enable "the unknowing" to respond correctly.

Your own teachers, like those at Central, probably used a great variety of instructional methods. What worked for one teacher did not necessarily work for others. Yet, in thinking back, you will likely conclude that some methods were more effective than others in certain situations. ■

As we said in Chapter 4, we think that good teaching is good teaching and that there are no limits on where it can occur. But all teaching and teachers are not alike. Individual teachers, like those at the imaginary Central Junior High, have their own particular ways of delivering instruction, evaluating instruction, and interacting with their students. This diversity makes the field of education exciting, and it is one of the intangibles that make teaching so rewarding.

As we've indicated in earlier chapters, there are more similarities than differences between students in special education and those in regular education classes. But if students are similar, if good teaching is good teaching, and if individual teachers vary, what is special about special education?

Four factors make teaching students who are exceptional different from teaching students who are not exceptional:

- Although many of their educational experiences are like those of their age-mates, students receiving special education have individualized education programs; their agemates do not.
- Some students who are exceptional have special learning needs. They receive instruction in skills that their agemates develop without special instruction.
- Although teachers in regular and special education do many of the same things, certain instructional methods are used more with students who are exceptional than with students who are not.
- Some students need special instructional adaptations to grow, develop, and prosper from schooling.

In this chapter, we talk about these aspects of teaching students with disabilities and special gifts and talents. As you're reading, remember that specific individual educational plans, learning needs, methods, and instructional adaptations may be different in special education. Yet most of what we do for students with disabilities can and should occur in the regular classroom as well.

Goals, Objectives, and Outcomes

The fundamental goal of schooling is to help students develop the skills they need to function in society. Those skills relate to content areas (reading, mathematics, science, language arts), to specific jobs, and to affective or social behaviors (developing trust, building relationships, coping with frustration and stressors, handling joint decisions and interpersonal conflicts, working for delayed gratification). Teachers and other people who work in schools help students develop these skills.

Instruction in regular education is designed to help students achieve competence in a variety of broad areas of knowledge. The goals and objectives of regular education reflect society's values. For example, children are told they have to go to school so they can learn to read, write, and do math, and grow up to be independent productive citizens. In 1990 then-President George Bush and the nation's governors specified six national education goals, which have remained during the Clinton administration. The goals were specified by Bush in a proposal entitled America 2000, and again specified by President Clinton and the U.S. Department of Education in Goals 2000: The Educate America Act. Two goals were added. The goals that are to be met by the year 2000 are listed in Table 15.1.

When parents, teachers or other professionals, or students themselves believe students need help to meet these broad educational goals, special education is one option. The broad goals of instruction in special education are the same as they are in regular education; the specific goals may be different.

Point of View

Outcomes-based Education

There is a major shift taking place in American education, a shift away from focusing on the process of education to focusing on its outcomes or results. Outcomes-based education (OBE) is the driving force. In a number of states, instead of completing certain numbers of courses to graduate, students must now meet specified graduation outcomes.

The shift toward outcomes-based education is much like the total quality management movement in business and manufacturing. It reflects a belief that the best way for individuals and organizations to get where they are going is first to determine where they want to be and where they are—then plan backwards to ascertain how they can move from where they are to where they want to go. Those who argue for outcomes-based education believe that major improvements in the educational system will occur if, and only if, we get widespread agreement on what the outcomes ought to be and then hold schools and school personnel accountable for pupils' achieving those outcomes. Opponents worry about who will decide on the important outcomes and how students, schools, and districts will be held accountable for achieving them, which forms a basic debate about the purpose of education in America.

Outcomes are statements about what students should know and be able to do as a result of their education, and the rhetoric on outcomes includes the notion that they will be achieved by all students. The terms *outcomes, standards,* and *goals* often are used interchangeably, and there is much disagreement about their meanings and applications. The terms also are used indiscriminately to refer to different types of results: content outcomes, student performance outcomes, and school performance standards. *Content outcomes* describe what students should know and be able to do in particular subject areas. *Student performance outcomes* describe how and at what level students must demonstrate knowledge and skills. *School performance standards* (sometimes called school

delivery standards) define the quality of education schools must provide for students to meet content and/or performance outcomes.

There are two principles that guide instruction within an outcomes-based-education model: (1) Instruction should be driven by clearly defined outcomes that all students must demonstrate, and (2) schools must provide opportunity for *all* students to reach the learning outcomes. The first principle implies that instruction should not be curriculum-driven, as is so often the case. Instruction should be tailored to help students achieve specific outcomes rather than make it through a specific book or piece of content material. The second principle implies that outcomes are constant and that the amount of time a student takes to reach them will vary. The overall implication is that schools will be organized on factors other than time. In practice, outcomes-based education requires a major shift in thinking about the purposes of education and about the ways in which schools are organized. As Spady (1992) has stated:

> What OBE means is that you start with a picture of what you want a kid to do that really matters and you build the curriculum you feel you need to accomplish that outcome. So in the purest sense, the outcome-based model has no curriculum until you know what the outcomes are. Until you know what the outcomes are, you don't know what to teach the kids. (p. 2)

A handy way to think about outcomes-based education is to recognize that outcomes are the goals of instruction. Instruction involves adjusting the amount of time, or the ways in which students are taught so that they can accomplish the designated outcomes. The process involves frequent assessment of the extent to which students are achieving goals or outcomes, and adjustment of instruction for students who are not.

(continued on next page)

Outcomes-based Education *(continued)*

Major approaches identified as outcomes-based education include John Champlin's Outcomes-Driven Developmental Model (ODDM), as reflected in the organization of instruction in Johnson City, New York, and William Spady's High Success Network (HSN) Strategic Design Model, as reflected in several communities in Colorado and Arizona and in several state-level (for example, Pennsylvania) models. When school systems shift to an out-comes-based approach they usually go through a period of extensive consensus building among teachers, parents, members of the business community, community agencies, and so forth on the valued outcomes of schooling. Once there is widespread agreement on the valued outcomes of learning, all school experiences and instruction are restructured to attain the valued outcomes.

Increasingly, the definition of goals in special education is being tied to the movement toward **outcomes-based education** (see the detailed explanation in the Point of View).

A model of educational outcomes

Using an outcomes-based approach, the National Center on Educational Outcomes (NCEO) at the University of Minnesota has been engaged in the development of a conceptual model for students with disabilities. The center has convened many groups of stakeholders (people like legislators, policymakers, teachers, parents, business executives, school administrators, and representatives of advocacy groups who have a stake in the outcomes of education for students with disabilities) to come to agreement on the major desired outcomes of education for students with disabilities. Agreement has been reached on the major outcome domains shown in Figure 5.1. This conceptual model illustrates that instruction takes place within a context (resources may differ in different places; for example, there may be more money for instruction in Montgomery County, Pennsylvania, than in International Falls, Minnesota). Educators provide services to students, and these result in outcomes. The stakeholder groups who participated in the development of the NCEO model have identified the most important outcomes for students completing school as those specified in Figure 5.2. Interestingly, those who specified important outcomes for students with disabilities indicated that the outcomes should not differ from those for students without disabilities. In other words, the valued outcomes shown in Figure 5.2 are valued for *all* students.

The most valued outcomes

The outcomes specified in Figure 5.2 do not include all of the possible outcomes of schooling. Rather, they are the outcomes the stakeholders valued most. The stakeholders indicated, for example, that they would like to see students complete their schooling (among other things) competent in communication (they did not care whether students communicated verbally or with sign language); able to cope effectively with personal challenges, frustrations, and stressors; physically fit; and aware of the significance of voting and the procedures necessary to register and vote. Stakeholders made it very clear that they

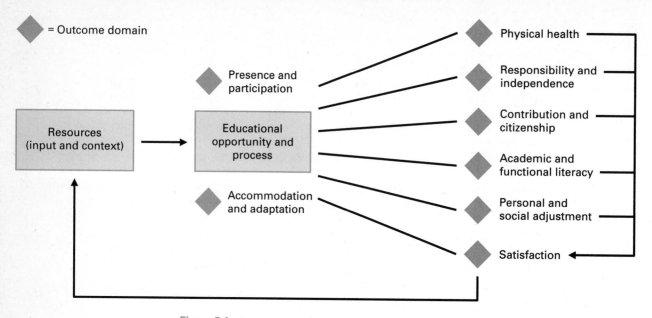

Figure 5.1
Conceptual Model of Outcome Domains
Source: Ysseldyke, James E. et al. *Educational Outcomes and Indicators for Students Completing School.* Copyright © 1993 National Center on Educational Outcomes. Used with permission.

would like to see schools and the nation gathering data on the extent to which all students are accomplishing these important outcomes.

Alternatives to Help Students Meet Goals and Outcomes

Within any classroom some students already have developed the skills being taught, others need help developing those skills, and still others need to be taught a set of prerequisite skills before they can learn the content others are learning. Put simply, students develop skills at different rates. Instruction in all classrooms must be adjusted to accommodate these individual differences so that all students reach the desired outcomes. Teachers try to match the level of instruction to the level of skill development of different learners in their classes. They modify and adapt the prescribed curriculum to meet the unique needs of their students.

Matching instruction to needs

When teachers need help accommodating a student with special learning needs, they can turn to special education. Why? Because the objectives of instruction in special education focus on meeting the needs of students who are exceptional. That instruction serves six purposes: development, enrichment, acceleration, remediation, compensation, and prevention. It is guided by an individualized education program that clearly defines the special learning needs of each student.

Six purposes of special education

An extensive knowledge base has been derived from research in the psychology of learning and development on how individuals develop skills. The

Presence and participation

- Is present in school
- Participates
- Completes school

Accommodation and adaptation

- Makes adaptations, accommodations, or compensations necessary to achieve outcomes in each of the major domains
- Demonstrates family support and coping skills

Physical health

- Makes healthy lifestyle choices
- Is aware of basic safety, fitness, and health care needs
- Is physically fit

Responsibility and independence

- Gets about in the environment
- Is responsible for self

Contribution and citizenship

- Complies with school and community rules
- Knows the significance of voting and procedures necessary to register and vote
- Volunteers

Academic and functional literacy

- Demonstrates competence in communication
- Demonstrates competence in problem-solving strategies and critical thinking skills
- Demonstrates competence in math, reading and writing skills
- Demonstrates competence in other academic and nonacademic skills
- Demonstrates competence in using technology

Personal and social adjustment

- Copes effectively with personal challenges, frustrations, and stressors
- Has a good self image
- Respects cultural and individual differences
- Gets along with other people

Satisfaction

- Student satisfaction with high school experience
- Parent/guardian satisfaction with the education that students received
- Community satisfaction with the education that students received

Figure 5.2
Important Outcomes for Each Outcome Domain
Source: Ysseldyke, James E. et al. *Educational Outcomes and Indicators for Students Completing School.* Copyright © 1993 National Center on Educational Outcomes. Used with permission.

component skills students must learn and demonstrate to perform complex behaviors have been studied, and the merits of learning skills in different sequences have been compared. The process of teaching students a set of progressively more difficult skills to enable them to demonstrate the complex **Developmental instruction** skills or abilities necessary to meet instructional objectives is called **developmental instruction.**

Some students make very rapid progress in regular classes. They are able to read earlier than many of their peers. Their arithmetic, writing, and language skills are more developed than those of their classmates, or they demonstrate

Enrichment

Acceleration

Remediation

Examples of remedial
instruction

Compensatory instruction

special talents in art or music. To meet their special needs, their teachers adjust instruction (see Chapter 7). **Enrichment** is the simplest approach. Classroom teachers enhance the educational experiences of these students by adding materials and activities to the curriculum; the educational setting remains the same. **Acceleration** is another way to meet the needs of students who are gifted and talented. In accelerated programs, students progress through a curriculum at a faster pace than their peers. They may spend less time drilling and practicing, or they may skip one or more grades to accommodate their heightened academic skills.

When students don't make expected progress in regular classes, many receive **remediation**—instruction designed to repair or correct basic problems or difficulties. In much the same way that doctors treat patients with medication, teachers give their students remedial instruction. A student can be taught specific skills (such as reading or math skills) to remediate deficiencies in skill development, or specific deficits in abilities (memory, perception of sounds) can be addressed in remediation.

By the time they are in high school, most students have learned to do basic math with high degrees of accuracy. In earlier chapters we talked about Larry Williams, a high school teacher of students with disabilities. Many of Larry's students have trouble with multiplication. Fred was having difficulty multiplying two-digit numbers. In watching the way Fred did his calculations, Larry noticed that he had not developed the skills to add the interim products together to produce the correct answer. Larry knew that trying to teach Fred to multiply two-digit numbers would be unproductive until he taught him to add the intermediate products correctly. This process of going back to remedy skill deficits is the kind of instruction that takes place in resource rooms and in the regular classroom. Earlier we also mentioned our friend Kim Bazan, who is an elementary education teacher with several students with disabilities in her classroom. One of Kim's students who was having trouble reading proved to have deficits in prerequisite reading skills; she confused some letters of the alphabet. Kim worked with her to develop accurate letter recognition before trying to teach her to read new material.

Instruction also can be **compensatory**. The word comes from compensate, which means "to make up for." If you don't own a car, you may compensate for it by taking buses, riding a bike, or getting rides from friends who do own cars. People who do not have the use of their legs compensate by getting around in wheelchairs; some of those who have lost the use of their voices compensate by writing what they want to say. Usually, compensatory treatments are used only when it's impossible to remediate a condition or when it's easier to compensate for the condition than to remediate it. Many educational methods are compensatory. Teaching students who are blind to communicate using braille, teaching students without arms to write holding a pencil in their toes, teaching deaf students to communicate using sign language and finger spelling—all are forms of compensatory instruction. Arranging for students who have difficulty reading or writing to take oral examinations, using "talking books" with students who have visual impairments, and tape-recording lectures for students who have difficulty taking notes also are forms of compensatory instruction. Compensatory instruction is designed to help students overcome the effects of disabilities that cannot be corrected.

Prevention

A final objective of instruction is **prevention**. Researchers have spent much time studying why students fail to achieve. They have identified individual students' characteristics, home and family characteristics, the ways in which schools are organized, and teaching procedures as factors associated with student failure. They also have identified instructional practices that, if taken into consideration in teaching, might foster the development of skills and competencies in more students. When school personnel know which academic skills and social behaviors students must have in order to acquire more complex skills and behaviors, and when they know what interferes with skill development, they are in a position to develop curriculums and interventions to prevent failure in school.

Head Start

A good example of a preventive intervention is the Head Start program, which was instituted in the United States in the 1960s. Head Start, a preschool program for children from low-income families, was developed in response to the high incidence of school difficulties and failure among these children. It offers intensive preschool instruction in an attempt to alleviate later problems. Head Start and other early-childhood prevention programs will be discussed in more detail in Chapter 14.

Faced with deciding which objectives to pursue, teachers have many options. They can teach to foster the development of skills, to enrich or accelerate the learning of content and skills, to correct or compensate for skills that have not been learned, and to prevent learning problems. These objectives are not unique to special education, but they are more evident in the instructional experiences of students who are exceptional than they are in the education of students who are not exceptional, and they are more evident in special education programs than in regular education programs.

Individualized Education Programs

IEPs

How are all of these different kinds of instruction organized and delivered to students with special learning needs? An *individualized education program (IEP)* is a written statement that describes what teachers and other professionals will do to meet the special learning needs of a student who is exceptional. As we noted in Chapter 3, IEPs are legally required for students with disabilities and are useful for those who are gifted and talented as well. An IEP is written for one particular student, and at any time only one IEP is used to guide the special education of that student.

Using an IEP

Kim uses an IEP to plan daily lessons and activities for managing, delivering, and evaluating Phyllis's instruction. She finds it helpful when sharing information with other teachers who work with Phyllis, the blind student discussed in Chapter 4. The IEP is also a source of information for Phyllis's parents and other professionals who provide services at school and at home. Her parents use it to know which teachers to talk to about their child, to get ideas about things they might work on at home, to keep a record of the programs and services Phyllis is receiving at school, and to help them know what to look for or what questions to ask when they visit Phyllis's school. The information in Table 5.1 will help you understand what an IEP is.

Most school districts have forms that are used for IEPs (see Figure 3.1 on page 69). The forms may differ from district to district, but the information described in the following sections should be a part of all IEPs.

IEP specifies condition, services, people responsible

Special Education and Related Services   An IEP must list the special education condition the student exhibits (for example, mental retardation, deafness) and the setting in which the student is to be educated. It should list the name(s) of the person(s) responsible for the program and the school where the program(s) is held. Related services (such as readers for a student who is partially sighted, counseling for a student with emotional difficulties, special transportation for a student with health impairments) and the names of the people responsible for them also should be listed on the IEP if they are part of a student's special education program. The IEP must also include a description of the transition services to be provided for a student who is older than 16 years.

IEP specifies time in regular classroom

Participation in Regular Education   Students who are exceptional should be educated in environments that are as much as possible like those experienced by nondisabled students. How much time a student will spend in regular education classes and the subjects studied there should be listed on the student's IEP, along with teachers' names.

IEP specifies dates

Time Frame for Implementation of the IEP   The date the program or service will begin (the initiation date), the length of time the program will continue (the anticipated duration), and the month and year the program will be reviewed (the review date) should be listed on the IEP. Most IEPs have places to indicate the date the program was written and the date parents and teachers and other professionals agreed to the information in the document. A space also is provided to indicate any disagreement among participants.

IEP specifies present levels

Present Levels of Functioning   The IEP should identify areas of special learning needs. Included are a description of current levels of performance and the source of that information (for example, a score of 115 on the WISC-III). An IEP should describe what a student can do ("Bobby read 47 words a minute with 80 percent accuracy in his basal reader") and may describe what a student cannot do ("Five days of independent observations indicate that Phyllis is unable to move freely around school without the help of a classmate"). Sometimes present levels of performance are listed simply as test scores (for example, a grade-equivalent score of 3.7 on the Reading Recognition subtest of the Peabody Individual Achievement Test–Revised).

IEP specifies goals and objectives

Goals and Objectives of the Special Education Program   One or more general statements describing what is expected in each area of special learning need should be included in the IEP. Annual goals describe what a student is ex-

Table 5.1   Individualized Education Program:
A Closer Look

An individualized education program is a written statement that

- describes the special education program for an exceptional student.
- describes in general terms what an exceptional student can do (his or her present level of functioning).
- describes the specific direct and indirect services the student will receive while in the special education program.
- describes how much time a student will spend in special and regular education classes.
- lists the dates on which special education will begin, end, and be reviewed.
- describes what an exceptional student is expected to learn and how progress will be evaluated.
- lists the people who developed the plan and indicates their agreement with its content.

An individualized education program is not

- a daily lesson plan that describes each little thing that will happen to a student while in a special program.
- a report written by a psychologist or educational diagnostician to describe a student's strengths and weaknesses.
- an agreement that promises all services that are needed will be provided or that guarantees that services that are provided will work.
- a ticket to unlimited mainstreaming or to full-time placement in a special education program.
- inflexible.
- a substitute for a report card or other daily, weekly, or monthly progress reports.
- a formal contract that places legal obligations on the people who develop it or the parents and professionals who agree to it.

pected to do after a year in the special education program. The following is one of the annual goals listed in the IEP of one of Larry's students:

An annual goal

> William will improve his reading comprehension skills from a grade equivalent of 5.0 to a grade equivalent of 6.0 as measured by the Woodcock–Johnson Reading Mastery Test–Revised.

Short-term objectives identify the steps that should be mastered to reach an annual goal. Suppose an annual goal is "Arnell will demonstrate mastery of multiplication skills as measured by the Mathematics Computation subtest of the Peabody Individual Achievement Test–Revised." The following are examples of appropriate short-term objectives:

Sample short-term objectives

- Arnell will perform basic multiplication problems (zero to nine multiplications) using number lines with 80 percent accuracy.
- Arnell will recite multiplication times tables for any multiple through twelve times twelve with 80 percent accuracy.
- Arnell will multiply any two-digit number by any one-digit number that doesn't require carrying with 80 percent accuracy.
- Arnell will multiply a one-digit number times a two-digit number that requires regrouping (carrying and renaming) in one column with 80 percent accuracy.
- Arnell will multiply a one-digit number times a three- or more-digit number with regrouping required in more than one column with 80 percent accuracy.

IEP specifies evaluation process

Evaluation Procedures and Criteria By the end of the year or periodically during the year (for example, after a specified number of short-term objectives have been mastered), Kim decides how well her students with disabilities are doing. All IEPs describe how progress will be measured and specify how much or how well a student must do. Evaluation procedures identify specific tests, observations, and interviews that will be used to measure progress (for example, the Mathematics subtest of the Peabody Individual Achievement Test–Revised or a five-minute time sampling on ten consecutive days). Evaluation criteria define standards that are used to measure progress (for example, 80 percent of the time, ten minutes each day of the week, or 90 percent accuracy).

IEP includes signatures

Signatures When an IEP is complete, parents (or guardians) must give their permission for the special services described in it to begin. Teachers and other professionals who prepare the IEP, parents, and the student usually sign it to indicate that they were at the meeting in which it was developed or that they agree with its content.

Other Information The information we just cited is required by law for students with disabilities. Teachers and administrators can include other information that makes the IEP even more useful:

Useful additions to the IEP

- How parents are expected to participate
- Language spoken in the student's home
- Health or medical information
- Management programs being used to control the student's behavior
- Special testing considerations
- Special requirements related to graduation from high school
- Student's daily or weekly class schedule
- Emergency information for use in contacting parents

Providing an IEP to guide the educational experiences of a student who is exceptional is one way special education is different from regular education. Having an IEP does not mean a student must be educated in a special environment. The better the program, the more likely instruction can be delivered in an environment as much like normal as possible.

Areas of Special Learning Needs

The goals and objectives contained in IEPs provide an indication of the areas in which students with disabilities have special learning needs. Primary areas of special learning needs, sample instructional goals, and examples of IEP objectives are shown in Table 5.2. As you look at the table, remember that all students need to learn the skills identified in each of the listed areas. Students who receive special education want to learn and should be taught the same content as their friends and peers in regular education. What makes some students special is that their current levels of functioning indicate that they have not learned the skills on their own or under ordinary conditions of instruction, or that they have special learning needs that require special instruction. Special education

Table 5.2	Special Learning Needs of Exceptional Students	
Area	**Sample Instructional Goals**	**Examples of IEP Objective**
Preacademic skills	Visual tracking Auditory discrimination Visual discrimination Visual memory	. . . will identify similarities and differences in visually presented stimuli . . . will demonstrate 90% accuracy on Frostig worksheets assigned
Academic skills	Reading, writing, arithmetic, science, social studies, civics, calculus, computers	. . . will pass all tests at Basic 4 level with 80% or better score
Social skills	Self-management Peer interactions Disruptiveness Verbal/nonverbal noises	. . . will sit attentively and listen for five consecutive three-minute time periods . . . will raise hand to ask questions during class lessons.
Language skills	Verbal communication Speech production Sentence structure Grammar/syntax	. . . will complete Units 4–9 of fourth-grade language program . . . will complete supplemental units of *Language Step by Step*

(continued on next page)

Table 5.2	Special Learning Needs of Exceptional Students (continued)

Area	Sample Instructional Goals	Examples of IEP Objective
Mobility skills	Physical independence Obstacle detection Cognitive maps	. . . will travel independently from homeroom to lunchroom . . . will identify three critical points for unaided trip to library
Independent living skills	Dressing Dining out Checkbook balancing	. . . will put boot on correct foot with assistance from Freddie . . . will calculate daily balance with 95% accuracy for one month
Vocational skills	Preemployment interview Employment interview Arrive at work on time Use machines safely	. . . will identify appropriate job listings in classified ads . . . will complete job application without assistance
Leisure skills	Dancing, singing, bicycling, swimming, softball, fishing, camping, hiking, board games, computer games	. . . will play electronic bowling for ten minutes with Phyllis . . . will complete "Scrabble" game with three other students without having a temper tantrum

helps them learn the skills that they have not or would not learn without the help of special teaching methods.

Special Teaching Methods

The actual content of an IEP depends on the special learning needs of the student being served. If you looked at one hundred IEPs, you'd find many similarities in the information in them. If you watched regular and special education teachers working with students who are exceptional, you'd notice many similarities in the ways they put the information in the IEPs into practice. The special teaching methods we describe next illustrate the diversity of approaches that are used to meet the special learning needs of students who are exceptional in regular and special classrooms. But there is no magic in these methods. They are simply used more often when teaching students who are exceptional because special education is needed to help these students learn what they could not learn without it.

Precision Teaching

Precision teaching is one of the ways in which teachers plan, use, and analyze the effects of instructional methods to improve students' performance. The approach involves continuous evaluation of students' progress toward meeting instructional objectives and always focuses on improving skills. It is a five-step process:

Steps in precison teaching

1. The teacher pinpoints the target behavior.
2. The teacher or student counts and records the baseline rate of the behavior, a measure of performance before teaching begins.
3. Using this baseline information, the teacher writes a short-term objective.
4. The teacher tries an instructional method, recording and evaluating changes in the student's behavior.
5. If the evaluation indicates that the student's performance is inadequate, the teacher changes the instructional method.

Teachers who use precision teaching usually record each student's progress on a special record called a *standard behavior chart,* but some simply use graph paper to keep track of changes in behavior.

Ability Training

Training in preacademic skills

When students need instruction in preacademic skills (for example, differentiating visual or auditory stimuli and remembering them), their teachers use **ability training** to organize their special education experiences. For example, if a student has a problem seeing the differences among geometric shapes, letters, or numbers, the teacher would assign activities that require matching a figure with one like it. If a student has a problem differentiating the *sh* and *th* dipthongs or the vowel sounds of *a* and *e,* the teacher might assign tape-recorded activities to give the student practice. Often ability training involves this kind of practice in an area where a student has difficulty. But it is also an effective way to teach students to use their own strengths to compensate for their ability deficits. For example, a child with poor auditory discrimination could be taught using a whole-language approach.

Direct Instruction

Larry believes that his actions as a teacher should be directly and functionally related to the goals of instruction. For example, if a student has not mastered math skills involving division or is not able to use tools to assemble a product, he arranges teaching activities to provide systematic, guided instruction in division facts or tool use. This approach is called **direct instruction,** and it relies on task analysis to identify the component steps of the skill that needs teaching. Initial development of the direct instruction model is typically attributed

Basics of direct instruction

to Siegfried Engelmann, Wesley Becker, Douglas Carnine, and Russell Gersten of the University of Oregon.

Attack strategy training is a form of direct instruction in which students are taught small steps of a skill and rules for putting the steps together, so that they can use the strategy for any problem like those they have solved (Lloyd, 1980). For example, in solving a multiplication problem like 2×4, students might be taught to read the problem and say "Count by two, four times—'two, four, six, eight'—then repeat the last number in the sequence as the solution to the problem." Once learned, the same strategy can be used to attack similar problems $(3 \times 4, 4 \times 2,$ and so on).

The process works like this:

Steps in attack strategy training

1. Analyze the curriculum content to determine the class of skills to be taught.
2. Devise a strategy for attacking problems that require the application of the skill being taught.
3. Analyze the attack strategy to decide how to teach it.
4. Teach the attack strategy and evaluate performance.

Learning Strategies Training

Teaching students how to learn

Students with disabilities sometimes are trained to follow a step-by-step procedure to acquire teacher-presented content. **Learning strategies training** teaches students how to learn content and how to demonstrate their knowledge. For example, Larry taught several of his students to use a three-step paraphrasing procedure represented by the mnemonic "RAP" (Schumaker, Denton, & Deshler, 1984). They Read a paragraph, Ask themselves about the main idea and two supporting details, then put (or Paraphrase) the information into their own words. The focus of learning strategies is learning content to complete teacher-assigned tasks. They are taught to students using direct instructional techniques (Deshler & Schumaker, 1986; Schumaker, Deshler, Alley, & Warner, 1983). Deshler, Schumaker, and their colleagues have developed, field tested, and validated a learning strategies curriculum for adolescents with learning disabilities.

Students monitor themselves

Self-monitoring is a technique in which an individual acts as an observer for his or her own behavior and records the observational data. Lloyd, Landrum, and Hallahan (1991) report a scenario that illustrates self-monitoring. The scenario is reproduced in the Bring Your Learning to Life feature on page 137.

Students correct own errors

Self-correction is an approach used to teach academic content. For example, Okyere and Heron (1991) used self-correction to improve the spelling performance of students in regular education classes. Students were taught to compare their misspelled words to a model, identify specific types of spelling mistakes, correct their mistakes using proofreading marks, and write the correct sequence of letters for the work. The authors report that use of the procedure produces demonstrable, generalized, and lasting gains in performance.

Graham and Harris (1988) describe an application of learning strategies training to teaching students to revise essays composed on a word processor.

Bring Your Learning to Life

Training and Implementing a Self-monitoring Program

The following script illustrates a teacher's application of a self-monitoring program designed to get a student to pay attention.

"Edwin, you know how paying attention to your work has been a problem for you. You've heard teachers tell you 'Pay attention,' 'Get to work,' 'What are you supposed to be doing?' and things like that. Well, today we're going to start something that will help you help yourself pay attention better. First we need to make sure that you know what paying attention means. This is what I mean by paying attention." (Teacher models inattentive behaviors such as glancing around and playing with objects.) "Now you tell me if I was paying attention." (Teacher models attentive and inattentive behaviors and requires the student to categorize them.) "Okay, now let me show you what we're going to do. While you're working, this tape recorder will be turned on. Every once in awhile, you'll hear a little sound like this:" (Teacher plays tone on tape.) "And when you hear that sound quietly ask yourself, 'Was I paying attention?' If you answer 'yes,' put a check in this box. If you answer 'no,' put a check in this box. Then go right back to work. When you hear the sound again, ask the question, answer it, mark your answer, and go back to work. Now, let me show you how it works." (Teacher mod-

els entire procedure.) "Now Edwin, I bet you can do this. Tell me what you're going to do every time you hear a tone. Let's try it. I'll start the tape and you work on these papers." (Teacher observes student's implementation of the entire procedure, praises its correct use, and gradually withdraws.)

The Next Day

SCENE: A classroom of students engaged in various activities. One teacher is walking about the room, preparing for her next activity. Some students are sitting in a semicircle facing another teacher and answering questions she poses. Other students are sitting at their desks and writing on papers or workbooks. Edwin is working at his own desk. The teacher picks up some workpages that have green strips of paper attached to their top.

TEACHER: (Walking up to Edwin's desk.) Edwin, here are your seatwork pages for today. I'm going to start the tape and I want you to self-record like you have been doing. What are you going to ask yourself when you hear the beep?

EDWIN: (Taking papers.) Was I paying attention?

TEACHER: Okay, that's it. (Turning away.) Bobby, Jackie, and Anne; it's time for spelling group. (Starts a tape recorder and walks toward front of room where three students are gathering.)

EDWIN: (Begins working on his assignments; he is continuing to work when a tone comes from the tape recorder. Edwin's lips barely

(continued on next page)

Training and Implementing a Self-monitoring Program *(continued)*

move as he almost inaudibly whispers.) Was I paying attention? Yes. (He marks on the green strip of paper and returns to work. Later, another tone comes from the tape recorder. Edwin whispers.) Was I paying attention? Yes. (He marks on the green strip of paper and returns to work. Later as the students in one group laugh, Edwin looks up and watches them. While he is looking up a tone occurs.)

Was I paying attention? No. (He marks the strip of paper and begins working again. He continues working, questioning himself when the tone occurs, and recording his answers.) (p. 202)

Source: Stoner, et al. (eds.). *Interventions for Achievement and Behavior Problems.* Copyright © 1991 by the National Association of School Psychologists. Reprinted by permission of the publisher.

An application for revising essays

They have students go through the following steps in revising essays:

- Read your essay;
- Find the sentence that tells what you believe—is it clear?
- Add two reasons why you believe it;
- SCAN each sentence (Does it make Sense; Is it Connected to my belief; Can I Add more; Note errors);
- Make changes on the computer; and
- Reread the essay and make final changes. (p. 509)

Graham and MacArthur (1987) found that when they used this approach students made two to five times as many revisions and their essays improved in overall quality.

Study Skills Training

Students with disabilities often lack the organizational and study skills needed to respond to academic task demands, and they experience difficulty acquiring those skills. "Study skills are systematic procedures that students initiate to complete such complex tasks as skimming, determining relevant information, taking notes, and studying material for a test" (Gleason, Colvin, & Archer, 1991). Gleason and Archer (1989) conducted a survey of junior high content area teachers in San Diego to ascertain their ratings of study skills necessary for success in their classes. Table 5.3 lists those teachers' ratings. Teachers also indicated that using work time, listening, following directions, and preparing for tests were behaviors that students with mild disabilities did not perform.

Helping students acquire study skills

Archer and Gleason (1989) developed a set of training exercises to teach study skills to students in grades 3 to 6. The intervention is used to educate students

Table 5.3   Study and School Behaviors Needed in Classes:
A Teacher Survey

| Study or School Behavior[a,b] | Percentage Responding[c] | | | | | |
| | Not Critical | | | Critical | | Combined |
	1	2	3	4	5	4 and 5
Asks for help when needed.	0	1	5	33	60	93
Listens during lectures/discussions.	0	1	6	25	67	92
Attends class regularly.	0	2	7	33	58	91
Comes to class with proper materials.	0	2	8	27	63	90
Utilizes independent work time in class effectively.	1	2	6	33	57	90
Is ready to work at beginning of class sessions.	0	3	9	37	51	88
Turns work in on time.	0	4	7	31	57	88
Socializes only at appropriate times.	2	2	9	32	54	86
Prepares for tests.	3	1	11	27	58	85
Reads and follows written directions independently.	0	3	19	36	41	77
Answers written questions independently.	3	4	21	38	34	72
Is punctual to class.	0	9	18	32	40	72
Works well with other students.	3	4	32	36	25	61
Reads textbook independently.	8	11	20	30	30	60
Determines meaning of words in context.	4	8	28	28	32	60
Utilizes effective test-taking strategies	10	8	26	32	24	56
Volunteers pertinent information in class discussions.	3	7	34	34	20	54
Writes complete sentences.	15	11	23	22	30	52
Scans materials for specific information.	9	9	30	29	23	52

(continued on next page)

Table **5.3** Study and School Behaviors Needed in Classes:
A Teacher Survey *(continued)*

Study or School Behavior[a,b]	Percentage Responding[c]					
	Not Critical			Critical		Combined
	1	2	3	4	5	4 and 5
Writes legibly.	5	11	33	35	16	51
Skims written material for main ideas.	15	10	27	34	14	48
Turns in neat papers.	5	10	40	29	15	44
Takes notes from lectures/discussions.	13	14	32	23	17	40
Writes clear paragraphs.	21	14	27	22	16	38
Proofs papers for punctuation and spelling errors.	21	17	25	21	15	36
Maintains a neat and organized notebook.	23	16	27	23	10	33
Decodes longer words (multi-syllabic words).	23	14	30	19	12	31
Utilizes reference materials (e.g., dictionary, encyclopedia).	27	17	26	18	12	30
Takes notes from written materials.	19	20	33	17	11	28
Utilizes library resources (e.g., card catalogue).	32	10	31	19	8	27

[a] Remaining school and study skills were rated 4 or 5 by fewer than 25% of the teachers. Thus, they were omitted from this table.
[b] Study/school behaviors have been reordered in descending order of percentage of teachers judging the behaviors critical to classroom success by marking 4 or 5.
[c] Percentages were rounded and as a result do not always add to 100%

Source: Stoner, G. et al. (eds.). *Interventions for Achievement and Behavior Problems.* Copyright © 1991 by the National Association of School Psychologists. Reprinted by permission of the publisher.

in gaining information from content area textbooks (surveying chapters, self-questioning, attending to maps and graphics that accompany content, answering questions about what they read, writing summaries of materials they have read, taking tests) and organizing information (notebook organization, assignment calendars, preparing neat papers). The authors specify a set of procedures for teaching social skills (most of them parallel strategies we discussed in Chapter 4) and illustrate ways to promote generalization and transfer.

Cognitive Skills Training

Some of the IEPs for students in Kim's class contain objectives in areas like critical thinking, reasoning, and convergent and divergent thinking. Many teachers believe that students should be taught thinking skills as part of their schooling. The most widely recognized grouping (taxonomy) of educational objectives in the cognitive domain was developed by Benjamin Bloom and his colleagues (1956). Bloom's taxonomy identifies six levels of cognitive skills—knowledge, comprehension, application, analysis, synthesis, and evaluation—each more complex than the one before it (Clark, 1983). To teach *knowledge* skills, teachers expose students to aesthetic, economic, political, educational, and social aspects of the environment and to people with similar interests, and give them experience doing needs assessments (determining necessary information or principles for successful completion of a project) and organizing data. *Comprehension* and *application* skills include collecting information to use in decision making, working with people who share common interests, and developing original products. *Analysis* and *synthesis* skills include examining creative products, changing ways of thinking, comparing thinking patterns with others, and integrating knowledge using convergent and divergent thinking strategies. Identifying standards for making comparisons, developing decision-making skills, and making choices are *evaluation* skills.

Teaching students to think should be a goal of all teachers. Critical-thinking objectives are central to the IEPs of many exceptional students because they have enormous potential to improve students' lives and the lives of those who live and work with them.

Peer-mediated Interventions

Often teachers use classroom peers to provide instruction to students who are having difficulty. Remember from Chapter 2 that Chris and Pat studied with a "study buddy." Four peer-mediated interventions are cooperative learning, peer tutoring, classwide peer tutoring, and peer-directed behavior management strategies.

Cooperative Learning   Teachers can structure school activities cooperatively, competitively, or individually. In **cooperative learning** structures, a small group of students, usually fewer than six to a group, work together on an instructional task. There are several essential components of cooperative learning (Johnson & Johnson, 1994, pp. 81–94).

1. *Positive interdependence:* instructional goals are achieved through the participation of all group members—all for one and one for all.
2. *Individual accountability/personal responsibility:* group members share responsibility for the joint outcome. Each participant makes unique contributions to the group's goals, and individuals are held accountable by group members for contributing their fair share.
3. *Face-to-face promotive interaction:* "group members meet face-to-face to work together to complete assignments and promote each other's success"

> **Window on Practice**
>
> ### The Power of Cooperation and Teamwork
>
> The Killer Bees is a boys' high school basketball team from Bridgehampton, New York (a small, middle-class town on Long Island). Bridgehampton High School's total enrollment has declined since 1985 from sixty-seven to forty-one, with fewer than twenty males attending the high school. There have never been more than seven players on the team. Yet, since 1980 the Killer Bees have amassed a record of 164 wins and 32 losses, qualified for the state championship playoffs six times, won the state championship twice, and finished in the final four two other times. None of their players was ever really a star and the team members were never tall. Not one of the Killer Bees went on to play professional basketball. Although every Killer Bee graduated and most went to college, few had the talent to play basketball in college.
>
> How did the Killer Bees become so successful with so few players and no star players? There are at least three reasons why the Killer Bees consistently won against bigger, supposedly more talented, opponents. The first is that the Killer Bees' game was "team basketball." They won not by superior talent but through superior teamwork. The second reason is that team members adopted an incredible work ethic. They practiced 365 days a year on skill development and teamwork. The third reason was their versatility and flexibility in how they played their opponents. The source of the Killer Bees' focus on teamwork, hard work, and versatility was a richness and depth of purpose that eludes most teams. Their mission was more than winning basketball games. They were committed to bringing honor and recognition to their community and protecting and enhancing their legacy. They were also committed to each other. The commitment of team members was reciprocated by the community, whose members came to every game and relentlessly cheered the team on.
>
> It is the potential for such performances that makes cooperative groups the key to successful education. Teamwork can do for learning what it did for the Killer Bees' basketball performance.
>
> *Source:* Reprinted from D. W. Johnson and R. T. Johnson, *Learning Together and Alone: Cooperative, Competitive, and Individualistic Learning.* Fourth Edition, pp. 75–76. Copyright © 1994 Allyn and Bacon.

(Johnson & Johnson, 1994, p. 89). The students discuss assignments and help and assist each other.

4. *Interpersonal and small-group skills:* Students are required to learn the interpersonal skills they need to work effectively with one another.

5. *Group processing:* groups of students meet to review their work and to assess the quality of their interaction, receive group feedback, hold each other accountable and responsible, set goals to improve their effectiveness, see how effectively the entire class is functioning, and celebrate good performance.

Larry uses this technique to teach social studies to some of his students. First, he breaks an academic unit (say the Civil War) into several component parts (such as biographies of key people, major historical events). He then assigns each member of a cooperative learning team one section of the total project (for example, a ten-page written report, an oral report, a play).

Peer tutoring is a popular method of instruction in many classrooms. *Paul Conklin/PhotoEdit*

Students work independently to gather information, then meet to share their contributions with other team members and to plan the final product. Sometimes Larry assigns final grades to each student independently; at other times he awards the same grade to all group members.

Peer Tutoring   For many years, questions like "Why can't Johnny read?" have motivated teachers to search for something within their students that causes them to fail. Recently, the concept of opportunity to learn has shifted the blame for academic failure from the student to interactions within the classroom. Research findings that students typically spend little time actively engaged in academic tasks support the development of instructional methods that can increase opportunities to learn (Delquadri, Greenwood, Whorton, Carta, & Hall, 1986; O'Sullivan, Ysseldyke, Christenson, & Thurlow, 1990; Ysseldyke, O'Sullivan, Thurlow, & Christenson, 1989).

Students as tutors

One of those methods is **peer tutoring:** A student is assigned to teach a classmate or peer under the supervision of a teacher (Greenwood, Carta, & Maheady, 1991). One resource room teacher incorporated peer tutoring into his sixth-grade instructional program. His objectives were to review and practice basic math facts and increase the self-confidence, responsibility, and interpersonal interaction skills of his students. He paired students from regular third and fourth grades who were having difficulties remembering their number facts, with special class students who needed review on the same academic content. The tutors spent two weeks practicing effective teaching techniques (planning lessons, providing supportive or corrective feedback) before they worked with their "students." On Monday and Wednesday of each week, the older students planned their lessons. On Tuesday and Thursday, they tutored for thirty minutes. On Friday, they evaluated their own performance and that of the student they had tutored. Periodically, the classroom teacher evaluated the progress of all the participating students and changed the program as needed.

Peer tutoring for the entire class

Classwide Peer Tutoring   **Classwide peer tutoring** is an instructional alternative in which students supervise one another's responses to academic tasks. Kim uses this approach twice a week during math. She divides the class into two teams, then pairs the students on each team. Each pair of students creates a set of flashcards by copying single-digit number facts onto a set of index cards. The problem goes on one side of the card, the answer on the other. Then the students actively practice the facts for twenty minutes. During the first ten-minute session, the "teacher" shows the problem sides of the index cards and the "student" provides the answers. During the second ten-minute session, the students change roles. During both sessions, the "teacher" provides corrective ("No, two plus two equals four") or supportive ("Yes, three plus two equals five") feedback. After the tutoring sessions, Kim tallies the total points for each team and records the results on a graph in the front of the room.

Peers help modify behavior

Peer-directed Behavior Management Strategies   Peers can also be used to assist in managing individual student's behaviors. Suppose, for example, that Willis spends a lot of time out of his seat when working with groups of children. The teacher can indicate to the group that the group will receive a reward or privilege if Willis remains in his seat. The group can be asked to help Willis by encouraging him to remain in the group and in his seat. Specific criteria can be set ("If Willis is not out of his seat more than three times during the group work session . . ."). The encouragement and support of the group can be a powerful incentive for behavior change.

Behavior Therapy

Behavior therapy, which is commonly used in working with students with disabilities or those who are gifted and talented, is the process of systematically arranging environmental events to influence behavior. It assumes that antecedents (environmental events or actions that occur just before a particular behavior) and consequences (which happen just after the behavior) can be used to increase, decrease, or maintain behaviors. Teachers may change antecedents or consequences to attempt to change behavior.

Changing antecedents and consequences

Behavior therapy is based on the principles of respondent and operant conditioning. *Respondent conditioning* ties a reflex response to a new stimulus.

Principles of respondent conditioning

- Innate responses (reflexes) follow specific triggering stimuli. For example, a puff of air near your eyes causes you to blink. The frequency of the response is directly related to the frequency of the triggering stimulus.

- New stimuli can come to trigger innate responses through the process of conditioning. By continually pairing a stimulus that evokes a response with a new stimulus that does not normally evoke the response, the new stimulus comes to evoke the response when presented alone.

Operant conditioning is the systematic application and removal of rewards and punishments to increase wanted behaviors and to reduce unwanted behaviors. Behavior therapy approaches based on operant conditioning typically follow five steps:

Steps in operant conditioning

1. Specifying a target behavior and a plan for measuring it
2. Identifying levels of the behavior before intervention
3. Selecting reinforcers (rewards or punishments) and formulating a plan for systematically applying them
4. Implementing the plan
5. Evaluating the effects of the intervention

Using desensitization

Teachers use many different respondent and operant techniques to meet the learning needs of students who are exceptional. For example, Larry uses *desensitization* to help students overcome test anxiety. At the beginning of the year, he noticed that Marsha, Pat, and Andrea became very nervous just before tests and quizzes. The announcement that there was to be a test or quiz, or the distribution of the test or quiz, triggered anxiety in Marsha, Pat, and Andrea. Now before an exam, he has them do some relaxation exercises, in which they alternately tense and relax the muscles in their hands, arms, legs, and feet. He also has them do some deep breathing and some "positive self-talk" ("If I mess this up, I can always make it up on the next quiz," "This only counts for 5 percent of my total grade"). His records of their performance before and after the desensitization exercises indicate that the technique has improved the students' performance on tests and quizzes.

Using a token system

Another teacher at Larry's high school designed a *token system* to improve students' behavior on bus trips. She identified target behaviors that her students needed to change (entering the bus screaming at the driver, shouting across people to talk to a friend). Then she listed the target behaviors and dollar amounts that could be earned for them on the first page of a checkbook. She gave each student a checklist that had the behaviors on the left side of the page and the days of the week across the top. She talked to the bus driver, who agreed to check the students' behaviors after each trip. Just before lunch each day, she had the students calculate the money they had earned and gave each of them a personal check in that amount. The students kept track of their earnings in their own checkbooks (which gave them needed practice in basic mathematics). Periodically, they were allowed to write checks in exchange for coupons that could be used at off-campus restaurants for lunch.

Using contingency contracts

Kim uses *contingency contracts,* a technique mentioned in Chapter 4, with many of her students. Kim wrote a formal agreement for Bobby that specified the consequences of completing and not completing his homework. She described the behavior she wanted him to change (not completing homework assignments) and identified things that she wanted to use as reinforcers (discount coupons for a fast-food restaurant). Then she wrote up a contract that stated that Bobby would earn one point for each homework problem he completed.

When he earned twenty points, he could trade them for a coupon for a free order of french fries. It wasn't long before Bobby started asking for his homework assignments right after lunch.

Using a response cost technique

Another fifth-grade teacher in Kim's school uses *response cost* to improve behavior during art class. Her students had asked if they could listen to music while they worked on their projects. She identified a set of appropriate and inappropriate behaviors and posted them on a chart in the front of the room, then made the music contingent on the students' behavior. Now she tunes a radio to an FM rock station and plays it softly while students work on their projects. If a student misbehaves, she gives the student a warning. After three warnings, she turns off the radio. When six students demonstrate appropriate behaviors, she turns it on again.

Counseling Therapy

Some teachers and many related service professionals focus on students' interpersonal problems. Many of these professionals structure classroom activities to accommodate the social and emotional problems of their students with techniques called **counseling therapy.**

Types of counseling therapy

A number of different practices are used in this approach. For example, in *reality therapy,* the initial objective is to help students identify the problem and ways to rectify it (Glaser, 1965). In *client-centered therapy,* the teacher creates a warm, permissive environment that encourages students to express themselves and to develop their own problem-solving strategies (C. Rogers, 1951). In this kind of interaction, the teacher avoids making evaluative statements of any type. *Transactional analysis (TA)* identifies communication patterns between individuals, then changes them to improve interpersonal relationships. Transactional analysis teaching techniques include contracts, discussions, and specific assignments on how to interact.

Crisis therapy and the life space interview

One of the most widely discussed approaches to counseling therapy is called *crisis therapy* (Redl, 1959). Like other therapies, the focus here is on building supportive therapeutic relationships, but the point at which the therapy begins is an actual life event, not a therapy session removed from the real world. A key element of crisis therapy is the *life space interview,* which Redl describes as "the type of therapy-like interview that a child may need around an incident of stealing from the 'kitty' in his club group but that would be held right around the event itself by the group worker in charge of that club, rather than by the child's therapist—even though the same material would probably later come up in therapy too" (pp. 40–41). The nature of the life space interview depends on its objective. If a teacher simply wants to help a student get through a critical event or crisis, then on-the-spot emotional first aid is the appropriate strategy; if the intervention target is longer-term learning, then a clinical exploration of life events is appropriate. The student's willingness to take part in the interview as well as the time frame in which it occurs also helps determine which strategy a teacher can use.

To deal with the crisis immediately, the teacher should be sympathetic to and understanding of the student's fears, anger, and guilt, but firm about the need for rules and standards of behavior. The objective is to bring the student back to the task at hand. In clinical therapy, the details of the critical incident are used to teach new behaviors or ways of reacting in similar situations. For example, by pointing out that each time Mark calls Sally a certain name, he is likely to get the same reaction, Larry helps Mark regulate the future consequences of his behavior. By offering or having Mark suggest new ways to talk to Sally, Larry helps Mark develop more appropriate interpersonal skills.

Teaching new behaviors

Social Skills Training

Some teachers take a direct instructional approach to improving students' interpersonal relationships. Critical elements of social skills training are a definition of the problem or target behavior, an assessment of the current levels of the problem, and the development and implementation of systematic procedures for teaching new behaviors or improving old ones (Hughes & Ruhl, 1989). Sabornie (1991) indicated that it is important for social skills teachers to teach behaviors that students can acquire relatively easily, that can be used readily in encounters with others in and outside classrooms, and that are powerful enough to elicit positive responses from others. The skills taught should enhance the social competence of those who receive treatment. Friendship skills (greetings, joining and leaving activities), social maintenance skills (helping, cooperating), and conflict resolution skills (compromising, persuasion) are common goals of social skills training. Principles of direct instruction—task analysis, modeling expected behavior, corrective and supportive feedback, and independent practice—are central to the process.

Teaching social skills

Published programs designed to provide students with training in social skills include the ACCEPTS program (Walker, McConnell, Holmes, Todis, Walker, & Golden, 1983), Skillstreaming the Elementary School Child (McGinnis & Goldstein, 1984), Skillstreaming the Adolescent (Goldstein, Sprafkin, Gershaw, & Klein, 1980), and the Walker Social Skills Curriculum (Walker, Todis, Holmes, & Horton, 1988).

Special Instructional Adaptations

Marc Buoniconti was paralyzed from the neck down in a football accident. But within four years, the young man became a dean's list student at the University of Miami, using a voice-operated computer that managed everything from answering the telephone to turning on the lights. He exercised daily at the university's medical center, using a high-tech bicycle that electrically stimulated his legs. Buoniconti proved there is life after a serious football injury (M. Rogers, 1989).

Voice-operated computers and other instructional adaptations can be used by students with disabilities to modify the way they participate in instruction and other activities of daily living. Even though many of these modifications help students with disabilities succeed in regular classrooms, their number

A great variety of
adaptations

and variety are evidence of another way special and regular education are different.

In this section we describe some of the instructional adaptations commonly used with students with disabilities to improve their communication and mobility. Later chapters on teaching students with specific disabilities say more about these adaptations. We briefly describe them here to show the range of available devices and to illustrate that many of them are used by students with different disabilities.

Adaptations for Communication

To be successful in school a student must be able to communicate with teachers and other students. Many people with disabilities have special learning needs in the area of communication. For example, some need large-print books to read. Others need special equipment on their telephones to "talk." Still others need some sort of modification to take tests.

From boards to
synthesizers

Communication Boards and Electronic Communication Aids   Communication boards are used by students who cannot speak. These boards have letters and symbols on them. The students point to the letters and symbols to communicate. You may have seen a student in a wheelchair with a board, much like a large tray, mounted on the chair. In many settings, the boards are being replaced with electronic communication aids that use voice synthesizers. These devices range from simple machines that produce prerecorded speech to sophisticated miniature computers with extensive vocabulary and high-quality speech output.

Advances in hearing aids

Hearing Aids   Perhaps the most widely known adaptive device is the modern hearing aid, a device that amplifies sound. Hearing aids can be worn behind the ear, in the ear, on the body, or in eyeglass frames. Technological advances have made hearing aids smaller, lighter, and more powerful. Audiologists or other specialists usually recommend the type of device that is best suited to meet the needs of a particular individual.

Classroom Amplification Systems   These systems are used to increase the communication abilities of groups of students with special communication needs. Most use a microphone to link the teacher to the students, who wear receivers that often double as personal hearing aids.

Closed captioning

Telecommunication Devices   One way those who are deaf communicate is by translating verbal messages into written form. The simplest method, of course, is pencil and paper; closed captioning on TV and telecommunication devices that allow people who are deaf to talk on the telephone are more sophisticated methods.

Closed captions for TV—a band of words running across the screen much like subtitles in a foreign-language film—summarize dialogue or plot. Many films and videos are also available with closed captioning. Commercially produced TVs now come equipped for closed-captioned broadcasts and tapes.

Phone adaptations

Telecommunication devices are small keyboards and transmitter/receivers that are connected to a normal telephone by an acoustic coupler. To make a call, you hook your phone to the device and call another person with a similar device. When the connection is established, a message appears on a small screen or mechanical printer on your machine. Then you type what you want to say, which is translated and printed on the printer connected to the other person's phone. The Americans with Disabilities Act requires that public telephone companies offer translation services so that a user of a telecommunication device can communicate with a person who does not own such a device. In recent years, moreover, many people with hearing or speech impairments, just like nondisabled people, have begun to use computers with fax modems to send and receive fax messages or electronic mail. These kinds of technology allow people with disabilities to communicate freely with the whole world.

E-mail

Braille In the early 1800s, Louis Braille developed a system of reading and writing that uses arrangements of six raised dots to represent letters, words, and numbers. Almost two hundred years later, it is still being used by people who are blind or who have severe visual disabilities. Although the braille system is complex, students who are blind can read much faster using it than they can using raised letters of the standard alphabet.

Learning braille

Most youngsters who need braille are introduced to it very early in school. They usually are taught a set of contractions rather than letter-by-letter representations of the words they read. Generally students take about two years to become proficient readers of braille (consider that nonexceptional students usually take the same amount of time to become proficient readers of print). Children who read braille have traditionally learned to write using a brailler, a six-keyed device that creates raised-dot words. Older students use a slate and stylus to punch out braille dots because they are smaller and quieter than a brailler.

Computer braille technology

Computer technology now exists that will translate braille into print and vice versa. Students can use this technology to translate their textbooks or reading assignments into a format they can read. There is also computer technology to enable students to take notes, type papers, and take tests in class. Students can use editing software to read their notes, papers, or tests, and translate them into English so that sighted readers can read them.

Computers that speak

Synthetic Speech Many students with visual impairments use a computer-based device that converts printed words into synthetic English speech. A popular form of this device is the Kurzweil Personal Reader. It has brought independence and self-confidence to many people who have trouble reading any other way. Stevie Wonder uses this kind of machine. You can see what it looks like in the photo on the next page.

Reprinted with permission from Xerox Corporation.

Other computerized adaptations

Computers The computerized adaptations already mentioned—synthetic speech, braille translating devices, electronic mail—are just the tip of the proverbial iceberg. Computers are helping exceptional people do almost anything. A professional musician who is paralyzed, unable to speak or swallow, uses a computer music system to compose and play his work. An architect with severe cerebral palsy who cannot use her arms and legs produces elaborate maps with a mouth stick for computer-assisted drafting. For those with extremely limited physical mobility, there are computers that can be operated simply by moving the eyes. Computers help students with physical disabilities by controlling various ordinary objects in their environment, such as light switches. Because of the increasing multimedia capability of personal computers—for instance, the recent advances in soundboards and sound software—many high-tech adaptations are widely available at relatively modest prices.

Bring Your Learning to Life

Computer Software Increases Lynn's Independence

Lynn has limited control of her hands because of cerebral palsy. It used to take her an hour to complete a single-page homework sheet, even with her mother's help. Now, with the aid of a computer program called the Electronic Answer Sheet, she can do the work by herself in only twenty minutes.

The computer is more patient than any human could be. If Lynn makes an error, the computer's synthetic speech can tell her, "Oops, try again." This kind of immediate, specific, pleasant feedback reduces the emotional strain on Lynn and on her entire family.

Now a young woman, Lynn has been using the computer since age 7. The ability to work by herself has given her a greater sense of her own achievements. The computer has also helped her increase her intellectual mastery, and this, too, has fostered her independence. Now that her hand control is improving, she can do assignments by handwriting if she likes, but she continues to use the computer for much of her work.

Source: Based on an account in Rachel Wobschall and Erik Aasland. (Summer 1990). Technology as family support, *Impact, 3* (2). Minneapolis: Institute on Community Integration, University of Minnesota, p. 8.

Moreover, computers are powerful teaching machines and rewards for all students.

Facilitated Communication   Facilitated communication is a rather controversial method of aiding expressive communication with people who are nonverbal or whose expressive ability is limited. Rosemary Crossley, an Australian educator and founder of the Dignity Through Education and Language (DEAL) Communication Center in Melbourne, is the originator of the method. Her method was used initially with individuals with cerebral palsy. Later it was expanded to include individuals with autism, Down syndrome, and other developmental disabilities. In January 1990 Douglas Biklen began to use the method in the Syracuse, New York, schools with individuals labeled autistic. The premise of the approach is the belief that for people with autism or other severe expressive communication disabilities, the problem of communication may not be cognitive in nature, but related to difficulties in initiating communication and expression.

With facilitation, which is a kind of supported typing, people with communication disabilities can use a letterboard, typewriter, computer keyboard, or Canon Communicator to spell out words. The method involves initial hand-over-hand and/or arm support that helps the person isolate the index finger and creates a level of comfort allowing the person to initiate the movements. Mild resistance provided by the facilitator—pulling the hand back after each

Hand or arm support

selection—slows the person's movements and increases accuracy. Over time the level of physical support may be faded to a hand on the forearm or shoulder. Over time the person progresses from structured work such as fill-in-the-blank exercises and multiple-choice activities to open-ended, typed, conversational text. Critical to the success of this method is the encouragement, verbal assurance, and belief on the part of the facilitator that the person is a competent, intelligent individual with many ideas to express. Biklen's work suggests that, contrary to our previously held beliefs that people with autism demonstrate cognitive deficits, they demonstrate unexpected literacy and numeracy skills and produce natural, if not eloquent, language. As we were preparing this text, however, researchers were beginning to produce studies that challenged the claims made for facilitative communication.

Adaptations for Mobility

Accessibility

In recent years, society has demonstrated an increased awareness of the special needs of its citizens. It is almost impossible to go anywhere without seeing some evidence of this reality. Special parking places for people with disabilities are one example. College and university campuses, as well as most public buildings and city streets, have been changed by the addition of travel ramps and curb cuts that make them more accessible to people in wheelchairs. As a result of these changes, most people with disabilities are where they should be, participating in life with the rest of us. We discuss other adaptations in the following subsections.

Guide dogs

Animals   Guide dogs are used by people who are blind to help them move around. They generally are not available to people under age 16. (Most guide dog schools require that owners be 16 years old because of the responsibility of caring for an animal.) Less than 2 percent of those with visual disabilities use guide dogs. Hill (1986) suggests that these dogs walk too fast for elderly people with visual disabilities or people with physical disabilities, that most visually handicapped people have enough vision to enable them to get about, and that many blind people either do not like dogs or prefer other means of mobility. Dogs also are used to help those who are hearing impaired.

The long cane

Canes   Various types of canes are used by people with visual handicaps to help them get around. Long canes, orthopedic canes, and folding canes are all in use. The most common are long canes—aluminum canes that have a rubber grip, a nylon tip, and a crook. By systematically tapping the cane from side to side to keep track of sidewalks and steps and walls, people who have difficulty seeing can tell where they are.

Wheelchairs   When people's mobility is limited because they cannot rise from a sitting to a standing position or when those who use crutches need to carry things and move around, they generally use wheelchairs. Modern wheelchairs

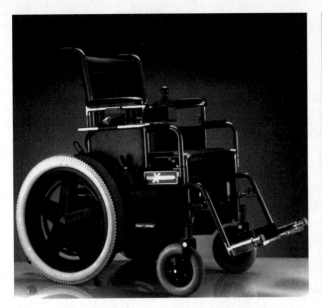 

Figure 5.3
Programmable Power Wheelchairs
Sophisticated design principles and technology enhance the comfort and functionality of modern wheelchairs.
Source: Photos courtesy of the manufacturer, Everest & Jennings.

Advances in wheelchairs

are made of lightweight metal, and have a durable seat and four wheels. The large back wheels have a special rim that helps make the chair move. Advances in technology have led to unbelievable changes in the sophistication of wheelchairs over the past decade. Motorized wheelchairs are computerized, operated by joysticks, with motor-mounted digital tachometers for instant communication with the computerized controller. The result is precise speed and tracking on all terrains and grades. We have illustrated two programmable power wheelchairs in Figure 5.3. The wheelchair on the left has large back wheels; the one on the right has smaller wheels specially designed for use on indoor carpet.

Adults who use wheelchairs to get around work in many different professions and can do most anything people who don't use wheelchairs can do. One of the teachers in Kim's school uses a wheelchair. He can't run up a flight of stairs, but he can and does play the guitar, lead an active social life with his family and colleagues, and teach fifth-grade students. Kim says that he has replaced the "can'ts" that handicap many people with the "cans" that many able-bodied people never achieve. Ron Anderson, a colleague of ours, uses a wheelchair to get around the university campus where he teaches an introductory course to undergraduate students planning to be teachers. There is an Annual Ms. Wheelchair America Pageant. The duties of the winner are numerous: "She will travel, visit advocacy groups, make public appearances and conduct television, radio, and print interviews. These include promoting

Replacing "can'ts" with "cans"

awareness of the need to eliminate architectural and attitudinal barriers, informing the able-bodied public of the achievements of physically challenged people across the nation" (Simmons, 1988, pp. 10–11).

Prostheses Some people with physical disabilities use special devices to increase their mobility. Artificial replacements for missing body parts are known as prostheses or prosthetic devices. These devices allow people with physical disabilities to function fully in society.

> Several years ago, Ivy Hunter was inducted into the International Models Hall of Fame, joining such modeling legends as Wilhelmina, Naomi Sims, and Cybil Shepherd. The honor was in recognition of her personal and professional achievements, achievements in personal courage, and professional commitment which far exceed those usually demanded of a fashion model: Ivy Hunter's right leg has been amputated.
>
> With a state-of-the-art natural-looking prosthetic leg . . . Ivy continues to model everything from swimwear and lingerie to daytime fashions and evening gowns at photo sessions, runway fashion shows, and in television commercials. . . . Ivy has learned to snow ski [and] has garnered several gold and bronze medals in the National Handicapped Sports and Recreation Association competitions. She also plays tennis, golfs, and water skis. ("Profile," 1988, p. 14)

Special Instructional Methods in Perspective

What's special about special education? This question has plagued us throughout our professional careers. We have never believed that the students in special education were very different from their friends in regular education. When we observed teachers in special and regular classrooms, we noticed that many of their methods were similar. They all planned instructional units, dealt with classroom disruptions, presented content, monitored their students' performances, and worried that there wasn't enough time in the day to get everything done. Because the similarities between regular education and special education teachers, students, or practices outweigh the differences between them, we began to wonder whether special education could be provided in a more efficient and productive manner.

Similarities between regular and special education

Sometimes, when we are considering alternatives to current practices, we think about what it would be like if regular teachers' first and foremost responsibility was to teach *all* students—if their primary goal was to take students where they are and move them forward, to reduce their need for special educational experiences. If students needed special help, their classroom teacher would provide remedial or compensatory instruction. If any students performed beyond expectations, their classroom teacher would enrich or accelerate their educational experiences.

Special instructional techniques (such as learning strategies and social skills training) would be considered appropriate for all students and would be provided as an academic content area by a specially trained teacher. If these techniques can help students learn, we'd like all students to have access to them.

IEPs for all students?

In the same way, it would be wonderful if *all* students had individualized education programs, both to improve instruction and to eliminate the stigma of being "different." Even though IEPs represent a positive difference between regular and special education, they sometimes reinforce stereotypes that operate contrary to the best interests of exceptional students. Having an IEP is like wearing a freshman cap, eating in a separate dining room, riding a special bus, going to a special class, and having a special teacher. It's a badge that reads "I am different." Most exceptional people that we know tell us they do everything they can to convey another message to people: "I am not different."

Class size an obstacle

The only legitimate obstacle to using special instructional methods in the regular classroom is the size of classes in most present-day schools. We would like to see an educational system in which the typical grade (120 students) is divided among five, not four, teachers. With fewer students, all teachers could spend more time on specialized instruction. We know they can; many are doing it in regular classes already. An alternative approach, one being used in some of the New American Schools Development Corporation's "Break the Mold" schools, is cross-grade grouping. Instead of assigning 20 third-graders to a third-grade teacher, 20 fourth-graders to a fourth-grade teacher, and 20 fifth-graders to a fifth-grade teacher, the school assigns 20 third-, 20 fourth-, and 20 fifth-grade students (total of 60 students) to three teachers who make decisions about how to group them for instruction. The students remain with the same teachers for a three-year period.

Cross-grade grouping

Special adaptations for all

We think special adaptations should become content areas of instruction, not methods for keeping students who are exceptional away from their peers. Why not teach second-graders braille so they can read what some of their exceptional friends have to say? Why not teach sign language to seventh-graders so they can communicate with a classmate who is deaf? Why not illustrate as early as possible the importance of making schools, libraries, and other public places accessible to all people who want to use them?

All education should be special. We would like to eliminate the differences that exist between special and regular education; we want our children and our children's children to learn in a single educational system where all education is special. The reasons for maintaining educational differences are becoming less and less easy to articulate and justify.

Chapters 7 through 13 provide specific tactics for working with special education students. In each chapter we focus the tactics on the specific characteristics of the group of students discussed in the chapter. In many cases, however, characteristics overlap—for example, many groups of special education students have social and emotional problems—and tactics therefore can overlap as well. A tactic we suggest for students with learning disabilities may also be appropriate for students with communication disorders or mental retardation. Keep that in mind as you read. You should use all the tactics we present as resources in working with all students in your classroom.

What Every Teacher Should Know

- Four elements make special education different from regular education: individualized education programs (IEPs), areas of special learning needs, instructional techniques, and instructional adaptations.

- Outcomes-based education (OBE) is a system in which a community decides the skills, knowledge, and behaviors with which they want students to complete school, and then all curricular activities are directed toward helping students achieve the outcomes.

- There are six kinds of instruction. *Developmental* instruction is the process of teaching students progressively more difficult skills to enable them to demonstrate the complex skills or abilities necessary to meet instructional objectives. *Enrichment* and *acceleration* are the objectives of instruction for students who are gifted and talented. *Remediation* is instruction designed to repair or correct students' basic problems or difficulties. *Compensatory* instruction helps students overcome the effects of handicaps that cannot be corrected. *Preventive* intervention is used with students who are at risk for academic problems, to stop those problems from becoming a reality.

- An IEP is a written statement that describes what teachers and other professionals will do to meet the special learning needs of an exceptional student.

- The methods used to teach students with special needs are not special in themselves; they simply are more evident in special education programs than in regular education programs. The methods now in use include precision teaching, ability training, direct instruction, learning strategies training, study skills training, cognitive skills training, peer-mediated interventions, behavior therapy, counseling therapy, and social skills training.

- Many instructional adaptations make it possible for students with disabilities to communicate well and to move around readily.

Projects

1. Obtain a copy of an IEP. Identify the long-term goals, short-term objectives, levels of current functioning, and procedures to be used in evaluating progress.

2. Interview a classroom teacher. Ask what special methods he or she uses to meet the special learning needs of exceptional students.

3. Obtain a copy of the graduation requirements in your state. To what extent are they based on numbers of completed courses (or earned credits) versus attainment of specific outcomes, goals, or objectives?

4. Obtain a list of expected educational outcomes, standards, or performances for your state. Compare your list to the outcomes listed in Figure 5.2. Are

yours more comprehensive, more specific, or about the same as the outcomes specified by the National Center on Educational Outcomes?

5. When you complete the exercise in activity 4, obtain specific wording on how students with disabilities are expected to achieve the outcomes in your state.

For Your Information

Books

Alberto, P. A., & Troutman, A. C. (1986). *Applied behavior analysis for teachers*. Columbus, OH: Merrill.
A description of how to use the techniques of applied behavior analysis in managing classrooms and delivering instruction.

Craig, E. (1972). *P. S. you're not listening*. New York: New American Library.
A compilation of teaching success stories.

Rosenberg, M. S., & Edmond-Rosenberg, I. (1994). *The special education sourcebook: A teacher's guide to programs, materials, and information sources*. Rockville, MD: Woodbine House.
This sourcebook helps teachers research new approaches and develop the most appropriate individualized instruction plans for their students.

Schloss, P. J., & Sedlak, R. A. (1986). *Instructional methods for students with learning and behavior problems*. Boston: Allyn & Bacon.
A basic text on instructional methods.

Sprick, R., Sprick, M., & Garrison, M. (1994). *Interventions*. Longmont, CO: Sopris West.
Contains a procedural manual and sixteen intervention booklets designed to help classroom teachers develop plans to decrease misbehavior and increase student motivation. The sixteen intervention booklets provide how-to information on topics such as managing physically dangerous behavior, restructuring self-talk, self-control training, teaching desired behaviors, and self-monitoring.

Stoner, G., Shinn, M., & Walker, H. (Eds.). (1991). *Interventions for achievement and behavior problems*. Silver Spring, MD: National Association of School Psychologists.
A compilation of chapters written by school psychologists on the design and implementation of interventions to improve academic functioning and student behavior.

Ysseldyke, J. E., Thurlow, M. L., & Gilman, C. (1993). *Educational outcomes and indicators for students completing school*. Minneapolis: National Center on Educational Outcomes.
A brief document containing a nationally developed set of educational outcomes and indicators for students completing school.

Ysseldyke, J. E., Thurlow, M. L., & Gilman, C. (1993). *Educational outcomes and indicators for individuals at the post school level*. Minneapolis: National Center on Educational Outcomes.
A brief document containing a nationally developed set of educational outcomes and indicators for students who have already completed school.

Ysseldyke, J. E., Thurlow, M. L., & Gilman, C. (1993). *Educational outcomes and indicators for early childhood (age 3)*. Minneapolis: National Center on Educational Outcomes.
A brief document containing a nationally developed set of educational outcomes and indicators for children age three.

Ysseldyke, J. E., Thurlow, M. L., & Gilman, C. (1993). *Educational outcomes and indicators for early childhood (age 6)*. Minneapolis: National Center on Educational Outcomes.
A brief document containing a nationally developed set of educational outcomes and indicators for children age six.

Organizations

RESNA
An interdisciplinary association for the advancement of rehabilitation and assistive technologies, RESNA publishes a journal called *Assistive Technology* along with a newsletter, books, and videos. Its national and regional conferences provide forums for discussing state-of-the-art adaptations. For more information, contact 1700 N. Moore St., Suite 1540, Arlington, VA 22209.

Technology and Media Division (TAM)
TAM is the division of the Council for Exceptional Children that is devoted to the effective use of technology. Besides holding an annual conference, it publishes *The Journal of Special Education Technology,* as well as a newsletter, a resource guide, and monographs on specific topics. For more information, contact Council for Exceptional Children, 1920 Association Dr., Reston, VA 22091.

National Education Association
Founded in 1857, NEA has more than two million members. It is both a professional organization and a union of elementary and secondary school teachers, college and university professors, administrators, principals, counselors, and others concerned with education. For more information, contact NEA, 1201 16th St. NW, Washington, DC 20036.

American Federation of Teachers
Founded in 1916, AFT has 790,000 members. An affiliate of the AFL-CIO union, AFT works with teachers and other educational employees at the state and local level in organizing, collective bargaining, research, educational issues and public relations. For more information, contact 555 New Jersey Ave. NW, Washington, DC 20001.

Computer Resources

ABLEDATA
A database with information on over 16,000 commercially available products for people with disabilities, ABLEDATA can be searched through the BRS system at many university libraries. A version for personal computers, called Hyper-ABLEDATA, is also available. For information on Hyper-ABLEDATA, contact Trace Center, CO-NET Coordinator, S-151 Waisman Center, 1500 Highland Ave., Madison, WI 53705.

Closing the Gap, P.O. Box 68, Henderson, MN 56044.
In addition to publishing a newspaper and resource guide, Closing the Gap maintains a database of information about hardware and software.

SpecialNet, GTE, 5525 MacArthur Blvd., Suite 320, Irving, TX 75038.
A computer network devoted primarily to special education, SpecialNet maintains bulletin boards focusing on telecommunications, assistive devices, and computer software.

Special Times, Cambridge Development Laboratory, 86 West St., Waltham, MA 02154.
A catalog free to educators, *Special Times* contains information from over one hundred publishers about software programs useful for students with special needs.

Journals

Assistive Technology
An applied, scientific publication in the multidisciplinary field of technology for people with disabilities. The journal facilitates communication among individuals working in all aspects of assistive technology including developers, researchers, clinicians, educators and consumers. For more information, contact Lawrence H. Trachtman, Editor, North Carolina Assistive Technology Project, 1110 Navaho Dr., Suite 101, Raleigh, NC 27609.

Instructor
A journal published by Scholastic, Inc., that includes practical information on teaching. Articles in the journal focus on application of specific techniques in teaching subject matter content. The publication office is P.O. Box 53896, Boulder, CO 80322-3896.

Instructor and Teacher
This journal contains articles written by personnel in public schools and in universities, and the content ad-

dresses practical methods any teacher can use in situations connected directly with curricula or student welfare.

Journal of Special Education Technology

The official journal of the Technology and Media Division of the Council for Exceptional Children. The journal includes policy papers and articles on advances in development and application of technology for individuals with disabilities. The journal is distributed by the Council for Exceptional Children, 1920 Association Dr., Reston, VA 22091.

Remedial and Special Education

This journal is devoted to discussion of issues involving the education of persons for whom typical instruction is not effective. Emphasis is on interpretation of research literature and recommendations for the practice of remedial and special education. For more information, contact PRO-ED Journals, 8700 Shoal Creek Blvd., Austin, TX 78757-6897.

The Reading Teacher

This journal is published by the International Reading Association and is a forum for current theory, research, and practice in literacy education.

Assessment Practices

- How is assessment used in the different phases of the special education process?

- What are the primary decisions that school personnel make using assessment information?

- What four methods are used to collect assessment information?

- What are the things educators and lay people worry about in assessment?

- What are the major assumptions underlying contemporary assessment practices?

- What guidelines should be followed in the assessment process?

Eleanor is not allowed to enter school because her performance on a test indicates that she is not yet "ready." Heidi is told to repeat second-grade because her performance on a set of tests indicates she has not yet mastered second-grade content. José is assigned to a class for students who are gifted, while Zeke is placed in a class for students with learning disabilities. Both placements were dependent on how the students performed on a set of tests. Ariel is admitted to Florida State University, but Clem is denied admission because his test scores are too low. Mark, an all-city basketball player, cannot attend a Division I college because his scores on the SAT are too low, even though his grades are high enough. Randy gets a scholarship because of his very high test scores. Kate earns a high score on a selection test; Esther does not. Kate gets a position with General Mills; Esther does not. Manuel wants to be a policeman, but the score he earned on the police exam places him 286th in line for hiring. This year the city expects to hire twenty-one police officers. ■

Emphasis on testing

For all of these young people, and others like them, testing can have a major effect on life choices and opportunities. American schools and society place considerable emphasis on test results. A recent report of the National Commission on Testing and Public Policy (1990) estimates that the nation's 44 million elementary and secondary students take 127 million separate tests annually as part of standardized test batteries mandated by states and school districts. An additional 125 million tests are given to these students over and above state or district requirements. American school children take more tests than any other children in the world.

Testing plays a major role in **assessment,** the process by which teachers and other school personnel collect information to make decisions about students. Historically in special and remedial education, and now increasingly in regular education, the focus of assessment is on the adequacy of student progress toward instructional goals or outcomes and on the extent to which students need special programs and related services. In addition to testing, we also gather data by observing students' behaviors, by interviewing students or those who work with them, and by reviewing collections of their work samples. The decisions we make about students are based on information obtained from all these sources.

Critical role of assessment

For students who are exceptional, assessment is especially critical because it helps educators decide who should receive special education services, the specific nature of instruction, and the extent to which students are making educational progress. In this chapter, we look at the ways assessment data are used to make decisions about students with disabilities and those who are gifted and talented, the ways in which information is obtained, and the particular type of information collected from different assessment activities. We also discuss standards for conducting assessment and some guidelines for best practice.

Assessment for Decision-making Purposes

The process of assessing students' special educational needs usually begins when a teacher or parent recognizes a need. Because of the complex system that has evolved in delivering special education services, students must be assessed before they are declared eligible for services. Students who are exceptional also are assessed as part of their daily educational programs, to determine what they already know and to keep track of their progress. Assessment is therefore a part of each phase of the special education process. The decisions that are made using assessment information are listed in Table 6.1 and are described in the following subsections.

Screening

Screening is the process of collecting data to decide whether more intensive assessment is necessary. School personnel have neither the time nor the resources to test all students to find if they have special needs; instead they screen them.

Early screening

Screening takes place at all levels of education. Children are screened before they enter kindergarten or first grade to determine their readiness in language, cognitive, and motor development, and in social and emotional functioning. They may also be given vision and hearing screening tests. They are tested, then their performance is compared to standards established by those who make the screening tests. For example, if two-thirds of the children who took the test when it was being developed scored three hundred points or better, children who score below three hundred could be considered "at risk." Test developers usually provide cutoff scores to help educators make decisions. These scores, called **norms,** are based on the performance of those who took the test sometime during its development. Formal statistical standards for normality and abnormality may be used, or the standards could be set by a state department of education or school district. Some students are denied school entrance if they score low on a screening test (parents are asked to hold the child back until she or he is ready to enter school), and sometimes low performance results in marking the child for observation and monitoring.

Later screening

Screening also is used throughout the school years to identify students who need extra attention because their performance or progress is markedly different from "normal" or "average." Cutoff scores for this type of screening are based on the average performance of students at various ages or grade levels. The scores of the norm group are used in making the decision whether or not more testing is necessary.

When students' scores indicate a special need, they may be referred for psychoeducational assessment—individually administered psychological and educational tests. These tests are used to determine the specific reasons for a student's performance on a screening measure. Usually they are administered

Table **6.1**	Decisions Made Using Assessment Information

Screening decisions
Decisions to provide special help or enrichment
Decisions to refer to an intervention assistance team
Decisions to provide intervention assistance
Decisions to refer for psychoeducational evaluation
Exceptionality decisions
Decisions about special learning needs
Decisions about eligibility or entitlement
Instructional planning decisions
Progress evaluation decisions
Program evaluation decisions
Accountability decisions

by school psychologists or other professionals working for the school district or service providers (private clinics, hospitals).

Implicit in screening is the notion that students' difficulties may go unnoticed if not checked. It is assumed, for example, that a student might have a hearing difficulty or cognitive deficit that will go unrecognized without screening.

Decisions to Provide Special Help or Enrichment

Performance on a screening test is only one basis for the decision to make a referral. Teachers also use classroom tests, daily observations, and interviews to decide whether a student is in need of special assistance. We consider the process of using data to make these decisions an assessment process. Provision of special assistance does not necessarily involve provision of special education services. Rather, as a "first line of defense" most teachers give special help to students who experience difficulty. The help may be in the form of tutoring, a study buddy, or adaptation of classroom materials and instruction. Recall from Chapter 2 that both Pat and Chris received special assistance in reading and math when they experienced difficulty. The help may be remedial (designed to correct a deficit or difficulty), compensatory (designed to make up for a disability), or enriching (designed to enhance regular classroom activities).

Special help as a first option

Referral to an Intervention Assistance Team

When the student does not make satisfactory progress, even with special help, the teacher may seek assistance from an *intervention assistance team (IAT),* as

More than ever before, teachers are helping students with special learning needs in classrooms as much as possible like those of their neighbors and peers. *Alan Carey/The Image Works, Inc.*

Role of the IAT

noted in Chapter 2. This team is usually made up of regular education teachers whose role is to help one another come up with ways to teach difficult-to-teach students. The IAT (sometimes called a teacher assistance team [TAT], mainstream assistance team [MAT], or school-wide assistance team [SWAT]) works as a problem-solving team. To determine whether to seek assistance from such a team, the teacher uses assessment information obtained as part of routine instruction/assessment, as well as information derived from monitoring the success of efforts to provide special help.

Decisions to Provide Intervention Assistance

Intervention at the prereferral stage

The interventions developed and put in place by intervention assistance teams are typically called *prereferral interventions* because they occur before formal referral for child study. At the time we wrote this text, prereferral interventions were required in two-thirds of states. The prereferral intervention (or intervention assistance) process has been put in place in states and local school districts in an effort to reduce referral for testing and overidentification of students for special education services. The process was instituted in response to the notion that many of the difficulties for which students were formally referred could be alleviated by adjusting classroom interventions. For example, Connecticut has a special project, called the Early Intervention Project: Alternatives to Referral, initiated in 1985 to address the misclassification of students as disabled. It is designed to intervene early in students' experiences of difficulty in an effort to alleviate problems. Sometimes the members of the intervention assistance team gather data through observation, interview, or testing. When they do so, they are engaging in assessment. In projects like the Early Intervention Project, team members receive formal training in assessment. The interventions suggested by intervention assistance teams may involve remediation, compensation, or enrichment.

Referral Decisions

Referral to the child-study team

When a student fails to make satisfactory progress, even with the help of an intervention assistance team, the student may be referred for formal psychoeducational evaluation. Referral usually is a relatively formal process involving the completion of a referral form and a formal request for a team of professionals to decide whether a student is sufficiently abnormal to require provision of special education services. The team of professionals is usually called a *child-study team*, although in some states and districts within states these teams go by other names (for example, IEP team, special education eligibility team). The team typically includes regular education teachers, special education teachers, one or more administrators, the student's parent(s), and related services personnel, such as the school psychologist, nurse, social worker, or counselor. Child-study teams make two basic kinds of decisions: decisions about exceptionality (whether or not the child has a disability or is gifted) and verification of special learning needs.

Exceptionality Decisions

Does the student meet state criteria?

To make an exceptionality decision the child-study team must decide whether a student meets the criteria for being declared eligible for service, as specified by the state in which the student lives. If, for example, the student must be shown to have an I.Q. score below 70 and deficits in adaptive behavior to be called mentally retarded, one or more team members administer tests to see if the child scores below the requirement. The team officially assigns a disability name. Teams decide whether students meet criteria for special education categories (e.g. mental retardation, learning disabilities...). Teams also decide whether youngsters are gifted and talented. Teams are required to gather assessment information, and it is illegal to base exceptionality decisions on a single test.

Decisions About Special Learning Needs

Does the student have special learning needs?

Child-study teams also make decisions about whether students have special learning needs. For example, they may document for students who are blind the fact that without instruction in braille or using large-print books the students can be expected to experience academic difficulties. They make formal statements that students have special learning needs that require special education assistance, including the kinds of assistance required. Increasingly, child-study teams rely on the data they receive from prereferral interventions with individual children. In fact, the purpose of prereferral intervention is twofold:

Bring Your Learning to Life

Collaborative Intervention Planning

The Intervention Assistance Team (IAT) at Madison Elementary School meets regularly to develop prereferral interventions for students. The team is comprised of regular classroom teachers and the special education resource teacher. Think about how the team works together to develop interventions for students. In planning interventions the team members use assessment information gained through observations, student interviews, teacher interviews, and students' work. Team members go through the following steps in the collaborative planning process:

- A teacher or teachers describe the concerns they have for the student. In doing so, they differentiate clearly between the student's actual performance and the kind of performance they want the student to demonstrate.

- Team members share information on how instruction currently is planned, managed, delivered, and evaluated for the student. They report the results obtained by use of *The Instructional Environment System-*

II (TIES-II) (Ysseldyke & Christenson, 1993), a system used to gather information about the student's instructional needs in the context of classroom and home environments.

- Team members arrive at consensus about a student's instructional needs.

- Team members use TIES-II to describe home support for activities taking place in the child's instructional program.

- Team members identify ways to involve the student's parent(s) or guardian and invite parents' assistance.

- Team members brainstorm ideas/options for intervention. All ideas are permitted, and their merits and limitations are not discussed.

- An intervention (or interventions) is (are) selected.

- Team members share resources and discuss ways they can work together to implement the selected intervention(s).

to try to alleviate difficulties and to document the techniques that do and do not improve student outcomes.

Decisions About Eligibility or Entitlement

Two conditions for eligibility

After the child-study team has specified a student's exceptionality and special learning needs, the team can proceed to declare the student eligible for (or "entitled" to) special education services. As we stressed in Chapter 2, the team must find *both* an exceptionality and special learning needs for the student to be eligible. If these conditions are met, the team will move on to develop an individualized education plan (IEP), a process that requires decisions about instructional planning.

Instructional Planning Decisions

Regular education teachers are able to take a standard curriculum and plan instruction around it. Although curriculums vary from district to district—largely as a function of the values of community and school—they are appropriate for most students at a given age or grade level. However, when students need special help to benefit from a standard curriculum, school personnel must gather data to plan special programs.

Types of planning decisions

As we illustrated in Chapter 4, three kinds of decisions are made in instructional planning: deciding what to teach, deciding how to teach it, and communicating realistic expectations. Deciding what to teach is a content decision, usually made on the basis of a systematic analysis of the skills that students do and do not have. Scores on tests and other information help teachers decide whether students have specific skills. Teachers also use information gathered from observations and interviews to decide what to teach. They obtain information about how to teach by trying different methods of teaching and monitoring students' progress toward instructional goals.

Progress Evaluation Decisions

Measuring progress

Teachers collect assessment information to decide whether their students are making progress. They may give unit tests, or they may have students keep portfolios of their work. They also rely on their observations of individual students' behavior, as well as their more subjective feelings and impressions of each student's work.

The best way to collect data for the purpose of evaluating individual students' progress is to sample the skills that are being taught. This allows teachers to measure the extent to which students have mastered content and to chart their progress toward meeting instructional objectives.

Program Evaluation Decisions

Is the program effective?

Assessment data also are collected to evaluate specific programs. The emphasis is on gauging the effectiveness of the curriculum in meeting the goals and objectives of the school. School personnel typically use this information for schoolwide curriculum planning. For example, schools can compare two approaches to teaching in a content area by (1) giving tests at the beginning of the year, (2) teaching two comparable groups two different ways, and (3) giving tests at the end of the year. By comparing students' performances before and after, the schools are able to evaluate the effectiveness of the two competing approaches.

Large-scale program evaluation

The process of assessing educational programs can be complex if a large number of students is involved and if the criteria for making decisions are written in statistical terms. For example, an evaluation of two instructional programs might involve gathering data from hundreds of students and comparing their performances using statistical tests. Program costs, teacher and student opinions, and the nature of each program's goals and objectives versus those of the curriculum might be compared to determine which program is more effective. This kind of large-scale evaluation probably would be undertaken by a group of administrators working for a school district.

A teacher's own evaluation

Program evaluations can be much less formal. When our friend Kim Bazan wants to know the effectiveness of an instructional method that she is using, she does her own evaluation. For example, recently she wanted to know if having students complete activities in their basal readers was as effective as having them use language experience activities. She compared students' written products using both methods and concluded that their language experience stories were better.

Accountability Decisions

America's public schools have come under increasing criticism in the past fifteen years. In 1983 the U.S. Department of Education issued a report, called *A Nation at Risk,* in which it raised a set of concerns about education in America and about the accomplishments of America's students. Increasingly, parents want reports on how students are doing in the schools to which they send their youngsters, legislators want to know how the schools are doing, and policymakers want data on the educational performance of the nation's youth. School personnel regularly administer tests to students, engage in portfolio assessment or performance assessment, and issue reports on the achievement of the students in their schools. This information is then used to determine **accountability**—the extent to which particular schools, administrators, or teachers should be held responsible for students' performance.

Holding schools and teachers accountable

Common Assessment Practices

Those who write about assessment practices use a number of terms to describe the practices. In addition, the terms sometimes change over time as new assessment practices are developed or old ones are modified. This section briefly introduces several common practices and the terms used to describe them.

Assessment based on the curriculum

Curriculum-based assessment is "a procedure for determining the instructional needs of a student based on the student's ongoing performance within existing course content" (Gickling & Havertape, 1981, p. 55). This kind of assessment includes direct observation and analysis of the learning environment, analysis of the processes students use to approach tasks, examination of students' products, and controlling and arranging tasks for students. Regular education teachers use performance on curriculum-based measures to decide which students are making satisfactory progress and which have special learning needs. Curriculum-based assessment also can be used for the other types of decisions described earlier, from screening through accountability. See the Point of View feature on page 170 for further discussion of curriculum-based assessment.

Point of View

The Value of Curriculum-based Assessment

Curriculum-based assessment, when conducted properly, can be an important tool for teachers and diagnostic specialists in a number of ways.

- *Analysis of the learning environment*   By careful examination of the learning environment, curriculum-based assessment helps to identify pitfalls that may be interfering with the student's learning. Such assessment can isolate problems with the instructional materials, with the ways in which instruction is organized or sequenced, with the manner of presentation (such as lecture or workbook), and with the grouping of students in the classroom.

- *Analysis of task-approach strategies*   By focusing on the student's task-approach strategies, curriculum-based assessment helps teachers identify basic learning skills that the student may need to develop.

- *Examination of student's products*   Through systematic examination of a student's work samples, curriculum-based assessment can spot particular error patterns.

- *Controlling and arranging student tasks*   By manipulating the ways in which materials are presented and the specific tasks that students are asked to perform, the curriculum-based assessment procedure helps teachers determine which approaches are most productive.

Choate, Bennett, Enright, Miller, Poteet, & Rakes (1987) list several reasons for using curriculum-based assessment:

- It complies with the procedural requirements of Public Law 94–142 for assessing students in need of special education.

- It is efficient.

- It is a valid, reliable basis for making decisions.

- It can be used to make different kinds of decisions (for example, screening, program effectiveness).

- It increases students' achievement.

- It helps teachers decide what to teach.

Diagnosing problems in instruction

Another common assessment practice is **instructional diagnosis,** which identifies the extent to which a student's poor performance is caused by poor instruction and indicates possible remedies for the problem. It consists of systematic analysis of the requirements of instruction, including the kinds of demands put on the learner. When educators engage in instructional diagnosis, they look at the skills required to complete instructional tasks and compare them to the skills students do and do not have. As we mentioned in Chapter 4, the process of breaking complex tasks into their component skills is called *task analysis.* For example, the teacher might break a complex skill, like brushing one's teeth, into its component skills. Task analysis is one part of instructional diagnosis.

How do students spend their time?

Academic time analysis is the study of how time is allocated in school. Borg (1980) reviewed a series of studies devoted to academic time analysis (Mann, 1928; Payne, 1904; Holmes, 1915). He found that contemporary educators allocate their time very differently from their predecessors (Table 6.2). Contemporary educators have developed new tools to engage in formal and

Table 6.2	Percentage of Time Allocated to School Subjects (Grade 2)			
Study	Reading	Mathematics	Other Academic Subjects	Nonacademic Subjects
Mann 6 cities 1862–1872	47	16	11	26
Payne 6 cities 1904	55	14	5	26
Holmes 50 cities 1914	42	9	7	42
Mann 444 cities 1926	48	10	7	35
Beginning Teacher Evaluation Study 1977–1978	28	12	3	57

Source: Adapted from W. R. Borg. (1980). Time and school learning. In C. Denham & A. Lieberman (Eds.), *Time to learn*. Washington, DC: U.S. Department of Education.

systematic analysis of how students spend their time in school. For example, Greenwood and Carta (1993) have developed a computer program called EBASS (Ecobehavioral Assessment System for Students) that educators can use to gather data on the exact amounts or proportions of time students spend engaged in academic work, inappropriate behavior, and so forth. They use this approach to report academic engaged time for individual pupils. They can also use it as part of a systematic assessment of how students spend their time in school, the specific inappropriate behaviors they demonstrate, or even the events that trigger appropriate and inappropriate behavior. The term *ecobehavioral assessment* is often used to describe the assessment of the relationship between contextual factors and student behavior.

The "bottom line" in assessment is improved instruction and instructional outcomes for students. As educators attempt to develop appropriate instructional interventions, they increasingly measure the extent to which the factors that lead to improved outcomes are occurring for individual students. When educators assess students' needs in the context of classroom and home envi-

Assessing the environment

ronments, and when they systematically appraise the presence or absence of components of effectiveness, they are engaging in *assessment of instructional environments* (Ysseldyke & Christenson, 1993).

Assessing outcomes

As the demand for accountability merges with the movement toward measuring school effectiveness in terms of specific outcomes, school personnel are being asked to engage in *outcomes-based accountability*—formal assessment of the extent to which pupils are meeting designated outcomes. An example of an outcomes-based accountability approach is the recently issued National Goals Report, an analysis by the National Education Goals Panel of the extent to which U.S. schools are meeting the six national education goals specified in federal legislation.

Data on performance

In addition, school personnel increasingly are engaging in performance assessment. *Performance assessment* involves gathering data on pupils' performance directly by having them work singly or in groups to perform tasks. Data are gathered on the quality with which tasks are completed, as well as on how students work together to perform tasks.

Collecting Assessment Data

Whether you teach or work with students in regular or special education programs, assessment will be a large part of your daily routine. It makes sense, therefore, to know something about the methods used to gather educational information and the kinds of information those methods provide. You also will need this knowledge because federal law requires that eligibility decisions be based not on just one source of information, but on multiple sources.

Methods for Collecting Data

We use four processes to gather information about students who are exceptional:

Four methods of data collection

Testing is the process of administering a set of items to obtain a score. A test is a collection of items designed to measure knowledge in a content area.

Observing is the process of watching an individual perform a set of behaviors to obtain information about the rate or duration of those behaviors. An observation is a record of performance.

Interviewing is the process of asking questions to obtain information about an individual's background, current levels of performance, and plans. An interview is a set of questions designed to provide information about a content area of interest.

Work sample assessment involves collecting the products of an individual's work. Because these products can be put into portfolios, this method sometimes is called **portfolio assessment.**

Teachers and other professionals use tests, observations, interviews, and work samples to make decisions about students. There are no fixed rules for deciding which assessment method to use. We choose the method that gives us the best information for the decision we are making. Suppose we are gathering data to decide whether a student is eligible for special education. For such a decision, most states require that an individual test of intelligence be administered, so we'd use a test. To evaluate a student's ongoing progress, we might use daily or weekly observations. In making screening and referral decisions, we might use rating scales or other types of interviews.

Tests

You've taken hundreds of tests over the years, so varied in form and content that they probably would confuse even the most able classifier. When confronted with large amounts of information, it is helpful to use categories to organize what we know. For example, grouping tests into formal and informal measures is a practical way to organize them; or we can group them by the way they are given, their format, their purpose, or their content.

Formal versus informal tests

Formal tests have standardized administration procedures and usually are produced by test development companies. They often are designed for use with large groups of people, but some are primarily for testing individuals. Tests taken at the end of the school year during elementary, middle, and high school are good examples of formal tests. *Informal tests* often are developed by teachers to measure knowledge in an area that was recently taught. Unit tests in science or social studies, weekly spelling tests, and fifteen- to twenty-item math tests are used by teachers to assign grades in academic content areas. Because these tests vary from year to year, usually are produced by the teacher just before they are given, and are administered without strict adherence to standardized procedures, they are thought of as informal measures.

Group versus individual administration

Another way to describe tests is according to the way in which they are administered. They can be group administered—given to an entire class at once—or individually administered—given to one student at a time. The primary advantage of group administration is that data can be obtained on an entire class in a relatively short time. Individual administration gives the examiner an opportunity to observe the student being tested more closely and to gather data on how the student earns his or her score.

We also can categorize tests according to the way the items are presented and responses are obtained. For example, on most tests, items are read to the students or the students are required to read the items themselves. Some tests require written responses in multiple-choice form; others require short answers or essays. Students give verbal answers on some tests; on others, they "perform" their answers, by choosing one item from several items, by putting puzzles together, or by performing some other physical action.

Categories of use

Tests differ in their intended uses. *Screening tests* are used to spot pupils who are making too little or too much progress compared to others or to the objectives of the curriculum. *Diagnostic tests* are designed to provide more specific information, usually in the form of a description of strengths and weaknesses in the development of a specific skill.

Tests also are either norm referenced or criterion referenced, names that describe the way in which test results are used, more than the actual format of the

Norm-referenced tests

test. When norm-referenced interpretations are made, the student's performance is compared to the performance of other students. **Norm-referenced tests** are standardized at the time they are developed; that is, they are given to a large number of students to obtain an index of "typical" or "average" performance. An individual's performance on the test is compared to that of a national or local sample of students of the same age or grade level. By definition, students who earn significantly higher or lower scores than their agemates or grademates are said to perform "abnormally." Students who perform very poorly on a test relative to others their age are said to be deficient in the area of performance; those who do much better than their agemates are said to be exceptionally proficient.

Criterion-referenced tests

Criterion-referenced tests give teachers a measure of the extent to which individuals or groups have mastered specific curriculum content. These tests also are called *objective-referenced tests* or *curriculum-based tests,* names that reflect what the tests are designed to do. These tests are developed by specifying the objectives or criteria to be mastered, usually in basic skill areas like reading and mathematics, then writing items to assess mastery of those objectives or criteria. The results indicate the degree to which the content or skill representing a particular instructional objective has been mastered; they are used to describe what each pupil has learned and needs to learn in a specific content area.

We also can describe tests according to the content of the items. In special education, tests commonly are used to assess intelligence, achievement, sensory acuity, perceptual-motor abilities, adaptive behavior, language functioning, and personality development. Scores on these and other measures can be found in the school records of virtually every student who receives special education services.

Observations

Active versus passive observation

Observations vary in the way information is collected. *Active observations* record ongoing behavior. When Kim sits beside Bobby and watches him do his math problems, she is using active observation. She also uses it when she records the amount of time he is out of his seat or the number of times he raises his hand to ask for help. When she looks at a product he produced last week, at test records, or at information in his cumulative folder, she is using *passive observation.*

Another way to describe observations is in terms of the action or product being observed. Classroom behaviors, academic tasks, vocational skills, interpersonal skills, and athletic performance are examples of actions or products observed in school settings. Like tests, observations also can be formal (using systematic procedures) or informal (using spontaneous data collection procedures).

Uses of observations

Teachers, other school professionals, and parents make observations as part of the educational process to gather the information needed to make decisions about students and programs. Observations provide different information than that available from tests and interviews. They are used when information is not available from other assessment sources or to verify information collected from those other sources. For example, in gathering data on a pupil's activity level we could ask the teacher to rate level of activity, or we could interview teachers or parents and ask them to describe a student's activity level. We could also observe his or her behavior. We use our observations to confirm and support information gathered from other sources (rating scales, interviews).

Interviews

Interviews can be given to a group of people or to one person. They can be given to people who know the person about whom information is being collected, or administered to the target individual directly. For example, Kim asks the parents of new students and the students themselves to complete a survey about attitudes toward school. She compares the responses of the parents with those of the respective students, then uses the information to decide how to motivate and teach each student.

Types of interviews

We also can describe interviews in terms of their form. Like tests and observations, interviews can be formal (predetermined, written down, and administered the same way each time) or informal (developed as the interview proceeds from initial questions). They also can be structured or unstructured. In a *structured interview,* we ask the same set of questions in the same way each time we use them. In an *unstructured interview,* the exact nature of the interview is not known before it is administered. We ask a question, and then, depending on the student's answer, we ask another question related to it. In all interviews, students respond orally or in writing.

Interviews can touch on any topic, from name, address, and phone number

An interview—asking questions to obtain information about a person's background, current levels of performance, and future plans—is a popular method of gathering assessment information. *Meri Houtchens-Kitchens/ The Picture Cube, Inc.*

to opinions about parents and pets. Larry Williams asks each of his students the following questions during the first days of the school year:

Sample interview to begin the school year

What is your favorite subject in school?

What is your least favorite subject in school?

When some students complete a project, they still want to work on it to make it better. How about you?

When some students receive a low grade, they try to improve it. How about you?

Some students try different ways to solve problems before giving up. How about you?

Some students really like school. How about you?

He uses the information from this brief survey to make decisions about which students to put together for group projects. He also thinks it helps him get to know the students a little better early in the school year.

Collected Work Samples or Portfolios

Movement toward reviewing portfolios

Many teachers now make extensive collections of the products of students' work. Besides reviewing individual products to see if students are performing tasks correctly, they review entire portfolios of products to make judgments about the extent to which students are making progress. As efforts are made to move away from multiple-choice tests to make decisions about students, more teachers are being asked to keep portfolios of students' work. State education agency personnel in some states (for example, Kentucky) are developing rules and procedures (called *rubrics*) for scoring and evaluating portfolios.

Behaviors Sampled by Assessment

Any assessment is just a sample

Any test, observation, interview, or work portfolio is just a sampling of the items that could be used to assess an ability, skill, or characteristic. For example, there are literally hundreds of items that could be used to assess the math achievement of fifth-grade students. Any test contains only a sample of these items. When we observe a student, we select what to observe and when to observe it. Obviously, we can't watch everything a student does at all times during the school day; any observation is a sample of the student's behavior. In the same way, the questions in an interview are just samples of those that could be asked. Remember this when you are collecting and evaluating information about students: What you collect is a sample of behavior, and the way you collect it controls the answers you get.

Intellectual Abilities

Testing intelligence

School personnel regularly use intelligence tests to identify the extent to which students demonstrate normal thinking and problem-solving skills. They are looking for discrepant scores, scores that are significantly lower or higher than the norm. Students who demonstrate lower levels of intelligence are thought to learn more slowly than their agemates; those who demonstrate higher levels of intelligence are thought to learn more quickly than their agemates. Both types of students are a challenge for regular classroom teachers. They do not fit easily into the organization, goals, and activities of the typical classroom.

Different intelligence tests sample different behaviors. The particular behaviors sampled by a specific test depend on the kinds of behaviors the test author thinks best reflect the performance being measured. Table 6.3 lists thirteen kinds of behaviors sampled by intelligence tests.

Observing intelligence

Observations also are used to assess intellectual abilities. As part of a psychoeducational evaluation, Kim was asked to record the number of four types of questions that one of her students asked during reading over a week's time. She also was asked to supply previously written products as evidence of the student's higher levels of thinking.

Informal observations gathered during the administration of a test can be very revealing. Kim told us about a school psychologist's experience testing one of her students. When asked general information questions on the intelligence test, the student consistently gave very expansive answers. For example, when asked which European first encountered America, he answered: "Some people say Christopher Columbus, some say Amerigo Vespucci, some people say Leif Erikson; actually, nobody really knows." When asked the sum of two numbers, the student supplied the answer and gave five more number sentences like it. When the testing was over, the psychologist commented that the student was the smartest child he had ever tested. His opinion was based not only on the student's score on the test, but also on his informal observations of the student's performance.

Interviews are another source of information about a student's intellectual abilities. Many school districts use screening checklists to identify students who may need special educational enrichment or acceleration. These rating scales usually are administered to parents or teachers, and contain items like these:

Sample rating scale for interview

Use the following scale (1 = strongly disagree, 2 = disagree, 3 = unsure, 4 = agree, 5 = strongly agree) to indicate the extent to which you agree with each of the following statements.

This student (My child) . . .

1. demonstrates superior thinking abilities.   1   2   3   4   5
2. demonstrates excellent memory for details.   1   2   3   4   5
3. demonstrates creative problem-solving skills.   1   2   3   4   5

Academic Achievement

We mentioned earlier that students, teachers, and parents need to know if progress is being made in academic subject areas of instruction. Achievement

Table 6.3 Kinds of Behaviors Sampled by Intelligence Tests

Nature of Task	Performance Required
Discrimination	Given a set of stimuli, the student is required to find the one that differs from all the others. The stimuli may be figures, symbols, or words.
Generalization	Given a stimulus, the student must select from among a number of response alternatives the one that is most like the stimulus. Both the stimulus and response alternatives may be figures, symbols, or words.
Sequencing	Given a series, the pupil must identify the one that comes next in the series.
Analogies	The individual must respond to an item of an A:B:C:? nature. The student must first identify a relationship between A and B, then identify from several alternative response items the one that has the same relationship to C as A does to B.
Motor behavior	The student may be required to walk, place geometric forms in a recessed form board, copy geometric designs, trace paths through a maze, and so on.
General information	The student is required to answer specific factual questions.
Vocabulary	The student is required to define words or to point to pictures that illustrate words read by the examiner.
Induction	The student is presented with a series of examples and required to induce a governing principle.
Comprehension	The student must give evidence of understanding directions, printed material, or societal customs and mores.
Detail recognition	Students are judged on the extent to which they recognize details in drawing pictures, find hidden objects in pictures, or recall details of a story.
Abstract reasoning	Students are required to state the meaning of proverbs, solve arithmetic story problems, and so on.
Memory	Several different kinds of tasks are used to assess pupil skill in remembering items, objects, details of stories, sequences of digits, and so on.
Pattern completion	Given a pattern, students must select from among response items the one that completes the pattern.

tests often are used to provide this information. There are literally hundreds of published achievement tests; we've listed some of them in Table 6.4.

Achievement tests

Achievement tests measure skill development in academic content areas. Some measure skill development in multiple content areas (say math and reading); others concentrate on one content area (for example, spelling). Any achievement test can be described using the framework in Table 6.4. For example, the Metropolitan Achievement Tests are group-administered, norm- or criterion-referenced screening tests that assess skill development in several content areas. The Gray Oral Reading Test–III is an individually administered, norm-referenced diagnostic measure that provides specific information on skill development in oral reading.

Table 6.4   Achievement Tests

Screening Devices

	Norm referenced		Criterion referenced	
	Single Skill	**Multiple Skill**	**Single Skill**	**Multiple Skill**
Group Administered	Gates–MacGinitie	California Achievement Test Iowa Tests of Basic Skills Metropolitan Achievement Tests (Survey Battery) Stanford Achievement Test Series	None	California Achievement Test Iowa Tests of Basic Skills Metropolitan Achievement Tests (Instructional Batteries) Stanford Achievement Test Series
Individually Administered	Test of Mathematical Abilities	Kaufman Test of Educational Achievement Peabody Individual Achievement Test–Revised Wide Range Achievement Test–III Woodcock-Johnson Psychoeducational Battery–Revised Kaufman Assessment Battery for Children Basic Academic Skills Individual Screener	None	Basic Academic Skills Individual Screener

(continued on next page)

Observations of achievement

Teachers use observations gathered while tests are being administered to help them understand a student's performance. They also use analyses of permanent products. For example, two students may earn exactly the same score on a mathematics achievement test, but demonstrate very different math skills on more detailed analysis of their written products. Consider the test performances in Figure 6.1. Bob and Jim each performed nine items correctly. Their scores could be represented as 60 percent correct or 40 percent incorrect. Similarly, if Bob and Jim were the same age, the number of correct items could be converted to age-equivalent scores, grade-equivalent scores, percentiles, quotients, standard scores, or other derived scores that are exactly the same.

Error analysis

However, even though Bob and Jim would receive the same score, Bob's performance on the test was different from Jim's. Using **error analysis,** systematic analysis of the kinds of errors a student makes, we can see, for example, that

Table 6.4   Achievement Tests *(continued)*

Diagnostic Devices

| | Norm referenced | | Criterion referenced | |
	Single Skill	Multiple Skill	Single Skill	Multiple Skill
Group Administered	Stanford Diagnostic Reading Test Stanford Diagnostic Mathematics Test	None	Prescriptive Reading Inventory Diagnostic Mathematics Inventory Stanford Diagnostic Mathematics Test	None
Individually Administered	Gray Oral Reading Test–III Durrell Analysis of Reading Difficulty Gates–McKillop–Horowitz Reading Diagnostic Tests Woodcock Reading Mastery Tests–Revised Tests of Written Language Test of Written Spelling 2 Test of Reading Comprehension Formal Reading Inventory Test of Language Development–2 Test of Adolescent Language–2	None	KeyMath–Revised Stanford Diagnostic Reading Test Standardized Reading Inventory	BRIGANCE® Diagnostic Inventories

Source: John Salvia & James E. Ysseldyke (1995). *Assessment* (6th ed.). Boston: Houghton Mifflin. Used with permission.

Bob seems to have mastered multiplication; Jim has not. This kind of analysis gives us more data for making decisions about a student's academic abilities.

Observations also can be valuable in deciding what to teach. For example, by observing how students read, teachers can uncover the errors they make and identify the factors that may be limiting their reading performance. Ekwall (1981) describes over twenty types of errors that students often make in reading and recommends ways to correct them. By recognizing and correcting specific types of reading errors, teachers are more likely to see improvement in reading scores than if they simply ask students to read without regard to the quality of the effort.

Interviews relating to achievement

Kim uses an informal interview to gain insight into factors that influence her students' performances in mathematics. She asks their opinions about the work in the textbook and their preferences for doing workbook assignments, teacher-made worksheets, or homework. She also asks questions designed to

Figure 6.1

Math Performance of Two Students on the First Fifteen Items of the Wide Range Achievement Test–III

Source: Test items from the Blue Form Arithmetic Subtest of the Wide Range Achievement Test–III by Gary S. Wilkinson. Wilmington, DE: Wide Range, Inc. Copyright © 1993 by Wide Range, Inc. Reprinted by permission.

Bob Jones $\frac{9}{15}$ correct $\frac{6}{15}$ incorrect

$1 + 1 = \underline{2}$	$\begin{array}{r} 5 \\ -1 \\ \hline 3 \end{array}$ ✓	$2 + 7 = \underline{14}$ ✓	$8 - 4 = \underline{4}$	$\begin{array}{r} 32 \\ 24 \\ +40 \\ \hline 90 \end{array}$ ✓
$\begin{array}{r} 9 \\ +3 \\ \hline 12 \end{array}$	$\begin{array}{r} 36 \\ -15 \\ \hline 11 \end{array}$ ✓	$3 \times 4 = \underline{12}$	$\begin{array}{r} 68 \\ +23 \\ \hline 81 \end{array}$ ✓	$\begin{array}{r} 7 \\ \times 6 \\ \hline 42 \end{array}$
$\begin{array}{r} 23 \\ \times 3 \\ \hline 69 \end{array}$	$\begin{array}{r} 33 \\ -17 \\ \hline 50 \end{array}$ ✓	$6 \div 2 = \underline{3}$	$4\overline{)16}$ with 4 above	$\begin{array}{r} 17 \\ \times 4 \\ \hline 68 \end{array}$

Jim Smith $\frac{9}{15}$ correct $\frac{6}{15}$ incorrect

$1 + 1 = \underline{2}$	$\begin{array}{r} 5 \\ -1 \\ \hline 4 \end{array}$	$2 + 7 = \underline{9}$	$8 - 4 = \underline{4}$	$\begin{array}{r} 32 \\ 24 \\ +40 \\ \hline 96 \end{array}$
$\begin{array}{r} 9 \\ +3 \\ \hline 11 \end{array}$ ✓	$\begin{array}{r} 36 \\ -15 \\ \hline 21 \end{array}$	$3 \times 4 = \underline{15}$ ✓	$\begin{array}{r} 68 \\ +23 \\ \hline 91 \end{array}$	$\begin{array}{r} 7 \\ \times 6 \\ \hline 48 \end{array}$ ✓
$\begin{array}{r} 23 \\ \times 3 \\ \hline 96 \end{array}$ ✓	$\begin{array}{r} 33 \\ -17 \\ \hline 16 \end{array}$	$6 \div 2 = \underline{8}$ ✓	$4\overline{)16}$ with 4 above	$\begin{array}{r} 17 \\ \times 4 \\ \hline 61 \end{array}$ ✓

assess their fears of math. She uses the last questions in the interview to estimate students' mastery of number facts, computation, problem solving, fractions, and other mathematics skills. Other teachers in her school use informal interviews to gain insight into the factors that facilitate or inhibit students' performance in reading. They find that students' answers indicate that they often are bored by basal reading activities, are confused by new words, and prefer to read silently. Kim asks her students to rank their word recognition skills when reading in science, social studies, health, and other content areas. She also asks them to rank the ways they remember words (sounding them out, using word parts, using meanings). Larry keeps a record of his students' responses to questions about their learning patterns and reading methods that have been effective in the past.

Teachers now talk about portfolio assessment. This usually consists of collecting samples of students' work—the stories they write, drawings, poems, samples of their mathematics problem solving. Portfolios can also consist of audiotapes or videotapes of student performances. They are collections of products used to demonstrate what a person has done and, by inference, is capable of doing. Portfolios were defined formally as:

> A portfolio is a purposeful, interrelated collection of student work that exhibits the student's efforts, progress, and achievement in one or more areas. The collection includes student participation in selecting contents, the criteria for selection, the criteria for judging merit, and evidence of student self reflection. The portfolio communicates what is learned and why it is important. (Paulson & Paulson, 1991, p. 1)

Sensory Acuity

Testing vision and hearing

Poor academic performance is sometimes caused by problems with seeing and hearing. Although severe sensory impairments are almost always diagnosed before a child begins school, tests of visual and auditory acuity are used regularly in assessments of students who are having difficulties in school. The simplest test of visual acuity uses the Snellen Chart. The individual being tested stands twenty feet away from the chart and tries to read it. An adaptation of the Snellen Chart, the Snellen E, is used to assess preschool students and those who are unable to read. The Titmus Vision Tester also is used to screen school-age children. An audiometer is used to assess hearing acuity. A pure-tone audiometer generates pure tones at different frequencies and at varying degrees of loudness.

Teachers also make informal assessments of sensory acuity by watching how students read and how they act when asked questions, and by asking them about how they approach tasks. Kim watches her students to answer these questions:

Can they see the chalkboard from their seats, or do they need to be closer to it to see or hear better?

Do they tilt their heads or squint when reading from textbooks and other printed materials?

Do they complain about itchy eyes or squint when focusing on different objects?

Do their visual skills differ in the classroom, on the playground, or in other areas of school?

Do they often ask for directions to be repeated?

Kim and Larry have developed an interview for use with students with special learning needs. They ask parents to complete a questionnaire about their child's visual and auditory abilities as a way of learning more about how to help the child succeed in school. A section of their interview form is shown in Figure 6.2.

Adaptive Behavior

There was a time when students were classified as mentally retarded on the sole basis of their performance on an intelligence test. In 1969, a report from the President's Committee on Mental Retardation indicated that many of these students demonstrated very normal behaviors outside of school. The phrase "six-hour retarded child" was coined to describe students who had been labeled mentally retarded in school but who were functioning normally out of school, in other environments. Because so much of performance on intelligence tests is based on general knowledge gained in school, it was reasoned that additional criteria should be used in the decision to classify a student as mentally retarded.

Defining adaptive behavior

In 1973 the American Association on Mental Deficiency (AAMD) modified its definition of mental retardation to include both subaverage intellectual functioning and deficits in adaptive behavior. It defined adaptive behavior as "the effectiveness or degree with which the individual meets the standards of personal independence and social responsibility expected of his age and social group" (Grossman, 1973, p. 11) (see Chapter 10). That definition was "legitimized" with the enactment of Public Law 94–142 in 1975.

Adaptive behavior scales

Adaptive behavior scales are not tests per se. Instead we use interviews with parents, teachers, or others familiar with the student to assess his or her behavior. For example, many adaptive behavior scales provide information about the student's self-help skills (eating, dressing, toileting), communication skills (imitating sounds, following directions), and occupational and social skills (using money, doing chores, playing games). A common measure of adaptive behavior is provided by the American Association on Mental Retardation (see Table 10.1 on page 310).

Understanding the environment

Assessing adaptive behavior is not an easy process. To evaluate the extent to which someone's behavior is adaptive—that is, normal in an environment—we have to identify the environment and understand the behaviors that are socially acceptable in that environment. There are two frames of reference for deciding whether a behavior is conforming: Is it deemed acceptable by most people, by a majority or public culture? Or, is it deemed acceptable by a few people, by a minority or private culture? Behaviors may be adaptive or conforming in the majority or public culture, and nonadaptive in a minority (race, religious belief) culture. For example, some adolescents dress in ways considered adaptive in a "punk" culture, while others dress in ways not adaptive to that culture. It is difficult to develop a standardized measure of adaptive behavior, simply because people's tolerance for particular behaviors depends on the type of behavior, the context in which it is exhibited, the status of the individual exhibiting the behavior, and the orientation (and presence) of the observer.

Figure 6.2
Sample Items from
an Interview Form

Visual Abilities

1. Does your child require any special considerations relative to the use of vision in the classroom? ____ If yes, what are they?

   _____

   _____

   _____

2. Does your child have trouble reading from the chalkboard? ____ If yes, what helps?

   _____

   _____

3. Does your child require special reading materials (for example, large-print books)? ____ If yes, what are they and do you have access to them?

   _____

   _____

4. Does your child wear glasses or use a magnifying glass or other visual aids? _____

Auditory Abilities

1. Does your child require any special considerations relative to the use of hearing in the classroom? ____ If yes, what are they?

   _____

   _____

2. Does your child use alternative communication systems (sign language, lip reading)? ____ If yes, which one(s)?

   _____

   _____

3. Does your child require special adaptations from speakers (slower pace, alterations of loudness)? ____ If yes, what are they?

   _____

   _____

4. Does your child wear a hearing aid? ____ If yes, is there anything special that I should know about it?

   _____

   _____

   _____

Language Development

For many students, poor academic performance is a function of immature or deficient language development. Tests exist for all levels of language development and functioning. They measure four components of language: phonology, morphology, syntax, and semantics (see Chapter 9).

Tests of language

Tests that are designed specifically to assess aspects of language require the student to provide language samples, which are then evaluated. Some tests also evaluate comprehension, with items that require the student to follow simple directions or to imitate words, phrases, and sentences. Language functioning also is a part of other tests, especially tests of intelligence and academic achievement.

Observations of language

Teachers also assess the language development of their students through formal and informal observation. They can count the number of specific classes of speech problems (part-word repetitions, whole-word repetitions) under a variety of conditions (reading, conversation), or they can assess fluency by counting syllables or words produced during a timed speech sample. They also can keep track of articulation errors ("wabbit" for *rabbit*), distortions ("bulu" for *blue*), and omissions ("pay" for *play*). Some teachers use videotapes, audiotapes, or written transcriptions to study their students' speech.

Background information about a student's language development generally is collected from parents using a structured-interview approach. A good interview does more than ask questions like "Does your child talk?" or "When did your child start to talk?"; it addresses how the child uses language. For example, the speech therapist in Kim's school gave her an interview form that contained the following questions:

Sample interview on language

1. Is speech easy to understand?
2. Is speech pleasant to hear?
3. Is speech linguistically appropriate?
4. Is speech labored in production?
5. Are content and manner of speech appropriate?

In assessing language development, usually a background interview comes first. Next, observations of the components of language development are completed as a basis for understanding how a student uses language in natural settings. Finally, standardized tests are used to provide information on selected aspects of language ability and to provide corroborative evidence for the strengths and weaknesses identified through other methods of assessment. Portfolios (collections of audiotapes or videotapes, samples of writing over time) could be used to assess language development.

Psychological Development

Psychological development is assessed by having students draw family pictures or self-portraits, answer open-ended questions about themselves, or respond to ambiguous pictures, drawings, or situations. These responses are evaluated for evidence of clinical or diagnostic pathology (for example, excessive fear of

Observing students perform carefully structured tasks provides valuable information when conducting educational assessments. © 1994 *Laura Dwight*.

Use of personality tests

death, aggressiveness, inadequacy). The use of personality tests in schools has diminished over the years. But in some schools, these tests are used extensively and may even be required to classify students as emotionally disturbed. In some districts, school psychologists conduct personality tests; in others, professionals in private practice are contracted by the school to assess students' psychological development.

Observations play an important part in the assessment of psychological development because inappropriate behavior is seen as an indicator of abnormal development. Any action can be the target of a formal or informal observation.

Measuring problem behaviors

The procedure is straightforward. First, the class of problem behavior to be observed is described in terms that can be counted. For example, the category of inappropriate behavior might include counts for not sitting in an assigned seat, looking out the window instead of at an assignment, talking without permission, and not completing assignments. Next, a system for measuring each target behavior is selected and applied. Finally, the counts are tallied and reported. Counts can be recorded in different ways:

Ways to count problem behaviors

Interval recording measures the number of time blocks in which a behavior or response occurs. For example, when Kim uses this method, she divides her observation period (say, ten minutes) into smaller intervals (say, thirty seconds) and checks whether the behavior she is monitoring occurs at any time during an interval.

Time sample recording measures the number of times a behavior or response occurs after a preset interval (for example, ten seconds or two minutes). When using time samples, Kim sets an interval period (such as every two minutes), then checks at the end of the interval and records whether the target behavior is occurring at that time.

Event recording measures the number of times a behavior or response occurs during a preset observation period. For example, Kim used event recording to count the number of times a student raised her hand during a thirty-minute observation period.

Duration recording measures the length of time over which a behavior or response occurs. When Kim and Larry use this method, they record the time a behavior starts and stops. Then they calculate the cumulative total time (for example, forty-eight minutes) for the observation period (such as sixty minutes) as a record of how long the behavior occurred.

Latency recording measures the time between a request for behavior and an actual response. When Kim and Larry use this method, they record the time they ask a student to perform a behavior and the time the student starts doing it.

Teachers' and parents' ratings are used extensively in assessing students who are thought to have emotional problems. These interviews vary considerably in form and content. For example, some require yes or no answers to questions about specific behaviors exhibited by the student being evaluated. Others use a Likert-type response format (1 = strongly agree . . . 5 = strongly disagree) to indicate the extent to which an item reflects the problems of the student being assessed. Most of the scales contain several dimensions of problem behaviors. The Revised Behavior Problem Checklist contains six: conduct disorders, socialized aggression, attention problems/immaturity, anxiety/withdrawal, psychotic behavior, and motor excesses (Quay, 1983). The Walker Problem Behavior Identification Checklist contains five (Walker, 1976):

Types of problem behaviors

Acting out   The student complains about discrimination or unfairness and becomes upset when things don't go the way he or she would like.

Withdrawal   The student has few friends, does not initiate interpersonal interactions, and does not engage in group activities.

Distractibility   The student is restless, continually moves, seeks attention more than other students, and easily loses interest in tasks and learning activities.

Disturbed peer relations   The student makes negative self-statements and comments that nobody likes him or her.

Immaturity   The student reacts to stress with physical complaints (stomach hurts, headaches) and cries easily.

Perceptual-Motor Development

Many educators believe that being able to translate sensory information into meaningful actions is important for success in school. For example, some special educators argue that a student who cannot copy a geometric design (a square or diamond, for example) has difficulty copying letters and numbers when working on academic tasks. Tests of perceptual-motor development require students to copy designs or perform other actions after being told or shown what to do.

Bender test

The Bender Visual Motor Gestalt Test is a good example of a perceptual-motor assessment device. It consists of nine geometric shapes that the student is asked to copy on a plain sheet of white paper. The reproductions are scored relative to four types of errors: shape distortions, perseveration, integration, and rotation. Errors are scored as shape distortions when a student's design is distorted to the extent that a representation of the original figure is lost. Perseveration errors are scored when a student fails to stop after completing the required picture. Integration errors result when parts of a design overlap or fail to meet. Rotation errors are scored when a student shifts a design more than forty-five degrees from the way it was presented.

Observations of perceptual-motor development

Kim uses observations to assess her students' perceptual-motor development. On the playground she keeps track of the way they walk, skip, and run around, and of their catching and throwing skills. When the students are working on art projects, she watches how well they color within the lines and use scissors. Many teachers also ask parents, other teachers, and students themselves about perceptual-motor skills. Students who lack these skills often are assigned to training programs. This practice is common with students classified as learning disabled, mentally retarded, physically impaired, or multihandicapped.

Standards for Good Assessment Practices

In addition to the kinds of behaviors sampled by tests, observations, interviews, and student portfolios, and the ways in which assessment data are used, you should understand the technical aspects of assessment practices—reliability, representativeness of performance, and validity.

Reliability: Is Performance Consistent?

Consistent results

Tests, observations, interviews and collections of student work samples should provide consistent measures of pupil performance. This means that different examiners, each using the same procedures with a specific student, should be able to obtain comparable results, and that the student should earn comparable scores on repeated administrations. Inconsistent performance sometimes can reflect different responses to different examiners or illness during one of the testing sessions, not just a problem with the test itself. But the value of a measure is very much a product of its reliability.

Reliability coefficients

Reliability is an index of consistency in measurement. Test, observation, interview, and work sample scores that fluctuate considerably on repeated measurement, either by different examiners over time or by separate administrations of the same measure, may not be reliable. Authors are supposed to include information in their technical manuals on the reliability of their instruments. Reliability is expressed as a coefficient, an index of the degree of relationship between scores earned on two administrations of a test. Reliability coefficients range from .00 to .99.

How high should reliability be? It depends on how we are using the scores. Two standards of reliability generally are accepted for use in educational decision making: *Group data*—When scores are being used for general purposes and are reported for groups, they should have a reliability of at least .60; *individual data*—When scores are used to make placement decisions about individual students, the minimum standard is .90. When a referral decision is being made, .80 is the accepted standard.

Representativeness: Does the Instrument Adequately Sample the Behavior?

An assessment instrument should include adequate samples of the behavior being tested. The more extensively an instrument samples the behavior, the better it is. Tests, observations, interviews, and portfolios cannot sample all aspects of a behavior, but they must sample enough to be **representative.** At the same time, procedures must be manageable in terms of time and costs.

Sampling appropriate behaviors

Representativeness also has to do with item content. To be technically adequate, an assessment instrument must sample the appropriate kinds of behaviors. This means math tests should include math items and reading tests should include reading items. It also means that observations should include different types of acceptable actions (for example, sitting in an assigned seat, maintaining eye contact when talking to another person, raising a hand before asking or answering a question). Further, it means that rating scales of adaptive behavior must contain more than a few items about independent living skills.

Validity: Does a Procedure Measure What It Is Supposed to Measure?

Suppose Kim developed a test to measure her students' skills in volleyball. If we wanted to use her test, how would we know whether it measured what she said it measured? It is Kim's responsibility to give us evidence of the test's **validity.** Validity can be demonstrated in many ways. For example:

Ways to demonstrate validity

Pupil performance on a measure of word recognition is shown to be highly related to performance on other measures of word recognition. Pupils who do well on one test of reading do well on other reading tests, or they simply read well.

People who earn high scores on a test of mechanical aptitude and who choose to become mechanics are shown to become successful mechanics; those who earn low scores do not.

Successful typists are shown to earn high scores on a measure of typing speed; bad typists do poorly.

People who have the best understanding of the content of this chapter earn the highest scores on a measure of understanding of the content of this chapter.

Window on Practice

Developing a Test

Would you like to develop a test, a test that could be published and then used by others? In most areas of human endeavor, whether art or technology, the product appears deceptively simple to accomplish. This is often the case with test development. If you try it, you may find the work arduous, but you can also find it interesting and stimulating.

Most professional test developers have had advanced training in a special branch of statistics called measurement theory. Your task of developing a test is facilitated by special training but also by the presence of certain character traits: Since your task requires attention to detail over a long period of time, it helps to become a compulsive neurotic. It also helps to develop a taste for delayed gratification, for the fruits of your labor may not be seen for years. Finally, you should strive to become a bit sadistic, a trait especially helpful when you must test young children for hours in order to gather important data.

Of course, you must have an idea for a test. Opportunities do exist. In the field of special education there are many potential areas of measurement for which no one has developed a good test. Your test might be the one that will help others. What would you like to measure? An aspect of school achievement? Adaptive behavior? Cognitive ability? Perhaps motivation or attention?

After you identify the area, other decisions remain. Is your test to be a clinical procedure administered to one subject at a time, or a group test that can be administered to an entire classroom? With which age range is the test to be used? Is the interpretation of an examinee's performance to be norm referenced (compared to peers) or criterion referenced (compared to curriculum objectives)?

Given the prerequisite personality characteristics for test development and an idea, what is next? The steps followed in test development are fairly standard and, in a sense, a form of engineering. First, the test design and specifications are prepared. Several more questions must be answered. How are the test questions to be presented (orally, read by the examinee, by pantomime)? What kinds of responses do you want from the examinees (written, oral, pointing)? What kinds of derived scores will the users of your test need (grade equivalents, age equivalents, standard scores, percentile ranks)?

Once you have designed the test, your second step is to prepare a pool of potential test items, usually at least twice as many as you expect to use in the final form of the test. (You'll be surprised how many of your favorite items prove inadequate once they are given a trial.) Keep in mind that your item pool is only a sampling of the knowledge or skills you want to measure; therefore, you must carefully analyze the area to be measured and then prepare a pool of items that represents a good cross-section.

Third, you conduct a series of small-scale tryouts, initially with only a small group of subjects. These tryouts allow you to polish the test administration procedures, improve item content and wording, and detect potential scoring problems. One outcome of this step is likely to be the realization that you need to develop even more items. Another possible outcome is you notice that you do not have enough easy items, or perhaps you decide you should measure one aspect in your test more thoroughly.

After this revision step, it is time to repeat the process of evaluating and editing your fledgling test again. This cycle will be repeated three or four times before you are satisfied that you have created a good draft of your test. Then you are ready to begin the process of standardizing the test.

Two goals are involved in standardizing a norm-referenced test. First, the test is administered under controlled, documented conditions that will be followed by subsequent test users. The second goal is to obtain normative data,

(continued on next page)

Developing a Test *(continued)*

which allow future users to compare the scores they obtain to the scores obtained by the subjects in your norming sample. The user of a standardized test usually wants to compare a person's performance on a test to the performance of others at the same age or grade placement. The people included in your norming sample must be carefully selected so that they provide a good cross-section of the population to which your test users want to compare their scores. This requires careful attention to factors such as a geographic distribution of your sample and personal characteristics such as race, sex, and socioeconomic variables. Finally, the test items are arranged in the final form from the easiest to the most difficult. The data from your norming study tell you that sequence.

Your users will expect you to provide infor-

mation about the reliability and validity of your test. The reliability information tells how precisely your test measures. The validity information tells how well your test measures what it is intended to measure.

Your last step is to prepare the testing materials, including the manuals your users need. This step makes all your efforts useful to others. The better you complete this part of your project, the easier it is for others to use your test in the way you intended.

And that's about all there is to it. That is, until it is time to revise your test.

Source: Richard W. Woodcock is an educational consultant and developer of the Woodcock–Johnson Psychoeducational Battery–Revised and the Woodcock Reading Mastery Tests–Revised.

Observations made during atypical or insufficient time periods by untrained or biased people of unrepresentative behaviors are not considered valid measures of a student's performance. Similarly, interviews conducted by people with little knowledge of the student being evaluated or by people with biased opinions are not appropriate sources of information for making decisions.

The Public's Concerns About Assessment

Those who develop tests and who administer and interpret them worry about the technical factors we mentioned in the previous section: reliability, representativeness, and validity. The general public does not typically think or talk about technical concepts like reliability, representativeness, and validity. Rather, they worry about test fairness, acceptability, and consequences. In this section we illustrate how the concerns of the lay public parallel those of test developers and users.

Fairness

We've all heard people talk about tests that were fair or unfair. Fairness is a fuzzy concept and a marker for a varied set of grievances. For example, when some people call tests unfair, they are arguing that the test is used to make unfair comparisons. You may have heard one of your friends make statements like "It is unfair to compare me to shorter people" or "It is unfair to compare

Haloed judgments

me to younger people." Some argue that tests are unfair when they include measures of things they have not had an opportunity to learn. Others use the concept of fairness in discussions of *haloed* or *stereotypic* judgments, judgments in which the decision maker is influenced more by a stereotype held for the student's race, gender, ethnicity, or background than by the student's actual performance and behavior.

Unfair content

Concerns about fairness also include those raised by students about content coverage of tests. You might have experienced what you thought was an unfair test: one in which the content tested was not, in your opinion, representative of the content covered in a class. This concern also includes objections raised by students who are tested on content they thought they would not be tested on. ("The prof said the test would cover only the lecture content, but it included content from the book.") Test developers go to great lengths to ensure that their tests are not viewed as unfair. They do so by trying to use representative groups for purposes of comparisons, and by trying to be sure that tests are valid and accurate measures.

Acceptability

Sometimes people argue that it is not fair to test them and to make judgments about them. Individuals who consider themselves professionals (including teachers) sometimes contend that they should not be tested or evaluated. They believe they, not others, should make judgments about their performance. In short, they find evaluation or testing unacceptable.

Is testing undemocratic?

Arguments about acceptability include the contention that testing is undemocratic and elitist. Some argue, for example, that colleges and universities should not use tests to make decisions about who gets into undergraduate or graduate programs. They contend that testing is not "authentic" and that all people should be admitted. Those who use tests to make selection or admission decisions contend that they do not have resources to admit everyone and that tests help them identify those for whom admission is appropriate.

Face validity

Many of the concerns people raise about acceptability are based on their judgments about face validity. *Face validity* refers to the extent to which a test looks fair. Of course, judgments about whether a test looks fair are just that—judgments. They are influenced very much by personal biases and beliefs.

Sometimes parents argue that testing their children is unacceptable. This contention may be an ethnic or religious contention—the argument that "_____ children should never be tested." This argument is often expressed by parents of students with disabilities. They make statements like "It is cruel to subject my child to this kind of [testing] experience."

Consequences

The general public worries about the consequences of testing, such as using tests to decide who graduates from school, who gets a job, who gets into college, who gets certified or licensed, and who gets a driver's license. Those who develop and use tests translate such concerns into concerns about accuracy and generalizability. They try to develop measures that provide accurate information that generalizes from one setting to another.

Assumptions Underlying Assessment Practices

Assessment is the basis on which professionals decide who should receive special education services, where and by whom those services will be delivered, the specific nature of instructional treatments, and the criteria used in evaluating the effectiveness of those treatments. In reaching their decisions, educators make certain basic assumptions about assessment procedures. To understand the use of assessment—and its possible misuse—you should be aware of these assumptions.

The Examiner Is Skilled

When students are assessed, it is assumed that the person doing the assessment is trained to establish rapport with the students and knows how to administer, score, and interpret the instrument used to collect the assessment information. To the extent that rapport is not adequately established and the instrument is administered, scored, and interpreted incorrectly, the results are not valid.

Establishing rapport

First of all, establishing rapport means making the student feel comfortable in the test situation and motivated to do her or his best. Suppose you wanted to remove Pat from a third-grade classroom to give him a reading test. It probably wouldn't be a good idea to enter the classroom and shout "Next victim." You certainly wouldn't march Pat down the hall to the testing room and say "Read." Instead you would talk to him about hobbies or TV shows or some other interest. Once you entered the testing room, you might have Pat draw pictures or tell a story to relax. Your task is to make the student feel comfortable. There are no rules for that; different techniques work with different students. However, remember that your main purpose is to test the student. Some examiners spend so much time getting the student ready for testing that when they get to the test itself, the student has lost interest.

Training the examiner

Second, an examiner must know how to administer an instrument. Obviously if an instrument is not administered correctly, the student's performance has little meaning. The amount and type of needed training vary with the type of assessment and its purpose. Special training is needed to administer, score, and interpret most individually administered tests. For many group tests, just reading the test manual is enough. Similarly, some observation instruments require formal training, while others can be completed simply by counting target behaviors. Very few interviews require extensive training, but most commercially available rating scales provide administration guidelines in their technical manuals. The gathering of portfolios of student work requires only that the teacher or student collect the work.

Scoring

Third, the examiner must be able to score the assessment instrument. In this age of machine scoring, teachers seldom have to worry about scoring group-administered intelligence and achievement tests, although they should check

Establishing rapport is an important part of the assessment process. *Charles Gupton/Stock, Boston, Inc.*

machine scoring when the results are suspect (for example, a gifted student's scores are below average, or the best reader in the class performs poorly). Most individually administered tests are scored by the examiner. All tests should include information about scoring in the test manual. Extra care should be taken when compiling scores on observations. Inaccurate counts of observed behaviors can result in misinterpretation of the extent of a student's skills or problems.

Interpretation

Finally, the examiner must know how to interpret the student's performance. For some procedures this means simply reporting the student's scores. For others, it means learning how to interpret the score.

Future Behavior Can Be Inferred from Present Behavior

The second assumption underlying any assessment is that future behavior can be inferred from the present behavior that is being measured. We have said that all tests, observations, interviews, and portfolios are samples of behavior. If we were trying to predict performance on the assembly line in an automobile plant, for example, the best assessment would be to watch the individual working on the assembly line. In most instances, however, this isn't possible, so we would sample the target behavior in different ways. We'd choose a form of assessment that we believed would predict future performance on the target task.

Plausible prediction

To predict performance on an assembly line, we would not use a spelling test, but we could use a manual-dexterity test. Future behavior can never be observed, so any prediction about future behavior is an inference. Inferences have different degrees of plausibility, depending on the similarity between the behavior sampled and the behavior being predicted.

Assessment Is Relatively Free from Error

People who rely on assessment instruments tend to assume they are accurate. But educational, psychological, and behavioral tests, observations, work samples, and interviews are not perfect measures of skills, characteristics, or abilities.

True score versus error

On any day, a student can make a careless mistake on a test or assignment, or an answer may simply be a guess. The student's scores are inaccurate to the extent that careless mistakes are made and some answers are guesses. The scores that students earn on tests always are made up of two components: true score and error. To the extent that error is present, the score is inaccurate.

In observations and interviews, we also must be concerned about the extent of error present in scores. After Kim observes a student, she asks herself if the performance she recorded is typical of the student's behavior. Brown (1981) describes the following types of common errors in rating scales:

Common errors in rating scales

Errors of central tendency   Raters tend to avoid extreme points on a continuum, overusing the middle categories.

Errors of leniency   Raters often are generous in their ratings.

Severity errors   Raters also can be too stringent in their ratings.

Halo effect errors   Raters sometimes allow their general impressions and opinions to influence their ratings.

Logical errors   Raters sometimes assume characteristics or behaviors are related when they are not.

Obviously, what people say about another person does not always reflect what the other person does. When using observations or interviews, teachers should try to be aware of their own attitudes and preconceptions that may influence the process. Special care is needed with interviews because the respondent is the sole source of the information.

Students Have Comparable Acculturation

Acculturation, as we noted in Chapter 2, refers to the way a person's background experiences and opportunities shape his or her acquisition of the society's culture. The fourth major assumption in assessment is that the student being assessed has comparable, not necessarily identical, acculturation to those with whom the student is being compared—that the student being assessed has had experiences and opportunities to learn similar to those in the norm group. According to standards specified by a joint committee of the American Psychological Association, the American Educational Research Association, and the National Council on Measurement in Education, infor-

Acculturation of the norm group

mation is supposed to be included in technical manuals that tells users the precise nature of the group on whom an instrument was standardized. Sufficient information should be provided on the age, gender, grade level, socioeconomic status, and geographic region of the norm group so that others can judge the extent to which the student being assessed is like those to whom he or she is being compared. To the extent that students differ from the norm group, judgments based on comparisons are invalid.

Guidelines for Appropriate Assessment

Assessment is central to special education because students cannot receive special services or leave special programs without it. It also is the basis of planning, implementation, and evaluation decisions. Given the importance of assessment in the lives of exceptional students, you should know something about "best practices." Here are some guidelines.

Tailoring assessment to the student

There Is No One Way to Do It Right   There is no recipe for assessment—no single battery of tests, form of observation, specific rating scale, or portfolio of student products that can tell us everything we want to know about any student. Remember that assessment is the process of collecting data for the purpose of making decisions about students. Only if all students had the same kinds of problems could there be one right way to assess them. Assessment activities must be tailored to the individual and to the nature of the instructional setting.

Avoiding a "search for pathology"

There Is No One Cause of School Problems   One of the major failings of current assessment practices is that many of those practices are driven by a "search for pathology." Students with academic and behavioral problems are assessed because somebody thinks there's something wrong with them. Sometimes there is; students do have sensory, communication, physical, emotional, and intellectual difficulties that are significant enough to interfere with learning. Those problems may be so evident that assessors can assume they are the primary problem.

But often the problems students experience in school have to do with instruction and the goals or demands of the school. Problems occur in a context: home, classroom, or home–school relationships or interactions. Assessors need to operate from a broad perspective, looking beyond the student to take into account the context in which difficulties arise.

Going beyond description

Assessment Must Do More than Describe Problems   Sometimes school personnel spend far too much time searching for and describing students' problems. They gather extensive information, develop elaborate profiles, and write lengthy descriptions of students' dysfunctions, defects, deficits, and disabilities. Then they share these descriptions with parents, colleagues, and school administrators. This process seldom benefits students. It is our job to solve their problems and develop their competence. Unless assessment prac-

Bring Your Learning to Life

The Hypothetical Word Processing Test

Suppose you are the personnel manager for a large industrial firm that does business around the world. Part of your job involves hiring word processors. You regularly require applicants to take a word processing test, which includes typing from handwritten English and from dictation. You score the test for both speed and accuracy. Sounds pretty simple, doesn't it? You expect the test to provide representative, valid results that will help you decide whom to hire.

But even if you give each applicant the same test, you need some basis for evaluating the performance. So you have to standardize your test—that is, you develop a set of norms according to which applicants' performances can be evaluated. There are many groups on which such a test could be standardized; for example, any of the following:

1. All high school seniors in your local school district.
2. All high school seniors in your local school district who have been enrolled in a business curriculum and who have taken at least one full year of word processing classes.
3. A representative national sample of high school seniors who have been enrolled in a business curriculum and who have taken at least one full year of word processing classes.
4. All the people who, over a three-year period, have applied for employment with your company.
5. All the people who, over a three-year period, have applied for employment as word processors with your company.
6. Persons currently employed as word processors in your company who have better than satisfactory performance evaluations from their immediate supervisors.

The nature of the group you select for standardizing the test will influence your judgment of individual applicants. An applicant might look very good compared with high school seniors but poor compared with currently employed, successful word processors.

Consider what will happen to an excellent typist who has never worked from a dictation device. Such a person might do very well on the typing-from-handwriting portion of the test but not as well on the part that includes dictation. If your norm group consisted of experienced word processors, that person's overall score might not meet your standards.

Consider the fate of an applicant who recently emigrated to the United States from China. This applicant, whose spoken English is excellent, types very fast but makes several spelling errors on both portions of the test. (Your test, remember, is in English.) If your norm group included few new immigrants, this applicant might be eliminated, even if your company does extensive business in China and needs more word processors who can type both English and Chinese.

If such problems can occur with a simple word processing test, imagine the difficulties with the complex, multidimensional instruments used in educational assessment. That is why tests are supposed to include detailed information about the norm group on which they were standardized. If a student's acculturation differs substantially from that of the norm group, the test is not a valid basis for comparison.

tices facilitate the development of competence in students, they are of limited value.

The goal: improve instruction

Assessment Should Be Directed at Improving Instruction   The ultimate goal of assessment is to identify problems with instruction and to lead to instructional modifications. A good share of present-day assessment activities consist of little more than meddling. Many professionals gather data simply because they find those data interesting, which isn't enough. We must use assessment data to improve instruction.

Frequent assessment

Assessment Should Occur Often During Teaching   Good teachers constantly assess students and programs. It is impossible to be sure about the best ways to teach students, so teachers choose an approach (their best guess), then measure the extent to which progress is made. The only way to determine the effectiveness of instruction is to collect data.

Relevance to the problem

Assessment Should Concentrate on Relevant Variables   For whatever reasons, much of current assessment is irrelevant to instructional decision making. Diagnostic personnel regularly administer intelligence tests, achievement tests, and other tests without thinking about the reasons for testing students. They conduct comprehensive interviews that bear little relation to the problem they are trying to solve. These practices are inappropriate and unnecessary. We don't always need information on cognitive functioning, general achievement, or personality functioning to improve instruction for students who are failing in school. The most relevant variable to look at when students have problems is the extent to which teaching is occurring. When students fail to read adequately, it may be because they have had little instruction in reading. Large numbers of students may fail to do well in mathematics because they seldom practice doing numbers. Although it is often important to assess the learner and the nature of instruction, the way to begin any assessment is by evaluating the extent to which instruction has occurred and to which the learner has played an active part in it.

Many teachers and school psychologists think they must look at literally every area of functioning to "uncover" a child's problem. They are wrong. Assessment should be directed toward identifying factors that can improve instruction. The classroom is clearly the place to start.

The usual environment

Assessment Should Occur Where the Behavior Occurs   To the extent possible, data on student performance should be collected in the environment where that performance occurs. If a student's performance in mathematics is of concern, math performance should be assessed in the classroom where it is a problem, with the materials the student uses in that classroom. This approach allows much less room for inference than removing the youngster from the class for assessment using a math test not related to the curriculum.

One of the authors of this textbook was once a school psychologist and, having been trained to do so, often tested students. As was common practice in those days, he would remove students from the classroom, then administer a number of reading tests. Later, when he would describe a student's "reading" to the classroom teacher, more often than not he would be told that the measure overestimated or underestimated the student's actual ability. Students perform differently in different settings with different people; the best place to assess performance is in the environment where a behavior occurs.

Tests Should Be Adapted to Accommodate Students with Disabilities

Major efforts are underway to include students with disabilities in all assessments without biasing the results against them (Ysseldyke & Thurlow, 1993). To accomplish this goal, modifications must be made in tests or in testing procedures. The following are some of the most important modifications that enable testing to provide a clearer picture of students' accomplishments:

Test modifications

Flexible scheduling   Tests can be administered during several brief sessions rather than a single lengthy one.

Flexible setting   Students can be allowed to take tests in a separate room with fewer or no people present rather than a large auditorium.

Alternatives for recording answers   Students with disabilities may be allowed to record their answers directly in a test booklet rather than filling in machine-scored answer sheets.

Alternative-print format   Students with visual disabilities can be given tests in large-print or braille versions.

Assessment in Perspective

Many teachers have been taught that it is their job to spot students who are having difficulty, and that they or someone else ought to spend time and effort identifying deficits or disabilities. Often they don't know what they are looking for, but the search itself is exciting. Currently a kind of test mania exists in many schools. Parents and teachers worry too much about overlooking students' problems. They worry that a problem left uncovered may irreparably damage a student. We don't agree. Serious problems become obvious early, usually well before a child begins school. The real danger is not in overlooking a problem but in identifying a disorder where one does not exist.

Test mania

Assessment is an ongoing part of the special education process. Assessment data are used to determine eligibility, the special education program, and the effectiveness of that program. The best place to collect assessment data is in the classroom, and we encourage you to make regular use of tests, observations, interviews, and student portfolios when you teach. We also encourage you to use the information you gather as a record of students' present levels of functioning, not primarily as an indicator of underlying problems.

Assessment in the classroom

Assessment is a process of collecting data for the purpose of making decisions about students. In this chapter we described the different kinds of decisions that are made. Many of the decisions made using assessment information are decisions that have a significant effect on individuals' life opportunities. Therefore, assessment is an activity that must be taken very seriously.

What Every Teacher Should Know

■ Assessment is the collection of information about a student for the purpose of making decisions. Assessment information is used to make the following kinds of decisions: screening, provision of special help, referral to an intervention assistance team (IAT), provision of intervention assistance, referral to a child-study team, exceptionality, presence of special learning need, eligibility or entitlement for special education, instructional planning, progress evaluation, program evaluation, and accountability decisions.

■ For students to be considered eligible for special education services, child-study teams must demonstrate that the students meet the eligibility criteria for the conditions of special education as specified in their state, and that they have special learning needs that require special education assistance.

■ Tests, observations, interviews, and portfolios are methods used to gather assessment information across a range of behaviors, skills, abilities, and characteristics. The information collected in the assessment process is just a sample, and it is controlled by the way in which it is collected.

■ Both lay people and assessors have concerns about assessment and the assessment process. Lay people tend to be concerned about fairness, acceptability, and consequences. Assessors tend to be concerned about reliability, representativeness, and validity.

■ A set of fundamental assumptions underlies current assessment practices; when those assumptions are violated, the results of the assessment are invalid.

■ Guidelines for appropriate assessment include the following: Assessment must do more than describe problems, should be directed at improving instruction, should occur often during teaching, should concentrate on relevant variables, and should occur where the behavior occurs.

■ Assessment practices are changing and being improved frequently, and it is wise to monitor these changes.

Projects

1. Obtain any commercial test. Write down five test items, then state the kind of behavior each samples.

2. List five kinds of behaviors that could be sampled in an assessment of intelligence.

3. Develop a class scrapbook on assessment practices by collecting articles on assessment from local newspapers and magazines. For each of the articles you collect, indicate the kind of decision-making activity in which assessment information is being used (for example, to make accountability decisions).

4. Visit an elementary school classroom. Pick any student at random and observe the student for an hour or two. Keep a tally of the number of twenty-

second intervals in which the student is (a) actively engaged in responding to academic materials and (b) doing something else. Write a summary of your observations.

5. Visit a local elementary school classroom. Pick a student at random and observe the student for two hours. During that time, record (a) the amount of time the teacher shows or tells the student what to do, (b) the amount of time the student spends demonstrating that he or she understands what is being taught, and (c) the amount of time the student is tested on mastery of what has been taught. Write a summary of your observations.

For Your Information

Books

Hammill, D. D., Brown, L., & Bryant, B. R. (1989). *A consumer's guide to tests in print.* Austin, TX: PRO-ED.
This text contains a set of reviews of the most commonly used educational and psychological tests. Each test is "scored" using a comprehensive rating scale. The text is useful to those who are trying to decide which of several tests to use in a domain.

Kramer, J., & Conoley, J. (Eds.). (1992). *Eleventh mental measurements yearbook.* Lincoln, NE: University of Nebraska Press.
The Mental Measurements Yearbooks contain critical reviews of the technical adequacy of commonly used tests. This is another source to consult before selecting and using specific tests.

Salvia, J., & Ysseldyke, J. E. (1995). *Assessment* (6th ed.). Boston: Houghton Mifflin.
A comprehensive textbook on psychological and educational assessment with a focus on issues and concerns in assessment of students with disabilities. The text includes basic information about testing and measurement, and extensive description of assessment practices in classrooms and out of classrooms. Most of the tests commonly used with students with disabilities are described and critically evaluated.

Sattler, J. (1988). *Assessment of childrens' intelligence and other special abilities.* San Diego: Author.
A textbook on assessment written primarily for psychologists, this text includes very good descriptions of use of major intellectual batteries. The text includes the latest research findings on specific devices and practices.

Ysseldyke, J. E., Algozzine, B., & Thurlow, M. L. (1992). *Critical issues in special education* (2nd ed.). Boston: Houghton Mifflin.
In Chapter 7 of this text the authors describe the major issues in assessment of students with disabilities. Topics include using tests to classify and place students, the use and misuse of intelligence tests, the push for a national achievement test.

Organizations

Council for Educational Diagnostic Services
An official division of the Council for Exceptional Children, its members include school diagnosticians, resource teachers, assessment specialists, school psychologists, and others whose professional employment involves assessment of students who are exceptional. For more information, contact Council for Educational Diagnostic Services, Division of the Council for Exceptional Children, 1920 Association Dr., Reston, VA 22091.

National Council on Educational Measurement
Membership in this organization includes university and test publishers; and educational measurement specialists and educators interested in measurement of human abilities, personality characteristics, and educational achievement. The NCEM publishes two quarterlies: *Educational Measurement—Issues and Practices* and the *Journal of Educational Measurement.* For more information, contact the NCEM, 1230 17th St. NW, Washington, DC 20036.

Association of State Assessment Personnel

Each of the fifty states and each of the territories has an assessment coordinator. Most assessment coordinators have staffs of individuals who run state testing programs and evaluate school districts. ASAP is a small organization whose members are the coordinators of state assessment programs and their staffs. For more information, contact the Association of State Assessment Personnel, Council of Chief State School Officers, 377 Hall of the States, One Massachusetts Ave., Washington, DC 20001-1413.

Journals

Journal of Psychoeducational Assessment

The focus of this journal is on tests and research conducted on tests. It is typical to find articles on the technical adequacy (reliability and validity) of a specific test, the use of tests to make decisions about students, or reviews of testing issues. For more information, contact the Editor, Bruce Bracken, Department of Psychology, Memphis State University, Memphis, TN 38152.

Diagnostique

This is the official journal of the Council for Educational Diagnostic Services, the Division of the Council for Exceptional Children that focuses on services to those who have diagnostic roles in school systems. The journal includes critical evaluations of specific tests, comparative studies of the "goodness" of competing tests in evaluating students with disabilities, and reviews of testing advances. For more information, contact the Council for Exceptional Children, 1920 Association Dr., Reston, VA 22091.

Journal of Educational Measurement

This is the official journal of the National Council on Educational Measurement. It is a highly technical journal in which authors publish articles dealing with the psychometric characteristics of tests. The journal also publishes critical reviews of tests. For more information, contact National Council on Educational Measurement, 1230 17th St. NW, Washington, DC 20036.

Instructional Approaches and Teaching Tactics for Students Who Are Exceptional

After Part II's overview of instruction and assessment, we are ready to discuss students in terms of the individual categories used in special education. The chapters in Part III consider the basic categories one by one.

At the heart of each chapter is a section on instructional approaches and teaching tactics. These sections are designed to be especially practical and easy to use in the classroom. The teaching tactics are specific, down-to-earth techniques for helping your students learn, and they are supplemented with tables of "top ten" tips as well as examples and vignettes from classroom experience.

In addition, the chapters in this part contain definitions of the categories, discussions of the students' characteristics, and succinct summaries of current trends and issues. Since the terminology for some of the categories varies from state to state, we try to offer perspective on the variation and the reasons for it.

Remember that the categories are not hard-and-fast divisions. Across all these groups, students are more alike than different, and techniques that prove effective for one group will likely be effective for others.

We'd also like you to keep in mind that teaching and learning are reciprocal behaviors. Though we generally write from the teacher's point of view, the student's perspective should never be neglected. The teaching tactics we present have proved to be practical classroom guides precisely because they reflect the best available research on ways to influence learning.

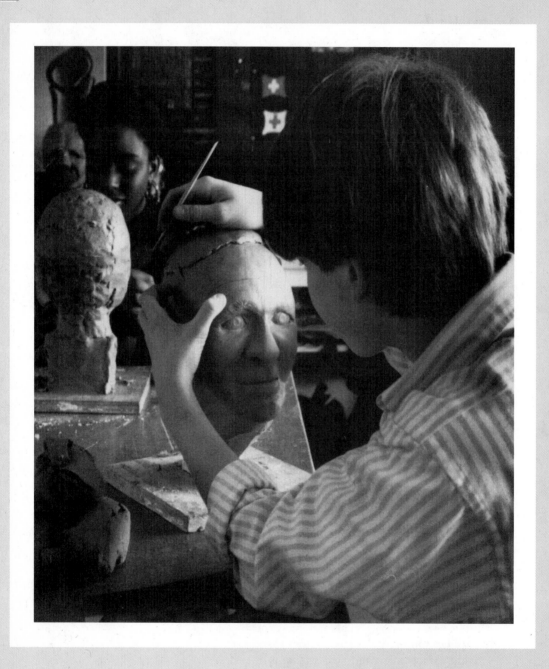

7

Teaching Students Who Are Gifted and Talented

Focusing Questions

- What definition is used for students who are gifted and talented?

- How many students who are gifted and talented receive special education?

- What are the primary characteristics of students who are gifted and talented?

- What instructional approaches and teaching tactics are appropriate for students who are gifted and talented?

- What special problems concern people working with students who are gifted and talented?

Lenny is one of those students whose abilities baffle his teachers. At 10 years of age, he scored a perfect score of 800 on the math portion of the Scholastic Aptitude Test. He set a record with four perfect performances on the American High School Math Exam, and he won a gold medal at the International Math Olympics. But his abilities go beyond mathematics. He has taken honors in violin and piano competitions, played on a championship basketball team, and earned a 4.0 grade-point average in college courses he took while still a full-time high school student. When he enters Harvard at the age of 16 as a sophomore, there is little doubt that his academic career will be an outstanding success.

Sarah is the best chess player in her class, in her school, and in her hometown. When she finishes the tournaments planned during her third-grade school year, she may be the best chess player in the country. Like few of her peers, Sarah is good at everything that takes place in school. Her teacher struggles to keep a step ahead of her, especially in math, but she enjoys the challenges that Sarah provides for her and the other students. She knows the school principal plans to offer accelerated coursework to Sarah in a few years, and she hopes her new teachers will think highly of the work she has done with her.

Nicholas had always been an excellent creative writer. Most of his teachers described him as the "most gifted writer" they had ever taught. By the age of 12, he was writing pieces that most teachers thought were characteristic of much older students. For the first quarter of his eighth-grade year, Nicholas was an excellent student. His teachers were surprised when his parents decided to enroll Nicholas in a special school. They were not surprised because the school was for gifted students but because they thought Nicholas was happy at his present school. When they asked Nicholas's parents why he was moving, they said he was "bored" with school and didn't enjoy what he did there. They said Nicholas tolerated the work he was assigned because he didn't want his teachers to feel bad. They also described Nicholas's real passion, a biography of Eleanor Roosevelt that he was working on every day after school. Nicholas's teachers described an instructional approach in which students "buy back" school time they were supposed to "spend" in one way so they can spend it in another, and asked his parents to give them a chance to try it before making the school transfer. After a month's participation in this "curriculum compacting" project, Nicholas decided to stay in his neighborhood school. ■

The category of "gifted and talented" includes young people with advanced abilities in the arts. *Karen Preuss/The Image Works, Inc.*

Gifted, creative, and *talented* are terms teachers use to describe students like Lenny, Sarah, and Nicholas. Some people use *genius* to refer to them because their strengths are far beyond even those of their peers who are perceived as really smart, bright, or artistic. These are people who can solve problems in traditional and nontraditional ways and who demonstrate consistently high performance in areas requiring considerable mental ability. They are also people who come up with novel solutions that are characterized as "creative," "imaginative," "outstanding," and "brilliant" by very talented judges in their respective fields. These people are recognized and considered exceptional because of the contributions they make and the performances they demonstrate. Widely acknowledged figures from the past and present whose contributions are considered far beyond the ordinary include Maya Angelou, Celestino Beltram, Alexander Calder, Marie Curie, Charles Darwin, Albert Einstein, Duke Ellington, Sigmund Freud, Martha Graham, Harvey Itano, Ynez Mexia, Alwin Nikolais, Sir Isaac Newton, Pablo Picasso, Srinivasa Ramanujan, Chu Shin-Chieh, Igor Stravinsky, Andy Warhol, and Laura Ingalls Wilder. Many believe today's students who are gifted and talented will also make outstanding contributions as they progress through life.

Definition

Although a large number of the students in any school are thought to be very "smart," only a few are formally identified as gifted and talented. The term is used to designate people who are intellectually, creatively, academically, or otherwise superior to a comparison group of peers or older agemates. The term **gifted** is usually used to refer to people with superior intellectual or cognitive performance, while the term **talented** is usually used to refer to people who show outstanding performance in a specific area such as the performing or visual arts. The terminology typically used in the professional literature to describe students who are gifted and talented is presented in Table 7.1. Notice that the terms are generally more positive than those sometimes associated with categories of disability. Notice also that some terms—the positive as well as the negative—may reinforce tendencies to stereotype students who are gifted and talented.

Unlike the other categories covered in this book, gifted and talented is not included in Public Law 94–142 or the Individuals with Disabilities Education Act. Separate legislation, the Gifted and Talented Children's Education Act of 1978 (Public Law 95–561), gives states financial incentives to develop programs for students considered gifted and talented. The legislation includes the following definition of gifted and talented children:

> The term "gifted and talented" means children, and whenever applicable, youth who are identified at the preschool, elementary, or secondary level as

Definitions of gifted and talented

Federal legislation

Table 7.1	Terms Often Used in the Literature to Describe Students Who Are Gifted and Talented

abstract thinker	intuitive
advanced comprehension	less willing to cooperate or
bookish	compromise
cooperative	motivated
creative	natural leader
daydreamer	persistent
divergent thinker	precocious
disruptive	prefers to think in generalities
erratic	problem solver
evaluative	responsible
flexible	self-critical
good memory	spontaneous
happy-go-lucky	sensitive
highly verbal	understands quickly
high tolerance for ambiguity	unmotivated
immature	willing to take mental and
intelligent	emotional risks

possessing demonstrated or potential abilities, that give evidence of high performance capability in areas such as intellectual, creative, specific academic, or leadership ability, or in the performing and visual arts and who by reason thereof require services or activities not ordinarily provided by the school. (Section 902)

In the past twenty years, many state and federal policies have supported widespread public interest in setting up special programs to serve students who are gifted and talented. Nevertheless, many of the programs that were prevalent in the 1970s and 1980s have been cut back as a result of budget problems (Larsen, Griffin, & Larsen, in press). Today, a modest federal program, established by the Jacob K. Javits Gifted and Talented Students Act of 1988, supports demonstration projects, a national research center, and national leadership activities, with priority funding going to efforts to serve "gifted and talented students who are economically disadvantaged, speak limited English, or have disabilities" (Office of Educational Research and Improvement, 1993, p. 18).

Variations in state definitions

State Department of Education personnel write definitions and criteria for identification of students as gifted and talented (Gallagher & Coleman, 1992). In some states the definition and criteria include both gifted and talented, in others the two conditions are differentiated. For example, the Maryland definition of gifted and talented reads

> An elementary or secondary student who is identified by professionally qualified individuals as having outstanding abilities in the area of general intellectual capabilities; specific academic aptitudes; or the creative, visual or performing arts. A gifted and talented child needs different services beyond those normally provided by the regular school programs in order to develop his potential. (Annotated Code of Maryland 8-201, 202)

In Louisiana the conditions gifted and talented are given separate definitions:

> Gifted children and youth are those who possess demonstrated abilities that give evidence of high performance in academic and intellectual aptitude.
>
> Talented is possession of demonstrated abilities that give evidence of high performance in visual and/or performing arts.

The concept of need

Note one other distinction in the definitions. The Maryland definition specifically includes the notion of educational *need,* but the Louisiana definitions do not include it. The concept of educational need is prominent in other state definitions, criteria, and regulations and is central to definitions you will learn about for other categories of exceptional students. The *Minnesota Standards for Services to Gifted and Talented Students* (1988) includes an appendix with a list of characteristics of gifted and talented students and a description of the educational need related to each characteristic. The *Minnesota Standards* also include descriptions of individual students who are gifted and talented, to serve as examples of students who should be identified. We include three of these descriptions here to help you see the types of students identified in definitions of gifted and talented.

Chu Now a high school student, this Vietnamese immigrant came to the United States at age nine. He learned to speak English. His fifth grade teacher noticed his artistic and musical abilities and he was encouraged to develop these talents. Chu loved designing intricate paper patterns and enjoyed learning. His teacher noticed a very mature sense of humor. Although new to the English language, his humor was dry and he understood the nuances of language missed by many of his age-peers. He was particularly advanced in mathematics and was fascinated with computers.

Encouraged by a mentoring teacher in junior high, Chu succeeded in learning to program a computer and won three national contests sponsored by a national computer firm. There were outlets for his talent. His coursework included independent study and frequent communication with his teacher/mentor who shared his interest in computers. Chu's interest in economics was sparked by a community volunteer who sought him out and provided additional support.

His exceptional ability in computer science was supported by individualized attention at his school. Chu was lucky. The high school in his attendance area has a technology focus. The mentoring teacher happened to share his interest and donated her free time to work with him. The community volunteer heard about Chu and wanted to help. He needed support, the tools to learn, an educational climate which recognized and valued his talent, and outlets for his work. His talent in computer science was appropriately matched with his school program. At the heart of this program was the mentoring teacher who devised an individualized plan to challenge him.

Annette Annette is a highly creative and artistic fifth grader. Her family is very supportive, although they are somewhat bewildered by her disorganized, erratic approach to school work in contrast to her sister, who is well organized and a "teacher pleaser."

Her greatest skills and most intense interests are in art and writing. Annette draws incessantly, often instead of doing assignments. She seldom takes the initiative to write a story, although when she receives a writing assignment, she begins with gusto and proceeds far beyond normal expectations. She does not cooperate with all school tasks. She complains about "old facts" (things she already knows), and she is excited by new information.

Annette's life is marked by passionate involvement with drawing, creative fantasy, and a wide interest in a variety of subjects. Her peers respect her drawing skills and sense of humor. Her passionate discourses command their attention, but she is not a sought-after playmate. She changes the rules of the game to use her creativity and her peers regard this action as cheating. Annette lacks athletic skill.

She has been identified for a gifted and talented program designed to challenge her abilities. Annette's classroom teacher also provides special challenges which involve her artistic and creative ability.

Elmer   When he entered kindergarten Elmer was reading at a third grade level. In mathematics he was able to read numbers in the trillions and he could add and subtract. He took pride in recalling populations and land sizes around the world. His kindergarten teacher provided him with more difficult work in reading and mathematics. Elmer still thought kindergarten was a waste of his time.

His kindergarten year was also a year in which he formed his opinion on abortion, divorce, world peace, and war. Elmer became depressed and talked about wishing he were dead.

Elmer was withdrawn from school and his mother taught him for first and second grade. At the end of second grade, his family moved to a new school district which would provide an individualized plan and allow for some acceleration. At his new school he was given a battery of achievement tests and scored consistently at the eighth and ninth grade levels.

Currently a fourth grader, Elmer is enrolled in science and mathematics classes with eighth graders. His language arts instruction is provided with a tutor. He attends the remaining classes with other fourth graders. His mental health began to improve when he began to receive a more correct academic diet.

However, Elmer still notes many days of feeling bad about himself and the world. He is very introspective. He receives less encouragement and fewer pats on the back than other children. People assume that someone with his ability has it "all together." His parents continue to be concerned about his mental health. They have arranged for psychological counseling and have actively sought an intellectual peer for him. Elmer is an "at risk" student and his psychological and cognitive growth continue to be a serious concern. (pp. 2–3)

Prevalence

Of the approximately 45 million students who attend U.S. elementary and secondary schools, professionals estimate that 3 to 5 percent are potentially gifted and talented. During recent school years, more than 2 million (4.4 percent) students in grades K through 12 participated in gifted and talented programs (Office of Educational Research and Improvement, 1993). In some states, providing services to students who are gifted and talented is mandated by law, while in others it is left to the discretion of local school districts. There is considerable variability among states in the numbers of students who are identified **Varying numbers of** as gifted and talented and who receive services. For example, in North Dakota **students served** 0.7 percent of the students are identified as gifted and talented, in Tennessee 1.7 percent, in Iowa 1.8 percent, in Hawaii 9.2 percent, and in New Jersey 9.9 percent. This variability from one state to another is a function of differences in definitions, regulations, criteria, and resources (Office of Educational Research and Improvement, 1993).

Regardless of the definition being used or the availability of resources for providing services to students who are gifted and talented, every teacher has some students who could profit from a special program because of superior abilities in academic and other areas. If you are concerned about how to identify students who are gifted and talented in your classroom, you are not alone. Many teachers share this feeling, but in most classrooms it is unnecessary. Even though some students with high potential may not be doing well academically, most students who are gifted and talented identify themselves by their performance on academic tasks and related activities.

Characteristics

In the sections that follow we describe the cognitive, academic, physical, behavioral, and communication characteristics of students who are gifted and talented. When you observe students consistently exhibiting these characteristics, the likelihood that they are gifted and talented is strong. Students suspected of being gifted and talented may exhibit many, but not all, of these characteristics and sometimes they exhibit concomitant problems as a result of them. Representative characteristics and potential problems of students who are gifted and talented are presented in Table 7.2.

Cognitive

Rapid generalization and quick comprehension of abstract concepts and complex relationships are cognitive traits commonly associated with giftedness. All learning, "bookish" or otherwise, involves generalization. Although children, adults, and animals generalize in the process of learning, students who are gifted and talented do so more quickly, on the basis of fewer experiences, and more extensively.

Students who are gifted and talented can quickly understand abstract symbols and can uncover complex relationships among the symbols they learn. They differ from other students in the degree of abstractness of the symbols they learn very quickly and in the complexity of the relationships among symbols they learn. They generally have excellent memories and learn facts about concepts like diffusion, justice, homogeneity, and positivism more rapidly and easily than their peers. They comprehend complex relationships like balance, symbiosis, photosynthesis, and equality easier than most of their classmates and many students who are older. Sometimes all these abilities cause problems such as boredom, resistance of conventional instruction, and peer alienation.

One of the cognitive traits regularly associated with giftedness is creativity. There has been much debate about whether creativity is an intellectual trait. Some children and adolescents who earn high scores on intelligence tests also earn high scores on measures of creativity. Yet creativity is not a characteristic of all gifted students, and not all those who perform well on measures of creativity also perform well on intelligence tests. Educators often distinguish two types of thinking: convergent and divergent thinking. Students who perform well on measures of **divergent thinking** are usually thought of as creative. They demonstrate fluency (produce many words, a variety of associations, phrases,

Identifying students who are gifted and talented

Ability to generalize

Understanding abstractions and complex relationships

Creativity

Convergent and divergent thinking

| Table 7.2 | Characteristics and Related Problems of Students Who Are Gifted and Talented | |

Area	Characteristics	Potential Problems
Cognitive	Outstanding memory Much information Higher-level, abstract thinking Preference for complex and challenging tasks Simultaneous thinking Unusual information-processing abilities Creativity	Boredom with pace of instruction Impatience Perceived as showoff by peers and other students "Too many" questions Resistance to conventional approaches to instruction
Academic	High performance Ease in learning even complex content High problem-solving ability High content mastery	Alienation from peers Expectations from parents for achievement in all areas Resistance for repetitive tasks Classroom disruption when work is complete
Physical	Discrepancies between physical and mental abilities	Limited development of other than mental abilities
Behavioral	Unusual sensitivity to needs of others Sharp sense of humor Unusual intensity Persistent, goal-directed orientation	Especially vulnerable to criticism High need for success Perfectionism Intolerance and rejection from peers Perceived as stubborn
Communication	Higher levels of language development Excellent listening and speaking vocabularies	Alienation from peers Perceived as showoff

and sentences), flexibility (offer a variety of ideas and alternative solutions to problems), originality (use rare responses and unique words), and foresight (see alternative solutions ahead of time). Those who perform well on measures of **convergent thinking** (measures of reasoning ability, memory, and classification) are thought to show high academic aptitude. The traits can be either independent or overlapping. Most often, they overlap: Those who perform well on measures of creativity also perform well on traditional aptitude measures.

Renzulli's model Joseph Renzulli is an educator who has repeatedly challenged school personnel to broaden their thinking about giftedness, adding to the concept of giftedness the notion of task commitment (dedicated practice, desire to carry out important work, perseverance). Renzulli (1979) described giftedness as represented by the intersection of three cognitive traits: above average ability, creativity, and task commitment. This conception of giftedness is illustrated in Figure 7.1. According to Renzulli, a major characteristic of individuals who are gifted is consistent high-level performance on tasks.

Academic

Superior academic achievement

People who are gifted are often first recognized for superior achievement in one or more school subjects. Their performance in mathematics, language arts, science, social studies, or other academic content areas is generally well above average (which means representative of the top 5 to 10 percent) when compared to their agemates. Often they demonstrate superior abilities in creative and other areas as well (such as photography) and sometimes excel in very specific aspects of a field of study (for example, portrait photography, photojournalism). Learning even complex content comes easier to these students than it does to their peers.

Problems of some students

Not all students who are gifted and talented perform well in school. Often their superior abilities create interpersonal problems with peers (such as not wanting to be different and thus trying to be as "normal" as possible). A major line of national research has addressed the problem of gifted students who drop out of school or perform very poorly in school. It has been argued that students who are gifted often drop out of school because the instruction is not challenging enough. As a result, they are not motivated to perform well in school, are victims of poor teaching, and learn to underachieve. The paradox is that students usually are not formally identified as gifted and provided special education services for gifted students unless they perform well academically. In most states students have to perform significantly above grade level academically, in addition to earning high scores on intelligence tests, to be considered gifted.

Different performance levels in different subjects

Students who are gifted and talented also do not perform at high levels in all school subjects, which sometimes causes problems when parents and others expect uniformly high achievement. For example, it repeatedly has been shown that students who are gifted perform especially well on measures of paragraph meaning, social studies, and science, but that their performance on measures of mathematics is more often at or slightly above grade level. This finding is understandable. Many children learn to read independently of school experience, and once they learn basic decoding skills, they can read very high-level texts. Most students' progress in mathematics is limited by their exposure to or formal instruction in mathematics skills. Gallagher (1985) provides an explanation for this observed difference in performance:

> Once the basic skills of reading have been learned, there are almost no additional barriers that need to be surmounted before the youngsters can go ahead, often on their own, in rapidly improving their breadth of knowledge and skill. Their performance on achievement tests, linked to reading, requires no further learning of skills.

Figure 7.1
Renzulli's Three-Ring
Conception of Giftedness
Source: N/S-LTI-G/T, *What*
Makes Giftedness, Ventura
County Superintendent
of Schools Office, Camarillo,
CA 93012. Used with
permission.

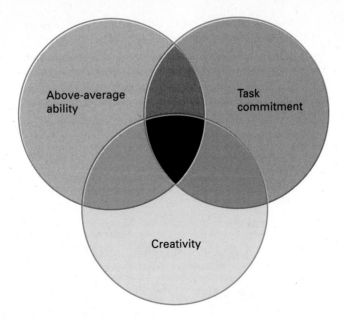

However, in the area of arithmetic, achievement is measured by the student's ability to progress through a series of a well-defined hierarchy of skills. Thus, the third-grade child, in order to attain a score in arithmetic computation at the sixth-grade level, would not necessarily have to have great depth of mathematical knowledge but merely knowledge of such arithmetic operations as subtraction of fractions or long division. (p. 39)

Physical

Physical stereotypes

There is a generally held stereotype of students who are gifted as gangly and physically uncoordinated. No evidence exists for this contention, but "pop" culture and contemporary trends (such as the image of a "nerd") sometimes perpetuate it. Terman and Oden (1951) reported the results of their longitudinal study of gifted children and stated that "the average member of our group is a slightly better physical specimen than the average child" (p. 23). But even when gifted students are similar in appearance to other students, the stereotype may affect people's perceptions and expectations. For example, many people who are gifted and talented complain that it is difficult to live a "normal" life when everybody expects you to do *everything* well simply because you do *something* well. Others argue that their "average" physical and athletic abilities are looked down on when compared to superior abilities in other areas (for example, cognitive or academic skills). Gallagher (1985) illustrates the point that gifted students are not always physically different with an example:

If the approximately three million children of twelve years of age were lined up on the interstate highway from New York, they could form a line extending all the way to Chicago. If a teacher then drove from New York to Chicago, he could get a reasonably good picture of the physical characteristics of the children. Suppose that the youngsters whom we have called academically gifted children tied red bandanas around their necks; we could then get some general impression of whether, *on the average,* they tended to be larger or heavier than the other children without bandanas.

If someone came to the teacher after this interesting drive and asked him or her what he thought about the physical characteristics of gifted children, the teacher might very well say, "Well, I thought they were a little bit heavier than the other children." At the same time, however, the teacher would remember the very thin, scrawny boy east of Toledo who, although he had a red bandana around his neck, didn't fit the general statement that the teacher had just made. (pp. 32–33)

Behavioral

Behavioral stereotypes

Most professionals argue that it is not meaningful to describe or be concerned about the social abilities or the emotional adjustment of children and young adults who are gifted because they vary so widely. Nevertheless, there are many stereotypes of the behavioral characteristics of students who are gifted and talented. Most prevalent is the notion that these students are "eggheads" who do not get along well socially with their peers and classmates. Often people think of students who are gifted as social isolates, and even as weird. Most research contradicts this stereotype, finding that students who are gifted and talented are socially popular and enjoy relatively high social status, but concomitant problems related to their needs and abilities to succeed do exist.

Unique social and emotional needs

Students who are gifted and talented have unique social and emotional needs that teachers should be aware of and work toward meeting. The affective demands of these students include the need to be stimulated through association with peers and through interaction with adult models, and the need to learn to accept their own abilities. Students who are gifted also need to learn to accept their roles as producers of knowledge and creative works; they need to develop habits of inquiry and research, and independence in investigation. It is not uncommon for students who are gifted, and who are not sufficiently challenged by their teachers and the educational experiences they are given, to remain socially aloof, to do just enough in school to get by, and to avoid the difficulty of meeting high teacher and parent expectations.

Communication

High-level communication

Students who are gifted and talented typically communicate at a higher level than their chronological-age peers. They tend to associate with and communicate with other children and adolescents who communicate at their level. Imagine you are listening to student conversations about economic issues in a high school class. Groups can carry on conversations about similar topics at different levels; for example, one group might be talking about the cost of living and about whether they will ever make enough money to live comfortably. Another group might be interested primarily in economic policy, and discuss the ways in which the laws of supply and demand affect the cost of living, the availability of goods, and so on. Because students seek their own levels in communicating, students who are gifted and talented often enjoy conversations with adults or older peers more than other agemates. This has an effect on natural social groupings in and across classrooms and is important to consider when grouping students for instructional purposes. It is also a source of potential problems when students who are gifted and talented are seen as showoffs and alienated by their classmates and peers.

Instructional Approaches and Teaching Tactics

The history of efforts to develop gifts and talents in students is usually traced to the Greeks, who, in working toward full development of the talent of the ablest among their population, established programs for students who were intellectually superior. In today's educational system, students who are gifted and talented are served through two kinds of instructional approaches: enrichment, and acceleration or advancement. General tips for working with students who are gifted and talented using these intervention approaches are presented in Table 7.3.

Table 7.3   Top Ten List of Tips for Teachers of Students Who Are Gifted and Talented

1. Provide alternative instructional activities addressing student interests and preferences, celebrate diversity.
2. Provide guest speakers, field trips, practical demonstrations, and other enrichment activities.
3. Model higher-level thinking skills and creative problem-solving approaches.
4. Develop instructional activities that generate problems requiring different types of thinking and solutions.
5. Allow students to move through the curriculum at their own paces.
6. Identify advanced content and assign independent reading, projects, worksheets, reports, and other enrichment activities.
7. Provide opportunities and an environment for sharing novel ideas and solutions to practical problems.
8. Allow students who are gifted to have input in deciding how classroom time is allocated.
9. Provide and encourage independent learning opportunities.
10. Eliminate material from the curriculum that students have mastered.

To meet the needs of some students, teachers provide enrichment activities that extend their educational experiences *E. Glasgow/ Monkmeyer Press.*

Enrichment programs

The term **enrichment** is used when teachers provide experiences or activities that are beyond the standard curriculum. Early efforts to educate students who were gifted and talented consisted entirely of enrichment efforts; one of the earliest formal enrichment programs was established in the Cleveland public schools in 1922. Students in enrichment programs are given more work or they are given assignments that extend their knowledge beyond what their peers are learning. They usually stay in their assigned classrooms and typically are enrolled in the same grade as their agemates. Enrichment can involve more than within-class tinkering with the curriculum. Students who are gifted can attend special programs at other schools, or they can be allowed to participate in university programs that help extend their learning.

Acceleration programs

Gifted students also have been treated by **acceleration** or **advancement,** sometimes characterized by double promotion, skipping grades, or advanced enrollment in higher-level coursework. This instructional approach is generally one of changing placement (and thus curriculum or level) rather than modification within a placement. In 1867, the St. Louis public schools began a practice of "flexible promotion." This very early effort to provide advancement for students who were gifted and talented allowed them to be promoted early. More recent evidence of advancement is provided in school districts like the Minneapolis public schools, where elementary, middle, and high school students who are gifted and talented are allowed to take courses at the University of Minnesota. In other districts, they participate in after-school classes at the university as evidence of acceleration and advancement.

Point of View

National Association for Gifted Students
Policy Statement on Acceleration

The practice of educational acceleration has long been used to match appropriate learning opportunities with student abilities. The goals of acceleration are to adjust the pace of instruction to the student's capability, to provide an appropriate level of challenge, and to reduce the time period necessary for students to complete traditional schooling. When acceleration has been effective in achieving these goals, highly capable individuals are prepared to begin contributing to society at an earlier age. Although instructional adaptations, such as compacting, telescoping, and curriculum revision, which allow more economic use of time are desirable practices for exceptionally talented students, there are situations in which such modifications are insufficient in fulfilling the academic potential of all highly capable children. Personal acceleration is called for in these cases.

Personal acceleration involves moving a student through the traditional educational organization more quickly and includes such practices as grade skipping, concurrent enrollment in two grades, early entrance into kindergarten or college, credit by examination, combining three years of middle school into two, acceleration in particular content areas, and dual enrollment in high school and college. Students may be accelerated in one discipline or across disciplines.

Research documents the academic benefits and positive outcomes of personal acceleration for carefully selected students. Decisions about the appropriateness of personal acceleration and the extent of acceleration for a given student should include examination of student preferences and disposition relative to the decision, the student's intellectual and academic profile, and social readiness. Other factors which enhance the success of personal acceleration are positive attitudes of teachers, timeliness of the decision, parent support, and the careful monitoring of new placements with a clearly articulated option to return to the earlier setting without penalty.

Opportunities to learn must be offered to all children. Accordingly, highly able students with capability and motivation to succeed in placements beyond traditional age/grade parameters should be provided the opportunity to enroll in intellectually appropriate classes and educational settings.

Source: National Association for Gifted Children, Policy Statement on Acceleration, November 6, 1992.

Enrichment Tactics

Enrichment introduces students to topics and methods of learning not ordinarily available in the standard curriculum. Enrichment tactics can be separated into three subgroups:

Types of enrichment tactics

1. Those that provide students with opportunities to practice and polish skills and content materials that are part of the regular curriculum

2. Those that extend knowledge in content areas that students have studied in the regular curriculum

3. Those that introduce knowledge and skills that are not part of the regular curriculum

Here are some ways to help students who are gifted and talented enrich what they have learned.

Fostering creativity

■ **To practice and polish skills in writing: Use open activities to foster creativity.** At a writing center, write the following categories across a sign, poster, or chalkboard. Provide ten items in each category; four examples follow:

Character	Goals	Obstacles	Results
1. Larry Johnson	1. Fame	1. Disability	1. Graduated
2. Bo Jackson	2. Wealth	2. Publicity	2. Quit Yankees
3. Brooke Shields	3. To be athlete	3. Temper	3. Superstar
4. Michael Jackson	4. College degree	4. Competition	4. Famous

Provide the following directions on a task card:

Directions for Creative Writing Activity

1. Write down your phone number. For example, 555–2214.
2. Drop the first three digits. For example, 2214.
3. Use the last four digits to match the items in each of the four categories. For example, 2214 would be Bo Jackson, Wealth, Disability, Famous.
4. Write whatever story comes to your mind (fact or fiction) using the items your digits match.

Changing location

■ **To practice and polish skills in mathematics: Change the location for learning.** Students at the primary level find facts fun to learn if they must work them out lying on the floor with a flashlight and reading them off the bottom of a table. Older students enjoy taking assignments outside to be completed.

■ **To practice and polish number facts: Combine sports and math.** After the students have mastered basic math facts, relate them to team and individual statistics. For instance, teach students how to compute batting averages, shooting percentages, or won/loss records, and have them keep stats for their favorite teams during appropriate seasons.

Problem-solving games

■ **To practice and polish mathematics performance: Use problem-solving games for application.** Prepare a set of index cards that contain open-ended math problems (see illustration).

Challenge students to use the six boxed numbers once with any math operation (addition, subtraction, multiplication, division) to arrive at a solution as close as possible to the target solution (560). Award points based on proximity to the target solution and have students create their own problems to share with other classes or their classmates.

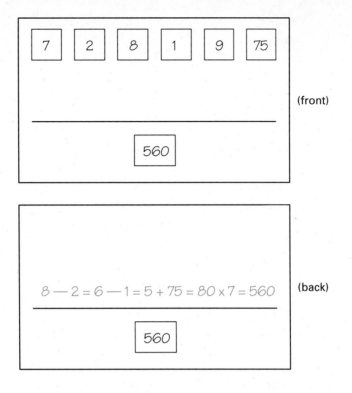

Student research activities

■ **To practice and polish mathematics performance: Use surveys and research methods.** Prepare a list of questions that require the use of estimation and inference. Place each question on an index card (see illustration) with space for a prediction, a description of a method(s) that could be used to arrive at a solution, and a solution. Have students work in teams conducting research to answer the questions. Compare and contrast the solutions found by using different methods.

Field Research Card

98–001

Research question: How many bricks are on the outside structure of the school building?

    Prediction:

    Method:

    Solution:

Sample research questions:

1. How many books are in the school library?
2. How many students' shoes have laces?
3. How close can you get to a bird?
4. How many names are in the white pages of our phone book?
5. How many pieces of popcorn would fill a file cabinet?
6. How many people in school have blond hair?
7. How many people in the city live in brick houses?
8. How many people in the city drive white cars?
9. How many people in school have fall birthdays?
10. How many teachers in school are over 40 years old?

Free-time activities

■ **To extend skills in all academic areas: Use free-time activities to apply learning.** For example, a map reading center can be used to extend mathematics and social studies by stressing solving problems that involve travel. Have students use maps and atlases to plan trips and/or solve problems such as the following:

■ Find where you live on the map. Make an *X* with your pencil. Find a place that is twenty miles from your town.

■ Compute the distance from Springfield to where you live. If your car gets fifteen miles from each gallon of gas, how many gallons would it take to get to Springfield?

■ Find a town that is north of where you live. Circle it with your pencil.

■ Find a town that is south of where you live. Draw a line under it.

Describing observations

■ **To extend skills in creative writing: Prompt use of adjectives and adverbs.** Create a center in which students can develop different methods of observation: a close-up view, a panorama, looking at something through a pinhole in a piece of paper, looking through a concave or convex lens. Ask the students to describe different observations using adjectives and adverbs. Provide a thesaurus and a dictionary. To vary the format of this activity, have students record their impressions on a tape recorder.

On-line computer services

■ **To extend skills in creative writing: Use on-line computer services to learn about other students.** Have students use computer networks (for example, Internet) to find students in other cities, states, or nations to become pen pals for sharing information about their school and life experiences. Prepare personal information sheets on students' backgrounds and special interests when sending or receiving communications on the network. Have students keep records of cities, states, and nations that are part of their creative writing network.

Computer data resources

■ **To extend research skills: Use computer data resources.** Have students choose a topic of interest to them and research it through electronic databases at the library or via computer bulletin board services. As the end product of their research, have them create a computerized multimedia presentation for their classmates or for parent–teacher night.

On-line computer services help teachers meet the needs of students with advanced skills. *Bachmann/Stock, Boston, Inc.*

Arts enrichment

■ **To extend knowledge in social studies: Mix history and the arts.** Illustrate lectures on periods of history with centers depicting artwork from that period. For instance, lessons on American history during the 1920s can be accompanied by an in-depth look at the art of the Works Progress Administration. Encourage students to read about literature, fashion, drama, and architecture from periods of history that are being studied.

Career awareness

■ **To extend knowledge in any content area: Provide career awareness.** Invite people who are actively involved in different careers to meet with the students, not only to talk about their professional fields but also to discuss the specialized methods and tools they use to accomplish their work tasks.

■ **To extend knowledge in any content area: Allow students to add to the curriculum.** Have the students who are gifted and talented review curriculum content to identify outdated information or possible new topics.

Science through literature

■ **To extend knowledge in science: Use literature to develop student interest in science.** Many works of literature, particularly science fiction literature, introduce scientific concepts and discoveries that students can learn about in greater depth. The following is an example of a task card at a center designed to follow up on scientific descriptions found in the science fiction story "Zero Hour" by Ray Bradbury. The center would be appropriate for students who are gifted and talented in any grade.

"Zero Hour"

Ray Bradbury

In this science fiction story, technology of the future is described. Using magazines and journals provided (such as *Discovery, Science Digest, Omni,* and *Smithsonian*), list scientific breakthroughs you believe will affect the world and its population. Choose a few of these breakthroughs and describe how they will affect us. Then group your findings together in categories (for example, methods of communication, travel, satisfying needs, defense). Create labels for each group of technological discoveries in these different areas. For instance, travel may be affected by a group of discoveries entitled "Time Travel" or "Solar Power."

Human resources

■ **To extend knowledge into new areas: Introduce new topics in the classroom.** Using literature in such magazines as *National Geographic, Science Digest,* and *Natural History,* have students who are gifted and talented select a new topic each month and create a learning center based on that theme.

■ **To extend knowledge into new areas: Use human resources.** Create a volunteer, mentor, or community resource file for the class. Have the "human resources" do class presentations describing their professional preparation, activities, and goals. Have them also describe current trends and future needs in their respective areas as a way to introduce students who are gifted and talented to real-world applications for new knowledge. Have students plan the file, locate resource people, interview them, and develop resource file entries.

Ideas for book reports

■ **To extend knowledge into new areas: Use book reporting to stretch learning beyond the regular curriculum.**

1. Use book reporting to extend knowledge; have students

   a. Make a list of things that would make their book better.

   b. Make a list of the interesting words in the book and tell why they are interesting.

   c. Make a list of ten words that tell about the story, and then decide which one of the words tells the most.

   d. Make a list of three different opinions that others might have about the book and the reasons for each opinion.

   e. Write alternative endings to the story in the book.

   f. Write descriptions about the book from the point of view of their favorite character(s) in the book.

2. Use book reporting to encourage forecasting; have students

   a. Predict what someone who reads the book in the future will say about it.

   b. Predict what some historical person would have said about the book if that person had read it.

   c. Predict what a character in another book would say about the book.

    d. Predict what someone older would say about the book.

    e. Locate and list cause-and-effect relations in the story.

    f. Write what might happen in a second version of the book.

Books and drama

3. Use book reporting to encourage dramatic talent; have students

    a. Write or tell how the book is the same as or different from their life.

    b. Present a play based on their book.

    c. Give a class report as they think one of the characters in the book would present it.

    d. Read their book (or a part of it) to a group of younger children.

    e. Give a report to the class the way the author of the book would give it.

Books and art

4. Use book reporting to encourage artistic talent; have students

    a. Draw a series of pictures to retell the sequence of events in their book.

    b. Make an original cover for their book.

    c. Use crayon, chalk, and paint to illustrate a favorite part of their book.

    d. Make a bulletin board display for their book.

    e. Make a comic strip of their book.

    f. Make a poster to "advertise" their book.

    g. Make a diorama based on their book.

    h. Make a mural illustrating their book.

Research in the real world

■ **To extend knowledge into new areas: Use research to solve problems that gifted and talented students might encounter in the real world.** For example, have them plan a family vacation or do some catalog shopping as a way to extend what they are learning in math and social studies.

Task Card

Plan a family vacation. Record the dates you plan to travel, where you plan to go, and how you will get there. Calculate the cost of travel, lodging, and other items.

Task Card

Select a wardrobe for a week's vacation. Calculate its cost, including taxes and shipping charges.

Provide all necessary materials for this activity, such as maps, vacation guides, and catalogs.

Drama and problem solving

■ **To extend knowledge into new areas: Use drama to enrich problem-solving skills.** Have students who are gifted and talented list and describe alternative solutions to a problem, the obstacles to those solutions, and the methods needed to remove those obstacles. Next, have them create sociodramas in which a protagonist must develop a plan of action and overcome specific obstacles to implement the plan. Records, videos, filmstrips, books, and other resources can be used to find examples of protagonists who have fought obstacles to solve specific problems.

Acceleration Tactics

Acceleration involves placing a student in contact with instruction that would normally be encountered at higher grade levels. Acceleration requires structured teacher planning and record keeping to determine areas of the curriculum in which students show particular strengths. The major arguments against acceleration are that moving students ahead does not help them apply knowledge and that it involves merely presenting material students inevitably will study anyway. Acceleration, such as skipping a grade and concurrent enrollment in high school and college, is usually considered an administrative practice rather than an instructional practice to be implemented by a classroom teacher, but here are some ways to use acceleration with students who are gifted and talented.

Alternative assignments

■ **When giving classroom assignments, have students who are gifted and talented start by completing the most difficult items first or by taking a pretest.** Allowing students to complete standard work more quickly reduces the likelihood of boredom and provides opportunities to accelerate individual learning processes. If they demonstrate mastery of the skills being practiced, provide alternative assignments that introduce more advanced material. For example, if students pass a spelling test with a score of 90 percent or higher, have them bypass regular workbook activities and the end-of-week test by selecting one or more of the following alternative activities.

1. Working with another student who also passed the pretest, find ten new words from other textbooks in the room. Study the words together and give each other a spelling test using the new words.
2. Using weekly spelling words and new words, create the smallest set of sentences that you can using all the words.
3. Create a crossword puzzle and key using the weekly spelling words and new words.
4. Create a set of categories into which all the words will fit.
5. Create a set of greeting card messages using all the words.
6. Create riddles with the weekly spelling words and new words as answers.

In addition, use diagnostic instruments in the basic skill areas (for example, reading, language skills, mathematics) to determine which students have mastered grade-level skills and competencies in specific curriculum areas so that more advanced content can be provided.

Bring Your Learning to Life

Instructional Acceleration

Lenny is the student introduced at the beginning of this chapter who has won awards in diverse areas and will enter Harvard when he is 16. Professionals in the school system where Lenny lives recognize that special programs require flexibility to accommodate the varying skills, abilities, and interests of students who are gifted and talented. When planning for individual students, they think in terms of combinations of programs rather than single types of programs. Lenny had the following program alternatives available to meet his needs for instructional acceleration:

Cluster grouping   Students with high ability are placed together in one classroom rather than spread among teachers at a grade level.

Interest grouping   Students with similar abilities and interests are provided opportunities to work together during regular school hours.

Multiage classes   Students with similar abilities are taught together in one classroom rather than spread among teachers at different grade levels.

Grade skipping   Students with high ability are allowed to skip a particular grade and advance to the next.

Telescoping   Students with high ability are placed together in a multiage classroom with the intention of completing two years of work in one academic year.

Acceleration classes   Students with high ability are provided opportunities to enroll in coursework at higher grade levels, at other schools in the system, and at colleges and universities.

During his school career, Lenny skipped several grades, completed third and fourth grade in one year, and always was part of a cluster grouping plan initiated when his superior abilities were first identified. During the last school year, he took advanced calculus at the local university along with other freshman courses.

Resources for multiple levels

■ **Develop units or use resources with multiple starting points and multiple activities.** These will allow students to start and continue their work at different levels according to their abilities, experiences, prior learning, and interests. **Programmed learning,** introduced through commercially designed materials, involves diagnosing students by preestablished instruments and programming them into learning resources at a point at which they demonstrate content mastery. These materials offer skills and objectives prearranged and sequenced on a continuum from simple to complex. **Instructional packages** are less structured; the students select and explore a variety of materials based on interest, selected goals, self-pacing, and individual leveling. As students use programmed learning or instructional package materials, record the skill they have mastered.

Bring Your Learning to Life

Curriculum Compacting Emphasizes Strengths of Gifted Students

In the opening of this chapter, we told you about Nicholas, whose parents almost enrolled him in a special school.

Nicholas's teachers were sympathetic to his feelings of boredom and his passion for writing. They decided to use curriculum compacting as an instructional alternative in his school program. First, they pretested Nicholas in every area of the semester's content. After analyzing his performance, they decided that Nicholas would have an hour a day available for his own work. They arranged for him to use his free time to work on his biography of Eleanor Roosevelt in the library at school.

They also provided free time opportunities for him to spend time with upper-grade teachers who were teaching students about biographies as part of their literature programs. They contacted a local author and provided opportunities for him to review Nicholas's book and discuss ways to improve his writing skills. In explaining the special program to Nicholas's classmates, his teachers stressed the criterion that had to be demonstrated (content mastery) and offered the same opportunities (intensive work on a project of their choice) to all of them. None took advantage of it.

■ **Use advanced tests and curriculum materials.** Obtain sample copies of textbooks and curriculum materials at many different levels to provide challenging and appropriate instructional materials in a variety of subjects.

A classroom talent pool

■ **Develop a talent pool in your classroom.** Encourage individual students to become "experts" or "consultants" on a particular concept, skill, or subject. Have the students prepare a book of "yellow pages" advertising their expertise. Provide a mailbox or separate mailboxes in which students can put questions they have written for the experts. Questions and answers can be recorded, if the students wish. During a group free period (such as just before lunch or before leaving school), the teacher can call on the student experts to share their questions and answers with the class.

Compacts allowing students to "buy" time

■ **Use *curriculum compacting* to provide opportunities for acceleration experiences.** Allow students to "buy" time for acceleration activities when they have demonstrated competence. For example, if a student obtains a score of 90 percent or better on a writing test, he might earn "free time" to work on an independent writing project. If a student demonstrates mastery on a math pretest, she is permitted to buy time doing problems from advanced placement tests. The key to this form of compacting is identifying specific skills students who are gifted and talented have mastered and allowing them to complete alternative activities instead of practicing what they already know.

Current Trends and Issues

Intelligence tests

Public schools did not have widespread programs for gifted and talented students before the development of the first intelligence tests. One of the earliest to be used in the United States was the Stanford–Binet Intelligence Scale, developed by Louis Terman and Maude Merrill. In describing usage of this test, Terman talked about giftedness and gifted people—those who scored in the top 2 percent of the population. Over time, this was operationalized as a score 2 standard deviations above average (standard score of 130 or above) on other intelligence tests. Today, most educators define giftedness by saying that students who are gifted and talented are those who score above 130 on an intelligence test.

Broadening the concept of giftedness

In 1972 an effort was made to broaden the concept of giftedness, and in a report to Congress Sidney Marland offered this definition of children who are gifted and talented:

> Those identified by professionally qualified persons, who, by virtue of outstanding abilities, are capable of high performance. These are children who require differentiated educational programs and services beyond those normally provided by the regular program in order to realize their contribution to self and society. Children capable of high performance include those with demonstrated and/or potential ability in any of the following areas:
>
> 1. General intellectual ability
> 2. Specific academic aptitude
> 3. Creative or productive thinking
> 4. Leadership ability
> 5. Visual and performing arts. (1972, p. 10)

Debates about criteria

Since the early work of Terman, professionals have debated the definition of giftedness and the specific criteria used in assessment of students as gifted. The debates sound very similar to those you will encounter over definitions and criteria used to identify students with disabilities. For example, professionals debate about the criteria for deciding when students do and do not evidence leadership ability, about the standards to be employed in deciding the extent to which a student demonstrates potential ability as an artist or a performer, and about the age at which giftedness can be identified.

Moving beyond intelligence tests

Debates about assessment and identification inevitably involve considerations of intelligence and its value in identifying students who are gifted and talented. Intelligence test scores have dominated selection and placement practices because they are easily used to set cutoffs and to make decisions about who is gifted (for example, individuals with IQ scores of 130 or higher). Recently, the concept of intelligence has been extended to represent more than a score on an intelligence test. Arguing that there are at least two types of giftedness—schoolhouse giftedness measured by performance on tests and creative-productive giftedness evidenced by development of original materials and products—Renzulli (1986) downplayed the importance of intelligence test scores as primary identification measures. Robert Sternberg (1985) argued that giftedness had three aspects. The first is cognitive and internal to the individual. The second is experiential, relating thinking to personal experience to solve problems. Third, a gifted individual may be superior in adapting to, shaping, and selecting experiences. For Sternberg and Davidson (1986a), giftedness comes in several varieties:

> Some gifted individuals may be particularly adept at applying the components of intelligence, but only to academic kinds of situations. They may thus be "test-smart," but little more. Other [individuals who are gifted] may be particularly adept at dealing with novelty, but in a synthetic rather than an analytic sense: Their creativity is not matched by analytic power. Still other [individuals who are gifted] may be "street-smart" in external contexts, but at a loss in academic contexts. Thus, giftedness is plural rather than singular in nature. (p. 9)

Multiple intelligences

Howard Gardner (1983) proposed a "multiple intelligences" (MI) theory in which all normal individuals are capable of at least seven independent forms of intellectual performance: linguistic, musical, logical-mathematical, spatial, bodily-kinesthetic, interpersonal, and intrapersonal. He believed that each could be developed to high levels and that each should be considered in identification efforts.

Clearly, nobody really knows what giftedness is, and there are no objective measures of it. This doesn't matter too much when members of society value giftedness as "arguably the most precious natural resource a civilization can have" (Sternberg & Davidson, 1986, p. ix). It causes problems only when groups of people are overlooked as identification practices are implemented.

Girls and giftedness

The number of girls identified as gifted declines with age, which has caused some professionals to wonder what happens to them (Silverman, 1986, p. 43). One explanation is that behaviors that are valued and measured in gifted identification practices (such as risk taking, competitiveness, and independence) are not fostered in the socialization of girls. Without them, creativity, achievement, and leadership are limited and girls are overlooked in identification practices. Stereotypes and other social factors also work against girls. Our friend Kim Bazan noticed it with Kevin and Chelsea, two of her best students in math. As part of his special education program, Kevin was "pulled out" for three periods a week with the "math specialist." Kim thought Chelsea should also participate. When she asked her principal about it, the principal said she didn't think girls needed math enrichment because eventually their aptitudes for it were replaced by interests and abilities in areas related to "softer stuff," like writing, language, and the arts. Kim pointed out to her that women have been successful in greater and greater numbers in professions traditionally pursued by men largely because schools were no longer fostering such stereotypes. She talked to other teachers and, with her principal's support, started an after-school enrichment program for girls who were gifted in math.

Giftedness and disabilities

When giftedness is associated mainly with high scores on intelligence tests or other unitary criteria, people with limited ranges of performance on these measures are at a disadvantage. Communication disorders, differences in na-

Although underrepresented in programs for gifted and talented, students from minority cultures often demonstrate academic or leadership gifts just like their peers. *Richard Hutchings/PhotoEdit.*

tive language, physical disabilities, learning disabilities, and emotional disabilities can influence individuals' scores on any test. Because of the limitations of most tests and theories of giftedness, they have not been particularly helpful in identification of people with disabilities who are gifted and talented.

People from some groups also slip through the cracks when singular conceptions of intelligence or giftedness are used for identification. Several categories of students are particularly neglected in programs for top students. These include children from some minority cultures and from families experiencing economic disadvantage, students with high IQ scores who do not achieve in school, and students with artistic talent (Office of Educational Research and Improvement, 1993; Reichert, 1987; Saccuzzo, Johnson, & Guertin, 1994). For example, in recent data compiled by the federal government, only 9 percent of students participating in programs for the gifted and talented were in the bottom 25 percent relative to family income (compared to 47 percent from the top 25 percent), and fewer than expected students from African-American, Hispanic, and American Indian families participated (Office of Educational Research and Improvement, 1993). Schools in some states are discouraged from serving these students by rules and regulations that force them to use specific IQ cutoff scores or levels of performance as a basis for identification. Most states encourage the use of test scores because they are easier to determine and "safer" than more subjective and comprehensive measures. Practices based on such principles are often seen as unsatisfactory because of their effects on important, underrepresented groups of students.

Groups neglected in programs for students with gifts and talents

There are no simple solutions to problems facing those who teach students who are gifted and talented (Gallagher & Coleman, 1992; Reichert, 1987; Reis & Purcell, 1993). If you teach, you will have some of these students in your classroom. You may be challenged to make the educational alternatives available for such students work for individuals sometimes overlooked in traditional efforts to reach students who are gifted and talented. Here are a few tips:

Tips for teachers

- Use multiple measures of ability when identifying students for gifted and talented programs.
- Hold high expectations in all content areas for all your students.
- Acknowledge the concept of multiple intelligences and strive to support the "expert" in all your students.
- Avoid sexist, cultural, class, and ethnic stereotypes and discuss them regularly with your students.
- Design career development activities that include successful people from varied groups.
- Expose your students to positive role models from traditional and nontraditional groups.
- Form support groups for students with similar interests.
- Have students read biographies of gifted people from traditionally underrepresented groups.

Gifted and Talented in Perspective

Important teaching practices

In general, teachers of students who are gifted and talented must pay attention to the pace at which these students learn, the depth at which they are allowed to explore topics, and the extent to which the students' own interests are incorporated into lessons and learning activities. There is no magic in deciding where these effective teaching practices are implemented. Everything written about teaching students who are gifted and talented stresses the importance of modifying the curricular content beyond presentation of simple facts, rules, and details to identification of complex generalizations, issues, and solutions to problems. Classroom teachers of students who are gifted and talented generally gain time for extension activities by modifying regular classroom assignments, involving students in independent or group activities, and structuring assignments to allow content enrichment. Their hope is the same as that of other teachers—that their efforts to meet the individual needs of their students will enable them to lead productive and valuable lives.

Effects of educational reform

A climate of educational reform has engulfed America's schools. Calls for richer and deeper experiences for students are seen as ways to combat our loss of economic competitiveness in the world. New organizational structures are placing teachers and schools under increasing pressure to produce outcomes and bolster evidence of accountability. More and more children are coming to school from diverse ethnic and linguistic backgrounds, forcing teachers to place more importance on the context of their work than ever before in history (Ogbu, 1992). This climate of interest and action will have a positive effect on educational programs for the nation's most talented students if communities value intellectual and artistic accomplishment and support schools and teachers in fostering it. For this communitywide support to occur, education professionals who see the need have provided direction for some serious educational reform (see Office of Educational Research and Improvement, 1993).

Establishing high standards

First, challenging curriculum standards must be established, and the responsibility for challenging students who are gifted and talented to achieve them must be shared by teachers and other members of society. As state and local education agencies develop standards for student performance, they must ensure that ceilings for performance are raised for students who are capable of the highest levels of achievement.

Making opportunities available

Second, opportunities that meet the needs of children who are gifted and talented must be available. These experiences must be provided inside and outside of school buildings, and be diverse enough to accommodate the varied skills and talents of these students. Providing in-depth work to extend knowledge in core curriculum areas, accelerating the rate at which core curriculum is presented and mastered, enrolling in special classes that enhance interests in specific areas, and providing work experiences within the local community are examples of how new opportunities will be provided.

Extending efforts to younger children

Third, teachers, parents, and other professionals must look for strengths and potential in younger and younger children. Schools and community agencies must work with parents to help them learn, and provide ways to nurture their children and help them achieve in school. Schools need to extend their spheres of influence to preschool programs in the community; such efforts should be directed at ensuring that strengths identified in preschool are extended into elementary, middle, and high school programs.

Reducing barriers for cultural and economic minorities

Fourth, opportunities for children from minority cultures and from families experiencing economic disadvantage must be expanded. Barriers to achievement that are common for many of these children must be overcome. Hindrances to participation in programs for students who are gifted and talented that are currently experienced by many of these children must be eliminated.

A vision for schools of the future

Finally, schools of the future must adopt a vision that fosters a richer curriculum for all students, supports each student's potential, and encourages teachers to develop their own talents and those of every student. Toward this goal, the following perspective on "excellent schools" describes what education for all students should be (Office of Educational Research and Improvement, 1993, p. 29):

■ All children progress through challenging material at their own pace. Students are grouped and regrouped based on their interests and needs. Achieving success for all students is not equated with achieving the same results for all students.

■ Diversity is honored in students' backgrounds as well as in their abilities and interests. The classroom, school organization, and instructional strategies are designed to accommodate [and value] diversity and to find strengths in all children.

- Students know that parents, educators, and other important adults in their lives set high expectations for them and watch them closely to ensure that they work to their ability and develop their potential.

- The community provides the resources needed to adapt and enrich the curriculum to meet student needs. School faculty and administrators ensure that community and school resources are matched with students' strengths and needs.

- Students gain self-esteem and self-confidence from mastering work that initially seemed slightly beyond their grasp.

- Students emerge from their education eager to learn and confident that they can join the intellectual, cultural, and work life of the nation.

Opportunity for all

Everybody wins in such schools. All students have similar opportunities for developing skills and demonstrating performance. All teachers are expected to nurture and support learning, and they are rewarded for doing so. All parents see growth in their children as a result of the teaching and learning that goes on in their schools. That's the way education should be, and society would benefit from it.

What Every Teacher Should Know

- Students who are gifted and talented are known more for their contributions and potential contributions than any other group of students.

- Terms used to refer to students who are gifted and talented are generally favorable, but these students may also experience problems in school, such as boredom, alienation from peers, and pressures to do well in all areas of performance.

- A variety of characteristics have been identified in students who are gifted and talented. Most reflect outstanding performance in cognitive, academic, behavioral, or related areas.

- For many students, giftedness does not extend across all school subject areas.

- Successful teaching approaches usually stress the attainment of higher levels of understanding, not just greater repetition of facts.

- Two primary types of instructional approaches—enrichment and acceleration—are used by teachers and other professionals to help these students be successful in school and later life.

- Continuing concerns for teachers and other professionals working with students who are gifted and talented are identification, cultural diversity, and the inclusion of populations that have been underrepresented in the past. Teaching students who are gifted and talented means being aware of these problems and their potentially detrimental effects on special education programs.

Projects

1. Imagine that you are a teacher with several students who are gifted and talented in your classroom. What decisions would you make to help these students be successful? What instructional approaches would be appropriate for working with them? What specific activities would you use to enrich a lesson you were teaching to your class on dinosaurs?

2. Attend a parents' group that is concerned with education of students who are gifted and talented. List the topics that are discussed. Interview at least three parents to obtain their overall impressions of the services provided by the school system to their children.

3. Write a brief paper explaining what you know about teaching students who are gifted and talented. Include the following information: definition, characteristics, prevalence, and interventions that could be used in any classroom to improve the educational program being provided.

4. Pick a topic that would be appropriate to teach a group of elementary, middle, or high school students. Plan an instructional presentation that you could use to teach basic content and extend students' knowledge and thinking skills related to the topic.

5. Think about two people who you think are gifted and talented. List five different characteristics for each person that support your opinion that they are gifted and talented. List five characteristics that illustrate similarities between these two people.

6. Review the names of Gardner's seven multiple intelligences. Think of ways you would identify students exhibiting one type and not the others. Think of people you know who have developed high levels of performance in one of the areas but not others. Write down your impressions of this theory and share them with a friend.

For Your Information

Books

Blume, J. (1993). *Here's to you, Rachel Robinson.* New York: Orchard Books.

Expelled from boarding school, Charles's return home proves disruptive especially for his sister Rachel, a gifted seventh-grader juggling friendships, school activities, and adolescent development.

Clark, B. (1983). *Growing up gifted.* Columbus, OH: Merrill.

An overview of education considerations for students who are gifted and talented, including identification and programming in elementary and secondary schools, and a chapter on areas of concern in gifted education.

Kerr, B. A. (1985). *Smart girls, gifted women.* Columbus, OH: Ohio Psychological Publishing.
A collection of case studies and other information about an often underrepresented group of students who are gifted and talented.

Parke, B. N. (1989). *Gifted students in regular classrooms.* Boston, MA: Allyn & Bacon.
An overview of identification, programs, and curriculum considerations, including case studies illustrating applications in different content areas (for example, mathematics, language arts, science, social studies).

Parker, J. P. (1989). *Instructional strategies for teaching the gifted.* Boston, MA: Allyn & Bacon.
Overview of cognitive, affective, and creative strategies with applications for content area instruction.

Smutny, J. F., Veenkner, K., & Veenkner, S. (1989). *Your gifted child.* New York: Ballentine.
Excellent book for parents, teachers, and other professionals interested in learning about identification, characteristics, and educational programs for students who are gifted and talented.

Wright, B. R. (1991). *The scariest night.* New York: Holiday House.
When her family decides to spend the summer in Milwaukee so that her adopted brother can perfect his genius at a special piano school, Erin finds herself concerned with jealousy and turns to a medium for help.

Organizations

American Association for Gifted Children (AAGC)
This is an advocacy group that supports parents, children, and educational programs. It promotes awareness and supportive activities for people who are gifted and talented. For more information, contact AAGC, 15 Gramercy Park, New York, NY 10003.

The Association for the Gifted (TAG)
A division of the Council for Exceptional Children (CEC), TAG encourages membership of professionals interested in program development and preparation activities related to educating individuals who are gifted and talented. TAG provides outlets for the exchange of ideas through a variety of resources, including a professional journal (*Journal for the Education of the Gifted*). For more information, contact CEC, 1920 Association Dr., Reston, VA 22091.

National Association for Gifted Children (NAGC)
Membership in this association includes parents, teachers, and other professionals interested in programs for people who are gifted and talented. With *Gifted Child Quarterly* and other resources, NAGC is a primary agency for information, materials, guidance, and networking advice for those working with the gifted and talented. For more information, contact NAGC, 1155 15th Street NW, Suite 1002, Washington, DC 20005.

Journals

Gifted Child Quarterly (GCQ)
This publication of the National Association for Gifted Children provides articles that describe research-based program evaluations, program descriptions, and other research-oriented activities. Articles published in GCQ are intended to further the knowledge base and to improve the lives of people who are gifted and talented. For more information, contact *Gifted Child Quarterly,* 1155 15th Street NW, Suite 1002, Washington, DC 20005.

Journal for the Education of the Gifted (JEG)
This journal is a publication of the Council for Exceptional Children's Association for the Gifted. Its purpose is to provide a forum for presentation of current research related to individuals who are gifted and talented, and to provide information about teacher training and programming. Articles published in JEG are intended to further the knowledge base and to improve service to individuals who are gifted and talented. For more information, contact James J. Gallagher,

Editor, University of North Carolina, 300 Nations Bank Plaza, Chapel Hill, NC 27514.

Roeper Review (RR)

This publication focuses on practical suggestions for improving programs for the gifted and talented.

Occasionally this journal publishes thematic issues in which all the articles address a central topic such as assessment or cultural diversity in gifted and talented education. For more information, contact Roeper City and County Schools, 2190 North Woodward, Bloomfield Hills, MI 48013.

Chapter

8

Teaching Students with Learning Disabilities

- What definition is used for students with learning disabilities?
- How many students with learning disabilities receive special education?
- What are the primary characteristics of students with learning disabilities?
- What instructional approaches and teaching tactics are appropriate for students with learning disabilities?
- How do learning disabilities relate to attention deficits and hyperactivity?
- What are some of the challenges and opportunities for educators in the field of learning disabilities?

Mark is a fifth grader with a learning disability. His school performance illustrates the pattern evident in most students with learning disabilities. He has had difficulty learning to read since the first grade. Now he can read third-grade material reasonably well, but he still has problems comprehending what he has read. His spelling is a little better than his reading, but his handwriting is still very messy and immature. Like most students with learning disabilities around the country, Mark spends most of his time in a general education classroom with his neighbors and peers. His teacher describes him as "likable and very interested in learning." She says his classmates sometimes complain about his constant questions and occasionally avoid him during independent activities, free time, and recess. She is working on improving Mark's peer relations. Mark is earning passing grades in math, science, and social studies with assistance provided by general and special education teachers in the forms of taped texts, modified tests, and a homework buddy.

"Hidden disabilities"

Puzzling is a term teachers use to describe students like Mark. Some people say these children have "hidden disabilities" because their strengths in some areas often mask or hide learning problems in others. You might remember a person in one of your schools who seemed quite bright, but who had trouble mastering information or skills that came easily to others. Some of these people, like Mark, had trouble reading; others did poorly in spelling. Still others could read and spell well but made frequent errors in math. These people are sometimes identified as students with **learning disabilities.** Teachers tell us that these children do not learn in the same ways or as easily as others their age. They say that these students have special needs that sometimes cause problems in large classes in which most other students perform reasonably well with only minor assistance. The goal of these teachers is to modify instruction so that all their students will learn.

Definition

Although no definition of learning disabilities is universally accepted, each state delivers services to students called learning disabled (LD) or one of its substitute terms (such as *perceptual and communication disorders*). Most states use the federal definition or a definition that will produce an "equivalent population." According to the latest federal guidelines implemented under the Individuals with Disabilities Education Act, *specific learning disability* means

Bring Your Learning to Life

Taped Text Helped Mark Compensate for His Reading Problems

Mark's teachers have found that tape recording passages from his content area textbooks is an effective way to help him compensate for his learning disability. They conducted an informal assessment to determine if he learned best with or without the actual text in front of him as he listened to the tape. He did better just listening.

Next, they decided what material to record and prepared the tapes. In some cases, they recorded only key sections of the text; in others, they recorded entire chapters and passages. Sometimes they added tips to the tapes to encourage Mark to review the material after critical sections or remind him to take notes on important parts of the lessons. One time they spliced comprehension questions in to provide practice recalling facts during the lesson; Mark reported that this strategy was very helpful. Whenever possible, the teachers had classmates do the actual taping during independent work times.

a disorder in one or more of the basic psychological processes involved in understanding or in using language, spoken or written, that may manifest itself in imperfect ability to listen, think, speak, read, write, spell, or to do mathematical calculations. The term includes such conditions as perceptual disabilities, brain injury, minimal brain dysfunction, dyslexia, and developmental aphasia. The term does not apply to children who have learning problems that are primarily the result of visual, hearing, or motor disabilities, of mental retardation, of emotional disturbance, or of environmental, cultural, or economic disadvantage. (CFR34, 300.7, b–10)

Criticism of the definition

When this definition was proposed, it was seen as vague and unacceptable to many professionals. Three problems were most troublesome. First, it separated the field into groups who supported the importance of identifying underlying causes of learning disabilities (such as psychological processing disorders) and those who did not. Second, the definition's reference to children alienated adults with learning disabilities. Third, professionals argued that the definition created confusion with its ambiguous "exclusion clause." Many professionals would have preferred a clear statement that learning disabilities can exist with other disabilities but cannot be the result of them.

Criteria for identification

To address some of these concerns, the U.S. Department of Education has also specified criteria to be used in identifying students with learning disabilities. First, the decision must be made by a team of professionals, each having different experiences with and assessment information from the child. The team must determine if the child does not achieve at a level judged appropriate in one or more of the following areas: listening comprehension, oral expression, written expression, basic reading skill, reading comprehension, mathematics calculation, or mathematics reasoning. In making this decision, the team searches for a discrepancy between academic achievement and intellectual ability in at least one area. A child is not identified as having a specific learning disability if the discrepancy between ability and achievement is primarily the result of another disability such as a visual, hearing, or motor disability; mental retardation or emotional disturbance; or perceived environmental, cultural, or economic disadvantage.

Expected versus actual achievement

Disagreement about criteria

The central indicator used to identify students with specific learning disabilities is a discrepancy between expected and actual achievement. Expected achievement is predicted using tests of intellectual ability, such as IQ tests. By comparing scores on IQ tests and achievement tests, professionals decide if variations in academic performance (for example, an ability to do math but not reading) are sufficient to justify special education. This criterion has been the source of considerable problems in the field because professionals cannot agree on the magnitude of the difference between expected and actual achievement that is necessary for a student to be identified with specific learning disabilities. Some states use one grade level and others use at least two; some states use 15 standard score points and others use 23 or 30. When the specific criteria vary, different numbers and types of students are provided special education services.

Despite the debate over specific criteria, students identified with learning disabilities are generally those who are performing poorly in some academic area. They show a discrepancy between actual performance and the level at which professionals and parents think they should achieve. They are the largest group of students receiving special education in America's schools.

Prevalence

About 4 percent of the population between the ages of 6 and 21 has received special education services under the category of specific learning disabilities in recent years (U.S. Department of Education, 1993). This is a large group (about 1 or 2 in every class of 25–35) of students. Of the 4.5 million school-age students who receive special education, nearly half (2.25 million students) are included in the specific learning disabilities category. Among students with disabilities, this is the largest group currently being identified and provided special education services. Most students with learning disabilities are served in general education settings (22.5 percent), where they spend less than 21 percent of the school day outside their regular classrooms, or resource rooms (53.7 percent), where they spend from 21–60 percent of the school day outside their regular classrooms.

The largest category of students with disabilities

Rapid growth in the category

Since the passage of Public Law 94–142, the number of students served in special education in the category of specific learning disabilities has more than doubled. The proportion of these students among all students with disabilities has also increased by over 100 percent. This level of increase has not occurred

Table 8.1	Percentage Distribution of Students with Specific Learning Disabilities (LD) in the United States		

State	All Disabilities[a]	LD[b]	LD as Percent of All Disabilities
All states	7.81	3.90	49.9
Alabama	8.99	3.56	39.6
Alaska	9.67	6.11	63.2
Arizona	6.38	3.78	59.3
Arkansas	7.62	4.33	56.8
California	6.55	4.00	61.1
Colorado	7.14	3.83	53.6
Connecticut	8.97	4.80	53.5
Delaware	8.56	5.25	61.3
District of Columbia	5.77	3.32	57.5
Florida	9.05	3.96	43.8
Georgia	6.28	2.00	31.9
Hawaii	5.05	2.91	57.6
Idaho	6.91	4.15	60.1
Illinois	8.30	4.06	48.9
Indiana	8.14	3.39	41.7
Iowa	8.35	3.93	47.1
Kansas	7.13	3.13	43.9
Kentucky	7.72	2.65	34.3
Louisiana	6.38	2.78	43.6
Maine	9.07	4.21	46.4
Maryland	7.99	4.14	51.8
Massachusetts	11.21	4.10	36.6
Michigan	6.97	3.36	48.2
Minnesota	6.97	3.09	44.3
Mississippi	8.15	4.22	51.8

(continued on next page)

with any other condition. Actually, growth in the category of specific learning disabilities has occurred along with decreases in other categories. For example, the percentage of students with mental retardation has been cut in half since 1977 (see Figure 1.3 on page 19).

A state-by-state breakdown is presented in Table 8.1. For each state, the first column of numbers shows the percentage of school-age children with disabilities; the second column indicates the percentage who have learning disabilities; and the last column shows those with learning disabilities as a percentage of all those with disabilities. Look at the last column. Nationwide, students with learning disabilities make up approximately half (49.9 percent) of all those with disabilities. Yet, state by state, that percentage ranges from about 32 percent in Georgia to over 60 percent in Alaska, California, Delaware, Idaho,

Wide variation among states

Table 8.1 Percentage Distribution of Students with Specific Learning Disabilities (LD) in the United States *(continued)*

State	All Disabilities[a]	LD[b]	LD as Percent of All Disabilities
Missouri	8.33	4.26	51.1
Montana	8.15	4.71	57.8
Nebraska	8.49	3.89	45.8
Nevada	6.80	4.14	60.9
New Hampshire	7.78	4.63	59.5
New Jersey	10.48	5.54	52.7
New Mexico	9.02	4.45	49.3
New York	7.63	4.62	60.6
North Carolina	7.64	3.61	47.3
North Dakota	7.15	3.61	50.5
Ohio	7.78	3.01	38.7
Oklahoma	8.19	4.18	51.0
Oregon	8.03	4.36	54.3
Pennsylvania	7.50	3.39	45.2
Rhode Island	9.03	5.82	64.5
South Carolina	8.22	3.51	42.7
South Dakota	7.28	3.48	47.8
Tennessee	8.89	4.83	54.3
Texas	7.73	4.55	58.9
Utah	8.06	4.26	52.9
Vermont	7.55	3.72	49.3
Virginia	7.86	4.19	53.3
Washington	6.94	3.41	49.1
West Virginia	9.43	4.39	46.6
Wisconsin	6.77	2.23	32.9
Wyoming	2.77	1.51	54.5

[a] Percentage of school-age population (ages 6 to 21) receiving special education in all disability categories.

[b] Percentage of school-age population receiving special education in the category of specific learning disabilities.

Source: U.S. Department of Education. (1993). *Fifteenth annual report to Congress on the implementation of the Individuals with Disabilities Education Act.* Washington, DC: Author.

Nevada, New York, and Rhode Island. This variation occurs because, as we pointed out, the definition and the criteria for identifying learning disabilities vary from state to state. Nevertheless, the overall trend for learning disabilities—steadily increasing numbers in the category—holds true for most states.

The rapid growth in the numbers of students with learning disabilities has caused concern for people in special education. There are several explanations for the growth. In 1983 the National Association of State Directors of Special

Explanations for the category's growth

Education attributed the increase to (1) improved procedures for identifying and assessing students, (2) liberal eligibility criteria, (3) social acceptance/preference for the learning disabled classification, (4) cutbacks in other programs and lack of general education alternatives for children who experience problems in the general classroom, and (5) court orders making other classifications more difficult to justify. The impact of these factors differs from state to state, accounting for some of the percentage variation shown in Table 8.1. If we had to choose a single general explanation for the increase in the learning disabilities category—an explanation that best interprets school and social trends as well as the research we and others have conducted on this issue—we would say that fewer students were achieving at expected levels in general education and that identification with specific learning disabilities had become the preferred way to get help for them.

Characteristics

Students with learning disabilities may be identified at any age, but most are first noticed in early elementary school grades. One feature provides a basis for identification at any age: Teachers and parents become concerned when a child's school performance reflects a discrepancy between expected and actual achievement. It is illustrated in a bright, verbal child having difficulty learning the names of the letters of the alphabet, remembering the names of classmates, or learning to count to twenty. Teachers and parents also suspect learning disabilities when a child is performing well in reading but very poorly in math and handwriting, or when a student might do very well with written examinations but be unable to express ideas verbally. Often the discrepancy is reflected in scores on tests (for example, a fifth-grader performing at the third-grade level in mathematics or a second-grader whose reading level is below first-grade level). In addition to this primary feature, a number of other characteristics of learning disabilities have been identified. We have placed them into cognitive, academic, physical, behavioral, and communication groups.

Cognitive

Processing problems

Most professionals believe that students with learning disabilities have average or above average intelligence with specific cognitive, thinking, or psychological processing problems. These include problems remembering things, problems discriminating or differentiating visual or auditory perceptions, and problems developing and using cognitive strategies. Students having difficulty remembering what they have seen or heard will likely experience difficulty in school. Both visual and auditory memory problems have been associated with specific learning disabilities.

Perceptual problems

Students with learning disabilities may also experience perceptual problems such as left–right orientation, figure–ground differentiation, pattern discrimination, body image difficulties, symbol recognition, and auditory association (associating sounds with symbols). Professionals have had considerable difficulty, though, developing adequate measures of these tasks and even more

Students with learning disabilities look like other students but show discrepancies between ability and achievement scores on standardized tests. *Elizabeth Crews.*

difficulty showing that improving perceptual problems produces related improvements in academic performance.

Deficiencies in learning strategies

Students with learning disabilities are said to fail to develop and use cognitive learning strategies such as organizing learning tasks and learning how to learn. There is evidence that successful learners employ a set of self-monitoring and self-regulating strategies that are absent or deficient in students with learning disabilities. These students are said to lack awareness of the skills, strategies, and steps necessary to solve problems or complete tasks, and to have difficulty evaluating the effectiveness of what they do.

Academic

Students with learning disabilities perform more poorly in school than expected by their teachers or parents (on the basis of their experience working with the child, the child's past performance, or performance on an intelligence test). Generally, this discrepancy is identified by comparing performances on standardized achievement tests and tests of intelligence. A discrepancy between ability and achievement is the primary characteristic associated with this group of students, but there is considerable debate about just how poorly a student must perform before he or she is identified with a specific learning disability. This debate translates into other interesting (mostly philosophical rather than practical) debates, such as "Can students who are gifted and talented have specific learning disabilities?" and "Can a student with mental retardation have learning disabilities?"

Use of tests for identification

Physical

Students with learning disabilities look like students who do not have learning disabilities. Sometimes teachers of younger students report that they are clumsier and more awkward than their peers and that some demonstrate poor physical coordination and motor abilities. These children may have good large-muscle coordination but difficulties in fine-motor coordination. Many of the tests used by schools to screen for learning disabilities include copying and tracing exercises to help teachers identify younger students who need remediation in these areas.

Behavioral

Problems of inattention and hyperactivity

Inability to attend to tasks (attention problems) and high rates of seemingly purposeless activity (hyperactivity–impulsivity) are behavioral characteristics commonly associated with learning disabilities. Students must attend to what is going on, whether listening to a teacher lecture, keeping their place in a book they are reading, or shifting attention among tasks when classroom activities change. Students with learning disabilities may have difficulty coming to attention, focusing attention, and sustaining attention. The terms used to describe their behavior are terms like *inattentive, hyperactive, impulsive, daydreamer, overly energetic, erratic,* and *distractible. Inattention, hyperactivity, distractibility,* and *impulsivity* as well as *disruptiveness* and *immaturity* are terms that have been used in behavioral profiles of students with learning disabilities. Professionals working with these students are not sure whether these

Cause or result?

characteristics are causes for low academic achievement or the results of it, because many students with learning disabilities exhibit none of these behaviors at all and many students without learning disabilities do exhibit them. These characteristics also are associated with attention deficit–hyperactivity disorder (ADHD) and cause confusion for professionals making differential diagnoses with this group as well. We discuss attention deficit–hyperactivity disorder later in this chapter.

Social problems

Doing poorly in school is also related to problems with social behaviors and peer acceptance. Some of these characteristics include a lack of judgment in social situations (such as sharing personal information with strangers), difficulty deciding how others feel, interpersonal problems, problems establishing family relations, lack of social competence in school, and low self-concept.

Communication

Language difficulties

At the preschool level, language problems are the most common characteristics found in students with learning disabilities. Many of these children often do not talk as well as expected, do not talk like their older brothers or sisters did at the same age, or do not respond adequately to statements and instructions. These discrepancies between expected and actual language performance are also evident in older students with learning disabilities who may have difficulty listening, speaking, defining words, and formulating linguistic constructions.

Teachers, professionals concerned with speech and language problems, parents, and other professionals who work with these students often focus their efforts on these oral language difficulties. At other times, they focus their work on written language difficulties.

Instructional Approaches and Teaching Tactics

Use of direct instruction

The single, most fundamental characteristic of students with learning disabilities is a significant discrepancy between expected and actual performance in at least one academic content area. For this reason, academic instruction is the primary area in which students with learning disabilities require assistance. Effective teachers provide direct instruction for skills these students need to know, and organize their instruction to help these students use their strengths and make up for their weaknesses. They use the same components of effective instruction as other teachers but modify their instruction to remediate problems of their students with learning disabilities or to help them compensate for skills they have not mastered. Providing extra instruction to a fifth-grader who has not mastered his multiplication facts is an example of the kinds of remedial instruction needed by some students with learning disabilities. Administering unit tests orally is an example of how a teacher might help a student compensate for her learning disability in reading. A summary of general interventions used by teachers with students with learning disabilities is presented in Table 8.2.

Students with learning disabilities sometimes also need help with classroom behaviors such as task avoidance, inattention, and hyperactivity. Many have trouble organizing their time and using effective study skills; some have difficulty getting along with their peers. Improving behavior and social relations is also part of effective teaching tactics used with students with learning disabilities.

Improving Basic Skills

An imperfect ability to listen, think, speak, read, write, spell, or do mathematical calculations is a defining feature for students with learning disabilities. Improving these basic skills is a primary objective in teaching these students.

Reading

Analytical reading programs

Most elementary school programs rely on analytical approaches or experience-based, whole-language approaches when teaching students to read. In analytical programs, beginning readers are taught a systematic method for decoding words. Students are taught skills for attacking or breaking down words, then they practice their decoding skills with words at appropriate instructional levels. Some analytic approaches rely on word families (*at: cat, fat, rat, hat, sat*—"The cat sat on the hat of

Table 8.2 Top Ten List of Tips for Teachers of Students with Learning Disabilities

1. Provide alternative assignments to help students compensate for academic weaknesses.
2. Help students focus on relevant aspects of assignments.
3. Use concrete examples and demonstrations when teaching new content.
4. Provide opportunities for students to progress at their own rate.
5. Modify assignments to help students compensate for academic weaknesses.
6. Provide more opportunities for practice than those required by peers.
7. Provide instructional aids (for example, calculators, fact tables, spelling dictionaries) to help students compensate for academic problems.
8. Provide substitute materials with lowered reading level in content area instruction.
9. Modify tests and evaluation measures to compensate for learning problems.
10. Provide opportunities for self-monitoring.

Whole-language programs

the fat rat.") as the backbone for beginning reading instruction and the construction of meaning or comprehension from what is read. In whole-language programs, reading is integrated with other communication skills, especially writing. Students are taught reading skills by actually using them rather than by learning and practicing word identification skills. In a whole-language classroom, teachers model reading and writing by reading aloud and telling stories to their students. Students choose some of their own reading and writing topics, and varied reading materials are present in their classroom libraries. Whole-language instruction relies on reading and writing about actual personal experiences rather than contrived stories or assignments as its fundamental learning and meaning construction experience.

Throughout history, educators have debated the value of word analysis versus experience-based methods of reading instruction. On the one hand, effective, skillful readers must know how to identify words; on the other hand, reading meaningful texts certainly enhances reading instruction. Moreover, the view from the field is becoming more forceful:

> The research ... gives ample evidence that we do, indeed know a great deal about beginning reading. Yet the divisiveness over code-emphasis [analytic approaches] versus meaning-emphasis [experience-based approaches] rages on. Isn't it time to stop bickering about which is more important? Isn't it time that we recognize that written text has both form and function? To read, children must learn to deal with both, and we must help them. (Stahl, Osborn, & Lehr, 1990, p. 123)

Whatever general approach is used for reading instruction in your school, here are some specific ways to help students with learning disabilities.

Computers and word processing programs are being used to improve writing skills in many classrooms. *Martin R. Jones/Unicorn Stock Photos.*

Students create word lists

■ **To improve sight word recognition: Have students produce their own reading practice sheets.** Provide lists of simple words (for example, *need, cheer, light*) and have students make new lists by adding word parts to each root word (*needy, needed, unneeded, cheery, lightly*). To make the activity more fun and integrate it with math, challenge students to find a specified number of words (such as 10, 20, or 30) and have them keep track of their performance using weekly graphs. After the lists are completed, have students read theirs to a classmate. An alternative activity is to provide students with a word (such as *harvest*) and have them find other words by rearranging the letters (*vest, rest, tar, hat, hear, hare, tare, tear, rate, rats, vase, aster, earth, stare, hearts, starve*).

Computer practice

■ **To improve sight word recognition: Have students practice with computer programs.** Software like *Reader Rabbit* (The Learning Company) and *Word Munchers* (MECC) can help students learn decoding principles. Such programs provide repeated practice in formats that are highly motivating to some students.

Repeated readings

■ **To improve reading rate and comprehension: Use repeated readings of the same passage.** Select a passage of 50 to 150 words at a level that is easily read by all students. Have them read their passages orally three or four times and keep track of the time required for each repeated reading. Also have them read their passages silently at least once a day. The goal for many students with learning disabilities is simply to practice reading on a more frequent basis. Repeated reading with high degrees of accuracy is an effective means of accomplishing this goal.

Phonetic cues

■ **To improve reading recognition: Add cues to help students remember phonetic rules.** Marking long vowels or combinations (rēad, rēēd), crossing out silent let-

Bring Your Learning to Life

Test Modifications Helped Mark Compensate for His Reading Problems

Mark lives in North Carolina. Education personnel in his state believe that students with disabilities may need alternative test formats, aids, or a different test environment to demonstrate accurately their achievement strengths and weaknesses. There are guidelines in North Carolina that permit these special arrangements to be part of testing programs for students receiving special education; most states have similar guidelines.

Mark's teachers decided that he performed best when he took tests in a separate room away from his classmates. They arranged for him to complete multiple-choice unit tests in the library with supervision by the school librarian. When special machine-scorable answer sheets were part of the testing procedure, they allowed Mark to answer in the test booklet and later transferred his responses to the computer form. They broke longer test sessions into shorter ones and allowed some extra time for Mark to complete his exams. They also used a couple of alternatives to compensate for Mark's poor handwriting. On short-answer tests, they allowed Mark to dictate his answers to another student. On essay

tests, they arranged for Mark to use a computer and word processing program to record his responses. On classroom tests, they lowered the readability level of the items so Mark's reading problems were less likely to influence his performance.

Examples of Test Questions with Lowered Readability

Original Item
    Compare and contrast the super powers and lifestyles of Batman and Superman.
Revised Item
    How are Batman and Superman alike? How are they different?

Original Item
    Earthquakes are produced by what underground conditions?
Revised Item
    What causes earthquakes?

Original Item
    List four environmental requirements for the growth of spores.
Revised Item
    List four things spores need to grow.

---

ters (tak¢), and dividing words into smaller parts (com|·|pre|·|hen|·|sion) can be very helpful for some students. Make up assignments with 15 or 20 practice words and have students read them at home for additional practice.

Thematic units

■ **To improve reading comprehension: Use thematic units to encourage social interaction and integration of reading with other areas of instruction.** Reading activities such as vocabulary study, study guides, spelling, comprehension activities, and reading guides can be incorporated into a thematic unit on seasons, months of the year, holidays, outer space, farm animals, great literature, the continents, and other timely topics. An integrated thematic unit on outer space might include having children write stories; draw constellations and label them;

write narratives of a space creature; list facts about the earth and its features; experiment with light, air, and water; create illustrations of night and day in different parts of the world; and create a creature from another planet. The goals should be to increase interest and comprehension of content as well as practice reading while learning about an integrated topic.

Interactive computer materials

■ **To improve reading comprehension: Use interactive computerized reading materials.** A single electronic book can contain the text of a story, pictures, sound effects, and movie clips of important scenes. The multimedia elements provide extra clues for comprehending the text. Typically the student can "click" on an unfamiliar word to get further information about it, either visually or auditorily.

Writing to improve reading

■ **To improve reading comprehension: Use writing to improve reading.** Have students identify relevant facts and list them on a sheet after they have read a short passage. Have them prepare an abstract using the facts. Review the abstracts and original passage. The practice of recalling facts and preparing a rewritten summary improves comprehension. Preparing an outline of main ideas and supporting details after reading a passage accomplishes the same thing.

■ **To improve reading comprehension: Use prompts and cues to help students focus on relevant content.** Select a reading passage that describes a central character engaged in some activity and use the following questions as prompts for students to use while reading the passage:

Questions as prompts

> Who is the story about? Who is the central character?
> What does the central character do?
> What happens when the central character does it?
> What happens in the end?

Using a minitest

■ **To improve reading comprehension: Make a reading assignment into a minitest that provides practice answering comprehension questions.** Have the student read several sentences and answer questions about the information provided in them before reading the next section.

Example of Minitest to Improve Comprehension

Just about every Boy Scout learned what to do for a snakebite: Cut open the wound and suck out the venom. Detailed instructions showing how to cut the bite marks with a sharp knife and how to pull the venom out were included in the Boy Scout handbook.

> *Minitest 1*
> 1. What did Boy Scouts learn to do for a snakebite?
> 2. Where were detailed instructions for this?

I never knew a Scout who was bitten by a snake so I never knew if this would really work. I never tried it myself. I'm glad I didn't because now scientists say it is a bad idea to suck venom out of a snakebite.

> *Minitest 2*
> 1. When was the author bitten by a snake?
> 2. Should you suck the venom out of a snakebite?

Teacher modeling

■ **To foster interest in reading: Show students that reading is important and has value by reading to them.** Teacher modeling of appropriate reading behaviors also provides students with demonstrations of expression, fluency, interest, enjoyment, and variety. This helps students become more confident in selecting reading materials that meet their interest, skills, and needs.

Classroom centers

■ **To improve interest: Use centers to make classrooms engaging environments for students with learning disabilities in reading.** Classrooms that are "literate environments" teach students to value written words and encourage them to share language in ways that promote positive attitudes toward reading. Have a center for each content area of instruction: math, writing, reading, science, and social studies. Have manipulatives related to current areas of instruction at each center. Display books related to lesson themes and have plenty of writing materials available to encourage students to write or draw as a center activity. To encourage students to use print and recognize its importance in their lives, label the items in the center as much as possible. Through the use of centers, many teachers encourage students with learning disabilities to feel comfortable making choices, taking risks, and experimenting with print media rather than constantly trying to avoid them.

■ **To improve motivation and interest: Provide opportunities for students to read materials they can't refuse.** Use a variety of reading activities to capture students' interests and encourage reading practice. When selecting materials, remember that reading something is better than reading nothing and reading anything is better than not reading everything, even the most wonderful reading passages. Here are some examples of nontraditional reading materials that capture the interest of many students with learning disabilities:

Nontraditional reading materials

1. Have students bring in cassette or compact disc covers of their favorite stars. Build reading activities around information on the covers and lyrics provided by the artists to accompany their recordings.

2. Develop an interview sheet with questions about interests, hobbies, and special activities. Have students conduct interviews with each other. Create a scrapbook of completed interviews and have it available for students to read whenever they are interested in it.

3. Survey students to determine their ten favorite TV shows. Ask a group of students to prepare a summary of the results using a line graph. Have another group write a synopsis of the top ten shows. Distribute a copy of the synopsis to each student. Have students watch as many of the shows as possible and rate each one using a simple scale (for example, good, fair, poor). Have another group of students summarize the results of the class ratings and distribute a "guide for viewing" for other class members or classes to read.

Researching an author or artist

■ **To deepen interest in reading: Provide opportunities for older students to develop detailed knowledge about an author or famous person.** For example, have students select an author or artist who was misunderstood and read a book about his or her life. Then have them find short stories, films, or videos to provide additional information about the person. Have them provide a report detailing facts about the person's life, draw inferences about what the person's life was like and how it was reflected in the person's work, and describe how the person's life might be different today or at another time in history.

Math

Low achievement in mathematics is less common than low achievement in reading. Yet for many students with learning disabilities, computation and analytical reasoning are the major areas of learning difficulties. The following activities have been used to help students with learning disabilities in mathematics.

Cues and organizers

■ **To reduce distractions and improve accuracy: Provide cues and organizers to focus attention.** For example, mark student worksheets with vertical and horizontal lines and place math problems in the squares created by them. This helps students with learning disabilities keep track of their progress and find their place a little easier. Some teachers also use answer blocks and other cues to help these students complete math problems.

$$
\begin{array}{cccc}
\boxed{1} & \boxed{}\boxed{} & \boxed{} & \boxed{8} \\
23 & 547 & 62 & 9\overset{1}{2}3 \\
+\ 39 & +\ 293 & -\ 47 & -\ 781 \\
\hline
\boxed{6}\boxed{2} & \boxed{\ }\boxed{\ }\boxed{\ } & \boxed{\ }\boxed{\ } & \boxed{\ }\boxed{\ }\boxed{\ }
\end{array}
$$

Assignment modifications

■ **To focus attention and reduce distraction: Modify assignments.** Reduce the number of problems presented on a page if students are reluctant to complete a worksheet. Have them complete a longer sheet by finishing several smaller assignments with in-between breaks. For example, if a student has 20 math problems to complete, four or five mini-assignments of 4 or 5 problems each are more likely to be finished than one with all 20 problems on it.

Multiple opportunities

■ **To improve accuracy: Provide multiple opportunities for success.** Define mastery in a new way (such as 100 percent correct after being told a previous attempt has errors in it). Have students try to achieve mastery with less than three retries.

Manipulatives

■ **To improve knowledge of basic facts: Use manipulatives.** Beans, blocks, game chips, stickers, paper clips, and other small objects are useful in helping students learn relationships between numbers and what they mean.

Real-life applications

■ **To make math meaningful: Use real-life problems and applications.** Set up a class checking account and use it to help students with learning disabilities learn about money and math related to it (for example, adding and subtracting credits and debits). Have students write checks to be used in a classroom store.

Basic problem-solving concepts

■ **To improve problem solving: Teach basic concepts and have students practice using them.** For instance, teach students with learning disabilities to look for clues in word problems. Words such as *altogether, sum,* and *plus* usually mean the problem requires addition. *Spent, remains, left,* and *lost* are used frequently in subtraction problems.

Simplify structure

■ **To improve performance: Simplify structure and content of assignments.** Make complex work easier by changing words. Solving word problems can be difficult when the vocabulary and writing style being used are above students' reading levels. Reducing the number of words in a sentence from 15 or 20 to 5 or 6 can have a positive influence on the performance of students with learning disabilities. Reducing the reading level by changing words like *remainder* to *how many left* can also help these students.

Activities that are fun

■ **To improve interest and motivation: Use activities that make math fun.** Students with learning disabilities at all grade levels often report "hating" math. Effective teachers use "tricks" to keep these students interested in math calculations and their applications.

Left to Right Addition (a "tricky" way to add)

53	Start with the first number at the top of the left-
17	hand column and call it by its "tens name" (50).
24	Add each number in the left-hand column to each
+ 19	preceding number using the "tens names" and
113	continue down the ones column.

$(50 + 10 = 60 + 20 = 80 + 10 = 90 + 3 = 93 + 7 = 100 + 4 = 104 + 9 = 113)$

Written Language

Along with listening, speaking, and reading, written language is an important part of any language arts program. Because so many children have problems with reading, many also experience difficulties with writing or written expression in general. Teachers working with students with written language problems have found the following tactics useful.

Quantity before quality

■ **To improve written products: Focus on quantity before quality in written work.** Students with learning disabilities often produce minimal amounts of written work when asked to demonstrate their writing skills, or they produce large numbers of grammatical errors when their written work is evaluated. By encouraging students to write as much as possible without concern for errors, many teachers achieve quantitative improvements that become a source for qualitative changes in their instruction. For example, have students write as many words as they can as a brief, timed exercise. Provide an option that the words can be related, but don't require it. Provide an option that the words can be in sentence form, but don't require it. At the end of the work period, count the number of written words and record the performance on a chart or graph. Repeat the activity on the subsequent days and encourage students to improve their writing by producing more words, by writing more correctly spelled words, by writing more complete sentences, or by writing about a topic.

Checklists

■ **To improve written products: Use checklists to guide students before they write.** Simple features differentiate well-prepared written work from writing that causes negative impressions. Many students with learning disabilities do not know what these features are, and many others simply fail to attend to the mechanics of writing. Preparing a simple checklist for students to use to evaluate a report or writing assignment can improve the overall quality of their work. Decide which features are important. For example, some teachers are concerned about form as well as content. They want written products to reflect appropriate use of headings, references, and style. Others are more concerned about the visual appearance of written work, such as absence of unnecessary marks, clean erasures, and word or page limits. Whatever your pleasure, letting students know about it and helping them evaluate their work before turning it in will greatly improve their performance.

Targeted skills and self-monitoring

■ **To improve written products: Teach specific skills and have students monitor their written work.** Composition skills are teachable, and written products are improved by using them. Targeted composition skills (for example, use of action words, action helpers, or describing words) should be taught using teacher-guided practice lessons. Students should then be asked to monitor their own written products ("Did I use action words?" "Can I use more describing words?" "Did I tell how the action was done?").

Familiar words

■ **To improve spelling: Use familiar words for practice.** Teach students to look for familiar words as they think of correct spellings. Common sight words that have at least five rhyming words and a similar spelling pattern (*big: pig, rig, jig, dig,* and *fig)* serve as targeted spelling vocabulary. Have students read the rhyming words and teach them a simple rule to use when spelling them ("When words rhyme, the last parts are often spelled the same"). Give spelling tests using the rhyming words to improve the confidence of students with learning disabilities.

Using technology

■ **To improve written expression: Use computers and word processing tools**. Many teachers report that writing instruction is easier for students with learning disabilities when they use computers as the primary means for producing written products. Many of these students are more receptive to revising their work when they can do it with a word processing program, and the work produced on a computer is easier to proofread and edit for students and teachers. Using computer-assisted grammar checkers or spelling checkers is also appealing to students with academic problems commonly associated with learning disabilities. There are also software tools to help students brainstorm and organize their ideas before writing. Some programs guide students through the entire writing process, from brainstorming through revision. Desktop publishing software, which allows students to create newsletters and other in-class publications, can boost their motivation to produce high-quality final products.

Improving Classroom Behavior

Although inappropriate behavior is not a primary characteristic of students with learning disabilities, they often exhibit work habits that interfere with productive academic performance. Many years of school failure often cause students to have very limited study skills and self-management skills.

Work Habits

Given an opportunity to complete a school assignment, many students with learning disabilities respond with statements or actions that deter them from completion of the task. Task avoidance and nonattention can be improved by the following tactics:

Reward attention

■ **To improve attention: Reward students who are attending.** Before an independent assignment is distributed to the class, jot down several times to call for a work stoppage to pass out rewards for students who are working appropriately. Set the times at random rather than fixed intervals (say, 10:35, 10:41, 10:55 rather than 10:35, 10:45, 10:55). Start with small time intervals and gradually increase them as student behaviors improve.

Self-monitoring of behavior

■ **To improve attention: Use self-monitoring.** Teach students to monitor their own behavior. Prepare a tape-recorded sequence of tones spaced at intervals that reflect the target student's levels of attention (for example, 35 seconds, 45 seconds, 38 seconds; or 2 minutes, 3 minutes, 4 minutes). Have the student use the tape as a cue to make a self-monitoring response (when the tone sounds, the student responds to a checklist [see below] question: Was I paying attention?). Reward improvements in attending that result from self-monitoring.

Was I paying attention?

Morning

1 _____	2 _____	3 _____	4 _____	5 _____	
6 _____	7 _____	8 _____	9 _____	10 _____	of 10 = __ %
1 _____	2 _____	3 _____	4 _____	5 _____	
6 _____	7 _____	8 _____	9 _____	10 _____	of 10 = __ %

Afternoon

1 _____	2 _____	3 _____	4 _____	5 _____	
6 _____	7 _____	8 _____	9 _____	10 _____	of 10 = __ %
1 _____	2 _____	3 _____	4 _____	5 _____	
6 _____	7 _____	8 _____	9 _____	10 _____	of 10 = __ %

Cues to focus attention

■ **To reduce distractibility: Use cues to focus attention.** Place written or pictorial cues (such as "Start here ➜ " or "Continue working after a brief rest") at appropriate places in an assignment to help students with learning disabilities focus their attention and improve their behavior.

Reward other class members

■ **To reduce inappropriate behavior: Reward appropriate behavior in others.** Keep track of specific behaviors used by students to avoid doing work (for example, sharpening pencils, visiting rest room, staring out the window). Reward other class members when a target student is exhibiting a task-avoiding behavior. By observing that task avoidance results in the loss of something positive, many students with learning disabilities try to control their behavior in the future.

Daily report cards

■ **To reduce inappropriate behavior: Use daily report cards.** Inform parents that their child will be bringing a "report card" home each day. Have them call for a verbal report if the written report is ever "lost." Keep track of inappropriate behavior (such as nonattention) as well as appropriate behavior (such as time on task) and note improvements on graphs kept in the classroom and at home.

Study Skills

Many students with learning disabilities don't use study time effectively. They may have disorganized study skills or simply fail to listen carefully to directions or ask appropriate questions about assignments. To help students to use class time and study more effectively:

Budgeting time

- **Teach students to budget their time.** Develop a schedule that divides class periods into shorter time frames. Help students make a list of tasks to be finished during each time frame. Encourage students to develop their own time schedules and keep track of improvements in grades and classroom behavior on a classroom chart.

Signals for help

- **Provide signals for students to gain teacher attention.** Some students have not learned alternative strategies for getting a teacher's attention, so they don't bother to ask for help when they need it. Use signals or signs to help these students. For example, a small HELP sign that can be flashed when needed can be a useful means for a student with learning disabilities to let a teacher know he needs assistance. Encourage students to personalize their signs and they'll be more likely to use them.

The "worst" and the "better"

- **Practice and discuss appropriate school behavior.** Select a school situation related to studying (for example, forgetting an assignment) and discuss the "worst" thing that a student can do if it happens. Have students generate "better" solutions and keep track of efforts to practice them.

- **Use care when giving instructions.** State directions for assignments and classwork clearly and concisely. Include only essential information and have students repeat expected behavior (for example, fill in the blank with the right answer) before beginning to work.

Teaching organization

- **Teach students how to organize.** Show them how to set up an assignment book and how to arrange a notebook to be efficient. Periodically check notebooks and assignment pads and provide remedial instruction as needed. Don't assume students with learning disabilities have acquired these skills on their own or that they will learn them from one instructional session.

Group projects

- **Group students to encourage completion of assignments.** Have students work together on a project and accept completed work only when all group members have finished their assignments. Encourage students in a group to share effective work habits and study skills.

Improving Social Relations

Many students with learning disabilities have difficulty interacting with classmates and peers. They are not as effective as their peers in initiating and maintaining appropriate social relations. The problems often result from the behaviors of students as well as from the attitudes of others toward them. To improve social relations of students with learning disabilities:

Valuing diversity

- **Change attitudes with information.** Words and actions provide a model for student behavior. Knowledge about students with learning disabilities should be

Bring Your Learning to Life

Homework Buddies Helped
Mark Improve His Study Skills

Mark always had problems remembering assignments and completing homework on time. Because he was not the only one in his class who had this problem, his teachers decided to do something about it. They divided the class into groups of five students each. One student from each group was assigned to be team leader each day of the week. Near the end of each school day, the teachers called on the team leaders to contact their group members and review homework assignments and progress on long-range projects (for example, upcoming book reports, science fair projects). They used a simple checklist to keep track of what they were doing. Although Mark didn't always complete his homework, he did improve, and he enjoyed being part of the team and serving as team leader at least once a week.

Homework Checksheet   Week of _____

Team Name: _____

Team Members: _____
(Put initials in the spaces provided after homework check has been made)

Monday   _____ _____ _____
            _____ _____

Tuesday   _____ _____ _____
            _____ _____

Wednesday   _____ _____ _____
            _____ _____

Thursday   _____ _____ _____
            _____ _____

Friday   _____ _____ _____
            _____ _____

---

shared with classmates. Care should be taken not to provide excuses for inappropriate behavior or develop a sense of helplessness in students who are exceptional, but to encourage students to value diversity and accept each other as individuals with strengths and weaknesses.

Alternative ways to communicate

■ **Provide alternative means for communicating.** Some students with learning disabilities resist classroom discussions and interpersonal interactions because they are afraid of failure. Teachers overcome this resistance by providing variety in the ways students can communicate in their classrooms. For example, sometimes students talk into tape recorders about their problems rather than telling the teacher personally. Others profit from keeping interactive diaries with the teacher and their classmates.

Group activities

■ **Initiate group activities to foster socialization.** Arrange for a group spelling test and pair a withdrawn student with a more competent one. Have a rule that each group member (initially two people) must spell at least one word on the test. Gradually increase the size of the group and the amount of interaction required by each member.

Group activities help students with learning disabilities improve their social skills. *Tony Freeman/PhotoEdit.*

■ **Force interaction with structured activity.** Arrange for the socially isolated student to be the keeper of a desirable classroom item (for example, a favorite free-time game or record). Have students who want the item interact with the isolated student when they want to use it.

Demonstrating appropriate behavior

■ **Demonstrate and reward appropriate behavior.** A variety of appropriate social interaction skills can be taught to withdrawn students by having classmates demonstrate the behaviors to them. This is best accomplished by arranging for the behavior to be modeled and rewarded in the presence of the isolated child.

Varied, inclusive activities

■ **Provide opportunities for varied social activities.** Active participation of students in daily activities can improve interpersonal relations. Identify skills, hobbies, general interests, and individual experiences of all students (usually they are eager to share them). Plan group activities so that isolated as well as popular students are included.

Progress reports

■ **Share evidence of social interaction.** Keep track of improvements in interaction skills and send progress reports home on a regular basis.

■ **Highlight similarities as well as differences among students.** Sharing information on strengths and weaknesses helps all students. Many of the characteristics of students with learning disabilities are similar to the characteristics of other students in the classroom. Differences are only differences if students and teachers make them differences.

Window on Practice

"The Preacher" in the Resource Room

As a resource room teacher, I work with high school students who have learning disabilities. The majority of students in my class come from very poor economic environments. Many have no parental support and they haven't been taught social and moral ethics. Their academic needs often come second to their social needs. Along with meeting the academic and vocational needs of my students, I spend a great deal of time addressing their social needs and counseling them.

I teach my students to think for themselves, believe in themselves, and always be in tune with themselves. Throughout the year we take class time and have heart-to-heart talks about whatever they want to discuss. Some of the topics we've addressed this year include drugs, sex, the service, college, abuse, peer pressure, and cheating. My students call me "The Preacher" because they say I preach to them about everyday things of life that no one has sat down and discussed with them before. I don't mind the name—I think it's quite fitting. One of my students last year told me that I was the first teacher to care about him as a person, not just as a student.

The only difference I see between my job and that of a regular classroom teacher is I sometimes spend more time counseling than teaching because my students' social needs are so great. Don't get the idea that I skimp on covering the academic competencies I'm required to teach: I spend a great deal of time preparing my students so that they can do as well in their mainstreamed classes as in their resource room classes. But a lot of times I think educators overlook the social needs of students. If I need to address them during class time, then I'll do that because in the long run, I know that my counseling is going to be just as helpful to them as my teaching. The way I see it, a child can't be taught new tricks until he or she understands the old tricks—or, another way of putting it, a child can't understand where he's going until he understands where he comes from.

Some of the major concerns I have about educating exceptional students center on their teachers' willingness to listen to them and to help them make their own decisions. Many exceptional students are not informed about postsecondary opportunities, and those who are often get the information too late. They may

(continued on next page)

Learning Disabilities and ADHD

Focus on inattention and hyperactivity

Within the past few years, much professional and parental attention has been focused on problems associated with inattention and hyperactivity in children. The terms **attention deficit disorders (ADD)** and **attention deficit–hyperactivity disorder (ADHD)** have been frequently used. According to the American Psychiatric Association (APA), people with attention deficit–hyperactivity disorder show developmentally inappropriate degrees of inattention, impulsiveness, and hyperactivity. Associated features are said to include low self-esteem, mood instability, low frustration tolerance, academic underachievement, problems with social relationships, and temper tantrums. The disorder is said to be common, occurring in as many as 3 percent of children not currently classified and receiving special education. Because these same characteristics (attention problems and hyperactivity–impulsivity) are found in students with learning

Window on Practice

"The Preacher" in the Resource Room (continued)

find out that they can go to college and receive financial aid, but if this information is not available to them until late in their secondary education, there may not be enough time for them to prepare for a college program right after graduation. Teachers need to spend time ensuring that students are adequately informed about opportunities. Moreover, teachers need to listen more carefully to exceptional students expressing their career preferences and to work with them in selecting a course of study that will help them reach their goals.

Anthony Wolfe is one student who has helped me learn a lot this year. He has helped me understand that even I need to work on listening to students more. At the beginning of the past school year, Anthony wanted to take an Algebra I course and I talked him out of it, saying, "No, you go ahead and take the Competency Math course." Halfway through the year I started to think that I hadn't made the best choice for Anthony. At the end of the year I knew I'd made a mistake. Anthony was talking about going to college and he had discovered

that math requirements for college include Algebra I, Algebra II, and Geometry.

Anthony will have to attend summer school to pick up the math he needs for college. I limited Anthony by not listening to what he was trying to tell me. I realize that my students and I can learn a lot from each other. I usually tell them this at the outset of the school year because I want them to feel comfortable with me. I want to be of help to them in any way they need.

Students with learning disabilities can lead successful lives—they can go on to college if that is what they want to do. One of my primary goals as a teacher of exceptional students is to help them realize that it is okay to have a learning disability and to have to learn information differently. I hope they will learn to see that this disability does not have to control them, that they can use strategies to help them control it.

Mabel Hines is a resource room teacher of students with learning disabilities at Terry Sanford Senior High School, Fayetteville, North Carolina.

disabilities, recent professional concern has turned to differentiating learning disabilities from attention deficit–hyperactivity disorder, but little progress has been made.

Definitions of ADHD

There is no federal category or definition for students with attention deficit–hyperactivity disorder. The most widely accepted definition(s) appeared in the *Diagnostic and Statistical Manual for Mental Disorders* (DSM) of the American Psychiatric Association. The first categorization of characteristics that have become known as attention deficit–hyperactivity disorder appeared in DSM-II and was called "Hyperkinetic Reaction to Childhood" (American Psychiatric Association, 1968). In DSM-III, fourteen characteristics were organized into three groups—inattention, impulsivity, and hyperactivity (American Psychiatric Association, 1980)—which received considerable criticism because of the complexity created for professionals trying to differentiate among them. This led to a single list of fourteen characteristics associated with attention deficit–hyperactivity disorder in DSM-III-R (American Psychiatric

Activity and attention levels vary considerably in most classrooms and sometimes students are viewed as needing special education because of it. *Michael Dwyer/Stock, Boston, Inc.*

Association, 1987) and paved the way for the latest efforts to define attention deficit–hyperactivity disorder in DSM-IV (McBurnett, Lahey, & Pfiffner, 1993).

Characteristics associated with attention deficit–hyperactivity disorder are similar to those associated with learning disabilities (see Table 8.3). For example, inattention, hyperactivity, and impulsivity are key behavioral characteristics associated with learning disabilities and "clinically significant distress or impairment in academic functioning" is an analogous phrase for "significant discrepancy between ability and achievement." Moreover, interventions prescribed for students with attention deficit–hyperactivity disorder are often used with students with learning disabilities (for example, training or shaping appropriate behaviors, reducing inappropriate behaviors, creating stimulating learning tasks, and using varied instructional activities).

Professionals concerned with students with attention deficit–hyperactivity disorder offer the following "principles of remediation" for improving inattention, excessive activity, and impulsivity (Children with Attention Deficit Disorders, 1992):

Principles for teaching students with ADHD

Inattention

- Decrease the length of the task.

  Break one task into smaller parts to be completed at different times.

  Give two tasks with a preferred task to be completed after the less preferred task.

  Give fewer spelling words, math problems.

Table 8.3	Criteria for Attention Deficit–Hyperactivity Disorder

A. Either (1) or (2):

(1) Six or more of the following symptoms of inattention have persisted for at least 6 months to a degree that is maladaptive and inconsistent with developmental level:

Inattention

(a) often fails to give close attention to details or makes careless mistakes in schoolwork, work, or other activities

(b) often has difficulty sustaining attention in tasks or play activities

(c) often does not seem to listen when spoken to directly

(d) often does not follow through on instruction and fails to finish schoolwork, chores, or duties in the workplace (not due to oppositional behavior or failure to understand instructions)

(e) often has difficulties organizing tasks and activities

(f) often avoids, dislikes, or is reluctant to engage in tasks that require sustained mental effort (such as schoolwork or homework)

(g) often loses things necessary for tasks or activities (e.g., school assignments, pencils, books, or tools)

(h) is often easily distracted by extraneous stimuli

(i) often forgetful in daily activities

(continued)

Use fewer words in explaining tasks (concise and global verbal directions).
Use distributed practice for rote tasks, rather than mass practice.

■ Make tasks interesting.
Allow work with partners, in small groups, in centers.
Alternate high and low interest tasks.
Use overhead projector when lecturing.
Allow child to sit closer to the teacher.

■ Increase novelty especially in later time periods of longer tasks.
Make a game out of checking work.
Use games to over-learn rote material.

Excessive Activity

■ Do not attempt to reduce activity, but channel it into acceptable avenues.
Encourage directed movement in classrooms that is not disruptive.
Allow standing during seatwork, especially during end of task.

Table 8.3	Criteria for Attention Deficit–Hyperactivity Disorder *(continued)*

(2) Six or more of the following symptoms of hyperactivity–impulsivity have persisted for at least 6 months to a degree that is maladaptive and inconsistent with developmental level:

Hyperactivity

(a) often fidgets with hands or feet or squirms in seat

(b) leaves seat in classroom or in other situations in which remaining seated is expected

(c) often runs about or climbs excessively in situations in which it is inappropriate (in adolescents or adults, may be limited to subjective feelings of restlessness)

(d) often has difficulty playing or engaging in leisure activities quietly

(e) is often "on the go" or often acts as if "driven by a motor"

(f) often talks excessively

Impulsivity

(g) often blurts out answers before questions have been completed

(h) often has difficulty awaiting turn

(i) often interrupts or intrudes on others (e.g., butts into conversation or games)

B. Some hyperactive–impulsive or inattentive symptoms that caused impairment were present before age 7 years.

C. Some impairment from the symptoms is present in two or more settings (e.g., at school [or work] and at home).

D. There must be clear evidence of clinically significant impairment in social, academic, or occupational functioning.

Source: Excerpted from DSM-IV (1994).

- Use activity as reward.

  Give activity reward (errand, clean board, organize teacher's desk, arrange chairs) as individual reward for improvement.

- Use active responses in instruction.

  Use teaching activities that encourage active responding (talking, moving, organizing, working at the board).

  Encourage daily writing, painting, reading, responding to academics.

  Teach child to ask questions that are on-topic.

Impulsivity

- Give the child substitute verbal or motor responses to make while waiting and where possible encourage daydreaming or planning in the interim.

  Instruct the child on how to continue on easier parts of task (or do a substitute task) while waiting for teacher's help.

  Have the child underline or rewrite directions before beginning or give magic markers or colored pencils for child to underline directions or relevant information.

  Encourage doodling or play with clay, paper-clips, pipe cleaners while waiting or listening to instruction.

  Encourage note taking (even just cue words).

If you teach, you will likely have at least one student whose behavior is characterized by symptoms associated with inattention, hyperactivity, or impulsivity. Sometimes the student(s) will be identified with specific learning disabilities, sometimes with attention deficit–hyperactivity disorder, and sometimes with another condition. The federal category of "other health impairments" (see Chapter 13) may be used for a student with attention deficit–hyperactivity disorder. Sometimes the student will not be classified at all. Paying attention, listening, following directions, sitting still, playing quietly, waiting, concentrating, and remembering are difficult for many students, especially when what they are being asked to do competes with other more interesting activities (as far as they are concerned). Take heart, for although the research into these issues may be complicated, in actuality there's not much mystery here. Stimulating, active lessons often go a long way in focusing the attention and controlling the activity of *many* of these students.

Current Trends and Issues

As our discussion of attention deficit–hyperactivity disorder demonstrates, it has always been difficult for professionals to differentiate learning disabilities from other conditions. Originally, by defining learning disabilities as a specific condition, professionals hoped to reduce some of these problems. But since the beginning of the field of learning disabilities in 1963, it has been difficult to arrive at a definition that met with wide acceptance. When in 1977, federal officials specified a definition that focused on underlying psychological processing disorders and discrepancies between abilities and achievement, they were met with the following criticisms:

Definitional problems

1. All of us have "imperfect abilities" in some areas and thus can be considered learning disabled.

2. Underlying psychological processing disorders (for example, visual perception, figure–ground discrimination, memory) are difficult to assess. Some professionals do not believe they are appropriate targets for instruction.

3. People have trouble differentiating students with learning disabilities from students with emotional disturbance, mental retardation, or attention deficit–hyperactivity disorder, and learning disabilities can coexist with other problems.

4. Discrepancies between ability and achievement scores are technically inadequate, simplistic, and misleading, lead to a focus on single areas of disability, and are systematically biased against identification of students who earn low scores on intelligence tests.

5. Professionals can't agree on the magnitude of discrepancy necessary for identification with specific learning disabilities.

Changing definitions

Criticism of the federal definition led to formation of the National Joint Committee for Learning Disabilities (NJCLD), an organization made up of representatives from the major professional organizations in the field. In 1981 that committee proposed a new definition of learning disabilities that stressed the general nature of problems grouped under the term *learning disabilities*. In 1984 the Association for Children and Adults with Learning Disabilities adopted a definition that broadened the scope of the problem beyond academics. Most recently, yet another study group (one appointed by the National Institutes of Health) proposed to Congress a new definition of learning disabilities. The new definition extends learning disabilities to the area of social skills and makes an effort to express the relationship between learning disabilities and attention deficit–hyperactivity disorder.

Continuing debates

Professionals are not yet united on whether to include psychological process disorders or socioenvironmental influences or attention deficit disorders in the definition of learning disabilities. They also are not united in their stance on whether students who have other kinds of conditions (like mental retardation, emotional disturbance, blindness, or giftedness) can be included in the category of specific learning disabilities. Some have tried to address this lack of unity by indicating that there may be more than one type of learning disability.

Subtypes of learning disabilities

In the recent definitions, *learning disabilities* is considered an umbrella term. It is referred to as a "heterogeneous" condition or a "generic term." Some now propose specific *subtypes* of students with learning disabilities. For example, Chalfant and Kirk (1984) describe two kinds of students: those with "academic learning disabilities," like disabilities in reading, arithmetic, spelling, and writing; and those with "developmental learning disabilities," which are disorders or dysfunctions in the processes or abilities necessary to acquiring academic skills. These disabilities can include deficits or disorders in attention, memory, perceptual-motor functioning, perception, thinking, or language. James McKinney (1984, 1988) describes seven subtypes of students with learning disabilities. The first five subtypes include those with (1) attention deficits, (2) conduct problems, (3) withdrawn behavior, (4) low positive behavior, and (5) global behavior problems. McKinney's final two subtypes relate to students who behave normally but have elevated scores on measures of specific personality traits. Such subtyping is a relatively arbitrary process. We have found it difficult to use in any practical way, such as planning specific instructional interventions, and misleading to teachers.

Varying eligibility criteria   Definitions for specific learning disabilities vary from state to state. Sometimes eligibility criteria vary among school districts within states. This means that a student receiving special education services in one district could move to another and no longer be eligible for them. Finding the best definition is one of the challenges that continues to face professionals working with people with learning disabilities. Developing appropriate and effective programs for adults with learning disabilities is another.

Transition questions   Information on what happens to students with learning disabilities after school (for example, how many attend college, find successful employment, are successful in transition to adulthood) is relatively sparse. This area will likely become important in the future as the large number of students classified as learning disabled during the 1980s and 1990s age out of school. Studies show that adults with learning disabilities are often concerned about problems with social and occupational skills that are taken for granted by people who have been successful in school. Often they report anxiety about their jobs and believe they need to improve their interpersonal relations and recognize their limitations more than their colleagues, and work harder and longer. As the large numbers of students with learning disabilities grow up and leave school, support services for transition and the world of work will continue to grow in importance.

Learning Disabilities in Perspective

There are many competing viewpoints on how to define learning disabilities and about who is learning disabled. At the same time, there is agreement that these students do not perform as well as they might in school. There is also reason to believe they might have an internal cause of their difficulties, can have other disorders in addition to a learning disability, and need special education services. There is continuing debate in the professional literature about how best to define and identify students with learning disabilities, and there is considerable variability among states in the numbers of students identified and served in this category. Although very many traits and characteristics have been attributed to students with learning disabilities, and students who are identified as learning disabled do demonstrate many of them, no characteristics are universal and specific to the condition.

Lack of universal or specific characteristics   Many of the students who experience significant learning disabilities or disorders *do* demonstrate many of the cognitive characteristics we have described above. Yet not all students who exhibit learning disabilities show these characteristics. Moreover, many children who have no difficulty whatsoever learning in school (students considered normal) evidence the characteristics as well. Some students who are considered mentally retarded, emotionally disturbed, speech and language impaired, deaf, blind, and otherwise disabled show the same characteristics. Most characteristics associated with poor performance in school are not universal (evidenced by *everyone* who is said to be learning disabled) or specific (evidenced *only* by students who are said to be learning disabled). Use of liberal eligibility criteria sometimes leads to faulty reasoning:

Students with learning disabilities have memory problems.

McGillicuddy has memory problems.

Therefore, McGillicuddy is a student with learning disabilities.

By the same token, someone might offer the following reasoning:

Dogs like steak.

You like steak.

Therefore, you are a dog.

Inappropriate labeling

Inappropriate labeling created by misapplication of an overly simplified identification process and liberal eligibility criteria remains a fundamental concern for professionals in special education. Recall that the learning disabilities category increased by more than 100 percent since 1977. Although growth at similar levels is unlikely in the future, you can expect to find students with learning disabilities in every grade in any school where you teach.

What Every Teacher Should Know

- Learning disabilities is the most rapidly growing area in special education.
- The term was first used in 1963 to describe students having difficulties in school who had no other obvious disability.
- Although there is no one, universally accepted definition, students with learning disabilities exhibit significant academic difficulties that cannot be attributed to any other special education condition and that cause them to need extra assistance to be successful in school.
- A variety of characteristics have been identified in students with learning disabilities, but the most common is a specific and significant discrepancy between ability and achievement in at least one area of academic functioning.
- Learning disabilities are sometimes called hidden problems because children with them often have strengths that mask weaknesses in specific areas.
- Students with attention deficit–hyperactivity disorder exhibit many of the same characteristics as students with learning disabilities, and many of the interventions used with them are appropriate for these students as well.
- Many different types of instructional approaches and teaching tactics are used by teachers and other professionals to help students with learning disabilities be successful in school and later life.

Projects

1. Visit a professor at your school who teaches coursework in the area of learning disabilities. Obtain answers to the following questions:

a. What definition is used by school districts for identifying students with learning disabilities in [your state]?

b. How many students with learning disabilities are there in [your state]?

c. What special courses are taken by teachers being certified in learning disabilities?

d. What are some specific activities that teachers use to remediate reading problems of students with learning disabilities? What activities do they use for math problems? For written language problems?

2. Select a journal that focuses on students with learning disabilities. Browse the most recent issues in your library. Find at least three articles that describe specific teaching activities that you could use to improve the reading skills of a student with learning disabilities. Find at least three articles that describe specific teaching activities that you could use to improve the mathematics skills of a student with learning disabilities. Prepare a notebook entry summarizing each activity.

3. Contact a local, state, or national organization that focuses on people with learning disabilities. Identify the purpose of the organization, its membership, and its services.

4. Look in the Yellow Pages of your local phone book for people or agencies that provide after-school tutoring. Call several and ask about the services they provide and how they work with teachers to meet the needs of students with learning disabilities and their families.

5. Using Table 8.1 as a source, list the percentages of students with specific learning disabilities in your state and a few neighboring states. Compare the figures and come up with three reasons for any variation that you identify.

6. Contact the following organizations for materials on attention deficit–hyperactivity disorder and prepare a summary for your files.

Ask your librarian to order a copy of the videotape and/or books for use in keeping the campus community current on this common school problem.

- The Attention Deficit Disorder Association at the University of California at Irvine offers a free packet on ADD. Call (800) 487–2282.

- The Southeast Psychological Institute conducts workshops on ADD for both parents and teachers. Workshops are offered across the country. Call (800) 526–5952.

- Children with Attention Deficit Disorders publishes material titled *Attention Deficit Disorder: A Guide for Teachers*. To get a free copy, send a self-addressed, stamped envelope (use two stamps) to CHADD, 499 N.W. 70th Ave., Suite 308, Plantation, FL 33317.

- The Neurology, Learning, and Behavior Center offers a two-hour videotape, Educating Inattentive Children, featuring child psychologist Sam Goldstein and child neurologist Michael Goldstein. For a copy of the video, send $89.95, plus $3.50 for shipping to: NLBC, 230 S. 500 East, Suite 100, Salt Lake City, UT 84102, or call (801) 532–1484.

For Your Information

Books

Clarke, L. (1975). *Can't read, can't write, can't talk too good either: How to recognize and overcome dyslexia in your child*. New York: Penguin.
> A mother describes her life with her son's learning disability and the problems he faced from preschool to graduate studies; excellent handbook for parents of students with severe oral and written language problems.

Corcoran, B. (1976). *Axe-time, sword-time*. New York: Atheneum.
> On the eve of World War II, a young girl with a reading disability has to cope with family problems and her future.

Dwyer, K. M. (1991). *What do you mean I have a learning disability?* New York: Walker.
> A photographic essay told by Jimmy (10 years old), who thinks he is stupid. He is forgetful, awkward, and having problems in school. Excellent book for elementary school students.

Gilson, J. (1980). *Do bananas chew gum?* New York: Lothrop, Lee, and Shepard.
> Able to read and write at only a second-grade level, sixth-grader Sam Mott considers himself dumb until he is prompted to cooperate with those who think something can be done about his problems.

Ingersoll, B. D., & Goldstein, S. (1993). *Attention deficit disorders and learning disabilities*. New York: Doubleday.
> Realities, myths, and "controversial" treatments (for example, stimulant medications, sugar-free diets, EEG feedback, vitamin supplements) are described and discussed in this up-to-date reference book for parents, teachers, and others.

Lerner, J. (1993). *Learning disabilities: Theories, diagnosis, and teaching strategies* (6th ed.). Boston, MA: Houghton Mifflin.
> An overview of learning disabilities focused on the assessment/teaching process and including information on theoretical perspectives and instructional strategies.

Marek, M. (1988). *Different, not dumb*. New York: Watts.
> Second-grader Mike has reading problems because of a learning disability. Elementary school students will enjoy this book.

Simpson, E. (1979). *Reversals, a personal account of victory over dyslexia*. Boston, MA: Houghton Mifflin.
> An autobiography of a successful psychotherapist and writer whose early life was characterized by learning disabilities related to reading, writing, and spelling.

Organizations

Children with Attention Deficit Disorders (C. H. A. D. D.)
C. H. A. D. D. is an organization concerned with being the most comprehensive source of up-to-date information on attention deficit disorders anywhere in the United States. Parents, educators, and health-care professionals are among the groups receiving newsletters and participating in C. H. A. D. D. activities. For more information, contact CHADD, 499 NW 70th Ave., Suite 308, Plantation, FL 33317.

Council for Learning Disabilities (CLD)
Founded in 1968 as a division of the Council for Exceptional Children (CEC), CLD became an independent organization in 1982 when its membership voted to leave CEC to become a multidisciplinary group rather than an organization primarily of educators. It is one of the smallest organized groups in the field of learning disabilities, with about four thousand members. CLD

provides outlets for the exchange of ideas through an annual conference, news releases, and a professional journal (*Learning Disabilities Quarterly*). For more information, contact CLD, P.O. Box 40303, Overland Park, KS 66204.

Division for Learning Disabilities (DLD)

Founded in 1982 to replace the Division for Children with Learning Disabilities of the Council for Exceptional Children, DLD is an organization concerned primarily with educational issues. With over thirteen thousand members, CLD provides advocacy, inservice training, and outlets for the exchange of ideas through regional and national conferences, and a professional publication entitled *Learning Disabilities Research and Practice*. For more information, contact DLD, Council for Exceptional Children, 1920 Association Dr., Reston, VA 22091.

Learning Disabilities Association of America (LDA)

Founded in 1963 under the name Association for Children with Learning Disabilities, LDA is an organization concerned primarily with parental issues. It is the largest organized group in the field of learning disabilities, with over fifty thousand members. Known to be an effective advocate for children with learning disabilities, LDA provides outlets for the exchange of ideas through an annual conference, news releases, and professional publications. For more information, contact LDA, 4156 Library Rd., Pittsburgh, PA 15234.

National Attention Deficit Disorder Association (ADDA)

ADDA is a key information source for parents and other professionals interested in attention deficit disorders. ADDA provides outlets for the exchange of ideas through meetings, news releases, and professional publications. For more information, contact ADDA, P.O. Box 488, West Newbury, MA 01985.

The Orton Dyslexia Society, Inc. (ODS)

Founded in 1949 in honor of Samuel T. Orton, a physician who studied diverse language disorders, ODS is an organization that maintains a medical and educational focus that is broader than most other organizations related to learning disabilities. Its 8600 members are organized into local units concerned with written-language problems (that is, reading and writing). ODS produces two publications: the *Annals of Dyslexia* and *Perspectives on Dyslexia*. For more information, contact ODS, 724 York Rd., Baltimore, MD 21204.

Journals

Journal of Learning Disabilities (JLD)

This multidisciplinary publication contains articles on practice, research, and theory related to learning disabilities. It is not affiliated with any professional group. It includes reports of research, opinion papers, case reports, and discussions of issues that are the concern of all disciplines engaged in the field. For more information, contact Lee J. Wiederholt, Editor-in-Chief, *Journal of Learning Disabilities,* PRO-ED Publications, 8700 Shoal Creek Blvd., Austin, TX 78757-6897.

Learning Disabilities: A Multidisciplinary Journal (LDMJ)

A publication of the Learning Disabilities Association, (LDA), LDMJ publishes information of interest to parents, teachers, and other professionals concerned with children and adolescents with learning disabilities. For more information, contact Editor, LDMJ, LDA, 4156 Library Rd., Pittsburgh, PA 15234.

Learning Disabilities Quarterly (LDQ)

This journal is a publication of the Council for Learning Disabilities. Its purpose is to publish educational articles with an applied focus. The main emphasis of each paper is on learning disabilities, rather than on topics or studies that incidentally use students with learning disabilities or only indirectly relate to the field of learning disabilities. Papers falling into the following categories are generally published in this journal: reports of techniques in identification, assessment, remediation, and programming; interpretive reviews of the literature; papers advancing theory and the discussion of pertinent issues; reports of original research with an applied focus; and papers advancing practices in personnel preparation. For more information, contact Dr. H. Lee Swanson, Educational Psychology, 2125 Main Hall, University of British Columbia, Vancouver, BC, V6T 1Z5, Canada.

Learning Disabilities Research and Practice (LDRP)

This is a publication of the Division for Learning Disabilities. The purpose of the journal is to provide a forum for presentation of current research in the field of learning disabilities and a vehicle for dissemination of information important to practitioners in the field. Articles published in LDRP are intended to further the knowledge base in learning disabilities and to improve service to individuals with learning disabilities. For more information, contact Kenneth A. Kavale, Research Editor, LDRP, Division of Special Education, N238 Lindquist Center, University of Iowa, Iowa City, IA 52242; or Susan A. Vogel, Practice Editor, LDRP, Department of Educational Psychology, Northern Illinois University, DeKalb, IL 60115.

Teaching Students with Communication Disorders

- What are the two main types of communication disorders?

- How many students with communication disorders receive special education?

- What are the primary characteristics of students with communication disorders?

- What instructional approaches and teaching tactics are appropriate for students with communication disorders?

- What concerns should professionals address in deciding whether speech or language "differences" are a sufficient basis for special education?

Peggy speaks very clearly when her teacher calls on her for information, but some of the words don't sound exactly right when she answers. "Keep away fwom me you wascally wabbit" is one of her favorite sayings. Although this type of substitution is common for children in kindergarten and first grade, it is beginning to cause problems for Peggy because her classmates are making fun of the way she says things, and her parents and teachers are concerned that it is no longer appropriate for children her age.

Sally's teacher describes her speech as "just like a much younger child." She mispronounces words, omits sounds, and sometimes speaks too quickly to be easily understood. A speech-language pathologist described Sally's problem as a speech fluency disorder and recommended that she work on producing proper sounds more than other areas of speech or language. She encouraged Sally's parents to help by using sentences with word pairs that illustrate the importance of pronunciation and speech sounds (for example, "Did they present the present?" or "The graduate will graduate this spring") and by being models of proper articulation when they speak to her rather than calling attention to her dysfluencies.

Irving is a high school student with a stuttering problem. Although his written work is outstanding, Irving is reluctant to volunteer answers in class, participate in group discussions, or give oral presentations. His stuttering is much worse when he is talking to people he doesn't know.

Grammatical errors (such as "she run to store") and immature language usage (such as "go now") are the most representative characteristics of John's language. He seldom uses complete sentences and often mixes, incorrectly uses, or omits parts of speech in his written and expressive language. He has a poor speaking vocabulary, and his language problems are beginning to cause serious problems with his peers. ■

Many students receiving special education have communication disorders. Some have such severe impairments that they need assistive devices such as computerized speech aids to communicate with other people. Most, however, like Peggy, Sally, Irving, and John, have somewhat milder impairments. The category of communication disorders includes people whose problems in producing speech or using language symbols interfere significantly with their ability to communicate. In most school districts, speech-language pathologists work collaboratively with classroom teachers to provide services to students with communication disorders.

Definition

Types of communication disorders

There are two types of **communication disorders:** those that affect speech and those that affect language. Problems with producing speech sounds (articulation), controlling sounds that are produced (voice), and controlling the rate and rhythm of speech (fluency) are generally considered **speech disorders.** Problems with using proper forms of language (phonology, morphology, syntax), using the content of language (semantics), and using the functions of language (pragmatics) are generally considered **language disorders.**

The American Speech-Language-Hearing Association (ASHA; 1982) has developed formal definitions of each speech disorder:

Speech disorders defined

Articulation disorder is defined as "the abnormal production of speech sounds" (p. 949). When a youngster says, "The wabbit wan don the woad," or "poon" for "spoon," or "gog" for "dog," he or she may be using spoken language appropriately but is not producing sounds correctly.

Voice disorder is defined as "the absence or abnormal production of vocal quality, pitch, loudness, resonance, and/or duration" (p. 949). Individuals with voice disorders sometimes sound very hoarse, or speak very loudly or in a very high or low pitch.

Fluency disorder is defined as "the abnormal flow of verbal expression, characterized by impaired rate and rhythm which may be accompanied by struggle behavior" (p. 949). S-saying th-the f-first s-sound o-of a-a w-word and th-then s-saying th-the w-word illustrates this problem.

All other communication problems are considered language disorders.

Types of language disorders

The American Speech-Language-Hearing Association (1982) defines three kinds of language disorders, specifically problems related to form, content, and function. Language *form* refers to the utterance or sentence structure of what is said—phonology, morphology, and syntax. Language *content* refers to meanings of words and sentences, including abstract concepts—semantics. Language *function* refers to the context in which language can be used and the purpose of communication—pragmatics. Problems can be *receptive* (related to hearing, listening to, or receiving language) and *expressive* (related to producing or expressing language).

Language form

Phonology is concerned with the smallest units of language (phonemes or speech sounds); morphology is concerned with the smallest units of meaningful language (morphemes or words and parts of words); and syntax is concerned with combining language units into meaningful phrases, clauses, or sentences (grammatically correct language). Problems with phonology, morphology, and syntax are evident when students are unable to differentiate sounds (/b/ versus /p/); words (cat or cap); or grammatically correct sentences ("John go to the movies" versus "John goes to the movies"); or produce appropriate sounds, words, or sentences.

Language content

Semantics is concerned with word and message meanings (vocabulary, comprehension, following directions). Problems with semantics are evident when students are unable to identify appropriate pictures when word names are provided ("Find the grapes"), answer simple questions ("Are apples fruits?"), follow directions ("Draw a line over the third box"), tell how words or messages are similar or different ("How are apples, oranges, and pears alike?"), or understand abstract concepts ("What is love?").

Language function

Pragmatics is concerned with the use and function of language in varying settings (that is, following social conversational rules). Problems with pragmatics are evident when students are unable to use language in social situations to express feelings, create or understand images, give or request information, and/or control actions of listeners.

Criteria for identification

Professionals use a number of criteria to identify students with communication disorders, and they may be concerned with receptive as well as expressive problems. Identification of speech problems is usually accomplished by listening to oral reading or speech samples or asking students questions. Most language disorders are identified by poor performance on language tests or from analyses of written and oral schoolwork.

Prevalence

Second largest group with disabilities

Students with speech and language problems are the second largest group of students with disabilities; they are the third largest group of students receiving special education. During recent school years, about 1 million children with speech and language problems were served (U.S. Department of Education, 1993). This figure represents about 22 percent of all students with disabilities; it is 1.7 percent of all school-age children and adolescents. Over the past ten years, the number of students with communication disorders has fallen somewhat as more and more students with learning disabilities were identified (see Chapter 8). Students with speech and language disorders are the most highly integrated into general classrooms of all groups of students with disabilities. In recent school years, more than 90 percent were served in regular classroom placements (78.9 percent) or resource rooms (13.9 percent).

Highly integrated

The percentage of students with disabilities identified with speech and language impairments in each state is presented in Table 9.1. As the table shows, the distribution across the states ranges far above and below the national average of 22 percent—from less than 10 percent in New York and the District of Columbia to over 30 percent in North Dakota, New Mexico, Mississippi, Kentucky, and Indiana. This variation is due to changes in numbers of students classified with other disabilities and differences in the extent to which communication disorders are viewed as part of special education.

Table 9.1   Percentage Distribution of Students with Communication Disorders (CD) in the United States

State	All Disabilities[a]	CD[b]	CD as Percent of All Disabilities
All States	7.81	1.73	22.2
Alabama	8.99	1.95	21.7
Alaska	9.67	2.15	22.2
Arizona	6.38	1.20	18.8
Arkansas	7.62	1.16	15.2
California	6.55	1.46	22.3
Colorado	7.14	1.08	15.1
Connecticut	8.97	1.47	16.4
Delaware	8.56	1.08	12.6
District of Columbia	5.77	0.44	7.6
Florida	9.05	2.55	28.2
Georgia	6.28	1.38	22.0
Hawaii	5.05	0.82	16.2
Idaho	6.91	1.27	18.4
Illinois	8.30	2.04	24.6
Indiana	8.14	2.62	32.2
Iowa	8.35	1.37	16.4
Kansas	7.13	1.80	25.3
Kentucky	7.72	2.35	30.4
Louisiana	6.38	1.63	25.6
Maine	9.07	2.11	23.3
Maryland	7.99	2.17	27.2
Massachusetts	11.21	2.40	21.4
Michigan	6.97	1.50	21.5
Minnesota	6.97	1.27	18.2
Mississippi	8.15	2.57	31.5
Missouri	8.33	2.00	24.0
Montana	8.15	1.90	23.3
Nebraska	8.49	2.14	25.2
Nevada	6.80	1.44	21.2
New Hampshire	7.78	1.51	19.4
New Jersey	10.48	3.02	28.8
New Mexico	9.02	2.72	30.2
New York	7.63	0.75	9.8
North Carolina	7.64	1.60	20.9
North Dakota	7.15	2.19	30.6
Ohio	7.78	2.01	25.8
Oklahoma	8.19	1.89	23.1
Oregon	8.03	2.02	25.2

(continued on next page)

Table 9.1	Percentage Distribution of Students with Communication Disorders (CD) in the United States (continued)		

State	All Disabilities[a]	CD[b]	CD as Percent of All Disabilities
Pennsylvania	7.50	1.91	25.5
Rhode Island	9.03	1.61	17.8
South Carolina	8.22	2.18	26.5
South Dakota	7.28	2.06	28.3
Tennessee	8.89	2.11	23.7
Texas	7.73	1.43	18.5
Utah	8.06	1.33	16.5
Vermont	7.55	1.68	22.3
Virginia	7.86	1.71	21.8
Washington	6.94	1.34	19.3
West Virginia	9.43	2.49	26.4
Wisconsin	6.77	1.33	19.7
Wyoming	2.77	0.73	26.4

[a] Percentage of school-age population (ages 6 to 21) receiving special education in all disability categories.

[b] Percentage of school-age population receiving special education in the category of communication disorders ("speech or language impairments").

Source: U.S. Department of Education. (1993). *Fifteenth annual report to Congress on the implementation of the Individuals with Disabilities Education Act.* Washington, DC: Author.

Characteristics

Federal guidelines do not separate speech and language problems. This causes state departments not to differentiate students with speech problems from those with language problems in their counts of students requiring special education. Yet students with speech problems demonstrate different communication characteristics than those with language problems. Speech problems are evidenced in the production of speech (for example, misarticulations, abnormal flow of expression), and language problems are evidenced in the form, content, and use of receptive and expressive language (for example, vocabulary, grammar). Caseloads of speech-language pathologists consist primarily of students who receive services for articulation or language disorders (less than 5 percent of their caseloads comprises students with voice and fluency disorders).

Bring Your Learning to Life

Identifying John's Communication Disorder

John's teacher was concerned about his communication problems and referred him to her school's diagnostic team. In collaboration with a speech-language pathologist and a special education teacher, the team planned an evaluation of John's speech and language functioning. They used this information to decide if his problems were serious enough to warrant special education.

Speech Evaluation

John's classroom teacher completed a series of checklists used by the speech-language pathologist to provide information about the seriousness of speech problems. Here's an example of some of the items on it:

Student _____

Age _____

Grade _____

Teacher _____

Date of evaluation _____

1. General Questions
   a. Can you understand what this student is saying? If not, give examples illustrating problems.
   b. Does this student sound like other students in your room? If not, give examples illustrating differences.
   c. Is what this student says appropriate to the situation in which it is said? If not, give examples illustrating problems.
   d. Does this student struggle when communicating? If so, give examples illustrating problems.
   e. Are there other indications of speech or language problems? If so, give illustrative examples.

   f. Does this child's communication interfere with his or her participation in the classrooms or socialization within the school environment?

2. Articulation (producing sounds)
   Which of the following sounds does this student usually produce correctly?

   ___ /w/ as in *waiter*   ___ /t/ as in *table*

   ___ /f/ as in *father*   ___ /m/ as in *mother*

   ___ /h/ as in *house*   ___ /b/ as in *balloon*

   ___ /r/ as in *rat*   ___ /l/ as in *lady*

   ___ /ch/ as in *church*   ___ /sh/ as in *show*

   ___ /th/ as in *think*   ___ /th/ as in *those*

3. Voice Quality (controlling sounds)
   What does this student's voice usually sound like?

   ___ pleasant   ___ not pleasant

   ___ quiet   ___ not quiet

   ___ hoarse, raspy   ___ not hoarse, raspy

   ___ nasal   ___ not nasal

4. Fluency (controlling rate and rhythm of speech)
   What does this student's speech usually sound like?

   ___ few hesitations, repetitions, or added sounds

   ___ some hesitations, repetitions, or added sounds

   ___ many hesitations, repetitions, or added sounds

Language Evaluation

The speech-language pathologist administered some formal and informal tests to provide information about the seriousness of

(continued on next page)

Bring Your Learning to Life

Identifying John's Communication Disorder *(continued)*

John's language problems. The following are some of the tests with which she evaluated John's use of language form, content, and functions.

1. Form (phonology, morphology, syntax)
   Goldman–Fristoe Test of Articulation
   Photo Articulation Test
   Test for Auditory Comprehension of
      Language
   Test of Language Development

2. Content (semantics)
   Assessment of Children's Language
      Comprehension
   Peabody Picture Vocabulary Test–Revised

3. Function (pragmatics)
   Observations of conversations with adults
      and peers
   Role-playing conversations in different
      situations

Pragmatics checklist (illustrated below)
How often does this student engage the following language functions appropriately?

Function	Very Seldom	Some-times	Very Often
		Frequency	
Greets others	1	2	3
Responds to requests	1	2	3
Relays messages	1	2	3
Asks for favors	1	2	3
Expresses feelings	1	2	3
Expresses disagreement	1	2	3
Compliments others	1	2	3
Expresses affection	1	2	3

Cognitive

Two competing views

There are two schools of thought about the extent to which students who have speech and language problems show cognitive difficulties. According to one of them, some students do have cognitive difficulties; they perform poorly on intelligence tests, particularly on verbal intelligence tests. Their development of cognitive skills (identifying similarities among objects or concepts, understanding sentences and words)—which is heavily dependent on language—is hampered by their language problems. The competing view holds that students with communication disorders have normal or average intellectual functioning but appear deficient because their speech and language problems affect their performance on intelligence tests.

It may be that difficulties communicating cause cognitive difficulties, or it may be that cognitive difficulties cause communication difficulties. The re-

Bring Your Learning to Life

John's Individualized Education Program Focuses on His Problems

After the school's diagnostic team determined that John's language problems were serious enough to justify special education, they prepared an individualized education program (IEP) to guide the delivery of these services. Here are selected components of John's IEP:

Annual Goals

1. By the end of the school year, John will use correct grammar in his spoken language 90 percent of the time. Person responsible: Speech-language pathologist.

2. By the end of the school year, John will increase his spoken vocabulary score on the district language test from the 35 percentile to the 55 percentile. Person responsible: Speech-language pathologist.

3. By the end of the school year, John will improve his use of articles, personal pronouns, adjectives, and proper verb tense to a level at least the same as 80 percent of his classroom peers. Person responsible: Classroom teacher using specifically prepared lessons with assistance from speech-language pathologist.

Regular Class Participation

John will spend instructional time for all academic subjects in the regular class.

Related Services

1. John will receive special education services from a speech-language pathologist for 30 minutes every other day.

2. John's teacher will be provided with consultation from the speech-language pathologist on a weekly basis and as needed.

search is not clear. We believe that the causation may run in either direction, depending on the individual student. The close relationship between communication and cognitive development can make it difficult to determine a student's actual needs.

Academic

School is a verbal-symbolic environment. Throughout the school years, especially in kindergarten and first grade, academic performance is highly dependent on students' skill in listening, following directions, and comprehending. Students are expected to understand and act in response to verbal symbols and spoken language. Students who have speech and language problems usually experience difficulties in reading, social studies, language arts, and other subjects that depend heavily on understanding verbal and written communication skills.

Listening and comprehension skills

Physical

Individuals with certain conditions—cerebral palsy, cleft palate or other kinds of oral-facial disorders, and some types of mental retardation—may experience speech and language difficulties as well as physical problems. But for most students with speech and language impairments there is no specific correspondence between physical appearance or functioning and speech or language functioning.

Behavioral

Communication serves a social function. Students with speech and language difficulties, by the nature of their difficulties, often call attention to themselves. When a student's speech or language is obviously different from his or her peers, teachers, adults, and those peers behave differently toward the student. They may pay more attention to the way in which the student says something than to what the student says. Others may ridicule an individual whose speech is noticeably different, and this can cause emotional problems. Students who have speech and language difficulties may withdraw from social situations, be rejected in social situations, and ultimately, they may suffer from a loss of self-confidence.

Ridicule and rejection

Communication

The communication characteristics of students with speech and language disorders are a function of the specific kind of disorder. For example, students with speech problems related to articulation mispronounce words or parts of words; they may have difficulty being understood. But the nature of the problem can be very different for different students. Diane's articulation problem may be one of omitting sounds; Sam's, one of distorting sounds.

Voice problems

Voice disorders can appear in quality, loudness, or pitch. At times the disorder is of such magnitude that the student's speech irritates teachers and other students. You can imagine what it's like to have a child with a squeaky or a loud voice in a classroom.

Stuttering

Students with fluency disorders demonstrate interruptions in the timing or rhythm of their speech, which can frustrate both speaker and listener. The most common fluency disorder is stuttering. There are approximately 17 million stutterers worldwide—2 million in the United States. At one time, stuttering was attributed to psychological problems. Although this explanation has not been entirely cast aside, researchers suspect that a combination of biological, psychological, and environmental factors predispose a person to stutter. New evidence suggests that stuttering may be caused by a physiological breakdown of brain mechanisms or possibly by excessive tension in the vocal cords.

Students with language disorders may demonstrate difficulty combining sounds to form words or combining words to form structurally correct sentences. They generally have difficulty using language to express themselves or understand others (see earlier section on definitions).

Speech and language pathologists work with teachers to facilitate speech and language development of all students and not just those with communication disorders. *Michael Weisbrot and Family.*

Instructional Approaches and Teaching Tactics

Names for specialists

Students with communication disorders often receive special education from people trained to address speech and language problems. The name assigned to these people varies. The most common and accepted term over the years has been **speech-language pathologist**. This name causes some concern within the profession because it implies a medical orientation that often is inappropriate for people working in schools. As we were writing the book, "teachers of the speech and language impaired" was being used in some areas. This also causes problems. First, teachers don't like the word "the" in the title because it refers to the students as the disorder and not as students (violating preferred practice relative to terminology—see Chapter 1). It also places communication disorders in a class by themselves because no other specialized service has such a specific title. We decided to use "speech-language pathologist" as the term for people who work with individuals with speech and language impairments. They may be called something else where you live and work, and we may change the term in subsequent editions of the book. We are not that concerned about what they are called; our interest is in what they do to provide assistance to students and other teachers of students with communication disorders.

Certification

Speech-language pathologists hold a master's degree in communication disorders, and most have a certification of clinical competence from the American Speech-Language-Hearing Association. They are certified by state departments of education, much like special education and elementary, middle, and high school teachers. Speech-language pathologists conduct assessments and provide therapy based on their results. When they work in schools, they sometimes function as itin-

Table 9.2	Top Ten List of Tips for Teachers of Students with Communication Disorders

1. Integrate appropriate language development activities into all curriculum areas.

2. Create supportive environment where communication is fostered and valued.

3. Provide opportunities during regular instructional day for students to practice skills being learned in therapy.

4. Use areas of strength to compensate for weaknesses.

5. Value speech and language diversity.

6. Arrange activities in which students use language for different purposes (for example, oral book report, mock job interview, speech, surveys) with different audiences (for example, another class at same grade level, class at another grade level, parents).

7. Provide good speech models.

8. Provide opportunities during academic instruction for free exchange of ideas and discussions about what is being taught.

9. Organize classroom space with at least one area reserved for students to talk to each other.

10. Consider developmental levels before making referral for outside assistance.

Collaboration

erant specialists, spending one or two days a week in each building to which they are assigned. In larger districts, they may be assigned to just one or two schools. Increasingly, speech-language pathologists are working collaboratively with classroom teachers, helping them plan instruction for students with speech and language problems. This is particularly true in school districts emphasizing inclusionary programs in which students with disabilities are taught in the same classrooms as their neighbors and peers. A list of tips for classroom teachers working with students with communication disorders is provided in Table 9.2. The speech-language pathologist can offer advice and assistance in developing these general interventions. More specific suggestions for classroom activities are presented in the following sections.

Reducing Speech Problems

Speech disorders, primarily those related to articulation of speech sounds and, to a lesser extent, fluency of speech or unusual voice quality, are often targeted for speech-language pathologists as the primary instructional personnel who work closely with teachers to provide services in their classrooms. The goal for most of these teachers is providing good speech models, accepting environments, and opportunities to practice newly developed speech skills (Lewis & Doorlag, 1991). The following tactics will help you improve these areas of speech production in students with communication problems.

Modeling speech

■ **Provide good models of appropriate speech.** Speak clearly with appropriate pronunciation and encourage students to demonstrate appropriate speech without calling attention to a classmate's errors. For example, when Peggy jokingly told her teacher, "Keep away fwom me you wascally wabbit," the teacher responded by saying, "Oh no you don't, I'll get you you rascally rabbit," rather than pointing out the mistake.

Quantity first

■ **Focus on quantity more than quality of speech.** Many speech production problems tend to become worse when teachers and students call attention to them. Attending to the content of communication more than the carrier often helps speech problems from becoming more serious.

Plenty of practice

■ **Provide opportunities for practice.** Many students with speech and language problems receive special education from speech-language pathologists in settings other than their regular classrooms. Teachers who encourage these students to practice what they are learning in the special education settings find that problems improve more quickly. For example, when Sally was working with the speech-language pathologist on differentiating words by paying attention to syllable accents, her regular classroom teacher organized a classroom word game in which students picked the right word from orally presented clues (for example, "You bring me to a party? Am I present [prĕz´´nt] or present [prĭ zent´]?").

Reducing Language Problems

Language disorders are most likely to be the concern of speech-language pathologists working collaboratively with classroom teachers. Problems in receptive and expressive language involving proper use of vocabulary and grammatical structure are common in most classrooms. Many students with learning disabilities exhibit language problems. The following tactics will help you improve the use of language in students with communication problems.

Grammar through meaning

■ **To improve use of grammar: Focus on meaning.** Sentence meanings are influenced by the use of punctuation and intonation. Playing word and sentence games can help students with language problems see the value of grammar and inflection. Have students say the following words in at least two different ways that convey positive and negative meanings: *turkey, school, love, monsters.* Have students identify the multiple meanings evident in the following sentences and then have them construct some of their own:

> Let's talk turkey.
> The man decided on the train.
> They fed her dog biscuits.

Vocabulary through meaning

■ **To improve vocabulary: Focus on meaning.** Encourage students with language problems to ask about the meanings of words they don't understand. Encourage them to use words with meanings they do understand.

Acting out words

■ **To improve vocabulary: Combine gestures with verbal language.** Students with language problems may have difficulty understanding the meanings of prepositions, adverbs, and action verbs. By acting out the meaning of *through, over, quickly,* and *struggled,* John's teacher helped him to understand a story she was reading to her class. She also had all her students act out words like *wiggle, shake, bounce, tumble,* and *spin* as they were learning them.

Acting out words some-
times helps many students
with speech and language
problems better understand
their meaning. *Elizabeth
Crews*.

Write, write, write

■ **To improve written expression: Focus on quantity as well as quality in written work.** Encourage students to write as much as possible without concern for errors and use these products as a source for qualitative changes in their instruction. For example, place a picture (such as an art print, magazine page, book illustration) on each student's desk and have the class write about the picture. After two or three minutes, have each student pass what has been written and their pictures to a classmate. Have them read what was written by the previous writer and add to what was written during the next writing segment (two to three minutes). Continue until at least four students have written about the pictures and have them read by the final writer. Use the content in these stories as a basis for planning future instructional activities such as using details, expressing emotions, summarizing text.

Teach elements of grammar

■ **To improve written products: Teach specific skills and have students monitor their written work.** Grammar is teachable, and written products are improved by using it appropriately. Correct grammatic usage (for example, use of verbs, adverbs, adjectives, and proper tense) should be taught using teacher-guided practice lessons. Ask students to evaluate what they write ("Did I use verb tense appropriately?" "Can I use more adjectives or adverbs?" "Did I tell how the action was done?") and keep journals illustrating improvements in their written products.

Building blocks

■ **To improve vocabulary and word usage: Use familiar words as building blocks.** Teach students to use familiar words to make new words. For example, simply adding prefixes (for example, *foot, afoot* or *unable, unbeaten, uncertain, undo*) and suffixes (*quiet, quietly, quietness*) produces new parts of speech and new words to expand vocabularies. Give spelling tests on the new words to improve the confidence of students with language problems in using their new words.

Bring Your Learning to Life

Technology Helps John Improve His Language

John's teacher asked a colleague responsible for her school's computer lab to help set up a computer program to reduce John's language problems. Working together, using HYPERCARD™, they designed a program "stack" that allowed John to work independently on improving articulation, fluency, vocabulary, and other communication problems. The stack contained a series of on-screen "cards" that had content (e.g., pictures, fill-in sentences) on them and control buttons and instruction at the bottom (see illustration).

John used the program to practice new vocabulary words, subject–verb agreement, and other language skills that he was learning in speech therapy. The teachers also encouraged John to use appropriate grammar when he was speaking to his peers.

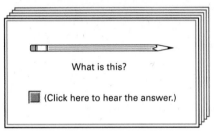

What is this?

■ (Click here to hear the answer.)

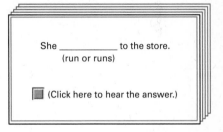

She _____ to the store.
(run or runs)

■ (Click here to hear the answer.)

Acting games

■ **To improve vocabulary and word usage: Use acting games to teach meaning.** Choose an action (such as "Stand in one place," "Move from place to place," or "Make your face ... "), and have students act out the meaning of appropriate words from their speaking and listening vocabularies. Here are some examples:

In One Place
bend, bob, bounce, collapse, contract, droop, expand, flop, hang, lean, rock, shake, stretch, wiggle, wobble

From Place to Place
amble, bop, crawl, dodge, evacuate, flail, gallop, hustle, limp, meander, prance, stamp, stumble, trot, wander

Make Your Face . . .
blink, chew, cringe, frown, glare, grimace, grin, groan

Make Your Legs and Feet . . .
drag, kick, shuffle, skuff, stamp, stumble, tap

Pantomime
calling, crowing, crying, falling, hiccupping, howling, humming, giggling, sneezing, snickering, whistling

Dramatize
boredom, conceit, contempt, disgust, envy, gratitude, happiness, horror, loneliness, shame, wonder

Word games

■ **To improve vocabulary and word usage: Play word games.** Use a few of the following riddles as starters; have students make up some of their own as practice in building expressive vocabularies and using language.

1. What is boring singing?	long song
2. What is a house mortgage?	home loan
3. What is a skinny hotel?	thin inn
4. What is a cheap medieval soldier?	tight knight
5. What is a chicken enclosure?	hen pen

Give students a word (*four*) and have them change one letter at a time to make another word (*five*) after a specific number of steps. Make the task more difficult by eliminating some clues.

Clue	Word
	four
bad smell	_____ (foul)
chickens	_____ (fowl)
aluminum _____	_____ (foil)
do not pass	_____ (fail)
all _____ down	_____ (fall)
ate too much	_____ (full)
_____ 'er up	_____ (fill)
storage space	_____ (file)
it's hot	_____ (fire)
	five

Give students a word (*fa*) and have them create new words by adding letters.

Example

Start with *fa* and change it to other words by adding letters to the initial consonant.

Clue	Word
	fa
cost, charge	_____ (fee)
before five	_____ (four)
picture _____	_____ (frame)
well-known	_____ (famous)
type of book	_____ (fiction)
after thirty-ninth	_____ (fortieth)
normal actions	_____ (functions)

More of these games can be found in *Games Make Alpha-Betics Fun* by John Dan and Karol Hicks (see the For Your Information section at the end of this chapter).

Praise for student accomplishments is a part of all successful speech and language programs. *David Young-Wolff/PhotoEdit.*

Reducing Interpersonal Problems

Students with speech and language problems often experience difficulties with interpersonal interactions as a result of their communication problems. The following tactics will help to overcome social and emotional problems often experienced by these students.

Genuine praise

■ **Praise accomplishments.** This approach is especially useful with students experiencing communication problems. Praise for genuine accomplishments is more effective than general, unspecified praise. Children with communication disorders are quick to recognize undeserved praise; they will view it as shallow and dishonest when it is delivered inappropriately. In judging when to praise, keep the student's past history and previous performances in mind; praise may seem appropriate and genuine to one student but greatly undeserved to another. The most effective praise is delivered when the student recognizes that it is in response to a genuine accomplishment.

Informative praise

■ **Convey information with praise.** Praise that provides specifics about a skill or accomplishment is more effective than praise that simply reflects status. For example, "Bill, that oral report was very clearly delivered" or "Thank you for slowing down when I gave you the signal we talked about" is more informative than "Bill, you received the highest grade in the class." Orient praise so that students can focus on their developing skills rather than on someone's approval of them.

Praising ability and effort	■ **Focus praise on ability and effort**. Praise that identifies a student's ability and effort as the source of success is most effective. The statement should indicate that success was achieved because skills were used to complete a task with the right amount of effort.
Timely praise	■ **Timely praise is better than heavy praise.** Students with communication disorders often overlook their own accomplishments. Stay alert for occasions when your students may not realize that they have completed a very difficult task; these opportunities for praise result in more powerful effects than when praise is delivered frequently without regard to appropriateness.
Avoid embarrassment	■ **Be careful to praise, not embarrass, students.** Not all of your students have the same reactions to praise, especially those who may be sensitive to public attention. Many students with communication problems find even simple recognition of their skills and abilities embarrassing; elaborate reactions to their behavior can be personally discomforting. Be sure that when you praise a student, it will be perceived as rewarding by the recipient. Bear in mind that private praise is more effective than public praise that is embarrassing.
Adapt praise to level	■ **Vary praise with developmental level.** Students learning new speech and language skills need more frequent praise than those practicing skills that have been acquired. Praise after a selected number of responses or a specified time period is appropriate for new learning. Intermittent praise—less frequent random presentations—is more appropriate for later stages of learning.
Group praise	■ **Generate praise for the entire group.** Students with communication problems often have a low self-concept and are reluctant to believe praise is true. To compensate, dispense praise to the whole group (or a select group) of children and in that context direct a specific "good word" to targeted students. Spend a minute or two quickly going around the classroom mentioning something positive about each student. Providing peers with comments like "nice handwriting," "beautiful shirt," "thanks for always being on time," and "great math today" may soften the extent to which students with communication disorders think they are singled out for specific praise for something they have done.
A joyful good-bye	■ **Praise the obvious.** Take a little time on certain days, just before the students leave for home, to point out some of the day's positive occurrences. This tactic can become a "joyful good-bye" for each student and provide a final opportunity to strengthen developing skills at the end of the school day.
Activities as praise	■ **Use activities as substitutes for praise.** A number of brief activities can be used to point out the positive qualities of a student. Careful selection of activities enables all students to benefit. The following examples illustrate verbal praise substitutes:
	■ *Teacher of the Day*—Each day select one student to be teacher. Have that student make all important decisions—such as time for recess and bathroom privileges—after consultation with the aide—the classroom teacher.
	■ *Student of the Week*—Each week a randomly selected student is the focus of peer praise. Classmates write down positive skills or characteristics of the target student; the teacher incorporates them into a letter to take home at the end of the week.

> ■ *VIP Bulletin Board*—Take a photo of a student and place it on a bulletin board with a list of positive statements. Leave space for students to add other positive comments.

Involving parents and family

> ■ **Communicate with parents to extend praise.** Involve the parents and other family members in instructional efforts. Have students with communication disorders use notebooks as diaries or scrapbooks of accomplishments. Buy several different sizes and types of inexpensive notebooks so students can make more individualized choices. Send the notebooks home and have family members sign them as evidence of recognition of the students' achievements. Have parents periodically select favorite passages and review the strengths of each with their children.

Current Trends and Issues

Speech and language problems are very common. Many more students demonstrated speech and language characteristics that caused concern for their teachers than those served in special education in recent years. Deciding when a child with speech or language problems is in need of special education and who should be responsible for providing it are difficult issues that teachers and other professionals face each school year. They also must decide whether language differences common in students from other cultures are an appropriate basis for special education.

Normal development or communication disorder?

Many teachers in the early grades report that some of their students speak like much younger children. Although this is common, it presents a problem when teachers are not exactly sure what to do about it. Being reluctant to speak can be a normal developmental stage or a symptom of a communication disorder. Having trouble finding the right word in a discussion can be developmentally appropriate or a symptom of a deeper communication problem. "Sloppy" speech, "lazy" speech, and "confused" speech can be appropriate characteristics at one stage of development or symptoms of communication problems at another. Although not providing services when they are needed is something that causes concern, not wanting to refer students too early is also an appropriate professional concern. There are no easy answers to either issue.

Cultural and dialectal differences

Given the increasing diversity of school populations, most classroom teachers teach students from different cultures. The language system used by many of these students is influenced by several factors, including geographic location, socioeconomic level, and ethnicity, and often results in "language differences" that must be addressed in school classrooms. When does a difference in speaking patterns constitute a cultural or dialectal difference, and when does it constitute a communication disorder? Again, the concern is that many students enrolled in special education classes or who receive speech and language services may be inappropriately placed. They may have no underlying communication problems, but only culturally, regionally, or developmentally appropriate differences in their speech and language.

Advances in technology have enabled many students with communication disorders to be educated with their neighbors and peers. *MacDonald Photography/ Unicorn Stock Photos.*

An imaginary scenario

    Imagine that you are placed in a German class with no knowledge or, at best, only a rudimentary knowledge of how to speak or read any foreign language. You are given an assignment to write an autobiography and present an oral report on it. You have been very successful in such activities in other settings. Your speaking and writing abilities are fine, but your first draft is unintelligible in any language. As a result of your clumsy and unacceptable skills, you are pulled out of the class and given a language test. Because of the poor results, you are placed in a special class to improve your language abilities. Your school career has been dramatically altered, perhaps inappropriately, but such a scenario is not as ridiculous as it may seem for children with dialectal differences. They may have been very effective communicators in their own cultures and may have learned language systems that were valued in those cultures. However, when the demands of a new educational experience require use of a new system, these children may be singled out and recommended for therapy.

    In addition to differences in communication that arise from diverse student backgrounds, teachers will increasingly encounter students who have severe communication problems in any language. More and more, such students are being included in schools and programs with their neighbors and peers. Advances in technology have already made it possible for these individuals to compensate for most types of speech and language disorders. For example, **Computer technology** personal computers can create synthetic speech to enable previously non-speaking children to "talk" using a keyboard, communication board, or other input device. The newer communication aids let users choose from a number of voices; alter the pitch and intensity of speech to convey emotions; and laugh, sing, and produce sound effects. In the not too distant future, the user of an electronic communication device may be able to design his or her own voice. These systems are constantly becoming more portable, less expensive, and better able to store vast numbers of words, sentences, and stories, enabling students with speech and language impairments to communicate more easily and effectively.

Communication Disorders in Perspective

The best-known story about a person with a speech disorder is that of the Greek orator and political leader, Demosthenes. He went down to the ocean, filled his mouth with pebbles, and shouted over the waves to cure his stuttering. In the eighteenth and nineteenth centuries, children with speech and language disorders usually were treated at clinics and hospitals. In 1908, the first public school class for children with speech disorders was established in New York. By 1910 the Chicago public schools were hiring "speech correction teachers," and by the early 1920s most large-city school systems had speech correction teachers on staff. In 1925 professionals in this field met and formed the American Academy of Speech Correction, known today as the American Speech-Language-Hearing Association. A primary function of this organization is certification of professionals other than teachers, who provide speech and language services.

Most students with speech and language problems are found in regular classrooms. Until the early 1980s, it was common for speech-language pathologists to remove students from classrooms and give them brief periods of speech and language therapy in another setting. In the last few years, however, a shift from direct to indirect services has been more prominent. Increasingly, speech-language pathologists work with general and special education teachers to devise ways to facilitate speech and language development in their classrooms—for all their students, not just for those with speech or language problems.

Large numbers of students with communication problems put a load on the educational system and also create issues related to deciding who receives special education and who is responsible for providing services to these students. Some professionals argue that speech and language specialists should be responsible for identifying and treating all communication disorders. Specialized training and controlled instructional environments are cited as advantages of such a system of service delivery. Disadvantages related to assessment and interventions provided out of the context of the regular classroom cause other professionals to support integrated models in which speech and language specialists are members of multidisciplinary intervention teams.

Who has the major responsibility for determining if a difference in communication skills is due to a disorder or simply a language difference? Who is responsible for correcting speech and language problems? There are no simple answers to questions related to who is best qualified to meet the needs of stu-

History

From direct to indirect services

Who provides services?

The Work of a Speech-Language Specialist

My name is Lynn Wilcox, and I am a speech/language pathology supervisor in rural Nebraska. For approximately half of my time, I am responsible for the professional growth and evaluation of fifteen persons who practice speech/language pathology and audiology in a county area. The other half of my time, I attempt to provide consulting and diagnostic support to those clinicians and to other special education team members working with children from birth to age 21 for the communication problems associated with whatever disability conditions we identify.

I love my job. I love the people I work with and work for. Those feelings are not expressed lightly, nor should they represent to you that my job is in any way easy. I could tell you that I have great responsibility to see to it that child change occurs, but that would be an unfortunate exaggeration. Actually, I am a cheerleader. I am a politician. And I am a loving manager. Finally, I strive to be a fair, firm, and friendly evaluator. I attempt to be aware of resources, techniques, materials, programs, services, and on and on. Much more though, it is my responsibility to be able to demonstrate and clearly explain to those I serve the areas I think the child needs help in and what they can do to implement improvement so they can see child change. I am a one-on-one inservice presenter who gets to coach the staff through a problem, direct their thinking a little, and enjoy watching their own excitement and the child's progress in relation to their efforts.

There are different supervisory styles. You may meet a supervisor along the way who functions differently from the way I do. My work is primarily directed toward the excitement of learning, and in that way I act primarily as a consultant to the clinician and very often to the resource teacher and the class teacher as well. I drop little nuggets about communication and how it affects class performance and test performance (particularly intelligence test performance) and offer suggestions about what things can be done to support a child in whatever setting to anybody that will listen, either by mandate or by interest. I am not very good at sitting and watching someone work. I have discovered that the people with whom I work appreciate having me participate in activities and sessions with them. Observing is a viable supervisory style. I do it briefly sometimes, although usually my supervision occurs in action.

Sometimes I work as part of the team diagnosing a child's problem. I have to be able to clearly state what the problems are from a communication viewpoint. I have to make that information relevant to the classroom and particularly clear and relevant to the child's parents. Then I either help write or provide ideas for writing educational plans that match the child's problems. I negotiate placement with administrators and other professionals who might see the child's problems differently than the way I see them. Sometimes I sit back while a clinician presents data and does the interpreting—oh, so important, that interpreting. Sometimes I am pleased because a clinician or a resource teacher or a parent really sees and understands how the child's communication fits into the scheme of things. Sometimes I am embarrassed by the lack of ability to interpret. I have to be careful not to wound clinicians and yet find a way to present uncomfortable information to them to make them want to learn instead of squashing their feelings just because I was embarrassed by their lack of preparation or information.

All in all, I spend about fifty or more hours every week doing something related to my profession. I am on call to each clinician at any time. In addition, I read, here and there, and call or write to those who replenish my own enthusiasm and my knowledge.

Maybe supervision can be done in a way that requires less dedication and less commitment. my personal philosophy is that I am willing to do more than I ask anyone else to do. I must be able to demonstrate any idea I present. I must understand my profession well enough to teach it to others.

Lynn Wilcox is a speech/language pathology supervisor from Hastings, Nebraska.

Joint effort needed

dents with communication disorders. We believe that the most successful approach involves a joint effort of speech-language specialists, bilingual education teachers, and general education classroom teachers. If students with speech or language problems leave your room for services, work with the speech-language pathologist to identify the best time for each student to be gone. During independent practice time, best subjects, or least favored regular class activities are better alternatives than during direct instructional times, subjects that require extra work, or favored activities. Try to keep a consistent schedule so students will know when to leave and what they will be missing each day. Provide cues (for example, a clock with times marked on it), but have students assume responsibility for being on time for special services. When students return, have a system (such as an assignment buddy or checking work folder) for getting them back with the regular program as quickly as possible. Recognize the need of each student with speech and language problems to receive special assistance, but try not to overgeneralize problems in other areas.

Labeling problems

Some of the terms used to describe students with communication disorders are listed in Table 9.3. Many of these terms have been used to describe students with other disabilities, and they tend to promote stereotyped thinking and negative impressions. We include them here as a reminder that, as with other types of disabilities, teachers and other professionals need to look carefully at the actual capabilities of students with speech and language problems, remembering the great diversity that can be hidden under a single label and the great disservice that can be done by lowering expectations as a result of the names assigned to children.

Millions with some impairment

Communication takes place constantly and is involved in every activity of daily living. Speaking and listening are the most common ways we communicate, but speech and language impairments affect more than 3 million Americans of all ages. These impairments range from mild to severe difficulty in producing speech sounds, in fluency, and in producing or understanding lan-

---

Table 9.3 Terms Often Used in Professional Literature to Describe Students with Speech and Language Problems

aggressive	impulsive
anxious	irritable
asocial	language delayed
competitive	language deviant
confused	language disordered
daydreamer	rigid
developmentally aphasic	shrewd
disruptive	shy
distractible	stubborn
dysfluent	submissive
erratic	unintelligent
frustrated	unmotivated
immature	uses baby talk

guage. Some people are unable to use speech at all. Regardless of where you work or what you do, you will encounter people with problems communicating. If you teach, some of these people will be your students. If you don't teach, some of these people will be your co-workers, neighbors, and peers. Because of the prevalence of speech and language difficulties, we end this chapter with a few suggestions for ways to improve communication.

Ways to improve communication

1. If a student, colleague, neighbor, or friend has a communication disability, learn all you can about it and ways to overcome it in your interactions.
2. Simplify information presented to people with communication disorders (for example, speak slowly in a normal tone of voice, use short sentences, use rephrasing, frequently check for understanding).
3. Present multiple forms of information.
4. Ask people with communication difficulties about their needs and ways you can overcome barriers to communication.
5. Show respect and sensitivity to individual differences and ask for help if you need it.

What Every Teacher Should Know

- Communication disorders related to speech and language are the second most common reason students receive special education.
- Speech disorders include problems producing speech sounds (articulation disorders), controlling sounds that are produced (voice disorders), and controlling the rate and rhythm of speech (fluency disorders).
- Language problems include difficulties using proper forms of language (phonology, morphology, syntax), using the content of language (semantics), and using the functions of language (pragmatics).
- Students with communication disorders often receive special education from speech-language pathologists, but sometimes people disagree about the relative responsibilities of these professionals and classroom teachers.
- General interventions for communication disorders include providing good models, an accepting classroom environment, and practice developing newly acquired speech skills.
- A continuing concern for teachers is differentiating true communication problems from cultural or dialectal language differences.

Projects

1. Volunteer to work in a setting where people with communication disorders are provided services. Participate for at least two hours on five different occasions. Describe the jobs you were given. Describe assistance you were provided by professionals working at the setting. Describe how you would

organize a volunteer experience if you were working in the same setting.

2. Draw a diagram illustrating how the following words or phrases are related to each other: *articulation, communication, content, expressive, fluency, form, function, grammar, language, pragmatics, receptive, semantics, speech, syntax,* and *voice.* Write a short paragraph that describes the diagram.

3. Ask a teacher of a student with a speech problem to share his or her instructional approaches.

4. Interview three professionals who work with people with communication disorders in three different settings. Ask them to describe what they do and any special methods they use to improve speech and/or language skills.

5. Select a journal that focuses on students with communication disorders. Browse the most recent issues in your library. Note the types of articles that are included (such as research, opinion, practical suggestions). Find at least three articles that describe specific teaching activities you could use to improve speech problems. Find at least three articles that describe specific teaching activities you could use to improve language problems.

For Your Information

Books

Bernstein, D. K., & Tiegerman, E. (1989). *Language and communications disorders in children* (2nd ed.). Columbus, OH: Merrill.
An overview of identification, causes, and intervention methods.

Brearley, S. (1989). *Talk to me.* Forestburgh, NY: A & C Black.
Children who are learning to communicate are portrayed using photographs and short passages. This is an excellent book for young readers.

Browning, S. (1973). *I can't see what you're saying.* New York: Coward.
A well-written story about a family's experiences with a child with aphasia, the inability to use words as symbols. Suitable for older readers, including adolescents and high school students.

Dan, J., & Hicks, K. (1987). *Games make alpha-betics fun.* Newport Beach, CA: Better Teaching Aid Publications.
A book of games that can be used to make language interesting and fun.

Hopkins, L. (1988). *Eating crow.* New York: Watts.
Croaker begins a friendship with a boy who does not speak. Elementary school students will enjoy this book.

Kemp, G. (1980). *The turbulent term of Tyke Tiler.* London: Faber.
A humorous English story about Tyke's friendship with Danny, a boy with a speech impairment.

Reed, V. A. (Ed.). (1986). *An introduction to children with language disorders.* New York: Macmillan.
An overview of language disorders, including information on assessment and intervention.

Riskind, M. (1981). *Apple is my sign.* Boston: Houghton Mifflin.
A young boy who is deaf and does not speak is sent to a special school in the early 1900s.

Shames, G., Wiig, E., & Secord, W. (1993). *Human communication disorders* (4th ed.). New York: Macmillan.
A comprehensive introductory text addressing key features of communication disorders. Recommended by the American Speech-Language-Hearing Association (ASHA).

Organizations

American Speech-Language-Hearing Association (ASHA)

This is the primary organization that supports parents, children, and educational programs for individuals with communication disorders. It promotes awareness and supportive activities, as well as preparation standards and competencies for speech-language pathologists. Members must hold the master's degree or equivalent with major emphasis in speech-language pathology, audiology, or speech and hearing science or the master's degree or equivalent and present evidence of active research, interest, and performance in the field of human communication. All members agree to abide by the code of ethics of the association. For more information, contact ASHA, 10801 Rockville Pike, Rockville, MD 20852–3279.

Division for Children with Communication Disorders (DCCD)

A division of the Council for Exceptional Children (CEC), DCCD encourages membership of professionals interested in program development and preparation activities related to students with communication disorders. DCCD provides outlets for the exchange of ideas through a variety of resources, including special publications and annual conferences. For more information, contact CEC, 1920 Association Dr., Reston, VA 22091.

International Society for Augmentative and Alternative Communication (ISAAC)

This group is devoted to enhancing the education, employment, and daily living of people with communication disorders. ISAAC produces a journal, *Augmentative and Alternative Communication,* and a newsletter; it also sponsors a biennial conference. For more information, contact ISAAC, P.O. Box 1762, Station R, Toronto, Ontario, Canada M4G 4A3.

Journals

Asha

This journal, published by the American Speech-Language-Hearing Association, pertains to the professional and administrative activities of speech-language pathology, audiology, and the Association. Manuscripts published in *Asha* may take the form of articles, special reports, news items, committee reports, reviews of books and materials, and letters. Articles are of broad professional interest and may be philosophical, conceptual, historical, or synthesizing. For more information, contact American Speech-Language-Hearing Association, 10801 Rockville Pike, Rockville, MD 20852-3279.

Journal of Speech and Hearing Disorders (JSHD)

JSHD is intended for professionals interested in disordered speech, language, and hearing, particularly clinicians who provide services to people with communication disorders and researchers who study the causes, assessment, and treatment of speech and language disorders. Articles, reports, and letters are published. For more information, contact Terry L. Wiley, Editor, *Journal of Speech and Hearing Disorders,* University of Wisconsin–Madison, Department of Communication Disorders, 1975 Willow Dr., Madison, WI 53706.

Journal of Speech and Hearing Research (JSHR)

This is a publication of the American Speech-Language-Hearing Association and pertains broadly to studies of the process and disorders of speech, hearing, and language. Experimental reports; theoretical, tutorial, or review papers; brief research notes describing clinical procedures or instruments; and letters to the editor are the primary types of material published in JSHR. For more information, contact John H. Saxman, Coordinating Editor, *Journal of Speech and Hearing Research,* Box 146, Teachers College, Columbia University, New York, NY 10027.

Language, Speech, and Hearing Services in the Schools (LSHSS)

This American Speech-Language-Hearing Association journal pertains to speech, hearing, and language services for children, particularly in schools. Articles published in LSHSS deal with all aspects of clinical services to children, including the nature, assessment, and remediation of speech, hearing, and language disorders; program organization; management and supervision; and scholarly discussion of philosophical issues relating to school programming. For more information, contact Wayne A. Secord, Editor, *Language, Speech, and Hearing Services in the Schools,* The Ohio State University, 110 Pressey Hall, 1070 Carmack Rd., Columbus, OH 43210-1002.

Teaching Students with Mental Retardation

Focusing Questions

- What definition is used for students with mental retardation?

- How are levels of retardation differentiated?

- How many students with mental retardation receive special education?

- What are the primary characteristics of students with mental retardation?

- What instructional approaches and teaching tactics are appropriate for students with mental retardation?

- What are severe disabilities?

- What instructional approaches are successful for students with severe disabilities?

- How can students with severe disabilities be successfully included in programs with their neighbors and peers?

Cecily is a high school freshman who had never taken classes with her peers before last year. She was born without a right hip, has poor vision and hearing, and has Down syndrome. Until last year, Cecily had always been in special education classes. When her parents proposed enrollment in her "home" high school, school officials were skeptical. The principal noted that there were no special classes in his school and no support system for Cecily. Nevertheless, the school agreed to give it a try. The experience was not easy. "Inappropriate questions," "Frustrated," "No friends," and "Always late for class" were words her teachers used to describe the first few weeks of school. Now, after a year, the experience is being called a "triumphant success." What happened?

Student volunteers and supportive teachers transformed Cecily's school experiences. Cecily's teachers adapted their lessons and tests for her and peer "buddies" provided assistance in every class. They helped her focus on what was expected in her assignments, held her to high expectations, and provided feedback on how she was doing. For the first time, Cecily tackled multiplication, division, word problems, and fractions. She gave a presentation in history class and read "The Odyssey," "To Kill a Mockingbird," and "Romeo and Juliet" in English class. Her previous school experiences represented the best offered to many students with mental retardation. Why hadn't Cecily made this kind of progress in her special education classes? Her father thinks it's simply because nobody challenged her to do it. ■

Mental retardation is a serious disability. People with mental retardation need special assistance to learn what many of their peers learn incidentally. Their learning problems also create obstacles in other areas of life that are often aggravated by prejudice and discrimination. With support from families, friends, teachers, neighbors, and peers, students with mental retardation, like Cecily, can be successful in school and lead happy and productive lives like everybody else. In most school districts across the country, this is happening in classrooms alongside neighbors and peers without disabilities.

Successful outcomes

After discussing students with mental retardation in the first part of this chapter, we briefly consider an overlapping group, students with severe disabilities. Although the terms are often confusing, those who are considered "severely" disabled generally have a substantial degree of retardation as well as other difficulties.

Definition

Variety of terms

Schools use a number of terms to label students with mental retardation: *mentally retarded, educationally retarded, educationally handicapped, mentally*

Bring Your Learning to Life

Career Education Goals Central to Cecily's Education Program

In addition to the regular content areas studied by her peers, Cecily's teachers are concerned about her success in career education competencies. The Individualized Education Program (IEP) that guides her special education contains long- and short-term objectives in some of the following areas:

Activities for Daily Living Success
   Life away from home
   Family and personal money management
   Child care and family living
   Personal hygiene
   Personal independence (food, clothing, shelter)
   Personal recreation and leisure
   Community living and responsibility
Activities for Personal-Social Success

Self-awareness, self-confidence, social responsibility
Social relations and personal independence
Communication and problem-solving skills
Activities for Occupational Success
   Job possibilities
   Job requirements
   Work habits
   Employment skills

Although achievement of these goals is important for all children and youth, students with mental retardation often need assistance learning what many of their peers learn without special help. Career education competencies are considered crucial for success in adulthood by students with mental retardation.

---

handicapped, severely handicapped, and *students with significantly limited intellectual capability.* Some states deliver services to students with mental retardation on a noncategorical basis without formally labeling them, although this is fairly uncommon.

Although there are several definitions used for this group of students, they typically reflect similar conditions: significantly subaverage intellectual and adaptive behavior functioning that adversely affects educational and life functioning. The American Association on Mental Retardation (AAMR) definition is representative (American Association on Mental Retardation, 1992):

AAMR definition

Mental retardation refers to substantial limitations in present functioning. It is characterized by significantly subaverage intellectual functioning, existing concurrently with related limitations in two or more of the following applicable adaptive skill areas: communication, self-care, home living, social skills, community use, self-direction, health and safety, functional academics, leisure, and work. Mental retardation manifests before age 18. (p. *iii*)

Limited functioning

The first part of this definition establishes mental retardation as a category of concern for people whose current levels of functioning are limited. Mental retardation is difficulty in learning and performing certain daily life skills as a result of substantial limitations in conceptual, practical, and social intelligence.

Intellectual functioning

The second part of this definition—"significantly subaverage intellectual functioning"—usually is translated as a score of 70 to 75 or below on one or more individually administered general intelligence tests. Test scores and other information are reviewed and evaluated by teams of professionals as a part of the process of diagnosing mental retardation.

Adaptive skills

The third part—that the individual also must demonstrate limited adaptive skills in key areas—is an important part of the definition. First, adaptive skill limitations must occur at the same time as intellectual limitations; intellectual functioning alone is insufficient basis for a diagnosis of mental retardation. Second, more than one area of adaptive skills must be limited to reduce the chances of making a mistake in diagnosing mental retardation. Finally, key skill areas central to successful life functioning are listed to facilitate the identification process.

Early manifestation

The last part of the definition indicates that mental retardation manifests itself before the age when individuals are typically expected to assume adult roles (the eighteenth birthday). From this perspective, mental retardation is viewed as a disorder of the life period characterized by the greatest expected development—namely, childhood.

Overrepresentation problems

There was a time when mental retardation was defined simply as significantly below average intelligence. Because low scores on intelligence tests could result from causes other than mental retardation (such as cultural differences, language differences), special classes were overpopulated with certain groups, such as socioculturally disadvantaged students and those from historical minorities. Parents, professionals, and students were not happy. With the addition of an adaptive behavior qualifier, definitions of mental retardation became more functional, and some of the overrepresentation problems were solved. The difference created by changing the definition is illustrated in Figure 10.1. Note that before the adaptive behavior qualifier was added, students with significantly subaverage intelligence were classified as retarded regardless of their behavioral functioning. Now, as the figure shows, a student fits the definition of mental retardation only if measured intelligence is significantly subaverage *and* adaptive behavior deficits are present.

Defining adaptive behavior

Whenever professionals try to define adaptive behavior, they come up against the same variables that make defining normal behavior difficult. The decision about the extent to which a person's behavior is adaptive is a subjective one; it depends largely on the standards of the individuals making the judgment and the environment to which the student is expected to adapt. There is no definition of adaptive behavior in the federal rules, but generally it refers to the way in which an individual functions in his or her social environment. The American Association on Mental Deficiency, now the American Association on Mental Retardation, defined adaptive behavior as

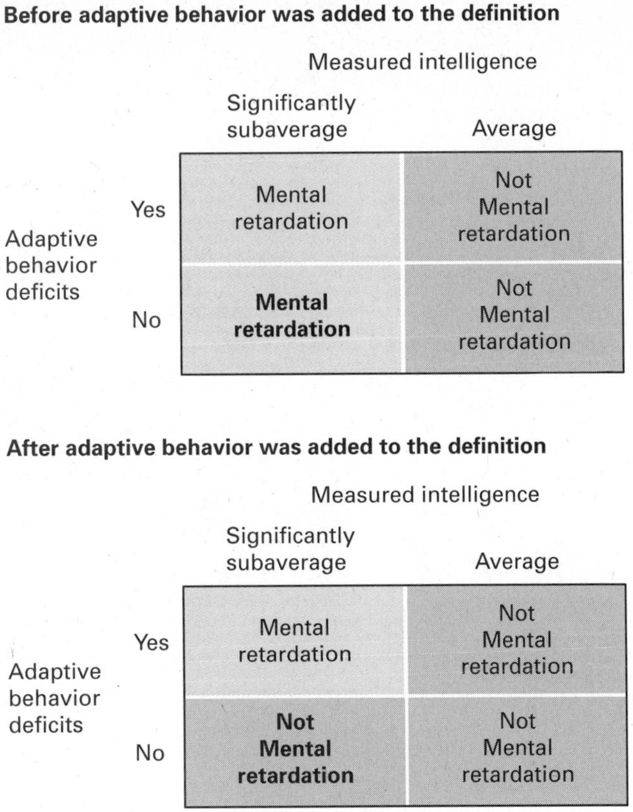

Figure 10.1
Effects of Adding Adaptive
Behavior to Definition of
Mental Retardation

Before adaptive behavior was added to the definition

After adaptive behavior was added to the definition

the effectiveness or degree with which the individual meets the standards of personal independence and social responsibility expected of his/her age and cultural group. (Grossman, 1983, p. 1)

The ten adaptive skill areas currently considered appropriate by the American Association on Mental Retardation are described in Table 10.1; being competent in these skill areas is appropriate for people with and without disabilities. Limitations in two of more of these areas are required for a diagnosis of mental retardation. Clinical judgments, environmental expectations, and potential support systems are considered when adaptive behavior is evaluated.

Adaptive behavior scales

There are dozens of adaptive behavior scales. They typically contain items related to self-care, communication, academic and social skills, home living, community use, health, safety, leisure, and work. The items usually require parents, teachers, or others familiar with the student's current functioning to respond to questions like these:

1. Some children are afraid of lots of things. How about _____ ?

   a. Is afraid of many things

   b. Is afraid of a few things

   c. Is not afraid of much

Table 10.1 Adaptive Skill Areas Evaluated in Diagnosing Mental Retardation

Area	Description
Communication	Communication includes the ability to comprehend and express information through spoken words, written words, graphic symbols, sign language, and manually coded English or nonsymbolic behaviors such as facial expressions, body movements, and gestures.
Self-care	Self-care involves skills such as eating, dressing, grooming, toileting, and personal hygiene.
Home living	Home living refers to daily functioning related to areas such as housekeeping, clothing care, property maintenance, food preparation, planning and budgeting for shopping, and home safety.
Social skills	Social skills include appropriate (for example, making friends, showing appreciation, smiling) and inappropriate (for example, tantrums, jealousy, public sexual behavior) social behaviors.
Community use	Community use refers to appropriate use of resources in the community, including transportation, shopping, obtaining services, worship, and using public facilities.
Self-direction	Self-direction refers to making choices related to learning and following a schedule, initiating appropriate activities consistent with personal interests, completing tasks, seeking assistance when needed, and resolving problems productively.
Health and safety	Health and safety refers to maintaining one's well-being, including having an appropriate diet, identifying, treating, and preventing illness, knowing basic first aid, and following rules and laws.
Functional academics	Functional academics include cognitive abilities and skills related to learning in school (for example, practical reading, writing, math, science, geography, and social studies).
Leisure	Leisure refers to recreational interests and skills related to them, such as choosing and initiating activities, taking turns, and using home and community activities alone and with others.
Work	Work relates to holding a job (part or full time) or participating in volunteer activities.

Source: Mental retardation: Definition, classification, and systems of support workbook, pp. 7–8. Copyright © 1992 American Association on Mental Retardation. Used with permission.

2. How does _____ get along with peers at school?
   a. not very well
   b. fairly well
   c. very well

People familiar with an individual's response to the daily demands of living in home, school, work, and community environments are best qualified to evaluate adaptive behavior.

Because expectations for different age groups vary, so do the criteria used to identify deficits in adaptive behavior at different ages. Grossman (1983) linked the criteria to developmental stages: During infancy and early childhood, deficits appear in

■ Development of sensorimotor skills
■ Communication skills (including speech and language)
■ Self-help skills
■ Socialization (ability to interact with others)

During childhood and early adolescence, deficits appear in all the areas just listed and/or

■ Application of basic academic skills in daily life activities
■ Application of appropriate reasoning and judgment in mastery of the environment
■ Application of social skills to participation in group activities and interpersonal relationships

During late adolescence and adult life, deficits appear in all the areas just listed and/or

■ vocational and social responsibilities and performance

The adaptive-behavior criterion is critical for identifying students with mental retardation. People who function adequately outside school are not considered mentally retarded, even if they perform poorly on intelligence tests. The adaptive-behavior criterion is also central to planning interventions for students with mental retardation. Instruction is directed at areas crucial to successful adaptation in schools, homes, and communities, not just typical academic areas (for example, reading, writing, arithmetic).

Levels of severity

Students with mild mental retardation sometimes are called **educable mentally retarded.** They represent more than 90 percent of all students with mental retardation (see Figure 10.2). Most of the states that offer special education services for these students use IQ scores between 50 and 70 as a partial basis for determining eligibility (these scores are more than 2 standard deviations below the mean). Intelligence test scores are used to differentiate other levels of mental retardation (see Table 10.2). Students with moderate retardation sometimes are called **trainable mentally retarded.** Students with moderate, severe, or profound retardation need ongoing assistance in most areas of practical living skills and are generally more dependent on others for care. Regardless of level of severity, today's students with retardation are receiving substantial

Figure 10.2
**Relations Between Mild,
Moderate, Severe, and
Profound Retardation**

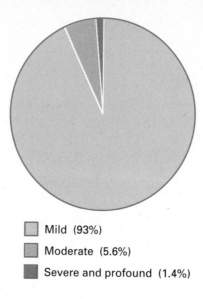

- Mild (93%)
- Moderate (5.6%)
- Severe and profound (1.4%)

portions of their instruction alongside their neighbors and peers without disabilities.

Prevalence

**State variations in
prevalence**

Of the 4.5 million school-age students receiving special education services during recent school years, approximately 554,000 were students with mental retardation. This number represents about 1 percent of all children and adolescents between 6 and 21. Individual states vary in percentages of the school-age population identified with mental retardation and receiving special education services. As illustrated in Table 10.3, the rates vary from highs of 2.52 percent in Alabama and 2.42 percent in Massachusetts to a low of 0.16 percent in Wyoming. Nationwide, approximately 12 percent of all students with disabilities are included in the category of mental retardation; the distrib-

Table 10.2 Levels of Retardation	
Severity	**IQ Range**
Mild	50–55 to 70–75
Moderate	35–40 to 50–55
Severe	20–25 to 35–40
Profound	below 20–25

| Table 10.3 | Percentage Distribution of Students with Mental Retardation (MR) in the United States |

State	All Disabilities[a]	MR[b]	MR as Percent of All Disabilities
All states	7.81	0.96	12.3
Alabama	8.99	2.52	28.0
Alaska	9.67	0.32	3.3
Arizona	6.38	0.59	9.3
Arkansas	7.62	1.75	23.0
California	6.55	0.37	5.7
Colorado	7.14	0.36	5.0
Connecticut	8.97	0.53	5.9
Delaware	8.56	0.91	10.6
District of Columbia	5.77	0.89	15.4
Florida	9.05	1.24	13.7
Georgia	6.28	1.46	23.3
Hawaii	5.05	0.51	10.1
Idaho	6.91	0.92	13.3
Illinois	8.30	0.91	11.0
Indiana	8.14	1.41	17.3
Iowa	8.35	1.59	19.0
Kansas	7.13	0.88	12.3
Kentucky	7.72	1.98	25.7
Louisiana	6.38	1.01	15.8
Maine	9.07	0.64	7.1
Maryland	7.99	0.50	6.3
Massachusetts	11.21	2.42	21.6
Michigan	6.97	0.82	11.8
Minnesota	6.97	0.95	13.6
Mississippi	8.15	1.03	12.6
Missouri	8.33	1.07	12.9
Montana	8.15	0.58	7.1
Nebraska	8.49	1.15	13.6
Nevada	6.80	0.48	7.1

ution across states ranges from about 3 percent in Alaska and New Jersey to over 20 percent in Alabama, Arkansas, Georgia, Kentucky, Massachusetts, and Ohio. One reason for this wide variation is that some states prefer to assign students to other special education categories such as learning disabilities. Another reason is that the adaptive-behavior criterion has been interpreted and implemented differently from one state to another.

Decline in numbers

Over time there has been a substantial drop in the number of students with mental retardation receiving special education in public schools, from approx-

Table 10.3 Percentage Distribution of Students with Mental Retardation (MR) in the United States (continued)

State	All Disabilities[a]	MR[b]	MR as Percent of All Disabilities
New Hampshire	7.78	0.35	4.5
New Jersey	10.48	0.32	3.1
New Mexico	9.02	0.48	5.3
New York	7.63	0.50	6.6
North Carolina	7.64	1.31	17.2
North Dakota	7.15	0.82	11.5
Ohio	7.78	1.67	21.5
Oklahoma	8.19	1.48	18.1
Oregon	8.03	0.58	7.2
Pennsylvania	7.50	1.22	16.3
Rhode Island	9.03	0.48	5.3
South Carolina	8.22	1.60	19.5
South Dakota	7.28	0.83	11.4
Tennessee	8.89	1.11	12.5
Texas	7.73	0.55	7.1
Utah	8.06	0.58	7.2
Vermont	7.55	1.04	13.8
Virginia	7.86	0.89	11.3
Washington	6.94	0.65	9.4
West Virginia	9.43	1.80	19.1
Wisconsin	6.77	0.37	5.5
Wyoming	2.77	0.16	5.8

[a] Percentage of school-age population (ages 6 to 21) receiving special education in all disability categories.

[b] Percentage of school-age population receiving special education in the category of mental retardation.

Source: U.S. Department of Education, (1993). *Fifteenth annual report to Congress on the implementation of the Individuals with Disabilities Education Act.* Washington, DC: Author.

imately 820,000 in 1976–77 to 554,000 in 1991–92 (about a 33 percent decrease). The decline in the number of students classified with mental retardation is believed due to a number of factors: stricter classification criteria (including adaptive behavior), court rulings controlling classification of minority students, and a tendency for both professionals and parents to classify students with mild learning problems as learning disabled rather than mentally retarded. The decreasing overall prevalence of mental retardation over time is also in part a function of medical and social advances in treating the factors that cause retardation. There are five general causes of mental retardation (American Psychiatric Association, 1987):

Causes of retardation

- Hereditary factors (inborn errors of metabolism, genetic abnormalities, chromosomal abnormalities). Down syndrome, a chromosomal abnormality, is the best known.
- Alterations of embryonic development due to maternal ingestion of toxins (alcohol, drugs), infections (maternal rubella), cerebral malformation, or unknown causes.
- Pregnancy and perinatal problems (prematurity, trauma, fetal malnutrition).
- Physical disorders acquired in childhood (lead poisoning, infections, traumas, brain disease).
- Environmental influences (psychosocial deprivation, sensory deprivation, severe neglect, malnutrition, complications of severe mental disorders).

Health improvements

A German measles vaccine has made major inroads in preventing maternal rubella, one cause of mental retardation in children. Phenylketonuria, an inherited metabolic disorder that can cause retardation, is being treated through diet. Efforts to educate women about the importance of good prenatal care have reduced the incidence of fetal malnutrition. With understanding of the environmental influences on retardation have come programs to improve conditions for those who are culturally disadvantaged.

Social class

Interestingly, the prevalence of mental retardation due to known biological causes is similar among children of all social and economic classes, except that certain causative factors, like prematurity and lead poisoning, are linked to poverty and lower social status. In cases in which no specific biological cause can be identified, mental retardation is evidenced by far more students from low than from high socioeconomic environments.

Placement options

Most (58 percent) students with mental retardation spend more than 60 percent of the school day in separate classes outside the regular classroom (U.S. Department of Education, 1993). These students are placed in self-contained special classrooms with part-time instruction in regular classes or in self-contained classrooms full time. Generally, the placements more commonly used for students with mental retardation are considered more restrictive than those used for most students with learning disabilities or communication disorders. Students with severe mental retardation are served in special day schools more often than their peers with other disabilities. The presumed need for and use of extended curriculum offerings (for example, career education, vocational training, teaching basic communication) are reasons for these differences; however, trends favoring inclusion of these students in general education classrooms are challenging such practices and beliefs.

Characteristics

Rate of learning

Early researchers in the field focused much of their effort on describing the characteristics of students with mental retardation. Primary indications include rates of learning that are slower than those of their peers and evidence of delays in most areas of development. For example, a 7-year-old child with mental retardation may be just beginning to demonstrate skills that his same-age peers demonstrated several years earlier, such as naming colors, counting numbers, and writing the alphabet. Similarly, whereas students with learning disabilities or communication disorders often display discrepancies in set performance in selected areas, students with mental retardation fail to meet expectations in several areas—cognitive, academic, physical, behavioral, and communication.

Overlapping characteristics

Mental retardation can also be a secondary condition, coexisting with another exceptionality. There is considerable overlap between the kinds of characteristics said to be evidenced by some students with mental retardation and those attributed to students with learning disabilities or behavior disorders. For example, students with mental retardation and those with learning disabilities are said to demonstrate attentional, memory, motor, and information-processing disorders. Students with mental retardation and those with behavior disorders are said to be anxious; to have temper tantrums; and to be overly aggressive, disruptive, dependent, and impulsive. It is almost impossible, then, to identify characteristics that are universal or specific to students with mental retardation. Representative characteristics and potential problems of students with mental retardation are presented in Table 10.4.

Cognitive

Cognitive problems

By definition, students with mental retardation show delayed cognitive functioning. A low score or set of scores on one or more intelligence tests is a diagnostic criterion of the condition and its severity (see Table 10.2). These students do not learn as effectively or efficiently as their agemates. Students with mental retardation are slow to generalize and conceptualize, and have very weak comprehension skills. They demonstrate limited short-term memory and have difficulty in discrimination, sequencing, and identifying analogies. They are less able to grasp abstract concepts than their peers. These cognitive deficits are considered the primary causes of their academic difficulties.

Academic

Retardation compared to learning disabilities

Students with mental retardation perform poorly in most academic areas, but at a level expected from their scores on intelligence tests. This is one distinction between mental retardation and learning disabilities. (Remember, students with learning disabilities show a discrepancy between their scores on intelligence tests and achievement tests.) Still another distinction is in the breadth of deficient performance. Students with mental retardation typically perform poorly in the majority of academic subject areas; students with learning disabilities often demonstrate specific areas of academic difficulty.

Physical

The physical appearance of most students with mental retardation does not differ from that of their peers, but some of their physical abilities (for example,

Table 10.4 Representative Characteristics and Concomitant Problems of Students with Mental Retardation

Area	Characteristics	Potential Problems
Cognitive	Limited memory Limited general knowledge and information Concrete rather than abstract thinking Slower learning rate	Inattention Inefficient learning style Difficulty communicating Prone to failure Standard teaching practices ineffective
Academic	Difficulty learning most academic content Limited performance in most content areas Limited problem-solving ability Limited content mastery	Limited attention, organizational skills, questioning behaviors, direction following monitoring of time and other school coping skills
Physical	Some discrepancies between physical and mental abilities	Performance often less than expected, based on physical appearance
Behavioral	Limited social and personal competence Limited coping skills Limited personal life skills and competence	Tardiness, complaints of illness, classroom disruptiveness, social isolation, inappropriate activity
Communication	Lower levels of language development, limited listening and speaking vocabularies	Trouble following directions, making requests, interacting, or communicating

gross and fine motor coordination, mobility) are deficient. Some students with mental retardation appear physically different from other students. Usually their retardation is a product of genetic rather than environmental factors. Nearly all of the genetic syndromes that result in mental retardation leave the individual with physical symptoms.

Those who have Down syndrome usually have a rounder face and shorter limbs than their agemates. They also tend to have some more specific physical differences, as explained later in this chapter. Klinefelter syndrome is a combination of physical abnormalities that typically result from aberrations in the sex chromosomes—pair 23 (the male has an extra X chromosome). These abnormalities become apparent only at and after puberty, and can include gynecomastia (development of female secondary sex characteristics), small testes, poor hair growth, and mental retardation. Microcephaly literally means "smallness of the head"; this also can be a physical sign of mental retardation.

Physical signs of particular conditions

Finally, neurofibromatosis (von Recklinghausen disease) is characterized by nerve tumor formation that can involve many parts of the body. If brain or spinal tissue becomes involved, mental retardation can result.

Mobility and movement

Most students with severe mental retardation have limited physical mobility. Many cannot walk, and some cannot stand or sit up without support. They are slow to perform physical movements (such as rolling over, grasping toys and objects, holding their heads up) that are easy for their peers without mental retardation.

Behavioral

Researchers have not been able to identify social and emotional characteristics specific to students with mental retardation, probably because each student is unique and interindividual variation is considerable, both in retardation level and in evidenced characteristics. By definition, individuals who are mentally retarded exhibit socially inappropriate behaviors; often they are both socially and emotionally immature. Inappropriate behaviors, antisocial behaviors, and odd mannerisms can lead others to reject those with mental retardation. Some people with severe or profound retardation have difficulty with independent living skills such as dressing, eating, exercising bowel and bladder control, and maintaining personal hygiene; often they must be cared for throughout their lives. People with severe retardation also often require special instruction involving adaptive devices (for example, specially designed eating utensils) or adapted learning sequences (for example, task-analyzed hierarchies) to learn these basic skills.

Inappropriate behaviors

Living skills

Communication

Conceptual development and language are closely related. Individuals who show delayed cognitive functioning typically show delayed development of language and communication skills. Students with mental retardation may have difficulty expressing themselves well enough to be understood. This is especially true of those with severe or profound retardation. Almost all students with severe mental retardation have limited abilities to express themselves or understand others. Many do not talk or use gestures to communicate; they often do not respond to communication from others. Those with mild retardation may demonstrate delayed comprehension as well as receptive and expressive language problems.

Language development

A Note on Down Syndrome

Down syndrome is a common type of mental retardation; it accounts for about 10 percent of all individuals with moderate and severe retardation. Down syndrome is a chromosomal abnormality. The nucleus of each human cell contains twenty-three pairs of chromosomes. In the most common type of Down syn-

Chromosomal differences

Window on Practice

A Parent's Perspective on Down Syndrome

My perspective on having a daughter with Down syndrome is unique. When I moved to Buffalo, New York, pregnant with my first child, my husband and I rented an apartment in a duplex downstairs from another couple who were also expecting their first child. In the short weeks before I gave birth, I became best friends with that other expectant mother, Lucy, and we looked forward to raising our children together. Little did we suspect that one month after my daughter Keller was born with Down syndrome, her son Michael would also be born with Down syndrome. Thus, my experience and attitude are colored by the fact that I have never felt alone or isolated as I know many parents of children with disabilities must feel. My friendship with Lucy has given me strength to take on more challenges than I might have taken on alone.

In our house Down syndrome was the norm. Keller was enrolled in an early intervention program, but I continued to treat her as a regular part of the family. At times I behaved as if I didn't realize she was different. When I went out, she went out. When she did something really goofy looking, I would laugh or get embarrassed. I had to keep my sense of humor and a kid with Down syndrome can be a source of real entertainment. Don't think for a second that I don't love my daughter with all my heart, but a part of loving her is accepting that she can bring me as much joy and laughter as any child brings to a parent.

When it came time for Keller to begin school, I looked at all the options our school system had to offer and, frankly, they were too segregated for me. Keller has always been treated as a regular member of our neighborhood. She had been functioning beautifully in our family, church, and the world in general. I was never quite happy with the separation in her preschool special education setting. No matter how much attention was heaped on her by teachers and professionals, it didn't make up for the fact that she wasn't included in the mainstream. How would she recognize normal and appropriate behavior if she was segregated from her peers? In the long run, I don't want her to be given special attention. I want her to be accepted and to meet her full potential. I didn't want to be the parent of a child with disabilities before I gave birth to Keller, but now I can't imagine my life without her. I suspected other people would feel about her the same way that I do if given the chance.

That's about all the rationale we had when Lucy and I asked our neighborhood school to give integration a chance for our kids starting kindergarten. It was not easy getting everyone to buy the idea, but we finally managed. Nor has it been easy to implement. The program has been in place for a year and I can't tell you how surprised and pleased I am with its success. Keller started writing her name spontaneously on her school work because all the other kids in the class did. She's learning age-appropriate independence and has impressed her teachers with how mature she has become. She's motivated to learn from her peers. She's been invited to birthday parties, friends call her on the phone, and her teacher reports she is quite popular in the class. It's a success for everybody involved: Keller and Michael, their classmates, their classmates' parents, the teachers, and the school in general.

I didn't know what a good idea integration would be until it happened. But then I didn't know what a good idea it would be having Keller as a member of our family. It's a good thing I wasn't given a chance to argue why I couldn't handle being the parent of a child with Down syndrome because I might have missed the opportunity to experience one of my greatest joys. And I'm not going to let our schools and school children miss the joy of knowing Keller and Michael either.

Charlotte Vogelsang is cofounder of Parent Network, an organization in Buffalo, New York, that advocates for children with disabilities.

drome, trisomy 21, the twenty-first pair has three rather than two chromosomes.

Physical characteristics

Some physical characteristics such as small stature, a relatively round face, and epicanthic folds (an extra flap of skin over the innermost corners of the eyes) are usually present in people with Down syndrome. These people often also have decreased muscle tone (hypotonia), hyperflexibility of joints, smaller oral cavities (causing tongue protrusion), and short, broad hands with a single palmar crease; they sometimes suffer heart, eye, respiratory, or ear problems. Identification in infancy is common. The level of retardation evident with Down syndrome is usually related to the age at which it was detected. Early identification and intervention results in less severe effects. Today many students with Down syndrome are being educated in regular classrooms with their neighbors and peers.

Early identification

Instructional Approaches and Teaching Tactics

Students with mental retardation need assistance learning the content and skills that many of their peers learn without special educational activities. Many of the tactics that are appropriate for teaching basic academic skills (reading, writing, and arithmetic) to students with learning disabilities (see Chapter 8), and communication to students with speech and language problems (see Chapter 9), are useful for teaching these same skills to students with mental retardation. These students also need special assistance relating what they learn to real-life experiences (that is, functional skills) and adjusting their approaches to learning activities (that is, school adaptive behavior). Effective teachers of students with mental retardation set high expectations for what they can achieve and focus their instruction on functional activities designed to promote success with real-life problems. A summary of general interventions used by teachers with students with mental retardation is presented in Table 10.5. Specific tactics for improving functional skills, school adaptive behavior, and leisure and work skills are discussed in the following sections.

High expectations

Improving Functional Academic Skills

Students with mental retardation respond to the same instructional methods as other students. They may require more time to achieve mastery, and typically require special instruction and extra practice to generalize what they have learned to settings other than the classroom. Sometimes they simply need to be taught how to approach academic tasks. For these students, basic academic skill instruction must go beyond basal readers and traditional worksheets. Effective teachers of these students design instructional and practice activities so that they relate to applications in everyday life, including home living and community use. Here are some ways you can do this.

Relating instruction to everyday life

Table 10.5 Top Ten List of Tips for Teachers of Students with Mental Retardation

1. Provide alternative instructional presentations using varied examples and focus on functional skills.
2. Provide opportunities for students to demonstrate understanding actively before moving to independent practice.
3. Provide more opportunities for practice than appropriate or necessary for classmates.
4. Use concrete examples when teaching new skills.
5. Provide supportive and corrective feedback more often than necessary for classmates.
6. Modify tests and evaluation measures to compensate for learning problems.
7. Evaluate students' performance and progress more frequently than appropriate or necessary for classmates.
8. Adapt instruction to the environments where what is being learned will be used.
9. Break lessons into smaller parts when teaching complex skills.
10. Be prepared to repeat teaching more frequently than necessary for peers.

Random checks

■ **To reduce task avoidance: Use random checks to monitor behavior.** Set an inexpensive kitchen timer to record the passage of randomly selected amounts of time during independent activities. Reward students who are working when the timer sounds.

Rewarding processes

■ **To improve task completion: Reward processes, not just products.** Completion of most classroom assignments can be broken into three main activities: starting, working, and finishing. With some students with mental retardation, simply getting started is a major accomplishment. Sometimes providing more frequent rewards, such as for starting and working, helps these students complete more work. Allowing them to select where to start and how much to do before a break can be helpful in improving the number of tasks they complete.

Practice with everyday materials

■ **To improve functional reading: Have students practice with everyday materials.** Use common community signs (for example, MEN, WOMEN, street names, business names); restaurant menus; selected sections of the newspaper (such as advertisements or sports); food labels; favorite foods; and names of toys or games, television shows, sports teams, or community helpers (such as mayor, sheriff, police) to create practice reading worksheets. Model the sheets on those being used with other reading materials, or make up some of your own. For example:

Put these streets in alphabetical order.

Redcoat Lane	1.	Allendale Lane
East Boulevard	2.	
West Boulevard	3.	
Allendale Lane	4.	
Sardis Road	5.	
Brentwood Drive	6.	
Randolph Road	7.	
Castle Street	8.	
Oldtowne Road	9.	
Walker Place	10.	

Using a phone book

■ **To improve functional reading: Practice with materials used in everyday living.** Using a local phone book, have students find numbers for classmates, teachers, friends, relatives, businesses, restaurants, movie theaters, and community agencies (such as sheriff and post office).

Computer puzzles

■ **To improve functional reading: Use computers to provide practice**: Place words from functional reading vocabulary into simple crossword or word-search puzzles produced with computer programs like *Crossword Magic* (Mindscape) or *WordSearch Deluxe* (Nordic Software). Have students prepare their own puzzles and exchange them with other classes in the school.

Word games

■ **To improve functional reading: Use games to practice word recognition.** Once students have learned a list of functional words, have them practice using them in games like Bingo or Concentration (see Figure 10.3). For bingo, have students prepare cards using words they are practicing. Select one student to be the caller and have others play bingo using poker chips, paper clips, or other markers to keep track of words as they are used. Have students decide the criterion for winning a game—straight line vertically, diagonal line, or four corners. For Concentration, have them put each word on two different index cards. Shuffle the cards and place them face down on a desk. Have students play the game by turning the cards over two at a time to find matches. Control the difficulty by the number of cards being used. Encourage social interaction by having two or more students play together.

Connecting writing to daily activities

■ **To improve functional writing: Use activities of daily living to practice writing, spelling, and handwriting.** Have students keep diaries of school activities, make lists of things to do and things that were done during the school day, practice taking telephone messages, complete job applications, order products from catalogs, write messages for parents describing upcoming school activities, and write letters to classmates as well as penpals in other classrooms, schools, states, and countries.

Computer math software

■ **To improve basic math facts: Have students practice with computer programs.** Use software like *Number Munchers* (MECC) to help students practice basic math operations (addition, subtraction, multiplication, and division). Keep records of performance improvements in accuracy and rate of completion for ten- and twenty-problem sets.

Figure 10.3
Examples of Bingo and Concentration

Bingo

Bobby's card

B	I	N	G	O
wait	walk	stop	street	job
help	cost	bill	safe	worker
work	hours	Free	wages	tax
check	bank	taxi	bus	boss
pay	store	food	enter	order

Jimmy's card

B	I	N	G	O
job	worker	tax	boss	order
street	safe	wages	enter	bus
stop	bill	Free	taxi	food
walk	cost	hours	store	bank
wait	help	work	check	pay

Concentration

Real-life math

■ **To improve functional math: Have students practice with real-life problems.** Everyday math skills are most commonly used in areas involving time, money, and measurement. Students with mental retardation need to practice these skills more than their peers. Prepare assignments on making change, keeping track of checking or savings account balances, doing comparison shopping, and keeping track of a weekly budget. Create problems on measurement (such as size of objects in the room, outside school, in the home) and time (such as telling time, using calendars, keeping schedules) to provide additional functional math practice.

Inclass field trips

■ **To improve functional math: Have students practice on classroom field trips.** A field trip is an experience designed to add to ongoing instructional programs. Most of the time, field trips are elaborate, well-planned visits to businesses, museums, or other places away from school. Inclass field trips can serve the same purposes. For example, functional-math field trips can provide experiences searching for specific information in newspapers or magazines in the classroom or at a local business (see Figure 10.4). The key is to have a specific set of activities for students to accomplish while on the field trip.

Figure 10.4
Inclass Field Trip Example

Field Trip Grocery Advertisement	Field Trip Grocery Store
Answer ☐ Find an item costing more than 45¢ but less than 89¢.	Answer ☐ Find two items whose prices are reversed (e.g., 69¢ and 96¢).
Answer ☐ Find three items that cost less than $1.00.	Answer ☐ Find three items whose total cost is less than $1.00.
Answer ☐ Find 5 items whose cost would be between $3.50 and $3.75.	Answer ☐ Find the price of three oranges and one grapefruit.
Answer ☐ Find something that costs less than $1.00.	Answer ☐ Find the price of a dozen large white eggs.
Answer ☐ Find two different items that cost less than $1.00.	Answer ☐ Find the price of the most expensive coffee in a can.
Notes: _____ _____ _____ _____	Notes: _____ _____ _____ _____

Bring Your Learning to Life

Task Analysis Helped Cecily's Teachers

Cecily's teachers were interested in making what they were teaching in science relevant to her daily life. They decided that first-aid skills were appropriate instructional objectives in areas related to personal hygiene and community living and responsibility. They located articles in professional journals that described procedures for teaching first aid skills to students with mental retardation (Stem & Test, 1989; Spooner, Stem, & Test, 1989). They used information in the articles to plan instructional units for Cecily and her classmates.

First, they identified important first aid skills: Communicating an emergency, applying a plastic bandage, and taking care of minor injuries. Second, they used task analyses presented in the articles to establish an appropriate teaching sequence to use with Cecily and to decide which skill to teach first (the least complex). They gathered baseline information on the extent to which Cecily was able to respond appropriately to mock situations involving first aid skills. Third, they taught each first aid skill using the demonstrate–demonstrate–practice–prove instructional model (see Chapter 4).

The teacher demonstrated the correct execution of the skill being taught. She then asked Cecily to demonstrate the skill. During this phase, she provided verbal praise (supportive feedback) for Cecily's correct responses and corrective feedback (verbal redirecting, another example, or physical guidance) for incorrect responses. When Cecily reached acceptable levels of performance (80 accuracy), the teacher had her practice the skills independently. She provided supportive and corrective feedback less frequently during the independent practice sessions. When Cecily had completed the instructional sequence, her teacher asked her to prove that she had learned the first aid skills by responding to mock situations without teacher assistance. She compared Cecily's performance before and after intervention to evaluate the effectiveness of the lessons and her instruction .

For the skill of communicating an emergency, Cecily's teachers used the following mock situation (Spooner, Stem, & Test, 1989):

> You and your friend are out at McDonald's eating lunch. Your friend is laughing and talking while eating and begins to choke on a piece of hamburger. He first begins to cough. Then he is unable to cough, breathe, or speak. What do you do?

For the skills of applying a plastic bandage and taking care of minor injuries, the teachers

(continued on next page)

Improving School Adaptive Behavior

Social skills, self-direction, self-care, and health and safety are among the school adaptive behaviors that are intervention targets for students with retardation. Improving the social repertoire of any student is not easy, and it is especially difficult for students experiencing adaptive behavior deficits. Here are some ways to address this area in your classroom.

Bring Your Learning to Life

Task Analysis Helped Cecily's Teachers *(continued)*

constructed similar mock situations. To evaluate Cecily's responses, they used these task analyses (Spooner, Stem, & Test, 1989):

Communicating an emergency

1. Locate phone
2. Pick up receiver
3. Dial 9
4. Dial 1
5. Dial 1
6. Put receiver to ear
7. Listen for operator
8. Give full name
9. Give full address
10. Give phone number
11. Explain emergency
12. Hang up after operator does

Applying a plastic bandage

1. Look at injury
2. Find bandages needed
3. Select proper size
4. Find outside tabs of wrapper
5. Pull down tabs to expose bandage
6. Find protective covering on bandage
7. Pull off by tabs exposing gauze portion
8. Do not touch gauze portion
9. Apply to clean dry skin

Taking care of minor injuries

1. Let it bleed a little to wash out the dirt
2. Wash with soap and water
3. Dry with clean cloth
4. Open plastic bandage
5. Cover with bandage (hold by the edges)
6. Call 911 if severe and no adult available

Finally, to judge the effectiveness of the lessons, Cecily's teachers plotted her progress on simple graphs like the following:

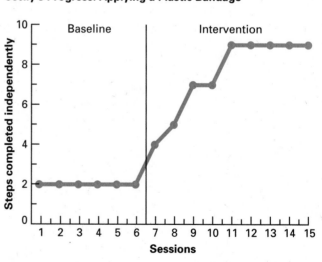

Cecily's Progress: Applying a Plastic Bandage

A play illustrating social skills

- **To improve social skills: Provide opportunities for practice** Create a "play" in which appropriate social skills are demonstrated in everyday activities (for example, greeting friends, working on group activity). Reward the "actor" for his demonstration. Be sure that students with mental retardation have opportunities to see the play and become actors.

Share experiences

■ **To reduce social isolation: Provide opportunities for sharing experiences.** Identify special interests and experiences for each of your students, and plan group activities to share this information and allow students to get to know each other better.

Help signals

■ **To improve self-direction and self-management: Provide signals for students.** Some students with mental retardation have not learned ways to let others know they need help. Some teachers create a signal system to replace unacceptable alternatives such as blurting out, wild hand waving, and not asking. For example, as we mentioned in Chapter 8, a small NEED HELP sign is a useful way for a student to get a teacher's attention without distracting others.

Best ways to react

■ **To improve self-direction and self-management: Have students practice and discuss alternative skills.** Select problem situations and discuss the best ways to react when faced with them. Have students generate, discuss, and practice as many alternatives as possible.

Card for self-monitoring

■ **To improve self-direction and self-management: Help students keep track of good behavior.** Place an index card on the corners of students' desks to keep track of appropriate behaviors such as completing assignments and asking for help. Periodically check the cards to be sure the students are monitoring appropriate behaviors. Have students with mental retardation share their self-reports with classmates and parents as a means of promoting positive self-concepts and pride in independent behavior.

Mock situations

■ **To improve self-care, health, and safety skills: Have students practice and discuss appropriate behaviors.** Create mock situations and have students generate, discuss, and practice appropriate solutions.

Improving Leisure and Work Skills

Being successful at work and knowing how to use free time are important adaptive behavior skills that are the focus of interventions for students with mild retardation. Work skills include following directions, being punctual, beginning assignments promptly, staying on task, and completing assignments; these are sometimes addressed with functional academic interventions. Leisure skills include functioning appropriately and independently during free time and participating in recreation activities that foster social skills.

Here are some ways to improve work skills:

Methods for improving work skills

1. Communicate to students that attendance and punctuality are important, and "practice what you preach."
2. Keep accurate records of attendance and punctuality, and provide special activities for students with perfect or improving records.
3. Have students monitor their own attendance and punctuality. Use daily journal entries or time cards as records for this self-monitoring activity.
4. Encourage students to be punctual by scheduling special announcements ("Anyone in his or her seat right now is eligible for a good behavior ticket") or providing special treats (piece of candy) for students who are on time for class.
5. Make special activities such as games, videos, and parties contingent on com-

Healthy competition should be part of the leisure skills curriculum for all students. © *Bob Daemmrich.*

pletion of assigned tasks. Start with a small number of tasks and gradually increase amounts of completed work to earn rewards.

6. Have students record and chart the number of assignments completed each day. Review the charts periodically and use them to make instructional planning decisions.

7. Break long assignments into shorter units. Provide rewards and support after completion of each smaller task.

8. Set liberal standards for task completion (such as one or two tasks a day) and gradually increase them after students with mild retardation develop appropriate work habits.

Here are some ways to improve leisure skills:

Methods for improving leisure skills

1. Identify the leisure needs of your students. Do they understand the concept of free time? Do they have basic leisure skills (for example, ability to play table games or interact with others)? Do they recognize age-appropriate leisure activities? Teach skills that have not been developed.

2. Incorporate recreation and leisure skills into existing instructional content. For example, have students call leisure businesses to obtain information as part of a social studies unit on community resources or use movie sections, recreation and parks brochures, or other leisure resources as reading materials.

3. Use leisure activities to reinforce classroom instruction. Teach students how to score a bowling game, figure won/loss records in sports, or calculate batting averages in baseball or field goal percentages in basketball. Create simple assignments for them to practice these skills.

4. Create problem-solving situations around leisure activities and discuss solutions to them. If it takes thirty minutes to walk to the bowling alley, what time should

Bring Your Learning to Life

Differential Grading Helped Cecily's Teachers

Cecily's teachers decided to use different systems when assigning inclass, homework, special-project, and report card grades. Sometimes they used simplified grades to reflect her performance: Pass/Needs Improvement/Fail, or Acceptable/Unacceptable. Other times they assigned a grade for achievement and another for effort. They also used combinations of three traditional grading systems:

1. *Grade-level appraisal.* Cecily's current grade level was identified, and her performance was compared to it.
   Cecily, Grade 7
   First Aid Grade Level 7
   First Aid Performance Grade A
2. *Performance-level appraisal.* Cecily's current grade level was identified, and her work behaviors rather than skill performance were compared to it.
   Cecily, Grade 7
   Reading Grade Level 3
     Reads independently: B+
     Asks for assistance: B

  Completes assignments
    independently: A
  Completes homework assignments: A

3. *Individualized appraisal.* Cecily's performance is evaluated using her individualized education program (IEP) goals and objectives.

Cecily, Grade 7

IEP Goal: By the end of the first semester, Cecily will demonstrate competence in key first aid skills.

Objective 1. Cecily will complete six steps in taking care of minor injuries with 100 percent accuracy. _√_ achieved _____ in progress

Objective 2. Cecily will complete nine steps in applying a plastic bandage with 100 percent accuracy. _√_ achieved _____ in progress

Objective 3. Cecily will complete twelve steps in communicating an emergency with 100 percent accuracy. _____ achieved _√_ in progress

you leave to be on time to meet your friends at 8:00? What alternatives do you have if you don't leave on time?

Students with mild and moderate mental retardation experience difficulties in many areas of school and life functioning. Instructional activities that work with these students aren't magical. In many ways, effective teaching of such students is the same as it is for all students (see Chapter 5). Whenever necessary, teachers modify their approaches to accommodate the special learning needs of their students. With this type of instruction, students with mild or moderate mental retardation can learn to overcome many of their problems, and can be successful and productive in school and life experiences. A key is the importance of high expectations: If we think we can, we will find a way; if we think we can't, we will not.

Severe Disabilities

Some students, particularly those with severe or profound levels of mental retardation, have disabilities so serious that they may be referred to in a separate group. As examples, consider these three young people:

> Andrew is in first grade. He gets around using a wheelchair. He has not developed language like his peers, and simple behaviors like feeding and dressing are extremely difficult for him.

> Thirteen-year-old Chris has never been in a "regular" classroom or neighborhood school. School district personnel thought Chris's behavior problems were too severe to be handled by general education teachers. But educational outlooks are changing. This year Chris will attend the same middle school as the other children living in the neighborhood. Teachers at the school will receive support from Chris's former special education teachers to make the transition go more smoothly.

> Stephanie is 23 years old. She spent most of her school career in a special day school for students with severe retardation. Now she is living in a small group home and working at a local fast-food restaurant where she clears tables and keeps the dining area orderly and clean.

In the not so distant past, students like Andrew, Chris, and Stephanie were not provided free, appropriate education like their neighbors and peers. There was a time when the lives of people with severe disabilities were thought hopeless. Today, school districts across the country are making serious efforts to develop effective ways to provide students with severe disabilities the same educational opportunities they provide to all other students.

Although there is no specific federal category for people who require intensive intervention or whose problems are especially severe, we can describe the way various professionals and organizations have discussed this group.

Definition

No federal guidelines

No definition for severe disabilities is included in federal guidelines for providing special education. However, the Association for Persons with Severe Handicaps (TASH) addresses the interests of people with severe disabilities, many of whom have traditionally been labeled with severe and profound mental retardation. The Association for Persons with Severe Handicaps (Meyer, Peck, & Brown, 1991: Document I.1, p. 19) has provided a widely accepted definition for **severe disabilities:**

TASH definition of severe disabilities

> These people include individuals of all ages who require extensive ongoing support in more than one major life activity in order to participate in integrated community settings and to enjoy a quality of life that is available to citizens with fewer or no disabilities. Support may be required for life activities such as mobility, communication, self-care, and learning as necessary for independent living, employment, and self-sufficiency.

Although people with any disability may be considered "severe," the label is usually reserved for a specific group of individuals. People in this group generally exhibit extremely low scores on intelligence tests (more than 3 standard deviations below average) and require special assistance because medical and physical problems, communication problems, and/or vision and hearing problems seriously limit the extent to which they profit from ordinary life experiences.

Prevalence

The prevalence for this group is difficult to determine because there is no universally accepted definition and current federal categories and data collection procedures do not include students with severe disabilities. Estimates range from 0.1 to 1 percent of the population, and it is generally agreed that this is an important group of students with disabilities in need of special education services. Most school districts in the country have programs for these students.

Curriculum Considerations and Instructional Approaches

Functional skills

The curriculum for students with severe disabilities emphasizes functionality, age appropriateness, and independence. Functional skills have applications in everyday life, including home living and community use. Using public transportation and purchasing items from vending machines are examples of functional skills that are appropriate for students with severe disabilities. All

Age-appropriate activities

students should participate in activities that are appropriate for their chronological age. For students with severe disabilities, this means learning functional skills and practicing them in natural environments in the presence of, or interacting with, peers without disabilities. Being independent, making decisions,

Independence

and participating in life's experiences are important goals for people with severe disabilities, just as they are for their peers.

Critical areas of instruction

Four areas of instruction are considered critical for students with severe disabilities: communication, self-care, mobility, and community living. Students who can communicate verbally or in writing are more likely to have a wider range of opportunities than their peers who are unable to speak or write. The development of self-care skills should begin early in the lives of students with severe disabilities because these skills represent a key stage in becoming an independent, functional person. Being able to get around in the environment also represents an important step in functionally independent, age-appropriate behavior. All these skills come together to support independent community living, including work and recreation.

Communication alternatives

Some students with severe disabilities are able to learn to understand spoken and written language; others may not learn these skills, even after extensive instruction. Alternative systems for communicating— sign language, communication boards, symbol boards, and electronic communication aids—enable these students to express their feelings in much the same way words and written messages enable their peers to communicate. Developing some form of communication is a key component of any instructional program designed to achieve functional, age-appropriate, independent behaviors.

Teaching self-care skills

Students with severe disabilities may experience delayed development of self-care skills that their peers without disabilities learn easily. For example, they often must be taught feeding, dressing, toileting, and grooming skills, such as hand washing, face washing, tooth brushing, and hair combing, with very specific instructional sequences before they acquire and use them as part of their daily lives.

Mobility, movement, and posture

Movement and posture are important to independence. They are linked not only to general health and comfort, but also to participation in school and community activities. It is not difficult to imagine how restrictive life would be if we could not move around easily in the environment or if we were unable to control our head, arm, or leg movements when sitting, standing, reaching and grasping, or walking. It is easy to see the importance of mobility and movement in the educational programs of students with severe disabilities. Adaptive equipment, such as the kind that facilitate appropriate body positions and movements, and physical therapy to improve flexibility, posture, and range of motion are critical components of instructional programs for many of these people.

Work skills

Functional, age-appropriate, independent community living requires mastery of basic vocational and recreational skills. Students with severe disabilities must be taught job-related vocational skills (such as following instructions, completing specific tasks, following rules) that their peers without disabilities often learn incidentally on the job. They require assistance finding, learning, performing, and keeping jobs. They also require assistance occupying them-

Leisure skills

selves constructively when they are not working. Students with severe disabilities may not learn appropriate and satisfying recreational skills without formal instruction.

A variety of instructional approaches are appropriate and effective in teaching communication, self-care, mobility, and community living skills to students with severe disabilities. Generally these involve increasing appropriate behavior or decreasing inappropriate behavior to facilitate functional, age-appropriate, independent living skills. The process teachers of students with severe disabilities use is the same process other teachers use; it includes the following steps:

Steps in teaching students with severe disabilities

1. Assessing current level of functioning (What can the student do relative to what is expected or desired?)
2. Defining the skill to be taught (What is the student expected to do or what will be taught?)
3. Arranging the conditions of learning (What sequence of steps will be used to teach the desired skill?)
4. Prompting or cueing responses (What verbal or physical messages will show the student what to do?)
5. Reinforcing responses (What feedback will be used to increase or maintain the student's behavior?)

Students with severe disabilities are being successful in neighborhood schools and their classmates and friends are sharing in the excitement of this integration. *Laura Dwight.*

6. Promoting generalization (What procedures will be used to ensure the behavior is exhibited in natural settings with peers and other people without disabilities?)

7. Evaluating performance (What information will be used to judge success?)

Successful inclusion

With instructional support, students with severe disabilities can be successful in school. Across the country, students with severe disabilities are attending neighborhood schools, interacting with their neighbors and peers, and participating in normal community activities. For example, in Vermont, students with severe disabilities have been receiving special education supports in general education classrooms since 1984, and it is working:

> At the beginning of the year, if I was making copies of something I might forget to count Jon: I just didn't deal with him. . . . When I count the kids in my class now, I've counted Jon. It just took me a while. (Giangreco, Dennis, Cloninger, Edelman, & Schattman, 1993, p. 359)

To ensure successful inclusion, school districts have adopted a number of principles when placing students in neighborhood programs:

Principles for placement

1. Place them in schools as close as possible to those attended by neighbors and peers.

2. Place them in age-appropriate schools.

3. Place them in schools and classrooms where principals and other personnel support inclusion.

4. Avoid placing them in schools with large numbers of students with other disabilities.

5. Avoid having their classes in isolated, nonacademic areas of the school.

Additional tips for including students with severe disabilities in school activities with their neighbors and peers are presented in Table 10.6; these suggestions are appropriate ways to facilitate inclusion of all students with disabilities.

Table 10.6 Top Ten List of Strategies for Promoting Interactions for Students with Severe Disabilities

1. Have students with severe disabilities use all school facilities at times their neighbors and peers use them.

2. Include students with severe disabilities in all regular school activities (for example, assemblies, graduation) available to neighbors and peers.

3. Include students with severe disabilities in field trips and fund-raising projects (for example, magazine sales, plant sales).

4. Include students without disabilities as aides in special activities (such as monitoring medication, physical therapy sessions) for students with severe disabilities.

5. Include students with severe disabilities in regular music, art, and physical education classes, as well as in homerooms and study halls.

6. Include students with severe disabilities in school improvement projects (such as arranging bulletin boards, planting flowers, decorating for parent night) with their neighbors and peers.

7. Include students without disabilities in activities designed specifically for students with severe disabilities (for example, Special Olympics).

8. Include students with severe disabilities in recess and extracurricular activities.

9. Include students with severe disabilities in all special classroom activities (publishing parties, holiday celebrations, birthdays).

10. Include students with severe disabilities in regular school jobs (for example, attendance monitors, cafeteria helpers, audiovisual assistants).

Source: "Top 10 List of Strategies for Promoting Interactions for Students with Severe Disabilities" adapted from "From Segregation to Integration: Strategies for Integrating Severely Handicapped Students in Normal School and Community Settings" by S. J. Taylor, JASH, 1982 8 (3). Reprinted by permission of The Association for Persons with Severe Handicaps.

Current Trends and Issues in Mental Retardation

Normalization

Deciding where students with disabilities should be provided educational experiences is not easy. It has been and will continue to be an important issue in special education, especially as it relates to mental retardation. The concept of **normalization,** as well as the least restrictive environment provisions of federal legislation, demands that the lives of people with mental retardation be as "normal" as possible. But as we mentioned earlier in the chapter, compared to other students with disabilities, students with mental retardation are more likely to receive educational services in more restrictive placements (U.S. Department of Education, 1993).

Debate about placement

Some professionals believe that these separate classrooms and special school programs represent the best placements for students with mental retardation. They claim that these settings provide the best opportunities for delivering the special instruction necessary for success. Others argue that separation from normal society is not good, and they promote full participation and integration of students with mental retardation in the same experiences as their neighbors and peers. There's no simple answer to deciding where special education should be provided. This issue, along with other concerns related to treatment, is continuously debated.

Prevention

Many causes of mental retardation are preventable; the President's Committee on Mental Retardation reported that more than half of all cases of mental retardation could have been prevented. There has been a continuing concern in this area of special education for prevention and early intervention. As illustrated in Table 10.7, many of the strategies for controlling mental retardation are simple; the issue is more one of why society has been so slow in implementing prevention strategies than of what should be done to prevent mental retardation.

Life after school

In addition to preventing and controlling retardation in young children before they enter school, professionals are concerned with the treatment of people with retardation who have left school programs. Not too long ago, many adults with mental retardation were segregated in institutions. Today, more and more people with retardation are living in natural environments, creating a need for people and services concerned with successful transition.

The ITP

Many students with mental retardation make the transition from school to job placements and work under the supervision of special education personnel. An *individualized transition plan (ITP)* is usually written as part of the student's IEP. While the IEP focuses on educational goals and objectives to be achieved during the school year, the ITP addresses skills—such as making leisure choices, being able to shop, and job placement assistance—and supportive services—such as vocational rehabilitation—required outside of school and in the future. The ITP lists transition services in attempts to coordinate assistance provided by outside agencies and the school. A typical ITP delimits instruction to be completed in the community and lists referral agencies for job placement and on-the-job services.

Graduation rate

In recent years, about 63 percent of students with mental retardation exited school by graduating with either diplomas or certificates of attendance (U.S. Department of Education, 1993). Compared to students with learning disabil-

Table 10.7	Top Ten List of Concerns for Professionals Interested in Preventing Mental Retardation

1. Obtaining proper medical care, as well as maintaining good maternal health and nutrition during pregnancy.
2. Preventing or treating infections during pregnancy.
3. Helping parents avoid sexually transmitted diseases.
4. Encouraging parents to plan and space pregnancies, as well as seeking genetic counseling and proper prenatal tests.
5. Ensuring proper nutrition, immunization, and general medical care for all children.
6. Keeping homes, vehicles, schools, and communities safe.
7. Creating appropriate educational programs.
8. Educating parents and providing support in parenting skills.
9. Protecting children from abuse and neglect.
10. Providing public education on causes of mental retardation.

ities or communication disorders, more students with mental retardation graduated through the certificate method. The percentage of these students who dropped out (about 22 percent) is slightly below that for all other students receiving special education (U.S. Department of Education, 1993).

Problems in transition

Follow-up studies have indicated that the majority of special education graduates do not make successful transitions from school to life as adults in their local communities. Many remain underemployed or unemployed despite participating in successful transition experiences. Professionals argue that this is due to a lack of decision-making skills and the unnatural experiences fostered by special education. This concern has spawned support for full participation of people with disabilities in natural settings in the community and for teaching them to make choices. **Self-determination,** also known as **self-advocacy,** refers to the ability to consider options and make appropriate choices at home, during school, at work, and during leisure time. It has become the battlecry of professionals, parents, and people with disabilities and probably will continue into the next century.

Self-determination

Mental Retardation in Perspective

Mistreatment in early societies

Mental retardation is one of the oldest categories of special education. Providing assistance to people with mental retardation and severe disabilities has come a long way. In early Greek society, infants were examined by a council of elders. If they were weak or disabled, they were left to die in the mountains. In early Roman society, children who were blind, deaf, or mentally dull were thrown by their parents into the Tiber River. Throughout early European and Asian history, people who were thought to be retarded were excluded from society. Present-day customs are very different.

Recent advances

Changes in the treatment of people with mental retardation came from the work of professionals who demonstrated that they could be helped and argued for humane treatment. In 1972, the Pennsylvania Association for Retarded Citizens (PARC) sued the Pennsylvania Department of Education, claiming denial of services to children with mental retardation. Based on the decision in *PARC* v. *Commonwealth of Pennsylvania,* the state's school districts were forced to locate, assess, and plan an appropriate educational program for students with mental retardation who had been excluded from school. The decision in PARC was one of the primary forces behind enactment of Public Law 94–142 (see Chapter 3). Through litigation and the activity of advocacy groups (among them, the Association for Retarded Citizens, the Council for Exceptional Children, and the American Association on Mental Retardation) and powerful people (such as the Kennedys and Hubert Humphrey), treatment and services for students with mental retardation and severe disabilities have improved dramatically. Today many people with mental retardation are taking control of their own lives. This movement, known as self-determination or self-advocacy, is one more example of the desire of people with mental retardation to be treated just like everybody else. As one group of professionals put it:

> The environments in which students with severe intellectual disabilities receive instructional services have critical effects on where and how they spend their postschool lives. Segregation begets segregation. We believe that when children with intellectual disabilities attend segregated schools, they are denied opportunities to demonstrate to the rest of the community that they can function in integrated environments and activities; their nondisabled peers do not know or understand them and too often think negatively of them; their parents become afraid to risk allowing them opportunities to learn to function in integrated environments later in life; and taxpayers assume they need to be sequestered in segregated group homes, enclaves, work crews, activity centers, sheltered workshops, institutions, and nursing homes. (Brown et al., 1989, p. 1)

Toward fuller inclusion

We would like to see fuller efforts at including people with disabilities in all aspects of life. Schools should serve all students, including those with mental retardation, and neighborhood schools are the best places for this service. Inclusive schools can offer a wide range of services for students with mental retardation as well as those in any other special education category. Responsibility for bringing these services to students rests with the entire professional staff, not just special education personnel. Significant progress has occurred in making inclusive schools a reality in today's educational system, but there is plenty of room for improvement. You can make this improvement happen.

What Every Teacher Should Know

- Mental retardation is one of the oldest areas in special education.
- The term refers to people who have difficulty learning and consistent delays in adaptive behavior and development.
- Professionals use scores on intelligence tests and measures of adaptive behavior as indications of learning and development.
- Academic instruction is the most common area in which teachers must modify what they do to accommodate students with mild mental retardation.
- The goal of education for students with retardation is preparation for adult life by teaching functional academic skills, adaptive behavior skills, and leisure and work skills.
- Instruction for students with mental retardation is more focused on everyday life experiences than it is for their peers.
- Students with severe disabilities exhibit extremely low scores on intelligence tests and require special assistance because medical and physical problems, communication problems, and/or vision and hearing problems seriously limit the extent to which they profit from ordinary life experiences.
- Students with severe disabilities require assistance with communication, self-care, mobility, and community living skills to be successful in everyday life.
- Employment is the single most important concern for those who work with adults with mental retardation and severe disabilities.
- History is full of incidents of less than favorable treatment of people with mental retardation and severe disabilities, but times are changing as a result of legal action and concern for normalization and inclusion.

Projects

1. Imagine that you are a teacher with several students with mental retardation in your classroom. What decisions would you have to make to help these students be successful? What instructional approaches would be appropriate for working with them? What specific activities would you use to adapt a lesson you were teaching to your class on measurement?

2. Attend a parents' group that is concerned with education of students with mental retardation. List the topics that are discussed. Interview at least three parents to obtain their overall impressions of the services provided by the school system to their children.

3. Check your local newspaper for evidence of bias, prejudice, or stereotypical thinking about people with mental retardation. Find articles and news stories that portray people with mental retardation favorably and write a letter to the editor supporting the work the newspaper did. If you find a

negative portrayal, write a letter "educating" the paper as to a better way to present information about people with mental retardation.

4. Contact a local, state, or national organization that focuses on people with mental retardation. Identify the purpose of the organization, its membership, and its services.

5. Look in the Yellow Pages of your local phone book for agencies that serve people with mental retardation. Call several and ask about the kinds of services they provide and how they work with school personnel to meet the needs of these students and their families.

For Your Information

Books

Bergman, T. (1989). *We laugh, we love, we cry: Children living with mental retardation.* Milwaukee, WI: Gareth Stevens.

A story about two sisters experiencing mental retardation. Excellent book for elementary school students.

Byars, B. (1970). *The summer of the swans.* New York: Viking.

The story of Sara, a fourteen-year-old with all the joys of adolescence, and how her life changes when her brother with mental retardation disappears.

Cipani, E., & Spooner, F. (1994). *Curricular and instructional approaches for persons with severe disabilities.* Needham Heights, MA: Allyn & Bacon.

An edited text addressing key areas of instruction for people with severe disabilities, including principles underlying behavior change, curricular domain, and key service delivery issues and approaches.

Edwards, J., & Dawson, D. (1983). *My friend David: A source book about Down syndrome and a personal story about friendship.* New York: Ednick Communications.

The first part of this book is a handwritten autobiography written by David Dawson, a man with mental retardation.

Garrigue, S. (1978). *Between friends.* New York: Scholastic.

Jill learns about retardation through her friendship with Dedi. Excellent book for upper elementary and middle school students.

Kaufman, S. Z. (1988). *Retarded isn't stupid Mom!* Baltimore: Paul H. Brookes.

What is it like to grow up with mental retardation? How do parents and families cope with the challenges and frustrations of daily life? Sandra Kaufman, with her daughter's assistance, describes joys and sorrows of raising a child with mental retardation.

MacMillan, D. L. (1982). *Mental retardation in school and society* (2nd ed.). Boston, MA: Little, Brown.

An introductory textbook describing definitions, levels of retardation, causes, and interventions.

Meyer, L. H., Peck, C. A., & Brown, L. (1991). *Critical issues in the lives of people with severe disabilities.* Baltimore, MD: Paul H. Brookes.

An edited text addressing six major resolutions passed by the Association for Persons with Severe Handicaps on critical issues of consequence for people with severe disabilities. Definitions and diagnosis, deinstitutionalization and community services, redefinition of a continuum of services, extensions of law and educational services, adult services, and life and death issues are addressed. Considered by many to be the primary book for those interested in people with severe disabilities.

Nobel, V. (1993). *Down is up for Aaron Eagle.* San Francisco, CA: Harper.

A mother's story of living and growing with a child with Down syndrome.

Robinson, N. M., & Robinson, H. B. (1976). *The mentally retarded child: A psychological approach* (2nd ed.). New York: McGraw-Hill.

An introductory textbook describing definitions, levels of retardation, causes, and interventions. Considered a classic by many professionals in mental retardation.

Shyer, M. F. (1978). *Welcome home, Jellybean.* New York: Macmillan.

A 12-year-old boy encounters major difficulties when his older sister with mental retardation comes home to stay. Excellent book for upper elementary and middle school students.

Snell, M. E. (1993). *Instruction of students with severe disabilities* (4th ed.). New York: Macmillan.

An edited text addressing key areas of instruction for people with severe disabilities, including assessment and functional skill intervention in key curriculum areas.

Organizations

American Association on Mental Retardation (AAMR)

Established in 1876, the American Association on Mental Retardation comprises physicians, educators, administrators, social workers, psychologists, psychiatrists, and others interested in the general welfare of persons with mental retardation and the study of causes, treatments, and prevention of mental retardation. The organization facilitates research and provides information for professional development. For more information, contact AAMR, 1719 Kalorama Rd., NW, Washington, DC 20009, (800) 424-3688.

Division on Career Development (DCD)

Founded in 1976, the Division on Career Development includes members of the Council for Exceptional Children who teach or in other ways work toward career development and vocational education of people with disabilities. The organization promotes research, legislation, information dissemination, and technical assistance relevant to improving life experiences of people with disabilities. For more information, contact DCD, Council for Exceptional Children, 1920 Association Dr., Reston, VA 22091.

Division on Mental Retardation and Developmental Disabilities

Founded in 1964, the Council for Exceptional Children's Division on Mental Retardation and Developmental Disabilities (CEC-MRDD) advances professional growth and research to promote programs for individuals with mental retardation and developmental disabilities. With 6800 members, including teachers, teacher educators, administrators, researchers, and other professionals, it is one of the largest CEC divisions. CEC-MRDD members receive professional journals, *Education and Training in Mental Retardation* and *MRDD Express,* and have access to other resources of interest to professionals working and living with people with mental retardation. For more information, contact CEC-MRDD, Council for Exceptional Children, 1920 Association Dr., Reston, VA 22091.

The Association for Persons with Severe Handicaps (TASH)

The Association for Persons with Severe Handicaps is dedicated to people perceived as having severe intellectual disabilities and seeks to build an inclusive society that values all people. TASH membership consists of people with disabilities, families, professionals, and community members committed to communities where no one is segregated and everyone belongs, new alliances that embrace diversity, eradication of injustices and inequities, research, education, dissemination of knowledge and information, legislation and litigation, and excellence in services. For more information, contact TASH, 11202 Greenwood Ave., N., Seattle, WA 98133.

The Association for Retarded Citizens (ARC)

The Association for Retarded Citizens was founded in 1950 as an organization for parents, professionals, and others interested in mental retardation. Work at local, state, and national levels promotes appropriate treatment, research, public understanding, and legislation for people with mental retardation. For more information, contact ARC, 2501 Ave. J, Arlington, TX 76011.

Journals

American Journal on Mental Retardation (AJMR)

This journal is published by the American Association on Mental Retardation. It is a scientific and archival multidisciplinary journal for reporting original contributions of the highest quality to knowledge of mental retardation, its causes, treatment, and prevention. Typical contents include (1) reports of original research on characteristics of people with mental retardation, individual differences in and correlates of such characteristics, and factors that alter them; (2) systematic reviews of and tightly conceived theoretical interpretations of research; and (3) reports of evaluative research on new treatment approaches. Annotated bibliographies, anecdotal case reports, descriptions of treatment procedures or programs, personal accounts, and descriptions of new test standardizations are not published. For more information, contact Dr. Stephen R. Schroeder, 1052 Dole Human Development Center, University of Kansas, Lawrence, KS 66045.

Education and Training in Mental Retardation (EMTR)

This publication of the Council for Exceptional Children (Mental Retardation and Developmental Disabilities Division) focuses on the education and welfare of persons who are retarded with research and expository manuscripts and critical reviews of the literature. Major emphasis of manuscripts appearing in this journal is on identification and assessment, educational programming, characteristics, training of instructional personnel, habilitation, prevention, community understanding and provisions, and legislation. For more information, contact Dr. Stanley H. Zucker, Editor, Special Education Program, Farmer 305, Arizona State University, Tempe, AZ 85287-2001.

Journal of the Association for Persons with Severe Handicaps (JASH)

This publication carries articles reporting original research, reviews of literature, and conceptual papers that address service delivery, program development, assessment, and intervention for people with severe disabilities. JASH is published quarterly by the Association for Persons with Severe Handicaps (TASH). For more information, contact TASH, 11202 Greenwood Ave., N., Seattle, WA 98133, or Jim Halle, Editor, JASH, Department of Special Education, University of Illinois, Champaign, IL 61820.

Journal of Intellectual Disability Research (JIDR)

Devoted exclusively to the scientific study of mental deficiency, this journal includes papers reporting original observations in this field. The subject matter covers clinical case reports; pathological reports; biochemical investigations; genetics and cytogenetics; psychological, education, and sociological studies; the results of animal experiments; and studies in any discipline that may increase knowledge of the cases, prevention, or treatment of mental retardation. For more information, contact Editor, *Journal of Intellectual Disability Research,* University of Wales, College of Medicine, 55 Park Place, Cardiff CF1 3AT, South Glamorgan, Wales, United Kingdom.

Mental Retardation (MR)

Published by the American Association on Mental Retardation, this is a journal of policy, practices, and perspectives in the field of mental retardation. As a publication with an applied focus, MR includes essays, qualitative and quantitative research articles, conceptual papers, comprehensive reviews, case studies, policy analyses, and innovative practice descriptions and evaluations. Style, methodology, or focus of an article is less important than its quality and contribution to knowledge about improving the lives of individuals with mental retardation. For more information, contact Dr. Steven J. Taylor, Editor, *Mental Retardation,* Center on Human Policy, 200 Huntington Hall, Syracuse, NY 13244-2340.

Research in Developmental Disabilities (RDD)

This journal publishes articles reporting original research, reviews of literature, and conceptual papers that address theory and behavioral research related to people with severe and pervasive developmental disabilities. RDD is published quarterly. For more information, contact Editor, RDD, Pergamon Press, Maxwell House, Fairview Park, Elmsford, NY 10523.

Teaching Students with Serious Emotional Disturbance

Focusing Questions

- What definition is used for students with serious emotional disturbance?
- How many students with serious emotional disturbance receive special education?
- What are the primary characteristics of students with serious emotional disturbance?
- What general instructional approaches and specific teaching tactics are successful with students with serious emotional disturbance?

Mrs. Luanne Jones had been a second-grade teacher for fifteen years. She had plenty of experience with children who became angry when their needs were not met or they were unable to do something; Sandy was different. Temper tantrums and sudden outbursts of anger that occurred when Sandy experienced frustration or failed to achieve a desired goal were a serious cause for concern in Mrs. Jones's class. Shouting obscenities, throwing things, screaming, crying, or trying to disrupt others were just a few of the ways Sandy would "throw a tantrum." Whatever form the tantrum took, it always interfered with productive interpersonal relationships and instruction.

Terry Peterson was a "living legend" at Magnolia Middle School. Everybody wondered what Terry would do next. Constantly asking questions, teasing other students, telling jokes, and generally disrupting the class were trademarks of a typical school day for Terry.

Avoiding social interactions or failing to participate in social events was a way of life for Bryce. As is true for other isolated and withdrawn students, sometimes Bryce's behavior provoked rejection and exclusion by classmates and peers. Social isolation, shyness, and/or general social withdrawal interfered with productive interpersonal relationships, and Bryce was often depressed and unproductive in school; truancy and failing grades were becoming serious problems. ∎

Violating expectations

Children like Sandy, Terry, and Bryce are sometimes described as having behavior problems or serious emotional disturbance. Their behavior violates expectations for what is accepted and causes concern for parents, teachers, or other children. For example, temper tantrums are common in very young children, but when they are part of the behavioral repertoire of older children and interfere with productive interpersonal relations, they become serious problems. Disruptions are common during most school days. When one student is responsible for more than expected or accepted numbers of disruptions, he or she may be seen as a behavior problem. Similarly, when social withdrawal occurs at an age when it is no longer appropriate and when it is adversely affecting school performance, it is a problem.

Terminology varies

Some of the problems associated with serious emotional disturbance are overt behaviors such as disruptiveness and tantrums. Others are more psychological problems; for example, anxiety, depression. For this reason, a variety of terms are used to refer to students who receive special education because their behavior violates what people expect and are willing to accept. In your state, they may be called students with emotional problems, students with behavior disorders, students with emotional and behavioral problems, students with learning and behavior problems, students with emotional handicaps, or students with serious emotional disturbance. We use **serious emotional disturbance** (SED) to refer to these students, because this term currently is accepted by the federal government and widely recognized as the umbrella term for overt psychological problems that are the basis for some students' receiving special education. Later in the chapter, however, we discuss changes that are occurring in the terminology.

Definition

Students with serious emotional disturbance are entitled to special education services. Although the states define and describe this category in different ways, most use federal guidelines that define "serious emotional disturbance" as follows:

Federal definition

> The term means a condition exhibiting one or more of the following characteristics over a long period of time and to a marked degree that adversely affects a child's educational performance:
>
> a. an inability to learn which cannot be explained by intellectual, sensory, or health factors;
>
> b. an inability to build or maintain satisfactory interpersonal relationships with peers and teachers;
>
> c. inappropriate types of behavior or feelings under normal circumstances;
>
> d. a general pervasive mood of unhappiness or depression; or
>
> e. a tendency to develop physical symptoms or fears associated with personal or school problems.
>
> The term includes schizophrenia. The term does not apply to children who are socially maladjusted, unless it is determined that they have a serious emotional disturbance. (Individuals with Disabilities Education Act, 1990)

With serious emotional disturbance, perhaps more than for any other category of special education, we are dealing with a definition that leaves much room for subjectivity and confusion. For this reason, the federal government may soon change both the category name and its definition.

What behavior is normal?

For now, there are no hard and fast rules or simple tests for deciding when problem behaviors constitute serious emotional disturbance. Consider the case of Susan, a 15-year-old who seems unhappy most of the time at school. Her classmates say she's in a "rotten mood" and avoid her. How do we judge the extent to which Susan's unhappiness is "general" and "pervasive," or normal? What about Luis, a third-grader who doesn't get along well with his classmates or his teachers? Is he showing "an inability to build or maintain satisfactory interpersonal relationships" or is he within the range of so-called normal behavior?

Social withdrawal, isolation, and depression are a part of serious emotional disturbance that is often difficult to assess. *Steve Takatsuno/The Picture Cube.*

Debate over standards

There is much debate over the standards used in deciding whether students are experiencing serious emotional disturbance. That debate focuses on the difficulty of measuring abstractions (such as unhappiness) as well as the definition's lack of specific behaviors that adversely affect educational performance. The debate is heightened by difficulties inherent in explaining inabilities to learn, and build or maintain interpersonal relationships. Further, it is difficult to determine whether a student's behavior is caused by serious emotional disturbance or some other disability.

Lack of dramatic indicators

Students who exhibit severely aggressive behavior or who are extremely withdrawn usually are easy to identify, but most students who are classified with serious emotional disturbance do not display dramatic indicators. Sometimes they are vulnerable to a particular teacher's tolerance for and ability to redirect their behavior. Sometimes they act belligerent or uncooperative because they simply don't understand English well enough to respond appropriately, even though they may understand enough to get by in nonacademic activities and settings. In essence, to be labeled with serious emotional disturbance a student must do something that bothers someone else (usually a parent or a teacher), then must be identified as seriously emotionally disturbed (or an equivalent term) by a sanctioned labeler (a physician, psychiatrist, psychologist, social worker, judge, or the police). These people try to be objective but differ in their perceptions of the seriousness and appropriateness of various behaviors; in their abilities to understand students of different cultural, ethnic, and social backgrounds; and in their views of how disruptive behaviors should be treated.

Prevalence

Relatively low prevalence

Short-term behavior problems are evidenced by most children and adolescents. Most students in our introductory classes are surprised to learn that the prevalence of serious emotional disturbance is relatively low. Of the 4.5 million school-age students receiving special education in recent years, about 400,000 were classified with serious emotional disturbance. This figure represents 8.9 percent of the special education students and 0.69 percent of the general school-age population (U.S. Department of Education, 1993). The prevalence of this group of students has been relatively constant over the last ten years.

Wide variation by state

There is considerable variation from state to state in the percentage of the school-age population identified as seriously emotionally disturbed. In Table 11.1, we list the percentages by state. Prevalence figures range from a high of 1.69 percent in Connecticut to a low of 0.03 percent in Mississippi. The percentages in the right-hand column, showing serious emotional disturbance as a proportion of all disabilities, also vary widely across the states, from less than 1 percent in Arkansas and Mississippi to 18 percent or more in Minnesota, Connecticut, and Georgia.

Four categories compared

Variation of this magnitude probably results from something other than variation in student behavior. You'll recall that categories we discussed in earlier chapters showed similarly wide disparities from one state to another. Table 11.2 compares the four most prevalent disability categories—learning disabilities, communication disorders, mental retardation, and serious emotional disturbance—to illustrate the percentage variations among five sample states.

Reasons for variation

As the table indicates, the percentages of students with disabilities assigned to each category vary markedly from one state to another. But the combined percentages for all four categories are nearly constant across all five states. Regardless of the ups and downs in individual categories, the four major categories together comprise 94 to 97 percent of students with disabilities. This pattern suggests that the variation across states has more to do with differences in definitions and classification practices than with differences among the student populations. Where serious emotional disturbance is a relatively small category, as in Arkansas and Mississippi, the students are being served in other categories.

Links to gender and age

In most states, the prevalence of serious emotional disturbance is related to gender and age. About 80 percent of the students referred for emotional and social problems are boys. Relatively few cases of serious emotional disturbance are reported in the early grades; there is a sharp increase and peak in the upper elementary grades, then there is a drop beginning in junior high and continuing through high school.

| Table 11.1 | Percentage Distribution of Students with Serious Emotional Disturbance (SED) in the United States |

State	All Disabilities[a]	SED[b]	SED as Percent of All Disabilities
All states	7.81	0.69	8.9
Alabama	8.99	0.55	6.1
Alaska	9.67	0.46	4.8
Arizona	6.38	0.41	6.4
Arkansas	7.62	0.04	0.5
California	6.55	0.20	3.1
Colorado	7.14	1.10	15.4
Connecticut	8.97	1.69	18.8
Delaware	8.56	0.81	9.5
District of Columbia	5.77	0.74	12.8
Florida	9.05	0.98	10.8
Georgia	6.28	1.26	20.1
Hawaii	5.05	0.43	8.5
Idaho	6.91	0.14	2.0
Illinois	8.30	0.97	11.7
Indiana	8.14	0.45	5.5
Iowa	8.35	1.10	13.2
Kansas	7.13	0.77	10.8
Kentucky	7.72	0.38	4.9
Louisiana	6.38	0.43	6.7
Maine	9.07	1.41	15.6
Maryland	7.99	0.49	6.1
Massachusetts	11.21	1.59	14.2
Michigan	6.97	0.81	11.6
Minnesota	6.97	1.26	18.1
Mississippi	8.15	0.03	0.4
Missouri	8.33	0.73	8.8
Montana	8.15	0.42	5.2
Nebraska	8.49	0.71	8.4
Nevada	6.80	0.38	5.6
New Hampshire	7.78	0.77	9.9
New Jersey	10.48	0.90	8.6
New Mexico	9.02	0.84	9.3
New York	7.63	1.14	14.9
North Carolina	7.64	0.64	8.4
North Dakota	7.15	0.28	3.9
Ohio	7.78	0.37	4.8
Oklahoma	8.19	0.24	2.9
Oregon	8.03	0.52	6.5
Pennsylvania	7.50	0.73	9.7
Rhode Island	9.03	0.76	8.4

Table **11.1**	Percentage Distribution of Students with Serious Emotional Disturbance (SED) in the United States (continued)

State	All Disabilities[a]	SED[b]	SED as Percent of All Disabilities
South Carolina	8.22	0.60	7.3
South Dakota	7.28	0.31	4.3
Tennessee	8.89	0.23	2.6
Texas	7.73	0.65	8.4
Utah	8.06	1.36	16.9
Vermont	7.55	0.68	9.0
Virginia	7.86	0.66	8.4
Washington	6.94	0.44	6.3
West Virginia	9.43	0.50	5.3
Wisconsin	6.77	1.00	14.8
Wyoming	2.77	0.17	6.1

[a] Percentage of school-age population (ages 6 to 21) receiving special education in all disability categories.

[b] Percentage of school-age population receiving special education in the category of serious emotional disturbance.

Source: U.S. Department of Education. (1993). *Fifteenth annual report to Congress on the implementation of the Individuals with Disabilities Education Act.* Washington, DC: Author.

Table **11.2**	Variations in Classification Among Five States: Students with Learning Disabilities (LD), Communication Disorders (CD), Mental Retardation (MR), and Serious Emotional Disturbance (SED) as a Percentage of All Students with Disabilities

State	LD	CD	MR	SED	Four Categories Combined
Mississippi	51.8	31.5	12.6	0.4	96.3
Arkansas	56.8	15.2	23.0	0.5	95.5
Minnesota	44.3	18.2	13.6	18.1	94.2
Connecticut	53.5	16.4	5.9	18.8	94.6
Georgia	31.9	22.0	23.3	20.1	97.3

Characteristics

Students demonstrate many different behaviors, and they are said to demonstrate many different kinds of behavior disorders. The magnitude of exhibited behaviors also differs. We skimmed the professional literature to identify terms associated with serious emotional disturbance. They are listed in Table 11.3. Some of the terms used to describe students in this category also are used to describe students with learning disabilities and students with mental retardation, as well as other students with disabilities; moreover, most of the terms are negative.

Schizophrenia

Children with schizophrenia are included in the federal definition of serious emotional disturbance. Schizophrenia is a condition characterized by a loss of contact with reality, bizarre thought processes, and extremely inappropriate behavior. The characteristics of this condition set it apart from more general types of serious emotional disturbance (see Table 11.4). People with schizophrenia often receive special education in clinical settings with assistance from a medical and/or psychiatric professional staff. Other cognitive, academic, physical, behavioral, and communication characteristics associated with serious emotional disturbance are described in this section.

Table 11.3 Terms Used in Professional Literature to Describe Students with Serious Emotional Disturbance

aggressive	immature
aloof	impulsive
annoying	inattentive
anxious	irritable
attention seeking	jealous
avoidant	manic
compulsive	negative
daydreams	obsessive
depressed	passive
delinquent	preoccupied
destructive	restless
disruptive	rowdy
distractible	schizoid
disturbing	self-conscious
erratic	tense
frustrated	truant
has short attention span	unmotivated
hostile	unsocialized
hyperactive	withdrawn

Table **11.4**	Special Characteristics of People with Schizophrenia and Other Psychotic Disorders

Lack of self-care and daily living skills

Lack of responsiveness to auditory and visual stimulation

Hallucinations and delusions

Very low scores on intelligence tests

Lack of social relationships

Serious speech and language problems

Self-stimulation (hand flapping, rocking, staring into space)

Self-injurious behavior (biting, scratching, hurting oneself)

Verbal and physical aggression toward others

Poor prognosis without early intervention

Cognitive

Memory and attention problems

Many cognitive deficiencies are attributed to students with serious emotional disturbance. These students are said to have poor memory and short attention spans, and to be preoccupied, overly active, and anxious, among other things. In general, students with serious emotional disturbance score slightly below average on intelligence tests, although the scores of individual students cover the entire range.

Academic

Adverse effect on performance

Most students with serious emotional disturbance do not do as well academically as we would expect from their scores on intelligence tests. Recall that a key component of the definition states that students with serious emotional disturbance exhibit characteristics which *adversely affect educational perform-ance.* This means they perform poorly on measures of school achievement. Recall that students with specific learning disabilities also perform poorly in at least one area of school achievement. Sometimes, when students evidence a sig-nificant disparity between the level at which they perform on intelligence tests and the level at which they perform on achievement tests, teachers question whether "emotional disturbance" or "learning disabilities" is the appropriate category under which to receive special education services.

Links between emotional and academic problems

Generally speaking, emotional problems can lead to academic problems, and academic problems can lead to emotional problems. When students are suffering emotionally, they can become very preoccupied and simply do not at-tend well to academics. Students who demonstrate behavior and emotional problems in school may be subjected to disciplinary actions (suspension and expulsion), which in turn limit their time in school and exposure to academics.

When students do not perform well academically, their perceptions of their own self-worth suffer. They can become withdrawn or aggressive, or their non-compliance may be labeled "isolation" or "aggression" when their teachers fail to understand that they may act that way because they don't understand English as well as their classmates. Students who receive low grades may give up and begin acting out. Of course, other factors (including life stressors like parental divorce, a move, loss of a parent or sibling) can lead students to experience both academic and emotional problems.

Physical

Most students with serious emotional disturbance are physically like other students. The exceptions are those with psychosomatic complaints (in which the physical illness actually is brought on by or associated with the individual's emotional state). Students who have serious physical problems can develop behavior disorders, especially when a physical disorder leads others to act negatively toward a student and the student develops low opinions of self-worth that are reflected in behavioral characteristics.

Behavioral

This is the primary area in which students with serious emotional disturbance are said to differ from others. The broad behavioral characteristics of these students are specified in the definition of emotional disturbance: an inability to learn, an inability to build or maintain satisfactory interpersonal relationships, inappropriate types of behavior or feelings, a general pervasive mood of unhappiness or depression, and a tendency to develop physical symptoms or fears. Many specific kinds of inappropriate behavior or feelings are said to characterize this population of students. In addition to the terms listed in Table 11.3, for example, these students are said to be sluggish, fixated, verbally abusive, too orderly, too conforming, disorderly, self-injurious, isolated, irresponsible, disobedient, shy, secretive, bossy, dependent, psychotic, and noncompliant.

Inappropriate behavior or feelings

Alternative classification systems

Some professionals have tried to organize the long list of behaviors said to characterize these students by developing alternative classification systems (subtypes). For example, one system describes conduct disorders, personality disorders, mood disorders, learning problems, neuroses, and psychoses. Another divides students with serious emotional disturbance into those with emotional problems (those who internalize, or keep problems to themselves and blame themselves for their difficulties) and those with social problems (those who externalize, or take out their problems on others and on society). There is no accepted, correct way to group these behaviors. We prefer a two-group system—emotional problems and social problems—because it is simple and makes sense relative to the concepts underlying the definition of serious emotional disturbance. Grouping behavior problems this way also provides direction for identifying appropriate instructional tactics.

How Bryce's Teachers Focused on Improving Social Interactions

Working collaboratively with a special education teacher, Bryce's teachers decided to gather data on the extent of occurrences of the following behaviors reflective of general social withdrawal:

■ Sitting alone at lunch or during recess or other activity in which other children are actively interacting

■ Failing to be selected by classmates as a team member or group participant

■ Failing or being rejected following attempts to socialize with classmates

■ Seldom volunteering answers or offering opinions during group discussions

Here's what they found for Bryce and a randomly selected classmate (in percentages that indicate how often each behavior occurred):

	Bryce	Shavon
Sitting alone	83%	35%
Peer selection	5	65
Peer rejection	75	28
Volunteering answers	3	82

They decided that the social withdrawal they were seeing required intervention. Here are a few things they tried:

■ They provided a tape recorder and note-book for Bryce to use to communicate with teachers. This was helpful because it reduced the need for Bryce to have face-to-face conversations. When the level of Bryce's communicating increased, the teachers encouraged more traditional interactions.

■ They paired Bryce with two competent classmates for a "group spelling test" and set a rule that each member of the group had to spell at least one word on the test. They gradually increased the size of the group and the amount of interaction required of each member.

■ They arranged for Bryce to be in charge of key classroom materials (for example, hall passes, headsets) so that other students would be forced to interact to obtain them.

■ They kept track of improvements in Bryce's social interactions and sent progress reports home on a frequent basis (initially every day, then at least twice a week, then weekly).

Communication

No universal
communication
problems

Although many students with serious emotional disturbance have language problems, there are no characteristics having to do with communication that are universal or specific to most of these students. Students who are considered schizophrenic sometimes do demonstrate abnormal language and communication skills. Many never speak, while others develop language and speech disorders like echolalia (parrotlike imitation of speech), illogical or disorganized speech, and inadequate comprehension of verbal instructions. These students represent a very small percentage of those classified as having serious emotional disturbance.

Instructional Approaches and Teaching Tactics

Students with serious emotional disturbance receive special education because they have emotional and social problems that require attention from teachers, parents, and other professionals if they are to be successful in school. **Emotional problems** stem from unproductive personal ways of managing stress or activities. Students with emotional problems may exhibit inappropriate types of behaviors or feelings, or a tendency to develop physical symptoms or fears. For example, one child's response to having to wait for lunch might be to become impatient, while another's might be to become very anxious. Anxiety, oppositional behavior, and temper tantrums are common emotional problems of students with serious emotional disturbance. **Social problems** are unproductive ways individuals respond in situations involving interactions with other people. For instance, students with social problems may be unable to maintain satisfactory interpersonal relationships. Disruptiveness, nonattention, irrelevant actions, and task avoidance are common social problems of students receiving special education for serious emotional disturbances.

Some general teaching tips are provided in Table 11.5; more specific tactics for reducing emotional and social problems are provided in the following sections.

Emotional problems

Social problems

Table 11.5 Top Ten List of Tips for Teachers of Students with Serious Emotional Disturbance

1. Establish rules for appropriate classroom behavior.
2. Establish consequences for inappropriate classroom behavior.
3. Praise students frequently for appropriate behavior.
4. Be consistent when using consequences for inappropriate behavior.
5. Teach appropriate behaviors and practice them every day.
6. Use preferred activities as rewards for good behavior.
7. Monitor behavior and post-performance records.
8. Reward good behavior models.
9. Teach students to monitor their own behavior.
10. Consider developmental levels before making referral for outside assistance.

Reducing Emotional Problems

A natural reaction to unknown or novel situations or things is apprehension or concern. A strong, unrealistic, and sometimes irrational fear is referred to as **anxiety**. Anxiety is a common characteristic of students with serious emotional disturbance. Being afraid of the consequences of their actions, being worried about daily life experiences, complaining or displaying physical symptoms in response to school activities, and changing speech patterns such as stuttering are some ways anxiety is exhibited by these students.

Anxiety is common

Understanding stress

■ **To reduce anxiety: Explore life events to understand stress.** Which events are stressful to students in elementary, intermediate, and high school? Knowing what bothers students can be the first step in dealing with stressful situations that affect their classroom performances.

Commonly identified stressors for elementary school students include

Stressors for elementary students

■ Family problems such as parental disapproval, insufficient time spent with parent(s), adjusting to stepparents and remarriage situations

■ Feeling different as a result of not having the same material things as others or low self-acceptance

■ School-related problems such as rejection by teachers, fear of failing, failing to meet parental expectations in regard to academic achievement

■ School-related problems in adjusting to different linguistic and cultural demands

■ Discipline-related concerns such as being afraid of punishment or believing parents and teachers are too critical

■ General concerns about simply doing something wrong or believing that something bad is going to happen

Stressors for intermediate-grade students include

Stressors for intermediate students

■ General adolescent concerns associated with adjusting to developmental changes, limited autonomy, low self-acceptance, or not understanding life's realities

■ Problems adjusting to different linguistic and cultural demands

■ Peer pressure associated with wanting to be accepted by friends; participating in activities like drugs, sex, and smoking; or doing things that cause discomfort

■ Family problems related to dealing with stepparents or siblings, or parents' misunderstanding; not feeling in control whenever parents set behavior restrictions; lacking the resources to be independent; or feeling that no one is listening

■ School-related problems such as not doing well academically, not seeing the relevance of school, or not adjusting to different teachers, students, and academic demands

Stressors for high school students include

Stressors for high school students

■ Dealing with the future and making decisions related to accepting responsibilities, relationships, and the uncertainties of life

■ Dealing with school-related problems such as getting good grades, taking courses to get into college, and teachers' misunderstanding

■ Social problems in adjusting to different linguistic and cultural demands or dealing with immigration at older ages

Window on Practice

A Survivor's Story

My name is Shannon C2 and I am a survivor. I am the middle child of three kids from a divorced family. As a child, I was abused sexually by a neighbor. I can remember my behaviors changing as the abuse was going on. I became more angry and violent toward males and did not care about my appearance. I never talked about the abuse to anyone—parents, peers, teachers, no one. It was something that was to be kept a secret, something I felt ashamed about.

I remember the transition into junior high school as being very difficult and scary for me. My dad entered law school around this time and was hardly ever home. My memories of when he was home are of his emphasis on "all work and no play." It seemed when my dad wasn't fighting with my mom, he was fighting with me and my sisters. I also remember feeling as if I did not fit in with my peers at this time. Their concerns were on dating and slumber parties and mine were on what it would be like when I got home. My grades at this point started to suffer. I went from a student who basically made all high grades to one who started receiving failing marks. At no point did a teacher of mine ever ask me if something was wrong.

At the beginning of my freshman year in high school, my parents were planning to get a divorce and my dad moved out of the house. The breakup of my parents was very traumatic for me. I lost all concentration and energy in school. My days were spent wondering and worrying about what was going to happen to me and my family. I fell into a deep depression. Sometimes I would go to my classes and just sleep all day. Some days I would doodle in half of my classes and cry in the other half. I remember sitting in my algebra class and just crying. I tried to keep the crying to myself, but I ended up hyperventilating. My teacher came over and asked me if I wanted to go to the restroom. He did not ask me if I needed to talk, go to the counselor, or just simply needed help. On another day, when I was once again crying, this same teacher came over

and patted me twice on the back without ever saying a word. Was what I was going through really that bad?

As my freshman year went on, my depression grew even deeper. I began to see my life as hopeless and worthless and I also felt helpless and powerless over my parents' divorce. I felt scared and could not see things as ever getting better, so I started trying to kill myself. I would make one attempt a week to kill myself. As I look back now, I remember having all the classic signs of suicide, yet not one of my teachers ever asked me how I was doing. Did they just not care? Or did they just not know, understand, or recognize the key signs?

At the end of my freshman year, I again attempted suicide, but this time I was caught by a family member. The next day I was admitted to a children's psychiatric hospital. While I stayed there, my parents' divorce became final and my mom received a job transfer to another part of the state 200 miles away. When I was discharged from the hospital, I went to a new home, a new town, a new school. The community was small and rural. I received counseling once a week, at a small outpatient counseling facility. My school counselor and teachers were aware of my having been in a psychiatric hospital. I had to face a thing called stigmas. I was called "crazy," "psycho," "loonbin," and "crackpot" by my peers. Even with my teachers and family there were labeling comments. These were very hard to deal with. No one ever told me that they weren't true, and after hearing them for awhile my self-esteem sank even lower. I began to believe these stigmas. I felt as if I would be institutionalized the rest of my life or that I was only destined to be a bag lady.

My grades remained low and my depression wasn't getting any better. After two years of just trying to make it through the day, I began to get real tired and hopeless again. I remember feeling so alone. I once again tried to kill myself and was placed back in the same psychiatric hospital where I had been two years earlier.

(continued on next page)

A Survivor's Story *(continued)*

After eight and a half months at the hospital, I was released and returned to my home. After being gone for so long, it was difficult readjusting to my family, my school, and my peers. I found that the stigmas were still there. Nothing had changed. Somehow I managed to graduate, which seemed to be a shock for my peers and some of my teachers, as they never thought that a "crazy person" could do this.

Presently, I am 21 years old and a junior at a university majoring in Human Services. I am also a grateful recovering alcoholic. The stigmas from high school and a feeling of aloneness continued as I entered college. The pressures of college life and education, combined with my own growing self-doubts as to any truths in those stigmas overwhelmed me. I came to the point where I used alcohol to mask and numb every feeling and memory I had. For two years, I bounced between surviving and being numb.

To my surprise, both my professor/advisor and my supervisor at the time seemed to actually care about me. They would ask me how I was doing, if I was okay, if I needed anything. They did not shy away from me when I was depressed; instead, they would ask me what was going on and actually talk and listen to me. This was scary for me because no adult figure in my life, outside of my family and a handful of hospital personnel, ever took the time to see how I was or even who I was. It was with the support of my professor/adviser and my supervisor that I was able to achieve sobriety.

Today, I have been able to come to terms with my past. However, when I get real tired and stressed, it is very easy for me to relive and feel those stigmas and remember how I was treated in school. It seems as if this will be something I will always have to deal with.

I was lucky—I survived. But does life for every kid with an emotional disorder have to be as difficult as mine was?

Source: Shannon C2 is a student at Northern Kentucky University and works at a runaway shelter.

- Dealing with peer pressure and not being accepted, being afraid of doing and saying the wrong thing, and dealing with the use of cigarettes, drugs, and alcohol
- Dealing with family problems like having different goals from those of parents, not having parental support, not having understanding parents, or having conflicts with stepparents.

Discussion, practice, role playing

- **To reduce anxiety: Discuss and practice other responses.** Have students talk about something that makes each of them anxious. Have them role-play ways to deal with each other's problems and then identify and practice ways to deal with their own problems. For students experiencing anxiety as a result of linguistic or cultural diversity, discuss differences that must be addressed when living in a different culture and have native language materials available for students to share with their peers.

Sharing with parents

- **To reduce anxiety: Share anxious moments with parents.** Find some stories about children's fears and have the parents read them at home as a special assignment. Ask the parents to discuss ways to deal with the problem after they read the story; then, have the student go over these during a discussion in school.

- **To reduce anxiety: Introduce new material gradually.** To some children, the introduction of new materials can be anxiety provoking. Have these students engage in a preferred activity before a new, less preferred one. Gradually introduce the new task while the student is still doing the more preferred one. Sometimes requesting that only a small amount of the new task be completed can aid in "sneaking" it into the daily activities. Sometimes introducing materials in a student's native language or letting students respond in their native languages reduces anxiety for students experiencing difficulties as a result of limited English language experience.

Ways to "sneak in" new materials

■ **To reduce anxiety: Share progress.** When a student does engage in an activity that he or she was previously anxious about, make a "big deal" of it. Special awards can be prepared for such occasions and carried home.

A "big deal"

Brief times, small units

■ **To reduce anxiety: Minimize the source of the problem.** Initially require that the student deal with the source of anxiety only for brief time periods. If schoolwork is producing anxiety, require small units of easily completed work and gradually extend the level of knowledge and the amount of work required for completion. Tips for helping students with school phobia are presented in Table 11.6.

Teaching stress management

■ **To reduce anxiety: Teach students how to handle their problems.** Many students with serious emotional disturbance have limited positive experiences dealing with stress or anxiety. They often simply have not been taught how to handle situations that cause stress or anxiety. Effective teachers address this problem directly. For example, if tests are producing anxiety, they teach students a few tips to make them better test takers (see Table 11.7).

Students sometimes become angry when they can't do what they want to do or when their needs are not met. Others become physically or verbally aggressive when asked to do anything and simply refuse to do it. **Oppositional behavior** or noncompliance means not doing what has been requested by another person. Arguing, blaming others, crying, throwing things, breaking pencils, and tearing up papers are examples of oppositional behaviors. A top ten list of tips for reducing oppositional behavior and noncompliance is presented in Table 11.8; other suggestions include the following:

Oppositional behavior

"Planned ignoring"

■ **To reduce oppositional behavior: Ignore it.** Of course, this should not be used if the problem behavior places the student and/or others in danger. Pairing "planned ignoring" with attention when the student is not engaging in oppositional behavior is also effective.

Table 11.6 Tips for Helping Students with School Phobia

1. Accept the students' fears, even though they may seem very irrational.
2. Discuss the students' fears and avoid arguing about them.
3. Have the students serve as assistants upon arriving at school.
4. Avoid allowing the students to return home once at school.
5. Make being at school especially rewarding.

Table 11.7 — Top Ten List of Test-Taking Tips for Students with Serious Emotional Disturbances

1. Be prepared (with pencil, eraser, pen, and paper as needed).
2. Review the entire test before answering any questions.
3. Estimate time needed for different parts of the test and develop a plan for completing it.
4. Answer easy questions first.
5. Use an outline of key points when answering essay questions.
6. Try to answer all questions.
7. Mark answers and write clearly.
8. Skip confusing questions and return to them later.
9. Trust first impressions, guesses, and responses.
10. Review the entire test before turning it in for credit.

Table 11.8 — Top Ten List of Tips for Dealing with Oppositional Behavior and Noncompliance

1. Use direct requests rather than questions to achieve compliance (for example, "I need you to start your work" is better than "Will you please start your work?").
2. Make a request close to a student rather than from across the classroom.
3. Maintain eye contact when making requests.
4. Give a request only twice rather than several times.
5. Make requests in a soft but firm voice rather than a loud one.
6. Give students time to comply with requests rather than expecting immediate responses.
7. Make more start requests ("Please start your work") than stop requests ("Please stop whining about the assignment").
8. Control negative emotions when making requests.
9. Make requests positive and descriptive rather than negative and ambiguous.
10. Reinforce compliance rather than ignoring it.

Source: Reprinted with permission of Macmillan College Publishing from *Teaching Behaviorally Disordered Students* by D. P. Morgan and W. R. Jenson. Copyright © 1988 by Macmillan College Publishing Company.

Aggressive behavior and temper tantrums are widely recognized behavior problems commonly associated with serious emotional disturbance. *Judith D. Sedwick/The Picture Cube.*

Lotteries

■ **To reduce oppositional behavior: Use lotteries to improve compliance.** Each time a student engages in appropriate behavior (such as not whining when an assignment is made), place a small ticket with his or her name on it into a "lottery" box. Periodically pick a ticket from the box and provide a small reward for the winner.

Rewarding others

■ **To reduce oppositional behavior: Reward appropriate behavior in other students.** Focus attention on students who quickly comply with requests and have them record their "good behavior" on charts that are prominently displayed in the classroom.

Temper tantrums

Many students with serious emotional disturbance are often frustrated by school activities; **temper tantrums** are a severe form of oppositional behavior that provides a relief from some of the frustration. Sometimes when they believe the likelihood of success at a task is limited, children use tantrums as attention-seeking behaviors. Similarly, if key people such as teachers and parents are responsive to a child only during or after a tantrum, the behavior may be reinforced and thereby continue.

■ **To reduce tantrums: Use cues to encourage alternative behaviors.** Teach students with serious emotional disturbance to give you a signal before a tantrum. Set up a policy with your school administrator to allow these students to leave your classroom to "cool down." When becoming frustrated, these students might simply ask to leave the room or take a walk around the school. If students

Options for cooling down

signal the need to express anger, provide a means for it to occur at recess; throwing a ball against the school wall, jumping rope, or just talking through the problem can be useful substitutes for a tantrum.

■ **To reduce tantrums: Have a plan.** **Reinforcement** is an event, object, or statement that results in an increase in the frequency of occurrence of a behavior. When the consequences of behavior result in increases in the behavior, they are said to be reinforcing. Like any other behavior, tantrums that are reinforced will be repeated. Discuss the importance of maintaining attention to tantrum behaviors with parents and other teachers. Encourage the student's parents to come up with a plan in which the tantrums can be punished in a positive way; this might include withholding some favorite activity as the result of a tantrum.

■ **To reduce tantrums: Let the class benefit from good behavior.** Have parents keep a record of tantrums at home. Set up a criterion by which the entire class can benefit from appropriate behavior of the student with serious emotional disturbance at home. For example, once the baseline number of tantrums is obtained, an extra half-hour of recess for the class can be made contingent on a 5 percent reduction in tantrums at home.

Reducing Social Problems

Students with serious emotional disturbance often exhibit behaviors or actions that result in annoyance or disturbance to others. This **disruptiveness** may be descriptive of physical and nonphysical behaviors. Physical disruptions involve body contact and include fighting, hitting, pinching, and tripping others. Nonphysical disruptions include making noises, name-calling, making faces, laughing boisterously, talking loudly, and acting in a way that causes others to laugh during otherwise solemn occasions.

Many school activities require sustained attention for successful completion. To do a math sheet requiring addition of single-digit numbers with sums under ten, a student must look at each item, compute the appropriate sum, and write the answers in appropriate locations. Not attending to any of the components of the task results in inadequate performance. **Nonattention** (distractibility) results when attention is drawn from the primary target to other more peripheral ones. Nonattention is a common social behavior problem that interferes with interpersonal relations and school progress of students with serious emotional disturbance.

Engaging in activities or actions not related to the task at hand is an example of **irrelevant activity.** Even if irrelevant activities are productive in themselves, they interfere with school progress because they limit the amount of time spent on relevant school tasks. The student engaging in irrelevant activities wants to clean the blackboard erasers during a group discussion or use soap and water to clean the desk during independent seat work in math. Irrelevant activities are of particular concern when they interfere with the work of others.

A common way of handling tasks that are not particularly interesting or appealing is to postpone them or elaborately prepare for them. This type of behavior is sometimes referred to as **task avoidance** or procrastination; think of all the term papers you could have written while you reluctantly got ready to write just one. Opportunities for task avoidance include a variety of behaviors related to beginning the task, actually working at the task, and completing the task. Task avoidance is a

Cooperative learning groups and team projects help reduce disruptiveness in many classrooms. *Elizabeth Crews.*

problem only when it results in individual nonproductivity and/or negatively influences the productivity of others. The classic example of task avoidance is demonstrated by the student who asks permission to sharpen a pencil so many times that the pencil is reduced to a worthless stub and the child then complains: "I can't do the work because I don't have a pencil."

Disruptiveness, nonattention, irrelevant activities, and task avoidance are common characteristics of students with serious emotional disturbance. Here are some ways to help them deal with these social problems.

Recording disruptions

■ **To reduce disruptiveness: Keep track of disruptions.** Clearly define the behavior that is disruptive. Place a small calendar-type chart on the disruptive child's desk and inform the child that each occurrence of the behavior during a particular day will be recorded on the chart. No other consequence should be applied. Generally, this simple counting of disruptive behavior significantly reduces the number of occurrences within two weeks. Students do not like records of their "bad behavior" kept as evidence that can be used against them.

■ **To reduce disruptiveness: Make being disruptive unpleasant.** Making a student engage in a disruptive behavior beyond the point when the student has decided to stop can effectively reduce future occurrences of the behavior. It is useful to arrange for the "extra practice" during an especially pleasant activity (for example, recess) that the child must miss to do the "disruptive exercise."

"Extra practice" of disruption

Bring Your Learning to Life

Tips from a School Psychologist Helped Mrs. Jones

Mrs. Jones asked the school psychologist in her school to help manage Sandy's temper tantrums. After observing in the classroom several times, Dr. Braitwaite made the following suggestions:

Ignore some behaviors to reduce them. If the temper tantrum does not place Sandy or others in physical or emotional danger, ignoring the tantrum may result in a decrease in its frequency. This practice should generally be paired with attention when Sandy is not engaging in the tantrum behaviors.

Avoid rewarding tantrums. Some of Sandy's tantrums are maintained by the attention received during or after the behavior. A time-out procedure can be a useful means of reducing the likelihood of reinforcing the tantrum. This can be accomplished by placing Sandy in another room during the tantrum or by rewarding students who are not having a tantrum.

Mrs. Jones tried the suggestions. She ignored minor tantrums and paid more attention to Sandy when tantrums were not occurring. Mrs. Jones didn't have a time-out room but used an alternative to punish Sandy's tantrums. She prepared a bulletin board with a card for each student tacked to it. On one side of the card she wrote IN and on the other side she wrote OUT. When her students entered the room Mrs. Jones had them "punch in" (turn card to the IN side), and when they left she had them "punch out." When Sandy (or any other student) was displaying inappropriate behavior such as a tantrum, Mrs. Jones "punched her out" and rewarded students who were "punched in." Sandy's tantrums decreased.

Team rewards

■ **To reduce disruptiveness: Use group contingency plans to change behavior.** The behavior of some students with serious emotional disturbance can be changed by two simple procedures. The first involves setting up teams within the classroom group. Tell the students that occurrences of disruptive behavior such as throwing objects, hitting others, shouting, and whistling will be noted during a certain time period (reading period, before lunch, or all day) and that the team with the fewest marks will earn a reward. Group members should be encouraged to support each other and periodically note when disruptive behavior is not occurring. An alternative group contingency plan can be established by having the most disruptive students be team captains and earn points for the team. The captain with the fewest disruptive marks earns a reward for each team member.

Avoiding public attention

■ **To reduce disruptiveness: Speak softly to change some behaviors.** Many students with serious emotional disturbance engage in disruptive behaviors to gain the attention of their teacher. When they are reprimanded for the misbehavior, the students often gain much desired public attention such as class laughter as well. Controlling the intensity of a reprimand so that only the target student can hear it may reduce the attention-getting aspects of the disruptive behaviors.

When using this strategy it is helpful to comment also on appropriate, nondisruptive behaviors.

Marking progress

- **To improve attention: Help students focus on what has been done.** Place small marks on written assignments (at the end of each line of work or after a specified number of problems) to help students see what they have done during independent work.

"Good behavior" rewards

- **To improve attention: Reward appropriate behavior.** Before making an independent assignment, tell students that you will be stopping them several times during the work period to reward those students who are attending to the task. Walk around the room while they are working and pass out "good behavior" tickets or place a count on the blackboard reflecting the number of students working when a "good behavior" check was taken.

Reinforcement linked to time periods

- **To reduce irrelevant activities: Reward students for not exhibiting problem behaviors.** Irrelevant activities, such as asking questions about inappropriate topics, can be reduced by providing reinforcement (a reward or recognition) when a student does not indulge in such activities during a particular time period. Initially, the time should be a brief interval; later, as the student reduces the level of inappropriate behavior, the time period can be extended. For example, providing a token for each thirty-second interval that a student does not ask an inappropriate question may be the best method for use early in a learning sequence, but extending the time to a five- or ten-minute period would be an appropriate goal if the procedure worked effectively.

Setting limits

- **To reduce irrelevant activities: Set limits on inappropriate behaviors.** Acknowledge the importance of all activities that students choose to do. Set up a system in which a specified number of activities is permitted during any one day; provide tickets that allow one occurrence of the activity, and give each student an individually determined number of the tickets. Behaviors that teachers permit in this manner often become less important to the children and rapidly decrease in rate of occurrence.

Reinforcement linked to limits

- **To reduce irrelevant activities: Link reinforcement to limits.** Sometimes problem behaviors that interfere with appropriate achievement-oriented behaviors (reading, writing, and so on) can be reduced by differential reinforcement techniques. For example, by reinforcing predetermined low rates of some behaviors, they can be kept at levels at which they interfere less and thereby become more appropriate. By setting "talk-out," "bathroom request," or pencil-sharpening limits on the basis of careful observations of a student's characteristic levels of each behavior and then rewarding the student for keeping at or below the limit, acceptable amounts of inappropriate behavior can be produced. Reminding the student each hour that targeted behavior is within the expected limits makes the initial trials more likely to succeed.

Teacher proximity

- **To reduce irrelevant activities: Change your position to change behavior.** The physical proximity of the teacher can have an impact on the extent and nature of a student's behavior. By moving closer to a student who is engaging in an irrelevant activity, a teacher can sometimes reduce the inappropriate behavior.

Small units of different types

- **To reduce task avoidance: Break large assignments into smaller units.** If an assignment is particularly long or unusually tedious, it is helpful to break it up into smaller units and divide the work time into different types of sessions. Some stu-

Bring Your Learning to Life

Dealing with Disruptive Behavior

Many of Terry's behaviors were disruptive. Teachers decided to keep track of them to try to bring them under control. They used a small index card to note occurrences of Terry's disruptive behaviors; each teacher was responsible for a different one. One teacher wanted to decrease the number of times Terry called out answers during a class discussion. He kept a 3" × 5" index card in his pocket and made a mark on it whenever Terry blurted out an answer. Terry quickly became interested in these actions and questioned the teacher's behavior. Mr. Keller simply indicated that he was keeping track of something he was thinking about. The number of "blurt outs" reduced to zero within a week. Incidentally, the behaviors of several other children also improved when Mr. Keller "kept notes."

dents with serious emotional disturbance like working on a tough assignment for fifteen to twenty minutes (sometimes less) and then taking a short break before completing the next portion.

Increasing payoffs

■ **To reduce task avoidance: Increase the payoff for doing work**. Prepare a series of reading passages that include important messages within them. For example, after several paragraphs of reading, a sentence such as "After you read this, come to my desk for a reward" or "After you read this, bring a pencil to my desk for a reward" could be inserted into the text. After several students have "found the treasure," point out to the others (especially the task-avoiding student) what happened. Let the student know that the same activity will be used again in the future, but don't provide rewards once the "secret" is out.

Planning alternative strategies

■ **To reduce task avoidance: Develop many plans for task completion**. Students with serious emotional disturbance who have problems involving task avoidance often are not good work planners; they seldom develop a plan before doing an assignment and almost never use one while doing their work. The value of plans can be illustrated by using homework as a target task. First, identify several comparable assignments for use in this activity. Next, plan several completion strategies with the student for getting the work done after school. For example, using blocks of time (4:00–5:00, 5:00–6:00, 6:00–7:00, and so on), develop at least three plans for when work, play, and other activities will be done. Have the student select one plan for use on the first day of the activity; contact parents to alert them to the plan. Have the student record the amount of time the assignment required and his or her accuracy. Repeat the procedure each day using a different plan and compare the effectiveness of the plans.

Current Trends and Issues

An issue that is generating considerable discussion is the contention that schools are underidentifying students with serious emotional disturbance. The concern is that students with behavior problems requiring special attention are not receiving services needed for success in school. This controversy has given some states the impetus to develop definitions that are more relevant educationally, to formalize and improve systematic procedures for identification, and to encourage alternative service delivery models (among them, school-based mental health services).

Too few students identified?

The appropriateness of terminology and definitions is a common concern in special education, particularly for serious emotional disturbance. For example, the currently accepted definition excludes students who are "socially maladjusted." Some professionals argue that this is a good idea, and others say it leads to underidentification of students and is merely a way to cut costs. The argument is complicated by the absence of any evidence justifying a separation of social maladjustment (delinquency and social deviance) from serious emotional disturbance (emotional and social problems). Further, because there is no generally accepted definition of social maladjustment, precisely what is being excluded is not clear.

Challenges to federal definition

Other aspects of the category's definition also have been challenged. Some professionals say the current definition's five criteria are not supported by previous or current research. The definition's reference to adverse effect on educational performance is often interpreted to mean only academics. Moreover, this is the only federal category, the critics point out, that incorporates a condition's severity as part of the definition.

Substitute terminology

As this book was going to press, a new substitute terminology and definition for this group of students had been proposed and was being seriously discussed by professionals in special education and mental health. Congress had directed the U.S. Secretary of Education to issue a Notice of Inquiry soliciting public and professional opinion on (1) the need to revise the current definition of serious emotional disturbance and (2) whether the term *emotional and behavioral disorders* and its related definition (see below) should be used in its place.

Proposed definition

The term "emotional or behavioral disorder" means a disability that is—

  (i) characterized by behavioral or emotional responses in school programs so different from appropriate age, cultural, or ethnic norms that they adversely affect educational performance (academic, social, vocational, and personal skills);

  (ii) more than a temporary, expected response to stressful events in the environment;

  (iii) consistently exhibited in two different settings, at least one of which is school-related; and

  (iv) unresponsive to direct intervention applied in general education, or the condition of the child is such that general education interventions would be insufficient.

The term includes such a disability that co-exists with other disabilities.

The term includes a schizophrenic disorder, affective disorder, anxiety disorder, or other sustained disorder of conduct or adjustment, affecting a child, if the disorder affects educational performance as described earlier.

Support for new definition

Those who favor a change have argued the virtues of the new terminology and definition: The proposed language includes a specific reference to age, cultural, and ethnic norms. It takes note of key skill areas. It includes widely recognized problems of mental health. Its insistence on evidence from multiple settings may help control biased decision making.

Whatever the merits of changing the definition, a new terminology cannot resolve all questions or correct all problems. As definitions are reworked, teachers should always keep the ultimate goal in mind: to improve special education and provide better services for students with disabilities.

Use of medication

Another current issue is the widespread use of medication in the treatment of behavior problems. Stimulants, minor tranquilizers, and major tranquilizers are drug groups commonly used with students with serious emotional disturbance. The goal in using any prescriptive drugs is to control behavior, but too often the side effects outweigh the advantages of compliance. In addition, students sometimes develop drug dependencies that are not physically or emotionally healthy. Of course, teachers and school personnel do not prescribe drugs. Physicians prescribe drugs and rely on teachers and school personnel to monitor the effects those drugs have on the problems that indicated the administration of medication. No single factor can be blamed if medication is

Using drugs to control behavior is a common, but widely debated intervention for students with serious emotional disturbance. *Elizabeth Hamlin/Stock Boston, Inc.*

abused in the treatment of children and young adults. The probability is very high that if you teach, you will have a student who is on medication. Your school-time monitoring can help physicians and parents decide whether a drug is working and whether its effects are beneficial or detrimental.

Serious Emotional Disturbance in Perspective

If you ask teachers what group of students they least prefer to have in their classrooms, they will probably say those with behavior problems. Discipline and classroom management consistently are ranked among the most serious problems and areas of greatest need in surveys of public and professional opinions about education. This continues to be true, despite the inclusion in teacher preparation programs of considerable knowledge about handling discipline problems. Teachers need help meeting the social and emotional needs of students, yet professional attention too often focuses on the appropriateness of a definition.

A serious concern for teachers

Time spent arguing about definitions is bound by a law of diminishing returns. There will never be a perfect definition for any category of special education. All current and former definitions can be (and most have been) criticized as too exclusive, too inclusive, too inadequate, too conservative, or too liberal to be useful to all people. Although a definition motivates practice, laboring over the definition should not *become* practice. Special education is an area of successive approximations. As long as people know whom the category is intended to include, the definition is adequate; it isn't perfect and it isn't useless, just adequate. At center stage should be deciding how to help students placed in special education because they meet the criteria implied or stated in the definition.

No perfect definition

The boundaries of serious emotional disturbance are fuzzy. Differences between this category and learning disabilities, mental retardation, or social maladjustment are not like those between sensory disabilities such as deafness and blindness. This is the most subjective special education category, and judgment is a key factor in evaluating and treating it.

Fuzzy boundaries

Typically teachers, school psychologists, and counselors gather data over a relatively long period before deciding whether serious emotional disturbance is an appropriate category for students experiencing problems in school. Often professionals from mental health and social service agencies are also involved in the identification and treatment of these students. Teachers are expected to work closely with outside-agency personnel to supply information during identification and intervention activities. But sometimes this information is limited by time, setting, and rater. Behaviors judged normal at one time in one educational or community setting may be judged abnormal at another time, in another setting, by a different judge.

Working with outside personnel

Although they may disagree about the extent to which certain behaviors are representative of serious emotional disturbance, classroom teachers do agree on one thing: Students who disrupt classes are not among their favorites.

Regardless, they are entitled to education and it should be provided in classrooms with their neighbors and peers. By providing teachers with support, this goal can and should be achieved. The adage "It's all in how you look at it" is appropriate for this category.

An existential philosopher might ask: If a tree falls in the forest and nobody hears it, does it make a sound? An existential professional in the area of serious emotional disturbance might ask: If a student exhibits a behavior and nobody is bothered by it, is it a problem? From this perspective, serious emotional disturbance and behavior problems are "in the eye of the beholder." For example, teachers provided the following varied illustrations of their experiences with students with serious emotional disturbance (Anderegg et al., 1993, pp. 24–25):

The eye of the beholder

> *Most Unforgettable Characters*
> The student who could lose his pencil while writing with it.
> The child who conversed with light bulbs.
> The kid who still fought while in a body cast.
> *Most Embarrassing Moments in the Classroom*
> "Hey Teach, I can see your bikini panty line."
> Saying "no" to former student visiting from prison.
> *Favorite Daydreams of Teachers of Students with SED*
> Sensory deprivation therapy.
> Instruments of torture.
> Giving directions once and having everybody follow them.
> Watching an administrator teach my class for a day.
> Lunch without kids.
> Indecent proposals... from an adult.

Although the content and tone of the preceding reflections are intended to be humorous and comforting, the message we want to leave you with is that students with serious emotional disturbance (or any other disability) are people with dreams, desires, disappointments, and deeds like everybody else. Although many find these students the most difficult to teach, many others find their antics interesting, exciting, and acceptable beginnings for the process of change that is part of any education. As the reflections suggest, some teachers may see the glass as half empty and some may see it as half full. In special education, especially when dealing with students with serious emotional disturbance, it really is. "all in how you look at it."

What Every Teacher Should Know

- Serious emotional disturbance is reflected in inappropriate behaviors that adversely affect educational performance.

- Although specific emotional and social behaviors are not specified in accepted definitions for this category, most professionals agree these students' educational performances are adversely affected by how they personally handle stress and challenges (emotional problems) and how they interact in other situations (social problems).

- Emotional problems of students with serious emotional disturbance include anxiety, oppositional behavior, and temper tantrums.

- Specific social problems include disruptiveness, nonattention, irrelevant activities, and task avoidance.

- Interventions for students with serious emotional disturbance generally focus on identifying stressors, rewarding appropriate behaviors, discouraging inappropriate behaviors, and coordinating school efforts with efforts in the home and community.

Projects

1. Make a list of behaviors that might be exhibited by an adolescent student who has especially high anxiety about developmental changes. Make a list of tactics you could use to reduce the student's anxiety and improve behavior in school.

2. Prepare a table illustrating the numbers of students with specific learning disabilities, communication disorders, mental retardation, and serious emotional disturbance in your state and a few neighboring states. (For data, see Tables 8.1, 9.1, 10.3, and 11.1.) Compare the figures and come up with three reasons for any variations that you identify.

3. Interview a teacher of students with serious emotional disturbance. Ask the teacher to describe the emotional and social problems evident in his or her classroom. Request recommendations of appropriate instructional methods to use in teaching in an elementary, middle, or high school. Ask the teacher to cite reasons students with serious emotional disturbance are successful or unsuccessful in school. Get the teacher's suggestions for special materials to meet the needs of students from diverse racial and ethnic backgrounds.

4. To help understand how people with emotional problems are treated, try one of these simulations and note reactions of people around you: Wear a heavy coat on a hot summer day; take a ride on public transportation and talk to yourself during the trip.

5. Make a list of rules you would want in your classroom. Describe the plan you would use if students failed to follow the rules.

6. Interview three professionals who work with people with serious emotional disturbance in three settings other than school. Ask them to describe what they do and any special methods they use to reduce social and emotional problems.

For Your Information

Books

Algozzine, B. (1994). *Problem behavior management: Educator's resource service*. Gaithersburg, MD: Aspen.

A comprehensive publication of up-to-date teaching tips and information describing a variety of instructional approaches appropriate for students with emotional and social problems.

Allen, C. (1985). *Tea with demons*. New York: Morrow.

Recollections of a 30-year-old housewife describing aspects of serious emotional disturbance. Excellent book for high school students.

Axline, V. M. (1964). *Dibs in search of self*. New York: Ballentine Books.

A true story about a troubled little boy as told by his therapist; "Dibs" has become a classic in the field of serious emotional disturbance.

Coleman, M. (1992). *Behavior disorders: Theory and practice* (2nd ed.). Englewood Cliffs, NJ: Prentice-Hall.

An overview of the field of behavior disorders with information on definitions, characteristics, prevalence, assessment, etiologies, and instructional practices. Focused heavily on educational programs and concerns.

Hayden, T. L. (1988). *Just another kid*. New York: Avon.

A teacher's description of one school year in a special education classroom for six students with serious emotional disturbance.

Heide, F. P. (1976). *Growing anyway up*. New York: Harper.

A young girl with serious emotional disturbance is alienated from her mother and finds adjusting to a new private school difficult. Excellent book for upper elementary and middle school students.

Long, N., Morse, W., & Newman, R. (Eds.). (1980). *Conflict in the classroom: The education of emotionally disturbed children* (4th ed.). Belmont, CA: Wadsworth.

A compilation of stories, opinion papers, and articles dealing with various aspects of serious emotional disturbance. Although somewhat dated, in many teacher preparation programs, this is a classic textbook for the introductory course.

MacCracken, M. (1973). *A circle of children*. New York: New American Library.

A compilation of stories about successful teaching experiences with students with serious emotional disturbance.

Morgan, D. P., & Jenson, W. R. (1988). *Teaching behaviorally disordered students: Preferred practices*. Columbus, OH: Merrill.

A practical methods book with information on assessment, behavior management, mainstreaming, and teaching academic and social skills.

Rhode, G., Jenson, W. R., & Reavis, H. K. (1992). *The tough kid book: Practical classroom management strategies*. Longmont, CO: Sopris West.

A resource of research-validated solutions designed to reduce disruptive classroom behavior.

Rosenberg, M. S., Wilson, R., Maheady, L., & Sindelar, P. T. (1992). *Educating students with behavior disorders*. Boston, MA: Allyn & Bacon.

Definitional matters; assessing and classifying disordered behavior; and methods for managing hyperactive, aggressive, socially withdrawn, and rule-breaking behaviors; as well as students with severe behavior disorders are discussed.

Snyder, Z. K. (1972). *The witches of worm*. New York: Macmillan.

A girl with serious emotional disturbance believes her selfish and destructive behavior is caused by witches. Excellent book for upper elementary and middle school students.

Organizations

American Orthopsychiatric Association (AOA)

For nearly seventy years, the American Orthopsychiatric Association (AOA) has brought together professionals in all disciplines devoted to mental health and human development. Members seek to apply a multidisciplinary perspective in addressing a broad range of issues affecting families, children, adolescents, adults, and school and community mental health. AOA believes its members have been innovators least likely to accept the status quo or to work contentedly within the confines of a single discipline; their activities result in annual meetings and professional publications. For more information, contact AOA, 19 W. 44th St., Suite 1616, New York, NY 10036.

Association for Behavior Analysis (ABA)

The Association for Behavior Analysis (ABA) is dedicated to advancing the science of behavior analysis and its application. The purview of ABA encompasses contemporary scientific and social issues, theoretical advances, and the dissemination of professional and public information about behavior analysis and behavior change. Activities of ABA include membership services, journal support, directories, newsletters (*The ABA Newsletter*), and an annual convention. For more information, contact Susan Goeters, ABA, 258 Wood Hall, Western Michigan University, Kalamazoo, MI 49008.

Council for Children with Behavioral Disorders (CCBD)

A division of the Council for Exceptional Children (CEC), formally affiliated in 1963, CCBD pursues quality educational services and program alternatives for children and youth with behavioral disorders, advocates for their needs, and emphasizes research and professional growth as ways to better understand serious emotional disturbance. The approximately 8,600 members include teachers, parents, and mental health professionals. Members receive *Behavioral Disorders, Beyond Behavior,* and the *CCBD Newsletter.* For more information, contact CEC, 1920 Association Dr., Reston, VA 22091.

Society for the Advancement of Behavior Analysis (SABA)

The goals of the Society for the Advancement of Behavior Analysis (SABA) are to provide instruction and training in behavior analysis and to disseminate information about behavior analysis that is useful to the public and beneficial to communities. SABA is concerned with research and practical applications of behavior analysis to the solution of community, educational, and social problems. For more information, contact Susan Goeters, SABA, 258 Wood Hall, Western Michigan University, Kalamazoo, MI 49008.

Society for the Experimental Analysis of Behavior (SEAB)

An organization concerned with research and practical applications of behavior analysis to the solution of community, educational, and social problems, the Society for the Experimental Analysis of Behavior (SEAB) exists primarily for the purpose of overseeing the publication of the *Journal of the Experimental Analysis of Behavior* (JEAB) and the *Journal of Applied Behavior Analysis* (JABA). The society does not hold annual meetings but does participate and subsidize panels and symposia at the annual meetings of the Association for Behavior Analysis. For more information, contact Devonia Stein, SEAB, Department of Psychology, Indiana University, Bloomington, IN 47405.

Journals

American Journal of Orthopsychiatry (AJO)

This journal is dedicated to public policy, professional practice, and knowledge production related to mental health and human development. Articles cover clinical practice, theory, research, and exposition. For more information, contact Milton F. Shore, Editor, AJO, 19 W. 44th St., New York, NY 10036.

Behavior Analyst (BA)

This is a publication of the Society for the Advancement of Behavior Analysis. Its articles cover various aspects of instruction and training in behavior analysis of use to the public as well as professionals concerned with improving behavior. For more information, contact Jay Moore, Editor, BA, Department of Psychology, University of Wisconsin–Milwaukee, Milwaukee, WI 53201.

Behavior Modification (BM)

This interdisciplinary journal publishes research and clinical papers in the area of applied behavior modification. The articles typically contain sufficient detail for readers to understand what was done, how it was done, and why the method of behavior change was selected. Assessment and intervention methods for problems in psychiatric, clinical, educational, and rehabilitation settings are included in most issues. For more information, contact Michel Hersen, Editor, BM, Nova University, Center for Psychological Studies, 3301 College Ave., Fort Lauderdale, FL 33314.

Behavior Therapy (BT)

This international journal is devoted to the application of behavioral and cognitive sciences to correcting clinical problems. Original research of an experimental or clinical nature that contributes to theory, practice, or evaluation of behavior therapy primarily constitutes each issue; case studies, clinical replication studies, book reviews, and invited papers are sometimes included. For more information, contact Lizette Peterson, Editor, BT, Department of Psychology, University of Missouri, 210 McAlester, Columbia, MO 65211.

Behavioral Disorders (BD)

The purpose of this publication of the Council for Exceptional Children is to publish research articles of interest to professionals working with students with behavioral disorders. Evaluations of interventions and position papers related to issues of interest to the field are among the more frequently published papers. For more information, contact Jo Hendrickson and Gary Sasso, Editors, BD, Department of Curriculum and Instruction, University of Iowa, Iowa City, IA 52242.

Beyond Behavior (BB)

A publication of the Council for Exceptional Children, this journal provides thought-provoking pieces, fiction, personal stories, and humor papers related to teaching and working with students with behavior disorders. For more information, contact Mary Kay Zabel, Editor, BB, Special Education, Buena Vista College, Storm Lake, IA 50588.

Journal of Abnormal Child Psychology (JACP)

This journal is devoted to studies of behavioral pathology in childhood and adolescence. Contents include empirical investigations in etiology, assessment, treatment in community and correctional settings, prognosis and follow-up, epidemiology, remediation in educational settings, pharmacological intervention, and other studies related to abnormal behavior. For more information, contact Herbert C. Quay, Editor, JACP, Department of Psychology, University of Miami, Coral Gables, FL 33124.

Journal of Applied Behavior Analysis (JABA)

This publication reports primarily on experimental research involving applications of the experimental analysis of behavior to solutions of problems of broad social importance. Technical articles relevant to such research, and discussion of issues arising from applications, are also published. The journal is published quarterly by the Society for the Experimental Analysis of Behavior. For more information, contact Nancy A. Neef, Editor, JABA, Graduate School of Education, University of Pennsylvania, 3700 Walnut St., Philadelphia, PA 19104.

Journal of Emotional and Behavioral Disorders (JEBD)

This multidisciplinary publication contains articles on research and practice related to individuals with emotional and behavioral disorders. It includes original research reports, reviews of research, descriptions of practices and effective programs, and discussions of key applied issues that are of interest to a wide range of disciplines. For more information, contact Dr. Michael Epstein, Editor, JEBD, Department of Educational Psychology, Northern Illinois University, DeKalb, IL 60115-2854; Dr. Douglas Cullinan, Editor, JEBD, Department of Curriculum and Instruction, North Carolina State University, Raleigh, NC 27695-7801; or PRO-ED Publications, 8700 Shoal Creek Blvd., Austin, TX 78757-6897.

Journal of the Experimental Analysis of Behavior (JEAB)

Published bimonthly by the Society for the Experimental Analysis of Behavior, JEAB includes primarily original publications of experiments relevant to the behavior of individual organisms. Review articles and theoretical papers also appear in this journal. For more information, contact Marc N. Branch, Psychology Department, University of Florida, Gainesville, FL 32611.

12

Teaching Students with Sensory Disabilities

Focusing Questions

- What are sensory disabilities?

- What definitions are used for students with sensory disabilities?

- How many students with sensory disabilities receive special education?

- What are the primary characteristics of students with sensory disabilities?

- What instructional approaches and teaching tactics are appropriate for students with sensory disabilities?

"I'm going to be a lawyer—I'm supposed to read the fine print. What a joke. I can't even read the large print." *Mary is legally blind and uses special equipment to help her read legal documents at the George Washington University law library.*

"I love softball. I'm hitting .425 and my kids think I'm a sports hero. I guess I am." *Tommy doesn't see well, but special adaptations like softballs with beepers and a closed-circuit television system to enlarge print help him lead a life much like his neighbors and peers.*

"To be honest, we were very concerned about placing Pat in the public school, but we couldn't be happier. It hasn't been a 'piece of cake,' but everything looks very promising right now." *Pat was born blind. Kindergarten could have been a major problem, but mobility and listening skill training smoothed the transition from a special education preschool program to her neighborhood school.*

"When I think about all the things that could be wrong with me, I think I'm pretty lucky. I've had a great time in high school and I'm going to college with my best friend. Right now, that's all I want." *Lee is deaf. An interpreter uses sign language to communicate what is spoken by others and to let them know what Lee has to say. A telecommunication device for the deaf (TDD) connected to the phone enables Lee to make and receive calls.*

"Ya know, growing up with Barry was just like growing up with Bobby. They both were royal pains. Hey, boys will be boys and sometimes they will be your brothers." *Barry is hard of hearing. His sister learned sign language and finger spelling so she could have private and public conversations with him.* ▪

Types of sensory disabilities

People like Mary, Tommy, Pat, Lee, and Barry receive special education because they have trouble seeing and hearing. Of the human senses, seeing and hearing are most important for translating external information to traditional learning, and these two senses are involved in what we broadly call **sensory disabilities**. More specifically, the term **visual impairments** refers to all degrees of vision loss. The term **hearing impairments** refers to all degrees of hearing loss. In this chapter, we provide an overview of these two areas of special education. As in the previous categorical chapters, we discuss current definitions, prevalence, and characteristics. We also review instructional approaches and tactics that are useful with students with these sensory disabilities.

Visual Impairments

History of programs

Students with visual impairments were among the first to receive special education services in the United States. The first institutional programs—the New England Asylum for the Blind and the New York Institution for the Blind—began in 1832. Five years later, the first residential school for students who were blind opened in Ohio. It was not until 1900 that the first day school classes for students with visual impairments were held in Chicago. In 1911 New York became the first state to make their education compulsory. In 1913 Boston and Cleveland started classes for students who were partially sighted. Until recently, it was common to place students with visual impairments in residential settings and day schools. Today, more and more students are being included in general education classes with their neighbors and peers and leading productive lives, both in and out of school, as a result.

Definition

According to federal regulations, a visual impairment is a problem seeing that, even with correction, adversely affects a child's educational performance. The term does not include people with normal or near normal vision, but does include people with low visual functioning (partial sight) as well as those who have only light perception or those who are totally without the sense of vision (Barraga & Erin, 1992). People with normal or near normal vision can perform tasks without special assistance. People with *low vision* may have difficulty with detailed visual tasks or may perform them at reduced levels of speed, endurance, or accuracy, even with assistance (sometimes these people are referred to as partially sighted). People who are *blind* or near blind have unreliable vision and rely primarily or exclusively on other senses.

Degrees of visual impairment

Visual acuity

Visual impairments are often defined in terms of visual acuity—the ability to see things at specified distances. **Visual acuity** usually is measured by having people read letters or discriminate objects at a distance of 20 feet. Those who are able to read the letters correctly have normal vision. Visual acuity usually is expressed as a ratio that tells us how well the individual sees. The expression *20/20 vision* describes perfect (normal) vision; it means that the person can see at 20 feet what people with normal vision see at 20 feet. A person with 20/90 vision needs to be 20 feet away to discriminate letters or objects that people with normal vision can read or discriminate at 90 feet.

How poor does visual acuity have to be before a person is considered to have a visual impairment? To address this question, the American Medical Association (AMA) adopted a definition of blindness in 1934 that is still used today. According to that definition, the criterion for blindness is

> central visual acuity of 20/200 or less in the better eye with corrective glasses or central visual acuity of more than 20/200 if there is a visual field defect in which the peripheral field is contracted to such an extent that the widest diameter of the visual field subtends an angular distance no greater than 20 degrees in the better eye. (Koestler, 1976, p. 45)

Field of vision

A person who needs to stand at a distance of 20 feet to see with correction what people with normal vision can see from 200 feet away is considered blind. The second part of the AMA definition is included so that people with a severely restricted **field of vision** are also considered blind. When looking straight ahead, a person with a normal field of vision is able to see objects within a range of approximately 180 degrees. Mary's field of vision is only 10 degrees, so she is able to see only a limited area at any one time, even though her visual acuity in that area is actually quite good. People with restricted visual fields sometimes say it is like looking through a narrow tube or tunnel. Other field of vision problems make it difficult to see things clearly in the central visual field but relatively easy in the peripheral field.

Eligibility standard

People who have a visual impairment but are not blind—those with low vision—are also eligible for special education services. These people have visual acuity greater than 20/200 but not greater than 20/70 in the better eye with correction. For most practical purposes, a student with a visual impairment is one who has visual acuity with correction of less than 20/70. In all cases, the standard is employed "with correction." This means that if the condition can be corrected with glasses or contact lenses, the student is not eligible for special education services.

Focusing problems

Many problems with visual acuity result from difficulties in focusing. In **myopia,** or nearsightedness, distant objects are blurred although nearer objects remain clear. In **hyperopia,** or farsightedness, the reverse is true: Distant objects are in clear focus but nearer ones are blurred. **Astigmatism** stems from irregular curvature in the eye's refractive surfaces, with the result that objects at any distance may be blurred or distorted. Obviously, conditions like myopia, hyperopia, and astigmatism can affect school performance; but since they are most often corrected before or during the school years, they are not generally considered visual impairments requiring special education services.

Problems of eye movement

In addition to difficulties with visual acuity and field of vision, students may have problems related to eye movement. **Ocular motility** problems affect the eyes' ability to move smoothly and focus properly. **Strabismus,** often caused by a malfunction of the eye muscles, involves an inability to focus both eyes on the same object. **Nystagmus** produces rapid, involuntary movements of the eye that interfere with focusing objects.

Emphasis on visual functioning

In recent years, rather than classifying students on the basis of vision tests that measured acuity, field of vision, or other physiological aspects of vision, teachers have begun to emphasize visual functioning—what the student can do with his or her vision. This shift in emphasis recognizes that all students who are blind or who have low vision are not alike in the way they use their vision. Currently it is more common for students with blindness or low vision to be classified in terms of the kinds of special assistance needed to be successful or the kinds of instructional approaches that are effective for them. From this perspective, students who are blind are those who must be educated through channels other than sight (using braille or audiotapes, for example). Students with low vision can use print materials but may need modifications such as enlarged print or use of low vision aids (magnification).

Prevalence

During recent school years, about 24,000 students with visual impairments received special education services; there have been notable decreases (about 12 percent) in the proportion of students served with visual impairments over the past ten years (U.S. Department of Education, 1993). This group represents about 0.04 percent of school-age children and adolescents and about 0.5 percent of students with disabilities. There is relatively little variation in the percentage of students identified in each of the states. In recent years, students with visual impairments had the second highest placement rate (42 percent) in general education classes; 23 percent were served in resource rooms, 20 percent in separate classes, and the remainder in separate school settings (U.S. Department of Education, 1993).

Many placed in regular classrooms

Characteristics

People with visual impairments receive special education because their vision after correction remains limited and may affect their development and achievement without intervention. Some possible signs of vision impairments are presented in Table 12.1. Not being able to see as well as neighbors and peers may result in a variety of other cognitive, academic, physical, behavioral, and communication characteristics if appropriate modifications and specialized instructional interventions are unavailable.

Table 12.1 Top Ten List of Potential Signs of Visual Impairments

1. Student frequently experiences watery eyes.
2. Student frequently experiences red or inflamed eyes.
3. Student's eye movements are jumpy or not synchronized.
4. Student experiences difficulty moving around the classroom.
5. Student experiences difficulty reading small print.
6. Student experiences difficulty identifying small details in pictures or illustrations.
7. Student frequently complains of dizziness after reading a passage or completing an assignment involving vision.
8. Student tilts head or squints eyes to achieve better focus.
9. Student uses one eye more than the other for reading or completing other assignments.
10. Student frequently complains of headaches or eye infections.

Cognitive   Cognition is largely a matter of developing concepts. Because many concepts are learned entirely through visual means, students with visual impairments have difficulty learning some concepts. Think for a minute about the difficulty of learning concepts like orange, circle, bigger, perpendicular, bright, and foggy with limited vision. Students who have visual impairments are not necessarily intellectually retarded, but they may perform poorly on most standard intelligence tests. The reason is the nature of those tests. Look at these items from intelligence tests:

What is a collar?

What is a pagoda?

Tell me another word for illuminate.

In what way are a radio tower and a police car alike?

Prior visual information would be helpful in answering such questions. Similarly, many subtests and items on intelligence tests require that students see the stimuli and responses: Students are shown pictures and asked to identify them; they are shown bead patterns and asked to reproduce them; they are shown visual stimulus arrays and asked to find the one stimulus that differs from the others. Performances on such items are greatly influenced by the visual capabilities of the people being tested.

Academic   Newland (1986) reported that "with the exception of unique problems of input and possibly a greater demand in processing, the fundamental learning procedures of blind children do not differ from those of nonimpaired children" (p. 576). The impact of visual impairments on academic performance is very much a function of the severity of the condition (that is, the degree of vision loss and causes) and the age at which the student's vision was reduced. We address some instructional characteristics and considerations in upcoming sections. Modifications for each student should be determined

individually using assessment data, not simply on the basis of vision status classification. With appropriate assistance, people with visual impairments achieve academic success just like their neighbors and peers.

The academic needs of students with visual impairments require a dual curriculum perspective that consists of the traditional academic content taught to their peers as well as disability-specific content needed for success in the tradi-

tional curriculum. Disability-specific skills for children and adolescents who are blind include those related to concept development and communication such as braille reading and writing, listening skills, use of a slate and stylus, use of an abacus for math, handwriting, and keyboarding. Additional skills may be needed that provide access to the traditional curriculum, such as tactual map reading skills and ability to use access technology like speech and braille access devices.

Physical   In terms of size and appearance, people with visual impairments are no different from those with normal vision. As children develop, however, low

vision and blindness may impact movement and the quality of motor skills.

Having a sensory disability doesn't mean you have to be educated in a self-contained special education classroom. *Bob Daemmrich.*

"Blindisms"

Imitation from visual observations, a primary method of learning for young children, may be absent for the child with a visual disability. In addition, information acquired by many children through "incidental learning"—unintended learning through observation—may be unavailable to many children with visual disabilities. Some children also develop repetitive stereotypic movements commonly referred to as "blindisms" such as rocking, eye poking, head rolling, and hand waving.

Orientation and mobility

Instruction in nonacademic disability-specific skills that encourage appropriate physical growth and independence should begin in early childhood and continue throughout a student's school career. Emphasis on orientation and mobility is an essential component. *Orientation* refers to the ability to know where one is in relation to the environment; *mobility* is the ability to move safely and efficiently from one place to another. Activities that provide and promote movement may discourage undesirable behaviors such as blindisms.

Behavioral   In general, there are few social and emotional characteristics specific to people with visual disabilities; however, low vision and blindness may influence a child's behavior. Nonacademic skills that may be affected include social skills, affective understanding, and nonverbal or body language behavior. In addition, the degree of independence in all areas of development affects a child's behavior and the behavior of others toward the child.

Social skills

Social skills are important to a child's overall success. Children need instruction and feedback in appropriate ways of interacting with others, such as initiating a conversation without eye contact, age-appropriate ways of sitting and standing, and facial expressions. Many students with visual impairments cannot see nonverbal forms of communication, so they miss out on the information and feelings displayed with a look, a nod, a smile, a frown, or a shrug.

Developing independence

Students with visual impairments can be taught to assert themselves from an early age to maintain and develop age-appropriate independence. It is important for children with disabilities to learn from their peers without disabilities. For developing healthy self-concepts, it is equally important for children with visual disabilities to learn from peers and role models with visual disabilities. Meeting behavioral needs of students with visual disabilities works best, not in isolation, but in the environment in which the behavior naturally occurs.

Communication   This is the major area in which students with visual impairments experience difficulty. To "read," for example, they sometimes have to

Adaptations for reading

use large-print books, special reading methods (braille), or recorded materials and readers. Many students with visual impairments are able to use special optical devices such as magnifiers, small telescopes, or glasses and contact lenses to help them perform better at tasks such as reading. Simple instructional

---

Table 12.2   Top Ten List of Tips for Teachers of Students with Visual Impairments

1. Reduce distance between student and speaker as much as possible.
2. Reduce distracting glare and visual distractions as much as possible.
3. Reduce clutter on classroom floor and provide unobstructed access to door and key classroom spaces.
4. Seat students near chalkboard or overhead projections, or give them the freedom to move close to areas of instruction.
5. Avoid partially opening cabinets, storage areas, and classroom doors; fully opened or closed doors are safer.
6. Use auditory cues when referring to objects in the classroom and during instructional presentations.
7. When presenting visually dependent materials, verbalize written information, describe pictures, and narrate nonverbal sequences in videotapes or movies. Use complete sentences to provide additional context.
8. Reduce unnecessary noise to help focus content of instructional presentations.
9. Keep instructional materials in the same place so students can find them easily.
10. Make sure glasses and other visual aids are functioning properly.

adaptations can also help them make up for their loss of vision. Some general interventions for students with vision impairments are presented in Table 12.2.

Choosing the literacy medium

A major area of emphasis critical to the literacy needs of students with visual impairments is determining an appropriate literacy medium based on an assessment of individual communication and learning skills. The decision to use braille or print (or a combination) for reading and writing may be an obvious decision for a child who is totally blind, but it can be a difficult one for a child with low vision. A sampling of factors that assist teachers in making this decision include preferences in using vision or touch to complete tasks, degree of vision, ability to read own handwriting, fatigue, and other disabilities. In addition, the use of large-print and auditory materials and tools should be based on a thorough and ongoing media assessment. Most teachers find that students with visual impairments prefer reading regular print with the assistance of an optical reader rather than large-print materials (Corn & Ryser, 1989).

Hearing Impairments

Moores (1987) notes that

> Although occasional references to education of the deaf may be found, no evidence exists of any organized attempt to provide for the deaf in the United States before the nineteenth century. Parents with the financial resources would send their deaf children to Europe to be educated. (pp. 56–57)

History of programs

The first permanent school for deaf students in the United States was established by Thomas Hopkins Gallaudet in Connecticut in 1817. The institution was called the American Asylum for the Education and Instruction of the Deaf and Dumb. In 1818 the New York Institution for the Instruction of the Deaf and Dumb was established, and in 1820 the Pennsylvania Institution for the Deaf and Dumb began. Only four more schools were established in the next twenty years (1820–1840), one each in Kentucky, Ohio, Missouri, and Virginia. In the next twenty years (1840–1860) twenty additional schools were established.

Gallaudet University

In 1857 the Columbia Institution for the Deaf and Dumb was established in Washington, D.C. This school eventually developed a collegiate and later a university unit, and is known today as Gallaudet University. It is the only liberal arts university in the world for people who are deaf. In 1869 day classes were begun for students who were deaf in Boston. These were the very first special education classes for students with any kind of disability. Today, people with hearing impairments lead productive lives and function successfully in general education classrooms and all walks of life. They believe that the only barriers to full access and acceptance by society are those erected by the attitudes of people without disabilities. Fortunately, partnerships and collaboration between hearing people and those who are deaf are going a long way toward overcoming these attitudinal obstacles.

Definition

There are two types of hearing impairments; they include people who are deaf and people who are hard of hearing. **Deafness** is a severe disability. People who are deaf have a hearing loss that prevents understanding speech through the ear. They have little functional hearing, even with a hearing aid, and they do not use hearing as their primary sense for gaining information. **Hard of hearing** is a less severe disability. People who are hard of hearing can process information from sounds and usually profit from amplification provided by hearing aids.

The federal definitions for these categories are brief and stress impact on educational performance:

> "Deafness" means a hearing impairment that is so severe that the child is impaired in processing linguistic information through hearing, with or without amplification, that adversely affects a child's educational performance (Individuals with Disabilities Education Act, 1990).
>
> "Hearing impairment" means an impairment in hearing, whether permanent or fluctuating, that adversely affects a child's educational performance but that is not included under the definition of deafness.

Eligibility for services under the categories of deafness and hearing impairment is based on degree of hearing loss. People with normal hearing can understand speech without a hearing aid. People who are deaf are unable to understand speech, even with the help of a hearing aid. Between normal hearing and deafness are various degrees of hearing loss.

There are two types of hearing loss: conductive and sensorineural. **Conductive hearing loss** is due to blockage or damage to the outer or middle sections of the ear. Conductive losses are generally considered to have less severe effects than sensorineural losses. **Sensorineural hearing loss** occurs when there is damage to the inner ear or auditory nerves.

Some causes of hearing loss are presented in Table 12.3. The cause is unknown in about half the people with hearing impairments. Sensorineural hearing losses are caused by viruses like rubella and meningitis for about 14 percent of the people with hearing impairments. Heredity and genetic factors account for about 13 percent of hearing impairments. Knowing the cause of a hearing problem helps teachers and other professionals decide on appropriate treatments. For example, children who are deaf at birth must be taught to communicate differently from children whose hearing loss is acquired after they have learned to talk.

We measure the ability to hear (auditory acuity) and hearing loss using two dimensions: intensity and frequency. People hear sounds at certain levels of loudness, or intensity. Loudness is expressed in decibels (dB); the greater the decibels, the louder the sound. A decibel level of 125 or louder is painful to the average person. Decibel levels from 0 to 120 are used to test hearing at different frequencies. Frequency, or pitch, is measured in hertz (Hz), or cycles per second. The frequency range for conversational speech is between 500 and 2,000 Hz. Both loudness and frequency can be measured with an audiometer.

Table 12.3 Some Causes of Hearing Impairments

Maternal rubella (5 percent)

> German measles contracted by a pregnant woman; depending on when illness occurs, typically results in sensorineural hearing loss

Meningitis (9 percent)

> Disease that affects the central nervous system; typically results in sensorineural hearing loss

Otitis media (3 percent)

> Infection of the middle ear and accumulation of fluid behind the ear drum; typically results in conductive hearing loss

Heredity (13 percent)

> More than 150 types of genetic deafness

Other causes at birth (22 percent)

> High fever, infections, trauma, birth complications, prematurity

Cause unknown (48 percent)

Hearing losses are most often described by the lowest decibel level that a person can hear. Moores (1987) used decibel levels in this way to define deafness and hard of hearing:

> A "deaf person" is one whose hearing is disabled to an extent (usually 70 dB or greater) that precludes the understanding of speech through the ear alone, without or with the use of a hearing aid.
>
> A "hard of hearing person" is one whose hearing is disabled to an extent (usually 35 to 69 dB) that makes difficult but does not preclude, the understanding of speech through the ear alone, without or with a hearing aid. (p. 9)

Students who are deaf are linked to the world of communication and information primarily through their eyes. Most of these students depend on some form of signing to express and receive information. Although most are educated in separate programs, many attend the same classes as their neighbors and peers (U.S. Department of Education, 1993). Typically, students who are hard of hearing are enrolled in general education programs and may receive selected special services such as speech and language therapy (Paul & Jackson, 1993).

Prevalence

During recent school years, about sixty thousand students with hearing impairments received special education services; there have been notable decreases (about 14 percent) in the proportion of students served with hearing impairments over the past ten years (U.S. Department of Education, 1993). This group represents about 0.11 percent of school-age children and adolescents and about 1.3 percent of students with disabilities. There is relatively little variation in the percentage of students identified in each of the states. Although almost 47 percent of students with hearing impairments were served in regular class or resource room placements, the largest single placement category (32.7 percent) for these students was separate classes (U.S. Department of Education, 1993).

According to the Office of Demographic Studies (1989–1990) at Gallaudet University in Washington, D.C., 63 percent of children in the United States who are deaf were white; 17 percent were black; 13 percent were Hispanic; and 7 percent were American Indian, Asian/Pacific Island, or other ethnicity. Christensen and Delgado (1993) believe that by the year 2000, many more school-age children with hearing impairments will be from African American, Hispanic, American Indian, and Asian/Pacific Island families because identification practices are improving and the numbers of children attending school from these groups are increasing.

Characteristics

Many traits or characteristics are attributed to deaf people in the professional literature. Unfortunately, most of them are negative. We say "unfortunately" because the use of negative terminology leads to negative stereotypes about those who are deaf. Moreover, the negative characteristics attributed to deaf people generally are not substantiated in empirical studies.

People with hearing impairments should not be stereotyped. The causes for hearing loss and the effects it has are simply too varied to lend credence to a typical case. People with hearing impairments have different learning styles and abilities. They do have one characteristic in common: Their ability to hear is limited and this disability may be reflected in other cognitive, academic, physical, behavioral, and communication characteristics.

Cognitive   There is considerable debate about the extent to which cognitive development is limited by hearing impairments. The environment of people who are deaf or hard of hearing is often qualitatively different from that of people who can hear. Much of what we think of as intelligence is developed through hearing and using language. It has been argued that people with hearing impairments do not think in an abstract way and that their intellectual functioning is limited. Moores (1987) puts the theories about the cognitive functioning of deaf students into perspective:

> The available evidence suggests that the condition of deafness imposes no
> limitations on the cognitive capabilities of individuals. There is no evidence

(Margin notes:)

Many placed in separate classes

Ethnic group percentages

Negative terminology

Avoiding stereotypes

Debate about cognition and hearing

Bring Your Learning to Life

Barry's Teachers Asked for Information About His Hearing Impairment

Barry's hearing problem was identified early in his life. With the assistance of doctors and other health professionals, his parents were able to start special education services during his preschool years. Barry came to school with complete records of his hearing ability and his ability to use speech and language. His teachers, concerned about what he could do, asked the following questions:

- What is the range of Barry's hearing in each ear?
- What will Barry's level of hearing loss mean in the classroom?
- How well is Barry using whatever hearing is available?
- How well does Barry understand speech

and language constructions?

- How well is Barry using speech in relation to his hearing loss?
- What steps should be followed to help Barry use his available hearing and continue to develop his speech and language?

To respond to these questions, the school system's audiologist and speech language specialist studied Barry's records and interviewed his parents. They also interviewed Barry himself and gave him some tests. With the information from these multiple sources, they provided thorough answers to the teachers' questions. The teachers were then able to plan Barry's school program to help him achieve continued success and independence.

to suggest that deaf persons think in more "concrete" ways than the hearing or that their intellectual functioning is in any way less sophisticated. As a group, deaf people function within the normal range of intelligence, and deaf individuals exhibit the same wide variability as the hearing population. . . . The great difficulty encountered by deaf children in academic subject matter is most likely not caused by cognitive deficiencies. In fact, it is safe to say that educators of the deaf have not capitalized on the cognitive strengths of deaf children in the academic environment. (pp. 164–165)

Paul and Jackson (1993) believe that differences in the cognitive performance of students who are deaf and of their hearing peers are more due to inadequate development of a conventional language system than to limited intellectual ability.

Academic   The severity of the hearing loss, the age of its onset, the socioeconomic status of the student's family, and the hearing status of the student's parents are related to the academic success experienced by students with hearing impairments. Children and young adults who have mild hearing losses generally perform better academically than those with severe losses. Students who are deaf from birth tend to have more difficulty acquiring academic skills than those who hear, then later lose their hearing. Students with hearing impairments from families of high socioeconomic status and those who have hearing parents tend to experience fewer academic difficulties than students from families of low socioeconomic status or those whose parents are hearing impaired.

Standardized scores versus functional ability

We cannot make firm generalizations about the ways in which students who are deaf and hard of hearing function academically. They do not perform as well as hearing students on standardized tests of reading and writing, and research suggests that children who are deaf have much more difficulty acquiring writing skills than they do acquiring reading skills. But research also suggests that the functional reading ability of students who are deaf is higher than that implied by the scores they earn on standardized achievement tests (Luetke-Stahlman & Luckner, 1991). Nevertheless, differences in language ability that result from deafness affect a student's ability to perform in traditional academic areas (Paul & Jackson, 1993).

Physical   Few physical characteristics are specific to those who are deaf or hard of hearing. The widespread belief that the individual compensates for deficiencies in one sense by developing extraordinary abilities in another is unfounded. People who are deaf or hard of hearing have senses of sight, smell, taste, and touch like their peers who do not have hearing impairments.

Functional hearing

A characteristic that does differentiate people with hearing impairments from their neighbors and peers is their functional hearing. *Functional hearing* refers to a person's ability to understand information presented orally and is related to how a person might be taught. For example, a person with a moderate functional hearing loss might not be able to profit from a normal classroom presentation and would require some instructional adaptation to be successful. Typically, functional hearing loss is categorized by decibel groupings (see Table 12.4) and related problems.

Behavioral   Generalizations about the social, emotional, and behavioral functioning of students who are deaf or hard of hearing are based on the performance of these students on standardized tests. But most of these tests are inappropriate for use with this group. Moores (1987) describes two perspectives on the social, emotional, and behavioral functioning of those who are deaf or hard of hearing: One is that people with hearing impairments are deviant and evidence many problems; the other is that people with hearing impairments are different and need access to services that encourage their optimal development. Based on a review of the research on the social and emotional functioning of people who are deaf, he concludes that

Most standardized tests inappropriate

> the evidence suggests that the social-emotional adjustment of the deaf is similar to that of the hearing, with great individual variation. Most deaf individuals cope with the reality of deafness as a life-long condition and lead normal, productive lives. This fact supports the contention that deafness itself has no direct impact, either negative or positive, on the development of a mentally healthy individual. (p. 180)

Table 12.4	Characteristics of Functional Hearing Losses
Less than 26 dB loss (normal)	No significant difficulty with faint speech
26–40 dB loss (slight)	Difficulty only with faint sounds
41–55 dB loss (mild)	Understands face-to-face speech and conversations at 3–5 ft.
56–70 dB loss (moderate)	Frequent difficulty with normal conversation and speech
71–90 dB loss (severe)	Understands only shouted or amplified speech
91 dB or more loss (profound)	Difficulty even with amplified speech

Recent evidence suggests that those who are deaf prefer to be with others who are deaf, that adults who are deaf tend to cluster in groups, socialize, and marry. There has been much discussion of *deaf culture,* a concept implying that people who are deaf experience and design their lives differently from the hearing people with whom they share the planet (Humphries, 1993). Accordingly, many people who are deaf see the experiences and signed language of deaf communities as the most important factors in their lives. People who are deaf teach one another how to function in society as well as how to get along with others. Sometimes, parents who are deaf want their children to be born deaf so they can share the culture.

Teachers need to be aware of deaf culture because it means that many children who are deaf add a dimension to the diverse backgrounds they bring to the classroom. But the extent of exposure to deaf culture will vary from student to student. For instance, deaf students from minority ethnic backgrounds may not have as many opportunities to experience deaf culture as those from majority groups:

Isolation of ethnic minorities

> It may be more difficult for African American, Hispanic, American Indian, and Asian/Pacific Island Deaf people to achieve a sense of community in the United States because of several factors: The social forces that isolate people of different races and ethnicity may isolate Deaf people of ethnic backgrounds from white Deaf communities as well. The forces that isolate Deaf children from Deaf adults may be even more effective among ethnic groups. There are few "models" of white Deaf people in the lives of Deaf children, and there are even fewer African American, Hispanic, American Indian, and Asian/Pacific Island Deaf role models in the lives of Deaf children. (Humphries, 1993, p. 14)

Debate about integration of people who are deaf

There is considerable debate about the importance of deaf culture and the effect on social development of integrating people who are deaf and hearing individuals. Most of the research supports integration. But, as with other dis-

Sign language helps people who are deaf develop and benefit from being a part of their own cultural group. *Deborah L. Martin/Unicorn Stock Photos.*

abilities, a continuing need exists to focus on critical factors, such as the qualifications, perceptions, attitudes, and demands of teachers as well as the content of the curriculum, within the integrated setting (Paul & Jackson, 1993).

Speech and deafness

Communication   Learning to speak is difficult if you can't hear. Paul and Jackson (1993) argue that "most deaf students have not learned either to speak or sign English at a highly competent level despite the advent and proliferation of signed systems . . ." (pp. 127–128). Largely as a result of this inadequate development of a primary form of English, many American students who are deaf experience difficulties in developing language and literacy skills needed for effective communication.

Communication problems can also seriously interfere with interpersonal relationships for students with hearing impairments who receive all or part of their education in general education classrooms. Their inability to communicate with other students can delay their language development. Moreover, that they communicate in ways that are different from those around them can inhibit their social interaction and development.

Personal interactions

Interaction is essential to language development, and much of language development and communication skills comes from the interactions of young children and their parents or other caregivers. The hearing parents of children who are deaf interact differently with their children than the hearing parents of children who are hard of hearing. Children who are deaf are often passive participants in communication, as their parents or caregivers bombard them with language stimulation and dominate the communication process. As a result, the vocabulary and syntax of children who are deaf grow slowly.

For teachers, it is useful to know the onset of hearing impairments. Children born deaf or those seriously hard of hearing are at a significant disadvantage in learning language. Some possible signs of hearing impairments are presented in Table 12.5; some general tips for teachers of students with hearing impairments are presented in Table 12.6.

Table 12.5 Top Ten List of Potential Signs of Hearing Impairments

1. Student experiences difficulties following oral presentations and directions.
2. Student watches lips of teachers or other speakers very closely.
3. Student turns head and leans toward speaker.
4. Student uses limited vocabulary.
5. Student uses speech sounds poorly.
6. Student shows delayed language development.
7. Student often does not respond when called from behind.
8. Student is generally inattentive during oral presentations.
9. Student constantly turns volume up on radio or television.
10. Student complains of earaches, has frequent colds or ear infections, or has ear discharge.

Table 12.6 Top Ten List of Tips for Teachers of Students with Hearing Impairments

1. Reduce distance between student and speaker as much as possible.
2. Speak slowly and stress clear articulation rather than loudness when speaking.
3. Reduce background noise as much as possible.
4. Seat student near center of desk arrangements and away from distracting sounds.
5. Use face-to-face contact as much as possible.
6. Use complete sentences to provide additional context during conversations or instructional presentations.
7. Use visual cues when referring to objects in the classroom and during instructional presentations.
8. Have classmates take notes during oral presentations for student to transcribe after the lesson.
9. Encourage independent activities and teach social skills.
10. Be sure hearing aid is turned on and functioning properly.

Window on Practice

Silence Is Not Empty

At the age of twelve I won the swimming award at the Lions Camp for Crippled Children. When my name echoed over the PA system the girl in the wheelchair next to me grabbed the box speaker of my hearing aid and shouted, "You won!" My ear quaking, I took the cue. I stood up straight—the only physically unencumbered child in a sea of braces and canes—affixed a pained but brave grin on my face, then limped all the way to the stage.

Later, after the spotlight had dimmed, I was overcome with remorse, but not because I'd played the crippled heroine. The truth was that I was ashamed of my handicap. I wanted to have something more visibly wrong with me. I wanted to be in the same league as the girl who'd lost her right leg in a car accident; her artificial leg attracted a bevy of awestruck campers. I, on the other hand, wore an unwieldy box hearing aid buckled to my body like a dog halter. It attracted no one. Deafness wasn't, in my eyes, a blue-ribbon handicap. Mixed in with my envy, though, was an overwhelming sense of guilt; at camp I was free to splash in the swimming pool, while most of the other children were stranded at the shallow end, where lifeguards floated them in lazy circles. But seventeen years of living in the "normal" world has diminished my guilt considerably, and I've learned that every handicap has its own particular hell.

I'm something of an anomaly in the deaf world. Unlike most deaf people, who were either born deaf or went deaf in infancy, I lost my hearing in chunks over a period of twelve years. Fortunately I learned to speak before my loss grew too profound, and that ability freed me from the most severe problem facing the deaf— the terrible difficulty of making themselves understood. My opinion of deafness was just as biased as that of a person who can hear. I had never met a deaf child in my life, and I didn't know how to sign. I imagined deaf people to be like creatures from beyond: animal-like because their language was so physical, threatening because they were unable to express themselves with sophistication—that is, through speech. I could make myself understood, and because I had a talent for lipreading it was easy for me to pass in the wider world. And for most of my life that is exactly what I did—like a black woman playing white, I passed for something other than what I was. But in doing so I was avoiding some very painful facts. And for many years I was inhibited not only by my deafness but my own idea of what it meant to be deaf. . . .

For the first few years my parents were as bewildered as I was. Nothing had prepared them for a handicapped child on the brink of adolescence. They sensed a whole other world of problems, but in those early stages I still seemed so normal that they just couldn't see me in a school for the deaf. They felt that although such schools were there to help, they also served to isolate. I have always been grateful for their decision. Because of it, I had to contend with public schools, and in doing so I developed two methods of survival: I learned to read not just lips but the whole person, and I learned the habit of clear speech by taking every speech and drama course I could.

That is not to say my adolescent years were easy going—they were misery. The lack of sound cast a pall on everything. Life seemed less fun than it had been before. I didn't associate that lack of fun with the lack of sound. I didn't begin to make the connection between the failings of my body and the failings of the world until I was well out of college. I simply did not admit to myself that deafness caused certain problems—or even that I was deaf.

From the time I was twelve until I was twenty-four, the loss of my hearing was erratic. I would lose a decibel or two of sound and then my hearing would stabilize. A week or a year later there would be another slip and then I'd have to adjust all over again. I never knew when I would hit bottom. I remember going to bed

(Continued on next page)

Silence Is Not Empty (continued)

one night still being able to make out the reassuring purr of the refrigerator and the late-night conversation of my parents, then waking up the next morning to nothing—even my own voice was gone. These fits and starts continued until my hearing finally dropped to the last rung of amplifiable sound. I was a college student at the time, and whenever anyone asked about my hearing aid, I admitted to being only slightly hard of hearing.

My professors were frequently alarmed by my almost maniacal intensity in class. I was petrified that I'd have to ask for special privileges just to achieve marginal understanding. My pride was in flames. I became increasingly bitter and isolated. I was terrified of being marked a deaf woman, a label that made me sound dumb and cowlike, enveloped in a protective silence that denied me my complexity. . . . I lied about the extent of my deafness so I could avoid the stigma of being thought "different" in a pathetic way.

It was not surprising that in my senior year I suffered a nervous collapse and spent three days in a hospital crying like a baby. When I stopped crying I knew it was time to face a few things—I had to start asking for help when I needed it because I couldn't handle my deafness alone, and I had to quit being ashamed of my handicap so I could begin to live with its consequences and discover what (if any) were its rewards.

When I began telling people that I was really deaf I did so with grim determination. Some were afraid to talk to me at any length, fearing perhaps that they were talking into a void; others assumed that I was somehow an unsullied innocent and always inquired in carefully enunciated sentences; "Doooooooo youuuuuuuuu driiinnk liquor?" But most people were surprisingly sympathetic—they wanted to know the best way to be understood, they took great pains to talk directly to my face, and they didn't insult me by using only words of one syllable.

It was, in part, that gentle acceptance that made me more curious about my own deafness. Always before it had been an affliction to wrestle with as one would with angels, but when I finally accepted it as an inevitable part of my life, I relaxed enough to do some exploring. I would take off my hearing aid and go through a day, a night, an hour or two—as long as I could take it—in absolute silence. I felt as if I were indulging in a secret vice because I was perceiving the world in a new way—stripped of sound. . . .

Silence is not empty; it is simply more sobering than sound. At times I prefer the sobriety. I can still "hear" with a hearing aid—that is, I can discern noise, but I can't tell you where it's coming from or if it is laughter or a faulty drain. When there are many people talking together I hear a strange music, a distant rumbling in my consciousness. But when I take off my hearing aid at night and lie in bed surrounded by my fate, I wonder, "What is this—a foul subtraction or a blessing in disguise?" For despite my fears there is a kind of peace in the silence—albeit an uneasy one. There is, after all, less to distract me from my thoughts.

But I know what I've lost. The process of becoming deaf has at times been frightening, akin perhaps to dying, and early in life it took away my happy confidence in the image of a world where things always work right. When I first came back from the Lions Camp that summer I cursed heaven and earth for doing such terrible wrong to me and to my friends. My grandmother tried to comfort me by promising, "Honey, God's got something special planned for you."

But I thought, "Yes. He plans to make me deaf."

Source: From Terry Galloway, "I'm Listening as Hard as I Can," Texas Monthly, April 1981. Adapted and reprinted with permission.

Deafness and Blindness

Students are identified as deaf and blind when they demonstrate both visual and hearing impairments and when their needs cannot be met in separate programs for students who are deaf or separate programs for students who are blind. In 1968 the federal government began funding programs for students who are both deaf and blind. In 1977 the condition was formally defined in federal rules and regulations. The following definition is currently accepted:

Federal definition

> "Deaf-blind" means concomitant hearing and visual impairments, the combination of which causes such severe communication and other developmental and educational problems that they cannot be accommodated in special education programs solely for children with deafness or children with blindness. (Individuals with Disabilities Education Act, 1990)

The common view of students who are deaf and blind is that they are totally deaf and totally blind, which is generally not the case. To be considered **deaf-blind,** a student must meet the criteria for being considered deaf as well as the criteria for being considered blind. Many students who meet these criteria have some functional hearing and vision.

Helen Keller

You probably know the story of Helen Keller, a person who was deaf and blind, who was taught by Anne Sullivan. To put the history of development of school programs into perspective, you should know that Sullivan began teaching Keller in 1887. Keller received her college degree in 1904, the first person who was deaf and blind to do so, some sixty-four years before the federal government began funding programs for students who are both deaf and blind.

During recent school years, about fourteen hundred students identified as deaf and blind received special education services (U.S. Department of Education, 1993). This number is very small, less than 0.01 percent of the school-age population, and although it has changed little in the last ten years, it may be far from accurate. We don't have a firm count of these students for two reasons: "Parents of such children tend to keep them out of circulation, and . . . once they are located, diagnosis of them is often ambiguous" (Newland, 1986, p. 577). Formal identification has increased over the years with the development of child-find programs—formal community and public school programs to locate young children with disabilities—but services for students who are deaf and blind are still among the least likely to be provided in general education settings, with more than 80 percent of the students receiving special education in separate classes, separate schools, or residential facilities (U.S. Department of Education, 1993).

Lack of firm numbers

Most in separate classes

The characteristics of students who are deaf and blind are a combination of those described for students who are deaf and students who are blind. In addition, these students exhibit more severe academic, social, and communication problems than students with a single impairment. This is especially evident in communication skills. Students who are blind can profit from verbal stimulation, and those who are deaf can profit from visual input. Students who are both blind and deaf rely primarily on other forms of stimulation, such as tactile feedback. Educational programs for these students focus on the use of adapted communication devices and mobility skills.

Communication problems

Instructional Approaches and Teaching Tactics

When the Rehabilitation Act of 1973 and the Education for All Handicapped Children Act of 1975 were passed, I believed wonderful things would happen for people with disabilities. I pictured disabled children finally going to school with nondisabled students of their age and grade. I pictured disabled and nondisabled children taking the same classes, reading the same books, and taking the same tests. I pictured them participating in the same clubs, sometimes becoming friends and other times not, getting into the same scrapes, and learning how to solve the same problems. I believed that the integrated education that had been atypical for me and other blind students of New Jersey in the 1950s and 1960s would be standard and unremarkable for this generation of disabled students. I assumed that today's high school graduates and college students would have experiences comparable to or better than my own of many years ago. . . . In the 1980s, I find that my expectations are only sometimes met. (Asch, 1989, p. 181)

In the 1990s, Adrienne Asch's dreams are still being only partially met in America's schools. Yet people across the country want to improve the lives of students with sensory disabilities, and the students themselves continue to hope for healthy and productive lives much like those of their neighbors and peers without disabilities. Toward this goal, students with visual and hearing impairments can best be helped by teachers who can eliminate barriers, improve communication, and foster independence.

Eliminate Barriers

Orienting the student

When our friend Larry Williams works with a student who is blind, he provides an orientation to his classroom. He points out the location of his desk, the student's desk, the learning centers, the computer, the pencil sharpener, and all the other places and things the student needs to know or asks about. He has found it helpful to introduce a few new things each day and always to start the student at his own desk as a point of reference for the orientation. Larry has found that introducing students with vision problems to the classroom environment and school space in a systematic manner helps them to "cognitively map" the physical space and function more effectively in it.

Like Larry, many teachers provide orientation and mobility training to students with visual impairments. This training is coordinated with any mobility aid that the student may use, such as a long cane. Regular assistance from a sighted person may also be needed.

Information processing

Another key concern for students with visual impairments is information processing. Listening skills training (see Table 12.7) can help students maximize their ability to acquire information by listening. For students with low vision, simple classroom adaptations such as additional lighting and use of high-contrast materials can also help. In writing activities, soft pencils, felt-tip pens, and dark-lined paper provide the best contrast. Teachers can divide extensive reading assignments into

Table 12.7   Interventions to Assist Students with
Vision Impairments

Orientation and Mobility Aids   Orientation is a mental map of our environment; mobility is the ability to get around in our environment. Guide dogs, canes, and assistance from a sighted person help people make up for orientation and mobility problems caused by vision impairments.

Listening Skills Training   Many students with vision impairments rely on listening as a primary means of obtaining information. Focusing on a single sound source, analyzing oral information, and focusing on key sound sources are among listening skills taught to people to make up for communication problems caused by vision impairments.

Braille   Some students with vision impairments need to learn to read and write using different methods. Braille is a communication system that uses raised dots on paper so people who are blind or who have low vision can read text by feeling it. Present-day technological advances enable computer text files to be converted to braille on special printers, and paperless braille devices convert information on computer screens to braille output.

Enhanced Image Devices   Many students with vision impairments learn to read using traditional methods with enlarged print. Closed-circuit television systems with a small camera and zoom lens, overhead projectors, micro-computers, telescopic aids, and other specialized equipment are used to enlarge text so that it is easier for people with low vision to read.

Audio Aids   People with visual impairments can hear what other people can read. Talking books, talking calculators, and devices that compress speech to speed it up and eliminate natural pauses are audio aids that help people with vision impairments make up for their limited sight.

Optical Character Recognition (OCR) Devices   Some students with vision impairments use a computer-based scanning device (e.g., Kurzweil Personal Reader) that converts printed words into synthetic speech. Recent advances in computer technology have greatly improved these devices. Often they now include small sensors that can be attached to microcomputers to help people who are blind or those with low vision learn from printed text.

short blocks of time to prevent eye fatigue. Reducing the amount of copy and drill work (if concepts are understood) may help students produce quality products.

Technological advances   Advances in technology are influencing the ways all students are taught. They are particularly relevant in methods used by people who are blind or who have low vision to access information that sighted people obtain visually (Schrier, Leventhal, & Uslan, 1991). Techniques using image-enhancing systems, synthetic speech systems, braille technology, and optical character recognition systems, separately or in combination, provide access to printed information for people with visual impairments.

Computer enhanced images and other technology provide opportunities for students with sensory disabilities to be successful in a variety of educational settings. *Bob Daemmrich/ The Image Works, Inc.*

Enhanced image devices

Improved access to print is provided by *enhanced image devices.* Personal computer software and hardware or closed-circuit television (CCTV) systems are used to achieve four- to five-times magnification that helps many people with visual impairments to read textual information more easily. The most basic computerized systems use word processing software to enlarge text being input or output for a letter, term paper, or written assignment; more sophisticated systems enlarge everything on the screen, including graphics. A closed-circuit television system uses a video camera to project the magnified image onto a video monitor or television screen. Some of the newer closed-circuit television systems are portable, which makes them particularly useful in environments where students need to move around while reading, for instance, to look up information or to examine labels on packages of food and medicine (Uslan, 1993).

Synthetic speech

Synthetic speech devices comprise a synthesizer that does the speaking and a screen access program that tells it what to say. The synthesizer can be a card that is inserted into a computer or an external device that is connected to a computer. The program is loaded into the computer's memory, and the keyboard or a separate keypad is used to input simple command instructions describing what the synthesizer is to do (for example, read a word, line, or paragraph). Using such a system, the student can access text from an electronic file and have the computer read it aloud. To many people, synthetic speech still has a robotic quality, but computers increasingly have humanlike voices. Many talking word processing programs, created to provide auditory feedback to children who are learning to write, can also assist students with visual impairments. Other talking devices such as clocks and calculators are becoming commonplace, and speech output will be a likely feature of many upcoming products.

Braille technology

Braille is the widespread system of representing letters, words, and numbers by patterns of raised dots. People with visual impairments who read braille are now using various types of high-tech, specialized equipment, including braille display technology, braille printers, and electronic braille notetakers. Braille display technology provides access in braille to information on a computer screen. These paperless braille devices are connected to computers and operate by raising or lowering a series of pins to produce braille codes for information shown on the computer screen. An advantage of paperless braille displays is that they allow the user to immediately learn the format of the information on the screen, thus helping with activities like proofreading (Schrier, Leventhal, & Uslan, 1991).

Braille printers convert information from computers. After being sent information to be brailled, they do the actual embossing of the braille code onto paper. These braille counterparts of ink printers use pins to produce the raised dots formerly done by hand.

Braille notetaking devices are small and portable, with keyboards for entering information and speech synthesizers or braille displays for providing information. People with visual impairments use these devices to keep track of what is going on in classroom presentations or meetings. Sometimes they transfer the information to larger computers to review it or print it on a paperless braille display or traditional printer.

OCR devices

Optical character recognition (OCR) devices convert print into electronic forms that can be accessed with other adaptive equipment. First printed information is scanned, and the images are converted to text using a computer and appropriate software. The text is then accessible using other adaptive devices, such as image enhancement, synthetic speech, or braille. Scanners may be hand held or separate machines that look like photocopiers. Some have bookedge options that facilitate scanning bound materials. Optical character recognition technology is becoming popular, and costs are decreasing largely because of its widespread use in business and industry (Schrier, Leventhal, & Uslan, 1991). Devices that recognize handwriting will soon be available at prices most people can afford, which will provide an additional avenue for people with visual impairments to use in accessing information.

Improve Communication

Profiting from oral communication is a key concern for students who are deaf or hard of hearing. Many people with hearing impairments rely on interpreters to help them communicate. Generally, they interpret in educational settings as well as for other activities such as conferences, workshops, phone calls, and presentations, or they serve as resources for others interested in interpreting (Luetke-Stahlman & Luckner, 1991). Oral communication, sign systems, total communication, cued speech, assistive listening, and telecommunication devices also help people overcome communication problems caused by hearing impairments (see Table 12.8).

Interpreters

Oral communication

Oral communication methods emphasize the development and use of skills in the areas of speech, speech reading, and residual hearing. The thrust of this approach is the use of oral English (in English-speaking countries) with all students with hearing impairments. Proponents of this method believe that the goal of edu-

Table 12.8	Interventions to Assist Students with Hearing Impairments

Oral Communication   An approach in which people with hearing impairments are taught to use speaking and residual hearing as their only means of communicating

Sign Language   An approach in which people with hearing impairments are taught to use manual gestures and body movements as their only means of communicating

Total Communication   An approach in which people with hearing impairments are taught to use oral and sign methods simultaneously as their means of communicating.

Cued Speech   An approach in which people with hearing impairments are taught to use visual cues provided by a speaker to decode what is being said

Assistive Listening Devices   Hearing aids, FM transmission and amplification devices, and audio loops are special types of equipment that help people with hearing impairments make better use of their residual hearing

Telecommunication Devices   Keyboards with screens or printers connected to telephones take advantage of vision to improve communication for people with hearing impairments; computer fax/modems and electronic mail are recent developments in this rapidly changing area

cation is the development of skills that foster full participation in mainstream (that is, hearing) society.

Sign systems

With *sign systems,* people with hearing impairments express ideas using manual and nonmanual body movements instead of speech. The manual aspects of this form of communication are displayed by shaping, moving, and positioning the hands. Nonmanual movements include other parts of the body—eyes, eyebrows, cheeks, lips, tongue, and shoulders—in the language being used. **American Sign Language (ASL)** is a widely recognized sign language that uses both manual and nonmanual movements. Finger spelling is a special form of sign system in which each letter of the alphabet has a finger sign used to spell words and sentences used in conversations.

American Sign Language

Total communication

Proponents of *total communication methods* advocate the use of all modes of communication. In this approach, oral methods and sign systems are used simultaneously. Sign systems that are used more prominently within total communication methods share three characteristics: They attempt to reproduce the words, word parts, and word order of English; they adapt signs from sign language systems; and they develop new signs as they are needed (Paul & Jackson, 1993).

Cued speech

Cued speech is another method that involves both oral communication and a

Hearing aids are part of a complete educational program for many students. *Stephen Frisch/Stock, Boston, Inc.*

Assistive listening devices

sign system. In cued speech, eight hand shapes are used in four positions on or near the face to accompany and augment speech. Each hand shape represents a group of consonants or consonant blends, and each facial position represents a group of vowel sounds that are used as cues to assist listeners who are speechreading.

Assistive listening and *telecommunication devices* take advantage of residual hearing or other senses to enable people with hearing impairments to communicate better. As we indicated earlier (see Chapter 5), hearing aids are the most widely recognized and used assistive listening devices. They are worn in the ear, behind the ear, on the body, or in eyeglass frames. Classroom amplification systems are another form of assistive listening device in which a microphone is used to link teachers to students who wear a receiver that often doubles as a hearing aid. When Barry was in preschool, his teacher used a classroom amplification system. Some of the children in his class had small receivers attached unobstructively around their necks. Each receiver was connected to a small earplug in one or both ears (depending on the degree of hearing loss). The teacher talked to the children using what looked like a regular microphone that hung around her neck. When she spoke to some of the children, she sometimes would have to get their attention by touching a shoulder or arm. Barry's parents thought the system worked rather well, even though Barry didn't need to use it.

TDDs

Telecommunication devices are small keyboards with screens or printers that can be connected to telephones. Telecommunication devices for the deaf (TDDs) and text telephones enable people with hearing impairments to make and receive telephone calls. When a call is made using these devices, the incoming and outgoing conversation appears on the screen or printer. Computerized fax modems and regular fax machines enable people with hearing impairments to communicate without speaking or hearing by using the phone system at their home, school, or work.

Among the three basic forms of communication systems—oral, sign, and total—no clear evidence has emerged to support the use of one method over the others (Paul & Jackson, 1993). Cued speech is used by a small percentage of students with hearing impairments, mostly from white, upper-middle-class families (Luetke-Stahlman & Luckner, 1991). Assistive listening devices are widely used, and advances in technology have made them lighter, smaller, and more sophisticated. Telecommunication devices have helped to break down long-standing barriers to communication for people with hearing impairments in employment and social interaction settings.

Foster Independence

Variety of interventions to foster independence

Students with sensory disabilities have a wide range of personal and social characteristics that can make them very dependent on others. Effective teachers encourage independent activities for these students. They teach social skills and listening skills as needed to foster a realistic balance between dependency and overdependency. Other strategies include

Allowing extra time for completion of tasks and using group activities to encourage socialization among regular and special students.

Learning to use special materials such as manual alphabets, sign language systems, and oral/manual communication activities to communicate effectively with students.

Working with other teachers who have suggestions for alternative classroom activities, materials, and instructional units.

These teachers are aware of the delicate balance that exists between needing special assistance and wanting to be normal. They are concerned with the impressions a student's special learning needs create, and they try to minimize the extent to which a student is treated negatively because of them.

Sensory Disabilities in Perspective

Sensory impairments can have serious educational implications. Students who are blind or deaf have unique educational needs that can be accommodated in general education classes with the assistance of other professionals, material and environmental modifications, and disability-specific curriculum content.

Attitudes an obstacle

Often the biggest obstacle to success, in any environment, has been the attitudes of teachers, neighbors, co-workers, and friends toward the capabilities of people with sensory disabilities. According to Dr. I. King Jordan, the first president of Gallaudet University who is deaf, an attitude that is making a difference in the nineties is that "[d]eaf people can do anything hearing people can do . . . except hear!" (cited in Singleton, 1992, p. 10). His words speak broadly for a movement toward empowerment in which people with sensory disabilities are taking control of their lives and are demanding active roles in decision making that affects them.

Empowerment movement

Likely to be the catch phrase of the 1990s, the "empowerment movement" has its seeds in the Civil Rights movement of the 1960s, the women's movement of the 1970s, and the technological revolution of the 1980s, which opened new avenues for communication and access for individuals with sensory impairments. It has broad implications for all people with disabilities. The following list, which includes suggestions for empowering people who are deaf, is relevant for other groups as well (Singleton, 1992):

- Encourage research on deaf history and the development of Deaf Studies programs to provide the deaf community a means of sharing their cultural identity with each other, their families, the community, and the world.
- Support pride in being deaf and encourage Deaf Awareness Day or Week activities.
- Recognize the deaf community as having a unique identity and a unique language–ASL (American Sign Language).
- Teach respect for difference among individuals.
- Place qualified people who are deaf in important leadership roles in programs and organizations for deaf people.
- Maintain a majority of deaf and hard-of-hearing persons as representatives on decision-making boards for programs affecting deaf people.
- Enforce all provisions of the Americans with Disabilities Act (ADA) to provide deaf, deaf-blind, and hard-of-hearing people with full access to society.
- Provide opportunities for socialization with other children or adults who are deaf.
- Educate parents about deafness and sign language so they can provide full communication to their child from birth.
- Increase the numbers of qualified deaf and hard-of-hearing teachers, counselors, and administrators in educational programs as positive role models.
- Require certified educational interpreters in mainstreamed programs.
- Provide full access to educational programs and employment training opportunities.
- Provide a tax deduction for the purchase of assistive listening devices such as Text Telephones and Braille TDDs.

Bring Your Learning to Life

Tips for Interacting Positively with People with Sensory Disabilities

Have you ever taken a different path to avoid a person who is blind? Raised your voice when speaking to a person who is blind? Stared at people using sign language? Most people have, largely because they have limited experience with people with sensory disabilities. Here are some tips for interacting positively with people with vision and hearing impairments.

- Speak first. Remember that you have the advantage in social and instructional situations. You can see the other person and the environment. You can hear the other person and the environmental sounds. Let the person with the sensory disability know you are there and happy to see them.

- Use natural language. Don't be afraid to say "see" or "look" around a person with a vision impairment. Use the person's name when speaking. Use a natural tone of voice and volume unless requested to change it by the person with the disability.

- If the person with a sensory disability indicates that he or she doesn't understand what you are saying, rephrase the mes-

sage and repeat it; be careful not simply to say the same words louder.

- Be precise when giving directions or describing things.

- Allow time for people with sensory disabilities to complete simple tasks; planning ahead will create more independence than doing it for them because you want it done quickly.

- Use outlines as guides and overhead projectors to avoid turning away from the class during oral presentations.

- During group discussions have one person speak at a time and use the name of the speaker to facilitate communication and understanding.

- Give individuals with a hearing or vision impairment the benefit of the doubt when making decisions about disabilities; don't assume problems just because a person doesn't see or hear as well as everybody else.

- Include placement in residential schools as an option for children who are deaf.
- Require individualized education programs (IEP) tailored to the child's individual needs after appropriate evaluations have been done by professionals trained in deafness. (p. 13)

In earlier chapters, we pointed out that few characteristics are specific to the conditions of learning disabilities, speech and language impairments, mental retardation, and emotional disturbance. We said that there are few educational interventions specific to these conditions, and we stressed the fact that implications for education need to be drawn from the behaviors students demon-

Differences between sensory disabilities and other categories

strate rather than from the names assigned to them. Sensory disabilities are a little different. Characteristics specific to these conditions affect functioning and have specific educational implications. People with visual and hearing impairments input and process sensory information in unique ways because they do not see or hear like people without these sensory problems. Knowing that a particular student is blind or has low vision, or is deaf or hard of hearing, is useful and important for planning instruction for that student.

Accommodations

The accommodations teachers and schools must make for students who demonstrate sensory disabilities are functions of the specific natures of their visual and auditory impairments. Many individuals with sensory disabilities function with very few modifications in their lives and the implications of living with a sensory disability can be minimal. Some modifications simply make sense. For example, when teachers see that lighting is inadequate for students with low vision, they provide additional lighting. Sometimes, they provide access to print materials through magnification or provide special writing materials like wide-lined paper and felt-tip pens, to help them complete assignments. They learn manual communication systems to improve information exchanges with students who are deaf. They learn how to identify and correct problems with assistive listening devices or other aids used by their students. They arrange classroom seating to reduce distractions and help students with sensory disabilities focus and obtain information from instructional presentations. In addition, many of these interventions may help students without disabilities.

Cooperating with other professionals

Classroom teachers of students with sensory disabilities also work closely with professionals serving in itinerant and consultative roles. Often, but not always, this means they are expected to communicate effectively and coordinate programs jointly with parents, paraprofessionals, specialists, administrators, and other professionals more than they would when working with students with other disabilities. Cooperative relations are essential when identifying strengths and weaknesses of students with sensory disabilities and when setting appropriate instructional objectives for them. Itinerant teachers and consultants often help teachers to understand the impact of vision or hearing loss on academic and social development, or help them learn more about the assistive technology needs (such as using hearing aids, interpreters, and braille technology) that are part of these students' lives. In addition, itinerant teachers provide disability-specific skill instruction to the students themselves, such as braille reading and writing and sign language. As key players in ensuring that educational needs of students are met, itinerant specialists must be involved in all phases of implementing students' education, including assessments, individual educational planning teams, and delivery of instructional services. The key for teachers to successful collaboration with these professionals is ongoing communication and up-to-date information.

Positive attitudes toward including students with sensory disabilities in classrooms with their neighbors and peers have improved their lives. Major technological advances have changed the ways and the extent to which students with sensory disabilities participate in and profit from schooling and other experiences. The future appears bright. Over the next ten years, new

Bring Your Learning to Life

Basic Troubleshooting for Hearing Aids

Like many students with hearing impairments, Barry came to school with an assistive listening device. At first, his classroom teacher worried about what she would do if the hearing aid failed. She believed that making sure the equipment was working was one of the most important things she would do during the day and decided it was her responsibility to be knowledgeable about the equipment that any of her students were using. She got in touch with the school system's specialists in hearing problems, and they provided the following "troubleshooting guide for people with hearing aids" based on information presented in Barbara Luetke-Stahlman and John Luckner's (1991) book.

Symptom	Possible Problem	Possible Solution
Hearing aid not working or not working well	Dead batteries	Check batteries or try new ones
	Batteries not properly placed	
	Earmold plugged with water or wax	Disconnect earmold, rinse with warm water, dry and/or clear with pipe cleaner or cotton swab
Hearing aid whistles or gives distracting feedback	Punctured or kinked tubing	Replace or straighten tubing
	Earmold not properly fitted in ear	Insert earmold properly
	Earmold plugged with water or wax	Disconnect earmold, rinse with warm water, dry and/or clear with pipe cleaner or cotton swab
	Receiver close to wall or other reflecting surface	Reposition student
Poor tone quality or distortion	Punctured or cracked tubing	Replace or straighten tubing
	Earmold not properly fitted in ear	Insert earmold properly
	Earmold plugged with water or wax	Disconnect earmold, rinse with warm water, dry and/or clear with pipe cleaner or cotton swab
	Receiver close to wall or other reflecting surface	Reposition student
	Microphone clogged	Clean microphone

(Continued on next page)

Bring Your Learning to Life

Basic Troubleshooting for Hearing Aids *(continued)*

The specialists also suggested a classroom "first-aid" kit for general hearing aid maintenance that contained the following items:

1. Battery tester
2. Replacement batteries
3. Pipe cleaners and/or cotton swabs
4. Forced-air spray cleaner
5. Toothpicks and set of tweezers
6. Small cleaning brush or toothbrush
7. Small roll of tape

The specialists encouraged the teacher to contact Barry's parents for additional ideas and to work closely with them if she spotted any problems with the hearing aid that required professional care or maintenance. While Barry was in her room, the teacher didn't have any problems with his assistive listening device, but she passed on what she knew to his next teacher.

technology, especially in the computer industry, will enable larger numbers of those with visual and hearing impairments to participate even more fully in educational programs.

What Every Teacher Should Know

- Students with sensory disabilities have impairments that affect how well they see or hear; overall, about 2 percent of students with disabilities have vision or hearing impairments.
- Those with vision impairments include people who are blind and those with low vision.
- Blindness and low vision are measured by acuity and field of vision.
- People with hearing impairments are referred to as deaf or hard of hearing.
- Hearing impairments are measured in units of loudness (decibels) and frequency (hertz).
- The cause is unknown for about half the people with hearing impairments; rubella, meningitis, otitis media, and genetic transmission are the main known causes.
- People are identified as deaf and blind when they demonstrate both visual and hearing impairments, and when their needs cannot be met in separate programs for people with visual or hearing impairments alone.
- People with sensory disabilities have specific educational needs; those related to vision impairments focus on information and environmental ac-

cess, and those related to hearing impairments focus on the learning and use of language.

■ With the exception of their hearing or seeing problems, people with sensory disabilities learn much like other people; with the aid of rapidly developing technology, they are participating more fully in classrooms with their neighbors and peers.

■ Often the greatest obstacles to success for people with sensory disabilities are the attitudes of people who live and work with them in school and other environments.

Projects

1. Draw a diagram illustrating how the following words or phrases are related to each other: *auditory acuity, conductive, deaf, decibel, frequency, hard of hearing, hearing loss, hertz, intensity,* and *sensorineural.* Write a short paragraph that describes the diagram.

2. Prepare a two- to three-page outline for a presentation to elementary school students on deafness. Answer the following questions as part of the presentation:
   a. What does it mean to be deaf?
   b. What do people with deafness or hearing impairments hear?
   c. What causes deafness?
   d. Are deaf people able to speak?
   e. If people are deaf, how do they learn to speak?
   f. Do people with hearing impairments hear better at some times than at others?
   g. Can people who are deaf use the phone and watch television?

3. Contact the American Federation for the Blind or similar local, state, or national organization that focuses on people with sensory disabilities. Ask for information on the purpose of the organization, its membership, and its services. Ask for information describing how technology is being used to improve services provided to people with sensory disabilities.

4. To help understand how people with sensory disabilities experience the world, try some of these simulations and note your reactions to them:
   Blindfold yourself and get ready for school as you would on any other day.
   Blindfold yourself and have a friend take you on a campus tour.
   Go to the middle of campus with a friend, blindfold yourself, and find your way home or to your advisor's office with your friend acting as a guide.
   Watch TV for one hour with the sound turned off.
   Watch TV for one hour with the sound very low.
   Have a conversation with a friend by using only gestures.

5. Do some research to discover how much TV is available in your area for people with hearing impairments. For a few days, look for evidence of closed captioning on local television programs or in local television guides. Prepare a graph illustrating the numbers and types of available shows (for example, drama, comedy, news, movies).

6. Try this activity to experience what it is like to have a frequency hearing loss. Write four sentences of eight to ten words each. Write them again, leaving out the following letters and letter combinations: *s, sh, ch, t, th, p,* and *f*. Try to figure out the words by reading them. Read the sentences to a couple of friends and have them figure them out. Try these sentences if you can't think of any:

   Those shells are cheap, but I still don't want them.

   Please put the food on the small shelf.

   Children, please wait before charging across the street!

   It takes two people to communicate, even if only one can hear.

   She sells seashells at the seashore.

7. Volunteer to work in a setting where people with sensory disabilities are provided services. Participate for at least two hours on five different occasions. Describe the jobs you were given. Describe assistance you were provided by professionals working at the setting. Describe how you would organize a volunteer experience if you were working in the same setting.

8. Provide child care for a family with a child with a hearing impairment for a total of six hours on several different days. Prepare a child care guide including things to remember when spending time with children with hearing impairments.

9. Find a telephone with a TDD (telecommunication device for the deaf) and make a call to the Council for Exceptional Children requesting information about divisions within the organization that provide services to people interested in students with sensory disabilities. The phone number is (703) 620-3660; tell the receptionist you want to use the TDD phone.

For Your Information

Books

Bergman, T. (1989). *Finding a common language: Children living with deafness.* Milwaukee, WI: Gareth Stevens.

   In a book suitable for young readers and filled with photographs powerfully illustrating children's personalities and moods, Tom Bergman shows that a disability should not be a cause for embarrassment, separation, or fear.

Cassie, D. (1984). *So who's perfect! People with visible differences tell their own stories.* Scottdale, PA: Herald Press.

   An excellent compilation of experiences of people with disabilities, including those who are deaf, hard of hearing, blind, and partially sighted.

Christensen, K. M., & Delgado, G. L. (Eds.). (1993). *Multicultural issues in deafness.* White Plains, NY: Longman.

   The deaf culture as well as populations of children

and youth who are deaf are among the topics discussed in this book.

Christian, M. B. (1986). *Mystery at Camp Triumph*. Morton Grove, IL: Whitman.

> After being blinded in an accident, Angie resents going to a camp for people with disabilities. She becomes involved in a mystery and develops confidence and independence as a result of the experience. Excellent book for upper elementary students.

Cohen, L. H. (1994). *Train go sorry: Inside a deaf world*. Boston: Houghton Mifflin.

> As a child, Leah Cohen put pebbles in her ears as make-believe hearing aids. She was raised on the grounds of the Lexington School for the Deaf, where her father is superintendent. In *Train Go Sorry*, she describes her experiences and provides valuable insight into the real issues in the deaf culture movement.

Greenberg, J. E. (1985). *What is the sign for friend?* New York: Franklin Watts.

> A children's book including common manual signs (such as those for *deaf, school, friend*) and illustrating that even though Shane is born deaf, he can do almost anything his hearing friends can.

Luetke-Stahlman, B., & Luckner, J. (1991). *Effectively educating students with hearing impairments*. White Plains, NY: Longman.

> Excellent resource illustrating key factors related to planning for and delivering instruction to students with hearing impairments. Chapter on working with others is particularly useful, as are those on teaching academics to students with hearing impairments.

Moores, D. F. (1987). *Educating the deaf: Psychology, principles, and practices* (3rd ed.). Boston: Houghton Mifflin.

> A comprehensive overview addressing key concepts related to definition, identification, causes, and treatments. Widely used and accepted as an introductory text on hearing impairments.

Moores, D. F., & Meadow-Orlans, K. P. (Eds.). (1990). *Educational and developmental aspects of deafness*. Washington, DC: Gallaudet Press.

> School and home aspects of deafness; a comparison of students from Israel, Denmark, and the United States who are deaf; and responses to hearing loss in later life are discussed.

Paul, P. V., & Jackson, D. W. (1993). *Toward a psychology of deafness: Theoretical and empirical perspectives*. Boston: Allyn & Bacon.

> A comprehensive overview of the impact of deafness on important aspects of cognitive, psychological, and social development. The book focuses on individuals with severe more than those with mild hearing loss.

Rezen, S. V., & Hausman, C. (1985). *Coping with hearing loss. A guide for adults and their families*. New York: Dembner Books.

> A sensitive treatment of the physical and psychological effects of hearing loss and how people cope with and overcome hearing problems.

Scholl, G. (Ed.). (1986). *Foundations of education for blind and visually handicapped children and youth*. New York: American Foundation for the Blind.

> Edited text addressing key areas related to sensory disabilities involving vision.

Schwartz, S. (1987). *Choices in deafness: A parents' guide*. Kensington, MD: Woodbine House.

> Trends in educating people with hearing impairments, as well as an overview and description of cued speech, oral communication, and total communication approaches are presented. Excellent resource for parents and teachers.

Smith, E. S. (1987). *A guide dog goes to school: The story of a dog trained to lead the blind*. New York: William Morrow.

> A book suitable for young readers, *A Guide Dog Goes to School* follows Cinderella as she is transformed from a frisky, friendly puppy into a loving and responsible companion capably leading her master, who is blind, along crowded streets and through bustling crowds.

Walker, L. A. (1985). *Amy: The story of a deaf child*. New York: E. P. Dutton.

> In her own words, Amy Rowley talks about her life with her friends and family, at school and at home. Illustrated with more than one hundred photographs, this is a wonderful portrait of a young girl whose parents went to court because they wanted her to have the same opportunities as her peers. At the end of the book is a series of photographs showing Amy signing common words.

Warren, D. (1984). *Blindness and early childhood development*. New York: American Foundation for the Blind.

An excellent resource including discussion of the effects of blindness on infancy, early childhood, perception, intelligence, and cognitive abilities.

Organizations

Alexander Graham Bell Association for the Deaf (AGBAD)

Parents, children, and educational programs are the focuses of this advocacy group. It promotes better public understanding of hearing loss in children and adults, promotes early detection of hearing loss and continued use of hearing aids, and promotes inservice training activities for teachers of students with hearing impairments. AGBAD encourages people who are deaf or hard of hearing to communicate using residual hearing, speechreading, and speech and language skills. This organization gathers and disseminates information on hearing impairment; collaborates with doctors, audiologists, speech/language specialists, and educators to promote educational, vocational, and social opportunities for individuals of all ages who have hearing impairments; and provides scholarships for students with hearing impairments to attend regular universities and colleges. For more information, contact AGBAD, 3417 Volta Place, NW, Washington, DC 20007.

American Council of the Blind (ACB)

This advocacy group supports parents, children, and educational programs. It promotes awareness and supportive activities for people with visual impairments. For more information, contact ACB, 1010 Vermont Ave., NW, Suite 1100, Washington, DC 20005.

American Foundation for the Blind (AFB)

The American Foundation for the Blind (AFB) is a leading resource for people with visual impairments, the organizations that serve them, and the general public. It is a nonprofit organization founded in 1921 and was recognized as Helen Keller's cause in the United States. AFB's mission is to enable people who are blind or those with low vision to achieve equality of access and opportunity that will ensure freedom of choice in their lives. For more information, contact AFB, 15 W. 16th St., New York, NY 10011.

Association for Education and Rehabilitation of the Blind and Visually Handicapped (AER)

This organization is dedicated to improving educational and rehabilitative services to people with blindness and visual impairments. It provides information and promotes better public understanding of vision problems in children and adults through publications such as *RE:view* and *AER Report* and other resources. For more information, contact AER, 206 N. Washington St., Alexandria, VA 22314.

Division for Children with Communication Disorders (DCCD)

A division of the Council for Exceptional Children (CEC), formally affiliated in 1964, DCCD is dedicated to improving the education and welfare of children with hearing, speech, and language disorders. Members receive the *Journal of Childhood Communication Disorders* and the *DCCD Newsletter* twice a year. For more information, contact CEC, 1920 Association Dr., Reston, VA 22091.

Division on Visual Handicaps (DVH)

A division of the Council for Exceptional Children (CEC), formally affiliated in 1954, DVH promotes appropriate educational programs for individuals with visual disabilities, as well as greater understanding of their concomitant life experiences. DVH has about one thousand members and provides outlets for the exchange of ideas through a variety of resources, including a professional newsletter (*DVH Quarterly*). For more information, contact CEC, 1920 Association Dr., Reston, VA 22091.

National Association of the Deaf (NAD)

The National Association of the Deaf (NAD) was founded in 1880 by deaf leaders who were concerned that deaf people were not included in the decision- and policy-making processes affecting their lives. The mission of this organization is to assure that a comprehensive, coordinated system of services is accessible to Americans who are deaf or hard of hearing, enabling them to achieve their maximum potential through increased independence, productivity, and integration. Membership includes deaf, hard-of-hearing, and hearing adults; parents of deaf and hard-of-hearing children; professionals who work with deaf and hard-of-hearing children and adults; organizations of, for, and by deaf and hard-of-hearing people; and other interested individuals. For more information, contact NAD, 814 Thayer Ave., Silver Springs, MD 20910.

National Federation of the Blind (NFB)

This advocacy group uses publication and other media to support parents, children, and educational programs.

A part of its mission is to improve the position in society of people who are blind. For more information, contact NFB, 1800 Johnson St., Baltimore, MD 21230.

National Information Center on Deafness

This center provides information on deafness and assistive technology for people who are deaf or hearing impaired. It also publishes fact sheets and other materials. For more information, contact Gallaudet University, 800 Florida Ave., NE, Washington, DC 20002.

Journals

American Annals of the Deaf (AAD)

This is a professional journal dedicated to quality education and related services for children and adults who are deaf or hard of hearing. Since 1847, AAD has served as a primary source of information and research on education, deafness, and related topics. In addition to four literary issues, subscribers receive the *Annual Reference Issue,* a comprehensive, detailed guide compiled by Gallaudet University researchers to schools and programs in the United States and Canada for people who are deaf and hard of hearing. For more information, contact Donald Moores, Editor, AAD, KDES PAS-9, 800 Florida Ave., NE, Washington, DC 20002.

Journal of Visual Impairment and Blindness (JVIB)

Published by the American Foundation for the Blind, JVIB is now a two-part bimonthly journal. Part one is the research publication, JVIB, which is the international, interdisciplinary journal of record on blindness and visual impairment that publishes scholarship and information and serves as a forum for the exchange of ideas, airing of controversies, and discussion of issues. Part two is the *JVIB News Service,* which is mailed with JVIB and is a newsletter digest of timely information and innovative ideas related to visual impairment. It is also a forum for discussions of current areas of interest and issues of controversy in the field. For more information, contact Mary Ellen Mulholland, Managing Editor, *Journal of Visual Impairment and Blindness,* 15 W. 16th St., New York, NY 10011.

Journal of Speech and Hearing Research (JSHR)

This publication of the American Speech-Language-Hearing Association pertains broadly to studies of the process and disorders of speech, hearing, and language. Experimental reports; theoretical, tutorial, or review papers; brief research notes describing clinical procedures or instruments; and letters to the editor are the primary materials published in JSHR. For more information, contact John H. Saxman, Coordinating Editor, *Journal of Speech and Hearing Research,* Box 146, Teachers College, Columbia University, New York, NY 10027.

Language, Speech, and Hearing Services in the Schools (LSHSS)

This journal is published by the American Speech-Language-Hearing Association and pertains to speech, hearing, and language services for children, particularly in schools. Articles in LSHSS deal with all aspects of clinical services to children, including the nature, assessment, and remediation of speech, hearing, and language disorders; program organization, management, and supervision; and scholarly discussion of philosophical issues relating to school programming. For more information, contact Wayne A. Secord, Editor, *Language, Speech, and Hearing Services in the Schools,* The Ohio State University, 110 Pressey Hall, 1070 Carmack Rd., Columbus, OH 43210-1002.

Rehabilitation and Education for Blindness and Visual Impairment (RE:view)

Formerly *Education for the Visually Handicapped,* this publication contains information for people concerned with services for individuals with visual disabilities, including those with multiple disabilities. Articles in *RE:view* describe useful practices, research findings, investigations, professional experiences, and controversial issues in education, rehabilitation teaching and counseling, orientation and mobility, and other services. For more information, contact Editor, *RE:view,* Heldref Publications, 1319 18th St., NW, Washington, DC 20036-1802.

The Volta Review (TVR)

A publication of the Alexander Graham Bell Association for the Deaf, this journal is published quarterly in winter, spring, summer, fall, and monthly in November. TVR contains articles that address research and practical concerns for people who are deaf. Articles in TVR are intended to further the knowledge base and to improve the lives of people who are deaf or hard of hearing. For more information, contact David F. Conway, Editor, *The Volta Review,* Alexander Graham Bell Association for the Deaf, 3417 Volta Place, NW, Washington, DC 20007.

13

Teaching Students with Medical, Physical, and Multiple Disabilities

"I can't believe I won the scholarship. I thought the story I wrote was good, but not that good." *Martin is a 17-year-old high school junior. He has cerebral palsy, a condition that restricts his speech and coordination. He uses crutches to get around school and a computer to help him communicate with his teachers and peers. All of his instruction is provided in classes with his neighbors and peers. A special education teacher supports Martin's teachers whenever they request help.*

"For years we went to the same school and it wasn't easy being the younger sister of the only person in the school with a disability. Everybody knew me as Bonnie, Mavis's sister. I thought I had to protect her and when she told me she wanted to take care of herself, life got a lot easier." *Because Mavis was born without feet, getting around is not easy for her. Although her sister wishes her family could do more physical activities together, she realizes it probably wouldn't happen even if Mavis didn't have a disability. After all, regardless of physical characteristics, family members don't always share common interests and disabilities don't have to control a person's life.*

"A lot of people would back away from me on the street. They would actually run away from me. People who associated with me were not treated much better." *Jeffrey didn't look different from the other boys in his class, nor did he act differently. But Jeffrey's medical condition was unlike anything any of his peers had ever experienced. Jeffrey had hemophilia—his body lacked a substance needed to make his blood clot. If he was cut or even bruised, the bleeding was very difficult to stop. Jeffrey took injections of the clotting substance to help him live a normal life; unfortunately, Jeffrey got AIDS from the injections and the disease caused serious problems, beyond the obvious, for him and his family.*

"I can't tell you how much being friends with Leslie has enriched our daughter's life. She truly is an exceptional child." *Leslie has a visual impairment, a hearing impairment, and physical impairments that make moving around school more of a challenge than a freedom. Karin lives in her neighborhood and has known Leslie all her life. Sometimes she wonders about Leslie's disabilities, but most of the time she is too busy with Leslie, doing what girls of their age do, to worry about it.* ■

Federal categories

In previous chapters, we described seven federal categories used to provide special education services. Students with specific learning disabilities, speech or language impairments, mental retardation, serious emotional disturbance, hearing impairments, and visual impairments, as well as those who are deaf and blind, account for about 95 percent of all students with disabilities in the United States (U.S. Department of Education, 1993). For students like Martin, Mavis, Jeffrey, and Leslie, however, there are five additional categories of special education under federally supported programs: Multiple disabilities, orthopedic impairments, other health impairments, autism, and traumatic brain injury. In this chapter we organize these categories into three groups: medical, physical, and multiple disabilities.

Grouping in this chapter

Under **medical disabilities** we discuss the federal category of other health impairments as well as special health problems that present challenges to school systems and teachers but for which no current special education category exists. Under **physical disabilities,** we discuss orthopedic impairments, autism and other neurological disorders that have physical effects, and traumatic brain injury. Because **multiple disabilities** is one of the current federal categories, we discuss it separately. The way we have grouped this last cluster of disabilities is somewhat arbitrary. It is based, however, on the central cause and/or primary characteristics of the disabilities that we discuss. The organization of topics for this chapter is presented in Figure 13.1.

Low prevalence

During recent school years, about 215,000 students with medical, physical, or multiple disabilities received special education services (Table 13.1 lists the percentage of students like Martin, Mavis, Jeffrey, and Leslie in the United States). They represent less than 5 percent of all students with disabilities, and about 0.4 percent of the school-age population. Their special education needs vary from supportive consultation provided by related services personnel to very specific assistance related to some medical conditions.

Figure 13.1
Relationship of Medical, Physical, and Multiple Disabilities to Federal Disability Categories

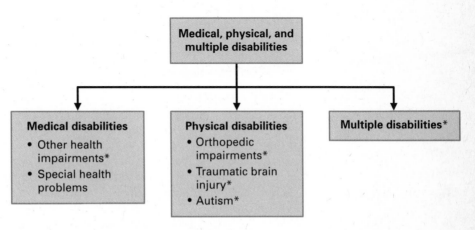

*Categories recognized by federal government

Table 13.1 Distribution of Students with Medical, Physical, or Multiple Disabilities in the United States

Disability Category	Number	Category as Percent of All Students with Disabilities
Multiple disabilities	98,402	2.2
Other health impairments	58,880	1.3
Orthopedic impairments	51,690	1.1
Autism	5,208	0.1
Traumatic brain injury	330	Less than 0.01
Combined	214,510	4.8
All disabilities	4,505,448	100.0

Note: Figures are based on children and adolescents between the ages of 6 and 21.
Source: U.S. Department of Education. (1993). *Fifteenth annual report to Congress on the implementation of the Individuals with Disabilities Education Act.* Washington, DC: Author (Table 1.2, p. 5).

Heightened interest and activity

Despite low prevalence, there has been heightened interest in medical, physical, and multiple disabilities over the past few years, and heightened activity in the fields of medicine and education to prevent and treat them. Improved medical care has increased the longevity of those with serious illness, adding to the visibility of their conditions. Also, the work of parents and advocacy groups has been especially intense on behalf of those with these low-prevalence conditions. The same legal and legislative initiatives that have had an impact on the delivery of services to those with higher-prevalence conditions have affected the education and treatment of those with medical, physical, and multiple disabilities. Those initiatives have brought these students into general education settings, increasing their visibility and interest in their conditions. Finally, the high costs of educating and treating these students have policymakers and educators examining all programs and services.

Medical Disabilities

Although extremely varied, medical disabilities have one thing in common: They are caused by disease or health problems prior to, during, or after birth. Federal guidelines place students with medical disabilities under the category of **other health impairments.** These students have limited strength, vitality, or alertness that adversely affects their educational performance. The causes include chronic or acute health problems such as heart conditions, tuberculosis, rheumatic fever, nephritis, asthma, sickle-cell anemia, hemophilia, epilepsy, lead poisoning, leukemia, or diabetes. For the most part, other health impair-

Other health impairments

ments involve chronic diseases that affect the whole body; students with attention deficit–hyperactivity disorder (see Chapter 8) are eligible for special education services under the "other health impaired" category if problems of limited alertness negatively affect academic performances.

The term *other health impairment* tells us little about the educational needs of students. The specific conditions included within the category usually can be identified objectively because of their medical symptoms. Asthma, tuberculosis, and sickle-cell anemia, for example, are medical problems that are identified by specific tests. Although the causes of asthma are unknown, the symptoms of labored breathing, shortness of breath, coughing, and wheezing have medical origins: tightening of the muscles around the bronchial tubes as well as swelling of the tissues and increased secretions in these tubes. Tuberculosis is caused by a bacterium that can be identified. Sickle-cell anemia is easy to identify by the shape of the individual's red blood cells (sickle shaped), which impair circulation and result in chronic illness, long-term complications, and premature death.

Identification by medical symptoms

Prevalence

During recent school years, about 59,000 students with other health impairments received special education services. This number represents about a 40 percent decrease from figures reported more than 10 years earlier (U.S. Department of Education, 1993). Students with other health impairments represent about one-tenth of 1 percent of school-age children and adolescents, and about 1.3 percent of students with disabilities. The percentages of these students vary little across the states.

Specific Impairments

Any disease that interferes with learning can make students eligible for special services under the category of other health impairments. This includes the diseases we describe below as well as others included in the federal definition (see Table 13.2). Students whose problems are due primarily to alcoholism or drug abuse are not classified with other health impairments or any other special education condition, even though they present special problems for students, teachers, parents, and other professionals.

Heart conditions

Heart conditions are not uncommon among young people. They are characterized by improper circulation of blood by the heart. Some of the disorders are congenital (present at birth); others are the product of inflammatory heart disease (myocarditis, endocarditis, pericarditis, rheumatic heart disease). Some students have heart valve disorders; others have disorders of the blood vessels. Very recently, students have been returning to school following heart transplants. When heart disorders or the medication necessary to treat them interfere with a student's ability to participate in normal activities, special education services may be provided as a short- or long-term support system.

Cystic fibrosis

Cystic fibrosis is a hereditary disease that affects the lungs and pancreas. Those who have cystic fibrosis have recurrent respiratory problems, and diges-

Table 13.2 Description of Selected Other Health Impairments

Condition	Description
Asthma	Chronic respiratory condition characterized by repeated episodes of breathing difficulties, especially while exhaling
Diabetes	Developmental or hereditary disorder characterized by inadequate secretion or use of insulin produced by the pancreas to process carbohydrates
Nephrosis and nephritis	Kidney disorders or diseases caused by infections, poisoning, burns, accidents, or other diseases
Sickle-cell anemia	Hereditary and chronic blood disease (occurring primarily in African Americans) characterized by red blood cells that are distorted and that do not circulate properly
Leukemia	Disease characterized by excessive production of white blood cells
Lead poisoning	Disorder caused by ingesting lead-based paint chips or other substances containing lead
Rheumatic fever	Disease characterized by painful swelling and inflammation of the joints that can spread to the heart and central nervous system
Tuberculosis	Infectious disease that commonly affects the lungs and may affect other tissues of the body
Cancer	Abnormal growth of cells that can affect any organ system

tive problems, including abnormal amounts of thick mucus, sweat, and saliva. Students with cystic fibrosis often spend significant time out of school. The disease is progressive and few who have it survive beyond age 20.

AIDS

Acquired immune deficiency syndrome (AIDS) is a very severe disease caused by *human immunodeficiency virus (HIV)* infection and transmitted primarily through exchange of bodily fluids in transfusions or unprotected sex, and by contaminated needles in addictive drug use. AIDS can also be transmitted to a child by an infected mother. AIDS is often used incorrectly as a catchall term for infection with the HIV virus. People with HIV infection do not necessarily have AIDS. AIDS is one stage of a series of stages in HIV infection.

Acquired means AIDS is not inherited (many diseases of immune deficiency are inherited), but acquired from some substance or microorganism outside the body. *Immune deficiency* means that the immune system has been weakened. A *syndrome* is not so much a disease as it is a collection of symptoms.

The symptoms of the AIDS infection include additional infections, developmental delays, central nervous system damage, motor problems, psychological problems, and death.

Teacher concerns

Many teachers are concerned about the risk of working with children with severe diseases such as AIDS. Generally people with medical disabilities require treatments to protect their health and the health of those around them. But extreme concern is usually unwarranted; a few general, common-sense considerations are all that is required beyond the ongoing medical treatment(s) being administered by physicians and other health personnel. Although the detailed medical guidelines for preventing transmission of HIV have changed over the years, Crocker and Cohen (1988) offered some tips that are still valid today for school situations:

Guidelines for school personnel

1. Transmission of HIV infection in the course of providing usual developmental services should not be a concern.

2. Activities and handling of people with HIV infection should involve normal interactions consistent with their developmental status and personal health.

3. Caution is required relative to susceptibility to other diseases by people with HIV infection.

4. Good hygienic practices appropriate in all situations of disease or infection require improved attention relative to HIV.

Washing

In general, hand washing is the most important way to prevent the spread of most infectious microorganisms. Any fresh bleeding cut or sore on a caregiver or person with HIV infection should be wiped free of blood and washed with soap and water or with a disinfectant such as bleach and alcohol (70 percent isopropyl). Gloves should be worn to cover cuts, sores, or torn cuticles when handling blood, feces, or urine and when cleaning open sores or surfaces soiled with blood, feces, or urine. Gloves are not necessary for schoolwork, therapy, feeding, diaper changing, physical examination, or developmental assessment. When in doubt about what to do in providing assistance to students with medical disabilities, consult the school nurse or other medical personnel for the latest information on best practices.

Use of gloves

Hemophilia

Hemophilia is a hereditary disease in which the blood clots very slowly or not at all. The disorder is transmitted by a sex-linked recessive gene and nearly always occurs in males. Those who have hemophilia bleed excessively from minor cuts and scrapes and suffer internal bleeding when they are bruised. In recent years, children with hemophilia and their families have faced increasing problems as a result of potential contamination of blood and blood products with the human immunodeficiency virus. (Jeffrey, the student we described at the beginning of this chapter, is one example; another is Ryan White, whose story is outlined in the Point of View feature.) Students with hemophilia should be protected from contact sports and school activities in which they might suffer a physical injury, but normal physical exercise should be encouraged.

Special Health Problems

Special health problems related to alcoholism and drug abuse are not considered disabilities under federal guidelines, even though they may adversely af-

Point of View

Ryan White Taught Us All Something

AIDS is a frightening disease. No cure has been discovered, and anyone who gets it is likely to become very ill and possibly die. Ryan White died from AIDS in April of 1990. His story was widely publicized as an illustration of the positive and negative ways in which people sometimes respond to children with disabilities.

In 1984, most people didn't know that Ryan was seriously ill. His mother told some school officials that he had AIDS in order to explain his many absences from school. In March of 1985, the local newspaper in Kokomo, Indiana, ran a story in which Ryan told how he and other people with hemophilia had contracted AIDS during their treatments. That story changed Ryan's life forever. In August of the following year, he was not allowed to reenter school. Although the school system suggested some alternatives such as home tutoring, Ryan's mother refused to go along with them, and his family filed a lawsuit to force the district to enroll Ryan in his regular school. The Ryan White story became national news and seriously divided the citizens of his hometown. Many supported the Whites, but many who were frightened and angry took it out on Ryan and his family and friends. When a federal court in Indianapolis ordered the school board to readmit Ryan, it was an empty victory. Many parents were still worried and angry; they refused to let their children play with Ryan or let him have a normal life.

A year later, his family moved to Cicero, Indiana, to escape the hostility and loneliness they experienced as a result of Ryan's illness. The citizens of their new hometown treated Ryan like any other child, and his trials became a source of inspiration for other people with AIDS and other health impairments. In 1988, Indiana's governor, Robert Orr, declared a Ryan White Day honoring Ryan, his family, and his school. Ryan died in April of 1990, but the last years of his life were filled with dignity and respect.

Ryan White's story illustrates difficult and complicated issues that surround all disabilities. Although much is known about them, sometimes the facts are simply not enough to prevent misunderstandings and mistreatments. Sometimes worry and fear preempt knowledge, and people with disabilities suffer. We are the future. If attitudes toward people with disabilities are to change, that change must begin with each of us. The senseless persecution of people with AIDS, mental retardation, serious emotional disturbance, learning disabilities, speech and language impairments, or any other perceived or real disability will stop only if we refuse to continue it.

Fetal alcohol syndrome

fect school performance. For example, *fetal alcohol syndrome* is evidenced in babies born to mothers who drink alcoholic beverages before and during pregnancy (Conlon, 1992). Children born with fetal alcohol syndrome have low birth weight and height, have unusual facial features, and evidence mental retardation. Some also have heart problems and varied learning problems.

Alcohol consumed during pregnancy affects the fetus because it crosses the placental membrane. This means that when the mother drinks, the fetus drinks. Some effects of drinking alcohol are decreased protein synthesis, impaired cellular growth, decreased production of essential metabolic products, and inhibited development of nerves (Conlon, 1992). These effects explain the growth retardation, abnormal physical appearance, and other problems of children with fetal alcohol syndrome.

Maternal cocaine addiction

Although not as common as fetal alcohol syndrome, *cocaine addiction* receives more press because it places pregnant mothers as well as their babies at risk for a variety of serious, sometimes life-threatening health problems. Problems for the mothers include seizures, shortness of breath, lung damage, nasal membrane burns, respiratory paralysis, cardiovascular problems, anorexia, and premature labor (Smith, 1988). Although data are limited, it appears that children born of cocaine-addicted mothers (referred to as "crack babies") experience a variety of problems with significant ramifications for success in school, including increased irritability, elevated respiratory and heart rates, neurological damage, low birth weight, and disturbed sleep patterns. Current information on the long-term effects of maternal cocaine addiction on children is equivocal: Some argue the effects are permanent and irreversible, and others believe the initial problems can be successfully treated without lasting damage. One thing is certain: More and more crack babies are being born, and concern for them and others with health impairments touches every school district in the country.

Medically fragile

Technology dependent

In recent years, new kinds of students have emerged with unique educational needs confounded by serious medical problems. Advances in health care have improved survival rates and created a population of children who have been called **medically fragile.** The Council for Exceptional Children (1988) defined this group as "those who require specialized technological health care procedures for life support and/or health support during the school day" (p. 12). A related, often overlapping group is that of students who are **technology dependent**—those who rely on life-sustaining medical equipment and complex nursing care to avoid death or further disabilities (Levy & Pilmer, 1992; Liles, 1993). According to the Office of Technology Assessment (cited in Liles, 1993), four separate groups of technology-dependent children have been identified, but the boundaries can be blurred:

Group I   Children dependent at least part of each day on mechanical ventilators (machines that help them breathe);

Group II   Children requiring prolonged intravenous administration of nutritional substances or drugs;

Group III   Children with daily dependence on other device-based respiratory or nutritional support, including tracheotomy tube care, suctioning, oxygen support or tube feeding;

Group IV   Children with prolonged dependence on other medical devices that compensate for vital body functions who require daily or near-daily nursing care. (p. 2)

Difficulties in labeling

The diversity of responses to medical problems sometimes makes it difficult to distinguish medically fragile or technology-dependent children from the larger group of children with special health problems and/or other medical disabilities. Generally, as the level of a child's disability improves and the intensity of medical intervention decreases, deciding what to call a child needing med-

While experts debate about who should be included in regular public school classrooms, children are showing them that it can and does happen for the benefit of all. *Michael J. Okoniewski*

ical assistance depends on the response to treatments. For example, should a child whose breathing problems improve over time be called technology dependent because he once needed a ventilator to overcome a medical problem in breathing? Similarly, a child may require minimal medical equipment but a great deal of nursing care (for example, for uncontrolled diabetes), while another may need specialized equipment but limited supervision (for instance, an older child needing overnight intravenous therapy). Although classification can present problems, three key components appear to be prominent in programs that successfully include children with medical disabilities and special health problems in school programs (Liles, 1993): clear and open communication to share information about resources and reduce fears, collaboration between school personnel and representatives from other agencies dealing with health care issues, and flexibility to accommodate the often highly individualized needs of this group of students.

Key program components

Physical Disabilities

Federal categories of physical disability

Physical disabilities are problems that result from injuries or conditions affecting the central nervous system or other body systems and their related functions. These conditions affect how children use their bodies. Federal guidelines place students with physical disabilities under the categories of "orthopedic impairment," "traumatic brain injury," and "autism." **Orthopedic impairments** involve the muscular or skeletal system, and sometimes the central nervous system; by limiting movement and mobility, they adversely affect a child's educational performance. **Traumatic brain injury** refers to a severe head injury that creates chronic physical problems that affect academic, behavioral, and interpersonal performances. **Autism** is a physical disorder of the brain that causes lifelong problems with communication, thought processes, and attention.

Orthopedic Impairments

Orthopedic impairments are the most common physical disabilities. They are conditions that generally involve the muscular, skeletal, or central nervous systems and affect movement and mobility. The term includes impairments caused by congenital anomalies (such as clubfoot and absence of some member), impairments caused by disease (such as poliomyelitis and bone tuberculosis), and impairments from other causes (such as neurological problems, cerebral palsy, amputations, and fractures or burns that cause contractures).

Prevalence During recent school years, about 52,000 students with orthopedic impairments received special education (U.S. Department of Education, 1993). These numbers have changed very little over the past ten years. Students with orthopedic impairments represent less than a tenth of a percent of school-age children and adolescents and about 1 percent of students with disabilities. Across the states, the percentages of these students show little variation.

Specific Impairments Orthopedic impairments limit muscular movement and mobility and differ in severity. Students who evidence mild impairments can function very well in general education classrooms with little or no special help. Those with very severe disabilities may need special furniture or devices, or the help of trained personnel.

Polio

Poliomyelitis is an acute communicable disease caused by the polio virus. The disease can be very mild, showing no apparent symptoms, to severe, with paralysis, muscular atrophy, and even fatal paralysis. Polio was first recognized in the mid-1800s and became epidemic in Norway and Sweden in 1905. The incidence of polio in North America, Europe, Australia, and New Zealand peaked during the 1940s and early 1950s. A vaccine developed by Dr. Jonas Salk became available in 1955 and virtually eliminated the disease. The Sabin vaccine, which can be taken orally and is more than 90 percent effective, is now the vaccine of choice. Today it is hard to appreciate how frightening polio once was. Still, occasional outbreaks of the disease occur, usually among groups who have not been immunized. The most recent in the United States was in 1979, among Pennsylvania's Amish population.

Muscular dystrophy

Muscular dystrophy is actually a group of birth disorders in which the skeletal muscles progressively atrophy; there are no neurological or sensory defects. Diagnosing muscular dystrophy depends on finding elevated levels of creatine kinase (CK) in the blood. This enzyme is released by dying muscle cells. Muscular dystrophy has four main forms:

Pseudohypertrophic (Duchenne's) type accounts for about 50 percent of cases and is found only in boys. The disease usually is diagnosed when the child begins to walk. The disorder is progressive: By the time they are teenagers, most of those who have the condition are in wheelchairs. Few live more than ten to fifteen years from the onset.

Facioscapulohumeral (Landouzy–Dejerine) type occurs in both sexes and weakens the shoulders and arms more than the legs. This form usually appears before age 10 but can start during adolescence. Early symptoms include the inability to pucker or whistle, and abnormal facial movements when laughing or crying. The disease is slower to progress than Duchenne's type, and many who have the condition live a normal life.

Limb–girdle dystrophy (juvenile dystrophy, or Erb's disease) follows a slow course and often causes only slight disability. Usually the disease begins between ages 6 and 10. Muscle weakness appears first in the upper arms and pelvis. Other symptoms include poor balance, a waddling gait, and an inability to raise the arms.

Mixed dystrophy generally occurs between ages 30 and 50, affects all voluntary muscles, and causes rapidly progressive deterioration.

Use of appliances

At this time there is no treatment to stop the progressive impairment associated with muscular dystrophy. Those who have the condition most often are helped by orthopedic appliances such as crutches, walkers, and wheelchairs, but use of these aids is discouraged as long as possible to maximize existing muscle strength. Exercise and physical therapy are also useful.

Juvenile rheumatoid arthritis

Juvenile rheumatoid arthritis is a disorder of the tissues that connect bones; there is no known cause. The three major types of juvenile rheumatoid arthritis are systemic (Still's disease, or acute febrile type), polyarticular, and pauciarticular. In the systemic form, the individual develops sudden fevers; rashes; chills; an enlarged spleen and liver; and swollen, tender, and stiff joints. Students with arthritis usually require only mild forms of special education intervention. Those who have severe forms of the disease may be incapacitated for long periods and require homebound instruction.

Osteogenesis imperfecta

Osteogenesis imperfecta is a hereditary disorder that leaves the child or adolescent with very brittle bones. The disease occurs in two forms. In the rarer form, fractured bones are present at birth, and the infant usually dies within a few weeks. In the more common form (called osteogenesis imperfecta tarda), the child develops fractures after the first year of life. Preventing injury is the usual treatment. Depending on the severity of the condition, children with this disorder either do not participate in contact sports or wear protective devices (pads, helmets) when they do.

Osteomyelitis

Osteomyelitis is an inflammation of the bone marrow that occurs more often in children than adults, and much more often in boys than girls. Usually it is the result of an infection coupled with trauma. It begins when a child is bruised in some way and at the same time has an infection. The infection finds

Special education means being provided with services that make learning and success in school more likely. © *James Shaffer/ PhotoEdit.*

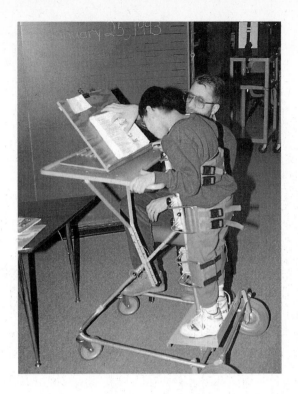

a home in the hematoma (swelling) caused by the injury, then spreads through the bone to other parts of the body. In children, the most common infections are in the bones of the arms and legs. Osteomyelitis also can result in underdeveloped bones.

Legg–Calvé–Perthes disease

Legg–Calvé–Perthes disease is a disorder that affects the head of the femur, the upper bone in the leg. Interrupted blood flow causes the head of the bone to degenerate; a new head forms that is misshapen, usually flattened. The disease occurs most often in boys ages 4 to 10. Those who have the disease show a persistent limp that becomes more severe over time. The disease can interfere with participation in typical classroom activities.

Limb deficiencies

Limb deficiencies, or loss of one or more limbs, may be present at birth (congenital) or occur later in life (acquired). A student may be born missing entire limbs or parts of limbs. Sometimes, because of an accident or illness that requires amputation, a student is missing one or more arms or legs. If the condition interferes significantly with performance in school, the student may receive special education services.

Craniofacial anomalies

Craniofacial anomalies are defects of the skull and face. Microcephaly (head circumference more than 2 standard deviations below average), hydrocephaly (accumulation of cerebrospinal fluid in the ventricles of the brain), and cleft palate (gap in the soft palate and roof of the mouth, sometimes extending through the upper lip) are forms of craniofacial anomalies that cause some students to receive special education. For example, one effect of microcephaly and hydrocephaly can be mental retardation (see Chapter 10). Conditions that involve the mouth or jaw usually result in some form of speech impairment. As a result, craniofacial anomalies can affect the ways people interact with individuals who have them.

The neurological system

The neurological (or nervous) system coordinates and directs various body functions (Batshaw & Perret, 1992). Its components are nerves and three subsystems: the central nervous system, including the brain and spinal cord; the peripheral nervous system; and the autonomic nervous system. Each component controls some aspect of behavior and affects how we deal with the world around us. An impairment of any part of this system makes us less able to adapt to the environment and may result in a variety of disorders. Neurological problems can affect the physical structure and functioning of the central nervous system, including the brain or spinal cord, or other components of the nervous system, resulting in neuromuscular problems. Some are genetic, others are due to infection or injury, still others stem from unknown causes.

Epilepsy

Epilepsy is a condition that affects 1 to 2 percent of the population. It is characterized by recurring seizures, which are spontaneous abnormal discharges of electrical impulses of the brain. *Petit mal* (or absence) seizures occur most often in children 6 to 14 years old and usually consist of a brief loss of consciousness (the eyes blink or roll, the child stares blankly, and the mouth moves slightly). Each petit mal seizure lasts from one to ten seconds; someone experiencing a petit mal seizure simply stares or shows small eye movements like fluttering of the eyelids. *Grand mal* (or tonic-clonic) seizures typically begin with a loud cry, brought on by air rushing through the vocal cords. The person falls to the ground, losing consciousness; the body stiffens, then alternately relaxes and stiffens again. Tongue biting, loss of bowel control, labored breathing, temporary cessation of breathing followed by rapid breathing, and blue to purple coloring of the skin can result. Grand mal seizures generally last for several minutes. Although they can be frightening, they are not dangerous.

Medication for epilepsy

Undiagnosed seizures can be mistaken for daydreaming or temper tantrums. Epilepsy can be controlled by medication that must be monitored to achieve optimal effects. Epilepsy medication has side effects of drowsiness, lethargy, intellectual dullness, coarsening of facial features, behavioral changes, and sleep disturbances that can also present problems in school. Teachers are important members of treatment teams by observing, recording, and reporting behavioral changes that accompany medical management of epilepsy.

Multiple sclerosis

Multiple sclerosis is a disease of older adolescents and adults. Because students with disabilities are now entitled to a free, appropriate education until age 21, you may come across this condition among your students. Multiple sclerosis is a disease in which the membranes of the brain and spinal cord progressively deteriorate. Those with multiple sclerosis have periods of incapacity and periods of remission, when symptoms are relieved and they can lead active lives.

Cerebral palsy

Cerebral palsy is actually a group of neuromuscular disorders that result from damage to the central nervous system (the brain and spinal cord) before, during, or after birth. There are three major types of cerebral palsy—spastic,

Bring Your Learning to Life

Information Helped Martin's Teachers Allay Concerns About Seizures

One of the characteristics associated with Martin's cerebral palsy was seizures. Although the seizures were being controlled by medication, Martin's teachers wanted information about what to do if he had a seizure at school. His doctor provided them with information describing the appropriate steps to assist a person experiencing a convulsive seizure:

- Prevent Martin from hurting himself. Place something soft under his head, loosen tight clothing, and clear the area around him of any sharp or hard objects.
- Do not force any objects into Martin's mouth.
- Do not restrain Martin's movements.
- Turn Martin on his side to allow saliva to drain from his mouth.
- Stay with Martin until the seizure ends naturally.

- Do not give Martin any food, liquid, or medication until he is fully awake.
- Be prepared to give artificial respiration if Martin does not resume breathing after the seizure.
- Provide an area, with supervision, for Martin to rest until fully awake.
- Be reassuring and supportive after the seizure is over.
- Although a seizure is not a medical emergency, occasionally one may last longer than ten minutes or a second seizure may occur. This requires medical assistance in a properly equipped facility.

Source: Reprinted from *Children with Disabilities: A Medical Primer,* Third Edition, by M. L. Batshaw and Y. M Perret. Copyright © 1981 Epilepsy Foundation of America. Used with permission.

athetoid, and ataxic—although the disorder sometimes occurs in mixed form and other grouping systems are recognized.

Spastic cerebral palsy is the most common, occurring in 70 percent of those who have the disorder. In its mildest form, spastic cerebral palsy can be detected only by a careful neurological examination. Severe spasticity leaves the individual rigid, with muscles tense and contracted. Athetoid cerebral palsy occurs in approximately 20 percent of those who have the disorder. The condition results in involuntary movements—grimacing, writhing, sharp jerks—that impair voluntary movements. Ataxic cerebral palsy is the rarest form, occurring in about 10 percent of those who have cerebral palsy. Its characteristics include disturbed balance, lack of coordination, underactive reflexes, constant involuntary movement of the eyeballs, muscle weakness, tremor, lack of leg movement during infancy, and a wide gait as the individual begins to walk.

Up to 40 percent of those with cerebral palsy also experience mental retardation, about 25 percent have seizures, and about 80 percent have impaired speech. Cerebral palsy cannot be cured, but proper management or treatment

Window on Practice

The Making of a Miracle

My 3-year-old son started preschool this fall. Soon after, he started riding the bus. Significant but routine events in the life of an American child—unless the child has, as my son does, cerebral palsy.

For parents of disabled children, every "routine" milestone reached is a miracle, bringing with it excitement, joy and, at least in this case, a small degree of trepidation. And this particular miracle will seem unusual to many readers because of its source. It was planted by the social activism of special-needs parents in the 1960s and 1970s. Its roots grew from special-education legislation. And its cultivation can be attributed in large part to the hard work and dedication of publicly funded educators, as well as parents and others who care. It is an example of the good that can and does spring from legislative policymaking and government spending.

Ben is a smiling, energetic, funny little boy (also quite handsome according to this unbiased source) who cannot walk, cannot sit up by himself, cannot reach his arms very far, cannot feed himself and can speak only in difficult-to-understand single words. His disability was caused by a congenital defect; a small "drain" in his brain is too narrow, resulting in a condition commonly called hydrocephalus or "water on the brain." Doctors gave him an auxiliary drain (a "shunt") when he was 6 days old, correcting the underlying problem but leaving Ben with brain damage that occured during pregnancy.

Trying to be a good parent—a challenge with any child—to a son who cannot communicate or learn the way typical children do can be a very frustrating and isolating experience. Not only do my husband and I have to attend to and contain our own feelings of guilt and grief; we also need to find ways to teach Ben things that typical children learn through their own physical independence. We are enormously proud of our Ben, but his birth drove home the reality that no matter how emotionally or financially independ-ent you are, there are some challenges you cannot face alone.

Enter the special-education system, mandated by state and federal law. Upon diagnosing Ben, doctors referred us to an early-intervention center (serving children from birth to 3 years) in our home state of Massachusetts. We were referred to another one when we moved to New Hampshire several months later in order for my husband to take a new job. These centers are staffed by some of the most creative, bright, warm and supportive people I have ever met. They helped us learn how best to teach Ben, how to motivate him and how to help him ex-plore the world around him. Just before he began school, Ben's case manager, an occupa-tional therapist, found a piece of equipment that helps him "crawl"—supporting his upper body on a sling so that his stronger legs can push the wheels attached to the sling's frame. Ben has begun to have the independent mobility that we had only dreamed of.

Prerequisites to success: Ben's preschool, run by our town's school system, is building on Ben's experience with early intervention. Although it has been some time since the school has had a child with Ben's level of physical dis-ability, the teachers and students have truly welcomed him to the school, a welcome that does not come cheap. Like all children, Ben needs a happy family life, a roof over his head, clean and appropriate clothes, good nutrition and caring teachers as prerequisites to success in school. But Ben's needs don't stop there. He requires a full-time classroom aide to help him move, play and eat with the other children. He and some of his classmates receive physical, occupational, and speech therapy so that they can reach their maximum development. The school will need to purchase special equipment. In a time of dwindling resources, educators, politicians and parents of typical children may well ask whether the expense is worth it.

I can answer with an unqualified yes.

(continued on next page)

Window on Practice

The Making of a Miracle *(continued)*

Obviously, it's worth it to my family—especially to Ben. No child deserves a disability and Ben should be able to dream of being anything he wants to be, just as we encourage other children to do. But it is also worth it to Ben's community and especially to his peers. Ben has the potential to be a citizen in the true meaning of the word, very possibly a self-sufficient one who will not, as an adult, need to rely on the government for all or most of his financial support. But more important, Ben will provide his peers with a window to a world few of them would otherwise see, teaching them acceptance, tolerance, perspective and creativity. He may also turn out (and I hope this for him more than anything else) to be a best friend to someone who really needs his friendship.

The early reports from preschool are amazing, especially when compared with what Ben was able to do just a year ago. Ben is happy, watching his classmates closely, and, in his fashion, participating in games, singing and story time. The other kids are curious about him, but once told that his muscles just don't work like everyone else's, they accept the information and figure out how they can play with him. They are happy that he likes to share his special equipment. The teachers and aides are warm, supportive and, most important, very enthusiastic about Ben.

This small miracle of a routine beginning is not the stuff of made-for-TV movies, where the child walks despite the dire predictions of all the doctors. It is a miracle created by activists through government. And it is a miracle that requires money; without the dollars, the network of professionals who create and develop the information and experience that will cultivate a little boy like Ben into an integrated member of our society simply wouldn't exist. And it is a miracle that few parents could afford to create on their own, no matter how willing they might be.

Sometimes government spending does make a difference. Sometimes it can create miracles.

Source: Maggie Wood Hassan, "The Making of a Miracle," *Newsweek,* Jan. 6, 1992. Used with permission.

limits further physical damage, improves functional skills, and offers opportunities for increased independence and successful life experiences.

Spina bifida

Spina bifida is a birth defect that is related to the development of the embryonic neural tube (the structure from which the brain and spinal cord develop) during the first trimester of pregnancy. One or more vertebrae push the spinal contents out, in an external sac. Usually the defect occurs in the lower back area, but it can occur at any point along the spine. Treatment is a function of the severity of the condition. An individual with a minor disorder may require no treatment and may be able to lead an essentially normal life. The most serious form of the condition is myelomeningocele. Here, a saclike structure that contains spinal cord membranes, spinal fluid, and a portion of the spinal cord protrudes over the spinal column. The condition usually is corrected surgically but results in some neurological impairment.

Spinal cord injuries

Spinal cord injuries occur when the spinal cord is traumatized or partially or totally severed. Spinal cord injuries are primarily caused by car or motorcycle accidents, gunshot wounds, or falls, although some may be caused by infections. People with spinal cord injuries experience partial or total paralysis; the

Table 13.3 Characteristics of Different Types of Paralysis

Type	Description
Monoplegia	One limb affected
Paraplegia	Lower body and both legs affected
Hemiplegia	One side of body affected
Triplegia	Three limbs affected, usually legs and one arm
Quadriplegia	All four extremities and trunk affected
Diplegia	Legs more affected than arms
Double Hemiplegia	Both halves of the body affected, with one side more than the other

effects depend on the amount of damage and its location. If the spinal cord is completely severed, complete paralysis occurs to a portion of the body. If the spinal cord is partially severed or damaged due to swelling or bleeding following a traumatic injury, partial paralysis occurs. Generally, parts of the body below the spinal cord injury are affected, and different terms are used to refer to the different types of paralysis (see Table 13.3).

Traumatic Brain Injury

According to recent federal guidelines, "traumatic brain injury" means an

> acquired injury to the brain caused by an external physical force, resulting in total or partial functional disability or psychosocial impairment, or both, that adversely affects a child's educational performance. The term applies to open or closed head injuries resulting in impairments in one or more areas, such as cognition; language; memory; attention; reasoning; abstract thinking; judgment; problem-solving; sensory, perceptual, and motor abilities; psychosocial behavior; physical functions; information processing; and speech. (Individuals with Disabilities Education Act, 1990)

Causes of traumatic brain injury

Common causes of head injury include falls, sports- and recreation-related accidents, motor vehicle accidents, and personal assaults, including child abuse (Michaud & Duhaime, 1992). Because the brain is part of the central nervous system, severe injuries to it may have neurological effects. Traumatic brain injuries include scalp and skull injuries, cerebral contusions (bruising of brain tissue), hematomas (blood clots), and concussions (loss of consciousness). The

Types of skull fractures

term does not apply to brain injuries that are congenital or degenerative, or induced by birth trauma.

Although scalp injuries sometimes result in considerable loss of blood, they generally have no neurological effects. Of more concern is an injury to the skull referred to as a skull fracture. *Skull fractures* are cracks or broken bones in the skull. They are classified according to both severity and location, and their effects can range from minor to severe. A *linear fracture* is a crack in the skull bones that is visible on an X-ray; these injuries are usually not associated with neurological problems and are considered less severe than *depressed fractures,* in which the skull bone is broken and presses against the underlying brain tissue. For example, a depressed fracture directly over the part of the brain that controls movement results in weakness of the opposite side of the body.

Contusions of the brain are bruises of the brain tissue that most often result from direct impact to the head. Their effects depend on the extent of the bruise and its location. *Hematomas* are swellings filled with blood. The effects of hematomas depend on their location and type.

Hematomas

Epidural hematomas form between the skull and the brain covering (the dura) and may be in arteries or veins. They may be associated with skull fractures that result from falls or from some other impact to the head. The classic sign of an epidural hematoma is a delay in the onset of any symptoms. When a child sustains the injury, the immediate neurological effects appear benign and harmless. As the hematoma enlarges and creates increasing pressure on greater areas of the brain, headaches, confusion, vomiting, and neurological deficits in strength and movement occur. Left untreated, this type of brain injury can be fatal; however, if surgery is performed before the effects are irreversible, the outcomes are very favorable (Michaud & Duhaime, 1992).

Subdural hematomas form beneath the brain covering, over the surface of the brain. The symptoms are more severe (among them loss of functioning), and the prognosis for recovery is much worse than for epidural hematomas. Subdural hematomas are usually the result of a major generalized injury to the brain.

Concussion

A brain injury sufficient to cause a brief loss of consciousness or amnesia is called a *concussion.* Usually, concussions are followed in minutes by a complete return to normal mental functioning, although some children experience periods of headaches, drowsiness, and confusion for several hours or even a few days. Most people recover from concussions in twenty-four to forty-eight hours.

Very low prevalence

Although traumatic brain injury is the number one killer and disabler of American youth, the type that results in children's needing and receiving special education is relatively uncommon. During the 1991–92 school year, the first-year data identified only 330 students with this disability (U.S. Department of Education, 1993). The primary physical problems associated with head injuries are treated by physicians, emergency room doctors, and other medical personnel.

What should teachers do about traumatic brain injury? They enter the treatment cycle during rehabilitation phases and aftercare. This means provid-

Role of teachers

ing assistance overcoming cognitive, academic, physical, behavioral, and communication problems, and other difficulties that result from the injury.

Teachers can also play key roles in preventing some head trauma that occurs at school from having more serious consequences (Michaud & Duhaime, 1992). Most head trauma is minor; it does not require treatment or result in serious consequences. If a child hits his or her head and does not become unconscious, no treatment is necessary unless symptoms of an epidural hematoma develop. Usually a little "tender loving care" cures minor "bumps on the head." If a child has a severe headache; loses consciousness; shows significant changes in speech or other bodily functions (for example, vomiting, continuous bleeding); or becomes lethargic, confused, or irritable after a head injury, then medical personnel should be contacted. If a child is momentarily unconscious and then resumes activities, he or she may have a mild concussion. Usually a neurological exam is recommended after such an incident, and parents are instructed to keep a close watch on the child's behavior, looking for delayed signs of complications, such as confusion or difficulty awakening from sleep. Finally, if a child remains unconscious after a fall or head impact, medical personnel should be called immediately.

Prevention

The National Head Injury Foundation (NHIF) supports the position that most traumatic brain injuries are preventable: The key to prevention is effective education, and the key to effective education is the organization's HeadSmart School program. HeadSmart Schools teach safe behaviors and effective coping strategies before unsafe behaviors and poor strategies become bad habits. The HeadSmart School program addresses the following areas:

HeadSmart program

- Pedestrian safety, such as how to walk safely in a crowded neighborhood or across a busy street
- Occupant safety, such as the proper use of safety belts and safety seats
- Tricycle, bicycle, and skateboard safety, such as responsible bike riding in traffic and use of safety helmets
- Playground safety, such as proper surfaces and safe sports equipment
- Avoidance of violence, such as child abuse and shaking of babies; the program stresses methods other than striking out for coping with life's frustrations

For more information, contact NHIF (see the For Your Information section at the end of this chapter for the address).

Autism

Autism defined

Autism is a rare disorder that affects multiple areas, including thought, communication, and behavior (Powers, 1989b). The National Society for Children and Adults with Autism (1977) defined autism as a biological syndrome (a complex combination of biological symptoms) manifested before thirty months of age and including disturbances of (1) developmental rates and/or sequences; (2) responses to sensory stimuli; (3) speech, language, and cognitive capacities; and (4) capacities to relate to people, events, and objects. All of the stated characteristics must be present for the diagnosis to be applied. Today, however, autism is usually recognized by a cluster of symptoms or characteristics as evidenced in the most recent federal definition:

> "Autism" means a developmental disability significantly affecting verbal and nonverbal communication and social interaction, generally evident before age 3, that adversely affects a child's educational performance. Other characteristics often associated with autism are engagement in repetitive activities and stereotyped movements, resistance to environmental change or change in daily routines, and unusual responses to sensory experiences. The term does not apply if a child's educational performance is adversely affected primarily because the child has a serious emotional disturbance. (Individuals with Disabilities Education Act, 1990)

Separation of categories

Until 1981 autism was included in the definition of severe emotional disturbance, but in that year the secretary of education moved autism from the federal definition of "severe emotional disturbance" to the category of "other health impairments." The decision to change categories was made in consultation with the National Society for Autistic Children and the National Institute for Neurological and Communicative Disorders and Stroke, and was based on evidence that autism was biologically rather than psychologically caused. Autism currently is a separate category in the federal classification system, and the 1991–92 school year was the first year in which data were collected on the number of children and youth with autism. About 5,200 students with autism were identified at that time (U.S. Department of Education, 1993).

Professional debate

The shift in categories reflects the recurrent debate among professionals about autism. Since Leo Kanner, a psychiatrist at Johns Hopkins University, first brought the disorder to public attention in 1943, professionals have debated the extent to which autism is a biological condition or the result of family, environmental, or psychosocial factors. Professionals do agree, however, that this is a complex, brain-based developmental disorder in which multiple areas of functioning are affected. Key symptoms of autism include failing to develop normal socialization patterns; disturbances in speech, language, and communication; unusual relationships to objects and events; unusual responses to sensory stimulation; developmental delays; and onset during the early years of life (Powers, 1989a).

Characteristics of autism

People with autism have difficulties relating to others. They exhibit impaired or delayed speech and language and often repeat words and phrases over and over again, as Dustin Hoffman's character did in the movie *Rain Man*. Some are over- or under responsive to sensory stimulation such as light, noise, and touch. People with autism may exhibit inappropriate social and emotional behaviors, and some students with autism engage in repetitive, stereotypic behaviors (for example, hand flapping, rocking) that interfere with productive academic and social activities. Many students with autism fail to develop appropriate behaviors related to play, recreation, and leisure. These severe and multiple problems make autism resistant to intervention and treatment.

Goals of treatment

The primary goals of treatment for children with autism include fostering normal development; promoting learning; reducing rigid, stereotypic behavior patterns; eliminating problem behaviors; and reducing family stress (Hart, 1993; Powers, 1989a; Reber, 1992). Programs that begin early in life are generally the most effective. Essential components of effective programs for children and adolescents with autism include emphasis on functional activities and skills needed to be successful in the real world, chronological age appropriateness of activities, instruction in both school and nonschool environments, and social integration to the maximum possible extent (Egel, 1989).

Sue Pratt, President of the Autism Society of America (ASA), believes that people with autism are entitled to the "highest quality of life possible and [should] be treated at all times with the same dignity and respect accorded to everyone else" (1988, p. 2). If you teach students with autism, you will probably meet professionals who believe that punishment is a necessary component of all treatment programs for these students. You will probably also meet professionals who believe that punishment should not be a part of any treatment program. A resolution by the ASA, offered to foster dignity and respect, suggests that strategies based on rewards for engaging in appropriate behavior or refraining from inappropriate behavior, rather than punishment, should be used as the first line of intervention with students with autism (Egel, 1989).

Rewards, not punishment

Prognosis

Not too long ago, the prognosis for people with autism was not good. Today, experiences like those available for people with other disabilities (such as group living homes) and increasing transition services (such as supported employment opportunities) are helping to make successful independent living more common.

Multiple Disabilities

Leslie Parsons was born with a visual impairment (she is legally blind), moderate hearing loss, cleft palate, muscular imperfection in her extremities, and ptosis (drooping) of the eyelids. She has some difficulty with tasks requiring muscle coordination and fine motor skills, as well as visual acuity. She wears a hearing aid, which is refitted periodically to accommodate her growth. Every few years, she has an operation to reduce the fluid in her ears. She has had two operations to tighten the muscles in her eyelids. Twice a week, Leslie works with a special education teacher. With the assistance of a device that enlarges and projects print onto a screen, Leslie can read and write independently; she is an outstanding reader.

Students with multiple disabilities like Leslie are included in current federal regulations governing special education. The category is used to identify two types of students: those with more than one disability and those with a primary disability and other secondary conditions. Before the 1978–79 academic year, students with multiple disabilities were not classified. Although they received special education services, they typically were classified as having one or the

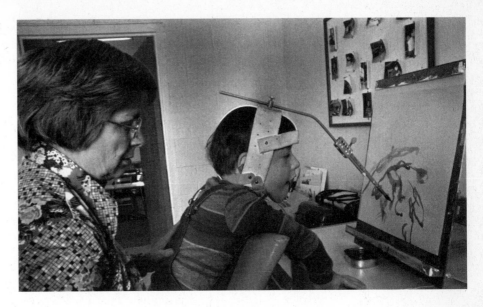

Multiple disabilities make it difficult but not impossible to be included in regular education programs.*George Bellerose/Stock, Boston, Inc.*

other of their disabilities. In 1977, the category was added to federal legislation and formally defined. Today, students with multiple disabilities have

Federal definition

concomitant impairments (such as mental retardation–blindness, mental retardation–orthopedic impairment, etc.), the combination of which causes such severe educational problems that they cannot be accommodated in special education programs solely for one of the impairments. The term does not include deaf-blindness. (Individuals with Disabilities Education Act, 1990)

Some of these students exhibit such a complex array of symptoms and conditions that identifying a primary condition is impossible. Others demonstrate a primary disability and a set of other conditions that are severe enough to interfere with placement in classes with students with a singular disability. Still others, like Leslie, receive special education support primarily in general education classrooms.

A fast-growing category

During recent school years, almost 100,000 students with multiple disabilities received special education (U.S. Department of Education, 1993). This group represented about 2.2 percent of all students with disabilities and was one of the fastest growing categories between 1979–80 and 1991–92. Over that period the number of students with multiple disabilities increased about 80 percent.

Explanations for growth of category

Why do the numbers in this category change so much? One explanation is that states do not use the same procedures in reporting the number of students with multiple disabilities. Another attributes the fluctuation to decreases in the number of children identified with mental retardation and other health impairments. Children initially identified with mental retardation or other health impairments may have been reclassified as having multiple disabilities due to recognition by school personnel and parents of related disabilities (for example, sensory impairments) that required special education. It is also possible that some children with mild sensory disabilities are profiting from technological advances that preclude the need for identification with multiple disabilities.

Medical advances

The number of individuals with multiple disabilities has also increased due to advances in medicine and medical technology. Improved prenatal care, lower infant mortality rates, and early diagnosis and treatment have contributed to the growing number of students with multiple disabilities. Medical advances save lives and thus prolong the lives of those whose functioning is significantly limited by multiple disabilities.

Students with multiple disabilities may be more severely impaired than their peers with single disabilities. For example, a student with blindness and mental retardation would likely demonstrate severe or profound retardation as opposed to mild retardation. A student with serious emotional disturbance and physical disabilities would tend to show more severe problems than a student with only physical disability. Every individual is different, but high expectations and special education help people with multiple disabilities live productive and successful lives.

General Characteristics

Students with medical, physical, and multiple disabilities do not demonstrate a precise set of common characteristics. Their behaviors and characteristics are usually specific to their particular impairments; however, some general cognitive, academic, physical, behavioral, and communication characteristics are relevant. Some of the more frequent characteristics that teachers encounter are summarized in the following sections.

Cognitive

Varieties of placement

The cognitive characteristics of students with medical and physical disabilities depend on their particular diseases or injuries. For example, some physical disabilities are accompanied by mental retardation. Students who have a disorder or injury and mental retardation receive special education services typically received by students with mental retardation. In the same way, students whose illness or injury causes learning disability usually receive learning disability services. An exception occurs when a physical disability is so debilitating that school personnel label a student as orthopedically impaired and place the student with others with similar impairments. School personnel usually make these decisions on the basis of available services and programs.

When a medical or physical condition does not result in retardation, the student usually is classified as orthopedically impaired or other health impaired, depending on the classification process used in the school district. These labels do not identify specific cognitive characteristics. Students with motor or speaking difficulties often have no cognitive impairments, as in the case of cerebral palsy.

Academic

Students with medical, physical, or multiple disabilities are more likely than their neighbors and peers without disabilities to experience academic difficulties. The problems are not always a function of academic skills, but of limited learning opportunities that translate into limited academic achievement. School attendance is a major consideration for some of these students. For example, students with orthopedic impairments may have their school day interrupted by physical and occupational therapy services. Students with other health impairments may not be able to last a full day at school or may miss school for long periods of time. When students' opportunities to participate in class are limited, they may miss academic content and their grades may suffer.

Moreover, medical and educational personnel are becoming concerned about the ways in which allergies and medications affect academic performance. For example, the most commonly prescribed asthma medication is correlated with inattentiveness, hyperactivity, drowsiness, and withdrawn behavior. There is considerable research under way on this topic, but the findings to date do not show a clear relationship between allergies and academic performance or between various medications and academic performance.

Physical

Physical problems are the primary difficulties faced by students with orthopedic handicaps or other health impairments. Their disorders may mean chronic illness, weakness, and pain, or these symptoms may be present only during acute phases. Some students with medical and physical disabilities develop extraordinary physical strength. Witness the outstanding athletic achievements and upper-body strength of many people who are wheelchair users.

Behavioral

There are no specific social or emotional behaviors associated with medical, physical, or multiple disabilities. The social and emotional behaviors evidenced by these students are functions of two factors: the specific nature of the condition and its severity. Reactions of parents and other caregivers as well as teachers and students also influence the social and emotional behaviors they exhibit in school, at home, and in the community.

Any physical disability affects the expectations that parents and others hold for the development of children. Most psychologists agree that the development of healthy social and emotional behaviors depends to a large extent on children's participation in positive interactions with and positive feedback

Limited opportunities to learn

Allergies and medications

Social interactions

from caretakers. Children with medical or physical problems that make them hyperirritable or nonresponsive may not have as many opportunities to interact positively with caretakers.

Effects of motor restrictions

Orthopedic impairments create obviously special problems. Most psychologists recognize the importance of movement in the development of social and emotional behaviors. Young children must move about to learn to be independent and to interact with other young children. Limited motor skills and self-help and self-care skills can limit students' social interactions. Being restricted from social and school activities also can impede the social and emotional development of students with medical disabilities such as heart conditions and cystic fibrosis.

Social development in autism

Disrupted social development is one of the distinctive features of autism. Individuals with autism often repeat verbatim what others say to them or carry on elaborate conversations that have little or nothing to do with their social context; they may exhibit aggressive behaviors, self-injurious behaviors, temper tantrums, and repetitive stereotyped behaviors (such as head rocking and ritualized routines). These behaviors tend to isolate students with autism from their peers, further limiting their social interaction and development.

Low expectations inhibit development

Many students with medical, physical, or multiple disabilities also have limited language and communication skills, which can restrict their social and emotional interactions with others. In addition, these students, like other students with disabilities, have to deal with the attitudes and expectations of others. When those expectations are low, they can inhibit social and emotional development. For example, many students with orthopedic or other health impairments demonstrate atypical or retarded behavior in response to the expectations of those around them. Those who experience chronic pain can develop emotional reactions to the pain. Those who are very ill must deal with the anxiety of death.

Communication

Wide range of communication abilities

The language and communication behaviors associated with medical, physical, and multiple disabilities are open to few generalizations. Think for a moment about the different forms of cerebral palsy and the degrees of severity within them. Many individuals with cerebral palsy have little language involvement; their speech and language skills are normal. Others are unable to communicate through normal channels. They must use special assistive, augmentative, and/or alternative systems to communicate. As an example, some students with cerebral palsy use communication boards (large lap-held or wheelchair-held boards that display letters, words, and symbols) to communicate with others.

Individuals with autism usually develop language very slowly. Many never develop functional speech, and those who do show various disturbances—echolalia (repetition of what has been said to them), saying words or phrases out of context, and voice disorders. They also have poor language comprehension, and difficulty following instructions and answering questions.

Bring Your Learning to Life

Heather Relearns Social Skills

Amy is a speech-language pathologist who works with adolescents and young adults who have sustained head injury. Heather is one of the people with whom Amy works. Heather had brain surgery to relieve seizures, and the surgery was necessarily invasive. We asked Amy the kinds of interventions she uses with Heather. She related that the primary deficit interfering with Heather's return to "normal" daily living is inappropriate social skills. Heather acts very inappropriately in social situations, and her interactions prompt others either to avoid her or to become very angry with her. If Heather believes a person's shoes look bad (and this includes most people's shoes), she tells them in no uncertain terms "Your shoes look like _____." Heather also has a tendency to pick a battle with anyone with whom she disagrees or whose actions she doesn't like. Heather has no friends, and she breaks records in making enemies.

One of the techniques Amy is using in an effort to improve Heather's social skills in verbal interactions is coaching. Amy regularly takes Heather into social settings, such as shopping at the mall and ordering food in a restaurant, where there are ample opportunities for Heather to interact with other people. Recently the two went to the mall. Amy tried on several pairs of shoes and a blouse or two, each time asking Heather what she thought of the appearance of the item. When Heather would tell her precisely what she thought (and there were few items she liked), Amy coached her to express her dislike in tasteful ways. After some training, Heather was at least modeling Amy's comments, making remarks like "I liked the black shoes better" or "The blouse fits too loose," rather than always saying "They look like _____."

At the conclusion of the visit to the mall Amy and Heather visited Mrs. Fields Cookies. Heather asked for a chocolate chip cookie with no nuts. As fate would have it, the young woman at the counter managed to pick up a chocolate chip cookie with nuts. Heather began "blasting" the young lady with comments like "You dumb _____. I said I didn't want any _____ nuts! How stupid can you be?" Amy intervened by saying to Heather "Let's see if you can talk to the lady in a different way that is kind." Heather replied "Oh, yeah that's right," and said softly "Excuse me, ma'am, but I believe I ordered a cookie with no nuts." The woman behind the counter looked confused, but gave Heather a cookie with no nuts.

Not all interventions are academic in nature. Rather, much good education takes place directly in the natural environment with immediate feedback on the correctness of performance. Amy has found that she has to provide Heather with immediate reminders of those instances in which she behaves inappropriately. Waiting causes Heather to forget instances of inappropriateness.

Instructional Approaches and Teaching Tactics

What related services must the school provide?

Based on guidelines established under Part B of the Individuals with Disabilities Education Act (IDEA) and Section 504 of the Rehabilitation Act (see Chapter 3), students with disabilities are entitled to a free, appropriate public education that includes specially designed instruction and related services. For students with medical, physical, and multiple disabilities, the related services are often needed to get them to school and help them stay there during the day and leave when they are ready to go home (Liles, 1993). If the service must be provided by a physician, it is not the school's responsibility. If the service could be provided by a teacher or assistant with minimal training, the school is almost always responsible for providing it. Who provides services between these extremes is generally determined during individualized education program (IEP) planning meetings.

Teacher's role in identification

Most students with medical, physical, or multiple disabilities are identified before school entry. Sometimes, however, the onset of their disabilities occurs during the school years. For these children and their families, teachers become valuable resources in helping to identify orthopedic impairments, other health impairments, or other disabilities. Signs they often recognize include limited energy, frequent absences, poor coordination, frequent accidents, speech or language difficulties, mental lapses, and acute or chronic complaints of pain.

Although some of the problems presented by students with medical, physical, and multiple disabilities can be serious, as a group they represent a relatively small number of students receiving special education. Even so, the chances are good that you will have a student with such a disability in your classroom sometime in your teaching career. Some general tips for teachers of these students are presented in Table 13.4; additional information about instructional approaches and teaching tactics is presented in the following pages.

Asking questions

The first step teachers of students with medical, physical, or multiple disabilities should take is to ask questions to learn about their needs (see Table 13.5). This information should be used to plan instruction and to inform other teachers and students of special considerations that must be taken into account in the classroom. Medical personnel, including the school nurse or the student's physician, can be helpful resources when gathering this information and conveying its essentials to others. Often, older students or siblings want to convey the information; this should be encouraged, but it is a good idea to go over the presentation with the student or sibling before the class hears it to ensure that abilities as well as disabilities are discussed.

Key areas of assistance

Some students with medical, physical, or multiple disabilities may need assistance with their medication while they are at school. Most schools have policies on administration of medication, and teachers should be familiar with them if they are being used to control medical or physical disabilities in one or more of their students. Students experiencing physical symptoms such as paralysis may need to be moved from place to place or positioned to profit from instruction. Others may have seizures and require assistance and care. Again, medical personnel, including physicians, nurses, physical therapists, and occupational therapists, are valuable resources for providing information and training in these areas. Key additional

Table 13.4	Top Ten List of Tips for Teachers of Students with Medical, Physical, and Multiple Disabilities

1. Ask questions about medical and physical needs.
2. Ask questions about ongoing medical and physical interventions (e.g., medications, physical therapy).
3. Learn to recognize signs of medical or physical distress.
4. Communicate information about needs and distress to all class members.
5. Keep classroom and school work areas accessible.
6. Keep work materials accessible and make adaptations when necessary.
7. Modify assignments to accommodate medical and physical needs.
8. Have emergency instructions and telephone numbers readily available.
9. Teach emergency procedures to all class members.
10. Recognize limitations but don't be ruled by them; hold high expectations for *all* students.

Table 13.5	Top Ten List of Questions for Teachers of Students with Medical, Physical, and Multiple Disabilities

1. Does student take medication? How often? How much? At school? Any expected side effects? Any other side effects?
2. When and how does student arrive at school? Any mobility concerns when at school?
3. Does student require assistance relative to classroom transitions? Any special concerns relative to wheelchair, crutches, or other prostheses?
4. Any verbal communication problems? Special communication needs and aids?
5. Any special considerations relative to written communication?
6. Does student require assistance relative to self-care activities (e.g., feeding, dressing, toileting)?
7. Any special equipment relative to self-care?
8. Does the student require positioning aids (e.g., pillows, braces, wedges)?
9. Any positions that are preferred for academic activities? Others?
10. Any other information teachers or other students should have to make educational experiences successful?

Source: Data from W. H. Berdine & A. E. Blackhurst (Eds.). (1985). *An introduction to special education.* Boston: Little, Brown.

areas for teachers of students with medical, physical, and multiple disabilities involve adapting instruction to accommodate individual needs, facilitating communication, and fostering independence.

Adapting Instruction

Removing architectural obstacles

Architectural obstacles that impede instruction for students with medical and physical disabilities should be removed or at least rendered manageable. For example, our friend Kim Bazan ordered a specially designed desk for a student in her room who needed a wheelchair to get around the classroom. Until it arrived, she placed the student's desk on concrete blocks to raise it to a comfortable level. She has also found it helpful to keep the classroom arrangement of desks, work areas, and materials as constant as possible. She tries to notify students of any changes in the physical structure of her room. She places students with physical disabilities at the ends of tables or rows of desks to make movement easier for them. When she teaches students with other health impairments, she becomes familiar with any special equipment or medical needs and periodically checks to be sure the students are safe and being successful at their assigned tasks.

Instructional adaptations required in school for students with medical, physical, and multiple disabilities vary greatly, depending on the type and severity of the individual's impairment. Some students require specialized assistance throughout the day. Others need support during specific activities only. Still others require only minimal adjustments, such as more time to finish an assignment or a modified response form, to be successful. Some common modifications teachers make to help students respond to academic tasks include:

Common adaptations

- Writing in a looseleaf notebook, spiral-bound notebook, or pad of paper, rather than on a single, loose sheet.

- Securing papers to work areas with tape, clipboards, or magnets.

- Limiting response options to single words or multiple-choice items that require minimal writing.

- Placing rubber strips or pads on work materials (rulers, calculators, science equipment) to prevent slipping during use.

- Using writing instruments that require less pressure to produce marks (felt-tip pens, soft lead pencils).

- Adding adaptive devices (rubber bands, plastic wedges, plastic tubing) to writing instruments to make them easier to grip.

- Using word processors, computers, typewriters, and calculators rather than handwriting for responses or calculations.

- Using study buddies in activities that require extensive writing.

Modifications that facilitate reading include book holders; reading stands for use while reclining, sitting, or standing; and automatic page turners that can be operated by people with orthopedic impairments with minimal mobility. Books on tape allow people who cannot hold books to enjoy a wide variety of reading material.

Mavis's Teachers Checked the School for Accessibility

Mavis's disability caused problems with mobility at home and at school. She brought her own wheelchair to school, but a physical therapist helped her teachers conduct an analysis of the school environment to determine its wheelchair accessibility and recommend necessary changes to foster Mavis's integration and success. They used the following questions as guidelines when checking the school for accessibility.

Sidewalks
Are there curb cuts that permit access?
Are they at least 48" wide?
Are they level, without irregular surfaces, bumps, or ridges?

Ramps
Are there ramps with handrails 32" high?
Is the grade of the ramp no more than 1" rise in every 12'?
Is there a nonslip surface present in all types of weather?

Doors
Is the opening at least 32" wide when the door is open?
Are floors level at least 5' in both directions from doors?

Are thresholds low enough (1/2") not to present obstacles?

Toilets
Is a stall available that is 3' wide by 4'8" deep with 33"-high handrails?
Are toilet seats 20" high and urinals 19" from the floor?
Are sinks, towel dispensers, and mirrors 36–40" from the floor?

Water Fountains
Are controls hand operated?
Is the spout in the front of the unit?
Are controls and spout 26–30" from the floor?

They found their school was very accessible, largely due to district implementation of guidelines required for employers established under the Americans with Disabilities Act.

Sources: Guidelines adapted from B. B. Greer, J. Allsop, & J. G. Greer. (1980). Environmental alternatives for the physically handicapped. In J. W. Schifani, R. M. Anderson, & S. J. Odle (Eds.), *Implementing learning in the least restrictive environment.* Austin, TX: PRO-ED.

Facilitating Communication

Communication devices

Some students with medical, physical, or multiple disabilities require special devices to help them communicate. The most common alternative methods for expressive language are communication boards and electronic devices with synthesized speech output. At the "high" end of adaptive technology, students use sophisticated equipment to create synthetic speech that teachers and classmates can readily understand. These electronic speech devices are usually operated by typing on a keyboard, by depressing a switch or key, or by touching a pressure-sensitive area of the device. In other cases, the simplest kind of equipment proves useful: Teachers construct boards with hand-drawn pictures representing specific things that the student needs to communicate. Students use the boards by pointing a finger, fist, or object toward the appropriate symbol. Some students who have restricted use of their hands use a head-mounted pointer or mouthstick to move around the communication board or electronic keyboard. Others use their eyes to localize letters, words, or symbols when communicating, and sometimes special overlays are used in specific content areas—for example, mathematics symbols and elements of the periodic chart for a high school chemistry test. Speech and language pathologists, parents, and medical professionals generally provide training in the use of such devices.

Writing aids

Computers with word processing programs and enhanced keyboards, and adaptive writing aids are used to facilitate written communication. Students with orthopedic impairments that cause muscle weakness, involuntary movements, and poor coordination benefit from hand splints or special pencil holders that help them grasp writing instruments. Sometimes they use slanted boards to support their arms when writing or heavy-weight paper with wide lines to allow extra space for written responses. Computers with keyboard adaptations or voice-activated input are increasingly popular as writing alternatives for students with physical disabilities.

Fostering Independence

A **prosthesis** is an artificial replacement for a missing body part, such as an artificial leg. An **orthosis** is a device that enhances partial functioning of a body part, such as

A prothesis is a device that enables a person with a disability to be independent and more successful in daily life. *Tom McCarthy/ PhotoEdit.*

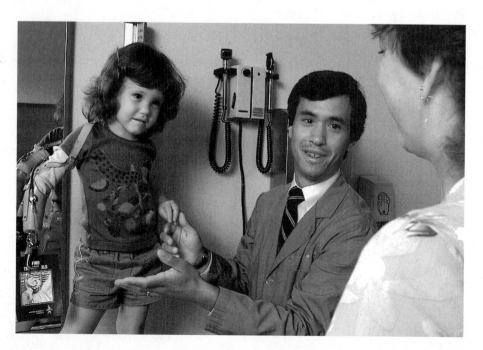

Bring Your Learning to Life

Martin's Teachers Adapted Instructional Activities to Assist Him

Martin's cerebral palsy caused him to have poor motor coordination and inadequate control of his muscles. He had difficulty writing and completing tasks requiring fine motor coordination. Here are some ways his teachers helped him to be successful in their classrooms:

- They taped his writing paper to his desk to keep it from moving if his hand or arm brushed it.
- They attached his pencil to his desk with a string so he could retrieve it more easily if he dropped it or knocked it off his work area.
- They designed many of his assignments so

that he could do them on a computer with a modified keyboard.

- They used a buddy system to get handouts and assignments to his desk.
- They used study buddies to provide him with lecture notes.
- They provided modified test questions that required short answers, true–false answers, or yes–no answers rather than elaborate, full-sentence responses.
- They gave him a little extra time to get ready for classwork, to complete classwork, and to get from one task or class to another.

Devices for daily living

a leg brace. An **adaptive device** for daily living is an ordinary item found in the home, office, or school that has been modified to make it more functional for a person with a disability; an example is a plate with suction cups to hold it to the table and a rim around it to keep the food from being pushed off it. Prostheses, orthoses, and adaptive devices help people become independent and more successful in daily life.

Taking advantage of residual functioning

Students with medical, physical, or multiple disabilities have certain skills and abilities, referred to as **residual functioning,** that should be used to help them become more independent. Prosthetics, orthotics, and adaptive devices often take advantage of this residual functioning. For example, an artificial hand is operated by muscles of the arm, shoulder, or back. A person with lower body paralysis uses his or her arms to get around in a wheelchair. Using residual functioning helps people with disabilities focus on what they can do rather than what they can't do.

Finding the right balance

Students with medical, physical, or multiple disabilities have a wide range of personal and social characteristics that can make them very dependent on others. Effective teachers help them and others see that their disability is just one aspect of their lives. They allow the students to talk about their limitations, but they encourage them to showcase their abilities as well. They use group activities to encourage socialization among students with disabilities and their peers. Like teachers working with students with sensory disabilities, these teachers are aware of the delicate balance that exists between needing special assistance and wanting to be normal. They are concerned with the impressions a student's special learning needs create, and they try to maximize the extent to which a student is treated positively because of them.

Current Trends and Issues

Like all other students, those with medical physical, or multiple disabilities are capable of achievement and deserving of respect. But basic decisions about their lives continue to trouble teachers, parents, and the students themselves.

Home care versus institutions

One basic decision concerns where the students should live—at home with their families or in hospitals or special residential facilities. Hospitals and many residential facilities offer full medical support. Yet most professionals agree that home care is more effective in promoting the child's psychological and emotional health. With the rapid introduction of sophisticated home care technologies, there is no reason to believe that natural home settings cannot be effective in promoting physical health as well.

According to Liles (1993), the effectiveness of home care is influenced by factors within the family, such as the abilities and attitudes of the family members, and factors outside the family, such as the availability of trained personnel and special equipment. "A crucial condition for effective home care is that the family wants the child at home and that it is willing and able to help care for the child or to accept and support a professional, full-time caregiver into the household"(p. 4).

Debate about inclusion

A related issue concerns where the child's schooling should take place. The trend in recent years has been toward greater inclusion of students with medical, physical, and multiple disabilities in regular schools and classrooms. Some critics believe that this practice creates problems because teachers are uncomfortable teaching such students. The critics argue that specialized skills are required to meet medical and physical needs and that the extra time required by some students jeopardizes the instruction being provided to others. They think it is more cost-effective to have special medical equipment centralized, rather than available at every school; they say the expense of making all schools accessible for a few students with medical and physical disabilities is difficult to justify. However, it was not long ago that arguments like these were used to segregate most students with disabilities into separate facilities.

Conditions for successful inclusion

Those who argue in favor of inclusion have helped identify important conditions necessary for it to succeed: (1) that teachers want children with medical, physical, and multiple disabilities at school; (2) that teachers are willing and able to teach and care for children; and (3) that teachers accept support from professionals with relevant expertise.

Barriers to overcome

To provide a free, appropriate public education to students with medical, physical, and multiple disabilities, a number of barriers must still be overcome. These include a lack of funding, a lack of public and staff awareness, inadequate services, inadequate personnel, teachers who don't understand the students' needs, and misinformation about their problems (Lynch, Lewis, & Murphy, 1993). Some strategies for overcoming these barriers are presented in Table 13.6; they can be used to overcome barriers to providing services to any students with disabilities, not just those with chronic health problems.

Table 13.6 Solutions to Barriers Faced by Children with Chronic Health Problems

District-Identified Solutions	Family-Identified Solutions
Change funding procedures to provide incentives for serving students with chronic health problems.	Improve schools in general so all students will benefit from higher-quality education.
Ensure school sites are accessible.	Improve home–school communication.
Designate responsibility for programs for students with chronic health problems.	Allocate funds for educating students with chronic health problems.
Support hiring of school nurses and make other medical personnel available to provide assistance with medical management to teachers and school staff.	Consider modifications in grading policies and procedures that are tailored to needs of students with chronic health problems.
Develop ways to hire teachers on nontraditional contracts to provide assistance after school in homes and hospitals.	Provide full range of service delivery options, including home tutoring and after-school services.
Use technology (e.g., telephone links, closed-circuit television) to provide instruction at home or in hospitals.	Make information on school and community services available to parents, families, and caregivers.
Increase contact with parents and develop resources to support them.	Serve as resource for parents, families, and other caregivers.

Source: Reprinted from "Educational Services for Children with Chronic Illnesses: Perspectives of Educators and Families" by E. W. Lynch, R. B. Lewis and D. S. Murphy, *Exceptional Children,* Vol. 59, pp. 210–220, table 3. Copyright © 1989 The Council for Exceptional Children. Reprinted with permission.

Medical, Physical, and Multiple Disabilities in Perspective

Advice for teachers

There is no magic in meeting the needs of students with medical, physical, or multiple disabilities. What parents say when asked for one piece of advice to teachers is revealing: Treat the child normally, be better informed about the illness and its implications, communicate with parents, remain hopeful, build the child's confidence and self-esteem, and be sensitive to the needs of the whole family (Lynch, Lewis, & Murphy, 1993). This advice is good for teachers of any students.

There is no reason to provide separate education for students with medical, physical, or multiple disabilities. With assistance, they can be successful in the same classrooms as their neighbors and peers. Evidence to support this belief is everywhere:

Examples of successful inclusion

- Although Martin needs some instructional adaptations, he requires very little other assistance during the school day. He has done very well in the traditional academic classes he has taken, and his grades are high enough that he will likely go to the college of his choice.
- Mavis is quick to point out the ribbons she has won at horse shows and to brag about the friends she has at school. She used to have a problem discussing her disability, but you would never know it now.
- Leslie's class took a field trip to a nature center. At first, Leslie was unhappy and wanted to go home because some of the animals were too far back in their cages for her to see. When she sat down on the ground and wouldn't take another step, her friend Karin didn't know what to do. Fortunately, the teacher said it was lunchtime and, as usual, Leslie had to be first in line. Leslie and Karin ate lunch with some other friends under a tall tree. After lunch, Leslie stuck watermelon pits on her cheeks and said she had chicken pox. Karin laughed so much her stomach hurt. On the bus ride home, as she put her head on Karin's shoulder, Leslie yawned, "It was a great trip, wasn't it?" Karin thought Leslie must like having a good friend like her—she knew she was lucky to have a good friend like Leslie.

Keys to success

For students with medical, physical, and multiple disabilities, the keys to success are the same as they are for other people with disabilities: fostering independence, providing supportive learning environments, and increasing communication, socialization, and employment skills; in short, treatment as much like neighbors and peers as possible. Discussing autism in particular, Holmes (1989) put it this way:

> The concept of "as if" is crucial to ensuring that young people are challenged to their full potential. The concept of "as if" is simple: if you treat an adult with autism *as if* he were capable of leading a productive adult life, the chances of him achieving that expectation are greatly improved. On the other hand, if you treat him *as if* he needs constant care, his skills and independence will decline. (p. 257)

This advice can easily be generalized to all people with disabilities (and probably to most without disabilities).

What Every Teacher Should Know

- Students with medical, physical, and multiple disabilities represent a relatively small percentage of students receiving special education.
- Students with medical disabilities include those with impairments related to disease, infections, or other medical problems. Many of these disabilities fall into the federal category of "other health impairments." Special health problems related to alcoholism and drug abuse, although not currently included in the federal categories, can also be considered medical disabilities.
- The terms *medically fragile* and *technology dependent* are being used to describe students who require specialized technological care or equipment for health support during the school day.
- Physical disabilities include orthopedic impairments, traumatic brain injury, and autism.
- Orthopedic impairments are disabilities generally related to mobility and movement. They include certain neurological conditions such as epilepsy and cerebral palsy.
- Traumatic brain injury involves a severe injury to the head or an anatomical abnormality of the brain.
- Autism is a rare disorder affecting multiple areas of functioning, including thought, communication, and behavior.
- The category of multiple disabilities includes people with more than one disability and those who have a primary disability along with secondary conditions.
- Students with medical, physical, or multiple disabilities have educational needs related to their specific conditions. Generally these needs focus on movement, mobility, communication, social development, and management of medical problems.
- Instructional adaptations for students with medical, physical, and multiple disabilities range from simple techniques to sophisticated, high-tech devices. Teachers should be prepared to adapt to students' individual needs.
- With assistance, many students with medical, physical, and multiple disabilities profit from instruction in the same classes as their neighbors and peers.

Projects

1. Find a journal or textbook that focuses on students with medical or physical disabilities. Browse the most recent issues in your library or review the table of contents of the textbook. Note the types of articles that are in-

cluded (for example, research, opinion, practical suggestions) in the journal. Check the references provided with the textbook. Find at least three articles that describe specific teaching activities you could use to help students with other health impairments be successful in your classroom. Find at least three articles that describe specific teaching activities you could use to help students with orthopedic impairments be successful in your classroom.

2. Imagine that you are a teacher with a student with cerebral palsy in your classroom. What decisions would you have to make to help this student be successful? What instructional approaches would be appropriate for working with this student? What specific activities would you use to modify a lesson you were teaching to your class on grammar and proper punctuation?

3. Diagram the content of this chapter and prepare a three-paragraph description of what you know about medical, physical, and multiple disabilities.

4. To help understand how people with medical, physical, and multiple disabilities experience the world, try these simulations and note your reactions to them:

    a. Use a pair of crutches to go between classes; take books, notebooks, and other items you would normally carry with you.

    b. Use a wheelchair to go from the center of your campus to the library. Locate a couple of books about medical and physical disabilities and check them out while still in the wheelchair. Do this without speaking.

    c. Strap one arm behind your back and go through a cafeteria line or make a retail purchase using only sign language.

    d. Have a conversation with a friend avoiding eye contact and repeating every other sentence said to you.

5. Look through the Yellow Pages of your phone book for the name of a physical therapist and/or speech-language pathologist. Contact these individuals and invite them to your class to demonstrate adaptive devices and/or prosthetics and orthotics needed by students with medical or physical disabilities.

6. Observe a professional, other than a teacher, who works with children with medical, physical, or multiple disabilities. Describe what you see and how it relates to classroom instruction.

For Your Information

Books

Aiello, B., & Shulman, J. (1990). *It's your turn at bat.* Breckenridge, CO: Twenty-First Century.

 The "Kids on the Block" puppets tackle cerebral palsy. Excellent for younger readers.

Aiello, B., & Shulman, J. (1992). *Friends for life.* Breckenridge, CO: Twenty-First Century.

The "Kids on the Block" puppets tackle AIDS. Excellent for younger readers.

Batshaw, M. L., & Perret, Y. M. (1992). *Children with disabilities: A medical primer* (3rd ed.). Baltimore, MD: Paul H. Brookes.

 An excellent sourcebook for parents or any professional for information about the medical needs of children with disabilities. Causes and effects, diagnostic and intervention strategies, and general information on how organ systems work (and what can go wrong with them) are described for common disabilities affecting children.

Bigge, J. L. (1989). *Teaching individuals with physical and multiple disabilities* (3rd ed.). Columbus, OH: Merrill.

A comprehensive examination of problems faced by people with physical disabilities, including chapters on assessment, instructional methods, and curriculum components.

Blume, J. (1974). *Deenie*. Minneapolis, MN: Bradbury. Instead of becoming a model, as her mother wishes, Deenie must cope with physical problems and wearing a spinal brace. Excellent book for upper-elementary and junior high school students.

Geralis, E. (Ed.). (1991). *Children with cerebral palsy*. Rockville, MD: Woodbine House.

Excellent resource for parents and others who want to learn about cerebral palsy. Includes chapters on diagnosis, assessment, treatment, early intervention, and family life, as well as an excellent resource guide with descriptions for national and state organizations providing support and additional information.

Greenfield, J. (1972). *A child called Noah*. New York: Harcourt Brace Jovanovich.

In 1969, *Life* published Josh Greenfield's account of life with his son, Noah. This book, although dated, is an excellent chronicle of five years of life with a child who would grow older but "not grow up" and for whom no cure was available.

Hart, C. A. (1993). *A parent's guide to autism*. New York: Pocket Books.

This is a well-written resource describing symptoms and types of autism, possible causes, therapy options, treatment alternatives, and other important information for parents and other professionals.

Hermes, P. (1991). *What if they knew?* New York: Harcourt.

Jeremy has epilepsy and must adjust to living with his grandparents. Excellent book for upper-elementary school students.

Howard, E. (1989). *Edith, herself*. New York: Macmillan.

At the turn of the century, Edith is sent to live with her married sister when their mother dies. Her life there is complicated by epileptic seizures. Excellent

book for upper-elementary and junior high school students.

Knowles, A. (1983). *Under the shadow*. New York: Harper.

Cathy becomes friendly with a boy who has muscular dystrophy. Excellent book for upper-elementary and junior high school students.

Krementz, J. (1992). *How it feels to live with a physical disability*. New York: Simon & Schuster.

Twelve stories of children aged 6–16 with medical and physical disabilities, with photographs illustrating aspects of daily living in extremely positive ways.

Martin, A. M. (1984). *Inside out*. New York: Holiday.

Jonno's younger brother, John, has autism. Excellent book for upper-elementary and middle school students.

Powers, M. D. (Ed.). (1989). *Children with autism: A parent's guide*. Rockville, MD: Woodbine House.

Recommended as a first book on autism for parents and families. Up-to-date information about diagnosis, treatment, daily living, education, and legal rights.

Reisner, H. (Ed.). (1993). *Children with epilepsy: A parents' guide*. Rockville, MD: Woodbine House.

Excellent resource for learning about epilepsy. Up-to-date information about assessment, medical treatment, daily living, and education.

Roberts, W. D. (1987). *Sugar isn't everything*. New York: Macmillan.

A story that presents the facts about diabetes for young readers. Excellent book for upper-elementary school students.

Rosenberg, M. B. (1983). *My friend Leslie*. New York: Lothrop, Lee, & Shepard.

A child's description and sensitive portrait of her friend with multiple disabilities and their first year at school. This book addresses many questions and feelings that are likely to spring up when children and adults meet a person with a disability for the first time.

Roy, R. (1982). *Where's Buddy?* Boston: Houghton Mifflin.

Mike must take care of his diabetic brother. Excellent book for elementary school students.

Slote, A. (1973). *Hang tough, Paul Mather*. New York: Harper.

Candidly and without sentimentality, Paul recalls from his hospital bed the details of his struggle with leukemia.

Umbreit, J. (Ed.). (1983). *Physical disabilities and health impairments: An introduction.* Columbus, OH: Merrill.

An overview with information on cause, treatment, prognosis, and educational implications of medical and physical disabilities.

Ylvisaker, M. (Ed.). (1985). *Head injury rehabilitation: Children and adolescents.* San Diego, CA: College-Hill Press.

An overview with information on cause, treatment, prognosis, and educational implications of head injuries.

Organizations

Autism Society of America (ASA)

The Autism Society of America (ASA) is a national organization of parents and professionals that was established to promote better understanding of autism, to encourage development of services, to support research, and to advocate on behalf of people with autism and their families. ASA provides information and referral services and publishes the *Advocate,* a bimonthly newsletter. For more information, contact ASA, 8601 Georgia Ave., Suite 503, Silver Spring, MD 20901.

Division for Physical and Health Disabilities (DPHD)

A division of the Council for Exceptional Children (CEC), formally affiliated in 1958, DPHD promotes quality programs for individuals with physical and/or health impairments. DPHD has about seventeen hundred members and provides outlets for the exchange of ideas through a variety of resources (*Physical Disabilities—Education and Related Services*), including a professional newsletter (*DPH Newletter*). For more information, contact CEC, 1920 Association Dr., Reston, VA 22091.

National Head Injury Foundation (NHIF)

The National Head Injury Foundation (NHIF) is a membership organization founded in 1980 by the parent of a person with a severe traumatic brain injury (TBI). Its mission is to improve the quality of life for persons with traumatic brain injury and their families and to promote the prevention of traumatic brain injury. Since its inception, the NHIF has grown to forty-four state associations with many support groups. It is the country's leading source for informational materials on traumatic brain injury. Members receive a quarterly NHIF newsletter as an update on association news, educational seminars, legislative efforts, the latest research, innovative community programs, international news, and NHIF events. For more information, contact NHIF, 1776 Massachusetts Ave., NW, Suite 100, Washington, DC 20036.

Organizations for Specific Impairments

American Cancer Society, 1599 Clifton Rd., Atlanta, GA 30329; (404) 320-3333.

American Diabetes Association, P. O. Box 25757, Alexandria, VA 22313; (703) 549-1500.

Arthritis Foundation, 1314 Spring St., NW, Atlanta, GA 30309; (404) 872-7100.

Association of Birth Defect Children, 3526 Emerywood Lane, Orlando, FL 32812; (407) 859-2821.

Epilepsy Foundation of America, 4351 Garden City Dr., Landover, MD 20785; (301) 459-3700.

Muscular Dystrophy Association, 810 Seventh Ave., New York, NY 10019; (212) 586-0808.

National Association for Developmental Disabilities Council, Suite 103, 1234 Massachusetts Ave., NW, Washington, DC 20005; (202) 347-1234.

National Association for People with AIDS, 2025 I St., Suite 415, Washington, DC 20006; (202) 429-2437.

National Center for Zero to Three, 2000 14th St. N, Suite 380, Arlington, VA 22201; (703) 528-4300.

National Foundation for Asthma, P. O. Box 300069, Tucson, AZ 85751; (602) 323-6046.

National Information Clearinghouse for Infants with Disabilities and Life-Threatening Conditions, Center for Developmental Disabilities, University of South Carolina, Bensen Bldg., 1st Floor, Columbia, SC 29208; (803) 774-4435.

National Multiple Sclerosis Society, 205 E. 42nd St., New York, NY 10017; (212) 986-3240.

National Society for Children and Adults with Autism, 621 Central Ave., Albany, NY 12206; (518) 459-1418.

Office for Developmental Disabilities Services, Health and Human Services, 349F Hubert H. Humphrey Bldg., 200 Independence Ave., SW, Washington, DC 20201; (202) 279-6085.

United Cerebral Palsy Association, 66 E. 34th St., New York, NY 10016; (212) 481-6300.

Journals

American Journal of Diseases of Children (AJDC)

AJDC provides information for physicians and other caregivers on current research developments and clinical findings on pediatric problems likely to occur in day-to-day practice. For more information, contact Editor, AJDC, American Medical Association, 536 N. Dearborn St., Chicago, IL 60610.

American Journal of Occupational Therapy (AJOT)

This journal provides articles that describe research-based program evaluations, program descriptions, and other research-oriented activities of interest to occupational therapists and teachers working with students with physical disabilities. Articles published in AJOT are intended to further the knowledge base and to improve the lives of people with physical disabilities. For more information, contact Elaine Viseltear, AJOT, 1383 Picard Dr., #301, Rockville, MD 20850-4316.

Archives of Physical Medicine and Rehabilitation (APMR)

This is the official journal of the American Congress of Rehabilitation Medicine and the American Academy of Physical Medicine and Rehabilitation. Its purpose is to publish reports of original research and clinical experience in physical medicine and rehabilitation, and diagnosis, therapy, and the delivery of rehabilitation care. For more information, contact James S. Lieberman, Editor-in-Chief, APMR, Suite 1310, 78 E. Adams St., Chicago, IL 60603-6103.

Brain Injury (BI)

All aspects of brain injury, including basic scientific research, causes, medical procedures, assessment methods, and rehabilitation interventions, are covered by BI. For more information, contact Henry H. Stonnington, Medical College of Virginia Hospitals, Virginia Commonwealth University, P. O. Box 677, Richmond, VA 23298.

Developmental Medicine and Child Neurology (DMCN)

This journal contains research articles and opinion papers of broad interest to those working with people with medical, physical, or multiple disabilities. It was formerly known as the *Cerebral Palsy Bulletin*. For more information, contact Editor, DMCN, Blackwell Scientific Publications, Osney Mead, Oxford, England OX2 0EL.

Journal of Autism and Developmental Disorders (JADD)

Devoted to all severe psychopathologies of childhood, JADD is not necessarily limited to autism and childhood schizophrenia. Experimental studies on the biochemical, neurological, and genetic aspects of disorders; implications of normal development for deviant processes; interactions between disordered behavior and social or group factors; research and cases studies on interventions; and studies related to diagnostic concerns fall within the scope of JADD. For more information, contact Eric Schopler, Editor, JADD, Department of Psychiatry, CB 7180 Medical School Wing E, School of Medicine, University of North Carolina, Chapel Hill, NC 27599.

Journal of Head Trauma Rehabilitation (JHTR)

Information on clinical management and rehabilitation of people with head injuries is included in this publication. Its contents are prepared for use by practicing professionals. For more information, contact Editor, JHTR, Aspen Systems Corp., 7201 McKinney Circle, P. O. Box 990, Frederick, MD 21701.

Physical and Occupational Therapy in Pediatrics (POTP)

This publication is designed for physical therapy and occupation therapy pediatric professionals working in hospitals, rehabilitation centers, schools, community settings, and health and human service agencies. It provides the latest clinical research and practical applications for professionals concerned with the physical and occupational needs of people with disabilities. For more information, contact Suzanne K. Campbell, Editor, POTP, Department of Medical Allied Health Professions, University of North Carolina, Medical Wing C221 H, Chapel Hill, NC 27514.

Rehabilitation Literature (RL)

This review and abstracting journal covers care, welfare, education, and employment of people with disabilities. Research papers, opinion pieces, and book reviews are among the typical contents. Most of the material in RL has broad applicability for professionals working in medical and allied health professions as well as schools and other community agencies. For more information, contact Stephen J. Regnier, Editor, RL, 70 E. Lake St., Chicago, IL 60601.

IV

Community and Professional Issues in Special Education

The first three parts of this book have provided an introduction to special education in today's classrooms. But for a full understanding of special education, it's important to look beyond the classroom to the broader educational, social, and political context. That is the purpose of Part IV.

Chapter 14 considers life-stage and community issues. Transition is one critical topic—how we help students progress from one stage of life to another, particularly from school to adulthood. Since many students need educational services before they reach school age, early intervention is another important subject. Chapter 14 also discusses the ways in which teachers can work with parents, families, and other professionals in the community to ensure that students receive the most effective services.

Chapter 15 broadens the perspective even further, placing special education in the context of long-term social, political, economic, and educational trends. We illustrate the influence of changing social values and economic factors. We show how the resources and priorities of special education are determined by shifts in public policy and by the actions of advocacy groups. Finally, we summarize the impact of current school reform movements, including the attempt to achieve national education goals. We hope that reflecting on such issues will help you become a full-fledged professional, ready to take an active and informed part in the educational process.

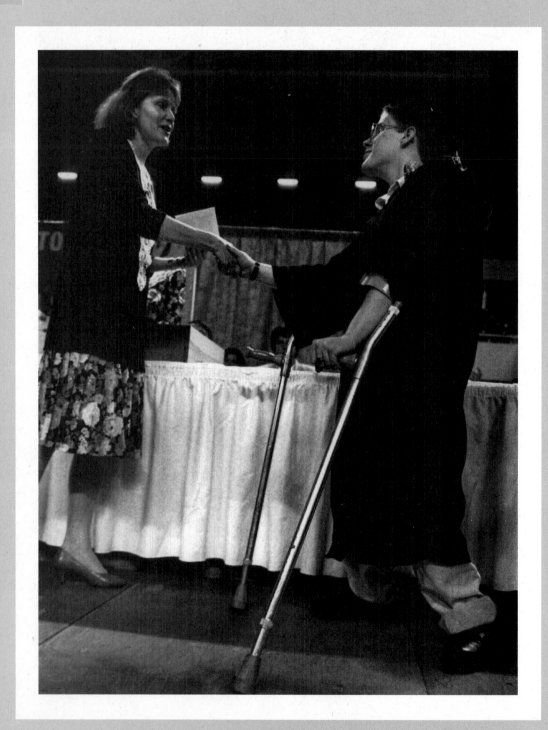

The Wider Context: Life Stages, Families, and Collaboration with Other Professionals

- What kinds of services are provided to children with disabilities and their families before they enter school?

- How do home-based and center-based programs differ?

- Does early intervention help alleviate later problems?

- What considerations do professionals need to take into account to help young children with disabilities make a smooth transition into school?

- How do students with disabilities exit school? How many drop out? How many graduate?

- What kinds of employment do individuals with disabilities achieve?

- What are the kinds of community living arrangements in which individuals with disabilities live?

- How can educators work with parents, businesses, and community agencies to enhance outcomes for students with disabilities?

Fred, a 1991 high school graduate, was born with developmental disabilities. There were no early childhood special education services in the early 1970s, but Fred's mother identified a teacher who was willing to provide preschool enrichment experiences to Fred for two hours a day three days a week. Fred attended self-contained special education classes during his school years but was mainstreamed for art and physical education. He also attended some vocational classes.

Transition planning for Fred began two years before he was to leave high school. By that time he had a county developmental disability social worker and a counselor from the state department of vocational rehabilitation services. He spent part of each school day at the county technical college, working on vocational skills in the technical center. Fred received training in the food industry careers program, where students learn food preparation, busing, dishwashing, and cleaning skills. This program helped provide him with the background necessary to find a job in his community.

As Fred's story illustrates, disabilities do not start and end when students enter and leave school. Besides, students with disabilities spend only about 20 percent of a twenty-four-hour day in school. If these statements were not true, we could probably end the textbook here. We'd assume that what students learn is a function of what we do to them in school. Instead, in this chapter we address some of the most exciting issues about working with students with disabilities: "life-stage" issues—early intervention and transition—and collaboration—working with parents, families and with other professionals. In short, we talk about aspects of the larger context of students' lives outside school that interact with and influence the actual instruction of those students. If you are going to be a teacher, you will have to give consideration to early intervention, transition, working with parents, and working with the broader educational community.

Importance of early experience

Educators and developmental psychologists recognize the importance of early development and early experience to later life success. In the first part of this chapter we describe the kinds of efforts now underway to intervene early in children's lives in an effort to prevent later school difficulties. We address the importance of such early intervention, especially in light of the major demographic changes taking place in society.

Planning for transition

In an age in which Americans plan everything, it should not be surprising to learn that major considerations are being given to planning for the successful transition of youngsters from home to school, and the transition of adolescents with disabilities from school to work. Much consideration is given to provision of skills that will enable students with disabilities to get jobs, to function in society, and generally to improve the quality of their lives. In the second part of this chapter we address the many transitions that students with disabilities must make during their lives.

Empowering parents

Parent and family involvement not only is a legal imperative, but also makes good sense. Over the past fifteen years or so, educators have talked a great deal about empowering parents and involving them in their children's educational programs. Very recently we have seen major efforts to make this happen, so we devote a section of this chapter to involving parents and to major considerations in working with them. It is also recognized that schools and school personnel cannot meet all of the challenges now confronting them without close working relationships with business and community leaders, and personnel

Collaboration

from community agencies and services. We describe current efforts to work in a collaborative manner to meet the concerns and challenges of the day.

Early Childhood Intervention

Our friend Kim Bazan recently told us an interesting story. It seems one of the kindergarten teachers in her school was finding that many of the students entering her class already had mastered the content she was prepared to present. Checking with some of the parents, she discovered that the local preschool programs had adopted a "firm stance on academics" in response to parents' requests that they better prepare children for kindergarten. The kindergarten teacher was considering restructuring the academic year in response to this new population of students with well-developed skills.

Rising numbers in preschool

By 1992, more than half of children ages 3 to 5 in the United States were enrolled in nursery school or kindergarten classes. The total number of children in preschool programs has risen steadily since 1970 and currently totals more than 6.5 million (U.S. Department of Education, 1993). By and large, these students are better prepared for school and much more advanced academically than students who started school five to ten years ago.

Greater need for early intervention

At the same time that there are more preschool programs, there are more students in need of the programs. Fetal alcohol syndrome and alcohol-related birth defects are on the rise. Babies born with AIDS are increasing in number each year. So are babies with medical problems resulting from their mothers' addiction to cocaine. Medically fragile infants are surviving through extraordinary medical interventions to face life with significant mental and physical impairments. Even children born healthy face the possibility of poverty, homelessness, or physical abuse. It is argued that we ought to intervene early in the lives of children to prevent later problems and to enable them to enter school ready to learn. As you will learn in Chapter 15, the first national educational goal is that by the year 2000, all children will start school ready to learn.

Federal laws and incentives

In 1968 the Handicapped Children's Early Education Assistance Act (Public Law 90–538) was passed. It was the first law that provided federal funds for in-

There are no boundaries on who can provide special education or where it can be provided. *Gaye Hilsenrath/ The Picture Cube, Inc.*

novative programs for preschool children with disabilities. By 1973 Head Start and other federally funded programs were required to keep at least 10 percent of their spaces available for children with disabilities. Public Law 94–142 mandated services for three- to five-year-olds by 1980, where state law already provided services for nondisabled children in that age group. It also provided incentive grants to states for improving early childhood special education programs.

In 1984, Public Law 98–199 made funds available to states to develop comprehensive services for children with special needs from birth to age 5. Two years later, then-President Reagan signed into law the Amendments to the Education for All Handicapped Children Act (Public Law 99–457). This legislation expanded services to children with disabilities who are under age 5. It mandated that schools must have on file for each preschool child with a disability an individualized family service plan (IFSP). As noted in Chapter 3, the IFSP is a kind of IEP (individualized education program) for young children.

The IFSP

Public Law 99–457 authorized the distribution of federal funds to help states provide special education to very young children and guaranteed a free, appropriate education to all preschoolers with disabilities. This public law also made special education for young children with disabilities compulsory, and parents became an important part of its educational program.

Direct and indirect services

Settings for early intervention programs differ, and the nature of services provided in the settings is diverse. When the services are provided to the child, they are called *direct services*, as we noted in Chapter 2; when they are provided to another person such as a parent who in turn serves the child, they are called *indirect services*. In the Window on Practice we list the diverse kinds of services provided to young children and their families in the Minneapolis Public Schools.

Window on Practice

Early Childhood Special Education Services in the Minneapolis Public Schools

The Minneapolis school system provides an example of the wide variety of early childhood special education (ECSE) services. The following services are provided in the Minneapolis Public Schools to children ages birth to 6.

Screening: Parents who have concerns about their child call the Minneapolis Department of Health (for children birth to 3-1/2) or the Minneapolis Public Schools (for children 3-1/2 to 6 years of age). School or health department personnel administer a brief screening test.

Evaluation: If the screening test indicates a need, a more extensive educational evaluation is conducted in the child's home, day care center, or school.

Sharing Meeting: Preschool educational services personnel meet with parents, share evaluation information, and develop a plan for meeting the child's need.

Service: Services for children birth to 3 may include home-based instruction, hospital-based instruction, consultation with caregivers in child care centers, ECSE play groups, parent support and education groups, and/or consultation with specialists. Services for students who are 3 and 4 years of age may include a school program for two to five half-days per week; ECSE services; family support and education; and direct or indirect services of speech and language clinicians, school nurses, occupational therapists, vision and hearing specialists, and physical therapists.

The diversity of services is illustrated in the following brief descriptions of programs at schools and community settings in Minneapolis. Note the efforts made to provide ECSE services to students with disabilities in settings with their nondisabled peers.

Anne Sullivan School: Children with hearing impairments and children with other developmental delays are given opportunities to participate with nondisabled kindergarten and first-grade students for physical education and story activities. Older students in this school often come to the ECSE class to serve as cross-age peers and work with the young children with disabilities.

Andersen Open School: Two ECSE teachers team-teach a class of ECSE students. A High Five program (preschool for five-year-olds) adjoins the ECSE room. Some activities are carried out jointly between the two classes.

Anwatin Early Childhood Center: Three- and 4-year-old students with disabilities come to this center from three to seven and a half hours per week. They work along with High Five students, kindergarten, and first- and second-graders. The goal is to develop and expand relationships among children through opportunities offered in physical education, guided play, meal times, and outdoor experiences.

Audubon Early Childhood Center: This center combines concepts of the neighborhood learning center, a full inclusion model, and a partnership with Head Start–Parents in Community Action. Students with early childhood special needs are placed in Head Start or High Five classrooms with public school and Head Start teachers. An ECSE licensed resource teacher provides direct and indirect services to children in these classrooms. Volunteer readers, puppet shows, and other activities in other classrooms give the youngsters opportunities to learn with typically developing children. Ratios do not exceed three special education students to seventeen regular education students.

Bethune School: There are two ECSE classrooms in this building, and they are team-taught. Children are integrated with existing kindergarten classes on an individual basis. Elementary students tutor and/or socialize regularly with ECSE students.

Four Winds School: The school houses an ECSE program in which young children are

(continued on next page)

Window on Practice

Early Childhood Special Education Services in the Minneapolis Public Schools *(continued)*

given opportunities to be integrated into activities in a High Five or kindergarten program.

Longfellow Early Childhood Center: This is a special center offering programs to students with ECSE needs from birth. Some of the services are provided in homes, some in hospitals, and others at community day care or preschool programs. The building houses four classes for three- and four-year-olds, and a young-three-year-old class. Students in these classes are integrated for socialization and language activities with High Five, kindergarten, and first-grade classes.

McKnight Early Education Center: This program is located in the Head Start building. High Five classes, ECSE classes, early child-

hood family education, and kindergarten are provided. Head Start, day care, and a program for homeless children are provided in the same location.

Pillsbury Math/Science Technology School: This school includes an ECSE class, and students are integrated on an individualized basis to participate in social and instructional activities with kindergarten children. First- and second-grade students participate weekly in a "Special Friends" project in the ECSE classroom.

Community Preschools: ECSE resource teachers provide direct and indirect services to students with disabilities placed in private preschools around the city.

Home-based programs

Some of the programs are **home based,** especially for very young (birth to 3) children. When this is the case, school personnel visit the home regularly either to provide direct services or to educate parents who in turn educate the young children. In some home-based programs, the visits occur weekly and are designed primarily to improve the parents' skills in working with their child. The type of service depends on the type of disability and the willingness of the parents to teach their child. Parents also receive indirect services in some home-based programs. Specially trained teachers make recommendations for training, organize groups of parents with similar concerns, and help parents monitor the progress of the intervention they are providing.

Hospital-based programs

Center-based programs

In other instances the programs are **hospital based** or **center based.** In hospital settings, the services may be provided directly to the child or to hospital personnel who work with the child. In center-based programs, parents bring their child to a center for direct or indirect services. The center may be at a hospital, school, day care center, clinic, or other facility. Once there, parents may work with their child under the guidance of specially trained professionals, or they may observe others working with their child. In some center-based programs, groups of parents meet to share concerns and provide support for one another. Other centers are organized primarily as referral sources for services available locally.

Advantages and disadvantages

For students who do not need to be hospitalized, the choice is between home-based and center-based intervention programs, both of which have advantages and disadvantages. At home, the child learns in a natural environment surrounded by family members who often can spend more time working with the child at home than they can at a center. Problems associated with transportation, care of other children, and general family disruption are minimized when special education is carried out at home. Home-based programs, however, have several disadvantages: Their success depends heavily on the parents' cooperation, children from poor homes or homes where both parents work are less likely to receive special education at home, and being at home limits opportunities for interaction with other adults and children.

A center-based approach provides varied types of help at a central location. Professionals from several disciplines (medicine, psychology, occupational therapy, speech and language pathology, and education) work together to assess and teach the child. The program benefits from periodic meetings to discuss progress and plan future interventions. The disadvantages of center-based intervention include the time and expense of transportation, the cost of maintaining a center, and the likelihood of less parent involvement.

Regardless of which approach is taken (and many professionals combine them), the curriculum generally is the same. We teach young children with disabilities to improve their language, motor, self-help, communication, preacademic, and cognitive skills. We also try to improve their self-concepts, creativity, motivation to succeed, and general readiness for social interaction in school.

JDRP

Table 14.1 lists and describes selected early intervention programs that have been approved by the Joint Dissemination and Review Panel of the National Diffusion Network, a federal panel that reviews project results and indicates which projects are effective enough to warrant replication and dissemination. The table indicates how the services are organized (center based, home based, parent training), the ages of preschool children served, and brief descriptions of the programs.

A generation ago, parents of preschool children with disabilities were offered very little help. Today, public special education is available for individuals from birth to age 21, and early childhood programs make up a rapidly growing area in special education.

Does Early Intervention Help?

Cost-effectiveness

Policy reports have regularly noted the cost-effectiveness and cost benefits derived from early intervention. For example, in 1991 the Committee for Economic Development stated:

> Quality preschool programs clearly provide one of the most cost-effective strategies for lowering the dropout rate and helping at-risk children to become more effective learners and productive citizens. It has been shown that for every $1 spent on a comprehensive and intensive preschool program for the disadvantaged, society saves up to $6 in the long-term costs of welfare, remedial education, teen pregnancy, and crime. (p. 28)

Table 14.1	Selected Early Intervention Projects Approved by the Joint Dissemination and Review Panel		
Project Name and Location	**Organization of Services**	**Ages**	**Description**
Cognitively Oriented Pre-Primary Experience (COPE), Devon, PA	Pre-primary curriculum/behavior-management program for preschoolers with varied learning needs.	3–6 years developmentally; pre-kindergarten, kindergarten, and early 1st grade.	Diagnostic/prescriptive. Curriculum based on assessment of skills and development at entry. Objectives pursued through individualized, small-group, and large-group instruction as well as free-inquiry situations. Teachers, paraprofessionals, and parents attend COPE workshop to learn how to use and integrate curriculum materials.
Early Prevention of School Failure (EPSF), Peotone, IL	Assessment program designed to prevent school failure and to identify developmental levels and learning styles.	4–6 years	Identifies child's developmental level in language, auditory, visual/motor areas, and learning style. Norm-referenced assessment instruments and observational procedures are used to create a portfolio of at-risk students. Literature-based reading and writing program, themes and unity, higher process thinking activities, and steps for teacher-directed instruction are applied strategically.
Family Oriented Structured Preschool Activity (FOSPA) ("Seton Hall" Program), St. Cloud, MN	A home- and center-based program for parents of preschoolers. Two hours once a week during the year before kindergarten entry.	Preschool–3 years	Program designed to train parents about child's developmental needs. Learning stations, classroom observation (formal and informal teacher/student interaction), and discussion groups are employed. Take-home activity kits to promote parent/child interaction.

(continued on next page)

Table 14.1	Selected Early Intervention Projects Approved by the Joint Dissemination and Review Panel *(continued)*		
Project Name and Location	**Organization of Services**	**Ages**	**Description**
High/Scope Preschool Curriculum, Ypsilanti, MI	Center-based intervention program based on application of the principles of Jean Piaget, a French psychologist.	Preschool children of all abilities	Needs/interests of child assessed. Teachers support children's decision making and problem solving. Room arrangement/schedule designed to stimulate active learning. Goal to develop physical, language, and thinking skills.
Kindergarten Integrated Thematic Experiences (KITE), San Francisco, CA	Center-based program for kindergarten–regular and academically disadvantaged students.	Kindergarten	Emphasizes cognitive, language, physical, and social-emotional development through interactive large- and small-group activities, both teacher-directed and child-initiated. Stimulates interest through game-like presentation and thematic approach. Can be implemented by teacher, whole school, or district.
Mother–Child Home Program (MCHP) of Verbal Interaction Project, Inc., Wantagh, NY	Home-based program to prevent educational disadvantage in children of low income/limited education parents.	2–4 years	Promotes cognitive and social-emotional health through positive play curriculum for parents and children. Twice-weekly demonstrations by instructors in home. Weekly guide sheets outline curriculum.
On the Way to SUCCESS in Reading and Writing with Early Prevention of School Failure (EPSF), Peotone, IL	Follow-up program designed to address special preacademic needs of K–2 students.	Post-kindergarten and 1st grade	Instruction/curriculum supplements regular classroom program. Direct instruction given daily for 20–30 minutes. Developmentally sequenced learning objectives form basis of curriculum. Parental involvement included.

(continued on next page)

Table 14.1 Selected Early Intervention Projects Approved by the Joint Dissemination and Review Panel *(continued)*

Project Name and Location	Organization of Services	Ages	Description
Parents as Teachers, St. Louis, MO	Home- and center-based parent/guardian education program.	Pre-birth (3rd trimester)–3 years	Primary prevention program, parent educators teach curriculum to families, regular home visits, group meetings, screening of child's development, access to parent resource center. Services offered through school district.
P.I.A.G.E.T. (Promoting Intellectual Adaptation Given Experiential Transforming) Project, Bethlehem, PA	Home- and center-based program for bilingual preschool children whose native language is Spanish.	Preschool and kindergarten	Diagnosis/prescription. Piagetian derived teaching strategies, parent education (to reinforce teaching strategies at home), and academic assessment of skills used to develop English language skills. Must include bilingual/bicultural professional/paraprofessional staffing.
Portage Project, Portage, WI	A home-based intervention program for children with disabilities and their families.	Birth–6 years	Home teacher works with parent on a regular basis to choose child's goals and plan how to teach developmental skills. Can also be used in connection with classroom. Instructional materials prepared and available for purchase.
INSITE Model, Logan, UT	Home-based program to identify multidisabled children with sensory impairment.	Birth–5 years	Identification and screening, direct services, support services, and a program management system are used to assist parents and their multidisabled children. Goals for the child include: achievement of meaningful interaction with other persons in the home, development of effective communication system, and acquisition of the highest level of independence possible.

(continued on next page)

Table 14.1   Selected Early Intervention Projects Approved by the
Joint Dissemination and Review Panel *(continued)*

Project Name and Location	Organization of Services	Ages	Description
Multi-Agency Project for Pre-Schoolers (MAPPS)	Home- and center-based intervention program for infants and preschool children with disabilities.	Birth–5 years	Curriculum and monitoring system for receptive and expressive language, motor development, self-help, preacademic skills, and social-emotional development.
Programming for Early Education of CHildren with Disabilities (PEECH), Champaign, IL	Center-based educational program for children with mild to moderate disabilities.	3–5 years	Individualized educational program designed on the basis of ongoing assessment. Teaching, learning environment, behavioral management, and family involvement are tailored to fit specific needs. Coordinator conducts training sessions with individual states to certify trainers.
SKI-HI Outreach, Logan, UT	A home-based diagnostic and intervention program.	Birth–5 years	Screening, audiological, diagnostic assessment services suitable for state or regional service. Curriculum for home program for hearing aid, communication, auditory, total communication, and language. Psychological, emotional, and child-development support provided for parents in home.
Early Recognition Intervention Network (ERIN), Dedham, MA	Curriculum/assessment to use for home- or center-based individual instruction.	3–7 years	Teaching adult organizes material and environment to meet individual child goals. Self-help/developmental concept and academic readiness curriculum suggests home and classroom modifications.

(continued on next page)

Table 14.1			Selected Early Intervention Projects Approved by the Joint Dissemination and Review Panel *(continued)*

Project Name and Location	Organization of Services	Ages	Description
Regional Program for Preschool Handicapped Children, Yorktown Heights, NY	A home- and center-based cooperative intervention program for children with disabilities.	3–5 years	Diagnostic/prescriptive teaching and intervention provided by teacher, teacher aides, and clinical team members. Transdisciplinary team shares in assessment, intervention, and consultation. Parent Involvement Model, volunteers, and group meetings to increase parent participation.

Source: National Diffusion Network. (1994). *Educational programs that work: Catalogue of the National Diffusion Network* (20th ed.). Longmont, CO: Sopris West. Used with permission.

Evaluations of Head Start

Head Start is the most widely publicized and publicly recognized early intervention for children. It is designed to be used with those who are economically disadvantaged. In a recent study of the extent to which Head Start helped children, Lee, Schnur, and Brooks-Gunn (1988) demonstrated that children who participated in Head Start showed significant short-term gains but were still behind their peers in absolute cognitive levels after a year in the program.

Haskins (1989) wrote a cautionary paper arguing that research has shown that model preschool programs and Head Start have an immediate impact on the cognitive test scores and social development of students, but that the gains diminish over the first few years of public schooling. He argues that "There is limited but provocative evidence that model programs may have positive effects on life success measures such as teen pregnancy, delinquency, welfare use, and employment, but there is virtually no evidence linking Head Start attendance with any of these variables" (p. 274). It may be very difficult to demonstrate direct links between preschool intervention and later life success, because it would be necessary to follow students for twenty or more years to answer the necessary cost-benefit questions. Most people would rather err in the direction of providing unnecessary yet nonharmful services than wait twenty years for evidence that the services had a beneficial effect.

Ypsilanti project

One of the most extensive evaluations of early childhood services was performed by analyzing the effects of the Ypsilanti Perry Preschool Project, a service for economically disadvantaged 3- and 4-year-old children in Ypsilanti, Michigan. It was shown that a substantial proportion of the costs for providing preschool services was recovered because children did not need such extensive special education support once they entered school. In addition, none of the graduates of the Perry Preschool Project required institutional placement. Perry preschool graduates were also shown to have higher projected lifetime earnings than similar children who did not receive the services. The evaluation showed that early intervention resulted in a savings per child of $14,819. Berrueta-Clement, Schweinhart, Barnett, Epstein, and Weikart (1984) reported that this amounted to a 243 percent return on original dollar investment.

Transition

Life is a series of transitions. People make the transitions from one class to another while in school and survive the transition between childhood and adulthood known as adolescence. People also move from one location to another, from one type of relationship to another, or from student life to work life. These transitions, although often stressful, are made without much difficulty by most persons. In the 1980s, however, professionals joined parents in realizing that not all individuals make transitions easily. This realization led to an emphasis on the transition process and the difficulties many individuals with disabilities had in successfully accomplishing transitions. Special efforts were deemed necessary to successfully "transition" the individual with special needs.

Types of transition

The transition from school to adulthood has received considerable attention from special educators. Schools are required by law to have transition plans for students with disabilities. The transition plans are for movement from school to work or other postschool environments. Moreover, individuals with disabilities make other critical transitions. For example, they must accomplish the transition from home into school in the first place and then negotiate numerous transitions within school. There are transitions from one grade level or type of school to the next, and unique transitions such as those from one type of school placement to another, one school to another, general to special education settings, and special to general education settings.

Transition into School

The first school-related transition of a young child is the transition from preschool into a formal K through 12 educational system. An important consideration at this time of transition is whether labels should be assigned to students with disabilities.

Should students be labeled?

It is not necessary to label students "disabled" to allow them to attend a preschool program for students with disabilities. Yet often the attendance in the program is a form of labeling. One of the authors of this text has had the experience of sitting in a teachers' lounge listening to a kindergarten teacher lament the fact that she was getting four children from the local preschool program for students with disabilities. Even before seeing or visiting with the children, she anticipated difficulty. Professional research literature tells us that when we expect students to experience difficulty, they often do so.

Variety of procedures

Thurlow, Ysseldyke, Weiss, Lehr, O'Sullivan, and Nania (1986) conducted a detailed case study analysis of what happened to young children as they left their preschool and entered kindergarten. The researchers found extreme variability in the transition process. In some districts, program staff visited with staff of the elementary program to which the student was going, discussing in detail the child's strengths and weaknesses and recommending techniques for teaching the child successfully. In one district, all information related to the child's participation in the early childhood special education program was deleted from the records, and the child was sent to the elementary school without indication of previous special education services. Seldom did those who served students with disabilities follow up on the performances of the children in elementary school.

Current information on how to ensure smooth transition of children from preschool to elementary school is not consistent. In particular, no evidence exists of the effects (whether positive or adverse) of informing kindergarten teachers that students have been identified as disabled. We do not know whether this awareness biases the teachers' expectations for the children's performance or whether it helps the children.

Transitions During School

Many transitions occur as children and youth get older—from smaller to larger classes, from smaller to larger buildings, and from having a single teacher all day to seven or eight teachers each day. Perhaps because these transitions seem to be made with ease, there has been limited research on them. Yet transitions probably are made more easily by children who are not disabled than by those with disabilities. Teachers need to work together to facilitate smooth transitions by students with disabilities.

Everyday movements and adjustments

Students with disabilities often move among school settings for their particular educational experiences. They may have to go to other rooms (or buildings) rather than spending an entire day with a single teacher. Students with disabilities usually are taught by more than one teacher, or they meet with a number of specialists: with an occupational therapist in the morning and a special education teacher in the afternoon, or with two special education teachers—one who specializes in academics and one who specializes in behavior. Students who leave regular classrooms have to adjust not only to dealing with more than one teacher, but also to entering and leaving curriculum activities when other students do not. In addition, they must explain to other students why they leave the classroom and for what purpose.

Adjustment within regular classroom

Students who do not leave the regular classroom but find themselves with the special education teacher inside it may not have to make as many transition adjustments as other students with disabilities, but the adjustments may still be considerable. When this type of integrated service is used by the special education teacher as another way to deliver typical special education (for example, using different materials, drilling basic facts), these students must learn to concentrate when others in the class are engaged in completely different tasks.

It is important that teachers give consideration to how students are going to make up work they miss when they leave a classroom to get special services. Much consideration must also be given to how the students will move among services.

Dropping out of School

We include a separate section on dropping out because so many students with disabilities end their school careers this way. Dropping out is a significant transition, perhaps the most negative of possible school outcomes. Schooling is compulsory by law; schools are expected to serve all children and youths.

How many children and youth end their school careers by dropping out? By the mid-1980s, researchers had shown that nearly 25 percent of all youths in America were dropping out of school. More than 200,000 students with disabilities left school each year. Research also demonstrated that dropping out was associated with negative personal outcomes such as unemployment, low income and lifetime earnings, limited cognitive growth, and limited scholastic achievement. **Federal statistics** Federal statistics on students with various disabilities and the circumstances under which they left school in the 1990–91 school year (the most recent year for which data are available) are shown in Table 14.2. During 1990–91, 23.3 percent of students with disabilities terminated school by dropping out. The categories with the highest dropout rates were serious emotional disturbance (37.2%), learning disabilities (22.2%), and mental retardation (21.6%). The picture on school completion for all students with disabilities is shown in Figure 14.1.

Personnel at SRI International (Wagner, 1991) conducted a follow-up of special education students and reported an even higher national dropout rate than shown in the table and figure: 32.5 percent over a two-year period. They supported the earlier finding that students with disabilities leave school more often than those without handicaps. Notably quick to leave are students with mild to moderate disabilities, especially those who have been declared emotionally disturbed. Major findings of the National Longitudinal Transition Study were the following:

Findings of the National Longitudinal Transition Study

- A sizable percentage of students with disabilities drop out of school—a significantly higher percentage than among typical students. The dropout problem is particularly acute for students with certain disabilities—those classified as having serious emotional disturbance, learning disabilities, speech impairments, or mental retardation.

- Dropping out of school is the culmination of a cluster of school performance problems, including high absenteeism and poor grade performance.

- A variety of student characteristics and behaviors are associated with poor school performance and a higher likelihood that students will drop out. For example, males were significantly more likely than females to have failed courses, and lower socioeconomic status was associated with several aspects of poor performance. Students who belonged to school or community groups had significantly better school performance and a lower probability of dropping out. Youth with discipli-

| Table 14.2 | Reasons for Leaving School for Students with Disabilities (Percentages for School Year 1990–91) | | | | |

Disability	Graduated with Diploma	Graduated with Certificate	Reached Maximum Age	Dropped Out	Status Unknown
All disabilities	45.7%	13.3%	2.0%	23.3%	15.8%
Specific learning disabilities	51.7	10.8	0.7	22.2	14.7
Speech or language impairments	41.3	9.1	2.3	17.1	30.3
Mental retardation	38.7	24.6	5.2	21.6	9.9
Serious emotional disturbance	30.8	7.9	1.3	37.2	22.9
Multiple disabilities	38.7	26.2	11.9	12.6	10.7
Orthopedic impairments	55.3	13.0	2.7	10.1	18.9
Other health impairments	48.6	16.4	2.2	17.4	15.4
Hearing impairments	56.8	16.4	1.5	12.2	13.2
Visual impairments	60.3	14.6	2.2	12.1	10.8
Deaf-blindness	52.8	17.6	7.0	14.1	8.5

Note: Percentages may not sum to 100 percent because of rounding.
Source: U.S. Department of Education, Office of Special Education Programs, Data Analysis System (DANS).

nary problems had poorer school performance on all measures. Understanding these risk factors can help schools target dropout prevention programs to students most prone to early school leaving.

■ Dropping out is not a function solely of student and family factors. There are significant relationships between aspects of students' school programs and student outcomes. For example, students who attended larger schools and those who spent relatively more time in regular education classes were more likely to fail courses. Students with disabilities who took occupationally oriented vocational training had significantly lower absenteeism and were significantly less likely than others to have dropped out of school. Schools can make a difference in their students' per-

Figure 14.1
Basis of Exit for Students with Disabilities Age 14 and Older: School Year 1990–91
Source: U.S. Department of Education, Office of Special Education Programs, Data Analysis System (DANS).

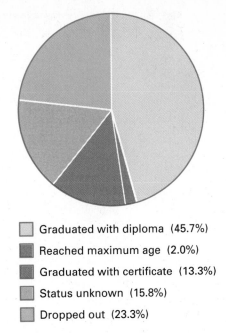

☐ Graduated with diploma (45.7%)

■ Reached maximum age (2.0%)

■ Graduated with certificate (13.3%)

☐ Status unknown (15.8%)

☐ Dropped out (23.3%)

formance. Schools can increase the likelihood that students will finish school. (Fourteenth Annual Report to Congress on the Implementation of the Individuals with Disabilities Education Act, 1992, pp. xxi, 81)

Averting dropout

Much can be done to avert dropout. In general, improved interventions early in the lives of those who experience difficulty in school are required. Table 14.3 lists dropouts' reasons for leaving and returning to school. The list gives us some insight into why students leave and the actions that might prompt them to return. Educators have been working since the mid-1960s to try to reduce the numbers of students, especially those with disabilities, who drop out of school. Nevertheless, they have not had much success.

Currently three model, federally funded programs exist to avert dropout. Each is targeted at the junior high school level, but the programs differ. The Partnership for School Success Project, a joint project between personnel at the University of Minnesota and teachers in the Minneapolis Public Schools, targets middle school students receiving special education services for learning and behavior difficulties. Efforts are made to promote positive connections between students' homes, schools, and communities by supporting students and families in these ways:

Partnership for School Success Project

- Academic support, including help with homework, helping students see the connection between their school experience and life outside the classroom, and aiding parents in preparing to take the GED

- Problem solving, including mediation between parents, students, and teachers; student skill building; and increasing communication between parents and teachers to prevent misunderstandings

Table 14.3 Dropouts' Reasons for Leaving and Returning to School

	Total	Male	Female
Reasons for leaving school			
School-related			
Did not like school	51.2%	57.8%	44.2%
Could not get along			
with teachers	35.0	51.6	17.2
with students	20.1	18.3	21.9
Was suspended too often	16.1	19.2	12.7
Did not feel safe at school	12.1	11.5	12.8
Was expelled	13.4	17.6	8.9
Felt I didn't belong	23.2	31.5	14.4
Could not keep up			
with schoolwork	31.3	37.6	24.7
Was failing school	39.9	46.2	33.1
Changed school, did not like			
new school	13.2	10.8	15.8
Job-related			
Could not work and go to school			
at same time	14.1	20.0	7.8
Had to get a job	15.3	14.7	16.0
Found a job	15.3	18.6	11.8
Family-related			
Had to support family	9.2	4.8	14.0
Wanted to have family	6.2	4.2	8.4
Was pregnant	31.0	0.0	31.0
Became parent	13.6	5.1	22.6
Got married	13.1	3.4	23.6
Had to care for family member	8.3	4.6	12.2
Other			
Wanted to travel	2.1	2.5	1.7
Friends dropped out	14.1	16.8	11.3
Percentage who . . .			
Plan to return and graduate	34.4	40.4	27.8
Plan to get a general equivalency			
diploma (GED)	59.1	52.9	66.0
Do not plan to return	4.1	3.5	4.8
Already have GED	2.4	3.2	1.5

(continued on next page)

Table 14.3 Dropouts' Reasons for Leaving and Returning to School (*continued*)

	Total	Male	Female
Reasons they would be likely to return to school			
Academics-related			
If it would improve			
reading skills	41.2	42.5	40.0
math skills	47.5	45.2	49.5
If I felt I could graduate	61.8	66.7	56.9
If I felt sure that I could get a good job after graduation	64.5	70.8	58.9
If I could take more job-related courses	51.4	59.6	43.8
If I felt sure I could get tutoring help to do better in school	48.3	49.8	46.8
School-climate-related			
If there were no gangs at school	13.7	12.2	15.3
If I felt safer at school	20.6	19.8	21.4
If I felt I belonged at school	47.9	51.1	44.8
If school was more interesting	62.7	72.7	53.4
If I could participate in sports or other activities	30.1	40.4	20.6
Family-related			
If I had a baby sitter	14.2	6.4	22.0
If child care were available at school	16.5	5.1	27.9
If I could attend classes at night or on weekends	49.2	38.6	58.9
If I didn't have to work to support myself or family	27.2	18.8	35.6
Other			
If parents were interested in my education	37.9	37.3	38.5
If friends went back to school	28.1	37.6	19.6

Note: Percentages based on dropouts from grades 8 through 10 who said the reasons applied to them.
Source: Reprinted with permission from *Education Daily.* (October 8, 1992). pp. 5–6. Capital Publications Inc., P.O. Box 1453, Alexandria, Va. 22312-2053, (703) 683-4100.

- Exploration of recreation and community service options, including opportunities for students to build social and recreation skills, and to be valued members of their community

- Monitoring each student's connections with his/her school, including looking for signs (for example, suspension, absenteeism, or failing classes) that the student and the school are moving apart. If signs appear, efforts are made to reconnect the youth and the school.

Belief Academy

Belief Academy, a joint project between faculty at the University of Washington and faculty in the Seattle schools, is located in two Seattle middle schools. Students sign contracts agreeing to stay in the program, and the project in turn has given the assurance that each student will successfully enter postsecondary education or be employed upon completing school. The program involves intensive academic instruction, using appropriate instructional procedures (much like those we described in Chapters 4 and 5), appropriate ethnic-sensitive curricula focusing on basic skills, and functional information. Students receive personal support through mentor relationships, prosocial activities, and Outward Bound experiences. Families receive support with social services, assistance in parenting, support from other families, and involvement in planning for their adolescent. Before students leave the middle school setting, they are directed into appropriate high school programs by assessing reading level, study skill level, and tenacity to study, as well as by discussing preferences with students and their parents. Triage decision criteria are used to help students and their families choose the best program for the student.

ALAS

The third model program is called Achievement for Latinos through Academic Success (*alas* means "wings" in Spanish). ALAS is a joint project between faculty at the University of California–Santa Barbara and teachers in the Los Angeles schools, and is focused on five spheres that influence student achievement and school continuance: students, teachers, school environments, parents, and community. In the student sphere, social problem-solving training is provided, as well as maintenance prompting for social problem solving. In the teacher sphere, teachers provide frequent feedback to students about classroom behavior and school assignments. The feedback is sent home in written notes to parents. In the school sphere, school bonding, perceived opportunity to receive recognition, and attendance accountability are addressed through specific interventions. In the parent sphere, parents receive training in school participation and home adolescent–parent problem solving and decision making. In the community sphere, school-based advocates help students and their parents negotiate school policies and procedures, and sustain due process protections. Advocates also serve the students and their families as liaisons to public agencies such as mental health and criminal justice.

To avert dropout will require additional supports like the special services and interventions used in Minneapolis, Seattle, and Los Angeles. Note that all of the projects recognize that interventions with parents, teachers, students themselves, community agencies, and peers are necessary to address the dropout issue.

Transition out of School

The ITP

A compelling need exists to improve the outcomes of youth with disabilities. In an effort to do so, in 1990 Congress added the requirement of specifying in a student's IEP the services that would be provided to aid the student's transition from school to adult life. This part of the IEP, known as the **individualized transition plan** (ITP), helps to focus educators' attention on outcomes and the preparedness of youth to assume productive adult lives. Section 602 of the Individuals with Disabilities Education Act defines transition services as

> a coordinated set of activities for a student, designed within an outcome-oriented process, which promotes movement from school to post-school activities, including post-secondary education, vocational training, integrated employment (including supported employment), continuing and adult education, adult services, independent living, or community participation. The coordinated set of activities shall be based upon the individual student's needs, taking into account the student's preferences and interests, and shall include instruction, community experiences, the development of employment and other post-school adult living objectives, and when appropriate, acquisition of daily living skills and functional vocational evaluation. (20 U.S.C. §1401[a][19])

Lack of employment

Employment and Financial Independence   When students with disabilities leave school, most are unemployed or underemployed. Only a third of people with disabilities between the ages of 16 and 64 are working, and of those working, three-fourths have part-time jobs (Wagner, D'Amico, Marder, Newman, & Blackorby, 1992). Employment is the single most important concern of those who work with older people who are disabled. School personnel report that adults with disabilities need vocational training, placement, and evaluation services more than they need transition or postemployment services.

Moving toward independence

The National Longitudinal Transition Study gathered data on the extent to which people who left school were moving toward independence within three to five years following school. Table 14.4 shows the percentages of students who were moving toward more or less independence over two measurement periods. The data illustrate that over the three to five years after leaving school, about half of students with disabilities were moving toward more independence. About 32 percent remained stable, while about 18 percent moved toward less independence. Note the differences among disability conditions in the percentages of individuals moving toward more independence. Categories in which the fewest students moved toward independence are deaf-blindness and multiple disabilities. Differences in movement toward independence are evident for students who graduated, aged out, and dropped out of school, with graduates consistently more likely to move toward independence than those aging out and dropping out.

Competitive employment

The most common work experience for people with disabilities is in sheltered and supported employment settings, not competitive employment. **Competitive employment** means that the individual's work is valued by the employer and is performed in an integrated setting with co-workers who are not dis-

Table 14.4   Fluctuation in Life Profiles of Youth with Disabilities, by Disability Characteristics

	Percentage of Youth Who:					
Youth Characteristics	Were Fully Independent (Profile 1) at Both Times	Moved Toward Greater Independence	Were Stable, Moderate Independence (Profiles 2–3)	Moved Toward Less Independence	Were Stable, Low Independence (Profiles 4–6)	n
All youth	4.0 (1.2)	50.0 (3.0)	16.0 (2.2)	18.3 (2.3)	11.6 (1.9)	1,706
Primary disability category						
Learning disabled	6.6 (2.3)	51.7 (4.7)	19.9 (3.8)	14.5 (3.3)	7.3 (2.4)	305
Emotionally disturbed	1.2 (1.3)	52.3 (6.1)	15.7 (4.4)	24.3 (5.2)	6.5 (3.0)	178
Speech impaired	2.8 (2.5)	53.4 (7.5)	17.4 (5.7)	19.4 (5.9)	7.0 (3.8)	118
Mentally retarded	.6 (.9)	46.1 (5.3)	8.2 (2.9)	23.8 (4.5)	21.4 (4.4)	242
Visually impaired	5.3 (3.0)	52.6 (6.6)	13.0 (4.4)	19.3 (5.2)	9.8 (3.9)	159
Hard of hearing	1.6 (2.0)	43.9 (7.8)	27.6 (7.0)	20.7 (6.3)	6.2 (3.8)	132
Deaf	3.6 (2.0)	49.0 (5.3)	18.2 (4.1)	25.7 (4.7)	3.4 (1.9)	233
Orthopedically impaired	.7 (1.3)	51.3 (7.8)	6.2 (3.8)	9.9 (4.7)	31.8 (7.2)	143
Other health impaired	.0 –	45.9 (10.2)	26.6 (9.0)	9.6 (6.0)	17.9 (7.8)	73
Multiply handicapped	.0 –	30.6 (6.8)	2.3 (2.8)	25.2 (8.3)	41.9 (9.4)	92
Deaf/blind	.0 –	25.2 (10.5)	11.6 (7.7)	18.6 (9.4)	44.6 (12.0)	31

Source: From *What Happens Next? Trends in Postschool Outcomes for Youth with Disabilities: The Second Comprehensive Report from the National Longitudinal Transition Study of Special Education Students* by Wagner et. al. Copyright © 1992 SRI International. Used with permission.

abled, and the individual earns at or above the federal minimum wage (Rusch, Chadsey-Rusch, & Lagomarcino, 1987). Despite the low percentage of adults who are disabled in competitive employment settings, most professionals agree that competitive employment should be the goal of all young adults with disabilities.

Competitive employment is a realistic goal for many people with disabilities. *Bob Daemmrich.*

Sheltered employment

Sheltered employment is work in a self-contained environment in which people who are exceptional are trained and paid for their output. Some sheltered workshops provide training for work that is performed outside the special setting. Other sheltered workshops are permanent work settings for the exceptional people who work there.

Supported employment is a relatively new concept that is designed for individuals with disabilities who need help finding, performing, and holding a job. Professionals who provide supported employment assistance to people with disabilities do one or more of the following tasks:

Professionals' role in supported employment

- Assist during job placement efforts (plan transportation, identify appropriate jobs, match skills to available jobs, communicate with social service agencies)

- Provide on-the-job training and help (train work skills, provide social skills and job-site training, work with co-workers) (The person who does this is usually called a **job coach.**)

- Monitor job performance (obtain regular feedback from employers, identify levels of performance and need for further training)

■ Provide evaluation and follow-up experiences (determine employer's satisfaction, communicate with employee periodically, help with future job placements)

Professionals in supported employment activities spend most of their time at the job sites where people with disabilities work. Supported employment specialists also spend time working with parents and exceptional people in training centers or at their homes.

People with disabilities are much more likely to find and keep jobs today than they were even a few years ago, largely because parents and professionals have worked to give them opportunities to become contributing members of society.

Needs for continued education

Continued Education   As people with disabilities grow older, their opportunities for education are restricted. The characteristics that lead them to special services during childhood often become barriers to education in adulthood. Adults with disabilities view their education and training service needs as less important than their employment and personal/social service needs. They don't realize that people with severe disabilities need further education services after school. For example, people with visual disabilities, medical or physical impairments, and multiple disabilities may have twice as many needs as people with learning disabilities, communication disorders, or serious emotional disturbance. In addition, individuals with sensory disabilities need professional readers or professional interpreters.

More and more students with disabilities are entering colleges, community colleges, vocational schools, and advanced technical schools with accessible and intensive programs for exceptional students. Many factors have contributed to the emergence of these specialized educational programs (Mangrum & Strichart, 1984):

Factors stimulating advanced programs

■ Many students with disabilities graduate from high school and are eligible to enter college; the support they received in elementary school and high school has been extended in many college programs.

■ The realization that college is a viable goal for students with disabilities has led many parents and professionals to advocate for special programs in colleges and universities.

■ The interest of exceptional students in advanced schooling has brought pressure on institutions of higher learning to develop programs to meet these students' unique educational needs.

■ There are not enough programs. Although more programs are available to students with learning disabilities than to those in other categories, the need for a greater number of continuing education alternatives is still apparent. Recognition of the situation is stimulating additional programs.

■ The movement toward open admission policies has led many students—who at an earlier time might have feared rejection—to seek enrollment.

■ With higher education enrollments dropping, students with disabilities are potential new consumers of postsecondary education; this financial incentive has stimulated program development for exceptional college students.

Community and Home Living Arrangements

Exceptional people are moving out into the world. The transition from school to work includes dealing with independent living responsibilities and residential needs. People with disabilities worry about where and with whom they will live. They wonder whether they will always have to live with their parents, whether they will ever have a room of their own, and whether they will be able to live in an apartment or home. Not long ago, people who were moderately and severely disabled lived primarily in large state hospitals and institutions. Institutional placement of people who were retarded, deaf, blind, or disabled in other ways was the primary means of intervention for over two hundred years. Today, large numbers of people with disabilities still live in institutional settings, but other options are available for those who do not wish to live at home with their families.

Group Homes   The practice of mainstreaming began when teachers and other professionals implemented the least restrictive environment (LRE) principle of Public Law 94–142 in public school settings and programs. In school settings, least restrictive environment means that students who are exceptional receive all or part of their educational experiences in classrooms that are as much like normal as possible. **Deinstitutionalization** is the implementation of the LRE principle in residential facilities. It moves people with disabilities out of institutions into smaller community-based settings that are as much like normal living arrangements as possible.

   Group homes are a fast-growing, community-based residential alternative for many people who are disabled. Group homes provide family-style living. They usually are located in residential neighborhoods near shopping and public transportation. The number of people living in each home varies from three or four to as many as fifteen or twenty. Generally, specially trained professionals serve as house parents for residents. Some group homes are primarily long-term residential placements. People in them are expected to develop independent living skills and often work outside the home in sheltered workshops or businesses in the community. Other group homes are intermediate-care facilities, where people who are disabled are supposed to learn the skills they need to move to more independent living arrangements such as foster homes and supervised apartments.

   Group homes are a very positive environment for the people who live in them. But they sometimes create controversy in their surrounding communities. Here's how one town in North Carolina reacted to plans for a small group home:

Some residents of Echo Farms, a golf subdivision in Wilmington off Carolina Beach Road, are trying to stop a home for the mentally retarded from locating in their neighborhood.

   At issue is the intended use of a brick house at 220 Dorchester Place. The owner, Charles Woodard of Goldsboro, plans to build an intermediate care facility for the mentally retarded.

   About 50 residents met Tuesday night for about two hours at the Echo Farms clubhouse. At the end of the meeting, representatives of the

Group homes are becoming primary choices for community-based residential alternatives for many people with disabilities. *Michael Weisbrot and Family.*

Homeowners Association said they were going to check into the situation. They also asked a lawyer who was present to check on whether Woodard had followed proper procedure before starting to work on the facility. . . . Mitwol [the lawyer] said he would make certain that Woodard had followed all procedures correctly.

"I think it would behoove all of you folks to hold his feet to the fire on this," he said. "If they didn't follow the rules, they're out." (*Wilmington Morning Star*, June 2, 1988, p. 1C)

Controlling this type of stereotyped thinking and discrimination remains a challenge for all of us.

Living in small groups

Alternative Living Units   Some states have organized small group homes of two or three residents as an alternative to more costly homes for larger groups of people with disabilities. An **alternative living unit** (ALU) is ideal for providing a more personal environment for training and an easier structure for supervision. The amount of service provided in these settings varies with the residents' needs. People with basic living skills may need a counselor to help with specific activities and tasks (like balancing a checkbook). Others may need someone to live in, to help with cooking, cleaning, and other activities.

Flexibility of ALUs

One advantage of this type of living arrangement is its flexibility: As residents' needs change, the amount and type of support they receive can be changed; they don't have to change facilities. Professionals who support the use of alternative living units also assert that they are easier to set up than group homes and attract less attention from neighbors.

Living with another family

Foster Homes   Some people with disabilities live with families who provide them a temporary home in return for reimbursement of their living expenses. Foster homes offer a number of positive life experiences for people with disabilities. Participating in normal family experiences, receiving personal attention, and developing close relationships with people who are not disabled are among the advantages. The primary disadvantage of foster homes is the difficulty of monitoring the quality of the experiences they provide.

Living on one's own

Independent Living   The greatest opportunity for independence and normal social interactions is provided by living in an apartment, mobile home, or other private residence. A goal of many professionals in special education is the movement of all people with disabilities to these kinds of independent living facilities. They argue that group homes and foster homes are too "institutional" to fit their ideal of normalization.

Independence—the greatest wish

Most adults with disabilities say that their greatest wish is to live independently. Some things that make independent living easier for those with disabilities are modified controls on kitchen appliances; adjustable countertops and furniture; accessible sinks, toilets, and showers; adapted door handles; room-to-room intercoms; and easy access to emergency medical, police, and fire services. Many personal and social services are available for adults with disabilities. Those who are emotionally disturbed need more family services, for example, and transportation needs are greater for those with medical, physical, and multiple impairments.

Mobility

One of the great challenges that people with disabilities face is independent mobility. Those who are not disabled often take for granted the independence that comes from being able to use automobiles, trains, airplanes, and buses. People with disabilities may have ambulation problems that make travel nearly impossible. If they are able to travel, they may be confronted by public places that are inaccessible. Adults with disabilities may be unable to obtain driver licenses, and they may have a limited circle of friends who can help them with transportation. It is critical that transition plans account for training and assistance to increase mobility.

Large-scale institutions

Institutions   For those who cannot or do not wish to live independently, in a group home, or in an alternative living unit, the option of a large-scale institution remains. Unfortunately, a residential institution housing as many as five hundred people might provide few opportunities for normal interactions. In recent years, professionals in special education have been critical of the care provided in the nation's residential facilities. They claim that residential placements violate the ideal of "life as much like normal as possible" that is at the core of Public Law 94–142. Parents do not necessarily agree: Surveys of their attitudes toward residential care are generally favorable.

Working with Parents

Not many years ago, parents were encouraged to place children with disabilities in institutions as early as possible. Today, they are encouraged to keep their

Parents as partners

children with special needs at home and, when they are old enough, to enroll them in neighborhood schools. Parents and families have become active partners in the special education process in ways that were unheard of 50 years ago.

Effects of Children Who Are Exceptional on Parents and Families

Parents' concerns

In the recent past, placing a child in an institution left many families with feelings of guilt and inadequacy. Now that normalization, least restrictive environment, and mainstreaming are available and are the treatments of choice, the families of those with disabilities must address different feelings and concerns. The parents of gifted children also face some of these concerns and others about the social, personal, and educational needs of their children.

Changes in the family

Whenever a child is born, the structure of the family changes. All families have to deal with that change, but the families of children with special needs face a special challenge. Some of their problems are unique; others differ only by degree. For example, the family of a child with special medical needs faces certain problems that families with healthy children do not face. Furthermore, although all families must think about their children's future, the families of those with disabilities have special concerns.

Parents' needs and feelings

At every stage of their child's life, the families of those who have disabilities must deal with special problems. Parents of a young child with a disability need accurate information about their child's condition. They have to decide what and how to tell relatives and friends about their child. They have to locate health and educational services. They worry about what others think about them and their child. They have to come to grips with their sadness, their guilt, and their anxieties. Brothers and sisters have to deal with feelings of jealousy, the loss of their parents' energy and time, new responsibilities, and their fears. They also worry about what their friends will think and say about their sibling with a disability.

Siblings

Starting school is a change in routine. Most children find it difficult to adjust to that change; exceptional children and their families find it extremely difficult. Parents are expected to participate in the educational program. They need to know about mainstreaming and the special class placement alternatives that are available in their community. Often they have to locate professionals who can give them help at home. In addition, they have to find after-school care and determine the extent to which they want their child to participate in extracurricular activities. Brothers and sisters may be embarrassed, frustrated, disappointed, and even angry when a sibling who is disabled is mainstreamed in their own school. Many siblings are expected to participate in special training programs and support groups that compete with other social and school activities. They also have to face the limitations that the disability may have on their brother/sister's future.

Adolescence

Adolescents with disabilities encounter increased peer rejection and personal isolation. They also often have special problems adjusting to the normal physical and emotional changes that occur during puberty. Parents may have to help them cope with their feelings and arrange out-of-school activities for them.

Problems of transition

Life after school presents a new set of problems for the individual with a special need and the family. Finding a job and a place to live can be special challenges for someone with a disability. The parents worry about how their child will manage and who will care for him/her when they are no longer able. Brothers and sisters may face financial responsibilities for their sibling who is disabled, and even forced to assume guardianship.

Concerns for children who are gifted

Parents of children who are gifted share many concerns with parents of other exceptional children. Many need help understanding the special needs of their gifted children. They worry that their children will be isolated, set off by their special abilities. Some need to be convinced that special education is appropriate and necessary. Others seek out special programs for their children. Although parents with unusually high expectations can create problems for their children and the teachers they deal with in school, these same parents can be welcome advocates in the early stages of developing programs for exceptional students.

Parent participation

Parents of students who are gifted can be eager to participate in their children's education. They typically want to know how to broaden their children's experiences, how they can help their children develop a love for learning and a willingness to take intellectual risks, and how they can become actively involved in making more services available to gifted students in their communities. Others worry that they lack the skills and knowledge to meet the special needs of their children and, like all parents, worry about the effects their mistakes will have on their children's lives.

Effects on the family

Are families adversely affected by the presence of children with disabilities? Most people believe they are. Yet the research on this issue is mixed. It is very risky to say anything about how students with disabilities affect their families. When researchers study the effects of children with disabilities on families, they find that the effects differ as a function of the disability (for example, deafness versus blindness) and the severity of the condition. Effects also differ according to parents' views about the extent to which their children measure up to cultural standards. The interrelationships among factors that influence the effects of children on families are very complex. Differing disabilities affect families in varying ways, and the same kind of disability may have radically different effects from one family to the next.

Changing times

Finally, it is important to keep in mind that the effects children with disabilities have on their families have changed significantly with the times. In the not too distant past, parents who chose to keep their children at home, rather than placing them in residential institutions, were subject to stigma. Now families are expected to keep their children with disabilities and to raise them at home. Institutionalization is the exception rather than the rule, and families are expected to assume responsibilities associated with raising those children. Contrary to the earlier reality, present-day parents who institutionalize children with disabilities are stigmatized, and families that choose to raise children with disabilities at home are very visible.

Parent involvement and support is an important part of any educational program. *Jerry Howard/Positive Images.*

Types of Parent Involvement

It is popular these days to talk about parent involvement. We regularly attend conferences at which we hear speakers calling for increased parent involvement and home–school collaboration as essential to solving problems that schools, children, and families face. Teachers tell us of the need to involve parents in their children's education. Parents sometimes talk about their desire to participate in the education of their children. But what does parent involvement mean?

Five kinds of parent involvement

There are at least five kinds of parent involvement (Epstein, 1992). In the first kind, parents fulfill basic obligations like providing for their child's health and safety, getting the child ready for school, and building the kind of home environment that supports learning. There is little contact with the school. In the second kind, the school creates certain minimal types of contacts between school and parent. The school communicates with parents about school programs, sends out report cards, and so on. In the third type of parent involvement, parents join activities at school by assisting the teacher and attending functions. A fourth kind of parent involvement is one in which parents participate in learning activities at home (for example, they initiate learning activities or monitor completion of schoolwork). Finally, in the fifth kind of parent involvement, parents participate in governance and advocacy activities at school, including PTA, parent study groups, and advocacy groups.

When professionals speak of increased parent involvement, they generally mean at least the third of these five levels, and often the fourth or fifth—in other words, involvement extensive enough that parents become genuine collaborators in their child's education.

Overcoming Barriers to Home–School Collaboration

Although professionals and parents readily acknowledge the importance of schools and homes working together, there are a number of barriers to home–school collaboration; some are listed in Table 14.5. To overcome these barriers, the school can do certain things to encourage parent participation:

Ways for schools to encourage parent participation

■ Parents are more likely to become involved in their children's educational programs if the school climate is open, helpful, and friendly. This can be accomplished by installing parent lounges and setting times when parents and teachers have lunch together, among other things.

■ Parents are more likely to become involved in the educational program when there is frequent, clear, two-way communication. They are also more likely to communicate when they are encouraged to comment on school policies and issues and to share in making decisions about programs.

■ Parents are more likely to become involved when they are treated as collaborators, rather than recipients of advice from experts. Active efforts must be made to involve parents, especially those who are considered very hard to reach. Schools in which administrators actively express and promote a philosophy of partnership are likely to have high levels of parent involvement. It is important to expect parents to work as volunteers, even after their children finish school.

■ Schools should provide written policies about how teachers are to involve parents in students' educational programs. Such documents might include statements of how parents and teachers are to work together, the ways in which administrators will support parent involvement, how teachers are to be trained to work with parents, ways to increase and improve two-way communication and networking, and methods for periodic evaluation of the effects of parent involvement.

Some ways in which you as a professional will be able to work to overcome barriers to home–school collaboration are

Ways for teachers to build home–school collaboration

■ Send home good news as often as you send home bad news.
■ Hold conferences with parents beyond those that are routine and scheduled. Work to make such conferences nonroutine.
■ Be sure to follow through on any communications with parents.
■ Provide parents with knowledge about how they can use your services, and ask parents to tell you how you can use them to further their childrens' education.
■ Contact parents by phone on a regular basis to let them know how their children are doing and to get their perceptions of how things are going in school. You should work very hard to reach parents who tend to be un-

Table 14.5	Barriers to Effective Home–School Collaboration

1. Parents feel anxious about surrendering their children to strangers who may have values different from their own and may inculcate in the children those values.

2. Teachers worry that parent involvement in decision making removes teacher independence and autonomy.

3. Sometimes teachers and parents will accede to their required responsibilities (as articulated by principals to diminish conflict and confusion); sometimes they will not.

4. Parents and teachers have inaccurate, often negative stereotypes of each other.

5. Because parents and teachers are busy, the pressure of having to get many things done in short periods of time interferes with effective collaboration.

6. Because many families have very low incomes, the financial pressures of making ends meet become primary to worrying about how their children are doing in school.

7. Parents are sometimes afraid to come to school because they do not view schools as safe environments.

8. Parents cannot always come to school because they cannot afford or have no access to child care for younger siblings.

9. School policies sometimes discourage home–school collaboration—for instance, in some schools union contracts specify that volunteers cannot be used for teaching functions.

10. Teachers and parents hold different views on who ought to be in charge of major decisions.

11. Parents and teachers sometimes attribute student failure or poor performance to different, mutually exclusive factors, which sometimes means they blame each other.

12. Many homes are socially stressed, and many students who experience difficulties in school are from socially stressed homes. The stresses may be such that they contribute to or exacerbate the difficulties students experience in school or take precedence over any difficulties students experience in school.

Sources: Henderson, A. T., Marburger, C. L., & Ooms, T. (1986). *Beyond the bake sale: An educator's guide to working with parents*. Washington, DC: National Committee for Citizens in Education; Imber-Black. E. (1988). *Families and larger systems:* New York: Guilford.

available, for it is precisely in such instances that obtaining parent involvement has dramatic effects on student behavior and academic performance.

Involving Community Agencies and Businesses

Different environments, different needs

It is critical that transition activities take into account the community in which the individual with disabilities will live. Students who live in rural environments will experience different needs than those who live in inner-city or large urban environments. Different kinds and degrees of social services may be available in the different settings, and it is important for those who plan transitions to coordinate the needs of the individual with the availability of mechanisms and agencies for meeting those needs.

Wide array of agencies

Students who receive special education services are those who also come to the attention of other agencies and organizations. Services for students in America are provided by a bewildering array of federal, private, state, county, and city agencies and organizations. Services include education, health care, transportation, welfare, housing, legal advice, and protection (fire and police). Collaboration between school personnel and those in other agencies is important so that "the right hand knows what the left is doing." Interagency collaboration can reduce redundancy of services and lead to improved benefits for individuals with disabilities.

Interdependence

Over the years agencies have become better at talking with one another and working together. They are currently more interdependent than independent. Teachers must work persistently to familiarize themselves with the services of other agencies and the ways in which their personnel help their students. Hodgkinson (1989) pointed to the ridiculous nature of failing to do so:

> It is painfully clear that a hungry, sick, or homeless child is by definition a poor learner, yet schools usually have no linkage to health or housing organizations outside those run by the schools themselves. (p. 1)

In the short time since Hodgkinson's observation there have been major steps in the development of close linkages among schools and service organizations. Interagency collaboration is especially critical at the time that students make the transition from school to the postschool environment. Adult service agencies provide vocational, recreational, social, and mental health services to individuals with disabilities. It is also important for school personnel and personnel from these agencies to work together early in students' careers so that they can plan postschool life and facilitate transition.

Business involvement

Involvement of business leaders is also important. The basis for a highly skilled workforce begins in the school years, with a range of quality educational programs and work-related experiences that allow students to reach high school graduation equipped to tackle the world of work, or to continue in some form of postsecondary education or training, or both. Wehman (1992) identified three reasons why it is important for school personnel to establish linkages with businesses and business leaders. First, local business personnel can help school personnel decide the extent to which the skills they are giving students are marketable. Second, businesses serve as training sites for students, and business leaders can provide school personnel with analyses of the kinds of experiences they can give students. Finally, since businesses may eventually employ students with disabilities, it is important that school and business personnel understand one another.

Business partnerships

Today's business leaders are working along with education leaders to improve linkages. More and more communities are developing ways to help students prepare for the move from school to work. In most states there are business partnerships, designed to connect education, employment, work, and learning.

Students with disabilities participate in many of the programs designed to prepare all students for technical careers. Many of these students learn challenging academic material in a real-world setting, where principles and ideas are applied to everyday problems and solutions. Some examples of programs that have resulted from close collaboration among educators and business leaders are highlighted below.

Apprenticeships

Youth apprenticeships are designed to expose students to work-day realities in areas such as health care, banking, insurance, hospitality, and retailing while they are still in high school. Participants spend part of each school week at work sites and the remainder of the week in the classroom. The on-the-job emphasis is on active learning. The employment connections give students a chance to try out actual working situations and gain work experience.

Linking high school with college

Tech-prep programs combine academic studies with job-related learning in a plan that links the final two years of high school with two years of college. People from industry join high school and community college teachers to develop curriculum, teach lessons, and monitor students at work sites. Students receive high-level training in math, science, language, and so forth, and enough training in technical skills to integrate the two and assume demanding technical employment.

Student businesses

School-based enterprises are individual or sequenced high school courses set up as actual student-run businesses. Sandwich shops, bookstores, print shops, child care centers, and construction firms are among the programs provided. Students study business operations and develop occupational skills.

In these ways and others, communities are experimenting with programs that provide challenging academics, allow students to learn in context, and give them the opportunity to explore and prepare for careers. The successful ones are built and maintained through close collaboration among teachers, parents, employers, and community leaders.

Key Elements for Success in the Wider Context

As you think about the wider context of schooling for individuals who are exceptional, you should consider the key elements of effective instructional programs—whether for very young children in early intervention settings or young adults in supported work environments—elements that are necessary.

Bring Your Learning to Life

Community and Business Collaboration Facilitated Fred's Transition from School to Employment

Because of collaboration among his teachers, school administrators, state and county officials, and people from the county technical college, Fred received substantial training in food services during his last two years in high school. Local business leaders were also involved in setting up this training program for students like Fred. Spending a few hours each day at the technical college, Fred learned vocational skills that were expected to give him a head start on finding employment after graduation.

Once Fred received his diploma, he was recommended for the McJobs program. Sponsored by the McDonald's chain of restaurants, McJobs is a structured eight-week training course for people with special needs. Since Fred had long envied people who worked at McDonald's, his favorite eating establishment, he jumped at the opportunity. He couldn't have been prouder when he got his uniform, especially the baseball-style cap.

He did well in McJobs, and he was hired as a regular employee at the local McDonald's. After a few months, the manager suggested that with training on more job stations, Fred could work more hours. The McJobs job coach spent an additional two weeks at the store to train Fred on additional job stations. He increased his work time to thirty-two hours a week at his dream job.

Fred's mother stated, "I never thought McDonald's would let Fred do as much as they have. He is a regular jack of all trades—he makes burgers, fries, nuggets, pies, everything in the grill area. He is now working breakfast as well as lunch, so he had to learn all those jobs too. When we got Fred, we were told that he was severely and profoundly retarded and would never walk, talk, or do anything. And now here he is supporting himself, and he loves his job."

Tailoring for individual needs

Individualized Planning   All services—from toilet training of young children in day care settings to job skills training and accommodations for adults—should be tailored to meet the specific needs of the individual. For example, if a young adult has difficulty with communication, detailed training in communication should be offered, including social skills training.

Normality and integration

Commitment to Normal Life Experiences   The educational experiences received by individuals who are exceptional should be as nearly normal as possible. Specific efforts need to be made to help individuals with disabilities become integrated into their communities, whether in a work environment or a preschool program.

Environmental considerations

Compatible Physical Environment   The physical environment in the home, at work, and at school should be made compatible with the person's prefer-

Point of View

Hush: It's Epilepsy

I wear a bright green hockey helmet and a quarterback's brown flak vest, and if you saw me walking down the street you'd do a double take. No, I'm not an escapee from a loony bin. I'm an epileptic. It took me almost 20 years before I was able to make that statement. Friends would say, "Shirl, you stare off, you walk off, you daydream." My reaction was always, "Are you nuts?" I casually mentioned these comments to Bory when we were married, in 1955, adding, "If I had a problem, I would know. Right?" "Right," he said.

I was behind the wheel of my Studebaker when I realized I *did* have a problem. It was 1957. I was driving on a one-way street in Chicago. Suddenly, I found myself staring at a car coming at me from the opposite direction. Fortunately, the car stopped short just a few inches in front of me, so no one was hurt. The driver pushed my car over to the side while I went to call Bory, who came to take me home.

We agreed something was not right and that we had better consult our family doctor. He referred us to a neurologist, who said I had epilepsy. Epilepsy? I didn't know anything about it, so I turned away to hide my shock and fear. The doctor asked if I understood. I pretended I did. He prescribed Dilantin (I've been taking it ever since), told me to take it five times a day and never to drive again, but gave me scant information about the drug. He never mentioned the complications it might cause. Not until my gums started to swell and bleed did I learn that this was one of the common side effects.

I read everything I could about epilepsy, did reams of research and even wrote a paper on the disorder for a course I was taking in college English. But I insisted on keeping my affliction a secret from almost everyone. If no one spoke about epilepsy, and some books referred to it as a sign of the Devil, why should I advertise it?

I had no idea my life would never be the same again and that I would be joining a battle that more than 2 million other Americans were

fighting. The few friends who knew my secret all said my life was going to be OK. It wasn't. I had 20 to 30 petit mal seizures every two weeks. I would suddenly and briefly lose contact with my surroundings, stare blankly for a few seconds or longer and never remember what had happened. But my main battle was with myself. My defense was simple: I went into the closet and closed the door.

Luckily, I had an understanding husband. In 1974 he was promoted to insurance executive, and we relocated to California. My seizures, however, got worse. As a company wife, I had to attend many social functions. At one unforgettable dinner party, I looked up from the table to find people staring at me. My hand was squeezing the roast beef and mashed potatoes on my plate, and I had wet my pants. I was mortified. I looked at the people, who were waiting for an explanation. I told them the truth. I had just had a spell. A few days later, Bory received a letter saying that because of my "nervous condition," I had been removed from his company health-insurance plan. That did it. I opened the closet door and came out.

During those episodes, I fell, bumped into things and broke ribs, a shoulder and my nose—not all at the same time. My neurologist ordered me to get something to protect my head and ribs. Our search for a helmet was easy. We found one that was light and secure in a medical-supply house.

My ribs were another matter. One of our friends, a policeman, had me try on his bulletproof vest. It would do the job, but I wouldn't be able to move about. We kept looking. Then, one day, while we were watching a Los Angeles Rams game at Anaheim Stadium, we saw the quarterback in the pocket, his offense running amok, letting the guy get sacked. We watched in amazement as he bounced back up. Bory looked at me and suggested I call the team. All I had to tell them was "I have epilepsy, I fall and need to protect my ribs." Don Hewitt, the equipment manager, didn't need to hear more. He invited

(continued on next page)

Point of View

Hush: It's Epilepsy *(continued)*

me to the Rams' locker room to rummage. He joined in the hunt and soon handed me a flak vest Joe Namath had worn during his Ram days. As 300-pound players wandered in and out, the team's seamstress altered it to fit my much smaller frame. Back home with my precious jacket, I tried it on and looked in the mirror. Facing me was a new woman with a helmet, flak vest and tinted glasses to keep out the glare. You can't imagine what it's like to walk into a library, supermarket, or business meeting wearing the sports equipment I have to put on every day. But it was that or break body parts.

Now I could do more than sit around the house. I was itching to get working again, so with my husband's encouragement, I studied for an insurance rep's license. I had not mentioned to the state that I was epileptic. During the exam, I had a seizure that disrupted the others. Needless to say, I flunked. I applied again, and this time the State of California lent me a hand. When I returned to take the test, there were two rooms, two monitors. One was filled to capacity. The other, mine, was empty except for the monitor. Despite a brief seizure, I passed the test. I was back in the business world.

Today, much to my surprise at 59, once I explain that I wear my "costume" for seizures I can't control and because it keeps me independent, people are very understanding. It was me who needed to stop condemning me.

I am grateful to doctors who have tried countless known and untried drugs; to an employer that doesn't care what I wear on my head, and to the State of California for opening doors for me without asking health questions. But my most profound thanks go to Bory, who always walks beside me, regardless of stares, and who one day four years ago put a computer with a modem on my desk. It not only made my day but also improved my life, because through the bulletin board, I now share my ups and downs with epileptics all over the country. I can finally say that although I have epilepsy, epilepsy no longer has me.

Note: Shirl Rapport lives in Anaheim, CA. She can be E-mailed on Prodigy at GHFB34E.

Source: From *Newsweek,* August 1, 1994. Copyright © 1994, Newsweek, Inc. All rights reserved. Reprinted by permission.

ences. If noise disturbs the young child or adult, then efforts should be made to find a quiet place to educate the individual. Special considerations should be given to how the physical environment—layout, shape, noise level, location—affects the behavior of the individual.

Remedial services

Commitment to Remedial Programming Even young children demonstrate uneven skill development and gaps in learning. The gaps in learning evidenced by older individuals with disabilities often keep them from functioning independently. Educational services should be designed to teach new skills and to fill in gaps in previously learned behavior or skills.

Behavior

Commitment to Encouraging Appropriate Behavior Success in preschool, school, or work environments depends much on the extent to which the individual demonstrates behavior that others consider appropriate. Both early education and transition activities should be directed toward reduction of inappropriate behavior.

Support throughout life

Lifelong Learning   Individuals with disabilities will likely need support and assistance in learning throughout their lives. Consistency and adjustment in providing services is critical for all ages.

The Wider Context in Perspective

The education of students with disabilities is a lifelong effort that involves co-operation and collaboration among school personnel, parents and families, community agencies, churches, and businesses. A significant part of the education and development of individuals with disabilities takes place before they enter school (early intervention) and after they exit school (postschool intervention). Disabilities do not start and end when individuals enter and leave schools. Educators need to be concerned about this wider context for schooling and actively involved in ensuring smooth transition at critical times in the lives of individuals with disabilities.

Focusing on the wider context

In this chapter we have talked about the transitions that occur when students enter and leave school as well as those that occur during the time they are in school. We have described efforts to intervene early in the lives of young children with disabilities, either to alleviate the disabilities or to prevent later and more significant difficulties. Although there are now more preschool programs than at any time in our nation's history, significantly more children need early interventions. There is overwhelming evidence that early intervention alleviates later school and developmental difficulties and results in improved outcomes for students, including those with disabilities. Educators ought to work very hard to ensure full funding of Head Start and to provide preschool experiences to all children with disabilities. It is a good investment. Moreover, increased efforts to improve educational services for students with disabilities are needed in elementary and middle schools to cut back on the large number of students who drop out of school. Waiting until high school to intervene is too late.

Promoting early intervention

Need to improve outcome

Educational outcomes for students with disabilities are not rosy. A large percentage drop out of school, most of those who complete school are unemployed or underemployed, and more work in sheltered workshops and supported employment settings than in competitive employment. This speaks to the need to improve educational services for these students, but also to the need to put more energy into improving transition planning. By working with business and industrial leaders, school personnel can learn to engage in better transition planning for youths with disabilities.

Collaboration: the basic theme

The theme this chapter emphasized was cooperation and collaboration. That same theme closes the chapter. There can be little doubt that improved educational outcomes for students with disabilities require improved instruction. Yet that is not enough; collaboration is equally necessary. Educators need to collaborate with one another in efforts to improve education for students with disabilities. They need to collaborate with parents to forge strong linkages between homes and families and schools. Finally, they need to collaborate with business and community leaders to develop ways to improve the results of education for students with disabilities. The significant challenges that confront

America's children cannot be addressed by educators (or parents, sociologists, psychologists, rehabilitation counselors, physicians and nurses, and so on) in isolation. Only by working together, and then working very hard, can we improve educational outcomes for the nation's youth.

What Every Teacher Should Know

- More than half of 3- to 5-year-old children attend nursery school or kindergarten classes. Although there are more preschool programs than ever before, more students are in need of them.
- Early intervention programs are either home based, center based, or hospital based.
- Head Start and other early intervention programs have been shown to be cost-effective and to save the nation money in the long run.
- Transitions occur at the time of school entrance, during school (from grade to grade, elementary school to middle school, and general to special education), and at the time students leave school.
- A large proportion of students with disabilities—roughly one-quarter to one-third—drop out before school completion.
- When students with disabilities leave school, most are unemployed or underemployed.
- More students with disabilities work in sheltered and supported employment settings than in competitive employment.
- An increasing number of students with disabilities are continuing their education in colleges or other advanced schools.
- Many adults with disabilities live independently. The trend toward deinstitutionalization has also promoted other community living arrangements such as group homes, alternative living units, and foster homes.
- There are at least five kinds of parent involvement, ranging from parental fulfillment of basic obligations but little contact with the school to intense involvement of parents in the schools their children attend. Teachers and other school personnel can help promote home–school collaboration.
- Business leaders, leaders from community agencies, and educational leaders increasingly have been working in partnership to improve educational outcomes for students with disabilities.

Projects

1. Consult the Yellow Pages of your local phone directory for a list of preschool programs. Contact the programs to obtain informational brochures. Use the brochures to complete a table like Table 14.1 Indicate the name of each program, the age range of students served, the kinds of students with disabilities included in the program, the organization of the program (for example, home based), and the kinds of services provided.
2. Divide your class into small groups and engage in a discussion of strategies

school personnel can use to enhance parent involvement in school programs. Indicate topics for small- and/or large-group meetings of parents.

3. Develop a list of ways in which school personnel can work with individual senior high school students with disabilities to ensure smooth transitions from school to postschool environments.

4. Develop a list of ways in which school personnel can work with individual preschool children to facilitate their smooth transition into school. Are there transition tactics that apply specifically to students with disabilities? Which tactics can be used with all children?

For Your Information

Books

American Council on Rural Special Education. (1988). *Rural transition strategies that work*. Bellingham, WA: National Rural Development Institute, Western Washington University.

Designed to assist educators in establishing rural transition programs. Contains descriptions of over fifty exemplary transition programs, strategies, and practices tested in rural areas.

Dunst, C. J., Trivetta, C. M., & Deal, A. G. (1988). *Enabling and empowering families: Principles and guidelines for practice*. Cambridge, MD: Brookline Books.

Written specifically for early intervention practitioners who work with families but who have not had extensive training in family systems assessment and intervention. The authors discuss ways to promote a family's ability to identify its needs and mobilize resources in a way that strengthens family functioning.

Lakin, K. C., & Bruininks, R. H. (1985). *Strategies for achieving community integration of developmentally disabled citizens*. Baltimore, MD: Paul H. Brookes.

A set of readings illustrating services to persons with severe disabilities in integrated settings. Guidelines and examples are offered on how to make integrated services more effective and how to improve public policies on residential, educational, and social/leisure services.

Meisels, S. J., & Shonkoff, J. P. (Eds.). (1989). *Handbook of early childhood intervention*. Cambridge: Cambridge University Press.

The text includes both theoretical and practical articles describing interventions for young children.

National Center on Education and the Economy, & American Society for Training and Development. (1989). *Training America: Strategies for the nation*. Washington, DC: National Center on Education and the Economy.

Provides background information on, and recommendations for, the development of a comprehensive strategy for improving job-related learning in the United States.

Rosenbaum, J. E., Stern, D., Hamilton, M. A., Hamilton, S. F., Berryman, S., & Kazis, R. (1992). *Youth apprenticeship in America: Guidelines for building an effective system*. Washington, DC: William T. Grant Foundation Commission on Youth and America's Future.

A reasoned discussion of the basis for a National Youth Apprenticeship System, this set of readings describes apprenticeships, school-based work experience, and apprenticeship as a model for learning. Guidelines for effective school–employer linkages are included.

Rosenberg, M. B. (1988). *Finding a way: Living with exceptional brothers and sisters*. New York: Lothrop, Lee, & Shepard.

A sensitive, warm, and straightforward exploration of the feelings of three children from different families, each the brother or sister of a sibling with a disability.

Rusch, F. R., DeStefano, L., Chadsey-Rusch, J., Phelps, A., & Syzmanski, E. (1992). *Transition from school to adult life: Models, linkages, and policy*. Sycamore, IL: Sycamore Publishing.

An edited book of readings on transition models and practices in selected states.

Taylor, S. (1991). *Life in the community: Case studies of organizations supporting people with disabilities.* Baltimore, MD: Paul H. Brookes.

A summary of community integration efforts in twenty-one states.

Villa, R., Thousand, J., Stainback, W., & Stainback, S. (1992). *Restructuring for caring and effective education: An administrative guide to creating heterogeneous schools.* Baltimore, MD: Paul H. Brookes.

This text provides strategies to respond to the unique needs of each learner and provide integrated classroom environments at the elementary and secondary levels. Included are guidelines for merging regular and special education, preparing staff and involving parents, encouraging student self-direction, managing classrooms, and structuring opportunities for collaboration.

West, L. L., Corbey, S., Boyer-Stephens, A., Jones, B., Miller, R. J., & Sarkees-Wircenski, M. (1992). *Integrating transition planning into the IEP process.* Reston, VA: Council for Exceptional Children.

Designed for educators to help students make smooth transitions from school to adult life by making sure the skills they need for successful employment, community involvement, postsecondary education, leisure pursuits, and self-advocacy are written into their IEPs.

Organizations

Association for the Care of Children's Health (ACCH)

An educational and advocacy organization, ACCH stresses the family's role in a child's life. With a membership of over four thousand, ACCH develops resources and training materials and cosponsors the National Information Clearinghouse described below. For more information, contact ACCH, 7910 Woodmont Ave., Suite 300, Bethesda, MD 20814.

National Information Clearinghouse for Infants with Disabilities and Life-Threatening Conditions (NIC)

Established in 1986, NIC provides a national information and referral system for services pertaining to infants and young children with disabilities. NIC specialists help families and professionals access local and national services in such areas as early intervention, parent support and training, assistive technology, and financial resources. NIC also produces bibliographies, fact sheets, monographs, and articles. For more information, contact NIC, Center for Developmental Disabilities, School of Medicine, Department of Pediatrics, University of South Carolina, Columbia, SC 29208.

Journals

Career Development for Exceptional Individuals

This journal is published by the Division of Career Development, Council for Exceptional Children, and focuses on vocational, residential, and leisure activities for children and adults with disabilities. For more information, contact CEC, 1920 Association Dr., Reston, VA 22091.

Early Education and Development

Published by Psychological Press, this journal publishes research and interventions in early education and development. For more information, contact *Early Education and Development,* P. O. Box 328, Brandon, VT 05733-1007.

International Journal of Rehabilitation Research Quarterly

This quarterly journal focuses on research studies in all areas relevant to rehabilitation of individuals with disabilities. For more information, contact International Society of Rehabilitation of the Disabled, Rehabilitation International, 432 Park Ave. South, New York, NY 10016.

Journal of Early Intervention

This is the journal of the Division of Early Childhood of the Council for Exceptional Children. It is a multidisciplinary journal aimed at professionals working in special education and related fields. For more information, contact Division for Early Childhood, CEC, 1920 Association Dr., Reston, VA 22091.

Topics in Early Childhood Special Education

This journal is published by PRO-ED, and each issue addresses a specific topic in early education and development. For more information, contact PRO-ED, 5341 Industrial Oaks Blvd., Austin, TX 78735.

15

The Impact of Public Policy: Social Trends, School Reform, and Special Education

■ How do social, political, and economic factors influence the practice of special education?

■ How is education generally funded, and how is special education funded?

■ What are the eight national education goals, and how do they guide education in America?

■ What are national education standards, and how do they relate to national goals?

■ Should educational standards be different for students with and without disabilities?

Earlier in this text you learned about Lenny, a brilliant student of mathematics, and Sarah, the best chess player in her hometown, perhaps in the country. We acquainted you with C. J. and Bobby, students with physical disabilities, one with and one without special learning needs. You were introduced to Terry Peterson, the "living legend" at Magnolia Middle School. And you read about Xong, the child who had migrated from Cambodia, had academic difficulties, and was referred for special education. Among these students, who should receive special education services?

What is education in America all about, and what are its goals? Should the goals be the same for Lenny, Terry, C. J., and Xong? Should the curriculum be easier for some of these students than others? Special education services are costly. Is educators' time and society's money better spent remediating Xong's language difficulties and experience deficits, or enhancing Lenny's outstanding math skills? Will society be better if Sarah builds her math skills to specialize in satellite telecommunications, or if we keep Terry out of jail? ■

Social change brings educational change

The delivery of educational services to students who are exceptional is a dynamic enterprise. Between the time we write this textbook and the time you read it, major changes will have taken place. Changes in society, legislation, general education, special education, related services professions, and community agencies bring about change in delivery of educational services to all students, including those who are exceptional. Education is a profession driven by social, political, and economic factors. When there are major changes in availability of resources, or in attitudes of the public toward education or toward people with disabilities, or in the federal government, there are changes in special education.

In Chapter 14 we discussed the wider context of special education in terms of parents and communities. In this chapter we widen the discussion even further, considering broad social trends, national school reform, and public policy. We look at the current scene in education with a focus on delivery of educational services to students who are exceptional. On occasion we take a historical glimpse at the origins of current activities, and we talk about questions that educators will face in the future.

Factors That Drive the Profession

Much of this text has described educational practices for students who are exceptional. On the broadest scale, however, special education is driven more by social, political, and economic factors. The following sections illustrate the influence of these factors.

Interacting factors

First, it's important to recognize that these factors do not operate independently; they interact with one another. The Head Start program is a program of intervention for disadvantaged preschool children that was created in 1965. Was Head Start a social, political, or economic innovation? Clearly the program had social origins and benefits: Providing educational opportunities for disadvantaged preschoolers improves their chances for success in later schooling and reduces the likelihood of their needing other special services. It also had political origins and benefits: Members of Congress and other political organizations fought to establish the program and continue to support it. In addition, it was influenced by economic factors: The costs of prevention have reduced later special service costs, and the program has added "producers" to society.

As you read this chapter, bear this in mind: There are no clear distinctions among the factors that influence special education. They work together to affect the ways in which special education is practiced.

Social Values and Special Education

How values govern resources

Many of society's resources are limited. People hold social values, opinions, and beliefs that influence how those limited resources are distributed. These social values affect who receives special education services; who pays for them; which services are provided; and where, when, and how they are delivered. Social values are not absolute. Different people hold different values or hold the same values to varying degrees. For some, education is a critical social value; for others, it is less important than a new civic center, good roads, or strong national defense. We voice our social values by voting in local, state, and national elections for candidates who believe as we do, and by forming or joining advocacy groups.

Changes in classification: the social backdrop

Social values are always changing. The general social climate—national and international—has a strong impact on educational policy. Social attitudes toward education in general and toward aspects of special education shifted radically, for example, after the Soviet Union launched the *Sputnik* satellite in 1957. Fear that the United States was falling behind the Soviet Union led to new programs to educate young children with disabilities, disadvantaged students, and gifted students. More recently, a major change has occurred in classification practices. As we explained in previous chapters, the number of students classified as mentally retarded has decreased in recent years, while the number classified as learning disabled has dramatically increased. This has not happened because of a sudden "cure" for mental retardation or an epidemic that resulted in learning disabilities. Rather, the overrepresentation of African-American students and other children of color among those labeled "retarded" led to legal challenges to the classification system. Many people became concerned about the stigma attached to retardation. Eventually the definition of mental retardation was changed, and fewer students were assigned to that category. Meanwhile, learning disabilities came to the fore as a designation with greater social acceptability. Because society could provide services for students with learning disabilities, use of that category increased.

Early intervention

The influence of social factors on special education is probably no more apparent than it is in the education of very young children (cf. Ysseldyke, Algozzine, & Thurlow, 1992). Early intervention has become the fastest growing area in special education. During the first part of the twentieth century, the education of very young children with special needs was a concern of a small, dedicated group of educators. Initially, private moneys were used to finance this effort, and preschool programs for children with disabilities were operated largely by independent agencies (like the United Cerebral Palsy Association) or parent organizations. Designed to provide relief for parents, these agencies were the first to provide educational services of direct benefit to young children. Interest in early childhood education revived during the 1960s, partly because Americans had entered a fierce scientific rivalry with the Soviet Union and partly because, as the post–World War II economy slackened, large numbers of women were entering the workforce and needed child care for infants, toddlers, and preschoolers.

Issues of the 1990s

Another factor was that an increasing number of students were not meeting the academic and behavioral standards of public schools. The Head Start program was a response to this shortcoming, a way to help disadvantaged children adapt to the educational program by giving them learning readiness skills. During the 1990s, early intervention programs are having to respond to even more complex social issues. More and more children are exposed prenatally to cocaine. Each year more babies are born with fetal alcohol syndrome. Many children now have to attend to their own needs, and increasing numbers get their basic nutrition from schools and service agencies. Society seems to relegate to schools important child care and child development functions previously performed by parents and families. Moreover, early intervention and elementary school programs often are expected to counteract the social effects of poverty, unemployment, racism, war, and drug use.

Political Factors and Special Education

A variety of political factors, closely related to social and economic factors, have significant effects on public policy for the education of students with disabilities. First, the general political climate influences public policy in special education. In a liberal or progressive political climate, special education services tend to become more available; the resources for delivering services are greater. In a conservative political climate, services become limited. During the 1960s, a liberal period, many federal programs were initiated for students with disabilities and disadvantaged students. In the late 1970s and 1980s, a conservative period, fiscal restraint was evident. Major questions were raised about the benefits of special education services, funding for programs was cut, and proposals to abolish the U.S. Department of Education were made.

Political climate

Parents and advocacy groups

Second, the political action of parents and advocacy groups shapes special education policy. As we noted in Chapter 3, class-action lawsuits have played a major role in the last several decades. The 1979 case of *Larry P.* v. *Riles,* for

Advocacy groups have made and continue to make important contributions to the lives of people with disabilities and their families and friends. *Bob Daemmrich.*

example, forced the state of California to stop using intelligence tests to place African-American students in classes for students with mental retardation. In 1993 the parents of such students again sued the California Department of Education, this time to allow their children to be given intelligence tests. It was argued that exclusion of the students from intellectual assessment might keep the students from being declared eligible for the benefits of services for students with learning disabilities. As these cases illustrate, the ramifications of legal action can be complex. Overall, however, parents and advocacy groups have used the court system to win educational rights for students with disabilities, as well as protection from abusive treatment and involuntary institutionalization.

Advocacy groups also have a direct influence on policymakers and legislators. The groups interested in special education range from broad-based organizations, like the Council for Exceptional Children and the American Federation of Teachers, to groups concerned with particular disabilities, such as the Learning Disabilities Association of America. The larger and more powerful groups wield political influence through their statements and publications. When the American Federation of Teachers issues guidelines for placement of students who are exceptional, educators throughout the country take notice. Many advocacy groups also employ lobbyists—experts who know how to disseminate information, sway public opinion, and bring pressure on important legislators. Advocacy groups often band together on issues. A group called Citizens Concerned about Disability, comprised of representatives of major professional associations and advocacy groups (usually each group is

Political influence of groups

Window on Practice

Case Study in Advocacy: Passage of Goals 2000

Goals 2000 is a federal education act that was signed in March 1994. (The contents of the act are discussed later in this chapter.) It is a good example of the power of advocacy groups. For instance, the original draft of the act listed six national goals, but the final law includes eight. Where did the extra two goals come from?

■ During debate on the bill, teacher groups argued that if they were to provide the up-to-date instruction implied by other passages of the act, they would need greater opportunities for professional development and training. Thus, a goal relating to teacher education and professional development was added to the law.

■ Both teachers and parents argued that students could not achieve the national goals without considerable parent involvement and strong linkages between homes and schools. For this reason, a goal concerning parental participation was added.

Other variations between the original and final drafts included the following:

■ The original draft had no specific language to indicate that the law applied to all American children, including those with disabilities. But parents of students with disabilities argued that the high educational standards specified in the act should apply to their children as well as others. In the end, such language was added.

■ The original bill mandated that states establish opportunity-to-learn standards (described later in the chapter). This provision reflected the belief that if we hold students responsible for achieving high standards, we should also hold schools and school personnel responsible for delivering the related instruction. But teacher unions and others actively opposed this requirement. As a result, in the law's final language, the opportunity-to-learn standards became voluntary rather than mandatory for the states.

■ The law's original version mentioned only certain academic subjects. The final version named a number of other subjects, because groups of teachers representing the omitted subject areas successfully lobbied for their inclusion.

These changes were neither unusual nor unexpected. Goals 2000 is merely one recent instance of the major role played by advocacy groups in formulating public policy on education.

represented by a person called a government liaison person), meets regularly in Washington, D.C., to have a voice in legislation and federal educational and mental health policy issues. The major educational laws of the past two decades—the laws that define special education as it exists today—are very much a result of such political influence by advocacy groups. So are the ongoing changes in classification, such as the recent establishment of autism and traumatic brain injury as separate federal disability categories.

Government agencies   Finally, certain government agencies protect or further the rights of individuals who are exceptional. For example, both the U.S. Office of Civil Rights and the Bureau of Indian Affairs have influenced the provision of services for those with disabilities. Thus, a federal or state bureaucracy can itself become an important political factor.

Economic Factors and Special Education

Funding special education

Who pays for special education? All education dollars come from federal, state, and local governments. Until recent decades, local governments provided the largest share. In the 1978–79 school year, however, the state share of funding rose above the local share (Stern, 1988), and the state contribution has remained higher ever since.

When it enacted the Education for All Handicapped Children Act, now the Individuals with Disabilities Education Act (IDEA), Congress assigned the responsibility for providing a free, appropriate public education to all children with disabilities to state and local governments. However, state educational agencies and local school districts get federal financial assistance in implementing the nation's special education mandates. Along with this financial help, the federal government provides supervision, policy support, and technical assistance.

Federal funding programs

The Office of Special Education Programs (OSEP) in the U.S. Department of Education administers two funding programs: The IDEA Part B State Grant Program and the Chapter 1 Program for Children with Disabilities. Under the IDEA Part B State Grant Program, funds are distributed to states according to the total numbers of students with disabilities reported as receiving special education and related services. State educational agencies conduct an annual child count on December 1 of the previous fiscal year and submit these counts to OSEP. Funds appropriated by OSEP during fiscal year 1992 amounted to $1.9 billion dollars. The average per-child allocation of federal funding was $419. An additional $143 million was allocated to support Chapter 1 funding for students with disabilities, amounting to an average of $524 per child. At least 75 percent of the funds that a state receives under the IDEA Part B State Grant Program must be distributed to local educational agencies and intermediate educational units to assist in the education of students with disabilities. Local education agencies must certify to the state that they are not using these funds to replace local funding, but to pay for excess costs of educating students with disabilities.

Federal review of state plans

The U.S. Department of Education attaches "strings" to such allocations. States must submit program goals, objectives, strategies, and priorities annually to the secretary of education for review and approval. The state plans are reviewed to spot deficiencies in service delivery. To receive its funding, the state must provide the assurance that it will implement corrected procedures during the forthcoming year and that all deficiencies in the plan will be corrected before the next grant cycle.

Site visits

On-site monitoring reviews are another important component of the federal program review process. Each state that receives financial assistance is visited about every three years by a monitoring team from the U.S. Department of Education. The team visits the state education agency and representative local education agencies. In addition to reviewing a state's written policies and procedures, members of the monitoring team solicit information from parents, the general public, advocates, and representatives of professional groups. They hold public meetings and solicit written testimony on the quality of service provided by the state.

The federal monitoring process produces a degree of uncertainty in educational funding; federal money is not automatic. Another source of uncertainty is the fact that education is only one among many social services that government provides. General and special education must compete for dollars with highways, sanitation, and other services. To the extent that members of society value special education more than other services, special education is financed more heavily. Special education also competes with regular education for financial resources. From all the funds provided for education, moneys must be allocated between general and special education. When a state increases the percentage of moneys allocated to special education, moneys allocated to general education typically diminish.

Government spending patterns influence public policy on the education of students who are exceptional, although those spending patterns also *reflect* public policy. If you want to know where the most research activity in special education will take place over the next five years, look at the research priorities established by the U.S. Department of Education. During the 1950s and 1960s, the federal government made mental retardation a priority, and centers for research on mental retardation were established across the country. As funding priorities changed, new centers were established, and old ones changed their names and expanded their missions. During the middle and late 1970s, institutes were funded to conduct research on learning disabilities and on early intervention. The 1980s saw less federal support for research on learning disabilities. Instead, support shifted to research on students with severe disabilities and transition services for older students with disabilities. In the 1990s, emphasis is on early childhood education. Decisions to shift research efforts often are motivated by economics: Researchers go "where the money is."

The overall pool of moneys available to provide special education services must be divided among all exceptional students. This creates competition for resources among the various categorical programs. If a fixed amount of money is available to educate students with disabilities, and if school personnel decide to spend a greater proportion of that money on educating students who are deaf, then less money is available for educating students with other exceptionalities.

Technical methods of funding allocation also influence special education services. State legislatures decide how much state money will be allocated to education of students who are exceptional, and they decide how the state moneys and the funds received from the federal government will be distributed to local education agencies. There are various criteria for these decisions.

Some states allocate funds according to the number of "teacher units." That is, for each school district, the state determines a reasonable number of special education personnel on the basis of community demographics; then the state

Competing for public dollars

Changing research priorities

Competition among categorical programs

Allocation methods

Funding based on "teacher units"

provides a certain percentage of those people's salaries. This method discourages schools from identifying large numbers of students with disabilities. More students mean larger special education classes, but not more money; hence, schools often develop informal policies that inhibit teachers from identifying students with special education needs.

Funding based on "pupil units"

Other states use a "pupil unit" method of allocation. This method is based on the assumption that it costs more to educate students with disabilities than students who are not disabled. The largest extra cost is for special education personnel; other costs include specially designed transportation, food services, equipment, and health and rehabilitation services. State departments of education typically pay school districts a subsidy for each student. In the per-pupil method of allocation, the state makes up for the extra costs of students with disabilities by increasing the subsidy for each such student. For example, if the state calculates that students with disabilities are 2.4 times more expensive to educate than those without disabilities, the state multiplies its subsidy by 2.4 for every student in the district who is classified as disabled. Average per-pupil costs vary from state to state, as do extra costs. The pupil-unit method seems fairer than the teacher-unit method. However, it encourages "bounty hunting" by school district administrators who may manipulate the number of students classified as disabled in order to increase the district's subsidy.

Adjusting funding according to disability condition

Some states, recognizing that certain disabilities require greater educational expenses than others, use different multipliers for different disability conditions. The state education department might decide that educating students who are blind costs twice as much as educating those with learning disabilities, and adjust the subsidies accordingly. Even this system can be manipulated; schools may label their students according to expected financial return rather than according to needs.

Growing financial burden

In times of financial prosperity, these economic considerations may fade. If money is not an issue, schools seldom attempt to limit services to students who are exceptional or to restrict the number of students declared eligible. For most public school districts, however, times have not been prosperous. Furthermore, the enrollment of greater numbers of students with severe disabilities in public education programs has increased the financial burden on the schools. Buildings and equipment must be modified, and new equipment and facilities purchased. Because schools must provide education and *related* services, they end up paying for communication boards, hearing aids, and other devices. As the financial burden increases, educators become concerned about the number of students receiving special education and who will pay the costs. There is a tenuous balance between society's desire to provide special education services and its ability to pay for them.

School Reform

As the previous sections indicate, social, political, and economic factors continually shift, and their total effect on education changes over time. Since the

Factors spurring reform

early 1980s, various factors have combined to spur a strong movement toward school reform. As we prepared this text, considerable reform activity was under way. Some of it was prompted by economic concerns, especially about the limited funding now available. Much of the activity stemmed from social and political concerns, particularly that the quality of schooling was not as good as society would like. Various reports identified areas in which America's schools were lacking, or in which American youth fell behind youth from other countries. The following sections describe efforts to establish national education goals, national standards, and opportunity-to-learn standards. We describe efforts to "restructure" schools and discuss the implications of all these efforts for provision of educational services to students who are exceptional.

National Education Goals

In 1983 the National Commission on Excellence in Education produced a report entitled *A Nation at Risk: The Imperative for Educational Reform*. The report was very critical of American schooling and called for a commitment to excellence—higher standards, more courses, more homework, more time in school, more time spent on academics, and more local and state responsibility for education. In 1984 President Reagan stated four national education goals to be reached by the year 1990:

Reagan's education goals

- To raise the high school graduation rate to more than 90 percent
- To raise scores on college admission tests above the 1985 average
- To make teachers' salaries competitive with entry-level business and engineering graduates' salaries
- To stiffen high school graduation requirements

Results of 1980s reform efforts

By 1990 the high school graduation rate was about 60 to 75 percent. (A range is reported because there is virtually no agreement on how to define and count dropout.) Scores on college admission tests had gone up slightly, while teachers' salaries had not become competitive with entry-level business and engineering graduates' salaries. Most states were stiffening graduation requirements, such as having students pass a test to graduate. Although admirable, the goals ignored the growing number of students who needed special education services.

In 1989 the National Governors' Association published a report entitled *Time for Results*. The report called attention to the need to improve school organization and policy as well as the quality of teachers; it recognized the needs of children at risk, especially those who were very young; and it addressed the need for early intervention.

REI

When educators were thinking deeply about reform in general education, the **regular education initiative (REI)** was proposed. Despite its name, it was a call from special education for reform in the way services were provided to students with disabilities. It involved responsibility shared by regular educators and special educators for students considered disabled, with the goal of breaking down barriers between the two educational systems and integrating students with disabilities more fully into the regular classroom environment. Debate about the initiative was heated among most special educators and parents. Some special educators worried about the need for their services if regular educators assumed responsibility for students with disabilities. Other special educators wondered whether they had the consultation skills required for the shared responsibility proposed by those who backed the initiative. Parents expressed concerns about due process rights and about whether their children would be educated appropriately. Personnel in general education knew relatively little about the initiative until years after debate about it had commenced.

Inclusion

As we noted in Chapter 2, the term *inclusion* or *full inclusion* recently replaced REI as the focus of debate. Although inclusion means different things to different people, the issue of responsibility has continued to be critical. Regular educators wonder whether they should assume responsibility for educating students with different disabilities, especially if little teacher training is provided.

A new set of national goals

Meanwhile, as the debates over REI and inclusion erupted, the reform movement in general education continued. In 1989 President Bush convened a meeting of the governors from the fifty states in Charlottesville, Virginia, at a "historic education summit" that resulted in a list of national education goals. The six goals were fleshed out with a set of national educational objectives and were specified in a press release from the White House (1990). The national goals were then specified in a proposal to Congress called America 2000. The national education goals were supported by Bill Clinton, who was governor of Arkansas at the time.

Goals 2000

When he became president, Clinton incorporated the six national goals into federal legislation as part of Goals 2000: The Educate America Act. Two goals were added as the legislation passed through Congress, and Goals 2000 was signed by President Clinton on March 30, 1994. The eight national goals are listed in Table 15.1. They focus on readiness for school, school completion, student achievement and citizenship, teacher education and development, mathematics and science, adult literacy and lifelong learning, the school environment (safe, disciplined, and drug-free schools), and parental participation in children's schooling.

School Readiness   The focus of the first education goal is readiness for school. Three educational objectives are associated with this goal:

Objectives for school readiness

- All children will have access to high-quality and developmentally appropriate preschool programs that help prepare children for school.

- Every parent in the United States will be a child's first teacher and devote time each day helping his or her preschool child learn; and parents will have access to the training and support they need.

- Children will receive the nutrition, physical activity experiences, and health care needed to arrive at school with healthy minds and bodies, and the number of low-birthweight babies will be significantly reduced through enhanced prenatal health systems.

Table 15.1   National Education Goals

Goal 1   School Readiness
By the year 2000, all children in America will start school ready to learn.

Goal 2   School Completion
By the year 2000, the high school graduation rate will increase to at least 90 percent.

Goal 3   Student Achievement and Citizenship
By the year 2000, all students will leave grades 4, 8, and 12 having demonstrated competency over challenging subject matter including English, mathematics, science, foreign languages, civics and government, economics, arts, history, and geography, and every school in America will ensure that all students learn to use their minds well, so they may be prepared for responsible citizenship, further learning, and productive employment in our Nation's modern economy.

Goal 4   Teacher Education and Professional Development
By the year 2000, the Nation's teaching force will have access to programs for the continued improvement of their professional skills and the opportunity to acquire the knowledge and skills needed to instruct and prepare all American students for the next century.

Goal 5   Mathematics and Science
By the year 2000, United States students will be first in the world in mathematics and science achievement.

Goal 6   Adult Literacy and Lifelong Learning
By the year 2000, every adult American will be literate and will possess the knowledge and skills necessary to compete in a global economy and exercise the rights and responsibilities of citizenship.

Goal 7   Safe, Disciplined, and Alcohol- and Drug-free Schools
By the year 2000, every school in the United States will be free of drugs, violence, and the unauthorized presence of firearms and alcohol and will offer a disciplined environment conducive to learning.

Goal 8   Parental Participation
By the year 2000, every school will promote partnerships that will increase parental involvement and participation in promoting the social, emotional, and academic growth of children.

Source: Goals 2000: The Educate America Act (March 31, 1994).

School Completion   The completion of high school is the focus of the second national education goal and its two objectives:

Objectives for school completion

- The nation must dramatically reduce its dropout rate, and seventy-five percent of the students who do drop out will successfully complete a high school degree or its equivalent.
- The gap in high school graduation rates between American students from minority backgrounds and their nonminority counterparts will be eliminated.

This goal sounds like one of the national goals voiced by Reagan in 1984, to be reached by 1990 ("to raise the high school graduation rate to more than 90%"). It similarly suggests nonrecognition of students with disabilities. The press release discussion of this goal (White House, 1990) suggested that it could be met by restructuring the public school system, and that "efforts to restructure education must work toward guaranteeing that all students are engaged in rigorous programs of instruction designed to ensure that every child, *regardless of* background or *disability* [italics added], acquires the knowledge and skills necessary to succeed in a changing economy" (p. 7).

Student Achievement and Citizenship   The broad notions of achievement and citizenship come together in the third educational goal, which specifies competence in English, mathematics, science, foreign languages, civics and government, economics, arts, history, and geography. It also specifies preparation for responsible citizenship. The five objectives associated with it are:

Objectives for student achievement and citizenship

- The academic performance of all students at the elementary and secondary level will increase significantly in every quartile, and the distribution of minority students in each quartile will more closely reflect the student population as a whole.
- The percentage of students who demonstrate the ability to reason, solve problems, apply knowledge, and write and communicate effectively will increase substantially.
- All students will be involved in activities that promote and demonstrate citizenship, good health, community service, and personal responsibility.
- All students will have access to physical education and health education to ensure they are healthy and fit.
- The percentage of students who are competent in more than one language will substantially increase.
- All students will be knowledgeable about the diverse cultural heritage of this nation and about the world community.

Assessment of outcomes

This goal focused on competency in various content areas and on the even broader goals of learning to use the mind to foster responsible citizenship, advanced learning, and productive employment. It reflected a move toward national and state-by-state assessments of educational indicators, which in turn created additional questions for professionals responsible for students with disabilities. Educators debated the extent to which students with disabilities could be included in state and national testing; they argued about whether students with disabilities could attain the goals; and they debated the absence of "functional skills" from the objectives.

Teacher training programs

Teacher Education and Professional Development   Goal 4 is one of the two goals added in congressional debate about Goals 2000. It specifies that teachers will have access to training programs designed to improve their professional skills. It also indicates that the purpose of this professional training is to enable students to reach the other goals and be prepared for the next century.

Solving problems is easier for students with disabilities when working with a friend. *Mimi Forsytn/ Monkmeyer Press.*

The objectives for this goal are that

■ All teachers will have access to preservice teacher education and continuing professional development activities that will provide such teachers with the knowledge and skills needed to teach to an increasingly diverse student population with a variety of educational, social, and health needs.

■ All teachers will have continuing opportunities to acquire additional knowledge and skills needed to teach challenging subject matter and to use emerging new methods, forms of assessment, and technologies.

■ States and school districts will create integrated strategies to attract, recruit, prepare, retrain, and support the continued professional development of teachers, administrators, and other educators, so that there is a highly talented work force of professional educators to teach challenging subject matter.

■ Partnerships will be established, whenever possible, among local educational agencies, institutions of higher education, parents, and local labor, business, and professional associations to provide and support programs for the professional development of educators.

Mathematics and Science   The fifth goal calls for U.S. students to be first in the world in math and science by the year 2000. Objectives associated with the goal are that

Objectives for math and science

■ Mathematics and science education, including the metric system, will be strengthened throughout the system, especially in the early grades.

- The number of teachers with a substantive background in mathematics and science, including the metric system, will increase by 50 percent.
- The number of U.S. undergraduate and graduate students, especially women and minorities, who complete degrees in mathematics, science, and engineering will increase significantly.

This goal targets two specific content areas for emphasis because of their significance in international business competition.

Adult Literacy and Lifelong Learning   The sixth goal moves the focus beyond the school setting to postschool outcomes. Its objectives are that

Objectives for adult literacy and lifelong learning

- Every major American business will be involved in strengthening the connection between education and work.
- All workers will have the opportunity to acquire the knowledge and skills, from basic to highly technical, needed to adapt to emerging new technologies, work methods, and markets through public and private educational, vocational, technical, workplace, or other programs.
- The number of quality programs, including those at libraries, that are designed to serve more effectively the needs of the growing number of part-time and mid-career students will increase substantially.
- The proportion of those qualified students, especially minorities, who enter college; who complete at least two years; and who complete their degree programs will increase substantially.
- The proportion of college graduates who demonstrate an advanced ability to think critically, communicate effectively, and solve problems will increase substantially.
- Schools, in implementing comprehensive parent involvement programs, will offer more adult literacy, parent training, and lifelong learning opportunities to improve the ties between home and school, and enhance parents' work and home lives.

This goal might be interpreted broadly as successful transition from school to work for students with disabilities. Yet the press release discussion of this goal spoke only of jobs that required more than a high school education, coordination of policies and programs to promote literacy, and greater access to college educations for those who were qualified.

Safe, Disciplined, and Alcohol- and Drug-free Schools   The seventh goal addresses the condition of the school environment. Objectives associated with it are

Objectives for improving the school environment

- Every school will implement a firm and fair policy on use, possession, and distribution of drugs and alcohol.
- Parents, businesses, and governmental and community organizations will work together to ensure the rights of students to study in a safe and secure environment that is free of drugs and crime, and ensure that schools provide a healthy environment and are a safe haven for all children.

- Every local educational agency will develop and implement a policy to ensure that all schools are free of violence and the unauthorized presence of weapons.
- Every local education agency will develop a sequential, comprehensive kindergarten through twelfth grade drug and alcohol prevention education program.
- Drug and alcohol curriculum should be taught as an integral part of sequential, comprehensive health education.
- Community-based teams should be organized to provide students and teachers with needed support.
- Every school should work to eliminate sexual harassment.

This broad goal is appropriate for all students.

Parental Participation   The eighth goal resulted from congressional debate on Goals 2000. It was argued that holding students responsible for achieving high standards required involving parents in their educational programs. The goal calls for partnerships between parents and school personnel to enhance the social, emotional, and academic growth of children. The objectives for this goal are that

Getting parents involved

- Every state will develop policies to assist local schools and local educational agencies to establish programs for increasing partnerships that respond to the varying needs of parents and the home, including parents of children who are disadvantaged or bilingual, or parents of children with disabilities.
- Every school will actively engage parents and families in a partnership that supports the academic work of children at home and shared educational decision making at school.
- Parents and families will help to ensure that schools are adequately supported and will hold schools and teachers to high standards of accountability.

Applying the goals to students with disabilities

In response to these eight national education goals, professionals responsible for educating students with disabilities must consider how the goals apply to those students. The goals are primarily academic; they say little or nothing about social skills, life skills, or functional skills. The ways the goals are being interpreted suggest that students with disabilities are not ready to learn, are not capable of achieving world-class standards, and are likely to drop out of school. Members of the disability community are voicing concern about what would happen to those they represent when schools focus intensely on the attainment of national goals. Are students whose developmental circumstances make it difficult for them to achieve the national goals to be excluded? Are they to be counted among the students who are ready to learn, who drop out, or who have world-class knowledge of math and science? If students with disabilities are not counted now, when will they count?

The best place for children with disabilities to be educated is with their natural neighbors and peers. *Laura Dwight.*

National Standards

National task forces, panels, and committees are encouraging the development of world-class standards for pupil performance, especially in basic skill areas. Goals 2000 specifies that Congress appoint a National Educational Standards and Improvement Council (NESIC). This group is responsible for certifying voluntary state-proposed standards for instruction. If a state requires that students meet specific graduation criteria or master specific mathematics content, for example, NESIC decides if the standards are appropriate.

NESIC

Standards are statements of criteria against which comparisons can be made. The term *standards* has several educational uses:

Types of standards

- as criteria for achievement level (performance standards)
- as desirable characteristics for action (delivery standards)
- as a necessary core of knowledge (content standards)

Discussion on national standards consistently stresses that the standards are for all students. Yet, the National Council of Teachers of Mathematics produced a set of math standards, for example, that did not indicate how they

Point of View

The Argument for High National Standards

The following paragraphs, excerpted from a report by the National Council on Educational Standards and Testing, present the case for establishing high national standards for all students. As you read this Point of View, ask yourself what the proposed national standards would mean for the inclusion process. Can the type of standards advocated here apply to students with disabilities? If not, how do we ensure that students with disabilities are included in the progress of educational reform?

In the absence of well-defined and demanding standards, education in the United States has gravitated toward de facto national minimum expectations. Except for students who are planning to attend selective four-year colleges, current education standards focus on low-level reading and arithmetic skills and on small amounts of factual material in other content areas. Consumers of education in this country have settled for far less than they should and for far less than do their counterparts in other developed nations.

High national standards tied to assessments can create high expectations for all students and help to better target resources. They are critical

to the nation in three primary ways: to promote educational equity, to preserve democracy and enhance the civic culture, and to improve economic competitiveness. Further, national education standards would help to provide an increasingly diverse and mobile population with shared values and knowledge....

Providing genuine opportunity for all students to achieve high standards is a national moral imperative. The standards that the Council proposes would apply to the entire education system. All students must have the opportunity to achieve them and to be assessed fairly on their attainment. To bring this about, equitable educational opportunities must be provided. High quality standards and assessments should mobilize educators and the public to reform schools, engage families and communities, create incentives for high performance, and provide genuine opportunity for all students.

Source: National Council on Educational Standards and Testing. (1992). *Raising standards for American education: A report to Congress, the Secretary of Education, the National Education Goals Panel, and the American people.* Washington, D.C.: National Council on Educational Standards and Testing, pp. 2–3, 40.

---

would apply to students with disabilities. Experts in mathematics say the proposed standards are appropriate but not feasible for students with disabilities.

Major standard-setting efforts now exist in most school content areas: math, science, geography, history, civics, English, and arts. Groups have been formed in the areas of health and physical education and foreign language learning. The Departments of Labor and Education are considering joint work on standards for work readiness.

Standards: inclusive or exclusive?

Can standards be established that are both challenging for students who are gifted and inclusive of students with unique learning needs? Different standards may need to be set for students with disabilities. If so, how do we avoid creating separate educational systems for students with and without disabilities? Does setting standards perpetuate the tendency to exclude students with disabilities from state and national assessments? How should standards be set, and who should set them?

Opportunity-to-Learn Standards

An important part of Goals 2000 is its encouragement for states to establish **opportunity-to-learn** (OTL) **standards:** the teaching and learning conditions necessary for all students to have a fair opportunity to learn, including ways of measuring the extent to which such standards are met. The OTL standards are to be developed by a task force and approved by NESIC. At the time we prepared this text, there was much debate about how opportunity to learn would be defined. Defining opportunity to learn as time spent in school has implications for students with disabilities who attend school for partial days. Defining it in terms of resources allocated to instruction suggests that students with disabilities get more opportunity to learn because their education costs more. Defining opportunity to learn as time actively engaged in instruction implies inequities in measuring engaged time, especially for students who spend limited time actively responding to instruction.

A basic question about opportunity to learn, regarding students with disabilities, is Should low functioning students get (a) the same amount of time as everybody else, or (b) the amount of time necessary for them to be successful? Ysseldyke, Thurlow, and Shin (1994) prepared an extensive analysis of the concept of opportunity to learn and its potential impact on students with disabilities. It is too early to speculate on the eventual impact of the legislation on this important concept. We encourage you to follow the debate on opportunity to learn and to consider its impacts on the education of students with disabilities.

School Restructuring

School restructuring is a specific approach to school reform. It is "A systematic approach that acknowledges the complexity of fundamentally changing the way schools are organized in order to significantly increase student learning. It shifts the focus of reform from mandating what educators do to looking at the results their actions produce" (National Governor's Association, 1990, p. 1). In restructuring, efforts are made to reorganize schools to produce better *results* for students. Major reforms currently are underway in general education. They are proceeding on a piecemeal basis, with more talk than action about reform. Examples of restructuring include site-based management (decision making at the school site rather than a central office), changing staff roles, implementation of a higher-order-thinking curriculum (emphasis on strategies for learning, for example, rather than on basic skills), and adoption of an accountability system. Excellence—successful preparation of students for adulthood—is the desired outcome of reform and restructuring.

Not all states have initiated such structural reform; some have been forced to change. In 1989, for example, the Kentucky State Supreme Court declared the entire state education system to be unconstitutional. Superintendents, local school boards, the state department of education, and essentially all educators were identified as part of the problem. The court ordered the revision of every aspect of the school system. Kentucky's response was to form a special task

Margin notes:
Defining opportunity to learn

A policy question

Examples of restructuring

Court intervention

force and several working committees to make recommendations. Legislators put together a school-reform bill that has been called a "roadmap to reform" and "one of the most comprehensive restructuring efforts ever undertaken by a legislature" (Walker, 1990). Features of the Kentucky reform, which was signed into law in April 1990, included:

The Kentucky reforms

- A system of rewards and sanctions for schools based on performance. Successful schools receive monetary rewards in the form of increased state subsidies. Unsuccessful schools are publicly identified and helped. Parents may use "choice" enrollment options to move their child out of an unsatisfactory school.

- Outcomes-based focus. New techniques will be used to assess student achievement. Schools will be assessed on student health, dropout and retention rates, and attendance, as well as on student achievement.

- Site-based management. Each district will have at least one site-based management school immediately, with all other schools phasing in by 1996.

Impact on special education

When such radical reform takes place, the effects on special education and those involved in it can be substantial. Teachers who participate in site-based management programs may find themselves helping to make basic policy decisions about special education: How should the school's available resources for special education be allocated? How many resource rooms should there be, and where? Who should teach? How should special education students be assessed? In such a climate, teachers must be flexible and prepared to adapt to new conditions. For example, changing staff roles may require that special education teachers serve students after school rather than pulling them out of mainstream classes, or a new accountability system may require teachers to prove progress in more rigorous ways than they've used previously.

Unified system

In some cases, too, restructuring may mean establishment of a *unified system*, in which the distinctions between regular education and special education are essentially abolished. Under such a plan, all students are merged into regular classes, and all educational funds are pooled. This kind of change can have profound effects on teachers who have exceptional students in their classrooms. In districts that engage in such radical restructuring, heavy demands may be put on teachers' resourcefulness and creativity. Concomitantly, though, teachers should have greater opportunities to contribute to fundamental improvements in their students' education.

Social Trends, School Reform, and Special Education in Perspective

Social, political, and economic factors change what happens in special education through their influence on current practice and on one another. When society's attitudes toward the education of students who are exceptional change, laws may be written or revised and funding patterns may change. When funding patterns change, social attitudes may change, and so on. The relationships among factors that influence special education are evident in the impact of Public Law 94–142. That law has led to many changes in educational practice,

Interrelationships among factors

Bring Your Learning to Life

Technology Helps Kim Bazan Meet New Roles and Keep Current

Our friend Kim Bazan, a classroom teacher, likes to keep up with new trends in education. She has read about education reform and the growing national concern for improving student outcomes. Moreover, some of the reform initiatives, including the movement toward greater inclusion, have taken hold in her school district. Kim is not sure where she stands on inclusion. On the one hand, she believes that all students should have the opportunity to be successful and that teachers should be able to teach anyone who comes through the classroom door. On the other hand, she knows that students with disabilities learn best when classroom opportunities are structured to support their learning needs, and that not all teachers are prepared to make such changes. Because she is assuming new roles as a result of public policy changes influencing special education, Kim believes the need for keeping current is more pressing than it ever has been in her career.

To find out more about different perspectives on inclusion, Kim recently enrolled in an interactive TV course offered by her state department of education and the community college in her area. She attended class at a local high school with several other teachers. The course was taught by a professor in another city. About seventy teachers at fifteen sites participated using TV monitors with split-screen technology and carefully designed course segments. Kim used her home computer to receive (download) assignments and send (upload) responses to the professor teaching the course. She also used it to communicate with other students in the class.

Kim also uses her home computer and Internet to keep in touch with us and other colleagues across the country for up-to-date information on tactics for keeping her students with disabilities in classes with their neighbors and peers. (Jim Ysseldyke's Internet address is YSSEL001@MAROON.TC.UMN.EDU; Bob Algozzine's is FCI00RFA@UNCCVM.UNCC. EDU.) From time to time she downloads information from electronic bulletin boards and shares it with her colleagues at school. When she needs information, Kim posts a message using E-mail or connects to her local library and searches the card catalog for new books. She recently attended inservice workshops that we provided to teachers in her area on strategies and tactics for effective instruction and simple ways to make teaching fun.

There is no question that special education is changing and that public policy changes are influencing teachers. Kim knows that keeping up means taking advantage of innovations in technology and teacher preparation methods. From living and working with students with disabilities on a daily basis, she has come to appreciate technology not as a magic potion but as a useful and important resource.

the effects of which probably won't be known for years. Most educators contend that students with disabilities are receiving a more appropriate education now than they were two decades ago. Yet, because there is no systematic collection of data on the outcomes of schooling for students with disabilities, we can't prove it. This reality is changing as more and more states and school districts collect data on outcomes of schooling for all of their students.

Special education means being provided services that make learning alongside neighbors and peers a reality. *Elizabeth Crews.*

Effects of Public Law 94–142 and IDEA

For decades, special education existed as a system parallel to regular education. With the enactment of Public Law 94–142 and the requirement that students with disabilities be educated in the least restrictive environment, special education became part of a continuum of delivering services to students. The law forged a new partnership between special and regular education. For the first time schools were challenged with educating new populations of students with severe disabilities, both younger (ages 3 to 5) and older (ages 18 to 21). With passage of IDEA in 1990, school personnel were confronted with educating students with disabilities birth to 21 and developing transition plans for these students to pass smoothly to the world of work. Schools were required by law to enter cooperative arrangements with other agencies to provide related services and to pay for those services. An era of interagency collaboration and cooperation was born.

Current reforms

Currently, with school reform, school restructuring, the establishment of national education goals, and the push for full inclusion, special education is changing further. Some districts are beginning to merge all types of education—regular, compensatory, and special—into a single system. In other districts, the ultimate impact of the reform movements is not yet known. The transformations raise fundamental questions about the long-term effects on the education of students who are exceptional.

Need for teacher training

One area that has felt the impact of ongoing changes is teacher training. To provide services to new populations of students with medical or physical disabilities, schools need specially trained teachers—teachers who can run portable respirators, use augmentative communication devices to communicate with nonoral children, clean out wounds, and bandage children with spina bifida. Regular education teachers, charged with the task of educating students with disabilities in the regular classroom, need inservice training. If schools do not have the financial resources to give them that training, teachers are faced with the task of providing services they are not trained to do and they develop job-related stress. Many change jobs; others leave the profession altogether.

There are various ways to meet the special learning needs of students. Are services being provided in the best possible way? As Biklen (1989) put it, "states could fund the education of all students without identifying any students or programs as special, but they do not. Persistence in funding labeled students or programs may reflect concern that students with disabilities would not receive much needed special services if unlabeled" (p. 9). Special education could be freed from the "stepchild" role it sometimes is forced to play. Its future could be different, if people learning about special education are encouraged to think differently about it. In 1983, Mary Moran wrote that "alternative futures can be imagined, if we free ourselves to question assumptions" (p. 36).

Toward a different future

Important decisions have to be made about the future of special education; many will be made by the students of today who will teach the students of tomorrow. This is your challenge, your social responsibility.

Closing Comments and Parting Thoughts

We close this text with some assumptions and tips for you to consider.

Two fundamental assumptions are driving the development of U.S. educational policy, and the way these assumptions are played out in practice will affect what happens to students who are exceptional. First, Americans assume we can have both excellence and equity in the education of students. This assumption has two premises. The first premise is that for our democracy and our economy to remain strong we need a well-skilled workforce. The kinds of skills needed to survive in our increasingly complex world are changing, but students still must have high-level skills. The second premise is that *all* students, including those with disabilities, must have the opportunity to learn to the same high-content standards. All students are capable of learning more than they now learn, and they have the capability of learning complex content. No one should be left out. At the same time, however, we don't always know precisely what to do with each student.

Excellence and equity

The second fundamental assumption is that schools cannot operate in isolation to get students to achieve important outcomes. This means that teachers, nurses, occupational therapists, psychologists, counselors, and social workers have to form alliances with other professionals to meet students' needs. The challenges students bring to schools are increasingly complex, and no one discipline can meet their needs in isolation. Inter- and multidisciplinary activities are required.

Alliances with other professionals

There are two ways to make major contributions to the instruction of students who are exceptional. First, lead in the appropriate instruction of these students. Strong leadership is needed to achieve broad moral obligations. Second, apply basic principles of effective instruction, such as those discussed throughout this book.

No magic can make your teaching life better. We hope something in this book will enable you to see people who are exceptional differently from your earlier conceptions. We hope we have helped you to become a better teacher. But prescriptions and advice have only limited value; teaching is hard work. The future is yours. We leave you with ten tips to use as you make the journey we call teaching:

Final tips

- Always deliver more than you promise.
- Keep records of methods that work.
- Be cheerful and enthusiastic, even when you don't feel like it.
- Dream big dreams but be known for what you do.
- Don't be afraid to make mistakes, but be sure to learn from them.
- Encourage every student to be an expert at something.
- Teach by this adage: You don't have to be sick to get better.
- Avoid paralysis by analysis.
- Teach students to tell the principal how much they enjoy being in your class.
- Never eat anything in the lunchroom covered completely with brown gravy.

What Every Teacher Should Know

- Special education is driven more by social, political, and economic factors than by actual changes in education.
- People's values, opinions, and beliefs influence how limited resources are distributed.
- The general political climate (conservative versus liberal), the political actions of parents and advocacy groups, and the work of legislatures and the courts have a significant influence on special education policy and practice.
- Services to students with disabilities are funded differently in different states, which influences who gets services and the nature of interventions.
- Goals 2000: The Educate America Act is a new federal law that specifies eight major goals to be reached by the year 2000, establishes a National Educational Standards and Improvement Council (NESIC) to oversee progress toward the goals, and specifies that states develop (on a voluntary basis) high content standards and assessment programs to measure progress toward the standards.
- Goals 2000 also requires that states develop opportunity-to-learn standards to assure that all students have a fair chance to learn.
- Some of the most far-reaching school-reform efforts involve school restructuring, an approach that stresses the need for fundamental change in the way schools are organized.

- Two fundamental assumptions underlie the development of current legislation on goals, standards, and assessments: (1) we can have both excellence and equity in the United States, and (2) schools cannot operate in isolation to get students to achieve the important outcomes.

Projects

1. Develop a list of actions you believe could be taken by elementary or secondary schools to lower the U.S. dropout rate. Then get together with a small group of classmates and compare your lists. Create one comprehensive list and reach agreement on the three actions you believe are the most important. Share and compare your group's list with your entire class.

2. Identify the way funding decisions are made in your state, and obtain a list of the percentages of students served in each disability category. Then get the percentages from two other states whose funding formulas differ. Discuss the extent to which the number of students served is a function of the ways funding decisions are made.

3. Find out the major educational goals of your state department of education and the activities of your state to meet those goals. How consistent are your state's goals with those listed in Goals 2000?

For Your Information

Books

Fullan, M. (1991). *The new meaning of educational change*. New York: Teacher's College Press.
 An excellent analysis of the school change process and a set of practical suggestions to effect change in systems.

Kirst, M. W. (1984). *Who controls our schools? American values in conflict*. New York: Freeman.
 A historical and political perspective on how schools are financed and governed.

Lane, J. L., & Epps, E. (1992). *Restructuring schools*. Berkeley, CA: McCutchan.
 National and international case studies and an analysis of challenges involved in restructuring schools.

McLaughlin, M. J., & Warren, S. H. (1992). *Issues and options in restructuring schools and special education programs*. College Park, MD: University of Maryland Policy Options Center.
 Explores the issues affecting decisions for delivering educational services to students with disabilities within the context of educational restructuring.

Sizer, T. (1992). *Horace's school. Redesigning the American high school*. Boston: Houghton Mifflin.
 A plan for secondary school reform proposed by a leading expert in the field of education.

Ysseldyke, J. E., Algozzine, B. A., & Thurlow, M. L. (1992). *Critical issues in special education* (2nd ed.). Boston: Houghton Mifflin.
 A critical analysis of major social, political, and economic issues in special education.

Journals

Journal of Disability Policy Studies

This journal publishes discussion, reviews, and research on a wide range of disability policy topics. For more information, contact Dept. of Rehabilitation and Research, University of Arkansas, 346 N. West Ave., Fayetteville, AK 72701.

Appendix A

Professional Associations Relevant to Special Education

This appendix lists organizations providing services to people with disabilities covered in each of the chapters of this book. Here we include information for individuals with disabilities and their families. These organizations are national, but most can put you in touch with regional, state, or local agencies with similar purposes.

The information was part of a directory of organizations compiled by the National Information Center for Children and Youth with Disabilities (P.O. Box 1492, Washington, DC 20013-1492) and distributed in the NICHCY *News Digest* (Vol. 3, No. 3, September 1993). It is in the public domain; readers are encouraged to copy and share it, providing credit to the National Information Center for Children and Youth with Disabilities. (Note: Some entries have been edited in order to keep them concise.)

General Information on Special Education

Access Unlimited
3535 Briarpark Drive, Suite 102
Houston, TX 77042
(800) 848-0311 (Voice, toll-free)
(713) 781-7441 (Voice, local)

Access Unlimited is a Houston-based nonprofit organization whose mission is to provide specialized computer resources to help youth with disabilities reach their full potential. To carry out this mission, the organization provides technical assistance to schools, organizations, and individuals that help children and adolescents with disabilities overcome barriers to learning through the use of computers. Access Unlimited also serves as a clearinghouse for information and training about adaptive computer technology to special education professionals, speech and occupational therapists, vocational and rehabilitation personnel, and families with youth who can benefit from this approach.

American Council on Rural Special Education
Dept. of Special Education
University of Utah
221 Milton Bennion Hall
Salt Lake City, UT 84112
(801) 585-5659 (Voice)
(801) 581-5020 (Text Telephone: TT)

The American Council on Rural Special Education (ACRES) is a membership organization of individuals and organizations interested in improving services for students with disabilities living in rural areas. A brochure on ACRES is available upon request. Members receive a newsletter, *RuraLink*, published every 6 weeks; the *Rural Special Education Quarterly*, which reports on practices, trends, and issues in rural special education delivery; and discounts on other ACRES publications. Through special interest groups, members can interact with individuals who share common interests and concerns. ACRES' Rural and Small Schools Library represents a collection of reports, monographs, teaching modules, and resource materials.

National Association of Private Schools for Exceptional Children (NAPSEC)
1522 K Street N.W., Suite 1032
Washington, DC 20005
(202) 408-3338 (Voice)

NAPSEC is a nonprofit association whose mission is to promote excellence in educational opportunities for children with disabilities by enhancing the role of private special education. It represents over 200 schools for both privately and publicly placed children. The organization serves as the national voice in Washington for educators regarding policies that affect children and youth with disabilities. Membership services include a free referral service to the public, governmental affairs seminars and educational conferences, a quarterly newsletter, and a monthly national issues service covering legislative initiatives, regulatory actions, educational issues, and judicial decisions. NAPSEC provides free referral for parents, educators, counselors, and others seeking placement options for students with disabilities.

National Clearinghouse for Professions in Special Education
Council for Exceptional Children
1920 Association Drive
Reston, VA 22314
(703) 264-9474 (Voice)
(703) 620-3660 (Voice/TT)

The Clearinghouse is concerned with the supply, demand, recruitment, and retention of qualified special education personnel. It provides information and services to promote an adequate supply of professionals to provide early intervention, special education, and related services to infants, children, and youth with disabilities. Staff collect, analyze, and disseminate information on current and future needs in special education and related services professionals. Information about career opportunities in the disability field is available, as is information about personnel preparation programs and sources of financial aid. A publications list is available upon request.

National Resource Center for Paraprofessionals in Education and Related Human Services (NRC)
25 West 43rd Street, Room 620N
New York, NY 10036
(212) 642-2948 (Voice)

The mission of the NRC is to promote an increase in the use of trained paraprofessionals in education and related services. The NRC disseminates information to employers, program managers, personnel developers, and paraprofessionals on such issues as skills and competencies needed by paraprofessionals, credentialing, new roles, career mobility, and funding sources. The Center also has information on pre- and in-service training models and training materials in use by state and local education agencies and by institutions of higher education.

Office of Indian Education Programs (OIEP)
Bureau of Indian Affairs (BIA)
MS 3512-MIB
18th and C Streets N.W.
Washington, DC 20245
(202) 208-6175 (Voice)

It is the mission of the Branch of Exceptional Education to assure that Indian children with disabilities who are between the ages of 5 and 22 and enrolled in Bureau-funded schools have a free appropriate education in the least restrictive environment in accordance with an individualized education program (IEP). This mission includes monitoring to assure the rights of the children with disabilities and their parents or guardians are protected; providing technical assistance to provide for the education of all children with disabilities; and assessing the effectiveness of efforts to educate children with disabilities.

Disability Information

Center for Children with Chronic Illness and Disability
Division of General Pediatrics and Adolescent Health
University of Minnesota
420 Delaware Street
Minneapolis, MN 55455
(612) 626-4032 (Voice)
(612) 624-3939 (TT)

Dedicated to the psychological and social well-being of children with chronic illness and disabilities and their families, the Center (1) conducts research to understand resilience and social competence across the childhood life span; (2) provides training for health, education, and social service professionals on resiliency and competency in children with disabilities; legal and policy issues; financing and insurance concerns for children and their families; and the special needs of children of color and their families; and (3) disseminates translations of the most current research. The Center has three publications: *Children's Health Issues,* which details resilience, ethnicity, and caregiving of children at risk; *Children's Health Briefs,* which publishes single articles on providing care for children and their families; and *Springboard,* the Center's newsletter.

Clearinghouse on Disability Information

Office of Special Education and Rehabilitative Services
(OSERS)
Room 3132, Switzer Building
330 C Street S.W.
Washington, DC 20202-2524
(202) 205-8241 (Voice/TT)

The Clearinghouse on Disability Information responds to inquiries on a wide range of topics, particularly in the areas of federal funding for programs serving people with disabilities, federal legislation affecting the disability community, and federal programs benefitting people with disabilities. The Clearinghouse refers inquirers to appropriate sources of information. The Clearinghouse also distributes a quarterly newsletter, *OSERS News in Print,* and other publications such as *Pocket Guide to Federal Help for Individuals with Disabilities, Summary of Existing Legislation Affecting Persons with Disabilities,* and *InfoPac* (an employment guide for people with disabilities). All services of the Clearinghouse are free.

National Council on Disability (NCD)

1331 F Street N.W.
Washington, DC 20004-1107
(202) 267-3846 (Voice)
(202) 267-3232 (TT)

The National Council on Disability is an independent federal agency led by 15 members who are appointed by the president and confirmed by the U.S. Senate. The overall purpose of the National Council is to promote policies, programs, practices, and procedures that guarantee equal opportunity to all individuals with disabilities, regardless of the nature or severity of the disability; and to empower individuals with disabilities to achieve economic self-sufficiency, independent living, and inclusion and integration into all aspects of society.

National Information Center for Children and Youth with Disabilities (NICHCY)

P.O. Box 1492
Washington, DC 20013
(800) 999-5599 (Voice/TT, toll-free)

NICHCY provides parents, professionals, and others with information and referral on issues of concern to children and youth with disabilities and their families. This includes information on specific disabilities, early intervention, special education, related services, transition planning, and other disability issues. Numerous free publications are available, including *Disability Fact Sheets, State Resource Sheets* (useful for identifying resources within each state), *Transition Summary* and *News Digest* issue briefs, and *Parent Guides.* NICHCY also has many publications in Spanish. A publications list is available upon request.

National Institute on Disability and Rehabilitation Research (NIDRR)

330 C Street S.W.
Washington, DC 20202
(202) 205-9151 (Voice)
(202) 205-9136 (TT)

Part of the U.S. Department of Education in the Office of Special Education and Rehabilitative Services, NIDRR provides leadership and support for national and international research on the rehabilitation of individuals with disabilities. NIDRR also studies developments in rehabilitation procedures. One of the most important aspects of research supported by NIDRR is integration of persons with disabilities into independent and semi-independent community life. NIDRR funds the National Rehabilitation Information Center (NARIC) and ABLEDATA (a database on assistive devices), and publishes *Rehab Brief,* a digest of research information.

National Maternal and Child Health Clearinghouse

8201 Greensboro Drive, Suite 600
McLean, VA 22102
(703) 821-8955, extension 254 or 265

The Clearinghouse distributes current publications on maternal and child health and human genetic issues. Publications cover such topics as pregnancy, nutrition, special health needs, chronic illness, and disabilities. A *Publications Catalog* is available from the Clearinghouse. Many items are free; this information is specified in the catalog. While most of the publications are written for a professional audience, the Clearinghouse welcomes calls from the general public and can provide referrals.

National Organization on Rare Disorders (NORD)

100 Rt. 37
P.O. Box 8923
New Fairfield, CT 06812-1783
(800) 999-6673 (Voice, toll-free)
(203) 746-6518 (Voice, local)
(203) 746-6927 (TT)

NORD acts as a clearinghouse, providing callers with information about thousands of rare disorders and bringing families with similar disorders together for mutual support. NORD also promotes research, accumulates and disseminates information about orphan drugs and devices, provides technical assistance to newly organized support groups, and educates the general public and medical professionals about diagnosis and treatment of rare disorders. NORD's "Rare Disease Database" is accessible via a computer with modem on CompuServe. Single written copies of disease information are available through a literature order form.

Office of Special Populations
National Center for Research in Vocational Education
University of Illinois Site
345 Education Building
1310 South 6th Street
Champaign, IL 61820
(217) 333-0807 (Voice)

The Office of Special Populations (formerly Technical Assistance for Special Populations Program, TASPP) works nationally to increase vocational program accessibility, quality, and availability for youth and adults from special popu-

lations. The Office of Special Populations conducts the following services and activities: (1) publication and production of papers and monographs, and presentations at conferences; (2) resource and referral service; (3) initiation and support of networks and professionals; (4) promotion of exemplary programs and adoption of model practices; and (5) collaborative activities with state and national organizations. These activities target all special populations in vocational education, including individuals with disabilities. A list of publications is available upon request.

Organizations for Families

Accent on Information (AOI)
Gillum Road and High Drive
P.O. Box 700
Bloomington, IL 61702
(309) 378-2961 (Voice)

ACCENT on Information is a computerized retrieval system containing information on products and devices which assist persons with physical disabilities. Also available is how-to information on such topics as eating, bathing, grooming, clothing, furniture, home management, toilet care, sexuality, mobility, and communication. For a nominal charge, a search of AOI's database is made on the caller's topic of interest. Callers then receive up to 50 of the most recent citations for each search. AOI has two sister services: (1) *ACCENT on Living Magazine,* and (2) ACCENT Special Publications, which publishes books of interest to persons with disabilities, along with a Buyer's Guide that lists equipment devices to assist persons with disabilities.

Access/Abilities
P.O. Box 458
Mill Valley, CA 94942
(415) 388-3250 (Voice)

Access/Abilities is a consulting, problem-solving firm dedicated to finding resources for a better life beyond functionality and independence. Local as well as national and international resources are available. This organization can provide information about accessible travel opportunities, aids and appliances, sports and recreation programs, good-looking clothing that really fits, shopping, and other customized services. It also offers consulting services concerning architectural barriers and accessibility.

Association for the Care of Children's Health
7910 Woodmont Avenue, Suite 300
Bethesda, MD 20814
(301) 654-6549 (Voice)

The Association for the Care of Children's Health (ACCH)

is dedicated to improving health care community response to the emotional and developmental needs of children. ACCH sponsors an annual conference for health care providers and consumers, as well as a Parent Network Meeting. Resources available from ACCH include books for adults; bibliographies and directories; patient and family education brochures; films and videotapes; and resources for children. ACCH also publishes *Children's Health Care,* a quarterly research journal; *Family Centered Care Network,* a tri-annual newsletter on family-centered care; *ACCH News,* a bimonthly newsletter for members; the *ACCH Advocate,* a biannual journal with feature articles and case studies; and an annual *Membership and Resource Directory.*

Beach Center on Families and Disability
University of Kansas
3111 Haworth Hall
Lawrence, KS 66045
(913) 864-7600 (Voice/TT)

The Beach Center on Families and Disability engages in research, training, and dissemination of information relevant to families who have members with developmental disabilities or serious emotional disturbances. The Beach Center's *Families and Disabilities Newsletter* is published three times a year. A descriptive brochure, the newsletter, and a catalogue listing many of the Center's publications are available free of charge upon request.

CAPP National Parent Resource Center
Federation for Children with Special Needs
95 Berkeley Street, Suite 104
Boston, MA 02116
(617) 482-2915 (Voice/TT)
(800) 331-0688 (Toll-free in MA)

The CAPP National Parent Resource Center (NPRC) is a parent-run resource system designed to further family-centered, community-based systems of health care for children with special needs and their families. The NPRC (1) supports effective parent/professional liaisons at all levels of health care; (2) identifies parent priorities and provides assistance and training to parents; (3) prepares written materials, training packages, workshops, and presentations on health care financing, special education, parent–professional collaboration, and other topics; and (4) provides technical assistance to parent training and information (PTI) projects, health agencies, and other parent projects.

Courage Center
3915 Golden Valley Road
Golden Valley, MN 55422
(612) 588-0811 (Voice)
(612) 520-0520 (Voice)
(612) 520-0401 (TT)

Courage Center is a nonprofit organization providing rehabilitation and independent living services for children and adults with physical disabilities and speech, hearing, and vision impairments, including ham radio and the transitional living program called Courage Residence. Services are offered in medical rehabilitation and education, camping, vocational training, sports and recreation, and transitional rehabilitation. Literature describing Courage Center's programs is available at no charge. Courage Center publishes a newsletter called *Meeting Ground* (principally for parents of children with disabilities). Subscriptions are free.

DIRECT LINK for the Disabled, Inc.
P.O. Box 1036
Solvang, CA 93464
(805) 688-1603 (Voice/TT)

DIRECT LINK is a public benefit organization that provides information and resources for any disability-related question. Responses are given over the phone or with a printed report. Special care is taken to find the closest local organization that meets the individual's needs. The LINKUP database contains over 11,000 organizations, including independent living centers, employment programs, support groups, device assessment centers, financial assistance programs, government offices, local affiliates of national organizations, community information centers, and agencies offering direct services to persons with disabilities and their families.

Family Resource Center on Disabilities
20 East Jackson Boulevard, Room 900
Chicago, IL 60604
(800) 952-4199 (Voice, toll-free)
(312) 939-3513 (Voice, local)
(312) 939-3519 (TT)

The Family Resource Center on Disabilities (formerly the Coordinating Council for Handicapped Children) is a coalition of parent and professional organizations that educates and trains parents and professionals on special education rights. Its information and referral service responds to mail and telephone requests for assistance, information, training, and support services. FRCD publishes manuals (such as *How to Organize an Effective Parent/Advocacy Group and Move Bureaucracies; How to Get Services by Being Assertive;* and *Special Education Manual*), pamphlets (such as *Does Your Child Have Special Education Needs?* and *How to Participate Effectively in Your Child's IEP Meeting*), factsheets, and a monthly newsletter.

Federation for Children with Special Needs
95 Berkeley Street
Boston, MA 02116
(617) 482-2915 (Voice/TT)
(800) 331-0688 (Toll-free in MA)

The Federation provides a number of services to families of children with special needs. Included in these services are information and referral, training, and education and support groups. The Federation is also the headquarters for TAPP (Technical Assistance for Parent Programs) and CAPP (Collaboration Among Parents and Health Professionals).

Federation of Families for Children's Mental Health
1021 Prince Street
Alexandria, VA 22314-2971
(703) 684-7710 (Voice)

The Federation is a national parent-run organization focused on the needs of children and youth with emotional, behavioral, or mental disorders and their families. Among the Federation's chief goals are to provide information about and engage in advocacy regarding research, prevention, early intervention, family support, education, transition services, and other services needed by these children and youth and their families. Publications, including *All Systems Failure,* are available.

National Coalition for Parent Involvement in Education (NCPIE)
1201 16th Street N.W., Room 810
Washington, DC 20036
(800) 999-5599 (Voice/TT, toll-free)

NCPIE is a membership coalition dedicated to the development of family/school partnerships in U.S. schools. It serves as an advocacy coalition for parent involvement issues and provides a forum for national organizations to share information regarding parent involvement in education. Because NCPIE membership includes the major education associations and advocacy groups in the country, it presents information on training, publications, and other services that promote community involvement, family education, family support, and school/family partnerships. NCPIE has published *A Guide to Parent Involvement Resources* (available through the National Council for Citizens in Education), which identifies resources and services available from NCPIE member organizations.

National Coalition of Title I Chapter I Parents
Edmonds School Building
9th & D Streets, N.E., Room 201
Washington, DC 20002
(202) 547-9286 (Voice)

This coalition is a grassroots organization committed to making the needs of educationally disadvantaged children a part of the national agenda. The coalition was formed in response to the Elementary and Secondary Education Act of 1965, Title I (Public Law 89–10). The organization provides a bimonthly newsletter, national and regional inservice training conferences, and on-site technical assistance workshops. It also provides a variety of information and training services designed to link parents with national and community resources devoted to children.

National Parent Network on Disabilities
1600 Prince Street #115
Alexandria, VA 22314-2836
(703) 684-6763 (Voice/TT)

The National Parent Network on Disabilities (NPND) is a nonprofit organization dedicated to improving the lives of children, youth, and adults with disabilities and their families. NPND is the first national-level umbrella organization designed to unite individual parents, family members, grassroots parents' groups, statewide parent centers, and coalitions. It serves as a national information, referral, and resource center. Among the services that NPND provides are legislative representation, reference and referral, national conferences, outreach to parents, materials development and distribution, and a database to link parents to local, state, regional, national, and/or international services.

Parents Helping Parents: The Parent-Directed Family Resource Center for Children with Special Needs
535 Race Street, Suite 140
San Jose, CA 95126
(408) 288-5010 (Voice)

Parents Helping Parents (PHP) is a comprehensive family resource center and parent training information center. The Center helps children with special needs. PHP provides information, support, and training on individual education

programs (IEPs), supplemental security income (SSI). Specific projects include developing manuals and program packets, conducting regional conferences and national workshops, and providing technical assistance to emerging Family Resource Centers. Individuals interested in starting a family resource center can contact the National Center on Parent-Directed Family Resource Centers at (800) 397-9827 (toll-free). All other callers would use the telephone number listed above.

Parent Training and Information (PTI) Centers
Parent Training and Information (PTI) centers exist in each state to assist parents of infants, children, and youth with disabilities. Although the activities of the PTIs vary from state to state, typically parents learn their rights under federal and state law and develop skills to help plan an educational program for their child. Speakers and workshops address parents' rights and responsibilities in special education, communication skills, transition from school to independent living, integration of students with disabilities, networking, advocacy, and parent/professional partnerships. PTIs have lending libraries, newsletters, and other materials. Call NICHCY at 1-800-999-5599, or contact the Technical Assistance for Parent Programs (TAPP) at (617) 482-2915.

Technical Assistance for Parent Programs (TAPP)
Federation for Children with Special Needs
95 Berkeley Street, Suite 104
Boston, MA 02116
(617) 482-2915 (Voice/TT)

The Individuals with Disabilities Education Act (IDEA), the federal special education law, establishes a grant program to support organized parent-to-parent efforts. The purpose of these programs, known as Parent Training and Information (PTI) Centers, is to enable parents to participate more effectively with professionals in meeting the educational needs of children with disabilities. The TAPP Project's primary responsibility is to serve the PTIs who are currently funded under IDEA. Grassroots groups in urban and rural settings are served through the developing Experimental PTI Project Initiative. PTIs seeking specialized help in the areas of Transition and Supported Employment are served through the SEPTA/TA Project. Parent organizations and groups meeting specific criteria set forth in IDEA may also receive assistance through TAPP.

Early Intervention

Activating Children Through Technology (ACTT)
27 Harrabin Hall
Western Illinois University
Macomb, IL 61455
(309) 298-1014 (Voice)

Activating Children Through Technology (ACTT) serves as a national distribution point for information on microcomputer technology designed for early childhood programs addressing all types of disabilities. Requests for information on microcomputer hardware, adaptive devices, and curriculum software are responded to verbally or with printed materials. Information and training services are available to professionals and families nationwide. Videotapes and software are available, as are a software catalogue and switch book and other written materials, including a curriculum called *Building ACTTive Futures.*

Family Enablement Project
300 Enola Road
Morganton, NC 28655
(704) 433-2877 (Voice)

This project provides technical assistance, consultation, and training to early intervention practitioners to enhance their ability to implement family-centered assessment and intervention services. Topics include family-centered principles and practices, effective help-giving relationships, parent/professional partnerships, family strengths, family needs/concerns, formal and informal sources of support and the resources these provide to families, and the Individualized Family Service Plan in the empowerment process. A publication list, a quarterly newsletter, and a reference guide are available upon request.

National Association for the Education of Young Children (NAEYC)
1509 16th Street N.W.
Washington, DC 20036-1426
(800) 424-2460 (Voice, toll-free)
(202) 232-8777 (Voice, local)

The National Association for the Education of Young Children is committed to improving early childhood program quality. A division of NAEYC, the National Academy of Early Childhood Programs, administers the only national, voluntary, professionally sponsored accreditation system for preschools, child care centers, and school-age child care programs. Another division of NAEYC, the Information Service, provides a national, centralized source of information about issues related to the provision of high-quality early childhood programs. A new division, the National Institute for Early Childhood Professional Development, provides resources and services to early childhood educators.

Transition

Association on Higher Education and Disability (AHEAD)
P.O. Box 21192
Columbus, OH 43221
(800) 247-7752 (Voice, toll-free)
(614) 488-4972 (Voice/TT)

AHEAD strengthens the professionalism, expertise, and competence of personnel working with postsecondary students who have disabilities. The Association has members throughout the United States and Canada representing residential and nonresidential campuses, and two-year and four-year institutions. AHEAD sponsors an annual conference and offers a number of publications, including a newsletter called the *ALERT;* a quarterly bulletin (*Journal of Postsecondary Education and Disability*); an annotated bibliography of information sources; proceedings of its national conferences; and guides such as *Reflections Through the Looking Glass, Testing Accommodations for Students with Disabilities, Peer Mentoring,* and *How to Choose a College.* An employment exchange in the field of disability support services is also available.

Center on Education and Training for Employment
1900 Kenny Road
Columbus, OH 43210-1090
(614) 292-4353 (Voice)

The mission of the Center on Education and Training for Employment is to facilitate the career and occupational preparation and advancement of youth and adults. The Center fulfills its mission by conducting applied research and using the full range of resources of The Ohio State University in evaluation studies. It also provides leadership development, technical assistance, and information services that pertain to education and training for work. Many publications are available related to preparing individuals with disabilities for training and employment.

HEATH Resource Center
American Council on Education
One Dupont Circle, Suite 800
Washington, DC 20036-1193
(202) 939-9320 (Voice/TT)
(800) 544-3284 (Voice/TT, toll-free outside DC)

The HEATH Resource Center operates the national clearinghouse on postsecondary education for individuals with disabilities. The Center, a program of the American Council on Education, serves as an information exchange about educational support services, policies, procedures, adaptations, and opportunities on American campuses, vocational-technical schools, adult education programs, independent living centers, transition, and other training entities after high school. HEATH publishes a newsletter,

Information from HEATH; several topical directories; and resource papers on aspects of education after high school for individuals with disabilities. Topics include accessibility, career development, classroom and laboratory accommodations, counseling, financial aid, functional limitations (vision, hearing, mobility, information processing), transition, vocational education, and vocational rehabilitation. Subscription to the newsletter and single copies of each publication are free. HEATH publications are also available on cassette or computer disk for those unable to read conventional print. In addition, HEATH staff respond to inquiries by mail and telephone.

National Center for Youth with Disabilities (NCYD)
University of Minnesota
Box 721
420 Delaware St. S.E.
Minneapolis, MN 55455
(800) 333-6293 (Voice, toll-free)
(612) 626-2825 (Voice, local)
(612) 624-3939 (TT)

NCYD was established as an information and resource center focusing on adolescents with chronic illness and disabilities and the issues surrounding their transition to adult life. NCYD's mission is to raise awareness of the needs of youth with disabilities and to foster coordination and collaboration among agencies, professionals, and youth in planning and providing services. Information specialists can conduct searches of the NCYD's National Resource Library database and can provide information about programs, training/education, and technical assistance. NCYD publishes a newsletter, *Connections,* a series of topical annotated bibliographies, *CYDLINE Reviews,* and fact sheets, *FYI Bulletins.*

National Rehabilitation Information Center (NARIC)/ABLEDATA
8455 Colesville Road, Suite 935
Silver Spring, MD 20910-3319
(800) 227-0216 (Voice/TT, toll-free)
(301) 588-9284 (Voice/TT, local)

NARIC is a library and information center on disability and rehabilitation. It collects and disseminates the results of federally-funded research projects, including commercially published books, journal articles, and audiovisual materials. The NARIC bibliographic database, REHABDATA, covers all aspects of the rehabilitation field. NARIC performs customized searches of REHABDATA for a nominal charge. The NARIC database is also available publicly through ABLE INFORM BBS (data number (301) 589-3563). Copies of documents cited in the database may be obtained for a photocopying fee. NARIC provides reference and referral services and publishes a free newsletter, *NARIC Quarterly.* Other free publications include brochures and resource guides.

President's Committee on Employment of People with Disabilities (PCEPD)
1331 F Street N.W.
Washington, DC 20004-1107
(202) 376-6200 (Voice)
(202) 376-6205 (TT)

The President's Committee is an independent federal agency whose mission is to help Americans with disabilities through employment. The Committee provides information, training, and technical assistance. Information programs include publications dealing with the Americans with Disabilities Act, employment issues, job accommodation, and data relating to people with disabilities. In addition to conducting a national conference on issues related to employment and empowerment of people with disabilities, the Committee also sponsors the Job Accommodation Network (JAN), a free service that provides information and consulting on accommodating people with disabilities in the workplace.

Transition Research Institute at Illinois
113 Children's Research Center
51 Gerty Drive
Champaign, IL 61820
(217) 333-2325 (Voice)

Transition Research Institute defines effective practices that promote the successful transition of youths with disabilities from school to adult life. The Institute is designed to address both the theoretical and practical problems of transition, and to organize and conduct a complementary set of activities including research, evaluation, and evaluation technical assistance. Many publications on transition are available.

Vocational Rehabilitation Agencies
Consult your local telephone directory for the office in your vicinity.

Vocational Rehabilitation is a nationwide federal–state program for assisting eligible people with disabilities to define a suitable employment goal and become employed. The state office provides callers with the address of the nearest rehabilitation office where persons with a disability can discuss issues of eligibility and services with a counselor. VR provides medical, therapeutic, counseling, education, training, and other services needed to prepare people with disabilities for work. The VR is an excellent place for a youth or adult with a disability to begin exploring available training and support service options.

Financial Assistance and Information

Funding Partnership for People with Disabilities
c/o Dole Foundation
P.O. Box 701
Merrifield, VA 22116-0701
(800) ADA-3885 (Voice, toll-free)
(202) 457-0318 (Voice/TT, local)

The Funding Partnership for People with Disabilities is a consortium of private grantmakers who foster the integration of people with disabilities into all aspects of American life. Funds are awarded to community coalitions to help people with disabilities. Criteria vary according to specific requests for proposals (RFPs). Coalitions must represent at least two of the following sectors: consumers; businesses; service providers; civic, professional, religious, and trade groups; unions; media; educational and job training institutions; independent living centers; government; universities; and independent research organizations. Coalitions should request an RFP before submitting formal applications.

Hear Now
9745 East Hampden Avenue, Suite 300
Denver, CO 80231
(800) 648-HEAR (Voice/TT, toll-free)
(303) 695-7797 (Voice, local)

Hear Now is a national, nonprofit organization serving children and adults with hearing impairments throughout the United States. Hear Now, in partnership with hearing health careproviders, provides hearing aids and cochlear implants to people with limited financial resources. Applications for assistance may be obtained by calling 1-800-648-HEAR.

Organizations Addressing Minority Concerns

Center for Minority Special Education (CMSE)
114 Phenix Hall
Hampton University
Hampton, VA 23668
(800) 241-1441 (Voice, toll-free)
(804) 727-5100 (Voice, local)

The Center for Minority Special Education (CMSE) was developed to respond directly to the Individuals with Disabilities Education Act (IDEA) mandate to "provide outreach services to minority entities and under-represented populations to assist them in participating more fully in the discretionary programs under the Act." The Center provides outreach services to minority entities defined as Historically Black Colleges and Universities (HBCUs) and other institutions of higher education serving at least 25 percent minority students (OMIs). The mission of the Center is to contribute to the advancement of a professional knowledge base and increase each institution's capacity to participate in federal, state, and local initiatives.

Clearinghouse for Immigrant Education (CHIME)
100 Boylston Street, Suite 737
Boston, MA 02116
(800) 441-7192 (Voice)

The Clearinghouse for Immigrant Education (CHIME) is a resource center to facilitate access to materials, organiza-

tions, and people concerned with the effective education of immigrant students. CHIME staff can provide specific information about relevant literature, descriptions of effective programs, names of organizations and experts, as well as more general advice and support. Information and referral are also available regarding the educational needs of immigrants with disabilities. A newsletter called *New Voices* is available.

National Clearinghouse for Bilingual Education (NCBE)
1118 22nd Street N.W.
Washington, DC 20037
(800) 321-6233 (Voice, toll-free)
(202) 467-0867 (Voice, local)

NCBE is funded by the U.S. Department of Education, Office of Bilingual Education and Minority Languages Affairs (OBEMLA), for the purpose of providing practitioners with information on the education of limited English proficient (LEP) students. NCBE information services are available to individuals or organizations responsible for or interested in the education of these students. Information about the needs of bilingual or LEP students with disabilities is also available, including the publication *Using Interpreters and Translators to Meet the Needs of Handicapped Lan-*

guage Minority Students and Their Families. A publication list is available upon request.

National Clearinghouse on Literacy Education (NCLE)
1118 22nd Street N.W.
Washington, DC 20037
(202) 429-9292, extension 200 (Voice)

NCLE is the only national clearinghouse for adult English as a second language (ESL) and literacy information. NCLE collects, analyzes, and abstracts documents for the ERIC database on literacy education for adults and out-of-school youth with limited English proficiency (LEP). Included in ERIC are research reports, instructional and assessment materials, program descriptions and evaluations, and teacher/tutor training guides. Educators can contact NCLE for free publications about working with LEP adults and out-of-school youth with literacy problems. NCLE publishes a newsletter and maintains a resource center that includes a database of over 700 literacy programs for LEP adults, families, and out-of-school youth.

Office of Minority Health Resource Center
Office of Minority Health, Public Health Service
U.S. Department of Health and Human Services
P.O. Box 37337
Washington, DC 20013-7337
(800) 444-6472 (Voice, toll-free)
(301) 587-1938 (Voice, local)

The Office of Minority Health Resource Center (OMHRC) identifies free and low-cost health-related information resources that target minority audiences. The Center focuses on HIV/AIDS, cancer, nutrition, men's health, homicide/suicide, infant mortality, and unintentional injuries. It maintains a database of minority health-related materials, organizations, and programs, and a network of active professionals who provide technical assistance. The Center has produced a series of fact sheets entitled *Closing the Gap,* which highlights current minority health issues and Center news. OMHRC also publishes a newsletter for health professionals. In addition, free single copies of research articles are provided. The Center provides services in Spanish and Asian languages.

Appendix B

Code of Ethics of the Council for Exceptional Children

We declare the following principles to be the Code of Ethics for educators of persons with exceptionalities. Members of the special education profession are responsible for upholding and advancing these principles. Members of The Council for Exceptional Children agree to judge and be judged by them in accordance with the spirit and provisions of this Code.

a. Special education professionals are committed to developing the highest educational and quality of life potential of individuals with exceptionalities.

b. Special education professionals promote and maintain a high level of competence and integrity in practicing their profession.

c. Special education professionals engage in professional activities which benefit exceptional individuals, their families, other colleagues, students, or research subjects.

d. Special education professionals exercise objective professional judgment in the practice of their profession.

e. Special education professionals strive to advance their knowledge and skills regarding the education of individuals with exceptionalities.

f. Special education professionals work within the standards and policies of their profession.

g. Special education professionals seek to uphold and improve where necessary the laws, regulations, and policies governing the delivery of special education and related services and the practice of their profession.

h. Special education professionals do not condone or participate in unethical or illegal acts, nor violate professional standards adopted by the Delegate Assembly of CEC.

Source: From the Council for Exceptional Children, Policy Manual (Reston, VA, 1993), Section 3, Part 2, p. 4. Used with permission.

Appendix C

Standards of Professional Practice of the Council for Exceptional Children

The following sections are excerpted from the Council for Exceptional Children's list of standards for professional practice.

Instructional Responsibilities

Special education personnel are committed to the application of professional expertise to ensure the provision of quality education for all individuals with exceptionalities. Professionals strive to:

1. Identify and use instructional methods and curricula that are appropriate to their area of professional practice and effective in meeting individual exceptional persons' needs.
2. Participate in the selection and use of appropriate instructional materials, equipment, supplies, and other resources needed in the effective practice of their profession.
3. Create safe and effective learning environments which contribute to fulfillment of needs, stimulation of learning, and self-concept.
4. Maintain class size and case loads which are conducive to meeting the individual instructional needs of individuals with exceptionalities.
5. Use assessment instruments and procedures that do not discriminate against persons with exceptionalities on the basis of race, color, creed, sex, national origin, age, political practices, family or social background, sexual orientation, or exceptionality.
6. Base grading, promotion, graduation, and/or movement out of the program on the individual goals and objectives for individuals with exceptionalities.
7. Provide accurate program data to administrators, colleagues and parents, based on efficient and objective record keeping practices, for the purpose of decision making.
8. Maintain confidentiality of information except when information is released under specific conditions of written consent and statutory confidentiality requirements.

Source: From the Council for Exceptional Children, Policy Manual (Reston, VA, 1993), Section 3, Part 2, pp. 4, 5, 7. Used with permission.

Parent Relationships

Professionals seek to develop relationships with parents based on mutual respect for their roles in achieving benefits for the exceptional person. Special education professionals:

1. Develop effective communication with parents, avoiding technical terminology, using the primary language of the home, and other modes of communication when appropriate.
2. Seek and use parents' knowledge and expertise in planning, conducting, and evaluating special education and related services for persons with exceptionalities.
3. Maintain communications between parents and professionals with appropriate respect for privacy and confidentiality.
4. Extend opportunities for parent education utilizing accurate information and professional methods.
5. Inform parents of the educational rights of their children and of any proposed or actual practices which violate those rights.
6. Recognize and respect cultural diversities which exist in some families with persons with exceptionalities.
7. Recognize that relationship of home and community environmental conditions affects the behavior and outlook of the exceptional person.

Relations with Other Professionals

Special education professionals function as members of interdisciplinary teams and the reputation of the profession resides with them. They:

1. Recognize and acknowledge the competencies and expertise of members representing other disciplines as well as those of members in their own disciplines.
2. Strive to develop positive attitudes among other professionals toward persons with exceptionalities, representing them with an objective regard for their possibilities and their limitations as persons in a democratic society.
3. Cooperate with other agencies involved in serving persons with exceptionalities through such activities as the planning and coordination of information exchanges, service delivery, evaluation and training, so that no duplication or loss in quality of services may occur.
4. Provide consultation and assistance, where appropriate, to both regular and special education as well as other school personnel serving persons with exceptionalities.
5. Provide consultation and assistance, where appropriate, to professionals in nonschool settings serving persons with exceptionalities.
6. Maintain effective interpersonal relations with colleagues and other professionals, helping them to develop and maintain positive and accurate perceptions about the special education profession.

Glossary

ability training Instruction in specific preacademic skills.

academic time analysis Systematic observation and recording of time students are engaged in responding to academic instruction.

acceleration Moving students through a curriculum more rapidly than their peers.

accountability Holding schools, administrators, teachers, and/or students responsible for students' academic performance.

acculturation Process of acquiring culture; in education, the term often refers to students' particular background experiences and opportunities.

adaptive behavior Behavior that meets the standards of personal independence and social responsibility expected of an individual's age and cultural group.

adaptive device An ordinary, daily item modified to make it more functional for a person with a disability.

advancement Changing a gifted student's curriculum or level by changing the student's placement, as by double promotion or skipping a grade.

aim line Graph showing progress needed for a student to achieve a particular goal.

alternative living unit (ALU) Supervised home for two or three exceptional students.

American Sign Language A sign language, widely used in the United States and Canada, that employs hand movements and other gestures.

Americans with Disabilities Act (1992) Federal law that extends civil rights protections to people with disabilities; it prohibits discrimination on the basis of disability in employment, state and local government services, public accommodation, transportation, and telecommunication services.

anxiety In psychology or medicine, a strong, unrealistic, and sometimes irrational fear; a common characteristic of serious emotional disturbance.

assessment Process of collecting data to make decisions about students.

assistive technology Equipment that improves or maintains the functional abilities of people with disabilities.

astigmatism Irregular curvature in the eye's refractive surfaces causing distortion or blurring of vision.

attention deficit–hyperactivity disorder (ADHD) A disorder involving developmentally inappropriate degrees of inattention, impulsiveness, and hyperactivity; also called *attention deficit disorder.*

autism Developmental disability significantly affecting verbal and nonverbal communication, social interaction, and educational performance; generally evident before age 3.

behavior disorder See *serious emotional disturbance.*

behavior therapy Systematically arranging environmental events to influence behavior.

blindness Absence of functional vision; often defined medically as visual acuity of 20/200 or less in the better eye, with correction, or a visual field of less than 20 degrees in the better eye.

braille System of representing letters, words, and numbers by patterns of raised dots.

category In special education, a grouping of exceptional students who are thought to share certain characteristics. Although professionals attempt to standardize the names and definitions of categories, there is significant variation from one state to another.

center-based program Program in which parents bring their child to a school, hospital, day care center, clinic, or other facility to receive direct or indirect services.

central nervous system Brain and spinal cord.

child-study team Group that determines a student's eligibility for special education and develops an individualized education program (IEP); typically composed of teachers, other representatives of the school district, and child's parents.

communication disorder Impairment in speech or language that interferes significantly with a person's ability to communicate. See also *language disorder* and *speech disorder*

compensatory instruction   Instruction that teaches a student to compensate for a disability; an example is teaching braille.

competitive employment   Employment in which the individual's work is valued by the employer and is performed in an integrated setting.

conductive hearing loss   A hearing impairment caused by blockage or damage in the outer or middle section of the ear.

consultative services   See *indirect services*.

contingency contract   Formal agreement between a teacher and a student specifying the consequences of the student's demonstrating certain behaviors.

convergent thinking   Thinking that involves reasoning, memory, and classification.

cooperative learning   Instruction in which students work together on a task in a small group.

corrective feedback   Feedback that informs a student about his or her mistakes and demonstrates the correct procedure.

counseling therapy   Intervention designed to uncover sources of problems or build new approaches to interpersonal relations through a supportive relationship between client and therapist.

criterion-referenced test   Test in which the individual's performance is interpreted relative to specific curricular objectives that have been mastered; evaluates a pupil's absolute level of mastery. Also called *objective-referenced test* and *curriculum-based test*.

curriculum-based assessment   Procedure for determining the instructional needs of a student on the basis of the student's ongoing performance in a content area.

curriculum compacting   System in which students can "buy" time for special activities when they demonstrate mastery in the required curriculum.

deaf-blindness   Category used to provide services to people who are deaf as well as blind. In the federal definition, deaf-blindness refers to "concomitant hearing and visual impairments" that cause such severe problems that they cannot be accommodated in special education programs solely for children with deafness or children with blindness.

deafness   Absence of functional hearing in both ears. In the federal definition, deafness means a hearing impairment so severe that the student is "impaired in processing linguistic information through hearing" and the student's educational performance is adversely affected.

deinstitutionalization   Implementation of the principle of least restrictive environment in residential facilities.

developmental instruction   Teaching students skills that are progressively more difficult to enable them to demonstrate the complex abilities necessary to meet instructional objectives.

diagnosis   Determining the nature of an educational task or problem; see *instructional diagnosis*.

direct instruction   Instruction in which teachers' actions are directly and functionally related to the goals of instruction; generally emphasizes systematic teaching of specific components of each desired skill.

direct services   Services in which special education personnel (including special education teachers, speech and language pathologists, and other professionals) work with students to remediate difficulties or to provide enrichment or acceleration.

disability   Medical, social, or learning difficulty that interferes significantly with an individual's normal growth and development.

disruptiveness   Pattern of behaviors that interfere with educational activities or cause annoyance or disturbance to others in the school.

divergent thinking   Thinking that shows fluency, flexibility, originality, and foresight.

Down syndrome   Congenital condition that results from a chromosomal abnormality and causes mental retardation.

due process clause   The part of the Fourteenth Amendment to the U.S. Constitution that forbids states from depriving anyone of life, liberty, or property without due process of law.

early intervention   Educational and other services provided before a child reaches school age or before school-related problems become serious.

educable mentally retarded   Term sometimes used for individuals with mild mental retardation.

education   Process of learning and changing as a result of schooling and other experiences.

Education for All Handicapped Children Act (1975)   First compulsory special education law; mandates a free and appropriate education for all students with disabilities between the ages of 3 and 21. Also called *Public Law 94–142*.

enrichment Enhancing the educational experiences of students with materials or activities that go beyond the standard curriculum; does not involve changing students' placement or educational setting.

equal protection clause The part of the Fourteenth Amendment to the U.S. Constitution that guarantees "equal protection of the laws" to all.

error analysis Systematic analysis of the kinds of errors a student makes.

evaluation The process by which teachers decide whether their methods and materials are effective on the basis of individual students' performance.

exceptional students Students who require special education because of their special learning needs. Exceptional students can have disabilities or be gifted and talented.

federal definition Definition of a term derived from U.S. government laws or regulations guiding provision of services to students with disabilities; many current federal definitions are included in the Individuals with Disabilities Education Act.

feedback Information provided to students about their performance.

field of vision Angular range within which a person can see objects without moving the eyes.

formative evaluation Evaluation that takes place during the instructional process.

gifted Having high intellectual or cognitive capabilities.

group home Residence that provides family-style living for a group of exceptional people.

hard of hearing Having significant difficulty hearing.

Head Start Federal program providing preschool education for students who are economically disadvantaged; the best-known early intervention program.

hearing impairment A hearing problem that adversely affects a student's educational performance.

home-based program Instruction or tutoring in the homes of students unable to travel to school.

hospital-based program Special education program provided to a student in a hospital, or to hospital personnel who work with the student.

hyperopia Visual condition in which near objects are blurred although distant objects remain clear; farsightedness.

inclusion Educating exceptional students—regardless of type or severity of disability—in regular classrooms in their neighborhood schools. Also known as *full inclusion*.

indirect services Services provided to regular classroom teachers and others to help them meet the needs of exceptional students; also called *consultative services*.

individual education program (IEP) A written document that includes (1) a statement of the student's present levels of functioning, (2) a statement of annual goals and short-term objectives for achieving those goals, (3) a statement of services to be provided and the extent of regular programming, (4) the start date and expected duration of services, and (5) evaluation procedures and criteria for monitoring progress.

individualized family service plan (IFSP) In an early intervention program, a document that details the child's present level of development, the family's needs related to that development, objectives of the program, specific services that will be provided to the child and family, evaluation procedures, and transition procedures to move the child from early intervention into a preschool program.

individualized transition plan (ITP) Part of the individualized education program that specifies services to be provided to aid a student's transition from school to adult life.

Individuals with Disabilities Education Act (1990) A reauthorization and renaming of the Education for All Handicapped Children Act; also includes a definition of transition services and specifications for individualized transition plans.

instructional diagnosis Effort to identify the extent to which a student's poor performance is caused by poor instruction and to determine possible remedies.

instructional package Instructional resources with multiple starting points and a variety of materials; a student can select materials suited to his or her interests, goals, pace, and level.

intervention assistance team School-based group designed to help teachers solve problems with individual students.

interviewing Asking questions to obtain information about an individual's background, current levels of performance, and plans.

irrelevant activity   Action not related to the task at hand.

job coach   Professional who provides employment assistance, in the form of on-the-job training and help, to individuals with disabilities.

label   Generally, a verbal cue that helps organize knowledge, perceptions, and behavior. In special education, labels are names assigned to behaviors, people, or the conditions people exhibit.

language disorder   Impairment that affects use of proper forms of language (phonology, morphology, or syntax), the content of language (semantics), or the functions of language (pragmatics).

learning disability   Disorder in one or more of the basic psychological processes involved in understanding or using language; may manifest itself in an imperfect ability to listen, think, speak, read, write, spell, or do mathematical calculations. Often identified by discrepancy between expected and actual achievement. Also called *specific learning disability*.

learning strategies training   Approach that teaches students how to learn content and how to demonstrate their knowledge.

least restrictive environment   Educational setting as much like the regular classroom as possible.

low vision   Vision sufficiently impaired that assistive technology or special services are required.

mainstreaming   Keeping exceptional students in the regular classroom whenever possible.

medical disability   Impairment caused by disease, infection, or another health problem; the term includes conditions listed in the federal category of *other health impairments*.

medically fragile   Requiring specialized technological health care for life support or health support.

mental retardation   Significantly subaverage general intellectual functioning that exists concurrently with deficits in adaptive behavior, manifests itself during the developmental period, and adversely affects the individual's educational performance.

mobility   Ability to move safely and efficiently from one place to another.

multicultural education   Education that attempts to provide equal opportunities for students from diverse cultural and ethnic backgrounds. Emphasizing the value of cultural diversity, it promotes positive contacts between groups and cultural enrichment for all students.

multiple disabilities   Combination of impairments causing educational problems so severe that they cannot be accommodated in special education programs designed solely for one of the impairments.

myopia   Visual condition in which distant objects are blurred although nearer objects remain clear; nearsightedness.

nonattention   Not paying attention to the task at hand.

normalization   Making the exceptional individual's life as normal as possible.

norm-referenced test   Standardized test in which the performance of the individual is compared to that of others who are of the same age or grade level.

norms   Standards against which performance is measured.

nystagmus   Condition characterized by rapid, involuntary movements of the eye that interfere with focusing.

observing   Watching an individual perform a set of behaviors to obtain information about the rate or duration of those behaviors.

ocular motility   The eye's ability to move smoothly.

opportunity-to-learn standards   Standards that establish conditions of teaching and learning necessary for all students to achieve specific knowledge and skills.

oppositional behavior   Not doing what someone else (such as the teacher) has requested; also called *noncompliance*.

orientation   Ability to know one's position in relation to the environment.

orthopedic impairment   Deficit in movement and mobility resulting from a congenital anomaly, disease, injury, or other cause and adversely affecting educational performance.

orthosis   Device that enhances partial functioning of a body part; for example, a leg brace.

other health impairment   Chronic or acute health problem that limits the individual's strength, vitality, or alertness and adversely affects educational performance.

outcomes   Specific results of the educational process; what students know and are able to do as a result of their schooling experiences.

outcomes-based education (OBE)   Education guided by the belief that curriculum should be based on desired outcomes rather than on predetermined subject-matter content.

peer tutoring   Students' teaching classmates or peers with teacher supervision.

physical disability   Impairment in movement, mobility, neuromuscular operation, or another mode of physical functioning; the term includes conditions in the federal categories of *orthopedic impairments, traumatic brain injury,* and *autism.*

portfolio assessment   See *work sample assessment.*

precision teaching   Teaching approach based on pinpointing the area in which a student needs to improve, continuously recording and evaluating progress, and modifying the instructional method as necessary.

prereferral intervention   Finding ways to improve a student's functioning in the regular classroom without referring the student for special education.

prevalence   Number or percentage of individuals evidencing a condition at a given time.

programmed learning   Instructional method that involves diagnosing students by preestablished instruments and programming them into sequenced learning resources when they demonstrate content mastery.

prosthesis   An artificial replacement for a missing body part.

Public Law 94–142   See *Education for All Handicapped Children Act.*

referral   First step in determining a student's eligibility for special education; process of requesting information or a professional evaluation to decide whether a student is eligible for special services.

regular education initiative (REI)   Contention that regular and special educators should share responsibility for students considered disabled, so that students with disabilities can be integrated more fully into regular classrooms; also called *general education initiative.*

reinforcement   An event, object, or statement that increases the frequency of a behavior.

related services   Supplemental services provided by trained personnel to help a student benefit from special education; these services include psychological testing and counseling, occupational therapy, school health services, and transportation.

reliability   Index of consistency in measurement; the extent to which results of the measurement can be generalized to different observers and different times.

remediation   Instruction designed to repair or correct deficits in performance by training students in deficient areas.

representativeness   Extent to which an assessment instrument adequately samples the behavior being measured.

residual functioning   Functioning that exists despite a disability; for instance, the remaining hearing ability of a person with a hearing impairment.

resource room   Room to which a student goes for part of a school day to receive special instruction or help with regular classroom work.

school-based enterprise   High school course, or series of courses, in which students operate their own business to learn occupational skills.

school restructuring   Approach to school reform that stresses the need for fundamental change in the way schools are organized.

screening   Collecting data to determine whether more intensive assessment is necessary.

self-contained class   Class taught by one teacher of students assigned there for the entire school day.

self-correction   Technique in which students identify and correct their own mistakes.

self-determination   Process in which exceptional individuals consider their own options and make their own life choices; also known as *self-advocacy.*

self-monitoring   Technique in which the student observes and records his or her own behavior.

sensorineural hearing loss   Hearing impairment caused by damage to the inner ear or auditory nerves.

sensory disability   Impairment in vision or hearing that adversely affects educational performance.

serious emotional disturbance   Condition in which a student exhibits one or more of the following characteristics over a long period and to a marked degree, adversely affecting educational performance: an inability to learn that cannot be explained by intellectual, sensory, or health factors; an inability to build or maintain satisfactory interpersonal relationships with peers and teachers; inappropriate behaviors or feelings under normal circumstances; a general pervasive mood of unhappiness or depression; or a tendency to develop physical symptoms or fears associated with personal or school problems. Also called *behavior disorder.*

severe disability   Disability requiring extensive, continued assistance in more than one major life activity.

sheltered employment Work in a self-contained environment in which the exceptional individual is trained and paid for output.

special class Setting outside the regular classroom for students to receive special education and related services.

special education Instruction for students with special learning needs.

specific learning disability See *learning disability*.

speech disorder Impairment in producing speech sounds (articulation), controlling sounds (voice), or controlling the rate and rhythm of speech (fluency).

speech-language pathologist Professional who provides special education services for students with communication disorders and works with teachers to enhance instruction in language.

speech or language impairment See *communication disorder*.

strabismus Condition characterized by inability to focus both eyes on the same object.

summative evaluation Evaluation that takes place at the end of the instructional process.

supported employment Use of professionals to help individuals with disabilities find, perform, and keep jobs.

supportive feedback Feedback informing a student that she or he has performed a task correctly.

talented Showing outstanding performance in a specific area, such as the performing or visual arts.

task analysis Breaking down a complex behavior or skill into its component parts or subskills.

task avoidance Avoiding performance of a particular task or assignment; may involve postponing the task or preparing for it over-elaborately.

teaching Systematic presentation of content assumed necessary for mastery within a general or specific area of instruction.

technology dependent Relying on medical equip-ment and complex nursing care to avoid death or further disability.

tech-prep program Program that combines academic study with job-related learning, linking the final two years of high school with two years of college.

temper tantrum Outburst of bad temper; a severe form of oppositional behavior sometimes manifested by students with serious emotional disturbance and other disabilities.

testing Administering a set of items to obtain a score.

token system Instructional approach in which students earn tokens, stars, points, or other prizes to exchange for things they want (like toys, free time, and so on).

trainable mentally retarded Term sometimes used for individuals with moderate mental retardation.

transition Student's movement from one life stage or educational stage to another, especially from school to adulthood.

traumatic brain injury Acquired injury to the brain caused by an external physical force, resulting in functional disability, psychosocial impairment, or both, and adversely affecting educational performance.

validity Extent to which a test measures what it claims to measure.

visual acuity Ability to see things at specified distances.

visual impairment Vision problem that, even with correction, adversely affects a student's educational performance.

work sample assessment The process of assessing a collection of products of an individual's work; sometimes called *portfolio assessment*.

youth apprenticeship Program in which a student spends part of each school week in a classroom and the remainder at a work site to gain actual work skills and experience.

References

Algozzine, B. (Ed.). (1994) *Problem behavior management: Educator's resource service.* Rockville, MD: Aspen.

Algozzine, B., & Mercer, C. (1980). Labels and expectancies for handicapped children and youth. In D. Sabatino & L. Mann (Eds.), *Fourth review of special education.* New York: Grune & Stratton.

Algozzine, B., & Ysseldyke, J. (1992). *Strategies and tactics for effective instruction.* Longmont, CO: Sopris West.

American Association on Mental Retardation. (1992). *Mental retardation: Definition, classification, and systems of support—Workbook.* Washington, DC: Author.

American Psychiatric Association. (1968). *Diagnostic and statistical manual of mental disorders* (2nd ed., DSM-II). Washington, DC: Author.

American Psychiatric Association. (1980). *Diagnostic and statistical manual of mental disorders* (3rd ed., DSM-III). Washington, DC: Author.

American Psychiatric Association. (1987). *Diagnostic and statistical manual of mental disorders* (3rd ed., rev., DSM-III-R). Washington, DC: Author.

American Psychiatric Association. (1994). *Diagnostic and statistical manual of mental disorders* (4th ed., DSM-IV). Washington, DC: Author.

American Speech-Hearing-Language Association. (1982). Definitions: Communicative disorders and variations. *Asha, 24,* 949–950.

Anderegg, M. L., Baker, J., Brewster, L., Cohen, J., Deanda, L., Donovan, M., Gaudes, Y., Gruenhagen, K., & Riddle, G. (1993). Top thirty. *Beyond Behavior, 5*(1), 24–25.

Archer, A., & Gleason, M. (1989). *Skills for school success (grades 3–6).* North Billerica, MA: Curriculum Associates.

Asch, A. (1989). Has the law made a difference? What some disabled students have to say. In D. Lipsky & A. Gartner (Eds.), *Beyond separate education: Quality education for all* (pp. 181–205). Baltimore: Brookes.

Banks, J. A. (1989). Multicultural education: Characteristics and goals. In J. A. Banks & C. A. M. Banks (Eds.), *Multicultural education: Issues and perspectives* (2nd ed.). Boston: Allyn & Bacon.

Barraga, N. C., & Erin, J. N. (1992). *Visual handicaps and learning* (3rd ed.). Austin, TX: PRO-ED.

Batshaw, M. L., & Perret, Y. M. (1992). *Children with disabilities: A medical primer* (3rd ed.) Baltimore, MD: Paul H. Brookes.

Beez, W. (1970). *Influence of biased psychological reports on teacher behavior.* Unpublished doctoral dissertation, Indiana University.

Berdine, W. H., & Blackhurst, A. E. (Eds.) (1985). *An introduction to special education.* Boston: Little, Brown.

Berrueta-Clement, J., Schweinhart, L., Barnett, S., Epstein, A., & Weikart, D. (1984). *Changed lives.* Ypsilanti, MI: High Scope Educational Foundation.

Biemiller, A. (1993). Lake Wobegon revisited: On diversity and education. *Educational Researcher, 22*(9), 7–12.

Biklen, D. (1989). Redefining Education. In D. Biklen, D. Ferguson, & A. Ford (Eds.), *Schooling and disability* (pp. 1–24). Chicago: National Society for the Study of Education.

Bloom, B. (1956). *Taxonomy of educational objectives. Handbook I: Cognitive domain.* New York: McKay.

Borg, W. (1980). Time and school learning. In C. Denham & A. Lieberman (Eds.), *Time to learn.* Washington, DC: National Institute of Education.

Brown, F. (1981). *Measuring classroom achievement.* New York: Holt, Rinehart & Winston.

Brown, L., Long, E., Udvari-Solner, A., Davis, L., VanDeventer, P., Ahlgren, C., Johnson, F., Gruenewald, L., & Jorgensen, J. (1989). The home school: Why students with severe intellectual disabilities must attend the schools of their brothers, sisters, friends, and neighbors. *Journal of the Association for Persons with Severe Handicaps, 14,* 1–7.

Campbell, P., & Olsen, G. (1994). Improving instruction in secondary schools. *Teaching Exceptional Children, 26* (3), 51–54.

Children with Attention Deficit Disorders. (1992). The teacher's challenge, *The CH.A.D.D.ER Box, 5*(7), 14–15.

Chinn, P., & McCormick, L. (1986). Cultural diversity and exceptionality. In N. Haring & L. McCormick (Eds.), *Exceptional Children and Youth.* Columbus, OH: Merrill.

Choate, J., Bennett, T., Enright, B., Miller, L., Poteet, J., & Rakes, T. (1987). *Assessing and programming basic curriculum skills.* Boston: Allyn & Bacon.

Christensen, K. M., & Delgado, G. L. (1993). *Multicultural issues in deafness.* White Plains, NY: Longman.

Clark, B. (1983). *Growing up gifted* (2nd ed.). Columbus, OH: Merrill.

Committee for Economic Development. (1991). The unfinished agenda: A new vision for child development and education. Washington, DC: Author.

Conlon, C. J. (1992). New threats to development: Alcohol, cocaine, and AIDS. In M. L. Batshaw & Y. M. Perret. (Eds.), *Children with disabilities: A medical primer* (pp. 111–136). Baltimore, MD: Paul H. Brookes.

Corn, A., & Ryser, G. (1989). Access to print for students with low vision. *Journal of Visual Impairment and Blindness, 83*, 340–349.

Council for Exceptional Children. (1988). *Report of the Council for Exceptional Children's Ad Hoc Committee on Medically Fragile Students.* Reston, VA: Author, Governmental Relations Committee.

Crittenden, J. B. (1993). The culture and identity of deafness. In P. V. Paul & D. W. Jackson (Eds.), *Toward a psychology of deafness: Theoretical and empirical perspectives* (pp. 215–235). Boston, MA: Allyn & Bacon.

Crocker, A. C., & Cohen, H. J. (1988). *Guidelines on developmental services for children and adults with HIV infection.* Silver Springs, MD: American Association of University Affiliated Programs for Persons with Developmental Disabilities.

Delquadri, J., Greenwood, C., Whorton, D., Carta, J., & Hall, V. (1986). *Exceptional Children, 52,* 535–542.

Deshler, D., & Schumaker, J. (1986). Learning strategies: An instructional alternative for low-achieving adolescents. *Exceptional Children, 52,* 583–590.

Edgerton, R. (1967). *The cloak of competence.* Berkeley, CA: University of California Press.

Egel, A. L. (1989). Finding the right educational program. In M. D. Powers (Ed.), *Children with autism: A parent's guide* (pp. 169–202). Rockville, MD: Woodbine House.

Ekwall, E. (1981). *Locating and correcting reading difficulties* (3rd ed.). Columbus, OH: Merrill.

Epstein, J. L. (1992). School and family partnerships: Leadership roles for school psychologists. In S. L. Christenson & J. C. Conoley (Eds.), *Home-school collaboration: Enhancing childrens' academic and social competence* (pp. 449–515). Silver Spring, MD: National Association of School Psychologists.

Ferguson, D., & Asch, A. (1989). Lessons from life: Personal and parental perspectives on school, childhood, and disability. In D. Biklen, D. Ferguson, & A. Ford (Eds.), *Schooling and disability* (pp. 108–140). Chicago: National Society for the Study of Education.

Foster, G., & Ysseldyke, J. E. (1976). Expectancy and halo effects as a result of artificially induced bias. *Contemporary Educational Psychology, 1,* 37–45.

Foster, G., Ysseldyke, J. E., & Reese, J. (1975). I never would have seen it if I hadn't believed it. *Exceptional Children, 41,* 469–474.

Friedman, J., & Gallo, N. (1988). Steve Largent has caught more passes than anyone, but without his home team he'd be incomplete. *People Weekly, 30*(22), 77–80.

Gallagher, J. (1985). *Teaching the gifted child* (3rd ed.). Boston: Allyn & Bacon.

Gallagher, J., & Coleman, M. R. (1992). *State policies on the identification of gifted students from special populations: Three states in profile.* Chapel Hill, NC: Gifted Education Policy Studies Program.

Gardner, H. (1983). *Frames of mind.* New York: Basic Books.

Giangreco, M. F., Dennis, R., Cloninger, C., Edelman, S., & Schattman, R. (1993). "I've counted Jon": Transformational experiences of teachers educating students with disabilities. *Exceptional Children, 59,* 359–372.

Gickling, E., & Havertape, J. (1981). Curriculum-based assessment. In J. Tucker (Ed.), *Non-test-based assessment.* Minneapolis: National School Psychology Inservice Training Network.

Glaser, W. (1965). *Reality therapy.* New York: Harper & Row.

Gleason, M., & Archer, A. (1989). *Critical school behaviors and study skills needed in junior high school content area classes.* Unpublished manuscript, University of Oregon, Eugene.

Gleason, M. M., Colvin, G., & Archer, A. L. (1991). Interventions for improving study skills. In G. Stoner, M. Shinn, & H. Walker (Eds.), *Interventions for achievement and behavior problems.* Silver Spring, MD: National Association of School Psychologists.

Goldstein, A. P., Sprafkin, R. P., Gershaw, N. J., & Klein, P. (1980). *Skillstreaming the adolescent.* Champaign, IL: Research Press.

Good, T., & Brophy, J. (1984). *Looking in classrooms* (3rd ed.). New York: Harper & Row.

Graham, S., & Harris, K. (1988). Instructional recommendations for teaching writing to exceptional students. *Exceptional Children, 54,* 506–512.

Graham, S., & MacArthur. (1987). *Improving learning disabled students' skills at revising essays produced on a word processor: Self-instructional strategy training.* Unpublished manuscript,

Gray, P. (1993, Fall). Teach your children well. *Time.*

Greenwood, C., & Carta, J. (1993). *Ecobehavioral assessment system software.* Kansas City, KS: Juniper Gardens Childrens' Center.

Greenwood, C. R., Carta, J., & Maheady, L. (1991). Peer tutoring programs in the regular education classroom. In G. Stoner, M. Shinn, & H. Walker (Eds.), *Interventions for achievement and behavior problems.* Silver Spring, MD: National Association of School Psychologists.

Greer, B. B., Allsop, J., & Greer, J. G. (1980). Environmental alternatives for the physically handicapped. In J. W. Schifani, R. M. Anderson, & S. J. Odle (Eds.), *Implementing learning in the least restrictive environment.* Austin, TX: PRO-ED.

Grossman, H. (Ed.). (1983). *Manual on terminology and classification in mental retardation* (rev. ed.).

Washington, DC: American Association on Mental Deficiency.

Haber, L., & McNeil, J. (1983). *Methodological questions in the estimation of disability prevalence*. Washington, DC: U.S. Government Printing Office (available from the Population Division, Bureau of the Census).

Hart, C. A. (1993). *A parent's guide to autism*. New York: Pocket Books.

Haskins, R. (1989). Beyond metaphor: The efficiency of early childhood education. *American Psychologist, 44*, 274–282.

Hill. (1986). Orientation and mobility. In G. Scholl (Ed.), *Foundations of education for blind and visually handicapped children and youth: Theory and practice* (pp. 315–340). New York: American Foundation for the Blind.

Hodgkinson, H. L. (1993). *A demographic look at tomorrow*. Washington, DC: Center for Demographic Policy, Institute for Educational Leadership.

Holmes, D. L. (1989). The years ahead: Adults with autism. In M. D. Powers (Ed.), *Children with autism: A parent's guide* (pp. 253–276). Rockville, MD: Woodbine House.

Holmes, H. (1915). Time distributions by subject and grades in representative cities. In S. Parker (Ed.), *The fourteenth yearbook of the National Society for the Study of Education. Part I: Minimum essentials in elementary-school subjects—standards and current practices*. Chicago: University of Chicago Press.

Hughes, C., & Ruhl, K. (1989). Social skills training. In B. Algozzine (Ed.), *Problem behavior management: Educator's resource service* (pp. 279–291). Rockville, MD: Aspen.

Humphries, T. (1993). Deaf culture and cultures. In K. M. Christensen & G. L. Delgado (Eds.), *Multicultural issues in deafness* (pp. 3–15). White Plains, NY: Longman.

Johnson, D. W., & Johnson, R. T. (1994). *Learning together and alone: Cooperative, competitive, and individualistic learning* (4th ed.). Boston: Allyn & Bacon.

Jones, B. (1988, Spring). Homey housing. *WAYS*, pp. 11–12.

Kirk, S., & Chalfant, J. (1984). *Academic and developmental learning disabilities*. Denver: Love.

Koestler, F. (1976). *The unseen minority: A social history of blindness in the United States*. New York: McKay.

Larsen, M. D., Griffin, N. S., & Larsen, L. M. (in press). Public opinion regarding support for special programs for gifted children. *Journal for the Education of the Gifted*.

Lee, V. E., Schnur, E., & Brooks-Gunn, J. (1988). Does Head Start work? A 1-year follow-up comparison of disadvantaged children attending Head Start, no preschool, and other preschool programs. *Developmental Psychology, 24*(2), 210–222.

Levy, S. E., & Pilmer, S. L. (1992). The technology-assisted child. In M. L. Batshaw & Y. M. Perret.

(Eds.), *Children with disabilities: A medical primer* (pp. 137–157). Baltimore, MD: Paul H. Brookes.

Lewis, R. B., & Doorlag, D. H. (1991). *Teaching special students in the mainstream* (3rd ed.). Columbus, OH: Merrill.

Liles, C. (1993). Serving children with special health care needs in school. *South Atlantic Regional Resource Center Newsletter, 3*, 1–10.

Lloyd, J. (1980). Academic instruction and cognitive behavior modification: The need for attack strategy training. *Exceptional Education Quarterly, 1*, 53–63.

Lloyd, J. W., Landrum, T. J., & Hallahan, D. P. (1991). Self-monitoring applications for classroom intervention. In G. Stoner, M. Shinn, & H. Walker (Eds.), *Interventions for achievement and behavior problems*. Silver Spring, MD: National Association of School Psychologists.

Luetke-Stahlman, B., & Luckner, J. (1991). Effectively educating students with hearing impairments. White Plains, NY: Longman.

Lynch, E. W., Lewis, R. B., & Murphy, D. S. (1993). Educational services for children with chronic illnesses: Perspectives of educators and families. *Exceptional Children, 59*, 210–220.

McBurnett, K., Lahey, B. B., & Pfiffner, L. J. (1993). Diagnosis of attention deficit disorders in DSM-IV: Scientific basis and implications for education. *Exceptional Children, 60*, 108–117.

McGinnis, E., & Goldstein, A. P. (1984). *Skillstreaming the elementary school child*. Champaign, IL: Research Press.

McKinney, J. D. (1984). The search for subtypes of specific learning diabilies. *Journal of Learning Disabilities, 17*, 43–50.

McKinney, J. D. (1988). Research on conceptually and empirically derived subtypes of specific learning disabilities. In M. C. Wang, H. J. Walberg, & M. C. Reynolds (Eds.), The handbook of special education: Research and practice (pp. 253–282). Oxford: Pergamon.

Mangrum, C. II, & Strichart, S. S. (1984). *College and the learning disabled student*. New York: Grune & Stratton.

Mann, C. H. (1928). *How schools use their time: Practice in 444 cities including a study of trends from 1826–1926*. New York: Teachers College Press.

Marland, S. (Ed.). (1972). *Education of the gifted and talented* (Report to the Congress of the United States by the U. S. Commissioner of Education). Washington, DC: U. S. Government Printing Office.

Meyer, L. H., Peck, C. A., & Brown, L. (1991). *Critical issues in the lives of people with severe disabilities*. Baltimore, MD: Paul H. Brookes.

Michaud, L. J., & Duhaime, A. (1992). Traumatic brain injury. In M. L. Batshaw & Y. M. Perret. (Eds.), *Children with disabilities: A medical primer* (pp. 525–546). Baltimore, MD: Paul H. Brookes.

Minnesota standards for services to gifted and talented students. (1988, April 22). St. Paul, MN: Minnesota State Advisory Council for the Gifted and Talented.

Moores, D. (1987). *Educating the deaf: Psychology, principles, and practices* (3rd ed.). Boston, MA: Houghton Mifflin.

Moran, M. (1983). Inventing a future for special education: A cautionary tale. *Journal for Special Educators, 19,* 28–36.

Morgan, D. P., & Jenson, W. R. (1988). *Teaching behaviorally disordered students: Preferred practices.* Columbus, OH: Merrill.

National Commission on Excellence in Education. (1983). *A nation at risk: The imperative for educational reform.* Washington, DC: U. S. Government Printing Office.

National Governors' Association. (1986). *Time for results: The governors' 1991 report on education.* Washington, DC: Author.

National Governors' Association. (1990). *State actions to restructure schools: First steps.* Washington, DC: Author.

National Society for Autistic Children. (1977, September). A short definition of autism. *Newsletter.*

Newland, T. E. (1986). Children with auditory and visual impairment. In R. Brown & C. Reynolds (Eds.), *Psychological perspectives on childhood exceptionality: A handbook* (pp. 556–589). New York: Wiley.

Nihira, D., Foster, R., Shellhass, M., & Leland, H. (1975). *AAMD Adaptive Behavior Scale.* Washington, DC: American Association on Mental Deficiency.

Office of Demographic Studies. (1989–1990). *Annual census of deaf children and youth.* Washington, DC: Gallaudet University.

Office of Educational Research and Improvement. (1993). *National excellence. A case for developing America's talent.* Washington, DC: U.S. Department of Education.

Ogbu, J. U. (1992). Understanding cultural diversity. *Educational Researcher, 21*(8), 5–14.

Okyere, B. A., & Heron, T. E. (1991). Use of self-correction to improve spelling in regular education classrooms. In G. Stoner, M. Shinn, & H. Walker (Eds.), *Interventions for achievement and behavior problems.* Silver Spring, MD: National Association of School Psychologists.

O'Sullivan, P., Ysseldyke, J. E., Christenson, S. L., & Thurlow, M. L. (1990). Mildly handicapped elementary students' opportunity to learn during reading instruction in mainstream and special education settings. *Reading Research Quarterly, 25,* 131–146.

PACER Center. (1991). "It's the 'person-first'—then the disability." Guidelines. Minneapolis: Author.

Paul, P. V., & Jackson, D. W. (1993). *Toward a psychology of deafness: Theoretical and empirical perspectives.* Boston, MA: Allyn & Bacon.

Payne, B. (1904). *Public elementary school curricula.* New York: Silver, Burdett.

Powers, M. D. (1989a). What is autism? In M. D. Powers (Ed.), *Children with autism: A parent's guide* (pp. 1–29). Rockville, MD: Woodbine House.

Powers, M. D. (Ed.). (1989b). *Children with autism: A parent's guide.* Rockville, MD: Woodbine House.

Pratt, S. (1988). Resolution discussed and concerns stated [Editorial]. *Advocate, 20*(4), 2.

Profile: Ivy Hunter. (1988, November/December). *A Positive Approach,* p. 14.

Quay, H. (1983). *Manual for the Revised Behaviors Problem Checklist.* Coral Gables, FL: University of Miami.

Rawlings, S. W. (1993). *Household and family characteristics: March 1992.* U. S. Bureau of the Census, Current Population Reports, p. 20–467. Washington, DC: U. S. Government Printing Office.

Reber, M. (1992). Autism. In M. L. Batshaw & Y. M. Perret. (Eds.), *Children with disabilities: A medical primer* (pp. 407–420). Baltimore, MD: Paul H. Brookes.

Redl, F. (1959). The concept of the life space interview. *American Journal of Orthopsychiatry, 29,* 1–18.

Reichert, E. S. (1987). Rampant problems and promising practices in the identification of disadvantaged gifted students. *Gifted Child Quarterly, 31,* 149–154.

Reis, S. M., & Purcell, J. H. (1993). An analysis of content elimination and strategies used by elementary teachers in the curriculum compacting process. *Journal for the Education of the Gifted, 16,* 147–170.

Renzulli, J. (1979). *What makes giftedness?* (Brief 6). Los Angeles: National/State Leadership Training Institute of the Gifted and Talented.

Renzulli, J. S. (1986). The three-ring conception of giftedness: A developmental model for creative productivity. In R. J. Sternberg & J. E. Davidson (Eds.), *Conceptions of giftedness* (pp. 53–92). Cambridge: Cambridge University Press.

Research and Training Center on Independent Living. (1990). *Guidelines for reporting and writing about people with disabilities* (3rd ed.). Lawrence, KS: Author.

Rogers, C. (1951). *Client-centered therapy.* Boston: Houghton Mifflin.

Rogers, M. (1989, April 24). Technology: More than wheelchairs. *Newsweek,* pp. 66–67.

Rusch, F., Chadsey-Rusch, J., & Lagomarcino, T. (1987). Preparing students for employment. In M. Snell (Ed.), *Systematic instruction of persons with severe handicaps* (3rd ed., pp. 471–490). Columbus, OH: Merrill.

Sabornie, E. (1991). Measuring and teaching social skills in the mainstream. In G. Stoner, M. Shinn, & H. Walker (Eds.), *Interventions for achievement and behavior problems.* Silver Spring, MD: National Association of School Psychologists.

Saccuzzo, D. P., Johnson, N. E., & Guertin, T. L. (1994). *Identifying underrepresented disadvantaged gifted and talented children: A multifaceted approach* (Vol. 1). San Diego, CA: San Diego State University.

Salvia, J., Clark, G., & Ysseldyke, J. (1973). Teacher retention of stereotypes of exceptionality. *Exceptional Children, 40*, 651–652.

Schain, S. (1972). Learning of low ability children and tutor behavior as a function of the self-fulfilling prophecy. Unpublished doctoral dissertation, University of Illinois, Champaign-Urbana.

Schrier, E. M., Leventhal, J. D., & Uslan, M. M. (1991). Access technology for blind and visually impaired persons. *Technology and Disability, 1*(10), 19–23.

Schumaker, J., Denton, P., & Deshler, D. (1984). *The paraphrasing strategy.* Lawrence, KS: University of Kansas Institute for Research on Learning Disabilities.

Schumaker, J., Deshler, D., Alley, G., & Warner, M. (1983). Toward the development of an intervention model for learning disabled adolescents: The University of Kansas Institute. *Exceptional Education Quarterly, 4*, 45–70.

Silverman, L. K. (1986). What happens to the gifted girl? In C. J. Maker (Ed.), *Critical issues in gifted education: Vol. 1. Defensible programs for the gifted* (pp. 43–89). Austin, TX: PRO-ED.

Simmons, R. (1988, November/December). Smart, beautiful: Ms. Wheelchair America Pageant. *A Positive Approach*, pp. 10–11.

Singleton, P. (1992). We can! Empowerment of people who are deaf … An empowerment agenda for the 1990s and beyond. *OSERS News in Print, 5*(2), 12–15.

Smith, J. (1988). The dangers of prenatal cocaine use. *American Journal of Maternal Child Nursing 13*(3), 174–179.

Spady, W. G. (1992, March). It's time to take a close look at outcome-based education. *Communique, 20*(6), 16–18.

Spooner, F., Stern, B., & Test, D. W. (1989). Teaching first aid skills to adolescents who are moderately mentally handicapped. *Education and Training in Mental Retardation, 24*, 341–351.

Stahl, S. A., Osborn, J., & Lehr, F. (1990). *Beginning to read: Thinking and learning about print, by M. Adams, A summary.* Champaign: IL: Center for the Study of Reading.

Stem, B., & Test, D. W. (1989). Teaching first aid skills in the classroom. *Teaching Exceptional Children, 22*(1), 10–12.

Stern, J. (1988). *The condition of education: Elementary and secondary education.* Washington, DC: National Center for Education Statistics.

Sternberg, R. J. (1985). *Beyond IQ: A triarchic theory of human intelligence.* Cambridge: Cambridge University Press.

Sternberg, R. J., & Davidson, J. E. (1986a). Conceptions of giftedness: A map of the terrain. In R. J. Sternberg & J. E. Davidson (Eds.), *Conceptions of giftedness* (pp. 3–18). Cambridge: Cambridge University Press.

Sternberg, R. J., & Davidson, J. E. (Eds.). (1986b). *Conceptions of giftedness.* Cambridge: Cambridge University Press.

Task Force on DSM-IV. (1993). *DSM-IV Draft Criteria, 3–1–93.* Washington, DC: American Psychiatric Association [limited circulation; obtain from American Psychiatric Press, Inc., 1400 K St., NW, Suite 1101, Washington, DC 20005].

Terman, L., & Oden, M. (1951). The Stanford studies of the gifted. In P. Witty (Ed.), *The gifted child.* Boston: Heath.

Thurlow, M. L. Ysseldyke, J. E., Weiss, J. A., Lehr, C. A., O'Sullivan, P. J., & Nania, P. A. (1986). *Policy analysis of exit decisions and follow-up procedures in early childhood special education programs.* (Research Report No. 14). Minneapolis: University of Minnesota, Early Childhood Assessment Project.

Turnbull, A. P., & Turnbull, H. R. III (1979). *Parents speak out.* Columbus, OH: Merrill.

U.S. Bureau of the Census. (1993). *Poverty in the United States: 1992.* Current Population Reports, Series p. 60–185. Washington, DC: U. S. Government Printing Office.

U.S. Department of Education. (1992). *Fourteenth annual report to Congress on the implementation of the Individuals with Disabilities Education Act.* Washington, DC: Author.

U.S. Department of Education. (1993). *Fifteenth annual report to Congress on the implementation of the Individuals with Disabilities Education Act.* Washington, DC: Author.

Uslan, M. M. (1993). A review of two low-cost closed-circuit television systems. *Journal of Visual Impairment and Blindness, 87*, 310–313.

Wagner, M., (1991). *School completion of students with disabilities: What do we know? What can we do?* Paper presented at the Annual Leadership Conference for State Directors of Special Education.

Wagner, M., D'Amico, R., Marder, C., Newman, L., & Blackorby, J. (1992). *What happens next? Trends in postschool outcomes for youth with disabilities: The second comprehensive report from the National Longitudinal Transition Study of special education students.* Menlo Park, CA: SRI International.

Walker, H. (1976). *Walker Problem Behavior Identification Checklist.* Los Angeles: Western Psychological Services.

Walker, H. M., McConnell, S. R., Holmes, D., Todis, B., Walker, J., & Golden, H. (1983). *The Walker social skills curriculum: The ACCEPTS program.* Austin, TX: Pro-Ed.

Walker, H. M., Todis, B., Holmes, D., & Horton, G. (1988): *The Walker social skills curriculum: The ACCESS program.* Austin, TX: Pro-Ed.

Walker, R. (1990, April 11). Lawmakers in Kentucky approve landmark school-reform bill. *Education Week, 10*(1), 34–35.

Wehman, P. (1992). *Life beyond classrooms: Transition Strategies for young people with disabilities.* Baltimore, MD: Paul H. Brookes.

White House. (1990). *National goals for education* (press release). Washington, DC: Author.

Wittrock, M. C. (1986). *Handbook of research on teaching* (3rd ed.). New York: Macmillan.

Yell, M. L. (1989). *Honig* v. *Doe:* The suspension and expulsion of handicapped students. *Exceptional Children, 56,* 60–69.

Ysseldyke, J. E., Thurlow, M. L., & Shin H. (1994). *Opportunity to learn and students with disabilities.* Synthesis Report 14. Minneapolis: University of Minnesota National Center on Educational Outcomes.

Ysseldyke, J. E., & Christenson, S. L. (1993). The instructional environment system–II (TIES II). Longmont, CO: Sopris West.

Ysseldyke, J. E., O'Sullivan, P., Thurlow, M. L., & Christenson, S. L. (1989). Qualitative differences in reading and math instruction received by handicapped students. *Remedial and Special Education, 10,* 14–20.

Ysseldyke, J. E., & Thurlow, M. L. (1993). A self-study guide to the development of educational outcomes and indicators. Minneapolis, MN: National Center on Educational Outcomes.

Ysseldyke, J. E., Thurlow, M. L., & Gilman, C. (1992). *Educational outcomes and indicators for students completing school.* Minneapolis: National Center on Educational Outcomes.

Ysseldyke, J. E., Algozzine, B., & Thurlow, M. L. (1992). *Critical issues in special education.* Boston: Houghton Mifflin Company.

Name Index

Subject Index